A HISTORY OF WOMEN
IN AMERICA

A HISTORY OF WOMEN IN AMERICA

JANET L. CORYELL
Western Michigan University

NORA FAIRES
Western Michigan University

McGraw Hill
Connect
Learn
Succeed™

The McGraw·Hill Companies

Connect
Learn
Succeed™

A HISTORY OF WOMEN IN AMERICA

Published by McGraw-Hill, a business unit of The McGraw-Hill Companies, Inc., 1221 Avenue of the Americas, New York, NY 10020. Copyright © 2012 by The McGraw-Hill Companies, Inc. All rights reserved. No part of this publication may be reproduced or distributed in any form or by any means, or stored in a database or retrieval system, without the prior written consent of The McGraw-Hill Companies, Inc., including, but not limited to, in any network or other electronic storage or transmission, or broadcast for distance learning.

Some ancillaries, including electronic and print components, may not be available to customers outside the United States.

This book is printed on acid-free paper.

1 2 3 4 5 6 7 8 9 0 DOC/DOC 1 0 9 8 7 6 5 4 3 2 1

ISBN 978-0-07-287813-4
MHID 0-07-287813-4

Vice President & Editor-in-Chief: *Michael Ryan*
Vice President EDP/Central Publishing Services: *Kimberly Meriwether David*
Publisher: *Christopher Freitag*
Sponsoring Editor: *Matthew Busbridge*
Executive Marketing Manager: *Pamela S. Cooper*
Senior Managing Editor: *Meghan Campbell*
Project Manager: *Erin Melloy*
Design Coordinator: *Margarite Reynolds*
Cover Designer: *Mary-Presley Adams*
Cover Credit: Left to right: *Jules Frazier/Getty Images; Quilt by Minnie Davisson Baringer and Bonnie Baringer Coryell Hatch; photo by Janet Coryell; Photograph of suffrage campaign workers in New Jersey; OJO Images/Getty Images*
Photo Research Coordinator: *Brian Pecko*
Buyer: *Nicole Baumgartner*
Media Project Manager: *Sridevi Palani*
Compositor: *Glyph International*
Typeface: *10.5/12 Janson Text LT Std*
Printer: *R. R. Donnelley*

All credits appearing on page or at the end of the book are considered to be an extension of the copyright page.

Library of Congress Cataloging-in-Publication Data

Coryell, Janet L., 1955-
  A history of women in America/Janet L. Coryell, Nora Faires.
    p. cm.
  Includes bibliographical references and index.
  ISBN 978-0-07-287813-4 (alk. paper)
  1. Women—United States—History. I. Faires, Nora Helen. II. Title.
  HQ1410.C675 2012
  305.40973—dc22
www.mhhe.com   2010042891

For Jim and David Smither, who also asked what
the women were doing;

For Linda Pritchard, feminist colleague, fabulous friend;

For our students, who want to learn and need to know.

BRIEF CONTENTS

Contents

LIST OF ILLUSTRATIONS

WHY WRITE A WOMEN'S HISTORY BOOK?

We wrote this textbook because we wanted to integrate the stories of American women into the national narrative that serves so many students as their understanding of American history. We wanted to show students that women have never stood on the sidelines, but have always been active participants in our nation's growth and development.

As you read this textbook, you will find women participating in virtually every aspect of American life. Instead of women's activities placed in boxes, supplements, or sidebars, we weave their lives and actions into a national narrative, providing enough historical context so that readers can recognize the institutions, events, and activities they are already familiar with, as well as explaining those they know little about. By integrating women's lives into the very heart of the country's narratives—particularly the political narrative—we hope you will be better able to see women where they were, rather than having women appear as mere appendages to events controlled largely or even exclusively by men.

Nearly forty years after the first formal courses in women's history were offered, historians of American women's lives continue to produce countless articles, scholarly monographs, websites, documentary films, conferences, and popular books. Most student textbooks in American history now include numerous mentions of women. Yet few of those textbooks truly integrate women. The national narratives of American history, chronological sequences of major events that revolve around and emphasize the political, economic, cultural, and social changes that have taken place since the 1400s, help make order out of chaos, an act essential to understanding history. Survey-level courses in college, in particular, give students a framework for understanding history by enlarging upon those narratives. Yet national narratives often leave out many important actors, mostly women.

Integrating women into American history requires that we pick and choose stories to illustrate specific events by asking ourselves what women were doing while the men were doing what the textbooks said was "important." We presume little or no substantial knowledge of American history on the part of the student reader, and we assume the value of including examples of women's activities from all over the nation. We use a narrative style and accessible language so that beginning students in women's history as well as American history can readily follow the stories as well as their context and meaning.

THEMES OF THE BOOK

Accessibility   One of the sad characteristics of education over the last quarter century is the decline in students' language skills, as well as in the number and kind of history courses required to graduate from high school or college, particularly survey-level courses in American history. Polls regularly decry Americans' lack of knowledge regarding their own history, and pundits draw upon our national narratives to prove their point. To meet these challenges, we use accessible language, telling the stories that attract so many beginning students to the field of history, and we cast a wide geographic and chronological net to incorporate what women's history scholars have found into a narrative that paints a more accurate picture of our history. This textbook challenges and enriches students' understanding of our national story, showing where, when, how, and why women mattered throughout the American past into the American present.

Comprehensive Coverage   Our students in midwestern and Southern schools have often complained that women's history textbooks have a bias toward the East Coast. As scholars of the history of the American South and the Midwest and as teachers of students in those states, we sought illustrations and examples that came from all over the country—our text features comprehensive geographic coverage throughout the chapters. We have been particularly careful to include women in specific geographic regions in our narrative, such as the American South, where women are often nearly invisible, even in other women's history textbooks.

Diversity   We seek to incorporate major ethnic groups as they arrive in the national narrative, from Native American and African women who appear earliest in the text to the major immigrant groups who occupy increasingly larger roles throughout the nineteenth and twentieth centuries. Our chronological coverage also reflects our goal to be as inclusive as we can be. We include substantial coverage of the centuries before the American Revolution when competing imperial powers struggled to control the continent—a struggle that had profound effect on women's lives, yet one that is often overlooked in other women's history textbooks.

FEATURES OF THE BOOK

Chapter Opener   Each chapter begins with a detailed outline to prepare you for the topics we have covered within. The outline is followed by a short vignette about a woman or a group of women to illustrate the chapter's themes.

Illustrations and Primary Source Boxes   Each chapter includes a few illustrations and primary sources that teachers can use to highlight issues or illustrate important events. The illustrations illuminate women's actions in both traditional and uncommon settings. The primary sources provide historical documentary evidence as examples of women's actions. Both can serve as the springboard for class discussions of how women were an integral part of the American nation as it developed throughout the centuries.

End-of-Chapter Material Each chapter ends with a set of thoughtful questions, called Think More About It, that reflect back on topics covered in the chapter. Instructors can use these questions for a study aid, for class discussion, or for paper prompts. We also include a list of additional readings, called Read More About It, that can direct students to some of the best works on topics covered in each chapter. A brief list, called "Key Concepts," given at the end of each chapter, contains the most important terms students will need to master to understand the chapter's major themes.

ABOUT THE AUTHORS

We began our studies of American women from other fields of historical study—politics, military, biography, and Southern history for Professor Coryell; ethnicity, migration, race, and class for Professor Faires. Starting from existing fields of study has informed our research and made us aware of the importance of making women's history a part of the whole of American history, not just a separate field of study. Women's history filled important gaps in our knowledge of the development of the entire nation, and with this book we hope to share this knowledge with you.

Janet L. Coryell

Nora Faires

ACKNOWLEDGMENTS

This project began with conversations between colleagues with adjacent offices about the difficulties we shared teaching American women's history. Those discussions led us to conclude that there was a real need for a textbook that took a new approach to the subject. Several years have passed since those initial conversations and along the way we have received substantial help and caring support, which we are happy to acknowledge: Patricia Rogers gave us a close and inspiring critique of drafts of early chapters; José Brandão and Gray Whaley provided useful comments on Native American history; Linda Borish and Barbara Speas Havira encouraged our efforts; and the Burnham-Macmillan Endowment Fund of the Department of History at Western Michigan University provided financial support, including some fact-checking by various graduate students. Many friends and colleagues outside our department helped us as well, including Deborah Evett, who read it all; Grace Coolidge, Fran Kelleher, Sue Schwarzlander, Carolyn Shapiro-Shapin, and Gretchen Galbraith from Grand Valley State University who provided answers about women in their fields of endeavor. Thanks also to Wendy Zieger, a researcher extraordinaire; Linda Pritchard, Jewel Spangler, and Rachel Koopmans; Holly Mayer, John and Ruth Ann Coski, and the entire Coryell/Smither clans who listened for years; the members of the Southern Association for Women Historians, particularly Elizabeth Hayes Turner, Sandra Treadway, Cynthia Kierner, Marjorie Spruill, and especially Cita Cook, who encouraged our inclusion of Southern women throughout the chapters, as she was tired of schlepping handouts to class to cover their history. Our thanks go as well to McGraw-Hill and its editorial support: Steve Drummond's enthusiastic reception to our ideas as he took our manuscript on board; Jon-David Hague, Sora Kim, and many others at the press who assisted us as well, most particularly Gail Terry, who did a brilliant editing job and saved us from more than a few sins committed by two noncolonialists; and Maureen Spada and Meghan Campbell, who shepherded us through the final months in the process. These fine folk all gave us their wisdom and advice; any errors that remain, in the end, belong to us.

Additional thanks to the following colleagues for their insightful reviews of the manuscript:

Catherine Allgor, University of California Riverside
Devon Atchison, Grossmont College
Nancy Baker, Sam Houston State University
Amy Bix, Iowa State University
Stephanie Cole, The University of Texas, Arlington
Christine Erickson, Indiana University Purdue University Fort Wayne
Lisa Levenstein, University of North Carolina, Greensboro
Carolyn Lewis, Louisiana State University
Clark Pomerlau, University of North Texas
Martha Saxton, Amherst College
Elizabeth Reis, University of Oregon
Alicia Tucker, Northern Virginia Community College
Julie Webber, Illinois State University

Chapter I

NATIVE WOMEN AND EUROPEAN ENCOUNTERS

The Lady of Cofitachequi

In the warm soft air of spring in 1539, Spanish explorer Hernando de Soto landed on the west coast of Florida, commissioned by the Spanish Crown to conquer the Indian lands that lay before him. His army of Spanish conquistadors, 600 men strong, marched inland searching for gold and other treasures from the natives of the region, and demanding food supplies and tribute before they moved on. By the following year the battle-weary Native peoples had turned over what they could—buckskins, freshwater pearls, food, and *tamemes* (burden-bearers), as well as Native women whom the Spanish would use as sexual slaves. They then urged the Spaniards to seek greater riches further north. Still in search of gold, de Soto and his men left their winter camp at Anhayca (modern-day Tallahassee) and headed east, then turned north toward what the Apalachee Indians promised would be a kingdom of silver and gold—the chiefdom of the Cofitachequi.

At the Wateree River, near present-day Camden, South Carolina, de Soto made camp and demanded to see the leader of the Cofitachequi, whom the Spaniards called the "Lady of Cofitachequi." Spanish accounts of her arrival describe her as a beautiful woman, a "chieftainess," carried to de Soto's camp on a platform covered with white cloth. She welcomed the conquistadors with animal skins, cloth, and freshwater pearls as gifts, and offered half the town—a

A NATIVE "FLORIDIAN" No image of the Lady of Cofitachequi exists. This drawing by John White, some fifty years after the Lady's adventures, illustrates a Native American woman from newly named Florida. Her body is covered in tattoos from her chest down and along both arms and legs, a common form of body art among Native Americans.

town she sought to discipline for not paying her the tribute she demanded as their ruler—for the army's use. She then withdrew, impressing the Spaniards with her regal bearing, while contemplating her next move in her diplomatic maneuverings with the invasion force. The Spaniards, meanwhile, recorded her visit, remarking on her intelligence. The "sensible and well-chosen" words she used amazed them, they reported, coming as they did from an Indian woman.

When the Lady returned, de Soto demanded gold. Instead, she gave him copper, mica, and more pearls, and showed him the town's temple, built atop one of the mounds characteristic of the many towns she ruled over in her chiefdom. The temple housed the remains of important families and town leaders, as well as ceremonial objects and treasures. De Soto's men ignored the sacred nature of the temple and seized the pearls that covered the tombs of the dead—200 pounds' worth—as the Lady calmly watched them and told them of greater treasures in the town where she resided, Talimeco, a name meaning "chief's town." She then disappeared, having decided that the Europeans were uncivilized barbarians incapable of practicing diplomacy. The Spaniards had given no gifts to her to reciprocate her generosity; they had desecrated the temple rather than showing proper respect; they had eaten through the town's supplies of corn that rightly belonged to her. She had tried diplomacy and it had failed. Resistance to such a large armed force was most likely futile. If she fled from the Spanish, then the towns under her chiefdom would refuse to release food supplies to de Soto when he marched in. With any luck, the Europeans would then starve, since they carried little food themselves.

The Lady's strategy worked momentarily. Hungry Europeans stole what little corn they could find, but it was not nearly enough for such a large force. They continued north, eventually finding the Lady's residence at Talimeco. They desecrated the temple there too, then ate through the granary. Finally, de Soto ordered his men to find the Lady of Cofitachequi. They did so, kidnapping her and carrying her with them as they moved toward the mountains in search of the elusive cache of gold so many of the Native men and women had told them of, in hopes that the Europeans would leave them undisturbed. After two weeks, the Lady escaped her captors, after telling them she needed to go into the woods "to attend to her necessities." She disappeared, along with her serving women and several enslaved members of de Soto's expedition.

Deprived of his captive's guidance, de Soto continued his explorations farther north. He then moved west, spreading disease and death in his wake, until his own death in 1542 in present-day Mississippi. Later chroniclers of early America hailed him as a major explorer, a "discoverer" of the Mississippi River. In contrast, little is known of the Lady of Cofitachequi after her unhappy encounter with the conquistadors. In significant ways, her story is emblematic of the position of Native women in the history of America. The Lady Cofitachequi is one of the first women to appear in American history as a discernible individual, exercising authority in ways many people do not associate with Native women. She ruled over thousands of Native Americans in a vast chiefdom that stretched from the Atlantic seaboard to the foot of the Appalachian Mountain range in present-day South Carolina. She received tribute payments from dozens of villages, usually in the form of corn, which she stored in massive granaries and distributed as gifts to cement political alliances or to supplement food supplies during times of poor harvest. Despite occupying a position of political power and leadership in her own right similar to that of European monarchs, she endures as a historical character primarily because her story is linked to that of male European explorers. They mentioned her in documents they created for their own use. Other than that, the Lady of Cofitachequi's story was barely preserved and rarely repeated, seldom mentioned even in regional studies or histories of Native Americans, and overshadowed by the stories of the men who destroyed so much of her chiefdom. She was relegated to the role of a little-known anomaly.

The Lady of Cofitachequi's story tells scholars much about the relationship between gender and political power among the southeast Indians. It also says a great deal about European perceptions of the lands they invaded and the leaders they met along the way. It tells very little, however, about the majority of Native women living on the North American continent in her time. Unlike the Lady of Cofitachequi, most Native women were not leaders, and they seldom appear in written records, aside from those documents left by European invaders. They are largely invisible despite their importance to the survival of their families and, in the case of the Lady, to the survival of their entire group. To patch together the stories of these ordinary women, historians have turned to the methods of anthropology, archaeology, and oral history. Scholars have analyzed clothing, pottery, and baskets, studied legends and songs, and unearthed the remains of houses and ceremonial grounds to illuminate the history of Native women.

American women's history begins with the stories of Native women living in distinct Native regional cultures. In all of these regions, women played important economic, social, cultural, and spiritual roles, though very few had the power of the Lady of Cofitachequi. While particular experiences varied greatly depending on where Native women lived and how their societies were organized, most shared common duties and significant patterns of daily life from birth through old age. As the Lady of Cofitachequi's story illustrates, Native women's lives began to change from their earliest contacts with the Spanish, French, English, and other European men and women as these Europeans sought to conquer, trade, and occupy Native lands. Encounters with Europeans dramatically disrupted not only the lives of many Native women but also the organization of their societies, and even their geographic locations. Europeans often related to Native American women based on images of them that they carried from their own cultures, rather than the realities of Native women's experiences.

NATIVE AMERICA

By 1500, at the point of exploration and contact with Europeans, some 10 million Natives inhabited the North American continent, living in over 500 distinct groups with different languages, living patterns, and economic systems. These diverse Native American groups (the term *tribe* was not used until much later) lived in what anthropologists have defined as seven major regional cultures: Eastern Woodland, Southeast, Southwest, Plains, California Inter-Mountain, Plateau, and Northwest Pacific Coast.

The physical environments shaped the social and cultural characteristics of the groups who lived in each of these regional cultures. Most significantly, the ease with which Native Americans could gather, prepare, and store food depended on the physical environment and largely determined whether the group could farm. If growing food and storing it for the winter season were possible, a group could settle in an area, plant gardens, harvest crops, and build substantial long-term housing. Consequently, within these regional cultures, societies can be divided roughly into three types: *horticulturalists*, who depended primarily on farming and lived in settled communities; *hunter/gatherers* (or *nomadic* groups), who relied more on hunting game or fish and gathering food from the wild, often over a broad expanse of territory; and *semisedentary* or *seminomadic* groups, who combined agriculture with hunting, fishing, and gathering.

A second important factor in shaping Native societies was whether they were *patrilineal* or *matrilineal*. These two terms refer to lineage systems, the ways ancestry was traced and resources were allocated. Patrilineal systems, based on one's male parent, were most common. But other groups used matrilineal, or female, lines of descent to define families and pass on land use, rights, and offices. In general, horticultural groups were more likely to be matrilineal because of women's importance in food cultivation. In most horticultural societies, men cleared the land of trees and shrubs to prepare for planting, but women did the farming, controlling food production and distribution. They planted, cultivated, harvested, and then prepared the food for eating or storage. Women made baskets and pottery with which to store and cook the food, then taught their daughters to do the same. Men hunted and fished during the appropriate seasons, since fresh meat was a welcome and necessary addition to the diet, but women were responsible for feeding the group winter and summer. Such an important role meant that horticultural societies afforded women more active roles in politics or public life, since power in societies such as these was linked to food production and control over land. In matrilineal societies, then, women generally exercised public forms of power along with their domestic duties.

Most matrilineal groups were organized by clan, with clan membership defined by one's kinship, determining where one lived, whom one could marry, and who provided care during sickness or old age. When a daughter married in matrilineal societies, she brought her husband with her to live in the village where her mother lived (a characteristic termed *matrilocal*), rather than moving to her husband's village or house (*patrilocal*). Women of matrilineal groups also controlled the land, building and maintaining the houses. The special importance of their labor—deemed "women's work"— gave women significant power. Women were often the guardians of group traditions and key to many groups' social and economic stability. Elite women in horticultural groups could rise to roles of leadership. The Lady of Cofitachequi was one such leader, as were other woman chiefs Europeans met in their explorations of the Southeast, an area with many matrilineal horticultural groups.

In contrast, most hunter/gatherer groups were patrilineal and male-dominated. Hunting required both upper-body strength, which most women did not possess to the same degree as men, and mobility, which limited most women as they began rearing and raising children. Patrilineal groups included those who lived in the Plains region, such as the Kansa and, later, the Sioux and Comanche. Such groups were invariably nomadic, following the deer, buffalo, elk, antelope, or other game. Because the men in these societies possessed the skills and tools to harvest game, they typically wielded more power than women. Women gathered nuts, berries, and grasses to add to the group's diet, but men provided the bulk of the food, making seasonal journeys to traditional hunting grounds.

Regional Cultures

The *Eastern Woodland* Indians lived in the northeastern half of the present-day United States and southeastern Canada, including the Great Lakes region and the Chesapeake Bay, as well as eastern North and South Carolina. Woodland Indians were primarily semisedentary. They grew corn, beans, and squash, gathered wild rice, and hunted deer and beaver. Most spoke an Algonquian language and were patrilineal, with names and property descending through the male line. Some groups led fairly simple lives—the Lenapé along the Delaware River, for instance, lived in portable wigwams, hunted for food, and grew maize (corn) and little else. Other horticultural groups had sophisticated and complex settlements with permanent structures. The most important of the Eastern Woodland Indians were the Iroquoians. Unlike other Woodland groups, the Iroquoians were horticultural and matrilineal, with descent following the female line. In what would become upstate New York, Iroquoians organized themselves into a sophisticated political group—the Iroquois Confederacy—that met regularly to keep the peace and regulate trade. They built permanent towns filled with longhouses, communal dwellings made of bark or logs that stretched several hundred feet in length and housed as many as 500 people. A senior woman served as a leader in each longhouse, and women had active political roles in Iroquoian society.

The *Southeast* Indians lived in present-day North and South Carolina, Georgia, Florida, Alabama, Mississippi, Louisiana, and eastern Texas. They spoke related languages known as Muskogean. Because of the long growing seasons and fertile soils, most Southeast Indians were horticultural. The Cofitachequi, who survived until 1700, were one Muskogean-speaking group. Two others of these complex and hierarchical groups in the Southeast were the Cahokia, moundbuilders of southern Illinois who had disappeared before Europeans arrived in North America, and the Natchez of Mississippi. The Cahokians left archeological remains that point to a thriving urban complex, some 10,000 to 30,000 strong. They sustained themselves on corn-based agriculture and extensive trade, from the Rockies to Ontario to the Gulf of Mexico. The Cahokians erected Monk's Mound, a hundred-foot-high ceremonial mound still visible near St. Louis today. Monk's Mound likely served as the physical and spiritual center of the

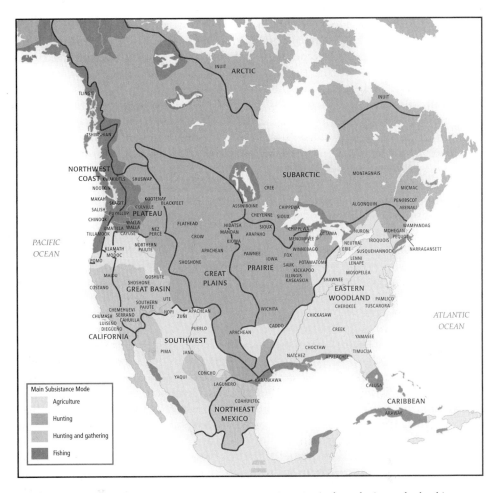

MAP OF NATIVE AMERICAN SUBSISTENCE MODES, C. 1400 Anthropologists and ethnohistorians divide Native American groups into regional cultures, usually defined by language or environment. This map of Native American regional cultures also shows the ways in which Indians supported themselves—agriculture, hunting, fishing, and so on—prior to European arrival.

group's ceremonies and took as many as 5 million labor-hours to build. Cahokia disappeared after A.D. 1400, most likely due to environmental causes, and little is known about women's lives within the group. Archeologists have discovered small statues of women at Cahokian digs, however, and art historians argue that the statues symbolize women's fertility, an important role for women in any agricultural community that requires laborers.

Historians know more about women among the Natchez, a group that survived European discovery, and thus appear in European written documents. The Natchez, who may well have been descendants of the Cahokians, also built permanent villages and constructed impressive earthen mounds for their ceremonies. A matrilineal group, they worshiped deities led by the god representing the sun, and were ruled by a male leader called the Great Sun. He was chosen, however, from the matrilineal line of descendants of a woman called the Woman Chief. The complex social order of the horticultural Natchez included elite and lower classes, and the group used captured enemies as slaves, as did many other Native American societies. The Natchez maintained their group identity into the eighteenth century, when they lost a war with France. Most of the war's survivors were enslaved and sent to the Caribbean "sugar islands" held by France.

The *Southwest* Indians lived in an area that stretched from present-day Colorado and Utah south to Arizona, New Mexico, and northern Mexico. This vast region is divided into three distinct climate zones. In the northern pine forests and high valleys lived the nomadic Hopi, as well as the seminomadic Zuni, who first hunted mammoth and later buffalo. In the cactus-covered deserts of southern Arizona and New Mexico, the horticultural Pueblo, descended from the Anasazi cliff-dwellers, built adobe towns in the cliffs, surrounding them with thick walls for protection from outsiders. In the desert lands that are today the border between Arizona and California, groups such as the Mojave, a patrilineal horticultural group, lived in huts along the Colorado River. There they farmed, relying on the annual flooding of the Colorado to water their crops, and stored their food in distinctive coiled pottery women created. Others in this region include the Navajo, a nomadic group turned horticultural after coming into contact with the Pueblo, from whom they adopted many farming techniques. The Navajo eventually specialized in raising livestock, and women wove sheep's wool into blankets that were traded widely. Both before and after European contact, the natives of this region migrated when living conditions changed or when their groups were scattered by natural disaster or warfare. As in other regions, they would then regroup to form new societies.

The *Plains* Indians, whose territory was in the center of the North American continent as it stretched from Canada to Texas, followed the buffalo on its annual migration south. Plains groups included nomadic hunter/gatherer groups such as the Blackfoot and Shoshone, as well as the Mandan, who were matrilineal and seminomadic. Some groups voluntarily migrated into the region, while others, such as the Dakota Sioux, the Cheyenne, and the Arapaho, were later pushed there by European invaders. These groups had originally been horticultural but eventually became more nomadic because of the Plains' scarce rainfall, which limited agriculture, and its large herds of buffalo, or bison, that provided a ready food source. Eventually, all of the Plains Indians became dependent on the buffalo for their food and their culture. After horses were introduced by the Spanish in the sixteenth century, Plains Indians grew more nomadic and often more warlike than in other regions of the country as they competed for buffalo. More hunting by male members of the group, coupled with a corresponding decline in farming by women, left women with a less powerful role within the economy of the group.

The *California Inter-Mountain* Indians lived in the lands south and west of the Rocky Mountains, in California, and along the length of the Baja Peninsula. The area's harsh climate—the northeastern part of the region had long winters and deep snows, the southern portions deserts and scrub land—prevented many Native groups from farming. Instead, the Utes, the Northern and Southern Paiutes, the Guaycuras, and other groups were hunter/gatherers who divided their tasks by gender: men hunted deer, elk, mountain sheep and small game; women gathered pine nuts, wild grains, bird eggs, and small animals such as caterpillars and locusts for sustenance. Life was often spartan, and storing food during winter was difficult, making women's skill at fashioning useful, durable—and beautiful—baskets critical to the survival of the group. Kinship ties, defined by patrilineal records and preserved by oral traditions, formed the basis for group organization in this area, and leaders typically used persuasion, rather than force, to build consensus and to retain their power.

The *Plateau region* Indians lived in the highlands of western Montana, Idaho, Washington, and Oregon, and southwestern Canada. Groups such as the Nimi'puu (called "Nez Percé"), Walla Wallas, Yakima, and Bitteroot Salish (called "Flatheads") lived as hunter/gatherers, traveling annually to the Plains to hunt bison. Men hunted; women dried salmon from the rivers and harvested camas (an edible lily bulb) and other root vegetables to eat during winter. In summer the group lived in longhouses covered by mats made of tule, a reedlike grass women harvested, dried, and wove; in winter their mats covered round houses sunk partly into the ground for warmth.

Northwest Pacific Coast Indians lived in the region stretching from southern Alaska to northern California. Food supplies from the sea were so readily available in the region that groups such as the Tlingit, Tsimshian, and Chinook did not need to grow crops, "farming" the sea instead. The bountiful food supply also encouraged extensive trade among groups in the region and later with European and Asian sailors. Similarly to farming communities, these hunter/gatherers established permanent villages where extended families resided in large houses. A male leader headed the political system, but matrilineal descent determined the clan and residence of each member of the group. Women, particularly among the Tlingit who lived near the Gulf of Alaska, were known as sharp traders, an economic skill that often provided them more power within the group as Native and then European traders sought their goods.

Geographic location had a powerful role in determining the development of different Native groups. Within those groups, women's activities varied due to the economic basis of the group—whether it was primarily horticultural, hunter/gatherer, or semisedentary. These varied economic activities also affected the organization of the society, whether descent was matrilineal or patrilineal, and usually affected women's power within the group.

The Life Cycles of Native American Women

Despite great variations in regional cultures and in the economic and social structures that existed on the American continent, the lives and work of most Native women typically revolved around interests common to women in many other societies: family, childbirth and child care, food preparation, health care, education, and the social and cultural activities of their group. Even with the changes wrought by European contact, the day-to-day existence of most Native women remained centered around their *life cycles* within their society. *Life cycle* refers to the stages of life an individual passes through from birth to death. For most women, the life cycle includes infancy and childhood; puberty and coming-of-age; sexuality, courtship, and marriage; pregnancy and childbirth; adult women's work; and spirituality and death. Looking at life cycle patterns over time, while bearing in mind the important and varied exceptions to them, helps in understanding the history of women in groups who share a geographic or cultural region.

Infancy and Childhood

In most Native societies, women had the primary responsibility for educating children, at least until they were mobile. After they could walk, mothers continued to be important, but members of the entire group took part in training the young to ensure the community's harmony, as well as passing along its traditions. This training included instruction in the culture and religion of the group in addition to practical tasks. Most groups divided

NATIVE CRADLEBOARDS   Many Native American women used cradleboards while walking or riding. This photograph of an Apache mother and her child, taken in 1906, illustrates the material objects women used that changed little over the centuries prior to contact with Europeans and that many groups continued to use in the centuries after contact.

labor by gender, with girls and boys learning different skills and cultural roles. Among Woodland Indians, for instance, girls played with dolls and learned to make buckskin clothing, first for the dolls, then for their families. They also learned how to make bark wigwams for shelter, to chop wood and gather berries for food, and to fashion the birchbark containers that they would use to store food for their families.

Both boys and girls were taught how to dress and adorn themselves in ways particular to their culture. Woodland children wore few clothes before puberty, boys and girls alike often wearing just a breechcloth with leggings to protect their legs. After that, they wore deerskin aprons decorated with beads, fringe, and carvings. They wrapped themselves in deerskin cloaks when it got cold, and covered themselves with bear grease in summer to keep mosquitoes away. In contrast, the Nootka in the Pacific Northwest wore conical hats, nose rings, and clothes women wove of shredded cedar bark to protect the group from the constant rains of that environment. Among the Chinook in the same region, a mother pierced an infant's ears shortly after birth and again after the child took a first step, celebrating such milestones with body decoration. Other groups decorated their bodies with tattoos, or used temporary body art created with paint made from roots that women gathered and prepared. Groups often fashioned jewelry from items they obtained locally or for which they traded; pearls, shell beads, copper, animal teeth, and bone beads were popular. Crow Indian girls decorated themselves, wearing jewelry made from elk teeth, a commodity often available from hunts in the Yellowstone River valley in which they lived, while young Hopi girls in the southwest, from a group who depended on squash crops for sustenance, marked their single status with special hairstyles called squash blossom whorls. Variations in dress and adornment were considerable, and reflected the groups' definitions of culture, beauty, and status.

Puberty and Coming-of-Age

Among Native women, *menarche*, the onset of menstruation, was the critical marker of the passage from childhood to womanhood. Many Native groups viewed menstrual flow as having spiritual power, presumably because girls bled every month yet remained healthy, whereas when men bled, from wounds or sickness, they often died. Many groups had legends to explain the phenomenon, and the power of menstruating women was respected and often feared in Native cultures. (See Primary Source 1-1.) Among the Yurok in northern California, menstruating women lived in isolation, not because they regarded themselves as dangerous, nor as somehow "unclean" (as many Europeans thought), but because they were at the height of their spiritual powers during menstruation, and such powers had to be respected. Such beliefs were common, but so were views that women's powers at such times could be dangerous. The Micmac of present-day Maine, for example, believed that if a menstruating woman touched a man he would lose the use of his limbs and be unable to walk; if she touched a gun, it would no longer function. The Chinook Indians who fished the

THE MENOMINEE EXPLAIN MENSTRUATION

Native Americans explained physical attributes by linking them to the natural and supernatural world. The Menominee, a group of Woodland Indians in present-day Wisconsin, offered the following explanation for women's menstruation. The story begins when Manabush arrives at his grandmother's home.

"Manabush was jealous of the attentions the Bear showed to Nokomis, his grandmother. One day, in a rage, he killed the Bear and went away. When he returned he noticed his grandmother had combed her hair and put on clean clothes. He suspected that someone had been there, but she made no reply which satisfied him. He went into the woods on the following day and again, when he returned, his grandmother had combed her hair and put on clean clothes. This went on for several days. Manabush suspected that it was the Bear who was visiting his grandmother, so he waited near the wigwam, very quietly. Soon, he heard the Bear coming along the trail, snorting and grunting. He made straight for the wigwam and entered it.

Columbia River feared nets would be unlucky if touched by a menstruating woman. Other groups thought that menstruating women had the power to cause sickness or make an illness worse. Many groups forbade sexual intercourse during a woman's menstrual period and often separated menstruating women and girls from the rest of the group. Potawatomi girls in the Great Lakes region were separated from their families at menarche, staying by themselves in the woods. They fasted part of the time, hoping for a vision. For a Potawatomi boy, having a vision was necessary to become an adult member of the group, but for a Potawatomi girl, having this experience was regarded as a special blessing.

Among the Navajo in the Southwest, the coming-of-age ceremony marking the onset of menarche was known as the *kinaaldá*. This ceremony included rituals of singing and praying, as well as visits by relatives and friends. For four days, a newly menstruating girl arose at dawn and ran toward the east. On the third and last evening, the medicine woman or medicine man joined the family for an all-night "sing"—a chant that seeks to restore harmony in Navajo cosmology. On the fourth day, the girl ran toward the east and when she returned home she ate a specially prepared corn cake, which she shared with the rest of the gathering. She was now ready for marriage.

Puberty and marriage were often closely linked. When a Woodland girl began to menstruate she often prayed to the manitou, or spirits, for a good husband and healthy children. In a ceremony at her parents' lodge, the *shaman*, or religious leader, placed food in her mouth then took it out before she could eat. Repeated three times, this ritual taught the girl patience and self-discipline as she finished her transition to adulthood. For the rest of her life, when she had her monthly flow, she would join other

"Manabush was furious. He got a piece of dry birchbark and lit it. With the torch in his hand, he crept up to the door of the wigwam, pulled the cover aside and saw the Bear with his grandmother. He threw the torch at the Bear and struck him on the back, just above the groin. Frantic with pain, the Bear rushed out, through the woods and down the hill to the stream. But the flames kept burning him, and finally he dropped dead. When Manabush came up to the dead body, he carried the carcass back to his grandmother's wigwam and said: 'Here, grandmother, I have killed a bear; now we can have something to eat.'

"His grandmother asked him how he killed the Bear, but he just mumbled something, not wanting her to know how the Bear had been killed.

"Then Manabush cut up the Bear and offered a piece to his grandmother, but she refused, saying: 'No, my grandson, I cannot eat this. He was my husband.' Angry, Manabush caught up a clot of the Bear's blood and threw it at Nokomis, hitting her in the abdomen. She replied: 'For that act your aunts will always have trouble every moon, and will give birth to just such clots as this.'

"And that is why Indian women menstruate every month."

Source: Adapted from Robert E. Ritzenthaler and Pat Ritzenthaler, *The Woodland Indians of the Western Great Lakes* (Prospect Heights, IL: Waveland Press, 1983), 146–147.

women in a menstrual hut, set apart from the others. Such menstrual huts were common. Among Pacific Northwest Indians, for example, women joined one another in isolation from the rest of their community, spending the time caring for one another, sharing stories, and teaching the young girls what it meant to become a woman in the group in which they lived.

Sexuality, Courtship, and Marriage

Rules regarding sexuality, courtship, and marriage varied greatly among Indian groups. Fortunately, rituals and stories told by Natives themselves survive, helping to explain some Indian societies' views about how to behave sexually and how to choose a proper mate. Among the Southeast Indians such as the Choctaw and Cherokee, for example, the story of the Deer Woman served as a cautionary tale. In it, a young man meets a beautiful woman—Deer Woman—whom he finds sexually attractive. He falls so deeply under Deer Woman's spell that he does not notice she has hooves instead of feet. He turns away from his group to follow her, wastes away, and dies. The tale suggests that marriage for purely sexual reasons is perilous. A mate should instead possess qualities that help provide for the family and enable one to take one's place within the community of Indians, not yearn for a creature from another land. Similar stories emphasizing that lust is dangerous for an individual and the community appear among the Dakota Sioux and some California Inter-Mountain groups.

Other than Native oral traditions, little reliable information exists about Indians' sexual practices prior to European contact. European writings about Native sexuality must be scrutinized meticulously, since the newcomers

AN APACHE GIRL'S COMING-OF-AGE   Apache girls faced a four-day ceremony to mark their coming-of-age. On the last day, a girl completing the ceremony was covered with paint to symbolize the completion of the task as well as her link to the Painted Woman, part of the Apache creation story. This modern photograph shows that the ceremony survives to the present day among Apaches who follow their ancient traditions.

viewed Indian life through the lens of Christian rules and Western traditions. Most such accounts severely criticize Native behavior, particularly because Indians' sexuality, including that of women, did not follow the rules that European clergy and most other Europeans claimed to uphold.

In most Native groups, for example, heterosexual intercourse prior to marriage was often customary. Among the Huron of the Great Lakes region, not only was sexual activity acceptable before marriage, it was encouraged. A tribal matchmaker brought young people together. If a young woman became pregnant, she selected the young man she liked best as the child's father. Such socially sanctioned freedom of sexual expression scandalized many European observers, whatever their private practices. At the same time, it helped explain the matrilineal nature of such groups: one always knew who was one's mother, but not necessarily one's father. Kinship defined through the mother's line therefore made more sense.

Europeans also found other sexual activities practiced by some Native groups shocking. These included *polyandry* (a wife having more than one husband) and *polygyny* (a husband having more than one wife), practices often used by groups in which there were shortages of marriageable partners. In such situations, these marriage forms afforded all adult members access to the companionship and sustenance that a spouse provided. Some Native societies also permitted marriages to be ended easily, recognizing that people often change their affections over the course of their lives or that some spouses might prove unworthy or incapable. Some Europeans also condemned the occasional use of Native women as "gifts" to honored guests. The women Hernando de Soto received from Southeastern Indians he encountered reflected a Native custom that openly acknowledged the pleasure that sexual activity could provide to visitors. Some sixty years later, English explorer John Smith claimed to be disturbed when, at a dance welcoming him to the Powhatan Indians' village in Virginia, thirty young women crowded around him, crying "most tediously," he said, "Love you not me? love you not me?" He viewed their behavior as immodest at best.

Another shock to European senses came from Native Americans' acceptance of those whose sexual identity was fluid. Europeans brought with them the conviction that gender identity was fixed: women were feminine, men were masculine. But in Native societies, some individuals had transgender identities, with men dressing as women and displaying characteristics associated with females in their group or with women donning male garb and taking on men's activities. The sexuality of these individuals varied, although most seem to have been heterosexual. Known to Europeans as *berdaches*, these transgendered individuals could be found in Native American groups from the Midwest to Florida and Mexico to Alaska. To the Europeans' discomfiture, berdaches usually were well-respected members of their society, regarded by themselves and their group as neither male nor female but as a third, distinct gender.

Native American courting rituals and marriage practices varied. In most groups, courtship highlighted the skill and talents of the person hoping to attract a desired partner. For instance, among midwestern Woodland Indians, young men played wooden courting flutes to seek the favor of a young woman. The societies made the men play the flutes outside the bounds of the village or camp, since parents thought the notes were so sweet a girl would be unable to resist the player if he were too close. Most young Native women combined practical and emotional considerations when they chose a husband. A good provider was important, but so was attraction and affection. The right background counted too: for many groups, all of the couple's relatives and the village's political and religious leaders—the *sachem* and shaman—had to approve of the marriage because it often united two clans as well as two individuals. Marriages among Indians with high status, such as the sons and daughters of leaders, were often made for political reasons, including strengthening an alliance between groups. Thus, parents could veto a marriage, tribal leaders could veto the marriage, and the young woman herself could veto a marriage. This ability to refuse a match put Native women in a relatively powerful position to shape their lives.

Many, if not most, Native societies had no formal marriage ceremony. Instead the couple went off on their own for several days and returned to the home of the groom's father, if the group was patrilocal, or the bride's mother, if it was matrilocal, to set up housekeeping. Marriages were often celebrated by an exchange of gifts between couples and families. In most cases these gifts were symbols of the future husband's ability to provide, and varied among the different types of Native societies. Among the horticultural Pueblo nations in the Southwest, which included the Hopi and the Zuni, giving gifts at marriage maintained the proper critical balance of obedience, respect, and hard work between the parties. At the wedding, the bride and groom covered each other with blankets. The husband received a bow, a spear, a club, and a hoe, representing his role in protecting the farm and growing corn. The wife received a grindstone, along with cooking implements and serving items, symbolizing her task to cook for her husband. Among the nomadic Hidatsa in the Plains, courtship was public but marriage was private, suggested to the prospective groom by his brothers and sisters. The groom-to-be then approached the prospective bride's parents to ask for her hand, knowing that he already had his family's support and carried with him their presents for the bride. After the delivery of the gifts, the marriage ceremony took place, entailing the exchange of still more gifts between the families and the wife and husband. In contrast, the Western Apache and other Plains Indians sometimes raided other Indian groups for women to take as wives, a process of coercion, not courtship. Such forced marriages, common in a number of Native groups in North America, sought to replace women members of the group who had been captured or killed, or who had died and were no longer available as sexual partners, domestic laborers, and producers of children to maintain the group's population.

Native marriages depended upon both parties fulfilling the duties required by their sex. Among some Eastern Woodland Indian groups, a couple lived for a year with the woman's family to prove the husband could provide adequately for the marriage and that the wife could run the household. In matrilocal societies, this arrangement also allowed the husband to demonstrate that he could get along with his wife's family. Once all were satisfied, wife and husband joined the group as a couple, and the village held a public feast to celebrate.

Not all Native marriages lasted. Some ended because the husband failed to provide sufficient meat or the wife failed to perform her domestic tasks adequately. Some wives and husbands simply did not get along. Among the Hidatsa in what would become North Dakota, aggrieved parties returned to their parents' lodges, while among the Pueblos the unhappy party simply moved out of the shared home. If the marriage ended amicably between two Cherokee, the parties divided blankets, but an angry wife might simply pile her husband's belongings in front of their door to indicate that the marriage was over. In most Native groups, neither party in a divorce suffered social stigma, although some groups did discourage divorce. The Yokuts of California used marriage as a way to expand their economic holdings through kinships, added by marriage. Ending a marriage threw those kinship links into disarray, so while unhappy wives could divorce their husbands, the practice was frowned upon since such an act had profound consequences on the kin networks that organized northern California Indian groups.

Pregnancy and Childbirth

Many Native societies believed that during pregnancy, childbirth, and breast-feeding, women had heightened spiritual powers and particular needs. Some groups also believed that, like menstruating women, those who were pregnant or had just given birth could be dangerous to men. Consequently, during pregnancy women were sometimes separated from the rest of society. Similarly, because Native groups understood that healthy children were vital to community survival, many taboos arose to help women give birth to healthy babies and to protect infants. For example, Chinook women were told that if they stayed in bed too long while pregnant their babies would take a long time being born, a taboo that produced healthier babies from mothers who got adequate exercise during pregnancy. A less effective taboo directed mothers not to wear necklaces, so that the child's umbilical cord might not wrap around its neck. The Great Lakes region Potawatomi had taboos against pregnant women looking at deformed people or animals, so that a baby would not be "marked" by the experience and be born with similar defects. Women were also warned that if they ate turtles the child would have a slow, jerky gait; if they consumed rabbits, the child might have fits. These taboos were common in numerous societies to provide explanations for birth defects and other natural, if undesirable traits.

In many societies, women gave birth alone or with female assistants. While some women sought privacy in the woods, other women used menstrual/birthing huts, small ones called *wickiups,* or larger ones similar to men's sweat lodges. Many groups told women not to show fear or pain while in labor, since doing so might affect the child's spirit of courage. The power of encouragement or spirituality aside, some groups developed effective methods to ease labor pains. Cherokee women drank tea made of the inner bark of a wild black cherry tree, and the Alabamas made a similar tea from the cotton plant. Both helped lessen the pain of childbirth. Among Woodland Indians, some women used a delivery rack, a pole suspended between two supports at chest height that women held onto as they knelt to give birth. After the baby was born, mothers often preserved a piece of the umbilical cord to give to their children as a safeguard against harm.

Methods for carrying newborns varied. Plains women used hide bags to transport infants. Eastern Woodland women used cradleboards, ingenious devices with cedar backs. Attached to the cradleboard's back was a hoop that fit over the baby's head. If the cradleboard flipped, the hoop prevented the child's head from hitting the ground. Mothers nursed babies while they were still on the cradleboard, and tied babies onto their backs while traveling. Swaddled on the board, babies used sphagnum moss as a diaper, which mothers discarded when it was soiled.

On average, Native women breast-fed their children for a long time, two to four years. This practice benefited the child and also served as a form of birth control, since intensive breast-feeding often, but not always, delays ovulation. Native groups needed to control birth rates or they would outgrow the resources available to the society, and then all would suffer from want or famine. Many groups forbade sexual intercourse while women were breast-feeding. In addition, Native women used other contraceptive methods, including herbs to induce miscarriages, abortion, and sometimes even infanticide. Native societies loved, cherished, and valued children, but the survival of the community was paramount.

Adult Women's Work

In most Native societies, women controlled the household, bearing and educating children, providing shelter, cooking food, and producing and distributing clothing. In horticultural societies they often also produced and allocated food. Women often worked in groups, socializing and sharing tasks. Their work was varied, as they traveled from garden to cooking fire to water source on a daily basis. Much of women's work was physically demanding as well, particularly clearing fields in horticultural groups, scraping animal hides, building houses, and harvesting such crops as tuckahoe, a tuber the Powhatan consumed. Paddling out to the tidal marsh where tuckahoe grows, a group of Powhatan women would surround the plants and dig at their tough root system to pry them out of the mud, a process that could take twenty minutes or more per tuber. Cleaning the tubers was actually painful, since the plant contained oxalic acid. Even the simple task of grinding dried or baked tuckahoe into flour took considerable pounding with a wooden pestle in a wooden mortar. Archeologists studying Native women's bones have found evidence of heavy musculature and arthritis, indicating how strenuous women's work was.

Labor was usually sex-segregated among Native groups, based on the belief that each gender contributed to the community distinctively. Specific tasks had corresponding spiritual rituals for each sex. Before undertaking a hunt, for instance, men conducted male-only ceremonies. Women likewise held exclusive ceremonies. Cherokee women, for example, chose the date to perform the Mature Green Corn Ceremony, a time of thanksgiving for the harvest that incorporated religious worship and socializing through dance, song, and feasts. Such interdependent ways of producing such an important commodity as food for the whole group meant that each gender had its own economic power within the society and neither could claim superiority over the other, since both contributed to the group's survival. Consequently, egalitarian notions of gender characterized many horticultural societies, and the interdependency between women and men was seen as a natural result of creation.

Adult women and girls provided shelter and built the houses in many groups. Among nomadic societies, these structures were occupied during summers; among sedentary groups they were lived in all year. Native house designs varied according to the raw materials available. In the Southwest among the Pueblo, for instance, men hauled timber to the village, where women erected the walls of the houses, plastered them, and then took possession of them. Some nomadic groups had homes of deerskins or buffalo hide laid across poles set into the ground in a circle, known as *tipis*. Others had more substantial houses, such as barrel vaults made of cut saplings covered with peeled bark and furnished with mats woven from straw and grass. Many societies also allotted to women the task of gathering the materials and making the tools for building, whether from stones and shells, or animal bones and teeth.

In nearly every Native American group, women did the farming. Women often fashioned the tools they used and participated in religious rituals to guarantee a fruitful harvest before planting the crops they would later harvest. Among the horticultural Woodland Indians, in May, June, and July, women tended crops of corn, beans, tobacco, squash, and sunflowers; they gathered berries and nuts as they ripened, and searched for and preserved herbs for medicines. Among the Chippewa and the Menominee in Wisconsin, women harvested the wild rice, a diet staple that grew in shallow lakes and streams. Men paddled the canoes while women knocked the rice into the boat, then cleaned it of twigs, barks, and leaves. The cleaned rice dried in the sun, making it possible to separate the grain from its husk, called the chaff. Women then tossed the rice from large birch bark trays into the air so that the chaff blew away in the wind. They stored cleaned rice in birch bark containers they had made, to be cooked and eaten later along with the other crops they raised. Native women also made all the implements for food production and storage: birchbark trays, wooden dishes, gourd ladles, turtle shell cups, and clay pots and baskets for storage. Basketry, in particular, reflected not only women's skill in creating useful and beautiful items, but also their horticultural training. They manipulated the plants they needed for baskets by pruning, burning, and weeding, as well as cultivating the soil to ensure an adequate supply of basket-making material.

As the seasons changed, women were responsible for packing up and moving nomadic households so that hunters could begin the annual search for deer, buffalo, and other animals that provided not only food, but the raw materials for clothing as well. Among Woodland groups, after men hunted and skinned what they caught, caring for animal hides became the province of women. They scraped off the flesh from the underside and the hair from the outer side. They softened the hide by soaking it in a mixture of water and deer brains, then stretched it out on a wooden frame. The tension produced by the frame on the hide further softened it, resulting in soft, strong, supple leather that women used to produce clothing, moccasins, and many other items.

In most societies that wove cloth, women did the weaving. In the Southwest, the Pueblo and later the Navajo became well known for the quality and beauty of their cloth. The Pueblo wove first with yucca fiber, combining it with rabbit fur and feathers to make robes and baskets. Later they incorporated cotton woven on small looms. Navajo women learned this skill from Pueblo men who married into their societies, the Pueblo men in turn having learned to weave with cotton and later with wool, after the Spaniards brought sheep to the region during the sixteenth century. In Northwestern groups, women wove blankets from dog fur and the hair of mountain goats, and made clothes from shredded cedar bark that shed water in the rainy environment. Other Indians wove fabric bags of nettle fiber, buffalo wool, flax, and hemp, creating geometrical designs that depicted animals or told stories. Besides blankets, robes, and *serapes* (a shoulder wrap),

Native weavers made sashes for the waist, garters to hold leggings in place, mats for floors, and bags for storage and carrying. Women processed cattails and sewed them into covers for wigwams. They wove coiled baskets from sweet grass; wicker baskets from willow, cedar, or the inner bark of the basswood, which was first boiled and pulled into strands. Woodland societies not only used looms, but also developed stitchery to decorate items, combining thread with dyed porcupine quills. Women flattened the quills by drawing them through their teeth, then dyed them, laid them in a pattern, and stitched over them with sinew thread to hold the design in place. When Europeans arrived and brought beads, these new products began to replace quills. By making decorative items or adorning everyday tools and garments, Native women expressed their love of beauty, their creativity, and spirituality, even as they fulfilled their daily duties to themselves, their families, and their nation. European traders would quickly seize upon these useful and beautiful items, using them as trade commodities as they ventured into the interior of the country.

Caring for the health of the community was another important area of everyday life, where women and men again played important and reciprocal roles. Women tended to be in charge of childbirth and the young; men usually took care of acute illnesses. The terms medicine woman, medicine man, and shaman all referred to a member of the group responsible for medical care. Many shamans supervised specialists, such as herbalists or midwives, and had apprentices—children who seemed to have a gift for healing. Most Native Americans believed that health depended on a person being in balance with the larger natural and spirit world. Thus to cure illness, a shaman had to discover why a patient was out of harmony and then restore the proper balance. Among Eastern Woodland Indians, shamans were usually men. They danced, performed rituals, and prayed to understand the patient's illness. Among the Great Lakes groups, women often cared for the sick through more hands-on methods; for example, they performed cupping (bleeding to relieve pain or pressure) and tattooing (striking the sore area with a garfish's long lower jaw, which was covered with needlelike teeth). In addition, in many of the hunter/gatherer groups, women were the herbalists, selecting, gathering, dispensing, and applying a wide range of medicinal herbs, including versions of modern medicines such as aspirin, digitalis, quinine, belladonna, cocaine, curare, and ipecac—all used in North America prior to the arrival of Europeans.

Politics was a part of everyday life for Native Americans, including women, with the political structure of a group reflecting the complexity of its society. The Mississippian Natchez, for instance, lived under the absolute authority of one man and had a hierarchy ranging from elites to workers to slaves. The Southern Paiute, by contrast, elected their leader, who ruled based on persuasion rather than force. Among Pacific Northwest coastal societies, status and ability to rule depended on one's ability to give property away as gifts to others in a ceremony known as the *potlatch*. Many Woodland groups had little political organization and uncomplicated social structures. Some Woodland Indians, however, had strong formal organizations that incorporated women as important actors. The best known was the Iroquois Confederacy, a social and political system that began before Europeans arrived, perhaps as early as 1142, and continued long afterward. The Confederacy formed to end a long cycle of violence among its five members—the Cayuga, Mohawk, Oneida, Onondaga, and Seneca. (See Primary Source 1-2.) Operating as a vital military alliance, the Confederacy operated democratically, with decisions made unanimously. Women played an important role in the Confederacy. Clan mothers selected representatives to the tribal meetings, nominated and removed chiefs, and controlled food production and distribution, which affected diplomatic decisions. Women could withhold food supplies or moccasins, both needed to pursue war or raids, if they disagreed with the political decision to go to war. Women also often determined the fate—death or adoption—of captives. Men spoke in clan meetings on political issues, but they had come to a consensus with the women in discussions before making decisions.

In another Woodlands group, the Cherokee, women also participated directly in political life, ruling on issues in their own council and awarding the title of "Beloved Woman" to those who served the group well. Beloved Women led the Cherokee Council of Women, worked to influence the rulings of the men's General Council, served as ambassadors or peace negotiators, and had the power to commute a death sentence for condemned prisoners. Women rarely served as sachems, governing chiefdoms and leading or accompanying men into battle. The Lady of Cofitachequi in the sixteenth century, and the seventeenth-century Virginia Colony's Queen of the Pamunkey, Cockacoeske, were two of a very few. Far more common were ordinary women who participated in political and military decision-making through their roles as provisioners, either supplying or withholding goods such as corn, moccasins, and snowshoes that were critical to carrying out political activities.

Spirituality and Death

For Native Americans, as for people the world over, spirituality and religion provided ways to understand and cope with the circumstances of their lives and the reality of death. Many Native societies developed elaborate *creation myths*—stories that explained where the group came from and its meaning in the cosmos, which scholars can examine to understand the status of women in a group. For example, the Iroquoian creation stories begin with the formation of the earth when a woman who has fallen from the Sky World gives birth first to twin boys, Good and Evil, and then to the "Three Sisters" of corn, beans, and squash. The Iroquois are matrilineal and accord women political power; their creation story reflects this. In contrast, in the creation story of the patrilineal Ottawa, men spring forth from the bodies of animals. The Creator then produces women to be helpmates to men. Among the Zuni of the Southwest, a society in which women and men shared equally in the power and organization of the group's duties, the creation story centers around Mother Earth and Father Sky sharing equivalent roles in fashioning the world and the people.

FOUNDING THE IROQUOIS CONFEDERACY

One version of the story of the Iroquois Confederacy's founding highlights the important role of women and reflects their high status in the matrilineal society in which they lived by describing their role in forming the Iroquois Confederacy.

"The Peace Maker travelled among the Iroquois for many years, spreading his message of peace, unity and the power of the good mind. Oral history says that it may have taken him forty some years to reach everyone. Born of a Huron woman who was still a virgin, the Peace Maker grew rapidly and one day announced that he had to journey forth to deliver a message from the Creator. He selected a white stone canoe to carry him to the Iroquois as proof of the power of his message. But he was met with much skepticism and the men that he came across refused to listen to him. After Jikohnsaseh [a woman chief] rejuvenated his spirit, he continued and was able to persuade fifty leaders to receive his message. He gathered them together and recited the passages of the Great Law of Peace. He assigned duties to each of the

Many Native American groups believed in an afterlife. Some Pacific Northwest groups believed in reincarnation, while the Mandans of North Dakota believed that babies who died before being named returned to "Baby Hill," a special place where they waited to be born again. Burial practices were important for Native peoples, although they varied so widely that few generalizations are possible. Some groups used the occasion to reinforce hierarchical divisions in the society, so that where and how members were buried reflected their age, rank, sex, and social standing. Women tended to have lower status than men, and their burial sites reflect this, being more modest than those of men. Funerals and burial sites of powerful women, however, affirmed their importance in the society. In one case, the deceased was a Mandan woman of great power, the mother of many children as well as a person who could call to animals to come near the Mandans so that they could be hunted and the group could be fed. Dressed in her finest clothes, her face painted red, and her body oiled, this powerful woman was wrapped in buffalo hide and placed on a scaffold. Her relatives mourned her for four days, sometimes cutting themselves with knives as expressions of grief. Her bones were buried, but her skull was preserved as part of the community's sacred ground, a marker of her importance to the group.

Mourning the dead took many forms, and could be used to reinforce group ideas of proper behavior for women. Among the Menominee, for example, mourning women were not allowed to harvest the rice or touch a child, for fear of doing harm. A widow would build a "spirit bundle" of her husband's belongings, including treasured items such as a lock of hair, leaders. To honor the role of Jikohn-saseh, he selected women as the Clan Mothers, to lead the family clans and select the male chiefs. Women were given the right to the chief's titles and the power to remove dissident chiefs.... Women are the connection to the earth and have the responsibility for the future of the nation. Men will want to fight. Women know the true price of war and must encourage the chiefs to seek a peaceful resolution....

"There was initial opposition to the plan of unity from a powerful Onondaga war chief whose name was Tadodaho. He was said to be the embodiment of evil, an individual who had woven snakes into his hair to intimidate all in his presence, and he had no interest in supporting a league dedicated to peace. The Peacemaker and Hayanwatah [his supporter and a skilled orator] despaired of ever converting him until they voiced their concerns to Jikohnsaseh, a woman chief of the Cat (or Neutral) Nation. She suggested that he could be won over by being offered the chairmanship of the Great League. When the nations assembled to make their offer, Tadodaho accepted. Jikohnsaseh, who came to be described as the Mother of Nations or the Peace Queen, seized the horns of authority and placed them on Tadodaho's head in a gesture symbolic of the power of women in Iroquois polity."

Source: Frederick E. Hoxie, ed., *Encyclopedia of North American Indians* (Boston: Houghton Mifflin, 1996), 299.

favorite beadwork, or blankets. At the end of the mourning year, she could ask her husband's relatives that they release her from mourning. If she had been sincere enough to satisfy them, they released her, held a feast, and accepted the contents of the spirit bundle. If they were not satisfied, the widow would have to continue carrying and adding to the bundle until they believed she had shown appropriate respect. Then, as in many Native societies after members completed their mourning to their collective satisfaction, the group symbolically "returned" to life with a feast to celebrate the departed soul's completed journey to the afterlife.

NATIVES ENCOUNTER EUROPEANS

Dozens of different rituals, beliefs, and ways of life existed among the hundreds of Native American groups inhabiting North America prior to European contact and colonization. Europeans who invaded the continent presented conflicting views of Native groups in their reports on their discoveries. Christopher Columbus, for example, reported that the Indians he first met were "children of nature" and had no religion, so he believed they would make good servants and could be easily converted to Christianity. He also reported stories he had heard, however, of ferocious cannibals, presenting a far more hostile image of Native Americans than did others. Many Europeans reported on the striking distinctions between themselves and the people they encountered. Simply put, Native Americans did not live in the same ways Europeans did. Because of this, many Europeans regarded them as not only strange and exotic, but also inferior, and, as Native groups organized their resistance to the invaders, dangerous. To Europeans, Native Americans quickly became subjects for conversion, colonization, conquest, rule, and, often, elimination.

Europeans' assumptions about gender played a key role in determining what they thought about Native Americans. Most Europeans took these assumptions for granted, regarding them as natural, and even divinely ordained. For example, Europeans thought of agriculture as primarily men's work because in Europe men did most of the tasks in the fields. When they saw Native women going about their everyday activities, such as growing corn, Europeans called them squaws, seeing these women as drudges doing work in the fields they thought the Native men ought to perform. They condemned Native men as lazy because they did not do the same labor of planting and harvesting crops that European men either did themselves or supervised other men doing. Europeans dismissed profound social and cultural differences as savagery. To the Europeans, historian Patricia Limerick wrote, "savagery meant hunting and gathering, not agriculture; common ownership, not individual property owning; pagan superstition, not Christianity; spoken language, not literacy; emotion, not reason."

Similarly, many Europeans concluded that Indian women who had sexual relations outside of Christian marriage were immoral, believed that Natives with multiple spouses were adulterous, and pronounced Native societies, on the whole, indecent. Such attitudes toward Native peoples were not surprising, given that most Europeans came to North America convinced of their own superiority and determined to remain so. For many Europeans, the more vulnerable or accommodating a Native group was to political domination, labor exploitation, religious conversion, and wholesale cultural transformation, the better. On the other hand, when a Native society resisted subjugation and conversion, Europeans believed they were justified in forcing that group into submission, even if they destroyed the Native society in the process.

In turn, most Native Americans regarded Europeans as rather odd. Natives thought Europeans had some very foolish ideas, strange behaviors, and bizarre modes of living. Europeans had repellant body odors and ate disgusting food, both overcooked and poorly seasoned. They ignored religious rituals that were critical in maintaining the balance between humans and nature. They did not give gifts, or if they did, the gifts were far less than they should have been, upsetting the balance between host and guest. They lived in houses that were dark, cold, and drafty. They did not know how to grow corn or how to harvest and store it so they could survive in the depths of winter. At the same time, Europeans arrogantly criticized the Indians' productive horticulture and snug housing. They ignored Native women designated as negotiators and refused to talk to them, speaking only to men. Most unfortunately for Native Americans, Europeans waged war incorrectly. Rather than waging war to exact revenge or replace members of their group as most Native Americans did, Europeans sought to drive people off the land and then claim it as their own. Europeans regarded

European-style farming and settlement as the only appropriate use of land. They fought for and seized territory already in use by Native women and men who were using it in ways Europeans did not recognize as valid. These territorial struggles were also cultural clashes that had disastrous consequences for Indians.

Europeans and the Columbian Exchange

What scholars refer to as the Columbian Exchange began in 1492 when Genoese explorer Christopher Columbus, sailing under the flag of Spain, brought people, animals, and European diseases to the New World. With virtually no resistance to diseases that had circulated for centuries in Europe, Native Americans died by the millions. They contracted sicknesses from exposure to Europeans and their microbes, and spread the diseases along extensive trade routes across the continent. Just a year after Columbus' arrival, influenza struck, probably beginning in Cuba and extending to the Florida peninsula. Smallpox followed in 1518 and spread rapidly and devastatingly along trade routes as far as the Columbian Plateau in the area of present-day Washington, Oregon, and Idaho. Archeological digs in the region suggest a massive, rapid depopulation. In 1531, measles spread north from Mexico. By 1619, a three-year epidemic of either bubonic plague or smallpox had killed an estimated 90 percent of the Indians in the area that would become New England. So few Indians were left in the region that the Pilgrims, arriving a year later, were convinced that God had cleared the land of what the English colonists called the "fearful savages" as a favor to their settlement. The immensity of this demographic disaster is difficult to measure. Scholars estimate that a hundred years after Columbus arrived, the Native population of North America may have been only 10 to 30 percent of what it had been before European contact. Millions of indigenous women, children, and men succumbed to the invisible enemy—germs—that the visible newcomers brought with them.

Indians were affected profoundly by the kinds of Europeans they encountered; by the goals Europeans had for themselves and for Natives; by the trade they conducted with Europeans; by Europeans' proximity and type of settlement; and by the cultural, economic, and governmental policies, including warfare, they both pursued. While numerous European nations attempted colonization, the greatest impact on Native American societies came from the major European nationalities who first colonized the New World: the Spanish, the French, the Dutch, and the English.

The Spanish

The earliest European arrivals in the New World were the Spanish, men whose monarch directed them to "conquer and settle and reduce to peaceful life" the land and its peoples. These conquistadors and Catholic missionaries first established colonies in the Caribbean and from bases there moved into Mesoamerica—present-day Mexico and Central America. There they established military forts and slave-gathering camps, outposts designed to capture local populations to labor in the silver mines that they had taken from the Natives. Beginning in Mesoamerica and moving northward up the North American continent, Spanish soldiers enslaved, kidnapped, and forced into service Native women and men. In 1542, when the Spanish forbade enslaving Indians, after some fifty years of Spanish incursions, disease, removal, and brutal working conditions, the Mesoamerican Native population and most of their world had been destroyed. The Spanish had annihilated the organized military alliances and populous cities of the Aztecs, all for the riches—gold and silver—that were transferred to Spanish treasure ships that traversed the Atlantic Ocean back to the mother country.

Pursuing the same practices in Florida, where Native people had less complex nomadic or semisedentary societies, was impossible. In terms of trade and exportation of resources, the area also had little potential, for, despite the pearls delivered by the Lady of Cofitachequi, de Soto's explorations in the 1540s had demonstrated that Florida lacked valuable minerals. In addition, despite the Crown's instruction that Spaniards convert the Natives to Christianity, the conquistadores had little success. De Soto's secretary claimed in his recollection that Native women were baptized more for men's "carnal intercourse than to instruct them in the faith." By 1565, when Pedro Menéndez de Avilés established the first North American colony at St. Augustine, he and the Spanish monarchy resolved to avoid the mistakes that had caused so much suffering and destruction and had cost the Crown so much money in Mesoamerica. Instead of enslaving the Native American population and setting them to work mining gold and silver to fill Spanish treasure ships, the Spanish Crown proposed instead the "missionization" of Indians in the southeastern region of North America. Roman Catholic priests would convert Natives to Christianity, and then force converted Natives to work at feeding and supporting the Spanish missions—a yearly obligation of all single men called the *repartimiento*. By converting and then performing punishing toil for the benefit of their conquerors, Natives could escape the eternal damnation the Spanish assumed would be imposed by their Christian God. The missions thus would serve the Crown's goal of establishing outposts to protect the treasure ships as well as "saving" the Indians from their fate.

By 1625, the missionization project in Florida had spread northward into what became modern-day Georgia, but it did not last. In the enclosed mission settlements, young Indian men, fulfilling the *repartimiento*, fell prey to outbreaks of disease and died, or carried the diseases back to their villages and infected their communities. Others fled, unwilling to fulfill the incessant demands of the Spanish. Young women, deprived of single men as marriage partners, did not have enough children to replace those who died, contributing to Native depopulation. As Floridian Native societies collapsed, Indians from the north invaded their lands, capturing any who remained and selling them as slaves farther north. By the end of the seventeenth century, the Spanish had largely abandoned their missions and the Native societies of Florida had all but vanished. Descendants of the Lady of Cofitachequi and others had succumbed to European diseases, warfare, and enslavement. By 1708, when the only Spanish mission left was the one in St. Augustine, the groups indigenous to Florida had disappeared, replaced by *mestizos* (people of mixed Spanish and Native descent) and by Seminole Indians who had migrated south from the Creek Indian lands in Georgia. The few survivors from Native groups in the area joined forces with others, forming new societies to protect themselves from the European conquerors.

In contrast to the southeastern debacle, the Spanish missions established in the Southwest and California proved much more long-lasting. Spanish explorer Francisco de Coronado surveyed the region in 1540, searching for the fabled Seven Cities of Gold. He did not find them, but instead discovered Pueblo Indian settlements along the Rio Grand River that flowed through the interior of present-day New Mexico. As de Soto had done in Florida, Coronado and his men ate most of the stored food of their Native hosts, raped many of the Indian women, massacred numbers of Indian men, then moved north, seeking riches to take back to Spain. Such conquistadors were followed or accompanied by Franciscan friars in charge of missionization. By the late sixteenth century, Spanish missionaries and soldiers moved into Pueblo country in New Mexico and Arizona. Determined to meet their goals of political control and religious conversion, missionaries and accompanying soldiers offered the Pueblo Indian groups Christian conversion. Those unwilling to convert were frequently subjugated; some were executed. As in Florida, the Spanish established the institution of the *repartimiento* to reinforce their power, requiring labor and time from the local Indians as a form of tribute payment. Native men were required to build houses for the Spanish, herd their livestock, and grow their crops; Indian women, meanwhile, did all the domestic labor for the soldiers and clergy as well as for their own families.

The Spanish also sought to enforce European notions of gender roles on the Native population. Pueblo women, for instance, had considerable power in these matrilineal horticultural societies because they were responsible for food production and controlled land use. They were used to choosing their own marriage partners and ending marriages without sanction from the group. The Spanish missionaries insisted that men should be the builders and the farmers, not women. They also taught Natives that monogamy and chastity were paramount moral values and that marriage was a lifelong commitment. As other European conquerors would do, the Spanish sought to impose not only their economic and gendered labor systems on Natives, but also their religious values. Pueblo Indians resisted, often subtly, preserving their culture in the *kivas* (religious centers) and village plazas, while adopting the outward forms of Christianity to appease the Spanish clergy and the military.

Spaniards also reshaped the environment and Native ways of life by introducing domesticated animals to the New World, notably sheep and horses. Sheep provided wool, which the Navajo and Pueblo used to weave blankets, serapes, and other items prized by Native groups with whom they conducted a lively trade. Native Americans throughout the Southwest and the Great Plains rapidly adopted horse riding, enlarging their hunting territories and changing their tactics of warfare. Over time, increased reliance on horses transformed formerly horticultural societies into semisedentary or nomadic groups, as different Native groups coped with the invasion of their lands. Such structural changes to their societies transformed Native women's lives. The status and economic power they exercised in horticultural communities diminished as the groups became more reliant on men hunting for food to sustain their new way of life.

The French

The French colonists who came to the New World were, like the Spanish, overwhelmingly male and Catholic. The French established settlements far to the north in the continent, where they took a different approach from the Spanish to the religious conversion of Natives. The main French missionaries to the Natives were the *Jesuits*, members of the Society of Jesus, a group dedicated since 1534 to spreading the Catholic faith to the unbelieving. They accompanied French traders to Native American settlements, learned indigenous languages, and adapted to Native ways of life, residing in their villages and eating their food. Jesuits believed willing conversion was more effective than forced imposition of a foreign faith.

French explorer Jacques Cartier had traveled up the St. Lawrence River in 1534 and claimed the land he traversed for his homeland. Calling the vast territory New France, the French allowed fishermen, traders, and missionaries into the region, but a permanent French settlement was founded only in 1608, when Samuel de Champlain built Quebec. Like other Europeans who came to the New World, the French wanted to find and take whatever valuable resources they could. In their case, the prime resource was fish, which they found in tremendous abundance in lakes, rivers, and especially along the Atlantic coast. The French also engaged in the increasingly important fur trade with the Indians for beaver pelts. European beavers, which had long been used to make hats, were hunted to near extinction by the seventeenth century. American beaver pelts replaced the overharvested European beaver and the trade in furs proved lucrative for the French as well as for some Native Americans.

The vast fur trade, stretching hundreds of miles from the Atlantic Ocean to the lands beyond the Great Lakes and the Mississippi River, had dramatic and long-lasting effects on Native groups. In exchange for harvesting beaver, many Indians had regular access to European products for the first time. Native women traded fur pelts for needles and woolen and cotton cloth to produce clothing, for steel awls to pierce deerskin used in making clothing and shelters, for glass beads to use for decoration instead of porcupine quills, and for iron kettles and pots to use as cooking vessels instead of the clay or birchbark they previously had made themselves. One Jesuit observer described the variety of trade goods available, listing the contents of the ships that arrived in 1620 at Tadoussac, in the Gulf of St. Lawrence. They held, he wrote, "cloaks, blankets, nightcaps, hats, shirts, sheets, hatchets, iron arrowheads, bodkins [thick needles], swords, picks to break the ice in winter, knives, kettles, prunes, raisins, Indian corn, peas, crackers or sea biscuits, and tobacco." Natives who obtained such goods in trade usually substituted them for familiar products, seeking to make their daily activities less arduous and time-consuming. Cooking in a copper kettle, lighter and more durable than clay pots, freed Native women from having to make pots that broke easily. Trading for corn and peas meant women no longer had to spend their time growing their own crops. Using wool to make garments meant not having to spend weeks curing animal hides and fashioning them into clothing.

The effect on the material aspects of Indian life was rapid and pronounced. Less obvious but no less profound was the impact such trade had on the practice of traditional skills that had served as the economic base of Native societies. As Indians embraced European wares, skills for self-sufficiency withered away in one domain after another: in planting and harvesting, fashioning clothing and housing, making tools for hunting, conducting ceremonies, and storing and cooking foodstuffs. At the same time, Woodland Indians pursued the beaver to near extinction, changing their hunting patterns to focus almost exclusively on beaver. Commenting on this transformation to a Jesuit missionary, one Indian joked that the power of the beaver to replace traditional Native activity was vast: "it makes kettles, hatchets, swords, knives, bread; in short, it makes everything."

As Native men spent more time hunting, away from their villages, women became far more dependent on themselves or on European traders for the goods they needed. Such disruption of traditional patterns had far-reaching effects on Native groups in the areas where the French traded and where a few eventually settled. The territory claimed by the French was vast: New France, by 1612, extended for miles along the northern and southern sides of the St. Lawrence River from the Atlantic west to the Great Lakes and beyond. *Voyageurs*, men employed by fur companies to transport pelts from Native hunters back to trading outposts, paddled their canoes thousands of miles through rivers and lakes. These were often the first Europeans that Native Americans encountered. Many *voyageurs* formed intimate relationships with Native women, some of which were long-lasting and affectionate, and others of which were short term and exploitative. As the numbers of marriageable Native men declined due to disease and warfare, more Native women married French voyageurs, trappers, and traders. Native women in these relationships often gained substantial material benefits, in the tangible form of goods the French brought into their country. Whether they were married to Frenchmen or not, Native women were targets for missionizing, and Jesuit priests succeeded in converting some to Catholicism. Notably, Kateri Tekakwitha, a Mohawk convert, eventually was beatified by the Catholic Church (her canonization as a saint is pending) and is regarded as a patroness of ecology and the environment. Other converts included the offspring of mixed marriages called *métis*, who would play important roles in the fur trade in the future.

Among Europeans who arrived in North America in the sixteenth and early seventeenth centuries, the French had the least hostile and destructive policies toward Native peoples. They extracted resources in vast quantities—fish and furs, primarily—from New France and incorporated Native men and women into the process of procuring these commodities. The French fur trade made Natives part of an international market economy that over time reached into the heart of the North American continent. Their actions transformed the daily lives of Native women and men and drew them, on very unequal terms, into a transatlantic system of exchange. By doing so, they wrought tremendous changes in the economies and cultures of Native societies.

The Dutch

The Dutch, the greatest trading nation in seventeenth-century Europe, viewed the New World as a golden opportunity to expand their commerce and holdings. By 1609, Henry Hudson, an English explorer working for the Dutch, had explored what became known as the Hudson River Valley as well as parts of Canada. Settlers soon followed, and by 1624 some thirty families had settled in the province of New Netherland. In 1629, eager to settle more Dutch in the area, the Dutch West India Company and the government of the Netherlands awarded patroonships—large landholdings—to patroons who promised to bring fifty settlers to the area.

Relationships between the Dutch and the Native Americans of the region centered around the fur trade. A prosperous trade developed up and down the Hudson River as Iroquois hunters brought beaver pelts down river to be exported to Europe. To guard access to the river and protect the trade, New Amsterdam, later New York City, was founded at the mouth of the river in 1625. Women traders, called "she-merchants," played an active role in the fur trade. Dutch law, unlike most European law, allowed women to enter contracts and conduct business. One of the most famous she-merchants was Margaret Hardenbroeck, who arrived in the city of New Amsterdam in 1659. Beside raising five children, she built an empire of trading ships and took furs to Europe, returning with finished products to sell. She became the wealthiest woman in the colony. Women also could be patrons. Colonist Maria Van Cortlandt Rensselaer, widowed at an early age, held onto her late husband's patroonship, despite attempts by his relatives to take over after his death. Some of the richest land of the colony, the patroonship was twenty-four square miles and included gristmills to grind grain and sawmills to process rich harvests of timber. Women also ran a number of different businesses. Tryntje Jonas, employed by the Dutch West Indies Company as a midwife for the colony, lived in a house the colony built for her practice. Sara Roeloef, fluent in English and Algonquian in addition to her native Dutch tongue, worked as a translator for leading businesses in the city.

The Dutch claimed the territory of Manhattan they first settled by giving trade goods to the Canarsies, a nearby Native American group. The Canarsies accepted the goods from the Dutch in exchange for the land despite the fact that they knew the territory belonged to another group, the Weckquaesgeeks. The Weckquaesgeeks made repeated unsuccessful attempts to oust the Dutch from Manhattan, but finally were annihilated in attacks by the Dutch in the 1640s. Having eliminated the Native American threat to their colony, the Dutch turned their attention to English interlopers in the region who were interfering with the trade between the Pequot Indians and the Dutch.

The Pequot Indians occupied land in current-day Connecticut and had established trading relations with the Dutch. Their colonial competitors, the English, sought more land and greater access to the Atlantic coast, and eventually attacked a Pequot fort near modern-day Mystic, Connecticut, killing hundreds by setting a fire that burned alive, not the Pequot warriors, but instead the women and children of the town. The bloody victory thus ensured English control over the region by destroying the Pequots and driving away the Dutch traders. By 1640 the English regularly used their Connecticut lands to sail south to the eastern end of Long Island, where they settled in communities such as Southold and Southampton. From those sites, they could take advantage of a small-scale war that had broken out between the Dutch and Indians on the western end of the island. The Dutch won that conflict and pushed the Indians off the island, but by the 1660s, English colonists took advantage of a series of wars between England and the Dutch and began raiding settlements in New Netherlands. In 1664, the Dutch colony fell to the British fleet. Despite a Dutch return to the area in 1673, the colony was transferred again to England at the end of the Third Anglo-Dutch War in 1674. Thus the Dutch lost their struggle to keep their American colony, just as the Swedes, rulers of a short-lived colony along the Delaware River, had lost their own settlement to the Dutch in 1655.

The English

Spanish, French, and Dutch influence on Native Americans' lives would pale in comparison to the English influence in the lands that would become the United States. While all the European nations established extensive trade with Native Americans and sought to convert them to their particular Christian practices and beliefs, the English were exceptional in seeking to establish colonies that would serve as outlets for a growing and impoverished population at home. This policy had drastic consequences for Natives Americans.

In the early seventeenth century the English began transplanting whole families to colonies along the Atlantic coast, housing them on lands used for millennia by various Native groups. As the English became more entrenched in North America, they undertook the wholesale removal of Native societies that stood in the way of their desire for land. Over nearly two centuries, they used various methods to get rid of the Indians. Knowing that Indians had little experience with and tolerance for strong drink, they provided them with alcohol in exchange for treaties, then broke those same treaties when they had outlasted their usefulness. The English removed Natives, particularly those who had converted to Christianity, to segregated communities and, eventually, to reservations. Occasionally they exterminated whole villages through warfare, using advanced European weaponry and tactics that killed men, women, and children. As was true of other European groups, the English, largely unwittingly and perhaps most disastrously, infected Indians with European diseases, demolishing Native

JOHN SMITH'S STORY
OF POCAHONTAS

John Smith's history of his days in Virginia contained a suspect tale of his relationship to chief of the Powhatan people and is the first recording of the tale of Pocahontas, a tale that assumed mythic proportions in American history. By using the dismissive word "wench" and describing a scene where a queen was required to serve him, Smith helped the Europeans understand that, despite the visible hierarchies in Indian society, Native Americans could still be regarded as inferior to white Europeans.

"At last they brought him to Werowocomoco, where was Powhatan, their emperor. Here more than two hundred of those grim courtiers stood wondering at him, as he had been a monster; till Powhatan and his train had put themselves in their greatest braveries. Before a fire upon a seat like a bedstead, he sat covered with a great robe, made of raccoon skins, and all the tails hanging by. On either hand did sit a young wench of sixteen or eighteen years, and along on each

populations. The English then established settlements on the virtually depopulated lands.

The first permanent English colony came in 1607 when a group of merchant adventurers landed in Virginia on a peninsula of land between the James and York rivers. They called the tiny settlement Jamestown, in honor of England's king, James I. In 1608, more colonists arrived, including the first two women at the site, a Mistress Forrest and her servant, Anna Burras. Jamestown settlers benefited from their proximity to the Powhatan Confederacy, an alliance of some thirty Native groups in the Tidewater region, who provided food to the hungry colonists. As the English demanded more and more food and supplies without extending the reciprocal gifts the Natives expected, however, the relationship between the two groups deteriorated. An uneasy peace was restored when a young woman named Matoaka, or Pocahontas, daughter of Chief Wahunsonacock (leader of the Confederacy and called Powhatan by the English), negotiated a resolution between the Indians and the colonists.

Captain John Smith, an early leader of the colony, later wrote a self-aggrandizing and influential book about his experiences in the Virginia colony, called *The Generall Historie of Virginia, New-England, and the Summer Isles*, and published in 1624. As ethnohistorian Helen Rountree has pointed out, Smith and other Elizabethan Englishmen leave much to be desired as reporters. Their patriarchal cultural assumptions and fear of Indian resistance to the English colonists provide what she characterizes as a "myopic emphasis on men's activities: war, politics, and religion." Women show up in the records primarily as purveyors of corn, which the colonists had to purchase to survive at Jamestown. However, Smith does tell one story, that of Pocahontas. (See Primary Source 1-3.) That story has become the most commonly told tale of the interactions between Native women side the house, two rows of men, and behind them as many women, with all their heads and shoulders painted red, many of their heads bedecked with the white down of birds, but every one with something, and a great chain of white beads about their necks. At his [Smith's] entrance before the king, all the people gave a great shout. The queen of Appamatuck was appointed to bring him water to wash his hands, and another brought him a bunch of feathers, instead of a towel to dry them. Having feasted him after their best barbarous manner they could, a long consultation was held, but the conclusion was, two great stones were brought before Powhatan: then as many as could laid hands on him, dragged him to them, and thereon laid his head, and being ready with their clubs to beat out his brains, Pocahontas, the king's dearest daughter, when no entreaty could prevail, got his head in her arms, and laid her own upon his to save his from death: whereat the emperor was contented he should live to make him hatchets, and her bells, beads, and copper; for they thought him as well of all occupations as themselves. For the king himself will make his own robes, shoes, bows, arrows, pots; plant, hunt, or do anything so well as the rest."

Source: *Complete Works of Captain John Smith (1580–1631)*, ed. Philip L. Barbour, vol. 2 (Chapel Hill: University of North Carolina Press, 1986), 150–151.

and white men in the days of contact. Smith's narrative of Pocahontas still permeates American culture and has contributed to popular views of Native American women that survive today.

During a hunt in December 1607, Powhatan's men had captured Smith and several other settlers. Smith wrote that he was brought before Powhatan, warriors placing his head on a stone as they prepared to execute him. At this critical moment, Powhatan's young daughter Pocahontas begged for Smith's life. When Powhatan refused, she persisted. According to Smith: "the Kings dearest daughter, when no intreaty could prevaile, got [Smith's] head in her armes and laid her owne upon his to save him from death: whereat the Emperour was contented he should live to make him hatchets, and her bells, beads, and copper." Saved from what was not a real but a mock execution, a practice devised to impress Europeans with Powhatan's power, Smith returned to Jamestown. As president of the colony, he erected a larger and stronger fort to protect the colonists, built more houses, planted crops, and traded successfully with the Indians. Injured by a fire in 1609, he returned to England, where he began to tell the stories that would make him a celebrity in his day and a famous historical figure in time.

Images of Native Women in Colonial Women's History

In popular memory, Pocahontas fades from view after her supposed rescue of John Smith, but her later life warrants a closer look. Pocahontas seems to have been a genuine favorite of her father and of Smith. In bridging the gap between the two groups these men led, she fulfilled an important

POCAHONTAS SAVES JOHN SMITH   One of the most striking images of Pocahontas, a young girl at the time of her alleged rescue of John Smith, is shown here in a painting commissioned by the federal government under the auspices of the Works Progress Administration (WPA) during the Depression (see Chapter 8). Here, Pocahontas tries to prevent two Indian warriors from clubbing Smith, while her father raises his hand to stop them. This romanticized image of the young woman with flowing hair, exposed breast, and graceful pose reinforced her role in American history as a noble Indian princess.

traditional role undertaken by many Native women, serving as a negotiator and mediator between the Native Americans and the English. She often brought food to the English fort at Jamestown, and it seems that she enjoyed the settlers' company, although after Smith's departure she visited less frequently. In 1613, Jamestown's new ruler, Captain Samuel Argall, used her continued association with the colonists against her. Argall kidnapped Pocahontas, demanding that her father release English prisoners that he held. Powhatan complied with a partial payment, and Argall moved Pocahontas to a new English settlement, Henrico (today's Richmond). A year later, Argall attacked the Indians, hoping to get the rest of the ransom. By then, Pocahontas had converted to Christianity and planned to marry Virginia planter John Rolfe. They married, a union that both Powhatan and the English approved of as a diplomatic measure that would restore peace between the English and the Powhatan Confederacy. In 1615, Pocahontas, who had taken the Christian name Rebecca, had a son. That year she and her family left for England, where Pocahontas was displayed to the English court. Arrayed in English clothes and jewels, she was hailed as a Native American princess. In 1617, as Pocahontas prepared to sail for home, she contracted a disease—most likely tuberculosis, measles, or smallpox. She died in 1617 and was buried in Gravesend, England.

The tale of Pocahontas has been retold often in American history, providing a story that served two primary functions. A curiosity for the English of her day, she also became a symbol of their hopes: the English wanted North America's Native population to be docile, eager to help the colonists, and easily rendered both thoroughly English and fully Christian. The story of her rescue of Smith, along with the facts of her marriage and conversion, her beauty and amiability, reassured the English that they would succeed in exploring and settling a land populated by people very unlike themselves, but educable in English ways and customs.

Her story also created an image of Native American women that has endured for centuries: that of the noble Indian princess. In 1616, while she was at the English court, Pocahontas had her likeness preserved in an etching by a Flemish engraver, Simon van de Passe. Reproductions of this etching and countless similar images of her reached a huge audience in both England and America. Over the centuries, her image appeared again and again in the material culture of America, in venues high to low. As early as 1808, her story became a piece of theater in the popular play *The Indian Princess* by James Nelson Barker. Carved into the U.S. Capitol rotunda in 1825 was a rendering of her saving Smith's life. More recently, the Walt Disney Company produced a feature-length animated film titled *Pocahontas* (1995). Aiming to present a story they deemed more respectful to Indians, the filmmakers acknowledged the Natives' respect for nature—and the English colonists' lack of it. However, the film also romanticized her relationship to white men and sexualized Pocahontas, turning her into a curvaceous, dark-skinned, wide-eyed, mature woman. The film and its surrounding commercialization, which included material goods from dolls to lunchboxes to bedsheets, enshrined Pocahontas as a benign, beautiful, and loving Indian princess and, as such, a fit object for elite white men's desire as well as corporation profits.

The Disney film did put Pocahontas in the midst of the action, seeking to convey what the company's project historians, William Rasmussen and Robert Tilton, said was "the essential element of the story" of her role in the early days of English colonization. She was "an individual of unusual energy and vision who influenced the course of history." Such a portrayal was reiterated in 2005, when a major film version of the Pocahontas story, *The New World*, appeared, starring a young Native American woman. Fifteen-year-old Q'Orianka Kilcher, of Quechua/Huachipaeri heritage, portrayed Pocahontas in a film that sought to portray her life more accurately. Filmmaker Terrence Malick used Native Americans as extras and incorporated recent historical research on Native American lives, as well as de-emphasizing the Smith rescue to present a more nuanced portrayal of the relationship between the English and Pochantas. Such continuing interest testifies to the unique place of Pocahontas in American popular culture, if not in the annals of American history. The saga of Pocahontas continues to hold the attention of Americans. Only one other Native woman has received anything close to comparable notice by scholars and the public: Sacajawea, famous for her role in the early nineteenth-century Lewis and Clark expedition that explored the interior of the country.

In stark and revealing contrast to the noble image of the Native American princess represented by Pocahontas and Sacajawea, the English developed a second enduring representation of Native women: the highly derogatory image of the squaw. The English mostly likely took this term from an Algonquian word *squáa*, meaning "woman." They used it indiscriminately, applying it to virtually all Native women they encountered. For them a squaw was a dirty, menial worker, almost a beast of burden, commanded to do lowly labor by the lazy men of their tribes. Observers who could not understand or did not approve of the sexual division of labor that differentiated European and Native societies filed reports and published travelogues that became important sources for the view that Native women served as little more than slaves to their slothful husbands. For many white men the squaw, thus devalued, seemed human enough only to be a target of their lust, a proper subject for sexual servitude as well as harsh domestic labor and casual or calculated violence. Thus can be explained de Soto's demand, referred to at the beginning of this chapter, for women, as well as slaves, gold, and other goods. All were commodities in the eyes of invading European men.

The simplistic and racist images of noble Native princess and filthy Indian squaw held sway over many Europeans and, later, Americans in their dealings with Indian women. Reinforced and elaborated over the years, these images helped to blind Europeans from seeing the realities of Native American women's lives and led to deep distortions and vast omissions in the historical record. There can be no single history of Native women, despite the stereotypes Europeans sought to cast across all Native American groups. Along with their commonalities, women lived in different Indian societies, at varying times, in various environments. Women encountered a wide range of Native and European groups, all with differing circumstances, beliefs, hopes, and experiences. Although individual interactions varied, in the end the Europeans' refusal to accommodate the people they encountered and their zeal to trade, own, and accumulate created a cycle of hostility and destruction. As diseases decimated Native groups in North America and as the Spanish, French, Dutch, English, and other Europeans pressed upon the remaining Native population from all sides, many Native Americans abandoned their customary lands, trying to get away from the colonizers. Others took up arms. While they won some battles, in the end Natives did not succeed in turning back the tide of European men and women determined to settle the New World their way.

THINK MORE ABOUT IT

1. Return to the opening vignette about Spanish conquistador Hernando de Soto and the woman he called the Lady of Cofitachequi. How does the story of this encounter exemplify themes important for

understanding Native women's lives and the encounters between Native women and Europeans?

2. Identify the seven regional cultures of Native peoples. Explain the differences among these regional cultures, paying particular attention to geographic locations, economic patterns, and lineage practices. Why did women in matrilineal horticultural societies tend to have more social and political power than those in other types of Native societies?

3. How did Native women's life-cycle patterns across these seven regional cultures lead to substantial resemblances in the conduct of their daily lives?

4. Various European groups and diverse Native groups both had gendered labor systems. What were the key differences between how most Europeans and most Native societies understood the appropriate economic activities for women?

5. Identify at least ten items that Native women in various societies produced for their groups. How did some of these patterns of production change after contact with various European groups? What effects did such changes have on Native women?

6. Think more about the stereotypes of Native women as either noble princesses or squaws and how these images have persisted in American culture. What do these stereotypes tell you about those who developed and sustained them?

7. What did you learn in this chapter that you did not know before? How does this new information help you understand the overall story of women in American history? What topics would you like to explore further?

READ MORE ABOUT IT

James Axtell, *The Indian Peoples of Eastern America: A Documentary History of the Sexes*

Carol Berkin, *First Generations: Women in Colonial America*

Colin G. Calloway, *New Worlds for All: Indians, Europeans and the Remaking of Early America*

Charles Hudson and Carmen Chaves Tesser, eds., *The Forgotten Centuries: Indians and Europeans in the American South, 1521–1704*

Patricia Limerick, *The Legacy of Conquest: The Unbroken Past of the American West*

Helen C. Rountree, *Pocahontas's People: The Powhatan Indians of Virginia Through Four Centuries*

KEY CONCEPTS

horticulturalist

hunter/gatherer

matrilineal

patrilineal

matrilocal

patrilocal

life cycle

shaman

sachem

berdache

potlatch

creation myths

Jesuits

noble Indian princess

squaw

Chapter 2

WOMEN COLONISTS IN SEVENTEENTH-CENTURY ENGLISH AMERICA

Lady Deborah Moody of Gravesend, New Netherland

WOMEN IN PUBLIC LIFE

THINK MORE ABOUT IT

READ MORE ABOUT IT

KEY CONCEPTS

Lady Deborah Moody, an English widow, arrived on the southwestern tip of present-day Long Island, New York, in July 1643. The land was empty, momentarily unoccupied by Europeans or Native Americans, but claimed by the Dutch. In 1645, this Dutch colony of New Netherland granted Moody a patent to the lands she and some friends had settled upon. There Moody built Gravesend, the only permanent colonial settlement planned and designed by a woman. The town was built around a sixteen-acre square. Two

REMBRANDT'S *YOUNG WOMAN AT AN OPEN HALF-DOOR* Rembrandt's portrait of a Dutch woman leaning out of a "Dutch" door in 1645 could very well resemble Lady Deborah Moody, given the fashionable attire and necklace worn by his subject. Lady Moody, as was true for many colonial women, no doubt tried to maintain as many of her home customs as possible, including her dress.

roads bisected the square, dividing it into four sections, with ten house lots on each. A one-acre commons anchored each section, and hundred-acre farms known as boweries radiated out in triangular form from the center of the village, for all the world like the spokes of a bicycle wheel.

Moody was born in London in 1586. Her husband, Sir Henry Moody, died when she was only thirty-three. Some twenty years later, she emigrated to the English colony of Massachusetts Bay after converting to Anabaptism, a Protestant religious sect that opposed the baptism of infants, then the custom in most Christian sects. Massachusetts Bay Colony, which claimed all of the lands known today as New England, tolerated very little difference of opinion in religious matters. Moody's beliefs conflicted with those of the Puritans in charge of Massachusetts Bay, and they regarded her, according to Deputy Governor John Endecott, as "a dangerous woeman." As did others, Moody left Massachusetts Bay to find a more hospitable home elsewhere in the New World. The director-general of New Amsterdam, William Kieft, allowed Moody to settle and organize Gravesend. Less concerned than the Puritans of Massachusetts Bay with creating a religiously monolithic colony, the Dutch allowed Gravesend's settlers to worship as they pleased within their homes, although public worship in the colony continued to be that of the Dutch Reformed Church, the official church of New Netherland.

Dutch tolerance of religious dissenters was one reason why Deborah Moody was able to organize Gravesend. Another reason was because she enjoyed more rights as a woman under Dutch law than she did under English law. Dutch law considered women partners with their husbands, rather than dependents. They were allowed to enter contracts as legal individuals even if married. They could own businesses and property, buy and sell goods and land, borrow money and make it. As surviving spouses, Dutch widows inherited half of their husbands' property outright, and could administer the rest on behalf of any other heirs. Dutch women active in business thus had long-standing legal rights to property. However, those same rights, as well as women's economic activities, were sharply curtailed when the Dutch lost the colony of New Netherland to the English.

The English brought to their new colony laws, customs, and traditions that affected the colonists' daily lives, especially women's lives. British law denied married women the freedom of action that Dutch colonial women had. By the time the English took power, Moody had passed from the scene but Margaret Hardenbroeck, used to conducting business as a she-merchant since her arrival in North America (see Chapter 1), watched the decline in the number of women actively involved in commerce. In 1655, New Netherland had 134 women working as independent traders. By 1700, after the English had been in control for a generation, the records listed no women as independent traders. No doubt many women still worked in the trading economy of the colonies, as well as in the transatlantic trade the Dutch were famous for. Until her death in 1691, for instance, Hardenbroeck still actively supervised a fleet of vessels, trading in wheat, fur, and even Native American *wampum* (oyster-shell beads used as money). As a woman colonist under English law, however, her daughter Catherine could not represent herself and protect her business interests in a court of law, having to rely instead upon her husband to do so. English laws regarding married women's rights limited their abilities to act as entrepreneurs, and affected all women colonists, regardless of their nationality.

Differences in women's legal status and their abilities to participate in the colonial economy reflected the control European powers sought to exercise over American spaces. All Europeans brought to their colonies their religious traditions, laws, and customs, affecting colonists' daily lives. The English were not the only colonists in North America in the seventeenth century, but the eventual success of the English colonies ensured the eventual dominance of English legal, social, and economic systems. British colonists who settled the vast region along the Atlantic seaboard carried their common cultural assumptions with them. These assumptions were affected by both environment and demography, and two distinctive regional cultures emerged in English America: one in the Chesapeake Bay area and one in New England. The rise of the tobacco economy in the Chesapeake region created a huge demand for labor, filled first by indentured servants from England, then by African slaves. As a southern slave society developed, with increasingly rigid laws to define and control slaves, the Chesapeake's high mortality rates and overwhelmingly male population had profound implications for white women's lives in the region as well. In New England, by contrast, the religious practices of Puritans, a remarkably healthy climate, and the immigration into the region of entire families and few slaves resulted in a different kind of English society there. While women colonists appear in historical records in unusual circumstances such as in times of war or when behaving in ways society considers inappropriate, for most colonial women, life within the household would continue to shape their everyday lives.

CULTURAL TRANSPLANTS

Over the course of the seventeenth century, the English came to dominate the eastern edge of North America with the exception of Spanish Florida. Other European powers never reached the numerical force that the English did, even though they maintained colonies in North America. Some colonies were made up almost entirely of soldiers manning forts, as was the case for the Spanish in Florida and the Swedes in short-lived New Sweden, later called Delaware. The French colonies in the New World stretched from the Atlantic Ocean to the Great Lakes and the Mississippi River Valley (including much of present-day Canada), but were populated almost entirely by men—trappers, traders, and Jesuit priests—with a few Ursuline nuns also serving as missionaries. French attempts to increase the number of settlers met with little success. New families were created as marriages took place between Native women and French traders, with important consequences for Native groups (see Chapter 3). The French government, however, refused to recognize such marriages because they were not performed by the Roman Catholic Church. To strengthen the colony, King Louis XIV (1643–1715) sent marriageable young Frenchwomen, known as *les filles du roi*, or "the King's Daughters," to the New World to marry French colonists. From 1663 to 1673, nearly 1,000 young women arrived in New France, courtesy of the royal government. They received dowries, then grants for marrying and having children. Eventually, settlers produced enough children so that New France became a series of small settlements rather than just a string of trading outposts, but eventually royal attention to New France waned and by the end of the seventeenth century only about 14,000 French citizens lived in New France.

During that same period, English immigration grew rapidly. By 1700, there were 250,000 English colonists in North America. The English often transported whole families to their colonies and seldom married Native Americans, preferring to wed other English colonists. They imported as well common assumptions about the nature of society and the proper, God-given roles of women and men. The numerical superiority of English settlers and the transplantation of their culture and laws meant English traditions would become prevalent in what would someday become the United States.

Western Christianity

Religious understandings about the proper role of women greatly affected the laws that were transported to the colonies, and the degree to which those laws were modified by the circumstances in which colonists found themselves. Many writers and preachers who explained Catholic and Protestant theology, including Anglicanism (the official church of England and its colonies) and Puritanism (the church of New England), emphasized that the original sin of Eve made all women untrustworthy. Eve's sin was to disobey God by enticing Adam to eat from the Tree of Knowledge. God banished the couple from the Garden of Eden as punishment. As a result of Eve's disobedience, most Christians believed that woman's proper place was within the household, under the authority of the husband. Theologians also cited the teachings of the early Christian writer Paul, who wrote in the New Testament that "women should keep silence in the churches." "Keeping silence" meant that women should neither teach, nor hold any authority over men. In 1645, Governor John Winthrop of Massachusetts Bay Colony made note approvingly of this patriarchal model, writing that "A true wife accounts her subjection [as] her honor and freedom, and would not think her condition safe and free, but in subjection to her husband's authority." Linking the governing of one's family with religious beliefs as well as with the civil government—the state—defined the early English settlements, as it did life in England. Throughout the colonies, the notion that civil government should be separate from the church was foreign to most colonists. Many colonists thought God had led them to the New World, and that the way to maintain His blessings on the venture was to be sure they did not turn their backs on His rulings once they had arrived. Those rulings, defined by Western Christianity, held that the patriarchy was the God-given plan for ruling both family and state.

Religion and politics, a source of unrest in the Old World, mixed more easily in the colonies. Virginia required heads of households in the colony to pay taxes to support the state church, the Church of England, but allowed dissenters to reside in the colony. Maryland, founded in 1632, allowed colonists to practice Catholicism. After that colony passed the Toleration Act of 1649, followers of other Christian sects could practice their faith there, as long as the practitioners agreed on the validity of the Trinity

ALBRECHT DÜRER, ADAM AND EVE The biblical story of Adam and Eve informed much of Western Christianity's interpretation of women's roles in society and their relationship to men. This 1507 painting by Albrecht Dürer portrays Eve with the apple and the serpent, next to the Adam she is about to tempt.

(the Father, Son, and Holy Spirit of Christianity). Pennsylvania, founded in 1681 by William Penn, served as a safe haven that permitted members of all faiths to practice their religion without fear of religious or political persecution. Even Quakers, a dissenting Protestant group often persecuted in other colonies as well as in England, were safe in Pennsylvania, as were Quaker women who could even be religious leaders.

Religiously minded colonial political leaders drew from church ideals to craft laws and define acceptable behavior for the governed. The belief that women should be subject to their husbands combined the ideas found in the Bible's book of Ephesians, that women are to be subject to their husbands as their husbands are subject to the church, with the more secular notion that the family was a "little commonwealth," where the leader ruled to benefit all those who were dependent upon him. The "familie is a little Church, and a little commonwealth . . . a schoole wherein the first principles and grounds of government and subjection are learned," wrote English clergyman William Gouge in 1622 in his work *Of Domesticall Duties*. The patriarchal, hierarchical family to which Gouge referred was the household, the basic unit of English society. It included wives, children, servants, apprentices, and other dependents, all of whom relied on the head of their household for both guidance and sustenance. An Englishman had authority over, as well as responsibility for, all within that household. Women within the household, he wrote, must be subordinate to their husbands. "She may do nothing against God's will, but many things she must do against her own will if her husband require her."

English Law

English civil law also defined acceptable behavior in the colonies, as well as defining political power in government. In England, men of property controlled government. Property ownership was the key to achieving political power, since people who owned property were believed to have a vested interest in ruling a society properly; that is, they would rule for the benefit of those with and without property. In addition, voting rights were limited by one's religion (voters were Protestant and members of the state church) and one's legal status (freemen could vote; servants and slaves could not). Only a very few men in England could vote or hold office.

In the new colonies, these restrictions continued to define the franchise. One of the earliest acts toward governing the colonists took place even before the Pilgrims, some of the earliest English colonists, disembarked in 1620. Onboard their ship, the *Mayflower*, the men of the colony signed Mayflower Compact, agreeing to obey the laws that the civil body of the Plymouth Colony, their New England settlement, would devise. No women signed the compact. Indeed, no women were allowed to vote or participate in politics in either seventeenth-century England or in its colonies, since women were not thought intelligent enough or moral enough to do so, even if they were property owners, Protestant, and free. Self-government was limited to men, who then governed the women in their lives for their own good. Any voting that men did supposedly benefited women, as men both represented and protected the interests of their dependents in their society.

In Plymouth Colony, government was at first limited to church members, so-called saints, as opposed to "strangers," meaning members of the colony who did not belong to the church. In Massachusetts Bay Colony, founded ten years later, only men who were shareholders in the company (who also had to be church members) could vote at first. Eventually, the franchise was extended to all men who were neither slaves nor indentured servants. These so-called freemen could vote for the governor and the ruling council. In Virginia Colony, voting was also restricted. There, beginning in 1619, only elite men who were both free and property owners could vote for their "burgesses," as the representatives to the colonial government were called. In the colony of Maryland, freemen quickly formed a two-house legislature to govern the colony. As other colonies formed, self-government continued to exclude certain individuals. All women—single, married, property owners or not—were unable to vote. Indentured servants also had no right to participate in politics until after they were freed. Once slavery was made lifelong and inheritable, slaves had no hope of participating in the formal political system. In these ways, the English colonies reflected the same limitations on voting that the mother country had.

Although the legal system did not transfer wholesale across the Atlantic, transplanted English laws served as the foundation for colonial laws. Each colony modified traditional English laws to fit their circumstances, imposing standards of acceptable behavior and greatly affecting women's lives in the new colonies. *Substantive law* found in the Mayflower Compact and in colonial charters, organized and governed the various colonies, defining colonists' rights and duties. *Statute law* spelled out legislation and regulations in legislative acts and, eventually, law books. Unwritten, *common law*, based on custom, tradition, and legal precedent, was accepted by the courts because its evidence was deemed apparent to all. A common-law marriage, for instance, was one where all in the community acknowledged a couple as married because all in the community could see a couple acting as if they were married. Another kind of law, and the one most useful to colonial women, was *equity law*. Equity law, practiced in chancery courts, supplemented or overrode other laws to protect constitutional rights and enforce duties. Used primarily by elite women who had the most access to any courts, equity laws could make the interpretation of statute law or common law more fair. For example, ordinarily under English law a woman's property became her husband's at marriage. A married woman could use equity law to protect her property and let her keep control of it after the marriage took place.

English laws were gendered, which meant that laws differed in the way they treated men and women. They also differed in the way they treated single women and married women. These differences meant that women were defined legally in different ways. Single adult women were defined as *feme sole*, a term meaning "woman alone" or "single woman." Single women had many of the same legal rights as men. They could participate in the economy, for example, by entering contracts, suing in court, owning property, and running businesses. They had no political rights to speak of, but neither did most men in the seventeenth century.

The majority of women colonists married, and once married, their legal status became *feme covert*. This meant that a wife was under her husband's protection and authority. Her legal identity was "covered" by her husband's. Under this English law referred to as *coverture*, wives ceased to exist as separate legal individuals. They underwent what was termed a *civil death* at marriage. Coverture was based on Christian interpretations of marriage. Under coverture, the "two become one," a reference to the book of Genesis and its description of marriage. The "one" that the two became was the husband, and the wife's civil rights—particularly her property rights—were defined by her husband's status, severely limiting her former freedom to act as a legal individual.

In practical terms, coverture meant that women had little or no control over "real" property, which was real estate, both land and buildings, and, in some colonies, slaves. If a woman did own real property, her husband could control it, administer it, improve it by building upon it—or not—and do to it pretty much as he wished. He could, however, sell land that she owned only if she agreed. As far as a woman's personal property was concerned, under the law of coverture she lost the legal ability to own personal items when she married. Once a woman married, she no longer owned her clothing, her bedding, her jewelry, her books, her pots and pans, and, in some colonies, her slaves. The ownership of her personal property passed to her husband and he could do with it as he would, including sell it, dispose of it, or use it as collateral for a debt. The last meant a woman might find herself evicted from her home and left without a bed to sleep in or pot to cook in if her husband's loan was called to be repaid and he had insufficient funds to do so.

Once married, a woman also lost the legal rights she had enjoyed as a *feme sole*. She could no longer sue or be sued or make a contract, not even a will that disposed of her property without her husband's consent. She could not act as a legal individual in her own right. Given the precariousness of colonial life, this lack of power for women could be quite troublesome, as some colonial authorities came to recognize. If a husband traveled on business, was captured by Indians, or deserted his wife, for instance, a woman could not run the family business because she was not a legal individual. English towns in the medieval era had similar issues and devised a legal device called *feme sole* trader, which allowed married women to act as if they were single for purposes of business. English colonists transplanted and used the same law, reflecting the reality of women having to survive in the colonies when the men in their lives were gone or otherwise indisposed. It was often used by women who had been deserted by their husbands. Since divorce by desertion was the most common form of divorce in colonial America, the ability of women left alone to carry on was critical. *Feme sole* trader status provided women with opportunities to take care of themselves.

Women who were married also enjoyed some legal protections designed in part to provide for them after the death of their mates. A married woman had *dower rights*—specific rights to some of her husband's property simply because she was married to him. Even if she had not contributed financially at the beginning of the marriage, dower rights acknowledged a woman's economic contributions to the household over the course of a marriage. A married woman received a set amount (usually one-third) of a "life interest" in all the real property her husband owned at his death. That meant she could use that property, called her *thirds*, during her widowhood. If the property was a farm, for instance, she could not dispose of it or sell it, but she could live there, take care of the children who would inherit it, stay on it even if the heirs wanted her to leave, harvest one-third of the crops produced on it and sell them to support herself, and spend one-third of the interest of her husband's investments if she needed cash. Life interests usually lasted as long as widows did not remarry.

In some English colonies, dower rights also included provisions to take care of a wife if a husband died without leaving a will. In such cases or when a husband left property to someone other than his wife and did not provide for her in his will, most colonies allowed a widow some support for herself despite any provisions in the will to the contrary. Decisions in these cases were sometimes made by chancery courts using equity law—those laws that made "fairness" possible. What was probably more important than fairness for the community leaders, however, was preventing widows from having to rely on the local government for poor relief. The care of destitute widows (and orphans) often fell on the towns or counties in which they lived. English Poor Laws, brought to the American colonies, called for taxes to supply the poor with the necessities of life. These laws also could require towns to hire out poor widows or women deserted by their husbands and left without means so they could earn their keep. Towns might even pay a family to take someone in if the destitute individual could not work for her keep, an expensive proposition. Thus, laws preserving some property for widows benefited the town as a whole.

Beyond the institution of a widow's thirds, inheritance laws were gendered in other ways. In some colonies, under the practice of *primogeniture*, the firstborn son inherited everything unless the father made a will declaring otherwise. In other colonies, sons automatically inherited twice as much as daughters did if the property owner died without a will. Property ownership was so fraught with peril for women at marriage that some elite women used premarital contracts to avoid the limits on property ownership that they faced when they married. These contracts were for the well-to-do, however, not for the common folks. Wealthy elite fathers would use them to try to preserve their daughters' property for grandchildren. By giving a daughter control of her own property, family holdings might be protected from wastrel husbands.

The English did not transfer laws dealing with government and property rights wholesale to America, but modified some and wrote others to meet the circumstances in particular colonies. What students of history must keep in mind, however, is that the laws of the land were not always enforced. A frontier community more than 3,000 miles away from England, beset by conflict with Native people and possessed of a tiny population struggling to survive, could not hope to put every law into practice. Nevertheless, the ideas expressed in those laws had lasting power in the American colonies, establishing an underlying framework that undergirded women's legal status in all the colonies.

REGIONAL VARIATIONS

English colonial settlements in the seventeenth century clustered along the eastern seaboard, with easy access to the Atlantic. From these areas ships could resupply settlers with provisions and settlers could eventually export raw materials to England, then import England's finished goods as part of the great trade system known as *mercantilism*. Under mercantilism, colonies were regarded as both sources for raw materials and markets for finished goods, existing to increase the wealth of the colonizing nation.

While English colonies had much in common, there was considerable variation early in the century between the two regions first settled. The first colonies England established in North America were founded primarily for profit by joint-stock companies, chartered by the monarch. Stockholders in the companies hoped for profits from gold and other precious minerals, along with trade items from the Indians and raw materials harvested from American forests, such as lumber for ship masts. The English were experienced in settling "plantations" as their earliest attempts were called, named the same as English plantations in Ireland after that country had been forcibly conquered under Elizabeth I. The so-called wild Irish the English had subdued in Ireland in the sixteenth century had a counterpart in the so-called wild Indians of America. The English mindset that viewed the Native Americans, like the Irish, as little more than beasts to be conquered would guide their policies toward the Native men and women of the New World throughout their colonies.

The Chesapeake

The earliest settlement at Jamestown, in the Virginia Colony, began in a region hostile to survival—swampy land, brackish water, and an organized military alliance of Native Americans. Despite attempts by Pocahontas to help the settlers keep the peace with the Powhatan Confederacy (see Chapter 1), by 1622 the Virginia Colony was under attack by Indians determined to rid their shore of the invaders. This attack failed, as did another in 1644, and the English foothold in the region known as the Chesapeake (which included the colonies of Virginia and Maryland) survived.

The first company of adventurers who arrived in the colony in 1607 numbered 108. All were men. Two women arrived the next year and several more in 1609, including one Temperance Flowerdew, who eventually married the colony's governor, George Yeardley. Flowerdew, unlike many others, survived the early years in the colony. Most of her acquaintances in Virginia died of deprivation during the horrible winter of 1609 to 1610, known as the Starving Time. Powhatan, whose own people faced starvation in the midst of a terrible drought, refused to supply the colonists with any of the corn his group had stored for the winter. Although the colonists had some food in reserve, it was stored at Point Comfort, a dangerous journey away from the protective fort. Women and children colonists could not safely make the trip, and the colonists were forced to stay within the fort during the harsh winter. Virginia had 500 colonists that fall; fewer than 100 were alive at the end of the winter. Surviving colonists told stories of eating all their animals, including cats and dogs, then vermin, then shoe leather. At least one man was executed after having killed and allegedly eaten his wife (see Primary Source 2-1). Conditions were so bad that the survivors planned to abandon the colony. Their plans changed in the spring of 1610 when new supply ships carrying 150 new colonists, again almost all men, arrived.

Determined to prevent another such calamity, new laws were passed to teach the new arrivals the importance of leaving the Indians alone to prevent retaliatory attacks, husbanding scarce resources to prevent starvation, and keeping the fort clean to prevent disease. Male colonists were forbidden

GEORGE PERCY'S A TREWE RELACYON OF THE PROCEEDINGS AND OCCURENTES OF MOMENT . . . IN VIRGINIA

George Percy, youngest son of the ninth Earl of Northumberland who would replace John Smith as president of the colony in 1610, *wrote another version of Virginia Colony's troubles. His work* A Trewe Relacyon of the Proceedings and Occurentes of

to "ravish or force any woma[n], maid or Indian, or other," a crime now punishable by death, and no one—"man or woman"—was allowed to run away from the colony and join the Indians. No one was allowed to steal from a garden or kill livestock for food without permission from the council. A laundress employed to wash the "foule linnen" of another was not to trade it for poorer quality linen. If she did, she would be whipped and "lie in prison" until she made restitution. Coercing colonists with such laws was necessary, argues historian Kathleen Brown, since the colony had so few married English women to provide sexual partners for the English colonists, to plan for food distribution and consumption, and to perform other necessary domestic tasks.

In 1614, the colony entered a new stage of development when John Rolfe, husband of Pocahontas, successfully grew a strain of tobacco that thrived in Virginia and could be marketed to England. Tobacco, usually smoked in pipes or used as medicine in the form of snuff, or powdered tobacco, was in great demand throughout Europe. By concentrating on the production and sale of this crop, Virginia moved from a precariously settled backwater to a profitable colony that required permanent, long-term settlement that needed even more men and women as workers and servants.

Servants and the Tobacco Economy

Tobacco, long a staple for religious and medicinal purposes among Native Americans, became known in Europe when European sailors returned with samples from the New World in the sixteenth century. By the end of the century, the palliative powers of the plant were promoted in literature such as *Joyfull Newes out of the Newe Founde Worlde: Of the Tabaco and of His Greate Vertues* by Nicolas Monardes, a Spanish physician who claimed tobacco would cure thirty-six ailments. Despite disagreement from opponents, including the English king James I who wrote *A Counterblaste to Tobacco* in 1604 to dissuade his subjects from the demon weed, tobacco proved popular, addictive, and increasingly expensive, as the Spanish sought to control its production and distribution.

Moment . . . in Virginia (1625) *relates the disappearance of one anonymous woman colonist.*

"And now famin beginneinge to Looke gastely and pale in every face, thatt notheinge was Spared to mainteyne Lyfe and to doe those things w[hi]ch seame incredible, as to digge upp deade corpes outt of graves and to eate them. And some have Licked upp the Bloode w[hi]ch hathe fallen from their weake fellowes. And amongste the reste this was most Lamentable That one of our Colony murdered his wife Ripped the childe out of her womb and threw it into the River and after chopped the Mother in pieces and salted her for his food. The same not being discovered before he had eaten Part thereof for the w[hi]ch Crewell and unhumane factt I adjudged him to be executed. . . ."

Source: From *Virginia: Four Personal Narratives* (New York: Arno Press, 1972), 267.

Spanish tobacco from its colonies in the New World was pleasantly fragrant, according to its devotees, and controlled by a Spanish monopoly. In contrast, Virginia-grown tobacco was harsh, and Europeans would not smoke it. Colonist John Rolfe began to experiment with Caribbean tobacco seeds, the same kind the Spanish tried to keep exclusively to themselves, under penalty of death, and grew his first successful crop in 1612. By 1616, he had developed an English version of tobacco that compared favorably to the Spanish product. He had married Pocahontas in 1614, no doubt having learned much from her about how to cultivate the tobacco plants that the Powhatan grew so successfully. Rolfe and Pocahontas traveled with their son to England to discuss the successful crop with British officials. Despite the king's dislike of the noxious weed, the market craved it, the taxes it brought to the treasury were substantial, and the Chesapeake colonies had finally discovered a money-making enterprise that ensured their continuation. By 1617, the colonies exported 20,000 pounds of tobacco; by 1629, over 750 tons left America for England.

Tobacco cultivation was labor-intensive; women and men both took part. Tiny seeds were planted in seedbeds, then thinned, then transplanted—a four-month process. When the plants were three or four feet high, they were trimmed and "topped" to limit the number of leaves they produced, ensuring quality. They had to be inspected weekly to remove side shoots called suckers, and daily to remove pests that could destroy the entire crop. Harvesting was done by the individual plant, since all ripened at different times. Leaves were individually hung to dry in tobacco barns, then sorted, twisted into ropes, rolled into balls, and placed in casks for shipment. Planting started in January; the crop was usually harvested in August or September.

Because it was so lucrative and successful, the tobacco crop determined the way of life in the Chesapeake. It produced a land-hungry society because it grew best in previously uncultivated soil, stripping the nutrients from the soil as it grew. Demand for land rekindled conflict with the Native Americans in the region, and led to the uprisings in 1622 and 1644. It also demanded massive amounts of unskilled labor, which meant indentured servants and slaves were imported by the Virginia Company and, after the

The TOBACCO - MANUFACTORY in different Branches.

Engraved for the Universal Magazine 1750 for I Hinton at the Kings Arms in St Paulschurch Yard London

SLAVES AND THE TOBACCO INDUSTRY   In this engraving, an African slave woman hangs the leaves to dry with her child (right), while another slave strips the leaf. The man in the center rolls the leaves together, while the man on the left winds the rolled leaves to prepare them into a tobacco rope for shipping. The ropes of tobacco were packed tightly into casks for export.

company lost its charter and the colony became a royal colony in 1624, by the Crown.

Many of the emigrants to Virginia and the Chesapeake were *indentured servants*, men and women who signed a document called an indenture that promised their labor for four to seven years in return for an employer paying for their passage across the Atlantic. England's high unemployment rate, burgeoning population, and food shortages in the sixteenth century had driven many into poverty. By the seventeenth century, American colonies were seen as one way out of that desperate poverty, and many emigrants were among the truly desperate. Colonist Jane Wenchman, for instance, was picked up by English authorities and charged with vagrancy, or being homeless. They sent her to America as a servant, a sentence that probably kept her from starving in England. Other women were forced into servitude when their husbands or parents died, or the businesses they worked for closed. Of all the people emigrating to the Chesapeake area over the course of the seventeenth century, 75 to 80 percent came as indentured servants, contracting with employers to work for a fixed number of years in exchange for the employer paying their fare.

Women who emigrated as indentured servants were prevented by law from marrying or becoming pregnant until their indenture was done. If servants violated the terms of their indenture, they could have their terms of service extended as punishment. Becoming pregnant was the most common violation for women. About 20 percent of the indentures contracted in the colony of Maryland, for example, were extended because the servant became pregnant. Some of these pregnancies resulted from forced sexual relations. Women in isolated colonial settlements found it particularly difficult to resist a determined master. Trying to prevent rapes, colonies passed laws that penalized a master who impregnated his indentured servant. The pregnant woman's extra term of service was then sold to a different master, so that her extra labor would not benefit the man who had sexually exploited her. Colonial governments also tried to identify the fathers of children born to indentured servants to force them to support the child. If their fathers could not be determined, children were apprenticed by local governments until they reached adulthood.

Indentured servants who finished their terms of service were released at the end of their years of service. Their employers furnished them with "freedom dues," which included clothes, sometimes a few acres of land, tools and a ration of corn to tide them over until they could find work for themselves. They also gained the right to marry. For many women emigrants, however, living conditions in the Chesapeake were so harsh that they died even before they finished their indentures, and their ability to marry and start their own families was sorely limited.

Slavery

While indentured servants often came to America under duress, they could look forward to the day when they would be freed from their obligations. Other women coming to the Chesapeake region in the early years of the seventeenth century did not have the same option. African women arrived in Virginia in 1619, when three African women and seventeen African men arrived on a Dutch ship that had taken them from a Portuguese slave ship. The women and men were traded to local planters in exchange for supplies. These Africans may have been regarded as indentured servants—that is, able to work off their service and become free over time. England did not yet have African slavery (and would not charter a royal slave trading company until 1672), but the French, the Spanish, and especially the Dutch traded in slaves, competing with one another to supply workers for the sugar, coffee, and tobacco plantations located in the islands of the Caribbean and the South Atlantic. Since these plantations primarily needed strong male laborers, the vast majority of slaves sent to the islands were men. There were, however, women forced into slavery as well—Africans captured by slave traders and brought to American colonies.

Over the course of the seventeenth century, slaves became a critical source of labor in the Chesapeake because of the labor required for the tobacco crop. Slavery as a lifelong status, rather than a temporary condition for a set number of years, was legally established in the 1640s and became an inheritable status soon thereafter. The first evidence of that change came in 1649, when a Maryland man left three slaves and "all their issue [children] both male and Female" to his heirs. In 1652 in Virginia, a young African girl was sold, and the bill of sale included the phrase that the sale of her self included "her issue and produce during her . . . Life tyme. And their successors forever." This kind of provision meant that children born to slaves were to be slaves themselves, and that slaves were "chattel," or personal property. Later court cases continued to define children of slave mothers as slaves, a legal view that helped maintain slavery in the English colonies. Laws that required fathers to support their illegitimate children, no matter who their mother, were ignored in favor of laws that ensured slaveowners would not be held accountable for impregnating slave women. Any children born to slave mothers who had been raped because they were slaves were the property of the owner. They were seldom acknowledged as his kin. Because slaveowners did not suffer any financial and few social repercussions, some owners sexually exploited slave women that they owned, often seeking to increase their supply of workers as the labor-intensive agriculture in the region continued to grow.

In the Chesapeake, women servants and women slaves all worked in the fields, laboring from sunup to sundown, first light until it was too dark to see, working for fourteen to sixteen hours in the summer. Many women, despite being exhausted after laboring in the fields all day, returned to their dwellings and turned to doing work for their own families: caring for children and the sick, cooking food, quilting bedcovers, and mending tattered garments. They also grew what crops they could to improve their family's meals, taught their children their history, and participated in religious rituals.

Demography and Family Life

The need for women in the Chesapeake, an overwhelmingly male region, was acute. Englishwomen provided necessary domestic labor in the realm of food preparation and storage, clothing, cleaning, and laundry, in addition to serving as sexual partners for Englishmen, many of whom had discovered that Native women were not interested in their attentions. In 1619, a shipload of fifty-seven women came into port at Jamestown. During the next three years, another ninety women arrived. Most came seeking husbands, who were in greater supply in Virginia than in England. Many had their passage paid for by men seeking wives or servants—120 pounds of tobacco each, six times the price for a young male indentured servant.

To provide wives for male English colonists, the company needed to provide incentives for women to come to America. The Virginia Company provided a "headright" to those who paid for the transportation of settlers—fifty acres of land to settle and farm. Englishwomen, most of whom could never hope to own land in England, could own acres of it in America, since the offer of a headright was extended to women settlers who paid their own passage as well. Women could also marry in the colony more easily than in England, where there was a shortage of marriageable men throughout the seventeenth century. Company authorities were anxious for both men and women to marry because married men and women caused less trouble in a society than did single people. Married women also provided domestic labor and produced children, both necessary for the growth and stability of the colony.

Most women who took advantage of the opportunities afforded by the Chesapeake colonies were deemed "respectable" by English society, an important characteristic for the colonies' organizers as they sought to create families in the New World. Ann Jackson, who traveled to America with her brother, was the twenty-year-old daughter of a gardener. Alice Richards came too, a widow at twenty-five. She had been recommended to the Virginia Company for passage in part because, a church official wrote, "shee hathe demeaned herself in honest sorte & is a woman of an honest lyef." While some women who came from England were young and married soon upon their arrival, 70 to 85 percent of emigrants in the first half of the seventeenth century came as servants and had to complete their service prior to marriage. For women, such a relatively late age at first marriage (in their midtwenties) meant they had fewer children, and despite the goals of the colonies' organizers, the population could not grow by natural increase. As a consequence, the Chesapeake remained "a land of newcomers," as historians Lois Carr and Lorena Walsh have documented.

English colonists in the Chesapeake were subject to high mortality rates, largely because of the environment. By 1649, more than four decades after the first settlement, only about 18,500 English lived in Virginia and 600 in Maryland, for instance, despite the large numbers that had emigrated there (perhaps 60,000 by then). Many contracted diseases such as malaria, imported into the region from infected immigrants who spread the disease to mosquitoes; others died from typhus and dysentery due to poor sanitation, and still others succumbed to salt poisoning from drinking brackish water. Women were particularly vulnerable to the harsh conditions, as pregnant women seemed particularly susceptible to malaria, and the additional rigors of childbirth in the wilderness cost many women their lives. Demographers estimate that a woman who reached the age of twenty in the Chesapeake region most likely would die by age thirty-nine, and usually from childbirth; men would live five to ten years longer. Native-born women, on the other hand, married at much earlier ages than did their immigrant mothers, since the native-born women were not indentured and did not have to wait to marry.

Because of what demographers call a *skewed sex ratio* of far more men than women in the Chesapeake through the end of the seventeenth century, wives were in high demand, and most native-born women married before age twenty-one. In 1625 in Virginia, 75 percent of the population were men, and by 1650, the ratio was six men for every woman. In 1650 in Maryland, there were 600 men but only 200 women. As late as 1698 in York County, Virginia, there were 487 men but only 309 women. It was so rare for a woman not to marry that when one unmarried woman died at a ripe old age in Virginia Colony, the *Virginia Gazette* newspaper reported the fact that she was unmarried as the lead to her obituary.

Marrying Native American women was seldom seen as an option for Englishmen. As the increasing English population sought ever more land to grow still more tobacco, relations with the Indians deteriorated. The Native–English marriage between Pocahontas and John Rolfe was one of diplomacy as well as affection and was an anomaly among the two populations. Most Native women regarded Englishmen contemptuously, deeming them poor providers and weak warriors. They saw Englishmen begging Natives for corn to survive the winters, then stealing from them if the grain was not forthcoming. They also saw Englishmen as lacking self-control. Oppossunoquonuske, a female *werowance* (or chief) related to Powhatan, used Englishmen's desires against them, luring them out of the Jamestown fort by promising them sexual favors from the women in her group, then ambushing them.

Englishwomen in the Chesapeake faced undreamt-of hardships, along with unknown opportunities. Life was spartan and dangerous, and homes were tiny dwellings. Attacks from Indians angry at the invasion of their lands were always a risk. Moreover, women's daily round of work was far different from that in England. The complex society they left behind presumed that most women's work was inside the house and in the kitchen garden, not in the agricultural fields. Women did conduct businesses in England, but their commercial activities were largely connected to the domestic world, such as brewing beer, making lace, sewing clothing, or helping their husbands run a tavern or inn. But in the colonies of Maryland and Virginia, where growing tobacco had become the main preoccupation, women worked in the tobacco fields alongside men, hoeing out the weeds, tilling the soil, picking off the tobacco worms, and harvesting the leaves. In England such fieldwork would have been the domain of men, but in the Chesapeake only wealthy married women could replace their own labor with that of servants or, later, slaves.

Any notions these early women colonists may have had that they could start the kind of businesses women ran in England, such as producing butter and cheese for sale, soon fell by the wayside as the English colonists planted tobacco everywhere, from house to barn and even in the streets. Not until late in the seventeenth century did the economy begin to diversify, and women began to employ their skills in home industry, such as spinning yarn and making clothing, as they continued to contribute to the family economy.

New England

While many Englishwomen migrated into the Chesapeake region as individuals, usually as indentured servants, in the New England colonies women most often migrated as members of families. Here, religious impulses played an important role in their reasons for migration. The New England colonies, which included Massachusetts Bay, Rhode Island, and Connecticut, all had early settlements founded by religious dissenters who sought a safe place to practice their faith. Several of these colonies, including the largest, Massachusetts Bay, formed religiously closed communities. The founders of this colony had dissented in England; in America they created intolerant societies in which all who settled were required either to belong to a single established church or, at the least, to conform to its rules and practices.

Thus religious tensions roiled the New World, as they did the old, with important consequences for the women who settled in New England.

Puritanism and Its Significance

In the sixteenth century England had undergone great upheaval over religious issues. King Henry VIII (1509–1547) split from the Roman Catholic Church and formed the Anglican Church (the Church of England), a Protestant sect that denied the pope's power over the members of the church. The Anglicans kept many forms of the Catholic religious service and hierarchy, but also incorporated many of the beliefs that Protestant groups elsewhere in Europe had developed after the Protestant Reformation began in 1517. Two were most important: the idea of the priesthood of all believers, meaning no priests were needed to mediate between people and God; and the second that scripture—the Bible—alone was adequate for ruling Christians, rather than including Catholic Church laws as well. The Reformation had been launched because of disagreements over theological questions as well as complaints about corruption in the Catholic Church. By the seventeenth century, religious dissenters in England and other countries formed still more Protestant denominations, including Presbyterians, Calvinists, Lutherans, and Anabaptists. The two most important dissenting sects in England were the Separatists, who sought to separate from the Anglican Church, and the much larger group, the Puritans, who sought to purify it. In addition, reform-minded Catholics struggled to bring the Protestants back into what they believed was the one true church.

Politics intersected with these religious divisions. In England, Henry VIII's elder daughter Mary (1553–1558) tried to reinstate the Catholic faith by force, but failed. After Henry's second daughter became Queen Elizabeth I (1558–1603), she carefully balanced the interests of Protestants and Catholics to preserve civil order. Under her successor, James I (1603–1625), England remained Protestant, but James I launched new controversies. To gain more power over his kingdom, he announced his belief in "divine right absolutism," an ideology that argued that monarchs were answerable only to God. As common as this belief was among European monarchs, it conflicted with a basic tenet of Protestant sects such as the Separatists and Puritans. They believed themselves subject first to God, then to their king. Because they believed this, they refused to join the Church of England. Since church membership was a requirement of the state, these dissenters were regarded with suspicion and often discriminated against. Members of these two groups searched for a way to live peacefully in England, but many refused to compromise their religious ideals. They were among the first British emigrants to the New World. Beginning in 1620, they settled in a region that came to be called New England.

The first group of English Separatists, known as the Pilgrims, arrived in 1620 off the coast of Massachusetts and settled in an area where diseases carried by earlier European explorers and traders had destroyed the local Native population. Determined to separate from the English church, the Pilgrims considered Anglican theology false, and viewed belonging to the

Anglican Church as a violation of biblical precepts. Persecuted for their views in England, in 1607 they had fled to Holland, attempting to make a way of life for themselves. After over ten years of economic discrimination by the Dutch, and wanting to raise their children speaking English, the expatriates left Holland for Virginia, where they hoped to found a settlement where they might practice their faith. Led by William Bradford, 101 settlers and soldiers left Holland aboard the good ship *Mayflower*. Eighteen women were among the passengers, three in their last trimester of pregnancy. Eleven girls also made the journey.

A storm pushed the *Mayflower* off course, and the Pilgrims landed not in Virginia but much farther north, in the cold waters off the coast of Cape Cod. There, the women spent the winter onboard ship, while the men built houses and storage facilities. The fresh air and hard work may have kept many of the men alive—only half of them died as compared to three-quarters of the women. By spring 1621, Plimoth Plantation had been built, but half the colonists were dead.

English colonists who settled north of the Chesapeake faced far harsher winters but, at first, they enjoyed more successful relations with Indians than did their southern colonial counterparts. Disease and starvation took a toll on the colonists, and the weather was so cold that the seeds the Pilgrims brought to plant for food did not germinate. With help from the Pokanokets, members of the nearby Wamponoag nation, as well as from Squanto (Tisquantum), a local Pawtuxet Indian who had learned English after being kidnapped by earlier explorers, the remaining Pilgrims survived. They also benefited from a peace alliance with the Pokanokets against the Narragansett Indians who lived to the south of the colonial

GEORGE HENRY BOUGHTON, *PILGRIMS GOING TO CHURCH* George Henry Boughton's early-nineteenth-century painting of Pilgrims walking to church in the woods of New England, with women and children protected by armed men preceding and following them, gives some indication of the perils English colonists saw around them. It also exemplifies the proper dependent role of Englishwomen—caring for children, protected by men.

settlement. The settlers harvested enough corn, furs, and lumber, that by 1621 they were ready to hold a celebratory feast that Americans commemorate today as the first Thanksgiving. The colony's relatively poor soil and lack of access to fishing grounds and furs limited its growth, however, and it was soon overshadowed by Massachusetts Bay Colony.

There lived the second major group migrating to New England—the Puritans. Like the Pilgrims, the Puritans were religious dissenters, striving to cleanse what they viewed as a corrupt Anglican church. Still, they were less radical in their critique of the Church of England than the Separatists—they thought the Church was salvageable. Like the Pilgrims, the Puritans migrated mostly as families, hoping to replant a purer version of England in a much larger and more successful colony, formed to the north and west of the Pilgrims in what is today Salem, Massachusetts. Some 1,000 religious dissenters arrived in 1630, and between 1630 and 1643, another 20,000 English emigrated to the Massachusetts Bay Colony to settle in small towns and govern themselves according to English law and Puritan religious tenets. They formed communities in what became parts of current-day New Hampshire and Maine, as well as Massachusetts. Led by men who held both religious and civil power at the same time, the Puritans established communities where the church was the locus of both spiritual and political power. Puritans believed that they had been chosen by God—they were "the elect"—to establish what Massachusetts Bay Colony Governor John Winthrop, quoting the Bible, called a new "Citty upon a hill" where the rest of the world could see how to live if they wanted God's blessings to be given to them.

Gender and the Social Order

With their goal of establishing a model community in mind, and aware, as John Winthrop said, that "The eies of all people are uppon Us," Puritans were concerned that colonists behave properly. They had a rigid sense of what constituted proper behavior for women, as well as men, and their laws and customs reflected these ideas. Many of those who settled in the colony but disagreed with the Puritan worldview found themselves hauled before the General Court, the ruling body for the Massachusetts Bay Colony. If they were found guilty of disobeying the colony's laws, including its religious doctrines, they could be banished from the colony—sent away from the community into the wilderness—or sentenced to death, punishments equal in their end results. In this way, the colony tried to remain true to its mission of reflecting God's design for all to see.

Some dissenters who left or were expelled from Massachusetts Bay Colony formed colonies of their own. Rhode Island, founded in 1636, owed its existence to Roger Williams. He believed in tolerance, the absolute freedom of religious conscience, and the absolute separation of church and state, so that government did not corrupt religion. Connecticut, the other New England colony founded by a religious dissenter, was formed by Thomas Hooker and others in 1637. Hooker believed in allowing all freemen, not just church members, to vote and govern themselves. He led one hundred followers to Connecticut to found a colony on those beliefs.

THE TRIAL OF ANNE HUTCHINSON

Gov. John Winthrop of Massachusetts Bay Colony met his match in Anne Hutchinson. Cowed by neither his intellect nor his position, Hutchinson took Winthrop to task in her trial in 1637, insisting her revelations from God were true. He banished her not only on the religious grounds of heresy, but also on the grounds she represented a threat to the community and was unwomanly in her behavior.

Gov. John Winthrop: Mrs. Hutchinson, you are called here as one of those that have troubled the peace of the commonwealth and the churches here; you are known to be a woman that hath had a great share in the promoting and divulging of those opinions that are the cause of this trouble . . . you have spoken divers things, as we have been informed, very prejudicial to the honour of the churches and ministers thereof, and you have maintained a meeting and an assembly in your house that hath been condemned by the general assembly as a thing not tolerable nor comely in the sight of God nor fitting for your sex, and notwithstanding that was cried down you have continued the same. . . . Therefore we have thought good to send for you . . . that if you be in an erroneous way we may reduce you that so you may become a profitable member here among us. Otherwise if you be

Another prominent dissenter was Mistress Anne Hutchinson. Born about 1591 in England, Hutchinson emigrated to America in 1634. A healer, midwife, and mother of thirteen, she was married to one of the wealthier settlers of Massachusetts Bay Colony. Despite Puritan views that women had no authority in biblical matters and should not teach men, she held discussion groups of both women and men in her home in the new town of Boston, each week talking over sermons by the Rev. John Cotton, a leading minister. During the course of her discussions, she argued that only Cotton and another minister, her brother-in-law John Wheelwright, were preaching properly in their sermons as they interpreted for their listeners the covenant of grace. Other ministers, she argued, preached improperly regarding what was called the covenant of works. In her view, Cotton and Wheelwright were correctly preaching that humans were saved from eternal damnation by God's grace—a gift of salvation—not by doing good works or behaving well. This was basic Puritan theology. But Hutchinson then claimed that she knew this because God had revealed it to her via "direct divine inspiration." The Puritans did not believe this was the way of God. Instead they believed that while the devil might reveal himself to humans, God never did so directly, but only through His Word (the Bible) as interpreted by ministers.

Thus not only was Hutchinson teaching both women and men and criticizing leading ministers and their preaching, she was also coming dangerously close to espousing a heretical doctrine known as *Antinomianism*. This doctrine held that Christians did not have to obey laws created by men, not even the moral standards of their culture, because God's grace had freed them from these strictures. Such a belief was a direct attack on the authority of ministers, the church, and the government—the whole of obstinate in your course that then the court may take such course that you may trouble us no further.

Mrs. Anne Hutchinson: ... if you do condemn me for speaking what in my conscience I know to be truth I must commit myself unto the Lord. . . . You have power over my body but the Lord Jesus hath power over my body and soul; and assure yourselves thus much, you do as much as in you lies to put the Lord Jesus Christ from you, and if you go on in this course you begin, you will bring a curse upon you and your posterity, and the mouth of the Lord hath spoken it.

Gov. John Winthrop: I am persuaded that the revelation she brings forth is delusion. . . . The court hath already declared themselves satisfied concerning the things you hear, and concerning the troublesomeness of her spirit and the danger of her course amongst us, which is not to be suffered. . . . Mrs. Hutchinson, the sentence of the court you hear is that you are banished from out of our jurisdiction as being a woman not fit for our society, and are to be imprisoned till the court shall send you away.

Mrs. Anne Hutchinson: I desire to know wherefore I am banished?

Gov. John Winthrop: Say no more. The court knows wherefore and is satisfied.

Source: "The Examination of Mrs. Ann[e] Hutchinson," in *Early American Writing*, ed. Giles B. Gunn (New York: Penguin Books, 1994), 159–169.

Puritan society. The charge of Antinomianism often was leveled at dissenters who challenged the authority of the churches or the clergy. Puritan civil and religious leaders agreed that this view undermined their power and challenged their authority in a way that threatened the entire community, particularly given the tenuous nature of the settlements of the New World.

In November 1637, Hutchinson was put on trial for heresy by the General Court, led by Gov. John Winthrop. (See Primary Source 2-2.) Her gender was critical in determining her fate. As a woman, she was held in contempt by Puritan leaders and their supporters for stepping out of the role the Puritans thought proper for women, which was to keep silent in the church and allow the men to teach. In a society in which religion was so closely linked to the state, her rebellion was against both. The trial transcript that survives of Hutchinson being questioned by Gov. Winthrop shows his anger with her not only for what he viewed as heresy, but also because she would not submit to male authority. Her behavior, Winthrop charged, was neither "comely in the sight of God, nor fitting for your sex." He was determined, he said to Hutchinson in front of the court, to "reduce you that so you may become a profitable member here among us. Otherwise if you be obstinate in your course . . . then the court may take such course that you may trouble us no further." Too many women, he said, were spending too much time at Hutchinson's meetings listening to too much talk dangerous to the colony.

Hutchinson resisted Winthrop's description of her activities and of her theological ideas, and resisted also any authority he claimed he had over her. She challenged Winthrop directly, asking "What law have I broken?" and demanding that he show her a Bible passage to support his views. Such assertiveness by a woman was contrary to English views of women's proper place, and Winthrop criticized her as being "more bold than a man." Persuaded that Hutchinson's revelations were no more than "delusion," Winthrop banished her. Away from the protection afforded by the colony, Hutchinson, the General Court no doubt hoped, would die. Instead she found friends and joined Roger Williams in Narragansett Bay, Rhode Island. She stayed there for a while, but then moved to Long Island where she died when Indians attacked her farm in 1643. On hearing the news, Gov. Winthrop seemed satisfied with her fate, writing rather nastily that her death was "a special manifestation of divine justice."

Mary Dyer, another dissenter who attended Hutchinson's Bible studies and was banished with her, suffered a harsher fate. After her banishment, Dyer became a Quaker. A Protestant sect begun in the mid-1600s in England, the Society of Friends, or Quakers, believed in individual interpretations of God's work in the world. Listening for the voice of God, the "inward light," speaking to the individual was a feature of Quaker religious services, or meetings. Both men and women could be blessed with that inward light, and both were expected to speak out in meetings if God directed them to. They had no ministers and no hierarchy. They also believed in sexual equality and tolerated other religions. Such radical ideas led Puritans to condemn and to persecute Quakers, and the sect was banned from Massachusetts Bay. Dyer, who had become a Quaker preacher, returned to preach her Quaker beliefs and was arrested. The General Court found that she had "denied our Lawe" and, citing her rebelliousness against that law, hanged her in 1660.

The stories of Anne Hutchinson and Mary Dyer provide a window through which to view English customs and law as they affected women in colonial New England. For the Puritans, as well as many other English groups, women were defined not only by their duties as members of the family but also by their deficiencies and their limits, both physical and mental. People believed women were weaker than men in wit, will, and physical capacity, and at the same time, were so driven by their emotions that they had to be controlled by social institutions, especially religion and law. Ideas that Puritans and other Protestant groups held regarding women came from Jewish and Christian teachings that blamed women for much that had gone wrong with the world since the beginning of time. Because Eve first sinned and then convinced Adam to do the same, all women were considered to be the "daughters" of the first woman, Eve, and forever morally inferior to men. Accordingly, every woman needed to have a man in her life to protect her interests, to see that she behaved, and to limit the damage she might do to society by her uncontrolled behavior. English custom also presumed that all women would have a man—father, husband, or son—to limit their behavior and that none would make their own way in the world. According to this view, women would be—and should be—dependent upon and submissive to men in the home, the church, and society. In New England, where religion played a larger role in society and where women were a greater proportion of the population than in the Chesapeake, such ideas about women and their roles in society held particular power.

Demography and Family Life

New England family life differed markedly from family life in the Chesapeake region. As noted, in New England women arrived primarily as part of family groups, rather than as single indentured servants or wives-to-be. Although more single men than single women came to the colony (estimates indicate three to four single men for each single woman), the majority of emigrants between 1620 and 1649 were married women and married men. English emigrants married other English emigrants—men in their mid- to late-twenties; women in their early twenties. The first native-born generation married even earlier, at average ages of 25.3 for men and 20 for women. Men and women lived longer in New England than in the Chesapeake, with life expectancies comparable to those of the mother country. For those women who lived to age 21, life expectancy in New England reached 55. If a woman survived until menopause, the end of her child-bearing years, she would probably live to a ripe old age in New England where, as early as 1644, colonist William Bradford of Plymouth remarked on the longevity of settlers.

Colonial women in New England bore lots of children. Those born in New England before 1650 had on average seven children, bearing the last at age 37. Over half of the infants born in colonial America in the seventeenth century reached adulthood and in the New England colonies, survival rates could reach 80 percent or more. The clean water and cold air of New England was conducive to good health, unlike in crowded London, where only 20 percent of infants reached adulthood in the same era.

Families in New England also tended to stay intact, unlike in the Chesapeake, where early deaths of adult parent often resulted in complicated stepfamilies. The majority of New Englanders married one spouse and lived with that person until death. Unlike the Chesapeake as well, by about 1650 or so, the population in New England was increasing by natural means, as women produced large families. New England's low infant mortality rate and long life expectancy allowed the role of grandparent to be invented, since so many adults lived long enough to see their children marry and bring forth the next generation.

The family was an important source of labor in the preindustrial world, and by 1700, the average colonial family size was seven children, a total that did not take into account the miscarriages and stillbirths women commonly suffered. Many women spent their entire adult lives in the throes of childbearing and child rearing. For example, one New Englander, Sarah Stearns, married Peter Place in December 1685. Their first child was born November 1686. Their eighth surviving child was born in June 1706. For twenty years, Sarah had been either pregnant, nursing, bearing a child, or recovering from childbirth, as well as enduring the difficult years of raising small children. This pattern of childbearing was not uncommon. The high birthrate doubled the population every twenty years in the healthier New England colonies, and would continue to do so for some time.

The natural population growth meant that New Englanders imported far fewer servants or slaves for their labor, resulting in a society very different than the one in the Chesapeake. While the Chesapeake became a slave society, New England was a society with slaves. The earliest slaves in New England were Native American women captured in warfare. African women slaves arrived at least as early as 1638. Unlike in the Chesapeake, where black women slaves worked in the fields, the majority of black slave women in New England worked in domestic settings. They did the drudge work for the colonial elites, particularly the laundry, as well as other gendered tasks such as sewing, knitting, caring for children, and cooking. When hired out by their owners, they continued their domestic work, earning money for their owners and themselves that might be used to buy their freedom. Slave women, isolated inside houses and on small farms, had few chances to form a community or a family as they might have had on the large farms or the plantations that soon characterized southern agriculture. By 1700, there were only 820 blacks counted in a Boston census; some 41 percent of them were women. New Englanders who had little need for slaves themselves did not hesitate to participate in the lucrative business of trading for slaves, however. Boston traders pushed their way into the market and by the 1670s were successfully importing African and West Indians to sell to southern planters.

The regional variations between Chesapeake and New England were pronounced by 1640, by which time troubles in England between King Charles I (1625–1649) and the Parliament drew their attention away from colonization efforts. Emigration to the colonies lessened. A civil war erupted in England over fears that Charles I would restrict religious liberty for Protestants, as well as over how much of a role Parliament should have in governing the country. From 1642 to 1646, Royalists or "Cavaliers" fought with Parliamentarians or "Roundheads," until the Puritan leader of the Roundheads, Oliver Cromwell, won and helped impose Puritan rule over England after Charles I was executed in 1649. Cromwell died in 1658, however, and two years later Charles II (1660–1685) became king, restoring the monarchy.

Colonial expansion by England resumed in this period, known as the Restoration. In 1662, Connecticut received its royal charter, as did Rhode Island in 1663. New Hampshire became a royal colony in 1679. Farther south, in a region deemed the Middle Colonies, New York (1664), New Jersey (1664), Pennsylvania (1681), and Delaware (1682) became proprietary colonies whose charters were awarded to the king's supporters. Proprietors had to succeed at their enterprise, however, or lose their proprietorship, as was the case for all but three of the thirteen colonies. In the Lower South, the colony of Carolina (1663) included what later became North and South Carolina, as well as Georgia, in the early eighteenth century. South Carolina became the most prosperous of the three, trading in deerskins, Native American slaves exported to the Caribbean, cattle, and eventually rice, a commodity so profitable and so labor-intensive that slaves imported from Africa eventually became the majority population in the colony.

In each American colony, patterns of settlement varied because of factors such as the kind of settlers who came—male or female, slave or free—as well as their religions, their countries of origin, the commodities they were able to produce for themselves, and those they could export to the mother country. As England took over colonies originally claimed by other nations,

English laws and customs took over as well. As the seventeenth century drew to a close, cultural life in all the colonies more closely reflected characteristics of English life. In particular, American colonial women's daily lives reflected those commonalities.

WOMEN'S DAILY LIVES

The most common gendered expectation the English had was that any woman in society would be a *goodwife*. The goodwife, or "Goody" in the language of the time (*Goody* was comparable to the title of "Mrs." today), was a married woman. She was expected to be submissive to her husband, obedient to the authorities, industrious in her housework, pious in her religion, silent rather than complaining, and a good mother and housewife. Despite these limits imposed by their gender, historian Laurel Thatcher Ulrich has shown that goodwives did take on male roles, filling in for their husbands as "deputy husbands" when necessary. They took over husbandly duties when men left the home for various reasons, such as to hunt, to settle land, or to ship out on a fishing or whaling trip. These occasions required wives to take actions to benefit the families, such as planting crops, running businesses, or buying products. Being a deputy husband, however, was a temporary occurrence. The vast majority of colonial women spent their daily lives engaged in the labor it took to build new homes for their families.

Historians of colonial women have relied not only on the documents in which women appear—diaries, advice books, court records, probate records, wills, church registers, tax lists, books of sermons—to learn about

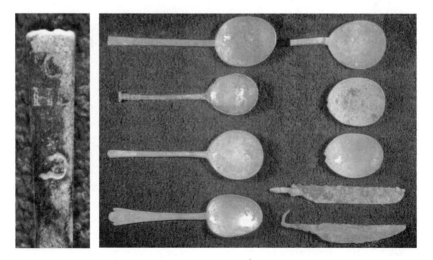

SEVENTEENTH-CENTURY LUXURY Spoons left behind by Lucy and Humphrey Chadbourne of South Berwick, Maine, between 1645 and 1690. Such items provide archeologists with information regarding the status of women within families: the spoon handle to the left is engraved with an *L* as well as an *H*. Including his wife's initial on such a luxury item as a silver spoon may have indicated that Humphrey Chadbourne saw his wife as a partner rather than simply a dependent.

their lives, but also on the material culture that survived them as well. Items women used often tell historians a great deal. These items include garments they wore, cloth they wove, jewelry they delighted in, storage baskets, candlesticks, and bed linens that filled their blanket chests, as well as archeological remains of their houses and gardens, and even their cemetery markers.

Colonial women, like Native American women, spent much of their lives surrounded by their families and caring for them. Evidence of women's daily life and work reveal much about their experiences of infancy and childhood, courtship and marriage practices, pregnancy and childbirth, and can all illuminate their past. However, as was the case with Native American women's lives, generalizations about colonial women's lives have to be made with caution. Many differences among women existed, depending on such factors as their European background, their husbands' occupation, their families' wealth, their proximity to the frontier, their religion, and their legal status. Even so, commonalities existed among women in the early colonial period, and there were common patterns of life for colonial women.

Infancy and Childhood

Children were precious commodities in the seventeenth century, and infant care was women's work. Women could learn about child care and feeding from advice books and sermons, but most colonial women no doubt learned to care for their infants from their own mothers or neighbor women. Breast-feeding was praised by physicians and ministers alike, as breast milk was thought to have not only high nutritional content but also considerable medicinal powers to keep babies healthy. Some critics viewed allowing an infant to suck for too many months as spoiling the child, one writing that the practice "doth them more mischief than the Devil himself." Mothers added solid food to babies' diets at anywhere from eight months to two years of age, depending on when children were weaned, a task often undertaken by sending a nursing mother on a visit without her child.

Childhood itself was perilous. Diseases such as measles, mumps, chicken pox, smallpox, dysentery, diarrhea, pneumonia, whooping cough, tetanus, and infections of all kinds killed children in these days before antibiotics and vaccines. Accidents injured and killed many as well. Colonial farms had cattle that could crush a small child, or sharp implements that could injure a careless one. In colonial houses with open fireplaces where fires were always burning, children suffered frequently from accidental scaldings and burns. In times of war between colonists and Native Americans, children were killed in the fray. Demographers' best estimates are that about 25 percent of New England children died before age five, with girls dying at a lower rate than boys.

English and Dutch writers in the seventeenth century emphasized the moral training of children from baptism on. Baptism gave a child a suitable name, one the family regarded as virtuous, so the child could be influenced from that day forward to live a virtuous life. Parents viewed children as blank slates or white paper upon which their lives would be written, and children needed parental guidance so that they could become morally strong adults. Child rearing methods varied from place to place, and often according to the parents' religious beliefs. Puritans believed that infants were inherently sinful and that their wills had to be broken through discipline, an outgrowth of the Puritans' belief in original sin ("In Adam's fall, we sinned all" was a lesson often repeated when training children to write). Like many other Europeans of the time, Puritans were strict disciplinarians and tended to treat their children as miniature adults, attempting to shape them into properly repentant individuals so that they too might achieve a state of grace. On the other hand, Quakers in the middle colonies of Pennsylvania, Delaware, and New Jersey raised their children less strictly. They believed children possessed a "light within" that could best be coaxed into full flower by gentle nurturing.

In the large colonial families that were the norm in the seventeenth century, caring for children was a gendered occupation. Mothers were the primary child care provider until children were old enough to begin chores that would train them in adult tasks. Across the colonies, childhood was meant to train children for their adult life. By the ages of seven or eight, boys and girls both undertook sex-segregated tasks. At that age, boys were *breeched*; that is, they began wearing short pants called breeches instead of the dresses they and their sisters had worn since infancy. Boys would be sent with fathers to the fields and the woods to learn to farm and to hunt, while girls worked with their mothers to learn the household jobs for which they would become responsible.

Children joined the work in the fields at planting time, when the crops needed cultivating, and at harvest times, as did both parents. Agricultural demands knew no gender boundaries and not until parents could afford servants, slaves, or hired workers could they hope to divide the many farm tasks into men's work and women's work. Responsibilities for children included caring for younger children, chores around the farm, and formal apprenticeships (mostly for boys), where children were sent out of the family to learn a trade in return for room and board. While some rules regarding apprentices postponed aspects of one's adult status until the apprenticeship was completed, children were generally considered adults at much earlier ages than in modern times.

Seventeenth-century education in the form of book-learning reflected regional variations as well. In New England, the emphasis was on religious instruction; in New Netherland, the content focused on the importance of international trade and commerce. In Pennsylvania, with its large Quaker population that believed in equality for women, education for girls and boys alike was more common than in other colonies. Schooling was accomplished at home as well as in dame schools (taught by women in their homes), and eventually at elementary schools and grammar schools (which usually did not admit girls). In all regions, some children were taught to read, write, and figure.

The first free public school was founded in 1639 in Dorchester, Massachusetts, outside Boston. The first Latin grammar school and the first college in America (Harvard, 1636) were in New England. Massachusetts

Bay Colony even passed a law in 1647 requiring that towns of fifty or more families hire a schoolmaster to teach boys and girls how to read and write. In Pennsylvania, a law passed in 1683 declared that all children must be able to read and write by age 12, and by 1689, the Quakers had started a public school for girls and boys. In the south, however, outside of Virginia where a public school was open in Elizabeth County by 1636, there were so few colonists in the seventeenth century that few schools existed. Elite whites, North and South, usually educated their children with tutors, while other whites' education was limited to that necessary for earning a living. Higher education in the south, beginning in 1693 at the College of William and Mary in Virginia, was limited to boys who would lead the colonies in the future. Literacy rates at the end of the seventeenth century, determined by whether one could write her name, were about 50 percent for New England girls, but only 10 percent for southern girls. With few opportunities for formal schooling, girls instead concentrated on learning tasks from their mothers that prepared them for their roles as wives and mothers.

Courtship and Marriage

Adulthood meant marriage for most white women in seventeenth-century America. Marriage was preceded by courtship. Stories of colonial courting practices nearly always mention the New England practice of *bundling*, when courting couples were placed in a bed with a board between them to prevent intimate contact. There, warm and cozy despite the frigid New England winter, the couple could chat all night long, learning enough about each other to decide if they wished to marry. Young men who wanted to marry usually sought their fathers' permission to begin courting. Young women weighed their suitors' economic as well as physical and emotional attributes. As had been the case in Europe, colonists married largely for economic benefits, in unions often arranged, or at least influenced, by parents. Children married when they had amassed enough goods to support themselves in a household. The man often brought land to the marriage; the woman usually brought household goods and utensils, even cattle and slaves, in what was termed a portion or *dowry*. Love and affection were a happy consequence, not the main reason for marriage. Seventeenth-century colonists believed that keeping one's wits and not being swept away by passion, romance, or courtly love made for a sound marriage.

That is not to say that romantic love did not exist among American colonists. It did, and it survives in poetic form. America's first poet, Anne Bradstreet, was born in 1612. She emigrated to America with her husband in 1630, living in Massachusetts Bay Colony with him and their eight children. She began writing poetry in 1632, and some of her work was published in 1650 when her brother-in-law appropriated a set of her poems and published them in England as *The Tenth Muse Lately Sprung Up in America, By a Gentlewoman of Those Parts* (see Primary Source 2-3). Bradstreet was quite embarrassed by the public notice, even writing a poem about her discomfiture at becoming a public figure. Poet she may have been, but public notice was not a woman's role.

Colonial historians estimate that 95 to 98 percent of all white women married. The institution of marriage was particularly important to the Puritans as a way for them to build families and, due to their religious beliefs, to provide the only legitimate outlet for sexual relations. Although the modern image of Puritans is that they were rather grim, so concerned with stopping fun that they never had any, the historical records tell a different tale. Puritans celebrated sex within marriage, and thought that a husband's duty was to satisfy his wife's sexual needs. One Middlesex County, Massachusetts, resident was, in fact, excommunicated from the church after refusing to have sex with his wife for two years. In another public record, in 1658, Benjamin Lane, answering the court's query, told the court he had not had sex with his wife, a claim she had made when requesting a divorce. The divorce was granted.

Outside marriage, sexual relations of any kind were considered both a sin and a crime. The influence and power of churches were important in determining which sin became a crime. Laws about property, particularly inheritance laws, depended on men knowing for certain who their true children were. Laws controlling sexual activity reflected those ideas. Sex outside marriage by an unmarried man and woman was termed *fornication*, and punished by fines or flogging (whipping). The two were also encouraged to marry, since sex did lead to pregnancy. Unmarried mothers were socially unacceptable; pregnant brides were not, and about one-third of all brides during the colonial period were already pregnant at marriage. If a married woman and an unmarried man had sex, that was known as *adultery* and was, in the early days of Massachusetts Bay Colony, punishable by death. Such a penalty was very rarely paid (historians have found only about six executions for adultery in colonial records). Most transgressors were instead punished by fines or lashes, or by serving time in the public pillory. This wooden structure provided miscreants with a seat, as well as holes in a board to imprison their hands and feet, stretched out in front of them. Offenders in the pillory were thus subject to public humiliation as well as discomfort.

Marriage was both a civil contract as well as a religious sacrament in some churches in the colonial period, just as it is today. Parental consent was required if one or both of the parties were under age, and the *banns* that announced the forthcoming marriage had to be posted or read in a public place three times to let the community know of the impending event, in case anyone knew of a reason it should not take place. Marriage ceremonies could be quite simple, held in church or before a magistrate, the bride and groom often clothed in nothing more than daily garb. Or they might be day-long affairs, such as the wedding of Frederick and Catherine Philipse, who married in New York in 1692. The wedding combined Dutch and English traditions: the bride wore an embroidered Dutch crown and petticoats of Asian silk. The party lasted for days and included an open house and visits by the bride and groom to all the surrounding relatives.

Once married, the husband was required by law to support his wife and family and to cohabit with them. The assumptions that the seventeenth-century English made regarding a woman's proper role as both

ANNE BRADSTREET, "TO MY DEAR AND LOVING HUSBAND"

Anne Bradstreet's work provides a lovely portrait of the more aesthetic side of American life in the very early settlement period. One of Bradstreet's most famous works is a love poem to her husband, published in 1678 after her death.

"If ever two were one, then surely we.
If ever man were loved by wife, then thee;
If ever wife was happy in a man,
Compare with me ye women if you can.
I prize thy love more than whole mines of gold,
Or all the riches that the East doth hold.
My love is such that rivers cannot quench,
Nor ought but love from thee give recompense.
Thy love is such I can no way repay;
The heavens reward thee manifold, I pray.
Then while we live, in love let's so persevere,
That when we live no more we may live ever."

Source: From *The Treasury of American Poetry*, ed. Nancy Sullivan (New York: Barnes & Noble, 1993), 1.

subservient and obedient to her husband occasionally came into conflict with the realities of married life. For example, accusations of neglect and physical abuse of wives occurred, and some colonies passed laws, beginning in the mid-seventeenth century, to outlaw physical abuse. Divorcing an abusive or unloved husband was possible in some colonies, but the methods of divorce varied greatly. Governor Peter Stuyvesant of New Netherland granted one man's petition for divorce. The General Assembly of Rhode Island granted a separation to the same man's wife. In Northampton County, Virginia, Mary Buckland's husband Richard had deserted her and lived with another woman with whom he had a child. The court not only granted the divorce, but also ordered Richard whipped and banished from the county.

Divorce or legal separation in the colonial period did not occur for light or transient causes, such as incompatability. People usually could divorce only by permission of the government—a long, complicated, and expensive process that often had as its goal the promotion of domestic and civil tranquility, rather than individuals' desires to rid themselves of partners with whom they were incompatible. In other words, for a divorce to be granted, a couple's problems had to be public enough to disturb the common welfare of the community. Far more often, when relationships failed, partners left their marriages by simply leaving. Desertion was the most common method of divorce.

Pregnancy and Childbirth

Pregnancy and childbirth among colonists were exceedingly common, and exceedingly dangerous for both mother and child. In the seventeenth century, maternal mortality rates (the percentage of women who died due to childbirth) on average were 1 to 1.5 percent of all births (compared to 0.0075 percent in the United States in 2000). Overall, one of every five adult deaths among women was related to childbirth, many due to dehydration, exhaustion, hemorrhage, or post-childbirth infections, known as puerperal fever. In both Europe and America, childbirth rates, combined with the environment, played a powerful role in determining life expectancy. In city centers such as London, crowding, poor sanitation, and disease resulted in an average life expectancy of only thirty-five to forty years. In the Chesapeake, bad water, disease, and harsh living conditions resulted in a similar life expectancy, while New England's environment was conducive to life expectancies in the low sixties for both women and men. Giving birth to children in difficult environments greatly affected the age at which a woman would die. Throughout the colonies, women had reason to fear childbirth.

Despite this fear, in an era when no reliable birth control existed, colonial women had lots of children. The average number of children per woman was between five and eight. Colonial women who wanted to limit the size of their families often had little success. People did not fully understand the mechanics of conception, except that sexual intercourse was definitely involved. Midwives were the source of birth control information. They might recommend breast-feeding, which tends to suppress ovulation, and can sometimes prevent a subsequent pregnancy, or douching with cold water immediately after intercourse. They also might recommend abstinence, the success of which depended upon a husband's cooperation, as did withdrawal of the penis prior to ejaculation—not a certain method, but one that was inexpensive and private. Midwives also knew of herbal medicines such as pennyroyal and mugwort that brought on menstruation, known as one's "courses." Surviving records from the period include sermons preached against abortion, making it clear that abortion was another method women used in their attempts to control fertility.

Pregnancy was a difficult time for colonial women and, as was true for Native American women, myths and superstitions abounded. Looking at a rabbit might cause the baby to have a hare-lip; looking at the moon might produce a "lunatic," since the moon was thought to have a role in causing insanity. Seeing a horrible sight could cause the child to be disfigured, as could a mother's longing for an unattainable item. For colonial women, pregnancy was a time of fear and sorrow as well as anticipation, when anything could go wrong and often did. A host of female relatives and friends attended the birth itself, offering comfort, experience, and company in a communal setting. The pain of childbirth was not eased by drugs, and women who complained were reminded of the sin of Eve, for which labor was seen as a fair punishment. Midwives attended births to help with the medical aspects, and, occasionally, legal issues. If a woman were unmarried, for instance, and the father of her child was not known, the midwife questioned the mother about the child's father while she was in labor. Local communities did not want to support unwed mothers and illegitimate children, so the midwife made every effort to determine the father's name when the woman was most vulnerable.

After childbirth, elite women might be confined to bed, sometimes for a month or more. The vast majority of women, however, resumed their chores as soon as they could and as best they could. Slaves and servants, including those impregnated by their masters, received little time off, and their health often suffered because of this. They might also find themselves separated from their children, who could be sold in the case of slaves, or bound out to service for a term of years.

Adult Women's Work

What colonial women did on a daily basis to survive in the new lands of America would wear out any modern-day citizen. Although differences existed in the amount and type of physical labor women did—rich women did less labor than poor women, and women with slaves or servants supervised more laborers than women who had no workers—almost all women worked hard, particularly in the early days of colonization. Whether paid or unpaid, the unremitting toil most women undertook contributed to the economies of the households, communities, and colonies through their labor.

Historians can only guess at the number or proportion of women who worked for wages in the colonial period. They do know from surviving court records and newspaper advertisements that, despite society's presumption that a woman would always have, and indeed ought to have, a man to take care of her, there were always some women who worked for money to support themselves. The most common business in which women made money was running a farm or plantation. The first record of female ownership of a farm run for profit, as opposed to being one run for simple subsistence, appears in Jamestown, Virginia, in 1610. Women wage earners often used their traditional role of caring for chickens and cows to produce eggs, milk, butter, and cheese which they sold in the marketplaces of their communities. They produced other goods as well: in 1653, Dionis Coffin brewed beer in Newberry, Massachusetts. Her daughter, Mary Coffin Starbuck, ran a store on Nantucket Island off the coast of Massachusetts. Starbuck also took full advantage of her Quaker religion's ideals regarding the equality of the sexes by working as a minister as well, although it is not clear whether she was paid for that task.

The growth of towns in the second half of the seventeenth century increased the complexity of the colonial economy and women's role within it. By 1700, Boston had a population of nearly 7,000; New York 5,000; and Philadelphia, 4,500. Southern towns were smaller: by 1690, Charleston, South Carolina, had a population of only about 1,200, and was still the fifth largest city in the colonies. In towns, the easiest way for women to make money was doing "women's work" for pay. In other words, women could expand their own domestic world to make money by taking in boarders, keeping a tavern, cooking, doing laundry, or running households for those who had no women available to do the labor that kept life going.

When women earned income in skilled trades, they usually did so as widows or as the wives of journeying husbands. Colonial women worked at all sorts of trades: milliners (making hats), dressmakers, blacksmiths, metalworkers, coopers (making barrels, tubs, and other containers), and printers. A few, like Mary Coffin Starbuck, even worked as ministers, but only among such sects as the Quakers and Moravians, since the Catholic Church and most Protestant denominations did not allow women to be religious leaders. Women were also midwives, shopkeepers, and teachers who ran dame schools. In agricultural communities, particularly in the southern colonies with their labor-intensive crop such as tobacco, women sometimes hired themselves out as day-laborers, performing many of the same tasks as male workers, although they were usually paid less. Young women and girls also served as apprentices, learning the trades by working for brewers, grocers, silk-stocking makers, as well as weavers, locksmiths, and wheelwrights, who made and repaired the carts and wagons that transported goods in the colonial world.

Women's paid work contributed to the family's economy and brought women into the larger market economy as well. But women also labored within the household, caring for their families and extended kin, as well as supervising others who lived with them, including apprentices, slaves, and indentured servants. Feeding, clothing, cleaning, and caring for the family's health occupied all women to some degree.

Most important was the preparation of food and its preservation for future use. On a daily basis, this task included both indoor and outdoor work, and it never ceased. Winter and summer women had to maintain a fire for heat and for cooking and had to maintain it from coals, since there were no matches. That meant a woman had to be able to bank the fire at night by raking ashes over the coals so they would survive overnight and could be used to ignite kindling the next morning. The fire burned constantly and was a safety hazard for women with long skirts and for small children who had not yet learned of its dangers. Open-hearth cooking, common throughout America until the eighteenth century, depended upon large pots suspended on iron hooks that swung out into the room so ingredients could be added. Fires were built from readily available wood, as colonists cut down America's forests to heat their homes and cook their food.

Women had kitchen gardens for growing herbs and vegetables. Herbs were used for both medicines and seasonings, and vegetables were used in the stews and soups that most people ate daily. Colonists favored crops they could store over the winter months: pumpkins, winter squash, and root vegetables, such as yams, turnips, beets, onions, leeks, carrots, and parsnips. Learning from their experiences after many of the seeds first brought over by colonists from England failed to germinate due to New England's cold climate, New Englanders imitated the local Indians who taught them how to grow corn. Both northern and southern colonists used corn as a staple to produce traditional English dishes such as bread, porridge, and pancakes, while they learned how to grow the wheat, oats, and barley they had raised in England.

Colonists also brought swine, cattle, and chickens with them. Women were in charge of the animals such as chickens and pigs, raising them, catching them, and killing them. They then cleaned or "dressed" them, plucking off the feathers and removing the innards. Cooking cleaned animals was the last of a long line of chores needed to move food from outdoors to the table, and cooking itself was a very demanding chore. The kettles and pots that hung on the hearth hooks weighed forty pounds or more.

At first, colonists had a monotonous diet. Most lived on soup and bread, salted meat or salted fish (before refrigeration, salt was used to draw out the moisture from foods that made them spoil), and corn cakes, which were flat biscuits made with cornmeal. As Indians taught colonists trapping and hunting methods, the settlers added lobster, oysters, clams, eels, turtles, crabs, seagulls, sturgeon, deer, rabbits, and turkeys to their diet. Most colonists drank what they drank in England: beer women brewed from grain, and eventually cider that women made after the apple trees they had planted matured. Virginia children after 1611 and New England children after 1624, when the first dairy cows were brought to America, had milk to drink. As they gathered, planted, and harvested fruit, colonists drank fruit juices made from native berries that usually got "hard" (i.e., they fermented into alcohol) before they were consumed. The liquids consumed by colonists were produced largely by women, as part of their traditional tasks.

Gathering and preparing adequate food supplies, particularly for the long, cold New England winters, meant the difference between life and starvation. In all the colonies, women salted meat and fish to preserve them (they had to soak the salt off and then boil the meat before eating it); they stored root vegetables in root cellars under or near their small houses; they dried squashes and fruits. Eventually, they would pickle vegetables and make relishes that added spice to their meals, but spices such as sugar, cinnamon, or nutmeg were luxury items until supply ships from Europe began to appear more regularly after the mid-seventeenth century. Food was fuel for the backbreaking work of settling the country. Masters were required to feed their indentured servants, and men and women who failed to provide their servants with adequate food could be hauled before the authorities and fined for their deficiencies.

Colonial women also were in charge of clothing their families. The wealthy purchased fine fabric, the poor coarse, but clothing was handmade, and women were the manufacturers of clothing. Keeping a family clothed meant constant labor, and it was rare to see a woman sitting without some sort of needlework occupying her, since making clothing was so time-consuming. Such labor-intensive work meant most people had very few changes of clothing. A woman might have three dresses, if she were lucky: one for formal occasions, such as church, one for everyday, and one to wear while another was drying. Elite women, who could purchase fabric and who might have servants or slaves to create elaborate gowns, had larger wardrobes, while poor women, servants, and slaves might have only a single garment.

Producing clothing allowed colonial women to indulge any sense of aesthetics that they retained in the midst of a hard life, and for most, handwork was their only "leisure" activity. What was especially pleasant for its practitioners was that women could do needlework outside the house in the fresh air, and could also do it while visiting with friends. Quilting, appliqué, patchwork, crewel work, and embroidery were common among women of all classes and races. But even handwork could be utilitarian; girls often used needlework samplers to show they had learned their letters, as well as to display their sewing skills.

The task of keeping anything clean in the colonial era was often a hopeless task. Seventeenth-century Americans were dirty. In a society without running water and without the custom of bathing, keeping a body clean meant washing a face and little else. The production of soap required a multistep process and resulted in a harsh product called lye soap, which reddened faces and cracked hands. Clothing was usually cleaned by brushing off mud and dirt as needed. When clothes had to be washed, they first were soaked in water, then beaten with feet, clubs, or arms, or rubbed on stones. Then the heavy, wet clothes were lifted out of the water, rinsed in more water, wrung, starched, dried—often by spreading them over bushes—smoothed with irons heated in the fire, and put away. When settlements became organized and self-sufficient enough to allow women to have the time to wash, wash days usually occurred once a month in summer and seldom if ever in winter, particularly in the northern colonies. The frequency with which one's clothes were washed quickly became a marker of economic and social class. If servants or slaves were available to do the wash, it was done more often, and the employer or slaveowner could wear more ornate clothing, which could be changed more often because servants or slaves did the dirty work.

Cleaning the house itself was another lost cause in the early part of the colonial period. The first houses in the country, made of materials called wattle and daub, were built of timbers and had earthen floors. Other dwellings were built into the sides of hills, and some early settlers used caves for shelter. In northern houses, fireplaces were first at one end, then in the center of the hall; in the southern colonies, fireplaces were built, with wooden chimneys, at one side of the one-room houses that first served as homes for the majority of colonists. At first windows were just holes left in the sides of the houses and covered with shutters, or they were filled with panels made of oiled linen to let in light while keeping out the wind. Glass windows began to appear in homes of the well-to-do after midcentury. In both the northern and southern colonies, most floors were first made of beaten dirt. Cleaning the house in the early years of settlement consisted of dumping the trash out the window into the side yard, or tossing it out the front door. (Trash dumps in the front yard might dismay modern sensibilities, but archeologists love them for the insight they provide into what colonists ate and how they lived in their rude homes.) Interior cleanliness for early colonists focused mostly on the beds. Colonists slept first on the floor, then on planks, then on rope beds, and finally on mattresses stuffed with cotton or straw. By spring, mattresses were filled with fleas, lice, and bedbugs. To clean them, women emptied out the stuffing and burned it, then restuffed the mattress with fresh matter.

In the later colonial period, as interiors grew more elaborate, women's work increased. Women cleaned walls by whitewashing them with lime mixed with water, an inexpensive kind of paint that also killed germs, although colonists did not know that. Glass windows were cleaned with water and lye soap, usually by servants or slaves, since houses with glass windows belonged to the well-to-do. Dust from unpaved roads, garden dirt, horse manure, and barnyard debris were all tracked into the house as most people lived in rural communities and were in and out of the house all day. As society became more complex and sophisticated in the south, wealthy families moved cooking tasks away from the main house into outbuildings, eliminating a source of dirt from the public rooms, such as dining rooms, that they added to their homes. In the north, cooking tasks remained in the main house, but the kitchen gradually shifted to the back of the house, confining greasier dirt to that smaller room.

Colonial housewives responsible for cleanliness probably were not dismayed by all the dirt in their houses. After all, dirt was a fact of life, most folks thought fresh air unhealthy, and no one associated dirt with disease. Colonists were more concerned about the last, as the diseases of three continents—Europe, Africa, and America—met in colonial America. The New World had a few diseases it shared with European arrivals as well, the most notable of which may have been syphilis. But by far, the majority of diseases killing off the intermingled populations were from Europe. The most common diseases colonists suffered from were those due to poor sanitation and water and those spread by respiratory means or contact: dysentery, typhoid, tuberculosis, scarlet fever, "fluxes" (which was any type of abnormal bodily discharge), "fevers" (which could be almost anything and often referred to malaria), smallpox, diphtheria, measles, and whooping cough. Elites, both women and men, used what few physicians existed in colonial society, but most physicians were so ignorant of biology that they wound up killing patients rather than saving them. Women healers were not usually known as physicians, but there is evidence of at least one woman who served as a doctor in the colonial period when little if any formal training was required to be regarded as such. Katherine Hebden, a Marylander, shows up in the historical record in 1644 when her husband went to court on her behalf against one Edward Hall. Acting as a physician, Hebden, claimed the suit, "did chiguery [surgery] upon the legg of Thomas Greenwell," one of Hall's servants, but Hall had not paid her for the operation. Hall had to pay the rest of Hebden's bill—190 pounds of tobacco. Hebden also prevailed in later court cases, a clear indication that the community regarded her as a doctor, not just an informal healer.

Katherine Hebden's status as a wage-earning physician is highly unusual. The majority of medical care was provided by adult women to their own families as a matter of course, and by women who worked as midwives.

Herbal medicines were the state of the art, along with the belief that the body had a balance of what were called *humors* that were out of balance when the patient was sick. Midwives and doctors both used bloodletting, blistering, purges, and emetics to clean out the body's various systems in hopes of rebalancing the humors and thus curing the patient. In most cases of ill health, however, women cared for their families themselves, doing the best they could.

WOMEN IN PUBLIC LIFE

The material world in which women lived in the seventeenth century has remained largely invisible in most history textbooks, despite its importance to everyday women. More commonly told has been the story of women in the public eye, women who became visible because they appeared in court documents or other public documents most historians use to write history and to understand women's roles in the early colonial period. Political women, women who played a public role in wartime, women who behaved badly, according to seventeenth-century society's expectations, were anomalies, but all are recorded in the public record as playing their parts in colonial history.

Women in Politics

Although women colonists were not allowed to participate in government, they no doubt followed the issues, and a few elite women occasionally involved themselves in political matters. The actions of one woman, Margaret Brent, offer a rare example of women acting in the political realm. In 1647, Brent asked the Maryland Assembly to be allowed to vote in the assembly proceedings. A single woman, she had arrived in Maryland in 1638. She was financially very successful, owning her own land, importing and selling servants, loaning money to new settlers, appearing in court when needed, and generally managing her considerable financial enterprises on her own. Brent was a trusted friend of the colony's governor, Leonard Calvert. When he died in 1647, Calvert's will made Brent executor of his estate, ordering her to pay all his bills. These bills included wages the colony owed to soldiers charged with protecting Maryland. Calvert had promised the soldiers that they would be paid, relying on not only his own wealth but also funds from the American estate of his brother, Lord Baltimore. But when Calvert died, Lord Baltimore was in England, unable to respond to the mounting crisis of hungry, unpaid soldiers threatening to mutiny. The Maryland Assembly could have raised taxes to pay the soldiers, but they did not want to do that, since they knew that Calvert had promised to pay the soldiers himself.

Given this stalemate and facing a possible rebellion by armed and hungry soldiers, Brent, as Calvert's executor, decided she had to act. She went to the Maryland Assembly. They transferred to her Lord Baltimore's power of attorney that his dead brother had held, so that she could sell Baltimore's cattle and thus raise funds to pay the soldiers. At the same time, Brent asked the assembly for the right to cast two votes: one for herself as a landowner in the colony; a second vote for her role as the representative of Lord Baltimore. The assembly and the governor refused her petition for the votes and, although Brent had successfully averted the crisis, Lord Baltimore was furious at what he regarded as her high-handed actions in selling off part of his estate. He eventually drove her from the colony, but the assembly complained to him that he had treated Brent unfairly. The assemblymen did "Verily Believe," as they told Baltimore in a letter, that his estate was safer "at that time in her hands then in any mans else . . . for the Soldiers would never have treated any other with . . . Civility and respect." Rather than criticism and "bitter invectives," wrote the members of the assembly, "She rather deserved favour and thanks from your Honour for her so much Concurring to the publick safety."

Brent's unusual freedom of action stemmed in part from her unmarried status and her wealth. Property gave women power, just as it gave men power, and the fewer the women in a community, the more power they could exercise. In the Chesapeake, in particular, the many colonial widows exercised considerably more power than did married women, but even married women could be given their husbands' power of attorney to act on their behalf. Colonel Francis Yeardley, for instance, appointed his wife Sarah to act as his attorney so she could conduct his business, presumably even before he traveled out of the colony. Such conveyances, as these were called, survive in the public records of the colonies as evidence that women did appear in public colonial life, in addition to working within the domestic world of the household.

Women in War

Because of the expanding settlements in the seventeenth century, the frontier between Native Americans and Europeans was never very far away. Indians traded with the English up and down the Atlantic coast and the rivers that provided passage into the continent's interior. By 1650 in New England, hunters had exhausted the local supplies of beaver and the English began demanding land in payment for the European goods that the Indians wanted. Soon, territorial conflicts arose between the English and the Indians, as well as between Native American groups who fought with their traditional enemies. The battles drove Native Americans from their homelands, usually farther west. The English then occupied those lands, building farms and settling towns.

The conflicting goals of Indians and English led to some of the bloodiest warfare in American history and including women as both leaders and victims. The Pequot War in New England in 1637, for example, pitted the English against the Pequot and resulted in the utter destruction of that group. Their defeat left the Wampanoag Indians as the major power in the area. Massasoit, the Wampanoag chief who had befriended the English in Plimouth Plantation as early as 1621, tried his best to maintain a peace between his group and the English. It was not to last as the English continued to encroach on Indian land. Finally, Massasoit's daughter-in-law Wetamoo, sachem of the Pocassets, allied her forces with Massasoit's grandson Metacomet, sachem of the Wampanoags and known to the English as King Philip. Another woman sachem, Awashunkes of the Sakonnets of Rhode Island, declined to join with them, preferring to side with the English with whom the group had strong trading ties. Other Native groups from the area, however, joined Metacomet and Wetamoo. Together they attacked the English.

King Philip's War lasted a year, from 1675 to 1676, and was, proportional to the population of the area, the bloodiest war in American history. Indians ambushed English soldiers and burned dozens of English towns. English militia marched against Indian villages and slaughtered men, women, and children. In February of 1676, Indians captured Mary Rowlandson of Lancaster, Massachusetts, a settler who later wrote a narrative of her captivity, which ended after nearly three months. (See Primary Source 2–4.) Her narrative became wildly popular, a best-seller of its time. For a time Rowlandson may have been the best-known woman in seventeenth-century colonial New England. Her narrative provided not only vivid descriptions of daily life with the Indians, but also the opportunity to spread her religious ideals, as she presented her captivity and eventual release as evidence of God's hand. An ordinary woman, Rowlandson became a historic figure when Native and English worlds collided and when a public record resulted.

Indian resistance in New England was matched by that in Virginia and led to a rebellion there. By the 1660s in Virginia, declining tobacco prices and a rise in taxes brought on hard economic times. Recently freed servants had trouble finding enough land to settle on. Settlers in the far western reaches of the colony, called the "backcountry," fought with Indians in the region, and the Indians fought back. As the violence escalated, settlers demanded that colonial authorities protect them. Nathaniel Bacon, a newly arrived settler, not only attacked nearby Indians without authorization, but also went to war against the Virginia governor Sir William Berkeley when Berkeley refused to send troops to aid Virginians on the frontier. Susquehannock Indians continued raiding farms, killing servants and overseers. Bacon believed that the colonial government should declare Indians to be "outlaws," that is, outside the protection of English law and therefore fair game for settlers who feared for their lives and property. He also believed that Berkeley and the elite group ruling through the House of Burgesses were "corrupt and irresponsible." Gov. Berkeley considered backcountry strife to be of little import. He was far more interested in preserving the general peace with the Indians, who were in fact protected at the time by English law.

Bacon had considerable support, not only for his attacks against the Indians, but also for his attacks against the eastern elites ruling Virginia. Women took part in this war as well. Sarah Grendon, a Bacon partisan, supported Bacon's Rebellion by spreading word of his ideas and his victories as well as criticizing Gov. Berkeley and his wife, Lady Frances Berkeley.

MARY ROWLANDSON'S CAPTIVITY NARRATIVE

Mary Rowlandson's record of her captivity in 1676 illustrates some of the Native American ways that English settlers still found disquieting over fifty years after colonization began.

"The first week of my being among them, I hardly ate anything; the second week, I found my stomach grow very faint for want of something; and yet it was very hard to get down their filthy trash: but the third week, though I could think how formerly my stomach would turn against this or that, and I could starve and dy before I could eat such things, yet they were sweet and savoury to my taste. . . .

Other women in the backcountry wrote letters, attended meetings of the rebels, and spoke out against the governor. The governor's wife did not sit idly by. In defense of her husband, Frances Berkeley traveled to England, explained her husband's actions to the king, then brought home three shiploads of troops to help put down Bacon's Rebellion in 1676.

Bacon, attempting to force Virginia authorities in Jamestown to attack the Indian raiders, successfully stood for election to the House of Burgesses. He then marched on the colonial capital, where he took four leading citizens, "the prime mens wives," hostage, using them as human shields while he built fortifications to place Jamestown under siege. According to Ann Cotton, a Virginia woman whose letter to a friend recorded the scene, Bacon made all four women stand atop his siege works while he strengthened them. He then allowed the women to leave. The governor's troops attacked his fortifications but the attack failed. Mistress Cotton facetiously suggested that the charms of the ladies had "plugged up the enemy's shot" and only an equally virtuous power would be able to defeat the enemy. After the governor's troops left, Bacon burned Jamestown. The conflict that had inflamed the entire colony ended unexpectedly a month later in October 1676 when Bacon suddenly died of the "bloody flux," an intestinal ailment, some four months before Lady Berkeley made it back with the English troops. Many of Bacon's women supporters were tried and sentenced to corporal punishment. Rebel Sarah Drummond, whose husband William was hanged for his part in the rebellion, lost the estate she ordinarily would have inherited. Harsh punishment for women rebels as for men seemed to be the case, and women were publicly criticized for the inappropriateness of their behavior—not as rebels so much as women.

Brabbling Women

Elite women, such as Lady Berkeley, did appear from time to time in colonial records. Widows, especially numerous in the Chesapeake, appear

"The chief and commonest food was Ground-nuts: They eat also Nuts and Acorns, Harty-choaks, Lilly roots, Ground-beans, and several other weeds and roots, that I know not. They would pick up old bones, and cut them to pieces at the joynts, and if they were full of wormes and magots, they would scald them over the fire to make the vermine come out, and then boile them, and drink up the Liquor, and then beat the great ends of them in a Morter, and so eat them. They would eat Horses guts, and ears, and all sorts of wild Birds which they could catch: also Bear, Vennison, Beaver, Tortois, Frogs, Squirrels, Dogs, Skunks, Rattle-snakes; yea, the very Bark of Trees; besides all sorts of creatures, and provision which they plundered from the English."

Source: From "The Sovereignity and Goodness of God . . . ," in *American Colonial Prose,* ed. Mary Ann Radzinowicz (New York: Cambridge University Press, 1984), 89, 96.

often in property transactions, wills, deeds, and lawsuits. Generally speaking, however, colonial women tended to appear in the military history of the English colonies as victims of attacks, as Rowlandson did, or, as in the case of Cotton's description of the wives, as hostages. Englishwomen most often showed up in public records when they deviated from the role of goodwife that English law and tradition had assigned them. Lady Berkeley appears precisely because she acted outside the common role most women held. While some admired her assertiveness, overall Lady Berkeley's actions were met with dismay. Her public speechifying against Bacon put Lady Berkeley into a category called "brabbling" women. Brabbling women were those who spoke in public, but whose speech and actions were termed disorderly by their society.

Other disorderly women showed up in public records if they were acting the role of the "wench," a woman who broke the rules, perhaps even broke the law and was caught. She might be a tavern keeper who sold drink illegally to Indians. She might be a prostitute. She might sass authorities, rather than obeying them. She might be lazy, she might skip church, she might be a "common scold," a woman who scolded others in public and indiscriminately. Communities arrested, tried, and punished women who slandered others or otherwise defied authority with fines and whippings. Punishments also included tying guilty parties to a chair on a pole near a pond and ducking them under the water. Women acting outside the role of goodwives, acting as politicians, speaking publicly in a society that said they should be silent, acting in ways that society thought they should not, all represented a threat to the hierarchy and to the authority of the government and of men.

Despite possible repercussions to themselves, women also used informal networks and gossip to affect people's lives and to exercise power by reporting on unacceptable behavior in ways that could punish others, usually by damaging their reputations. Authorities in colonial communities were well aware of the power of women's gossip in the small worlds in which they lived. A whispering campaign could degenerate rapidly into that most serious attack against women who did not live up to societal mores: an accusation of witchcraft.

Witches and Witch Hunts

Accusations of witchcraft were part and parcel of colonial life. Witchcraft was the use of "magic," power that the authorities declared came from a witch's association with the devil. The earliest recorded witchcraft accusation in the North American colonies was most likely the one in 1626 against Goodwife Wright, a midwife in Kecoughtan parish in southeast Virginia near present-day Hampton. Goodwife Wright was accused of foretelling the future and causing breast sores on a nursing mother. In 1647, in Windsor, Connecticut, Alice Young was convicted and executed, the first recorded execution of a witch in the colonies. Witchcraft accusations against women were also made in other colonies, such as Pennsylvania and New York. It was in New England, however, where witchcraft accusations appear most often. Four women were executed in New England for being witches between 1648 and 1649, including a "physic" or doctor, Margaret Jones, who was hanged in Boston in 1648. In 1649, Eunice Cole, a woman previously taken to court for mean-spirited and slanderous speech, came to trial on witchcraft charges in New Hampshire. She survived three trials, each time for "unseemly speeches" as well as "familiarity" with the devil. Cole had a truculent attitude that defied social norms for women, giving those who disliked her the ammunition to strike against her, a common fate for a number of assertive and aggressive women.

Witches were almost always women in colonial America, and nearly all of them exhibited behavior that did not fit the role model of a goodwife. Seventeenth-century colonists believed women accused of witchcraft were handmaidens of Satan, causing problems throughout their communities. Witches might sour milk, cause fevers, or sicken people. They might make their victims turn away from religion, turn away from their marriages, and commit all sorts of dastardly deeds. Accusations of witchcraft, which might rest on something as simple as an icy glare from an insulted neighbor, were based on perceptions of behavior and reputation, the sorts of things that women's networks of conversation and gossip could readily supply. Women's work, upon which everyone depended and which centered around the household, also made women more vulnerable to accusations of witchcraft. Women, after all, were the ones who usually milked the cows and took care of the sick. If milk turned sour or people died, who easier to blame than the woman in proximity? If people suffering found a woman whom they thought caused their trouble because she was a witch, they would then bring the accused witch to the authorities for them to do something about her. Authorities derived their ideas of what a witch was from works that described witches' behavior and appearance, such as *Malleus Maleficarum*, published in 1484. They also used books that recorded specific cases of witchcraft, such as Boston minister Cotton Mather's *Memorable Providences, Relating to Witchcrafts and Possessions*, published in 1689.

When it came to figuring out whether someone was a witch, the authorities thought about it differently than did the general population. Popular thought regarding witches was subjective. Claiming that a woman "turned me into a newt," for example, is an example of a witchly activity that is a subjective experience. A man who had been turned into a newt was the only one to experience it unless he was still a newt, which was unlikely, since he was offering testimony and newts cannot speak. Authorities tried not to be influenced by such personal feelings or opinions. Instead, they searched for objective evidence, using a scientific approach. An official might declare, for example, that a witch "weighs as much as a duck." The accused would then be weighed by the authorities to determine in fact whether she weighed as much as a duck. Once authorities selected the objective measure, they could act with legal and physical means to produce a conviction. They could also rationalize techniques usually forbidden, such as torture, to gain confessions from accused witches, since protection of the community was paramount.

In Salem, Massachusetts, witchcraft accusations and trials reached a frenzied peak in 1692. Between May and October, over 150 people, mostly women, but also some men and even a few children, were arrested and imprisoned on charges of witchcraft. Nineteen were convicted; eighteen were hanged, and one man was pressed to death by stones. The town seemed truly possessed—by hysteria, if not by witchcraft. The panic began when several teenage girls began having "fits" and accusing others in the community of bewitching them. As was the case elsewhere, the first women accused were women outside the social norm of a goodwife. Tituba, a slave of the Reverend Samuel Parris, started it all by telling fortunes and stories about voodoo practices in the West Indies where she was from. Accused of witchcraft, she implicated Bridget Bishop, a woman who fought with all three of her husbands, kept two taverns, and dressed less modestly than people thought she should. Next was Sarah Good, a homeless, destitute woman who was heard muttering angrily as she begged for work to support herself. Tituba was imprisoned and Good was hanged.

As the witch hunt continued, the accusations began to touch the kind of people less commonly accused, such as Rebecca Nurse, an elderly woman with four sons and well thought of by the community, but vulnerable to attack since she had not remarried to reestablish her proper role as a goodwife. She was hanged. Tavern owner John Proctor and his wife Elizabeth were also accused. Proctor, who criticized the witch-hunt vociferously after his wife was accused, was imprisoned, convicted of witchcraft, and hanged in August of 1692. Elizabeth was spared because she was pregnant. Most disquieting was the hanging of Salem's former minister, George Burroughs. Accused and brought to court from Maine, where he lived after leaving Salem, Burroughs insisted he was innocent and, on Gallows Hill, recited aloud the Lord's Prayer, something no witch was thought capable of. Such contrary evidence of conviction was enough to push the authorities toward doubt. One of the leading prosecutors, the

Reverend John Hale of Beverly, north of Salem, said shortly after his wife was accused, "It cannot be imagined that in a place of so much knowledge, so many in so small compass of land should abominably leap into the Devil's lap at once."

Once doubt appeared, the wheels of bureaucratic justice began to grind. Despite more deaths (an 80-year-old was pressed to death by heavy stones after refusing to acknowledge he was a witch, and six more women and two men were hanged), the hunt began to lose its ferocity. Newly appointed Governor William Phips ordered the end of the hunt. Inspired in no small part by accusations that touched upon his wife, Lady Mary Phips, the governor also required "clear and convincing" evidence to prove guilt. By May of 1693, those accused still languishing in jails were all freed.

The Salem witchcraft trials have long been the most visible sign of women in seventeenth-century America. Historians have puzzled over the witchcraft craze in Salem and surrounding Essex County for years, suggesting various interpretations. A psychological interpretation took into account that the accusing girls had such poor marriage prospects that they attacked any love interests to punish them for their unavailability. A physiological interpretation argued that a blight called ergot on the rye grain used to make bread the accusing girls ate gave them hallucinations interpreted as witchcraft. Other scholars argued that economic and social tensions were the cause of the hysteria. As the number of historians studying women and the impact of gender in history increased, historian Carol Karlsen thought to ask the question that no one had yet asked to that point: why were witches almost always women? Her interpretation centered around women who behaved in ways society found unsettling or dangerous. Such women might be accused of witchcraft as a way to maintain the male hierarchy in the face of a changing or chaotic world. More recently, historian Mary Beth Norton has argued that unrest along the colonial frontier's contested territory contributed greatly to the witchcraft craze, as colonists searched for supernatural explanations for colonial defeats in Indian wars.

All these explanations exemplify the way that historians work when trying to explain the past. None of them can reveal the whole story. All of them together allow pieces of the past to come to light. They also make clear the importance of including women in the history of the country. If witchcraft and accusations related to witches had much to do with property and economics, with wars against Indians lost by the colonists, with religion and spiritual understandings of people's place in the New World, they also had much to do with gendered expectations of how women were supposed to act in society and under the law. In the seventeenth century, the English saw the New World filled with possibilities. Interference with those possibilities, by competing colonial powers, by Native Americans, by women trying to bypass the social hierarchies designed to control them, by any forces at all, had to be met and conquered if the New World was going to pass into the control of the Europeans who desired it.

THINK MORE ABOUT IT

1. Return to the opening vignette about Lady Deborah Moody. One of the themes of this book is that the narrative of women's lives in what became the United States has not been one of continued, steady progress toward greater rights. How does her life and that of other Dutch women colonists demonstrate this point?

2. Define the legal idea of *feme covert*. How is the status of women under coverture different from that of *feme sole* and *feme sole* trader? Explain how English laws about women played an important role in the life of the British American colonies.

3. As tobacco became a successful crop, Virginia became a land-hungry society. Discuss how this land hunger shaped the lives of diverse women in the Chesapeake colonies. Be sure to consider the effects on Natives, the enslaved, indentured servants, and other newcomers to these colonies.

4. By the end of the seventeenth century, the New England and Chesapeake colonies had developed quite differently in terms of economy, society, and religion. What were the major consequences of these differences on women's lives? In what areas were women's lives similar in both parts of colonial British America?

5. In colonial societies of the seventeenth century, women were expected to live by a fairly strict set of social norms, some inscribed in law, others followed by custom, and many bolstered by religious beliefs. Using specific examples, outline the norms that were thought to govern women's conduct and describe the consequences to women who stepped outside these bounds. (One good place to start is by rereading Primary Source 2-2 on the trial of Anne Hutchinson.)

6. In what ways did women in the colonies contribute to the economic and social welfare of their households during the seventeenth century? Offer precise detail about these contributions. How did their position as active participants in colonial households mesh with their legal subordination to their husbands, fathers, or masters?

7. What did you learn in this chapter that you did not know before? How does this new information help you understand the overall story of women in American history? What topics would you like to explore further?

READ MORE ABOUT IT

Catherine Adams and Elizabeth Pleck, *Love of Freedom: Black Women in Colonial and Revolutionary New England*

Kathleen Brown, *Good Wives, Nasty Wenches, and Anxious Patriarchs: Gender, Race, and Power in Colonial Virginia*

Lois Green Carr and Lorena S. Walsh, "The Planter's Wife: The Experience of White Women in Seventeenth-Century Maryland"

Carol Karlsen, *The Devil in the Shape of a Woman: Witchcraft in Colonial New England*

Mary Beth Norton, *In the Devil's Snare: The Salem Witchcraft Crisis of 1692*

Terri L. Snyder, *Brabbling Women: Disorderly Speech and the Law in Early Virginia*

Linda Sturtz, *Within Her Power: Propertied Women in Colonial Virginia*

Laurel Thatcher Ulrich, *Goodwives: Image and Reality in the Lives of Women in Northern New England, 1650–1750*

KEY CONCEPTS

les filles du roi

original sin

substantive law

statute law

common law

equity law

feme sole

feme covert

feme sole trader

indentured servant

chattel slavery

skewed sex ratio

Quakers

goodwife

brabbling women

witchcraft

Chapter 3

FROM COLONIES TO NATION: THE EIGHTEENTH CENTURY

Anne Broughton of South Carolina

On October 14, 1715, Anne Broughton, the wife of Colonel Thomas Broughton, a South Carolina politician and owner of Mulberry Plantation and one of the finest mansions in the colony, wrote to her son, Captain Nathaniel Broughton. After telling him that his father's health was better as he recovered from the "flux" he had suffered since Nathaniel left to resume command of his militia company, she mentioned that she had heard little news about the "Charakees" [Cherokees], whom many in the colony feared were plotting war against the colonists. Some thirty miles northwest of Charleston, Anne Broughton relied on travelers to bring her the news. Having recently seen someone from Wassamassaw, nearer the coast, she felt reassured that the visitor "knowes nothing of" any pending attacks. Rumors were rife but, she supposed, "it is all false." Nevertheless, her postscript informed her son that his father "orders me to tell you to take care to keep out scouts every day." On April 15, the previous spring, the Yamasee War began, and she no doubt feared continuing attacks in the fall from the Indians allied against the English.

Despite the reassurance Broughton received from her visitor, this missive makes it clear that Broughton combined her domestic duties of caring for her sick husband with increasing concern given the political world about her. Since 1708, Mulberry Plantation on the Cooper River served as a trading center for Indians and whites. That trade was sorely interrupted by the Yamasee War, and the Broughtons opened the plantation as a refuge for those fleeing the bloodshed during 1715.

One of the bloodiest wars in American history, the Yamasee War nearly destroyed the colony of South Carolina. Indian allies included the Creek, Catawba, Apalachee, Chickasaw, Pee Dee, and other southeastern groups. Determined to avenge attacks by the colonists, the Native Americans killed 7 percent of the English population between 1715 and 1717, and many of the survivors fled, some to Mulberry Plantation, far more to the security of the forts of Charles Town (today Charleston). The Cherokee that Broughton referred to in her letter to her son allied themselves at first with the Yamasee, but later shifted their support to the English colonists. That alliance, combined with additional colonial troops from North Carolina and Virginia, helped to turn the tide against the Indians.

Englishmen and women, such as Anne Broughton and her family, had long traded successfully with the Indians of the region for deerskin, but by 1715, economic downturns, acts of violence, and continued cultural misunderstandings took their toll on the relationship between the English and the Native Americans. English traders extended credit for high-priced and unregulated trade goods, and some Indians, particularly the Yamasee, faced mounting debts as the supply of deerskins in the region dried up due to overhunting. By 1711, the Yamasee owed the English 100,000 deerskins for the trade goods they had received, with no means to pay the debt. In addition to taking advantage of the Indians, English captured and enslaved both individual Indians as well as large groups. They did not hesitate to use violence, particularly sexual assaults, on Native women. In the matrilineal societies of the Southeast such as the Cherokee and the Lower Creek, Englishmen's ideas of women's proper place clashed with Native American ideas. When English trader Phillip Gilliard, for example, kidnapped an Apalachee woman, got her drunk, locked her up, and kept her "against her Will for his Wife," his acts of violence against a Native woman horrified the Indians. In their matrilineal societies husbands did not beat their wives, nor force their sexual attentions on them, nor boss them around. Rather the opposite was true, at least as far as the English could see. Cherokee women, wrote trader Alexander Longe, "Rules the Rostt and weres the brichess," and would "beat thire husbands within an Inch of thire life" to assert their dominance within their family. Englishmen who assumed that Native American women needed to be controlled and dominated, in the manner of English women, found it difficult to moderate their behavior so they would not offend the Indians with whom they traded.

This cultural clash regarding women's role in society was one of many such clashes that flourished along the frontier. The frontier, as ethnohistorians have defined it, was a zone of cultural interaction where the ways of neither culture—in this case, English and Indian—have yet become dominant. Clashes along that frontier continued as the competition for control of the North American continent lasted over the course of the eighteenth century. In addition to struggles with Native Americans, competing powers—the French, Spanish, and English—strove to become the dominant European power. The sheer numbers of English colonists decided the contest. British immigrants to America imposed their ways of life, including the social classes prevalent in England, and expanded the institution of black slavery. Colonists imported European religious and philosophical ideas, transforming them into American versions, modified to fit the American landscape. By the end of the colonial period, Americans—women and men—were quite different from the European colonists who had preceded them. Those differences led to one last upheaval—the American Revolution—as Americans sought to disengage themselves from European control and form their own nation.

FRONTZIERS AND THE COMPETITION FOR EMPIRE

As Europeans moved into the interior of North America, the frontier shifted. Settlement moved inward from the East Coast as well as into the great Southwest, often forcing Native Americans from coastal regions into the country's interiors, where they, in turn, fought against resident Native groups. Cultural conflicts also accelerated as the pace of European invasion increased. Competing European powers fought with one another and the Native American populations for supremacy and control. These clashes took different forms in the geographic regions of the Upper Midwest, the Southwest, and the Southeast, and women's participation varied as well.

The Upper Midwest

In the eighteenth century, the interior of North America, bounded by the St. Lawrence River on the north, the Mississippi River on the west, and the Ohio River on the south, became a land where the British, the French, and the Native Americans all vied for supremacy over the region. French colonists and fur traders worked in this area of present-day Canada into the Great Lakes region. The importance of the fur trade to the relationships between the French and the Natives cannot be understated. In exchange for beaver fur pelts, the French brought items such as silk and "trade cloth" (which replaced deerskin for Native American clothing), metal tools, and cooking utensils. Indian men themselves hunted or guided French hunters—the *voyageurs*—to beaver grounds, then loaded the pelts into canoes that they paddled to the

MAP OF BRITISH AMERICA IN 1763 This map of Britain's thirteen American colonies in 1763 also shows the vast expanse of lands to the west of the Proclamation Line, drawn to limit colonial settlement. The British, French, Spanish, Indians, and colonists—men and women alike—traded throughout the western areas, in the middle ground of cultural intersections.

markets. Indian women tanned the hides to get them ready for market, and provided the food that both hunters and traders needed to survive. They also negotiated with the European men, translating and bargaining, thus controlling much of the trade.

To achieve maximum success, the French soon learned that they had to work within the cultural sensibilities of the Native community. The Native Americans used kinship ties to control the fur trade in the region. Access to hunting grounds was also limited to kin. Even selling the pelts was often limited to people with whom Indians had a kin relationship. Marriage was one way to build kin networks, along with adoption of captives taken to replace family members lost in conflicts. Thus, numerous French traders, eager to gain access to the trade, married Native women. Many of these marriages proved long-lived; others were primarily undertaken as a way into the fur-trading network. Either way, Native wives incorporated the French *voyageurs* into their tribes. Marriage meant not only access to the fur trade, but also protection for the traders as they traveled with their goods to Indian hunting camps. Children born of these French–Native unions were called *métis*. In matrilineal tribes, such as the Iroquois, *métis* children inherited their mothers' clan and their mothers' community, often becoming important leaders by serving as bridges between the Native American and European worlds. *Métis* worked as Europeans or as Native Americans, as the occasion required, negotiating in what historian Richard White has labeled the "middle ground" of cultural intersections.

Indians and Frenchmen also forged ties through the Catholic religion and particularly through its tradition of godparents. Catholicism attracted numbers of Native women (see Primary Source 3-1). Unlike Kateri Tekakwitha, the seventeenth-century "Lily of the Mohawk," who after her conversion had adopted a European style of living (see Chapter 1), most Native women who became Catholic merged European and Native religious traditions. For example, eighteenth-century Jesuit missionaries found that the Lakota Sioux understood God as the Great Spirit, a familiar figure in their cosmology. Native women, who often used oral traditions to transmit their group's history, used similar methods to promote their faith in family prayers and by telling the stories of the Gospel. Native women who became Catholic also might serve as lay practitioners within the church, since the frontier was so vast and priests so few that the priest assigned to a region might appear only once a year. In the mid-1700s, for example, Marie Madeline Réaume, daughter of an Illini woman, Simphorose Ouaouagoukoue, and a French fur trader and interpreter, Jean Baptiste Réaume, appeared in records as a lay practitioner near Green Bay, in present-day Wisconsin. Women such as Réaume led daily prayers, participated in Sunday services, and assumed the responsibility for religious practices within both the family and the larger group.

Of the Catholic traditions, one of the most important for women was that of godparent. Not only did Native women serve as godparents, but the kin networks of godparents played much the same role as the kin networks of Natives. Both were crucial to the fur trade. Réaume, for example, had her son baptized with two prominent traders as his godparents. She married off two daughters as well, one to a Three Rivers (Michigan) fur

A JESUIT MISSIONARY'S VIEW OF ILLINOIS WOMEN

Jesuit missionaries attempted to convert the Indian women and men they lived with to Christianity. Their reports back to their home offices or to other missionaries provide historians much information about Native American societies, albeit presented in a Eurocentric view that dismissed the Indians' culture and compared all they did to European standards of proper behavior and gendered notions of work. Gabriel Marest, a Jesuit missionary living in the Great Lakes region, wrote this 1712 account of how receptive Illinois Native American women were to Catholicism because of their work habits.

"The Illinois are much less barbarous than other Savages; Christianity and intercourse with the French have by degrees civilized them. This is to be noticed in our Village, of which early all the inhabitants are Christians; it is this also which has brought many Frenchmen to settle here, and very recently we married three of them to Illinois women.

trader, the other to a Montreal merchant. With those kin connections, her place and the place of her children within the fur trade was secure.

Security was sometimes very difficult to come by on the frontier. A global war for empire between the French and British from 1754 to 1763, known as the Seven Years' War in America, resulted in the transfer of control of the Great Lakes region and its fur trade to the British. Englishmen arrived in the region and attempted to trade with the Native Americans, but ignored the kin networks and the women who controlled them and, through those networks, much of the fur trade. The British viewed the fur trade as part of the man's world, and tried to establish a trade similar to that which they had on the East Coast as well as in the Pacific and Canadian Northwest, where Indian men brought furs to English markets. Their failures in the Great Lakes confused English traders who did not understand that if they were not kin, they were not welcome. Coming from a patriarchal hierarchy, Englishmen simply could not fathom why women would need to be part of the process. By 1767, the impact of their miscalculation had become clear: 85 percent of the traders in the Upper Midwest were still French, and the English who succeeded in the fur trade were the ones who had married Native women and had been adopted into the kinship system that was part and parcel of the trade network.

The Southwest

Control of trade along the Southwest frontier between Spanish Europeans and Natives was also contested. The arrival of the Spanish and their market economy had greatly changed the lives of Native Americans in the Southwest. The Spanish had implemented a forced labor system known as the *encomienda*, enforcing the rules with floggings, dismemberments, and hangings. The

These Savages do not lack intelligence; they are naturally inquisitive, and turn a joke in a fairly ingenious manner. Hunting and war form the whole occupation of the men; the rest of the work belongs to the women and the girls,—it is they who prepare the ground which must be sowed, who do the cooking, who pound the corn, who set up the cabins, and who carry them on their shoulders in the journeys. These cabins are composed of mats made of flat rushes, which they have the skill of sewing together in such a way that the rain cannot penetrate them when they are new. In addition to this, they are busied in working up the hair of the oxen and in making it into leggings, girdles, and bags; for the oxen here [bison] are very different from those of Europe; besides having a great hump upon the back, near the shoulders, they are also wholly covered with a very fine wool, which takes the place of that which our Savages would obtain from sheep, if there were any in the Country. The women thus occupied and humbled by work are thereby more disposed to accept the truths of the Gospel. It is not the same toward the lower part of the Mississipi, where the idleness which prevails among the women gives opportunity for the most shocking irregularities, and wholly indisposes them to the way of salvation."

Source: From *The Jesuit Relations and Allied Documents,* ed. Reuben Gold Thwaites, vol. 66 (Cleveland: Burrows Brothers, 1900), 231–233.

Franciscan friars, missionaries to the region, persecuted Native Americans for practicing their own religions, demanding tithes and tributes that impoverished many. In 1680, when drought and famine exacerbated the misery in the New Mexico region, many Pueblo, supported by some Apache groups, revolted. The warfare was particularly disruptive to women's lives, as they were captured by both sides to be adopted, converted, or used as slaves. Women were also promised as rewards: "The Indian who shall kill a Spaniard will get an Indian woman for a wife," promised one Indian leader, "and he who kills four will get four women, and he who kills ten or more will have a like number of women." The Spanish were driven from the area for twelve years.

Between 1692 and 1696, however, the Spanish reconquered the area, but resumed their rule with a lighter hand. They eliminated the *encomienda* and allowed Native Americans to practice their own religion instead of forcing conversions to Catholicism, hoping to resume a lucrative trade system again. Even so, the Spanish continued to encourage the Indians they encountered to live by Spanish rules. Near present-day Santa Barbara, Father Junipero Serra wrote to Spanish Viceroy Bucareli in 1773, asking for permission to award livestock to men who married the local Indian women to encourage European standards of behavior. To encourage Christian marriages, and fearful that the flock in Alta California would sin beyond redemption because of their sexual relations with Native Americans, Spanish missionaries also insisted that Spanish women settlers must migrate to the region along with the men. While some Europeans married Native women, others did not, preferring not to formalize relationships they had with Indians. Various results came from these unions: *mestizo* (mixed) children, sexually transmitted disease, *nuevos cristianos* (Christian converts), and angry European wives such as Dona Eulalia Callis, who sued her husband for divorce in 1785 after catching him in a compromising position with a young Yuma girl. Attempts to arrive at a compromise on cultural questions were at the heart of European and Indian interaction along the frontier, but on some matters people refused to compromise.

By the eighteenth century, warfare and, even more often, disease resulted in depopulation in the Southwest. The number of Pueblo villages, for example, declined from eighty to about thirty. As villages disappeared and men died in warfare, women's lives changed drastically. Pueblo women reassembled their families in smaller and fewer villages and took up trade to support themselves and their families. Their pottery became an important commodity in trade with the Spanish and with other Native groups. After the reconquest by the Spanish, some Pueblos fled north to begin life again among the Navajos in northern New Mexico. There, Pueblo men often not only married Navajo women, but also taught them to weave, providing another product to support that community.

Throughout the eighteenth century, the Southwest borderlands remained a region of cultural conflict and women stood at its center. For all the parties in the region, women's labor was indispensable. Women fed, clothed, and often sheltered the rest of the group by building homes. Women's labor enabled men to pursue hunting, trading, politicking, and warring. Moreover, just as sheep, goats, mules, horses, and cattle were all fair game to be captured for use as natural resources and market goods, so women in the Southwest region were also commodities to be captured, traded, adopted, or enslaved (although the last was more common in the Southeast and Pacific Northwest).

Even as the encounter with Europeans changed Native ways of life, women were still responsible for feeding and caring for their families. The Navajo and Pueblo became more sedentary, farming and raising sheep and cattle. The Apaches, Utes, Shoshones, and Comanches focused on horsemanship to increase their success at raiding the Spanish and Pueblo settlements. Those raids furnished the Comanches, ascendant in the region after 1700, with not only material goods, but more often female captives. The Comanche adopted some women and girls to replace lost family members, a common fate for war captives in many Native American groups. They also sold some women as slaves to the Spanish (despite its illegality) and to other Anglos. More often, and unlike African slaves, Indian slaves kept by their captors gradually became full members of the household, shedding their status as war captives. Still other women captives became wives. Adopted into the tribe, women could become *chore wives* as opposed to *chief wives*, if the tribe practiced polygamy. Chore wives did the heavy labor at the direction of the chief wife, who was usually a Comanche man's first wife.

Comanches took captive thousands, mostly women and girls—mostly Indian, but also hundreds of Spanish, Mexicans, and Anglos from the lands in which they lived: New Mexico, Texas, Colorado, Kansas, and Oklahoma. The precariousness of a woman's existence in the Southwest borderlands might best be illustrated by the life of Spanish colonist Mariá Rosa Villalpando, age 21, captured by Comanches in 1760. Taken from her infant son José, she was traded to the Pawnees, where she had another son, whom the group would have viewed as a full member of the group and as a

Pawnee. As his mother, Villalpando's status in the group rose and she may well have been regarded as a family member rather than a captive. In 1767, French trader Jean Salé dit Leroie, founder of the city of St. Louis, arrived at Villalpando's Pawnee village and began living with her, no doubt seeking to join the kin network to which she belonged so he could trade more effectively. Villalpando bore him a son, and in 1770, the couple left for St. Louis, where they married and had three more children. She stayed in St. Louis in 1792, when Salé dit Leroie returned to France. In 1803, José Villalpando arrived at his mother's door, only to be paid off with 200 pesos in exchange for relinquishing any claim to her estate, which presumably, she preferred to conserve for her children by her French husband. She had successfully negotiated the cultures of the Spanish colony she began her adult life in, the Pawnee group she had lived with, and her final years in the American city of St. Louis. She found, however, that family ties at birth could be broken by adoptive ties, by marital ties and children, and by forty-three years of living with outsiders.

Spanish attempting to rule the Southwest in the eighteenth century faced not only Native men who might kill them or capture their women to use as part of their warfare, but also Native women rebelling against foreign rule. In 1785, for instance, a Tongva Indian medicine woman named Toypurina led Indians in a revolt in southern California against the Spanish occupiers at the San Gabriel mission. Angry that the missionaries refused to let the mission Indians hold their native dances, Toypurina, allied with a chief named Tomasajaquichi and others, conspired to destroy the mission. Discovered before their attack could succeed, she was accused of being a sorceress and put on trial. She told the military court trying her, "I hate the padres and all of you for living here on my native soil . . . for trespassing on the land of my forefathers and despoiling our tribal remains." The attack failed, and the Spanish banished Toypurina to a mission farther north, where she was forcibly converted to Christianity. This imposition of a European religion upon a Native American is an example of how the frontier's middle ground could end. Spanish forces could not have done this successfully until that middle ground of cultural compromise that characterized the frontier declined in the late eighteenth century.

In the eighteenth century, the Great Southwest was a cauldron of competing forces. As the Spanish pushed farther north from Mexico, Europeans displaced Indians, some of whom in turn displaced other Indians. The arrival of the European market economy, forced labor systems, drought, warfare, disease, depopulation, and competing claims for limited resources, as well as Native resistance to such upheaval, all affected women's lives within groups struggling for survival in the region.

The Southeast

Competition with Europeans for scarce resources also affected Indians of the Southeast. In Mississippi, the Natchez, who had coexisted peacefully with the French since they began settling the region in the 1600s, struggled to contain those colonists after 1720. The French demanded the Natchez cede their

NATCHEZ WOMAN AND DAUGHTER French artists recorded the appearance of this Natchez woman and her daughter. Their lack of clothing shocked Europeans concerned with preserving women's modesty, but these garments reflected practical choices made by Native Americans, given the tropical climate of the lower Mississippi River Valley.

rich lands to them so that they could raise tobacco for export. By 1729, more than 400 free French settlers, 280 African slaves, and 28 soldiers occupied the lands near Fort Rosalie, located on the Mississippi River. When the commandant of the fort demanded yet another parcel of land for yet another French farm, the Natchez had had enough. On November 28, 1729, the Natchez warriors borrowed the guns of French settlers (a custom that had enabled the Natchez to hunt in the past) and proceeded to kill the Frenchmen. Over 200 French men, women, and children died in the deadliest attack by Native Americans in the colony's history. Reprisals followed, and other colonists in the area were captured or enslaved, as the Natchez spared the lives of some white settlers to replace the lost members of their own families.

French officials heard of the deaths at the hands of the Natchez, as well as of another quarrel between the French and the Yazoo Indians nearby. Fearing a general rebellion of Indians in the area, French soldiers persuaded their Indian allies, the Choctaws, to join them in an attack upon the Natchez. After a siege, the Natchez were defeated in February 1730. The survivors fled to other regions, some joining the Chickasaws and the Creeks. Natchez leader the Great Sun and his family, along with some 400 followers, were captured, taken to New Orleans, and sold as slaves to the island of Haiti. By 1731, the Natchez, a complex matrilineal group of considerable power, were no more.

Complete annihilation of a Native group was not uncommon in the years of colonization and settlement in the Southeast. In Spanish Florida, for example, none of the Timucuan-speaking tribes survived into the nineteenth century, and most were gone by the middle of the eighteenth. *La Florida*, or "Land of Flowers," as the colony was known to the Spanish, was the outpost of a nation weakened by European wars at home and raids by English and French forces abroad. Pirates, including two women, Anne Bonney and Mary Read, and the notorious Edward Teach, known as "Blackbeard," plagued the region as well.

The center of Spanish settlement was St. Augustine. The Spanish had made attempts to establish missions elsewhere in the first half of the seventeenth century, but most were in ruins by the eighteenth, destroyed by English colonists and their Indian allies who launched a war from the Carolinas against the Spanish in Georgia and Florida. Indians in the region died from European diseases, were killed in raids by Carolinians, or were enslaved and taken north to the English colonies. During the War of the Spanish Succession in 1702, known as Queen Anne's War in English North America, the English began a major invasion of Florida by attacking the fort at St. Augustine, hoping to drive the Spanish from the southern border of the English colonies. Fifteen hundred men, women, and children fled to the protection of the fort where they outlasted a siege imposed by the British until relieved by Spanish troops from Cuba. The British withdrew, but the Spanish would see them again and again over the next half-century.

The sore point for the English went beyond the competing land claims and control of Indians and their trade. The Spanish colony had very different laws regarding slavery and did not recognize escaped English slaves as the property of English owners. In fact, the Spanish sometimes offered freedom to black slaves who ran way from their English masters. When James Oglethorpe settled Georgia beginning in 1733, slavery was forbidden by law. But escaped slaves from the Carolinas fled through the Georgia backcountry and on to Florida, and after 1751, when slavery was legalized in Georgia, even more English-owned slaves fled to Spanish territory, causing more unrest between the English colonies and their Spanish neighbor.

Under Spanish law, slavery was regarded as an "unnatural" state for humans. Slaves possessed instead a natural right to liberty, including the right to appeal to a court to be assessed so that they might determine their value and save their money to buy their freedom, even if their owner did not wish to sell. Not only that, but in 1693 King Charles II of Spain had declared that English slaves who fled to Spanish territories were free. Spanish law not only gave African women enslaved by the English more and different rights than they had under English law as slaves, it also offered them more and different rights than they had under English law as women.

Spanish law classified women (along with children, invalids, and delinquents) as dependents who needed protection. Women were under the protection of their fathers or brothers until they died, married, or reached the age of twenty-five. Women could inherit, sell, and hold property from their parents and could not lose their property to the husbands' creditors. Women under Spanish law inherited equally with their brothers. Dower rights were more substantial than under English law as well. A Spanish widow inherited outright half the wealth earned during a marriage at her husband's death, instead of gaining the use of only one-third of her husband's property, as was the case in English law. Women could also enter into legal contracts under Spanish law, as long as they had their husbands' written permission or his power of attorney.

Free women could and did own, operate, and manage farms and plantations in *La Florida* and elsewhere, running businesses, suing creditors, and buying and selling property as they needed to. Slave women also had specific legal rights: conjugal rights, the right to not be separated from their children, and the right to personal security, which meant they had a legal way to escape a cruel master. They even had the right to medical care. Slave women could hold and transfer property, could sue in court, and had the right to *buen gobierno:* justice. They could also hire themselves out, keep their wages, save that money, and then buy their freedom, even if their masters objected. Filis Edimboro, a slave from Guinea, worked as a laundress for her owner, Don Sanchez, a wealthy cattle rancher, but also took in laundry to make the money to buy her freedom. She made and sold toys, baked and sold *tortes* (a kind of cake), and hosted community dances with her husband Felipe. Eventually she and Felipe used the court system to buy their freedom from Sanchez over his protests in 1794. Other enslaved women washed for Spanish soldiers, cooked, trained girls for domestic service, raised pigs for market, and made baskets. Surviving records of the courts of St. Augustine show numerous women, both free and slave, used the legal system to claim their rights and often their freedom.

For rural slave women on Spanish farms in Florida, access to the legal system was more limited, but since so few settlements existed outside of St. Augustine and Pensacola, "rural" was still fairly close to those towns. Rural women did field labor, cared for animals and children, cooked, cleaned, did laundry, wove cloth, sewed clothing for both the black and white families they cared for, and practiced midwifery. Many of these tasks could be turned into a money-making proposition, although a woman's pay was ordinarily less than a man's daily pay of half a *peso*, and several hundred *pesos* were needed to buy one's freedom.

Slave or free, marriage for women in Spanish Florida was their most common fate, and the law required the protection of those women dependents. The Spanish legal system and society commonly recognized even irregular relationships. Common-law marriage, for example, was recognized and necessarily so, given the scarcity of priests who could marry the colonists of Florida. So was concubinage, as well as children born out of wedlock and other irregular relationships, all acknowledged, along with godparenting, as part of the kinship system of the community. As long as men publicly acknowledged the relationships they had with women, the courts upheld the rights of the women and children of those relationships. The dependency that the law forced women into could be to their advantage, particularly in terms of financial support. Even racial differences did not limit recognizing relationships between women and men. Spain had had centuries of experience with Africans as parts of Spanish communities, and racial categories were less rigid than they were farther north. Miscegenation (specifically interracial marriage) was neither forbidden nor seen as deviant behavior as was the case farther north. Small wonder that English slaves fled to Florida and grew into a substantial community, complete with their own settlement, Santa Teresa de la Gracia de Mose, just north of St. Augustine. Just thirty-five miles away from the English colonial border, and regarded with fear and loathing by English slaveowners who feared a slave rebellion or the disappearance of their property south, the town was a target for an English invasion in 1728, and yet another in 1739.

The warfare that characterized much of the eighteenth century displaced and widowed women, who faced death, capture, rape, and enslavement, along with the loss of their husbands, families, and homes. Anne Broughton's letter to her son Nathaniel, warning him to keep a lookout, was no doubt echoed by thousands of other women. In the Upper Midwest, conflict escalated over the fur trade, where women's roles in defining kin systems were crucial. In the Southwest, Spanish intolerance for Native American beliefs and behavior led to unrelenting conflict. In the Southeast, widespread destruction of Native American groups had turned much of the competition on the frontier into a contest between the Spanish and English. Differences in Spanish law, particularly laws relating to slavery, attracted escaped English slaves to the Florida colony, where they might eventually free themselves. At the same time, English colonists who feared both slave escapes and slave rebellion, sought to limit the damage to their property rights by engaging the Spanish militarily over the course of the century.

THE BRITISH IN NORTH AMERICA

If one looks at a map of European possessions in North America by the eighteenth century, the French appear to be the dominant power. New France ranged from the mouth of the St. Lawrence River, covered all the Great Lakes, slid down the Mississippi River to New Orleans near the Gulf of Mexico, then west to present-day Texas and north up the Missouri River almost to Lake Winnipeg. Although estimates by geographers vary, by 1740, at its territorial height, New France had around 60,000 colonists in Canada, and perhaps another 20,000 in areas west of the British colonies, particularly near New Orleans. The British, on the other hand, had less land but nearly 1 million colonists, located primarily near the Atlantic, although they also occupied lands west to the Appalachian Mountain range that divided the continent north to south. In the same area remained approximately 200,000 Native Americans. Despite resistance by Native Americans and imperial warfare conducted by the

GOTTLIEB MITTELBERGER'S EMIGRATION TO AMERICA

Moving to America in the eighteenth century was fraught with danger. Ships often took four months or more to travel from their home ports to the customs offices in England then across the Atlantic, always dependent upon the winds and subjected to the storms that blew through the area in the summers. Women's descriptions of the trip are rare. The following is from a man who described the journey in 1750, particularly the difficulties suffered by women as they traveled in overcrowded ships across dangerous seas.

"[D]uring the voyage there is on board these ships terrible misery, stench, fumes, horror, vomiting, many kinds of sea-sickness, fever, dysentery, headache, heat, constipation, boils, scurvy, cancer, mouth-rot, and the like, all of which come from old and sharply salted food and meat, also from very bad and foul water, so that many die miserably. . . . Add to this want of provisions, hunger, thirst, frost, heat, dampness, anxiety, want, afflictions and lamentations. . . . The misery reaches the climax when a gale rages for 2 or 3 nights and days, so that every one believes that the ship will go to the bottom with all. . . . No one can have an idea of the sufferings which women in confinement [labor] have to bear with their innocent children on board these ships . . . many a mother is

---

French in both Europe and America, the sheer weight of numbers had much to do with the eventual dominance of the British in North America, as emigrants to the New World continued to swell the ranks. British immigrants continued to bring their ideas regarding the proper role of women, even as the country developed its own measures of graceful living, supported in great part by African slavery, as well as developing its own religious and philosophical ideas during the Great Awakening and the Enlightenment.

Expansion and Immigration

The Act of Union in 1707 formed the nation of Great Britain by uniting England and Scotland and turned the English colonies into British North America. While in the seventeenth century most emigrants to the English colonies came from England proper, in the eighteenth century increasing numbers came from other parts of Great Britain: Scotland, Wales, and Ireland, as well as from German-speaking areas such as Switzerland, Alsace, and regions within the Holy Roman Empire (western and central Europe).

One of the greatest impulses of the eighteenth century was migration, despite its difficulties. (See Primary Source 3-2.) People came to North America from every country in Europe, as well as from Africa and South America, with the majority coming from western Europe. The second largest group was made up of African slaves. Unlike seventeenth-century slaves, who came mostly from trade with Barbados and other Caribbean islands, eighteenth-century slaves were forced migrants transported directly from Africa. Importation of African slaves coincided with increased British

cast into the water with her child as soon as she is dead. One day, just as we had a heavy gale, a woman in our ship, who was to give birth and could not give birth under the circumstances, was pushed through a loophole [port-hole] in the ship and dropped into the sea, because she was far in the rear of the ship and could not be brought forward. . . .

"When the ships have landed at Philadelphia after their long voyage, no one is permitted to leave them except those who pay for their passage or can give good security; the others, who cannot pay, must remain on board the ships till they are purchased, and are released from the ships by their purchasers. . . . Every day Englishmen, Dutchmen and High-German people come from the city of Philadelphia and other places . . . and go on board the newly arrived ship that has brought and offers for sale passengers from Europe, and select among the healthy persons such as they deem suitable for their business, and bargain with them how long they will serve for their passage-money. . . . A woman must stand for her husband if he arrives sick, and in like manner a man for his sick wife, and take the debt upon herself or himself, and thus serve 5 to 6 years not alone for his or her own debt, but also for that of the sick husband or wife. . . . [If] a husband or wife has died at sea . . . the survivor must pay or serve not only for himself or herself, but also for the deceased."

Source: From *Gottlieb Mittelberger's Journey to Pennsylvania in the Year 1750 and Return to Germany in the Year 1754* (Philadelphia: John Jos. McVey, 1898), 20, 22–23, 25–26, 28.

settlement in the south and the continued expansion of labor-intensive agriculture, particularly the rice plantations in South Carolina. Between 1730 and 1770, over 200,000 slaves left the slave dungeons of Africa and survived the *middle passage*, the horrific journey to the American coast, traveling in packed slave ships across the Atlantic.

Voluntary and forced immigrants both filled the colonies along the Eastern seaboard and journeyed into the interior as well. Although only about 10 percent of America was urban by 1700, there were cities developing in America able to absorb many of those in search of more opportunities than existed in Europe. By 1750, Boston, Massachusetts, had 16,000 inhabitants; Newport, Rhode Island, 11,000; New York City, 25,000; Philadelphia, Pennsylvania, 30,000; and Charleston, South Carolina, 12,000. All these cities possessed large stately homes, substantial buildings, banks, an occasional paved street, and all the accouterments of modern eighteenth-century life. Wealthy merchants, both women and men, who sold the natural resources that others harvested from the American interior and shores to Europeans, and who sold goods manufactured in Europe to Americans, became the elites of the colonies. Artisans and their apprentices, innkeepers and small store owners, men and women alike, along with unskilled laborers, sailors, indentured servants, and slaves (African and Native American) made up the rest of the population of the cities.

Urban centers were home to women of various occupations. While most women were married, there were sizable single populations in cities. There a single woman could make a living as a seamstress, a milliner, a domestic servant, a shopworker, or by keeping an "ordinary," or tavern. The growing complexity of the American economy meant urban women did not have to get married to survive. As historian Karin Wulf found in her study of colonial Philadelphia, the urban economy provided women with options beyond those that came with marriage to produce income or supplement any capital they may have inherited. She cited the life and career of Hannah Breintnall. Widowed, Breintnall opened a shop and tavern in her forties, then began operating an optician's shop. By 1767, she was worth 30 pounds, an amount that put her in the top 10 percent of those paying taxes that year. When she died, she left a large estate of 161 pounds, having never remarried. Thus the typical rural pattern for women that included marriage and, if a widow, remarriage was not always the case in urban communities.

While in the seventeenth century the word *woman* was nearly interchangeable with *wife*, by the late eighteenth century in Philadelphia almost 20 percent of elite women were unmarried. In two New Jersey Quaker meetings, 23 percent of the women members were unmarried at the age of fifty. By the fourth quarter of the eighteenth century, one-third of the Jewish women in Philadelphia, New York, and Charleston remained unmarried. Changes in the domestic economy meant jobs developed that could support women, although barely, but some women remained single because of the warfare that was part and parcel of the eighteenth century, leaving both widows and single women bereft of mates in its wake. In Boston, for example, 25 percent of the adult women in the city were widows after the Seven Years' War that ended in 1763.

In addition to women who could not find marriage partners, the disinclined, particularly in the middle colonies, refused to marry for personal reasons. A 1731 poem, copied out by a single woman in her surviving journal, read in part "Two Kindest Souls alone must meet; Tis Friendship makes the Bondage sweet." Such sentiments indicated that she would not marry for financial reasons—she required a true friendship with a husband. Some women could now afford to think not only about the economics of marriage, but also about its psychological cost, since marriage was a bond rarely broken by divorce. There were regional differences in this view of marriage as a choice instead of a destiny as well, in part because of regional cultural expectations. New England traditionally regarded single women with some suspicion, and the South's growing slave culture that forbade slave marriages made marriage of white women a mark of racial superiority. The middle colonies, however, were so heterogeneous that imposing a cultural standard such as marriage for all became increasingly difficult. The cultural and economic diversity of the region meant more choices for women, and less censure for those who did not choose the domestic path.

The Rise of Gentility

The domestic path of marriage and children changed as well in its nature with what is termed *the rise of gentility* in the eighteenth century. As people became richer, social classes reasserted themselves and became the determinant of behavior and cultural norms. In other words, how one behaved and what was considered normal behavior was defined in part by what social class one belonged to, and social class was determined largely, but not exclusively, by one's wealth. To be "genteel," was to be socially superior, polite, accomplished, and refined, all possible for the wealthy and the educated who benefited from the improvements in transportation, intercolonial trade, and the consumer revolution that relied on importing manufactured goods from Europe. Farmers' wives, instead of going to work in the fields at harvest, could become wealthy enough to manage and direct the work of others. Urban women could become wealthy enough to purchase the items they needed to run their homes instead of having to make them. New possessions not only transformed people's lives, they provided visible ways to convey one's social status.

In practical terms, the rise of gentility transformed the spareness of existence that the colonists in the seventeenth century exhibited. In the eighteenth century, for example, houses began to have separate rooms with separate functions, such as kitchens and bedchambers. Colonists began to own and use separate glasses for wine and tankards for drink, instead of passing around a family mug. Furniture was upholstered or cushioned instead of hard wood. Clocks and portraits and mirrors hung on the walls of rooms where people dined instead of simply refueling. The genteel classes might have carpets, silver plate, chandeliers, brass door-knockers, china dishes, and pewter andirons that were polished to shine like silver. These new possessions meant new chores to be undertaken by the mistress of the house or, far more often among the genteel, by the servants and slaves: dusting, polishing, and cleaning dishes, tablecloths, and glassware. Even cooking changed: simple one-pot meals became instead multicourse meals with separate dishes that required new kinds of cooking techniques, stoves, utensils, and pots and pans to prepare.

The genteel classes maintained their distance from the others in their society not so much by the accumulation of these goods, but also by using them and by creating rituals associated with their use. Upper-class women, for instance, took tea at social visits with members of their own class, using tea services imported from England or China and sweetened with sugar from the West Indies, presented on mahogany tables by servants and slaves, accompanied by delicate cookies and treats, in rooms with draperies and wallpaper. Farm women, on the other hand, gulped down the beverage on a break from their ever-present chores in a one-room house with shutters instead of glass windows. Upper-class girls trained to become mistresses of a household after their marriage and studied French, dancing, embroidery, and music, while farm girls did domestic chores and poor urban girls learned a craft or trade so that they could contribute to the family income until such time as they were expected to marry or perhaps to care for themselves. In addition, while marriage for the lower classes remained based on proximity, physical desire, and economic gain, marriage among the upper class became ritualized, demanding a degree of restraint in pursuit, romance in the language used, and companionship as a measure of compatibility.

Even women bearing children were affected by the rise of gentility. Upper-class women had fewer children and took longer to recover after childbirth, lying in bed for perhaps as long as a month, while poor and rural women were on their feet as soon as possible. Infant care, from birth to weaning to child rearing, while constant for most women throughout their lives, was eased among the rich by the use of servants, particularly young women looking for jobs in urban areas or for wages to supplement their family's farming income. Indentured servitude declined over the century, and most of these domestic servants were now either free women, particularly war widows, or slave women. An entire class of American-born domestic servants was the result: some free, some enslaved, all subject to the demands of the household's mistress.

Economic mobility was possible in America, but wage rates remained at subsistence level, and were far worse for women than for men. Historian Gloria Main concluded that women who earned wages while working on farms in parts of colonial New England earned only 35 to 43 percent of what men did. The weekly rate for female domestic servants in New England in 1777 was the same as the daily rate paid a male farmhand, and female tailors earned only thirty-seven cents for every dollar male tailors made. Spinners in New England, a job traditionally occupied by women, made less than five cents per day. Pay rates for women in Chester County, Pennsylvania, were even lower. Many women, such as maidservants, might be given room and board as part of their compensation, but others could earn barely enough to get by. Owning their own small businesses, such as doctoring, sewing, midwifery, wet-nursing, and tavern-keeping, could lift women out of poverty and put them on the road to a more genteel way of life, but raising the capital to start that business was often impossible.

Black Women, Enslaved and Free

Regional differences in immigration had considerable impact on the lives of black women in the British colonies, particularly slave women. The continuing expansion of tobacco culture, the establishment of rice and indigo cultivation, and the development of slave codes affected their lives greatly. Over the course of the eighteenth century, as the number of slaves increased in the South, the region developed slave societies, rather than simply societies with slaves (see Chapter 2). Virginia and Maryland held the most people in bondage. In South Carolina, the 4,000 slaves in 1708 had risen to 40,000 by 1740. In Georgia, slavery had been illegal but the ban was lifted in 1751, when rice production began in the state, and 349 slaves were tallied. By 1770, there were 16,000, most doing the backbreaking work of rice cultivation. By 1750, 78 percent of American slaves lived in these four colonies.

Tobacco production spread from the Chesapeake into Delaware and North Carolina, and from the coastal areas west into the foothills of the Appalachian Mountains. Massive wealth was generated by tobacco and increasing numbers of slaves were imported from Africa to work ever-larger plantations. By the end of the seventeenth century, African slaves had begun to replace both white indentured servants and Native American slaves, a change that continued through the eighteenth century. By 1720, 25 percent of the Chesapeake's population was black; by 1740, 40 percent. The increase was due almost entirely to Africans, forcibly taken from their homelands to serve the growing American demand for labor.

These changes affected the daily lives of slaves as well as the relationships between owners and slaves. Early in the century, Chesapeake planters first imported twice as many African men as women, making it difficult for newly arrived immigrants to form families and reproduce the population naturally. The birthrate also plummeted when newly arrived Africans succumbed to European diseases and the unhealthy Chesapeake climate. Africans, who came from varying groups and spoke different languages, were segregated from white servants as well as from native-born plantation slaves. On larger farms and plantations, women and men, living in single-sex barracks, were kept from integrating themselves into society and forced to become dependent on their owners for all their needs—food, clothing, shelter, and even communication as the language barriers they faced made it difficult for them to form social ties.

Furthermore, as the number of white indentured servants declined, slavery became more onerous. In the seventeenth century, slaves and English servants alike seldom worked for their masters on Saturdays and Sundays. Most usually had a midday break. They usually worked less in winter and seldom worked in the evenings. By the eighteenth century, however, planters added duties, shortened or eliminated the midday rest, and worked their slaves from sunup to sundown, rather than at a specific task until it was done. They generally gave slaves only three holidays (Easter, Christmas, and Whitsuntide—also called Pentecost, observed the seventh Sunday after Easter). Planters also transformed the slaves' independent economy. Instead of slaves providing their own clothing and food, owners began providing minimal clothing and food. Owners viewed all of slaves' labor as their own, and the time a slave might spend making clothing or growing food in a personal garden was time spent away from her proper task of doing the owner's work.

As the tobacco culture spread to the foothills of the Appalachian Mountains in an area called the Piedmont, slave families were separated, often by great distances, as planters sought new lands on which to grow the lucrative crop. Slaveowners most often took young male workers to the Piedmont, needing them for the heavy work of clearing new lands, as well as harvesting lumber, running mills, and fishing, all of which produced goods for market along with the tobacco. When soils wore out and wheat or corn cultivation replaced tobacco, men were the ones to use draft animals to plow the lands for grain crops. The Piedmont was heavily male in population, and women left behind in more settled regions to the east had to get along without their husbands, sometimes for months or years on end. Not until tobacco cultivation lessened in midcentury did the ratio of men to women even out in the Chesapeake, allowing families to stay intact and communities to form.

Rice cultivation in South Carolina, in what was called the "Low Country," succeeded on large-scale plantations and benefited from the expertise brought by slaves who had grown the crop in West Africa. Men cleared the fields, and women weeded, hoed, fertilized, and helped harvest the crop. Rice fields had to have irrigation systems built and had to be flooded periodically. Males were more valuable for slaveowners, and a skewed sex ratio of twice as many men to women resulted. Here again, as had been true in the Chesapeake, the population was unable to reproduce itself naturally. Harsh working conditions in swampy lands where rice was grown contributed further to high mortality rates and low birthrates. Not until midcentury did slaves begin to form stable families. By then, South Carolinians shifted to the *task system* of work, freeing many slaves from dawn-to-dusk labor characteristic of the *gang system* tobacco planters had used. Planters discovered that their rice production increased when they assigned slaves their own quarter-acre to grow their own rice, digging ir-rigation ditches to flood the crop, building fences to keep it where it be-longed, cultivating it, harvesting it, threshing it. Slaves who completed their tasks for their owner could grow their own rice as well as other crops, leading to a lively, if illegal, economy selling the corn, fish, and poultry they raised. In the urban markets in Charleston, as well as in Savannah, Georgia, slave women came every Sunday to sell the goods they and their families had produced the previous days and weeks.

The increasing size of farms and slaveholdings changed slave women's lives in the South over the course of the eighteenth century. Owners exer-cised far more control over slaves' daily activities, and used far more coer-cion, than they had in the seventeenth century. By day, women worked alongside men in the fields, then stripped leaves from tobacco stems or shucked and shelled corn by night. Women continued to hoe, weed, and worm the tobacco by hand, and to hoe, weed, and help harvest wheat and rice. They also began to build fences, clean stables, and spread manure to fertilize the fields, tasks previously performed by male slaves. Other slave women, particularly as they aged on these larger farms, were likely to be given more domestic service, working as seamstresses and midwives, look-ing after children and the ill.

While larger farms meant harder labor for women slaves, they also gave women a greater chance to form families, particularly in the Chesapeake, where more women had been imported into the region and where the work regime and climate were less deadly than in the Lower South. The life cycles of slave women varied slightly from those of free women. They mar-ried at younger ages to older men, a reflection of the skewed sex ratio that had characterized the Chesapeake region for years. Slave women had fewer children than free women, with a longer period of time between children as they nursed their babies longer than whites did, and suffered from mal-nutrition and other conditions that often limited their fertility. They had enough children, though, that the population increased naturally, and by the 1730s, the number of imported Africans was smaller than the number of American slave babies born—a proportion that would continue to drop.

Slave children remained with their mothers until about age 7, when they were most often separated into single-sex groups to learn their work. More heartbreakingly, it was between the ages of ten and fourteen that children were most likely to be sold away from their mothers or hired out to other planters, sometimes for years. Despite the rise of large farms and plantations, the majority of slaveowners still had so few slaves that slave families were bound to be broken up over the course of their lives. Slaves struggled to preserve their families and to care for them as best they could. Along with poultry, eggs, and crops they raised, slaves often sold baked goods and baskets at town markets. The money they earned went for cloth, thread, and table goods such as dishes and utensils, but slaves also saved their money so they might buy their freedom someday. Masters approved of such entrepreneurship since it lowered the cost of keeping slaves (and, if slaves earned enough to buy their freedom, it reimbursed the owners for their capital investment). Some colonies forbade the practice of allowing slaves to participate in the market economy, but such laws were often ignored.

Slaves who complained of their working conditions or any injustices they had suffered had nowhere to appeal their masters' rule, as slaveowners became absolute rulers over their estates. Any organized resistance to slavery was particularly difficult for women, so often isolated on small farms or watched within white households. Most participants in eighteenth-century slave rebellions were men, but occasionally women appear in the histories. South Carolina's Stono Rebellion in 1739, for instance, where slaves killed some twenty whites in the colony while marching toward freedom promised by the Spanish government in *La Florida*, seems to have had no women participants. That uprising, immediately quelled by South Carolinians, was followed in 1741 by one in New York City, which started with some suspicious fires in March and April. New York had already lived through one slave rebellion in 1712, and whites' suspicions that another had begun were confirmed by a young white indentured servant girl, Mary Burton, who described to authorities a vast conspiracy to burn down the city. Burton, promised her freedom and 100 pounds, pointed to the black owner of the tavern she worked at, John Hughson and his wife. She also accused two slaves and a prostitute. They all denied the crime but were executed, along with twenty-one other black citizens of the city. When Burton continued to accuse more prominent New Yorkers, however, the hunt for arsonists and conspirators ended abruptly.

Such unrest among the enslaved people of British North America, nearly 500,000 total by 1775, left the gentry (the landowners and the wealthy) on edge, particularly in the South. Slaveowners sought new restrictions to control the growing black population. In 1705, Virginia codified its restrictions and laws regarding slavery with a slave code designed to clarify the mishmash of laws that had been passed during the previous century. Colonial Virginia law made slaves of "All servants imported and brought into the Country . . . who were not Christians in their native Country," as well as counting "all Negro, mulatto and Indian slaves within this dominion" as real estate, or property, rather than persons. Some new laws limited physical mobility—for example, slaves needed written permission from their owners to leave their plantations. Other laws limited social mobility—for example, "associating" with whites could leave slaves whipped, branded, or mutilated. As race grew to be one's defining characteristic in these slave societies, unscrupulous owners were not above claiming free servants to be slaves. Moll, a black servant in Virginia, had a master who threatened to carry her out of the colony "claiming her as a slave," even though she was a free black. Slaves resisted these limitations by various means, including breaking tools, procrastinating, killing domestic animals, burning food, and running away. The swamps and forests of the low country and the Piedmont provided hiding places for "maroons," the slaves who left their masters and formed communities of their own.

Northern slavery included Native Americans, as did slavery in the South, but most Northern slaves were African or children of native-born slaves. Northern slave women of all ages performed domestic tasks, since Northern agriculture did not require slave labor to be productive. In addition, Northern slaves were dockworkers, farm laborers, artisans, or workers in city shops. They were far more likely to be alone in the households of their owners, and far more likely to see few people like themselves. Only 10 percent of the populations of Boston, New York, and Philadelphia were black by the end of the colonial period, and only 20 percent of families owned slaves. Phillis Wheatley, the first African American to publish a book of poetry in the colonies, was imported into Boston in 1761 as a domestic slave for John Wheatley's wife, Susannah. Phillis Wheatley's life changed drastically when Susannah decided she would rather train Wheatley in Greek and theology than in cooking and cleaning. In 1767, Wheatley published her first poem; in 1773, she published *Poems on Various Subjects* to

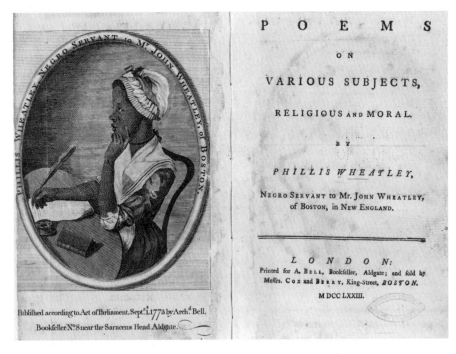

PHILLIS WHEATLEY'S *POEMS ON VARIOUS SUBJECTS* Phillis Wheatley's book of poetry, published in Boston in 1773, did not mention her personal history of slavery. Her portrait, drawn for her book of poems at the request of an antislavery noblewoman, the Countess of Huntington, was created by Scipio Moorhead, a man owned by the Rev. John Moorhead, a neighbor of the Wheatleys. As was the case with Phillis Wheatley, Scipio's talents were encouraged by the wife of the man who had enslaved him.

international acclaim. Freed by John the same year, Wheatley traveled to Europe, met Voltaire and George Washington, and returned to Boston to marry a free black man, John Peters, in 1778.

The free black community in Boston that Wheatley enjoyed was only one of several located in the urban areas in the country. By 1776, there were some 60,000 free blacks in America, 8 percent of the total black population. The largest free black community was in Philadelphia, where some of the earliest antislavery sentiments were articulated. Quakers were the first organized group to speak out against slavery. By midcentury, Quaker Anthony Benezet, a schoolmaster who taught free blacks and slaves at night, and his friend John Woolman conducted a campaign against slavery and for education of the black community. While the Quakers never fully incorporated African Americans into their meetings or their faith, by 1776, they would not allow Quaker members to attend the Philadelphia Yearly Meeting if they did not first free their slaves. Such beliefs were far outside the mainstream, however, and slave women continued to be held in bondage in every colony, while free black women continued to face various restrictions by the dominant white community.

Worldviews

The linking of political action to religious principle was nothing new for the Quakers, the third-largest religious group in the colonies, and an egalitarian religion that expanded the worldview of many an American. Quakers believe God is in everyone, and relied on particularly gifted members, including women, to sense God's direction for their meetings. These women were recognized by the sect as recorded ministers or public friends. They spoke out in meetings, the first group of women in their culture to take such a public role. Some women ministers even traveled as itinerant preachers, such as Esther Palmer. A worn, fragile manuscript survives of her work, describing how, from August 1704 until November 1705, she and three successive companions, Susanna Freeborn, Mary Lawson, and Mary Banister, journeyed some 3,230 miles from New England to the Albemarle Sound of North Carolina. In addition to horseback, they traveled by boat, canoe, and ferry as they crisscrossed the countryside. Despite innumerable hardships, bad weather, nonexistent roads, rough seas, and the possibility of attack by wild animals, Palmer and her companions were determined to share their "inner light" that they believed was given to them by God with others in the American colonies as they sought new adherents to their faith.

Quakers had enjoyed some success in widening the possibilities for women, and meeting a woman Quaker who "traveled in the ministry" did not unduly shock or surprise eighteenth-century Americans. Historian Rebecca Larson found well over 300 women ministers active in the 1700s. Sarah Kemble Knight, who kept a diary of her adventurous journey from Boston to New York in 1704, made reference to Quaker women, calling them "Limbertong'ed." Elizabeth Smith, from New Jersey, began preaching in 1745 at age 21 and wrote epistles for meetings as well as working for the New Jersey Society for Helping the Indians. Esther Peacock Clare emigrated from England to Philadelphia in 1714. Mother of seven, she preached because she wanted "to stir up Friends to their Duty in seeking unto & waiting upon the Lord." Seen as troublemakers and persecuted in the 1600s, Quakers were no longer regarded as a threat to the stability of colonies, a status best symbolized by Quaker Rachel Wilson's visit to Boston in 1769, lauded by the *Boston-Gazette* newspaper, a little over a century after Mary Dyer had been executed on Boston Common for her Quaker beliefs (see Chapter 2).

The growing toleration for different religious sects and an increasing emphasis on science and rational thought changed the worldviews of colonists in the eighteenth century. The ideas that sprang from the Great Awakening and the Enlightenment would have far-reaching effects on American women and men in the last quarter of the century.

The Great Awakening

The role of religion in the consolidation of the American colonies was a different one from the role it had played in the settling of those colonies. Puritanism in New England had declined in religious importance as more and more non-Puritans migrated to the region. Pennsylvania, settled by Quakers under William Penn, practiced a religious toleration that attracted not only Quakers, but also the Amish, Mennonites, Moravians, Dunkers, and Schwenkfelders, all Protestant religious sects persecuted in Europe. Scottish and Irish Protestants and French Huguenots (also Protestant) settled in the same region, as well as in Maryland, which tolerated Catholics, and in North Carolina, which was primarily Anglican but also home to Moravians, Lutherans, Reform Baptists, and a small community of Jews. In short, the American colonies, despite their established state churches, contained an agglomeration of religious sects that by the eighteenth century largely tolerated one another.

Varieties of religions in early America lessened the ability of any one sect to exercise a monopoly on religious sentiment in most communities. That did not mean Americans were not interested in religion. In fact, the first mass cultural movement in colonial America came in the form of a religious revival called the *Great Awakening*, which swept the British colonies between the 1730s and 1760s. Piety, many people feared, had declined, and too many Americans had turned away from God to pursue worldly interests. Leading figures of the Great Awakening such as the Reverend Jonathan Edwards's of Massachusetts, a Congregationalist, and the Reverend William Tennent of Pennsylvania, a Presbyterian, livened up their sermons with evocative descriptions of what happened to the damned, the most famous being Edwards' "Sinners in the Hands of an Angry God," wherein he likened sinners to spiders being suspended over a pit of fire by an angry Deity. From England came Methodist minister George Whitefield, an extraordinary preacher who became known throughout the colonies as he led huge outdoor meetings. Whitefield, originally an Anglican minister, stirred crowds with his eloquence. Jonathan Edwards wept through his whole sermon. Benjamin Franklin, a religious skeptic, was so impressed by Whitefield's sermon he emptied his purse into the collection plate and later published Whitefield's sermons.

The Great Awakening sought to appeal to people's emotions. Followers were urged to experience a personal conversion, turning away from the pleasures of this world and toward the salvation offered by God. By emphasizing the individual's connection to God, the Great Awakening prompted some reconsideration of women's place in religious communities. Some men, including prominent clergy, found these ideas about women threatening because they had the potential to disrupt the model of the household as a little commonwealth ruled by its head. While such criticism may have stifled many women, others, such as Sarah Osborn of Newport, Rhode Island, seemed to pay little attention. Osborn, born in 1714, joined the church in 1737 and founded a women's group that met with her in her home for more than fifty years. She taught school, cared for her two husbands, and published one of her letters on religious matters after a minister requested it. She opened her home to the African American community in the mid-1760s and enjoyed a lifelong reputation for piety despite her works in public. Her views on religion, not dissimilar to those expressed by Anne Hutchinson the century before, but treated with respect instead of claims of heresy, indicate the degree to which some of the country had changed in its view of women participating in religion's public realm.

The Enlightenment

The Great Awakening's emphasis on the importance of the individual in any relationship with God was matched by another movement also abroad upon the land: the *Enlightenment*. An intellectual and philosophical movement that grew out of Europe's scientific revolution of the sixteenth and seventeenth centuries, the Enlightenment emphasized reason instead of emotion, arguing that the intellect could discern God and God's laws within nature. The Enlightenment sought knowledge, freedom, and happiness rather than salvation, and its God was rational, not emotional. Deism, the faith of most of the founding fathers of the United States, came from Enlightenment views. God was not so much the supreme judge, angry at the sinners of the world, as a giant clockmaker who had set up the world with natural laws (discernible through the use of reason), wound it like a clockmaker winds a clock, and left it to run pretty much by itself, according to those laws. Laws of nature could be found not only in the natural world, but in the political world as well. Emphasizing reason rather than tradition, Enlightenment philosophers, called *philosophes*, argued against hereditary kingship and aristocracy solely based on birth, and for an orderly society where man's reason played a prominent role in determining man's role.

Women's roles in society came in for considerable discussion by Enlightenment thinkers. Enlightenment ideals held that men should be educated to participate in government and to be part of the "social contract," as

English philosopher John Locke put it, that was the agreement between the governor and the governed. An ideal society was one in which citizens could participate in the government, and participation required education so that those citizens would know how to participate to the best advantage of the nation. Such participating citizens were male. Because women were not considered candidates for citizenship by the majority of the *philosophes*, they needed little education. Locke's view of women was that their rights and powers rested in the domestic world, and that they had no political capacity. Jean Jacques Rousseau, the leading French *philosophe*, viewed women as largely (and appropriately) invisible with no political relationship to the state.

Only James Otis, a Boston lawyer and critic of the British government's rules regarding the American colonies, seemed to support educated women as part of the citizenry of a free nation. In his 1764 pamphlet *The Rights of the British Colonies Asserted and Proved* Otis argued, "Are not women born as free as men? Would it not be infamous to assert that the ladies are all slaves by nature? . . . If . . . all were reduced to a state of nature [i.e., if governments were no more], had not apple women and orange girls as good a right to give their respectable suffrages [votes] for a new King as . . . the politician?" For most Americans, the answer to this question was a resounding no. Women were not citizens, women should not be voters, women should not participate in politics. Their world was domestic and their interests should be confined to their families and children. Yet, there were always exceptional women who, because of their families, their wealth, or their communities, were able to educate themselves and take part in the larger world their brothers, husbands, and sons took for granted.

James Otis's sister, Mercy Otis Warren, was one such woman. Born in 1728 in Barnstable, Massachusetts, to Mary and Colonel James Otis, a lawyer and leading politician, Warren lived in an upper-class household that included servants and a black slave. As was true for most women, Warren was trained in the domestic and managerial tasks that would be expected of her when she married, and as a Congregationalist (née Puritan), she learned how to read and write as well. Unlike most girls, however, Warren received additional education. At age 10 or so, Col. Otis allowed her to accompany her brothers to their tutor, where she learned Greek and Latin literature, studied the great English writers such as Shakespeare and Milton, and explored history and politics. Her talents lay in the field of literature as she learned to express herself in compositions, letters, and eventually plays about the politics of eighteenth-century America. Mercy married James Warren, a Massachusetts politician, in 1754. Surrounded by politicians who would become the leaders of the American Revolution, and taken seriously by her brother James and his friends, Mercy Otis Warren published plays that predicted the American Revolution, a pamphlet that opposed the Constitution, a book of poetry dedicated to George Washington, and a three-volume work called *A History of the Rise, Progress and Termination of the American Revolution*. Her family's tradition of political involvement made her participation in the public world of politics possible.

For Eliza Lucas Pinckney, another exceptional woman, her father's wealth and her own education allowed her entrée into the public world of trade. Born in 1722 in Antigua, West Indies, Eliza Lucas grew up in a world of finishing schools and international travel. Her father George, a career British military officer, left Lucas in charge of three plantations in South Carolina at the age of sixteen, after her mother died and he had to return to his post in the Caribbean. Fascinated by the study of botany, Lucas began experimenting with indigo plants, searching for one that would produce a lasting blue dye without being too fussy about its growing conditions. She succeeded, producing the first commercially viable crop of the valuable plant in the colonies, then promoted the idea to South Carolina farmers, giving away plants and seeds. By 1748, two years after her experiments succeeded, indigo became second only to rice in its value to the colony. At age 22, Lucas married Charles Pinckney, a wealthy South Carolina politician and its first native-born lawyer, bore four children, and continued to experiment with crops, including figs, hemp, silkworms, and flax, on their three plantations near Charleston. Some forty slaves worked at Snee Farm, the plantation closest to Charleston that Eliza occupied most frequently, easing the workload so that Eliza was able to conduct her botanical experiments. By the time of her death, she was so highly regarded in the South that George Washington asked to serve as a pallbearer at her funeral.

Pinckney and Warren were the exceptions rather than the rule for women in eighteenth-century colonial America. But the War for Independence would draw thousands of ordinary women out of their domestic worlds as women coped with politics, warfare, and an aftermath that changed them from British subjects into American citizens.

THE AMERICAN REVOLUTION

The continued expansion of British North America into regions claimed by France led to warfare between the two nations between 1754 and 1763. At the end of the Seven Years' War, France had been driven off the continent of North America, and Britain controlled Canada as well as the lands west of the Appalachians to the Mississippi River. Administering those lands took considerable treasure and men, and Britain expected to be able to tax the colonies to help pay for their protection. The colonies, long used to what one British politician called "salutary neglect," as the British government failed to enforce many of the preceding century's tax laws, responded by protesting against any taxes imposed without a voice for the colonists in Parliament. "Taxation without representation is tyranny" became the cry of those determined to gain a voice in their government or break away from British rule.

The War for Independence

From 1763 on, a series of political events convinced many leading colonial politicians that Great Britain could not be trusted to treat them as

Englishmen, with all the rights and liberties that implied. At the end of the Seven Years' War, trying to appease Native American concerns regarding white settlers on their lands, the British forbade American colonists from traveling west of the Appalachians to settle, and instructed those who lived there to return. The proclamation stirred intense opposition, as did increased taxation on items such as sugar and tea, as well as restrictions on commerce in New England, including closing the port of Boston. "Patriot" women and men, those who supported American interests, took to the streets to protest Parliament's crackdown. The Daughters of Liberty, for example, marched with male protestors (called the "Sons of Liberty") in cities such as Boston, and helped burn tax collectors in effigy. Angry colonists sent delegates to meet in Philadelphia in 1774 to discuss their options. There, in July of 1776, after dissension escalated into armed conflict between British soldiers and American colonists in Massachusetts, the Continental Congress voted to separate from Great Britain and form the United States of America.

For most women, their involvement in the War for Independence was on the domestic front, in their homes and businesses, keeping both running while the men in the family were gone for soldiers, sometimes for years. Women could exhibit their patriotism through their actions as household managers and as consumers. One of the most powerful tools women had was an economic boycott against British-made goods. The eighteenth-century rise of gentility meant a rise in consumerism as Americans purchased British-made luxury items as soon as they were able. Consumerism and politics were intertwined as the British taxed the very items Americans most desired. As early as 1770, 126 women in Boston collectively announced they would boycott tea to frustrate Britain's collection of taxes that they feared would threaten American liberties: "We the Daughters of those Patriots who have and now do appear for the public Interest . . . do with Pleasure engage with them in denying ourselves the drinking of Foreign Tea, in hopes to frustrate a Plan that tends to deprive the whole Community of their all that is valuable in Life." Women in Charleston, South Carolina, did the same in 1774. As household managers, women could pour coffee instead of tea, create linsey-woolsey fabric instead of buying British-woven cotton, could weave homegrown crops into linens and bandages, could use herbal remedies instead of imported British medicines, and could even sell spun yarn to raise money. Spinning bees, where groups of women spun yarn in a social gathering, became political contests where women competed to see who could spin the most yarn for the cause. Boycotts and other economic activities provided an effective way for women to participate in the fight against the tyranny that Americans thought taxation represented.

Women, particularly those in urban areas, also raised and contributed funds and supplies. Such support meant buying *war bonds*, loaning the government money in hopes that they would win the war and pay them back. Some women even went door-to-door to promote bonds in the neighborhood. In Philadelphia in 1780, "An American Woman," Esther DeBerdt Reed, printed a broadside (an eighteenth-century political flyer) that laid out an organized plan for gathering contributions from American women. In addition to describing how best to send the donations to the army, Reed linked women's activities to the great women of the past, including France's Joan of Arc. The French were America's allies against the British as of 1778 and, wrote Reed, "We call to mind, doubly interested, that it was a French Maid who kindled up amongst her fellow-citizens, the flame of patriotism buried under long misfortunes: It was the Maid of Orleans who drove from the kingdom of France the ancestors of those same British, whose odious yoke we have just shaken off; and whom it is necessary that we drive from this Continent." Reed cited biblical examples and examples of Roman Republic heroines who not only forgot the "weakness of their sex" to build fortifications and dig trenches, but also paid the most painful price: sacrificing the company, comfort, and support of their husbands, their fathers, their sons to the national struggle for liberty.

These activities women took up as they needed to, could, or believed in. Not all women did all things. The war lasted a very long time, and covered a lot of territory geographically. As the war moved away or moved closer to one's geographic area, a woman's activity would change. But when the war was in their front yards, most women could not avoid getting involved. Temperance Wick, for example, had a horse British soldiers tried to requisition in 1781 in New Jersey. After she escaped from them, she hid the horse in her bedroom, muffling the sounds of its hooves with her featherbed. When the soldiers arrived, they never thought to check the bedroom, so they left the farm empty-handed.

Women were half the population of the country during the Revolution, and the list of women famous during or because of the war is long. There was the best known, Abigail Adams, wife of John Adams, a coauthor of the Declaration of Independence, a leading Boston lawyer, and a man who would become president in 1796. Abigail, left alone for much of their marriage, cared for the farm and their children while her husband was away in Philadelphia helping to form the country. To share their lives, she corresponded with her husband not just about the children and their measles, but also about the politics of the war and the new nation. In 1776, for instance, as John helped draft the Declaration of Independence, Abigail took issue with married women's status as *feme covert*, writing to him that he should not, in the new code of laws to be developed, "put such unlimited power in the hands of the Husbands. Remember," she continued, "all Men would be tyrants if they could." (See Primary Source 3-3.) A few years later, she reminded him in another letter to support education for women, saying, "you need not be told how much female education is neglected, nor how fashionable it has been to ridicule female learning." Abigail Adams's correspondence extended to Mercy Otis Warren as well, and the two women exchanged information on the war, as well as shared their longing to see their absent husbands. Adams wrote she felt "obliged to summon all my patriotism to feel willing to part" with her husband again as his service to the country continued. Warren agreed with her sentiment, yet pointed out to her younger friend, "Misery is the portions of Millions," and that they should not expect to "feel no interruption of Happiness." The Revolution

ABIGAIL ADAMS, "REMEMBER THE LADIES"

Abigail Adams had decided opinions regarding women's role in the new nation. She wrote to her husband John, as he labored in the Continental Congress in Philadelphia as one of the delegates charged with writing a declaration of independence to justify the American actions against England. In March 1776, a remarkable set of correspondence began between Abigail and her husband.

March 31, 1776: Abigail Adams to John Adams

"I long to hear that you have declared an independency—and by the way in the new Code of Laws which I suppose it will be necessary for you to make, I desire you would Remember the Ladies, and be more generous and favorable to them than your ancestors. Do not put such unlimited power into the hands of the Husbands. Remember all Men would be tyrants if they could. If perticular care and attention is not paid to the Ladies, we are determined to foment a Rebellion, and will not hold ourselves bound by any Laws in which we have no voice, or Representation.

"That your Sex are Naturally Tyrannical is a Truth so thoroughly established as to admit of no dispute, but such of you as wish to be happy willingly give up the harsh title of Master for the more tender and endearing one of friend. Why, then, not put it out of the power of the vicious and the Lawless to use us with cruelty and indignity with impunity? Men of sense in all Ages abhor those customs which treat us only as the vassals of your Sex. Regard us then as Beings placed by Providence under your protection, and in immitation of the Supreem Being make use of that power only for our happiness."

required explanation not only between friends, but also to the wider world, and women of words such as Warren participated from the beginning. Her 1776 farce, *The Blockheads; Or the Affrighted Officers*, poked fun at the British in response to General John Burgoyne's 1775 play, *The Blockade of Boston*. Phillis Wheatley wrote a poem to and about George Washington in 1776 in support of his efforts in the Revolution. Mary Katherine Goddard, a Baltimore postmaster and printer, printed the first Declaration of Independence that had the actual names of the signers on it in 1777.

Beyond the famous women were the women of ordinary means. Adams's role was in many ways typical of many middle-class women during the war: she managed the farm while her husband was away, although in her case, he was not a soldier, but a politician and diplomat. Poor women who had no farms to care for often followed their menfolk to war. There were two forces fighting for Americans in the Revolution: the colonial militia, comparable to today's National Guard, that was for home defense (ordinarily against Indians), and the Continental Army, led by General George Washington. The women who followed the army were called *camp followers*

April 14, 1776: John Adams to Abigail Adams

"As to your extraordinary Code of Laws, I cannot but laugh. We have been told that our Struggle has loosened the bonds of Government everywhere. That Children and Apprentices were disobedient—that schools and Colleges were grown turbulent—that Indians slighted their Guardians, and Negroes grew insolent to their Masters. But your Letter was the first Intimation that another Tribe more numerous and powerfull than all the rest, were grown discontented.—This is rather too coarse a Compliment, but you are so saucy, I won't blot it out.

"Depend upon it, We know better than to repeal our Masculine systems. Altho they are in full Force, you know they are little more than Theory. We dare not exert our Power in its full Latitude. We are obliged to go fair, and softly, and, in Practice you know We are the subjects. We have only the Name of masters, and rather than give up this, which would compleatly subject Us to the Despotism of the Peticoat, I hope General Washington, and all our brave Heroes would fight."

May 7, 1776: Abigail Adams to John Adams

"I can not say that I think you are very generous to the Ladies, for, whilst you are proclaiming peace and good will to Men, Emancipating all Nations, you insist upon retaining an absolute power over Wives. But you must remember that Arbitrary power is like most other things which are very hard, very liable to be broken—and, notwithstanding all your wise Laws and Maxims, we have it in our power not only to free ourselves but to subdue our Masters, and without violence, throw both your natural and legal authority at our feet—"

Source: The Book of Abigail and John: Selected Letters of the Adams Family, 1762–1784, ed. L. H. Butterfiled, Marc Friedlander, and Mary-Jo Kline (1975; reprint ed. Cambridge, MA: Northeastern University Press, 2002), 121–123, 127.

because they traveled with the troops and stayed in the camps to take care of their men before, during, and after battles. Camp followers have traditionally been thought of as prostitutes, but the reality is far more complex. The women who followed the armies did so to provide the services that the army needed but did not provide. In the days of the Revolution, for instance, there was no army medical department. There were no MREs (meals-ready-to-eat). There was no laundromat. Women provided these support services, making up an entire community, caring for the wounded, doing the cooking and laundry, and performing innumerable domestic duties.

In doing this, women also enabled men to fight more effectively and, in some cases, to fight period. Wives of some men, for instance, went because they had lost their lands to the British, lost their ability to care for themselves, or simply could not care for themselves and also their children by themselves. By traveling with the army, the husbands of those women could fight, earn some pay, provide their families with food and shelter, and care for them instead of worrying about them or deserting the army to care for them.

The needs of the army provided a check to the wholesale dismissal of the women, no matter how dangerous or inconvenient it was to have them near battlefields. Gen. Washington knew he would lose troops if he threw out women who had followed their menfolk to war, so he decided to deal with them by making them earn their keep and serve the army his way. He gave camp followers half-rations and regulated their behavior, limiting what they could do and where they could go. When he discovered escaped slaves and indentured servants in the camps, he tried to return them to their masters so that the masters would continue to support the war and so that the army would not be seen as a place of refuge. The British, on the other hand, offered freedom to all slaves, including women, who left for British lines and supported or fought for their side (half of Thomas Jefferson's slaves who fled to British lines were women).

Despite Washington's grudging toleration for the camp followers, he simply dreaded having women and their children around. They took up space, consumed scarce supplies, and presented a real danger to themselves because of their inexperience on the battlefield and in army camp. Occasionally, he would become frustrated enough to order the women home, but he always backed down when confronted with the reality of the army's resistance to losing their womenfolk. Soldiers would not support the war effort and fight well if they were worried about their families. In 1781, for example, Washington's aide-de-camp Alexander Hamilton learned of a soldier whose daughter had become a camp follower. When told to go home, she said she could not because "her mother had nothing for her to eat." So the leaders of the Continental Army bowed to the inevitable and let women stay. After all, it was their war too.

While most women associated with the army in the War for Independence served as a sort of support staff, some took on more unusual roles as spies and soldiers. Grace and Rachel Martin intercepted British riders, captured their plans, and turned them over to General Nathanael Greene in South Carolina. Anna Strong signaled messages to Patriots with laundry she hung out on Strong's Neck near New York City. Ann Bates took up as a peddler to infiltrate American camps to spy for the British. Sybil Ludington repeated Paul Revere's ride in 1777 in upstate New York. A sixteen-year-old, she was putting her siblings to bed the night of April 26 when word came that nearby Danbury, Connecticut, was being burned by the British. She convinced her father to let her ride to warn the militia in the surrounding forty-mile region. The men arrived in time to drive the British back to their ships, anchored in Long Island Sound.

Other women took action more directly linked to soldiering. Deborah Samson (or Sampson), for example, disguised herself as a man and enlisted in the Continental Army as Robert Shurtliffe in 1782. Fighting with the Fourth Massachusetts Regiment of the Continental Army, she was wounded at the battle of Tarrytown. Her identity was discovered in 1783, and General Henry Knox gave her an honorable discharge, despite her disguise. Ann Bailey also disguised herself, enlisting in the First Massachusetts Regiment. So successful was her disguise and so useful was her service that she was quickly promoted to the rank of corporal as "Samuel Gray." A single woman from Boston, Bailey may have enlisted because of patriotism or pay, but surviving records do not reveal her motive. Virginian Anna Maria Lane disguised herself to follow her husband into battle. When she was wounded at Germantown in 1777 and lamed for life, she was unmasked and discharged. She received a pension from the government in 1808 for her services that was double the size of any male veteran's pension.

Surviving records of women soldiers are few and far between, making it difficult to discover and interpret the histories of such women. Historians believe that women soldiers went to war for the same reasons men did: for the cause they were fighting for, but also for adventure, for excitement, or because their friends or relatives (particularly husbands) did. Most of the women who escaped detection as men did so because they bound their breasts and kept their clothes on. Since people seldom bathed in the eighteenth century and soldiers slept in their clothes, and since callow youths were common in warfare, it was quite possible for a young woman to pass herself off as a young, not-yet-bearded man. Thousands of women filed for pensions after the war, mostly because they lost husbands in the struggle, but some because they too had fought for the Americans as soldiers and needed support for themselves.

Women have always been involved in wars: as active citizens and leaders, as politicians and writers, as spies, as fighters, and, certainly most profoundly, as victims. Their involvement, however, has usually been portrayed symbolically, rather than detailed in its complexity. There are two images of women most common during the War for Independence: Betsy Ross, the seamstress, and "Molly Pitcher," the temporary soldier. These images served a dual purpose. The Ross image (a real seamstress in Philadelphia, but no one knows if she made the first flag or not) portrays a woman involved in helping make the new country, which is a patriotic good, but doing so in a very womanly way: sewing a flag. The subtext (that which is underneath the "text" in terms of meaning) is that domesticity (sewing) made politics (helping create a nation), a male activity, acceptable. Ross becomes a sort of patriotic goodwife.

The Molly Pitcher symbol is more of a problem. Molly Pitcher was a story based on the life of one, or possibly two, women during the war. Mary Ludwig Hayes took over for her husband at the battle of Monmouth, New Jersey. After her husband collapsed during the battle, Mary, who had been carrying jugs of water to the soldiers to cool the cannons, took over for him and continued to fire the cannon. Margaret Corbin also continued to fire artillery at a battle at Fort Washington, New York, after her husband could no longer do so. Corbin's record is more substantial, however, since Corbin wound up as the first woman with a Revolutionary War veteran's pension, thus providing historians with U.S. government proof of service to the army. She even has a monument at her burial site at West Point, New York. Having a woman work as a soldier, especially when the work was enough to grant her an army pension, is not exactly feminine behavior. But here again, the subtext was and is important. In both cases, the women were taking over for their husbands, the "real" soldiers. And in both cases, it was not their normal behavior, but the kind of heroic behavior heroines are allowed to do because they go back to behaving as they should afterward.

The Impact of the Revolution

The American War for Independence lasted from 1775, when the first shots were fired at Concord and Lexington, Massachusetts, until 1783, when the Peace Treaty of Paris was signed, turning over rule of the eastern part of the American continent to the Americans. The American Revolution lasted much longer. John Adams said it best years later: the revolution was in the minds and hearts of the people in the years before the war, when they grew aware of the "perpetual discordance between British principles and feelings and of those of America." America had been left alone too long by Britain, and trying to impose new restrictions on a nation long used to neglect and so different from the mother country was doomed to failure. The "radical change in the principles, opinions, sentiments, and affections of the People," said Adams, "was the real American Revolution." Most important among the changes were those that dealt with the values, ideas, and ideals about the interaction of government and society.

Having thrown off British rule, Americans had to reinvent their government from the ground up. The first attempt, the Articles of Confederation, was an abject failure by the mid-1780s. A weak central government and strong state governments, combined with massive geographic distances and a huge debt from the war, resulted in a country drowning in debt and unable to save itself because of the limits it imposed upon itself. Under the Articles, the central government could only ask states for contributions to the federal treasury, rather than tax the states or the people. The United States was in debt, with no way to solve its indebtedness. High taxes imposed by states to pay for the war led to foreclosures when poor farmers could not pay. In Massachusetts, an angry mob, led by Daniel Shays, marched on the federal arsenal in Springfield in protest. Such a protest, with its echoes of revolution, convinced state and national leaders they had to solve the crisis. They wound up designing a new government with a new constitution in Philadelphia in 1787. The new national government divided power into three branches: executive, legislative, and judicial. Male voters elected the male members of the House of Representatives; male state legislatures elected the male members of the Senate; and male electors, chosen by male voters, elected the male president. The male Senate approved the male president's nominations to the male judicial branch.

Nowhere in the new government did a role for women appear. This fact was not surprising, since at this time women did not have the right to vote in any national government anywhere. The American Revolution, however, had been an ideological revolution, not just a political one. Women experienced the war and participated in the war. For it or against it, women had opinions about it and about how to govern the country.

White Women and Citizenship

Many Americans wanted a return to British ways without the oversight of the British government. Much of the new American government that was formed was based on British laws and traditions, including the tradition of excluding women from politics. Despite Abigail Adams's request to her husband John, Americans maintained the legal status of married women as *feme covert*. Under the laws of coverture, a woman's political identification was dependent upon her husband's. Thus a woman was a Patriot or a "Loyalist," a supporter of the British, because of what her husband believed, not what she believed. If a Loyalist's property was confiscated during war when American Patriots took control of an area, the Loyalist's wife, under *feme covert* rules, would lose her dower rights, her "thirds." If she decided to be a Patriot and her husband was a Loyalist, she would keep her thirds, but also would be rebelling against her husband. Such a rebellion would mean disobeying her husband, a violation of the marriage vows. Under the laws of coverture, then, women would be forced to choose between patriotism and marriage. Probably there were very few women for whom this was the actual choice. But the question did raise the idea of the political identification for women in a republic, where one's political identification came from, in part, participation in the political system. For women without a vote, participation was limited. Without participation, women might feel they had little stake in the government. A new republic would survive only if the people supported it and felt they had a stake in its success.

One way women responded to both the war and to the discussion regarding patriotism and republican government was to embrace the concept of civic virtue. The idea of civic virtue came from the Greeks and the Romans. In the days of the Greek democracy at Athens, and later in the days of the Roman Republic, supporters of good government argued that private virtues should be extended into the public realm. Private virtues, such as industry, frugality, temperance, and moderation, would make the public realm—and government—more effective. Civic virtue was originally practiced by men. American Revolutionary ideology, however, called for women to apply civic virtue as they sought rules for their behavior in the new republic. The "Republican woman" was born: competent, confident, rational, thrifty, independent, self-reliant, not a slave to emotion, and not a slave to fashion. She contributed to the stability and longevity of the new republic by her virtuous behavior. Consequently, she was a useful citizen of the republic.

Such paragons of civic virtue came about through education. In the early years of the republic, Thomas Jefferson wrote that "If a nation expects to be ignorant and free in a state of civilization, it expects what never was and never will be." While Jefferson disdained education for women as unnecessary he promoted an educated citizenry otherwise. A literate, politically sophisticated constituency would understand what was needed for a strong republic based on representative government. Such a citizenry could be trusted to chose wise leaders. Americans feared tyrants guaranteed by hereditary leadership, and at the same time, they also feared radicalism. Shays' Rebellion had shaken them. Americans then watched the French people go through a upheaval similar to their own. Radicals in France promoted ideas that eventually would result in a bloodbath as the *ancien regime* was overthrown, aristocrats executed, and general mayhem and warfare ensued. By 1789, the French Revolution was in full force. Its excesses attracted Americans' attention. Some feared additional bloodshed if the

Plate V. A SOCIETY of PATRIOTIC LADIES, AT EDENTON in NORTH CAROLINA.

A SAD EFFECT IF "A SOCIETY OF PATRIOTIC LADIES" PROTESTS Americans were unsure what the result of politically active women would be. This cartoon, drawn after women in Edenton, North Carolina, signed a protest petition in 1775, leaves no doubt that the artist felt that women would behave badly if allowed to participate in politics.

mobs of common people such as those demanding liberty and equality in France were not controlled when or if they arose in America. Elites in America presumed they would rule to the benefit of all as they had done before the war; the lower orders presumed the war that they had helped win meant any rights gained from the Revolution belonged to them as well.

Including men from the lower orders into government would be radical enough. To include women as well, even as just a part of the educated citizenry, stretched the imagination of many. Since no one had lived under a government where women had political rights, and since only New Jersey allowed women to vote (until 1807), most Americans sought civic education for women rather than active participation by women. This helped define and limit women's education. The classical curriculum of learned men in the eighteenth century included Latin, Greek, rhetoric, philosophy, theology, mathematics, and science. Education for women had lesser goals: to strengthen women's position in marriage market, to prepare women for their natural vocation of domesticity and motherhood, and to teach women how to influence men and to raise virtuous children. Women's education was utilitarian: grammar, reading, penmanship, bookkeeping, geography, and history (considered "the anti-intellectual's compromise with higher learning"). No novels, no classics (Greek and Latin), no fiction: these taught women things they ought not to know or ought not to spend time on.

Civic organizations promoted the ideals of civic virtue and women's proper education: the Patriotic and Economical Association of Hartford, Connecticut, in 1786, for instance. Popular magazines and books promoted the ideals as well, with articles such as "The Advantages to Be Derived by Young Men from the Society of Virtuous Women," reprinted in 1788. Sermons in churches were published later as books for young women to read. An additional role model for white women in the early republic from about 1780 on through the early part of the nineteenth century developed: the *Republican Mother*. The Republican Mother served as a synthesis of ideas about women's nature, women's proper domain, women's education, and women's role in politics. Educational institutions such as Dr. Benjamin Rush's academy in Philadelphia, one of the leading schools for the elite women of the country, promoted the notions of Republican Womanhood and Republican Motherhood.

These roles served women and men both as socially acceptable ways to link women's desires to serve their country as patriots and to act as participants in the newly created republic with their task of raising virtuous children, particularly sons, who would support the republic. The roles also, not incidentally, avoided the full implications of Revolutionary ideology, which was the notion of self-government. Despite the Revolution, self-government remained a radical idea, particularly as it applied to women. Self-government, as explained by poet, essayist, novelist, playwright, and *Massachusetts Magazine* columnist Judith Sargent Murray, meant that women needed to develop their self-identity outside of marriage. A woman "should reverence herself," Murray wrote in 1784, lest she marry the first man who came along with flattery and sweet words. Part of developing self-identity was education, and that education should be equal, not inferior, to what young men received. In 1790, Murray published "On the Equality of the Sexes," pointing out that the desire to learn was not linked to one's gender, that there were men as dull and incurious as there were women desirous of learning. Equal educational opportunities should not be denied women with the explanation that women were inferior beings. They were not.

By the end of the revolutionary period, a real shift had occurred in ideas about women. Before the Revolution, most people accepted the ideas that women were the "weaker vessel," as they put it, that women were and should be subject to men in an order derived from God. They also believed society was best served by a hierarchy based on a monarchical pattern of government that consisted of God over all, the ruler chosen by God, men over women, women obedient to all. Most regarded that hierarchy as biologically determined, a view that could be proven by notions such as the divine right of kings.

Enlightenment ideas, which led to revolutions not only in America but also in much of Europe, questioned whether women's inferiority was due to biology or poor education. After the Revolution, Americans developed two views to answer that question. The first, which argued that women were not inferior but oppressed, came from writers such as the English theorist, Mary Wollstonecraft, who published *The Vindication of the Rights of Woman* in 1792. Wollstonecraft argued that women were equal to men and nothing should be denied women because of their gender. Her ideas were simply too radical to be accepted by most Americans, but some within the new republic did embrace them. In the city of Philadelphia, for example, where the new country had started in 1776 and where the Constitutional Convention was held a decade later, women interested in the larger questions regarding citizenship and service to the country read and commented on political debates in the newspapers. An active political community of women developed, attending theater plays on political topics, such as Judith Sargent Murray's *The Traveler Returned* and *Virtue Triumphant*, both of which argued for women's education and equality in marriage, as did another play, *Everyone Has His Faults*, by English playwright Elizabeth Inchbald. Popular magazines, such as *Lady's Magazine* and *Columbian Magazine*, published Wollstonecraft's and Murray's essays, allowing readers to respond in a public forum. Anyone could contribute their reaction, though not every letter was published. In one instance, the editor of *Lady's Magazine*, Charles Brockden Brown, informed a writer, "S.L.," that his submission to the magazine would not be printed because he had chosen to employ his pen in "degrading ideas of *female learning*," which the magazine favored. S.L.'s rejection was public: the dismissive letter was printed in the magazine.

Among public political women were those who supported the French Revolution as it continued in the 1790s. Numerous women approved of its newly republican government, its egalitarian notions regarding women, and the public reporting of women active in the politics of the new nation. French women protested, marched, rioted, petitioned the government to carry arms, and worked in organizations and on committees. One French-woman, Charlotte Corday, even committed political assassination, stabbing French counterrevolutionary Jean-Paul Marat in 1793, for his opposition to the Revolution. In addition to following the newspaper reports and books published about the Revolution (Martha Washington, for instance, purchased a six-volume history of the Revolution in 1793, and another volume the next year), American supporters might wear a fashionable French turban, or place a French cockade on their hats, or wear red, white, and blue sashes to show their support for the revolutionaries. American women adopted simpler styles of French dress, with simple fabrics and decorations that all citizens could afford to wear, rather than the silks and laces only the rich could buy. That others recognized the political nature of such fashionable statements could not be doubted, as a complaint by Philadelphia editor William Cobbett, publisher of *Porcupine's Gazette*, made clear in 1798. He complained about women displaying such sentiments along with their turbans. "For my part," he groused, "I would almost as soon have a host of infernals [devils] in my house, as a knot of these fiery frenchified dames.—Of all the monsters in human shape, a *bully in petticoats* is the most completely odious and detestable."

No doubt other cities were home to more such frenchified dames, as politically partisan women in Philadelphia were termed, but overall, most

Americans resisted women's formal political activity, preferring the role model of the Republican Mother over Republican Womanhood or, worse still, women's equality. Women's equality with men was an idea too far ahead of its time to survive. Republican Womanhood allowed women into the republic's public political world as participants, practicing their civic virtues. The Republican Mother ideal, however, led women citizens safely away from dangerous notions of equality for women promoted by radicals such as Murray and Wollstonecraft. Instead, it maintained that women were different and that political equality was not relevant to women. Women, held most people, had a separate sphere of activities from men: a "woman's sphere," defined by God and enforced by society. Political equality for women was unnecessary, since politics were not part of the woman's sphere. If women were better educated, however, their strengths, so different from men's, would shine. In fact, women would occupy a sphere that their biology destined them to occupy: the woman's sphere of rule over the heart, the spirituality of the family, and the home.

African American Women and Slavery

The practicality of the idea that men and women could be usefully employed in and defined by spheres of activity was one often limited by race because not all women were equal to other women. For African American women, most of whom were enslaved in 1783 when the war ended, the results of the Revolution were mixed and the idea of a separate woman's sphere was largely irrelevant.

Revolutionary rhetoric calling for liberty and equality led many Americans to question slavery, and one of the results was a rise in the number of manumissions, the legal process of freeing slaves from slavery. Northern states began to abolish slavery, either outright or gradually. In 1777, the Vermont state constitutional convention prohibited slavery; in 1780, Pennsylvania passed a gradual emancipation law that freed children of enslaved mothers at age 28. Similar laws were passed in Connecticut and Rhode Island in 1784, in New York in 1789, and in New Jersey in 1804. Massachusetts declared in its state constitution, passed in 1780, that "all men are born free and equal; and that every subject is entitled to liberty."

For Belinda, a slave in Massachusetts, the free black community that surrounded her no doubt gave her some of the impetus in 1783 to file a petition for reparations from her master, Isaac Royall of Medford, who had fled the colony at the start of the Revolution. Aided by local free black abolitionist Prince Hall, Belinda petitioned the court for a pension for herself and her daughter after Massachusetts outlawed slavery. Part of the petition described her capture in Ghana fifty years before and her parents' dismay: "Could the Tears, the sighs and supplications, bursting from tortured Parental affection, have blunted the keen edge of Avarice, she might have been rescued from Agony. In vain she lifted her supplicating voice. She was ravished from the bosom of her Country, from the arms of her friends, while the advanced age of her Parents, rendering them unfit for servitude, cruelly separated her from them forever!"

The ruling in favor of Belinda's petition came the same year as Elizabeth "Mum Bett" Freeman's suit against her owner, a Colonel Ashley of Sheffield, Massachusetts. She sued with the help of a prominent white local lawyer, Theodore Sedgwick Sr., using an argument that the new state's own Declaration of Human Rights, embedded in its new state constitution, was incompatible with slavery. The Massachusetts Supreme Court agreed. "The idea of slavery," it ruled, "is inconsistent with our own conduct and constitution; and there can be no such thing as perpetual servitude of a rational creature." The court's ruling that slavery was "repugnant" to the existence of the state's constitution allowed Freeman and others to sue or to simply walk away from their former owners. Antislavery societies began to form in the new states. Anthony Benezet, head of the first, the Society for the Relief of Free Negroes Unlawfully Held in Bondage, was succeeded in 1787 by Benjamin Franklin, a former slaveowner. The group was renamed the Pennsylvania Society for Promoting the Abolition of Slavery. By the end of the eighteenth century, antislavery societies were found in every state but those of the Deep South. Freedom from slavery was of utmost importance to slaves. As Freeman explained it: "Anytime, anytime while I was a slave, if one minute's freedom had been offered to me, and I had been told I must die at the end of that minute, I would have taken it—just to stand one minute on God's earth a free woman—I would."

In the Upper South, Virginia (1782), Delaware (1787), Maryland (1790), and the new state of Kentucky (1792), all passed laws enabling individual masters to free their slaves, instead of having to go to court or petition the state legislature to do so. Some owners availed themselves of the law, including a few who owned large numbers of slaves. Robert Carter, of Nominy Hall plantation in Virginia, wrote a deed of emancipation in 1791 that eventually freed several hundred slaves. George Washington freed his slaves in his will. Between 1782 and 1806 the number of free blacks in Virginia grew from 2,000 to 20,000.

Slavery did not end, however. The new Constitution had embedded slavery within it, keeping slave importation legal until 1808, and counting three-fifths of slaves when deciding a state's population to determine its representation in Congress. In 1793, Eli Whitney developed the cotton gin which made cotton easier to process for export. The rise of King Cotton in the South kept slavery alive, since cotton was at least as labor-intensive and as lucrative as tobacco had been (see Chapter 4). More cotton growers needed more slaves, and the institution solidified. In addition, the defeat of the British opened new lands for settlement in the areas that would become the states of Louisiana, Alabama, and Mississippi. Those rich agricultural lands encouraged the spread not only of cotton, but also of sugar cane and rice, labor-intensive crops as well. The more land under cultivation, the more pressure to keep slavery as part of the American republic. Finally, slavery supporters used a rise in scientific racism that agreed that blacks were biologically inferior to whites to justify slavery. Thomas Jefferson, for example, argued that "science" had shown blacks were inherently inferior and therefore unsuited to participate in a white republican government, this despite his long-term relationship with his slave Sally Hemmings, purportedly the mother of six of his children. The attendant horrors of slavery and its abolition would await another war.

For free black women within their own free black communities, the notion of Republican Motherhood or Republican Womanhood could not have meant as much as to free white women. Given the racism of the country, more important was the care of their own communities. To meet that need, free black women formed voluntary help associations. In Philadelphia, for example, the Female Benevolent Society of St. Thomas, founded in 1793, and the Benevolent Daughters, established in 1796, provided medical and burial expenses to members, as well as helping widows and children in the days before life insurance, social security, or welfare. Members had to pledge good behavior and many of the groups worked as self-improvement societies, as well as serving as schools for young girls and boys. Women also formed and joined antislavery societies, hired themselves out to earn a living, and saved money to buy their relatives. By and large, black women were far more concerned with the survival and well-being of themselves and their communities than concerned about being a Republican Mother.

Native American Women and Territorial Expansion

For Native Americans, the War of Independence was a war for survival. Some Native groups sided with the Americans, even against Indians allied with the British. Nan-ye'-hi, called Nancy Ward by whites, a Beloved Woman of the Cherokee, lost her first husband to a British attack in 1755. When the American Revolution broke out, she warned Americans of a planned attack against them by her cousin, Dragging Canoe. Most Native groups, such as the Iroquois, however, sided with the British during the war and were, according to one Iroquois, "thunderstruck" at their loss. In 1763, the British government had tried to limit American settlers to the lands east of the Proclamation Line, drawn roughly down the ridge of the Appalachian Mountains. That line was now gone: the British turned over control of the trans-Appalachian lands to the Americans as part of the Peace of Paris in 1783, but neither side bothered to invite the Native Americans who lived there to the peace table. Betrayed by their British allies, Indians were now faced with an ambitious nation that regarded them as a defeated enemy. In return, Native Americans viewed white settlers as a "plague of locusts," determined to occupy all their lands. Many warriors, determined to replace group members who had died, paid no attention to the peace and continued attacks on the Americans, even as new waves of white settlers moved into the region west of the Appalachians. Stories of attacks, past and current, portrayed Indians as merciless savages who deserved annihilation. Daniel Boone, a trader, hunter, and American militia leader, had to rescue his daughter Jemima in 1776 when she was kidnapped by Shawnee Indians outside Boonesborough, the town Boone had founded when he blazed an illegal trail across the Appalachians to Kentucky. Boone's exploits were widely reported, as was the rescue. The next year, Jane McCrea, a twenty-six-year-old from Fort Edward, New York, was kidnapped and killed by Indians allied with British forces. Her murder was also well publicized. In 1782, a Delaware Indian named John Montour arrived at Fort Niagara with four scalps and three young women captives, despite the suspension of hostilities between Americans and the British. Such events convinced many Americans that all Indians fought for the British (even though many, particularly in the Northeast, did not) and that Indians in general deserved no quarter.

A series of treaties between Indians and Americans turned over millions of acres to the Americans. Cherokee land cessions, for example, included most of Kentucky and Tennessee, as well as northern Georgia and Alabama—5 million acres in all. By the end of the war, their population had declined to 10,000 and they had lost three-fourths of their territory and half of their towns. More treaties netted more lands in the Upper Midwest as well, lands that would become the states of Ohio, Illinois, Indiana, Michigan, and Wisconsin—the Northwest Territory. As treaties were signed, oftentimes by Indians who had no authority to make them, groups were pushed out of their traditional lands and into those of their traditional enemies. Some formed new "intertribal" groups, made up of survivors of groups decimated by warfare and unable to replace those members who had died.

In the North, the Iroquois Confederacy was broken by 1800. The matriarchal systems that defined Iroquois daily life declined as the population did and as pressures from whites moving into their lands continued. In 1799, Seneca leader Handsome Lake combined surviving traditional Iroquois ways with Quaker ideas from missionaries and patriarchal ideas from English culture to arrive at a new religion and way of life for Iroquoians known as the Longhouse Religion. The Seneca, whose hunting range had shrunk from 4 million acres to 200,000, chose to survive by adopting this religion, which substituted men instead of women as heads of households and men instead of women as farmers. As the Iroquois declined in number, much of the traditional power women held within the community dissipated.

While the greatest immediate impact the American Revolution had on the lives of Native American women was geographic, trade between Native Americans and the British in Canada was also disrupted as Indians no longer trusted the British who had betrayed them with the Peace of Paris. In the Ohio Valley, the middle ground of trade and cultural coexistence fell before backcountry settlers determined to drive out the Indians and seize their lands. As the middle ground disappeared, so too ended the long traditions of Native American women as cultural brokers and negotiators. American government officials simply refused to deal with them. James Duane, the chair of the Committee on Indian Affairs for the Continental Congress, announced instead that Indians would be treated as dependent nations, and forced them to adopt American diplomatic protocol, which had no place for women negotiators or diplomats.

Staunch Indian alliances with the British during the war and their equally staunch resistance to Americans afterward led to years of warfare that displaced entire groups to such an extent that they gathered into multi-group communities. They formed new alliances, finding some protection in their union. The disarray and destruction of traditional group boundaries, hunting grounds, farming communities, and social structures meant, for many

Native women, a decline in their power, a shift in their traditional roles, the loss of young men with whom to form families, and years of unrelenting warfare and dislocation. Native women continued to trade and care for their families, but an increased American expansion west of the Appalachians greatly disrupted their traditional roles and unrelenting warfare left them with dwindling opportunities by the end of the eighteenth century.

THINK MORE ABOUT IT

1. Return to the opening story about Anne Broughton. Along with what you've learned in the rest of the chapter, what does the story demonstrate about the effect of the constant warfare of the eighteenth century on the lives of diverse women in the colonies?

2. Compare and contrast the impact that the expansion of the empires of the Spanish, French, and English during the eighteenth century had on Native women and their families.

3. At the beginning of the eighteenth century, slavery existed in various forms among Native societies and in various European colonies. By the end of the eighteenth century, a few of the newly created states of the United States of America had declared slavery illegal. But overall the institution of chattel slavery had become more widespread, entrenched, and cruel. Discuss the evolution of slavery during the eighteenth century, being careful to pinpoint the ways in which gender played an important role in this changing pattern.

4. How did the American Revolution affect women? This question is a popular topic for debate among historians of women and gender. As with most important historical questions, there is no simple or single answer. Develop your own answer to this question, being careful to consider the impact of the Revolution on diverse women throughout what came to be the United States of America.

5. During the eighteenth century, important currents of thought swept through parts of the American colonies and, later, the American republic. These include the new ideas of the Great Awakening and the Enlightenment; the radical concept of women's equality as citizens, and the much more accepted views of Republican Motherhood and Republican Womanhood; the fledgling movement for the abolition of slavery, as well as scientific and other justifications for slavery; and the acceleration of warfare against Native peoples. Examine at least two of these currents of thought in detail, demonstrating how notions of gender and women's proper place played a role in each.

6. The notion of Republican Motherhood presupposed that all women should be seen as a single entity—Woman—and that all women thought and behaved in similar fashion. Thinking broadly about differences among women in terms of background, economic situation, marital status, legal position, political view, and geographic location,

develop a portrait of women to whom this ideal might appropriately apply. For such women, what advantages did the concept of Republican Motherhood confer on them?

7. What did you learn in this chapter that you did not know before? How does this new information help you understand the overall story of women in American history? What topics would you like to explore further?

READ MORE ABOUT IT

Susan Branson, *These Fiery Frenchified Dames: Women and Political Culture in Early National Philadelphia*

James F. Brooks, *Captives and Cousins: Slavery, Kinship, and Community in the Southwest Borderlands*

Ramon Gutierrez, *When Jesus Came, the Corn Mothers Went Away: Marriage, Sexuality, and Power in New Mexico, 1500–1846*

Linda Kerber, *Women of the Republic: Intellect and Ideology in Revolutionary America*

Cynthia Kierner, *Beyond the Household: Women's Place in the Early South, 1700–1835*

Jane Landers, *Black Society in Spanish Florida*

Rebecca Larson, *Daughters of Light: Quaker Women Preaching and Prophesying in the Colonies and Abroad, 1700–1775*

Holly Mayer, *Belonging to the Army: Camp Followers and Community during the American Revolution*

Mary Beth Norton, *Liberty's Daughters: The Revolutionary Experience of American Women, 1750–1800*

Karin Wulf, *Not All Wives: Women of Colonial Philadelphia*

Rosemarie Zagarri, *A Woman's Dilemma: Mercy Otis Warren and the American Revolution*

KEY CONCEPTS

métis	Enlightenment
encomienda	Patriot
mestizo	Loyalist
middle passage	frenchified dames
gentility	Republican Womanhood
task system of work	Republican Motherhood
gang system of work	middle ground
Great Awakening	

WOMEN IN THE NEW NATION

Abigail Adams of Washington, DC

WOMEN AND POLITICS IN THE EARLY REPUBLIC

THE INDUSTRIAL REVOLUTION
New England Mill Girls
   Primary Source 4-1: Harriet Hanson Robinson Describes Life
   at the Lowell Mills
Industrialization in the South
Industrialization and the Market Economy in the Midwest
Women's Inventions

**NATIVE AMERICAN WOMEN AND THE MARKET
   ECONOMY**

**THE PLIGHT OF ENSLAVED SOUTHERN BLACK
   WOMEN**
   Primary Source 4-2: Harriet Jacobs, *Incidents in the Life of
   a Slave Girl*

THE REFORMING IMPULSE
The Second Great Awakening
Fields of Reform
Free Black Women and Reform
   Primary Source 4-3: Maria Stewart Challenges Fellow African
   American Women
Women and Abolition

THINK MORE ABOUT IT

READ MORE ABOUT IT

KEY CONCEPTS

In the cold gray dawn of March 4, 1801, President John Adams left the city of Washington, DC, some six hours before his successor, Thomas Jefferson, was inaugurated as the third president of the United States in the first year of the new century. Abigail Adams, John's wife and partner throughout his long political career, had left the month before, happy to depart both the White House and Washington City. The presidential home was unfurnished, cold, and damp, and the new capital city surrounding it, she wrote, was "the very dirtiest place I ever saw." Her view of the change in government was equally pessimistic. Jefferson and his Democratic-Republicans, supporters of agrarian ideals and a limited central government, had defeated her husband John and his Federalists, supporters of business interests and a strong national government. The outcome, she feared, would be mob rule and the eventual downfall of the infant republic.

In this prediction Abigail Adams proved mistaken. The "Revolution of 1800," when political power in the United States shifted from one party to another, foreshadowed a long tradition in the new nation. Across the world the transfer of political power from one group to another had often resulted in bloody uprisings, civil wars, and revolutions. But in the United States the democratic experiment worked, as Adams peacefully left office and his ideological opposite Thomas Jefferson became the country's third president.

PORTRAIT OF ABIGAIL ADAMS   Gilbert Stuart's portrait of First Lady Abigail Adams rests in the National Gallery of Art in Washington, a city she was only too happy to leave after her husband's defeat in the election of 1800.

On taking office Jefferson and his followers discovered an abiding truth about American politics: compromising with those who held other points of view and tolerating differences of opinion proved essential for the survival of the American experiment. Jefferson, the president who declared that the Constitution must be interpreted strictly and government power must be limited, would become the president who "stretched the Constitution till it cracked" in order to purchase the vast Louisiana Territory. He would also impose an economic embargo against Britain and France despite the Constitution's failure to explicitly grant him such a power. Jefferson represented the flip side of the ideological coin from Adams, but the political situation Jefferson found himself in when he took office necessitated compromise with his beliefs about federal power as he struggled to keep the new nation from being drawn into the warfare that had ravaged Europe since the days of the French Revolution. For him, the survival of the United States was paramount. For him, as for everyone in this new century, the United States had to decide how the country it had fought to create was going to survive.

But what form would the United States take? Abigail Adams believed, she wrote as her husband left office, that the "Halcion days of America" were already past. The new century brought new challenges: of national politics that needed to incorporate the ideology of the Revolution, of a national economy that struggled to incorporate changes wrought by industrialization and the expansion of slavery, and by reform-minded Americans who desired to build a better world. As the century dawned, Americans could reinvent themselves and their nation as they saw fit and as their circumstances permitted. Women's choices for reinvention, however, far more than men's, were constrained by their gender. They were also limited by their social and economic class, their race, their ethnicity, region, religion, and sexuality, as well as by the laws of the states and territories where they resided. Yet as American society felt its way toward its vision of a democratic republic, many women took advantage of opportunities to shape their own lives as well as the future of the nation.

WOMEN AND POLITICS IN THE EARLY REPUBLIC

The political revolutions that had transformed the British colonies into the United States replaced a constitutional monarchy with representative government. The same egalitarian ideology that led to war in America also led to prolonged unrest in Europe. Americans watched uneasily. The French Revolution had wracked the Continent for nearly twelve years. Now, its excesses—the mass executions, including that of King Louis XVI, the political refugees that flooded into America, the XYZ affair in which the French demanded bribes to deal with American ambassadors—were so apparent that many Americans turned from their former allies in disgust, fearing that those same excesses would show up in their own country.

The "fiery frenchified dames" of Philadelphia, followers of Judith Sargent Murray and Mary Wollstonecraft who had supported the French in the heady days of the revolution against the monarchy, suddenly seemed too radical to have a place in the discussion of women's roles in the new republic. Politics became a dangerous thing for women to aspire to, and few women dared to fight the social condemnation that came their way when they voiced public opinions on political matters. Instead, women of the new century used more traditional methods to influence politics.

One center for women's political activity was Washington, DC. The new capitol had to be built, literally from the ground up. Following the plan of the city laid out by French architect Pierre-Charles L'Enfant, slave and free workers constructed the city on swampy land located on the border between Maryland and Virginia in the early nineteenth century. The new city also had to be constructed socially as well as physically. Government ran not only within the buildings of marble and brick, but also in the social world that the women of Washington led. Martha Washington had held weekly receptions called *levées* in Philadelphia, the first capital city. Abigail Adams entertained congressmen at dinner parties at the new White House, despite being in the federal city for only about three months. The widowed Thomas Jefferson, on the other hand, proved distinctly uninterested in social events that politically connected women had held as a way to grease the political wheels in the capitol. Jefferson did not approve of political women at all, and when ambassador to France in the 1780s when the French Revolution began, called Frenchwomen "Amazons" and "meddlesome," and blamed Queen Marie Antoinette for plunging France into revolution. He bragged that American women had "been too wise to wrinkle their foreheads with politics." Jefferson's dislike of women in politics grew intense after his years in France. Even Abigail Adams, who had been a close friend for years, came in for criticism. At a January 1801 dinner party that the Adamses held to introduce the newly elected Jefferson to members of his own party, Abigail was amazed to find that he knew so few of them. She warned him that he needed to be aware of members of Congress because they might act contrary to his wishes if he continued to ignore them, but Jefferson, showing his customary disdain for women trying to involve themselves in politics, "laught out, and here ended the conversation," she wrote.

The administration of James Madison, the Democratic-Republican president who followed Jefferson in 1809, paid far more attention to women's opinions on political matters. Politicians used the social circle established and presided over by First Lady Dolley Madison to politick informally and to gather support for their positions in ways that they never could in the halls of Congress. Both domestic politics and international affairs were dealt with on the stage that was the President's House, as congressmen, diplomats, and city leaders attended Madison's social events. Dolley Madison excelled in creating an atmosphere that encouraged such activity. She furnished the White House in grand style, despite fears among some that she was contributing to an "aristocracy" that might corrupt the fledgling country by turning it into another England. She began by decorating a small sitting room where she could receive and entertain the ladies of Washington as they called on the president's wife, and by furnishing a large drawing room, where both Madisons could entertain diplomats and politicians in more formal events. As visitors arrived, they saw not a backwater shack in a swamp, but an elegant set of rooms that made the White House, as one historian wrote, "the focus for visitors of all nationalities and all classes." When they drank and ate from the president's table, they relaxed, feeling freer to suggest, to negotiate, to compromise, than they did in the more somber atmosphere of the government's official buildings. In the White House, elite women in Washington had a space and a place that allowed them to contribute to political discussion, and the first ladies who followed Dolley Madison continued the traditions she began, ensuring women at least an informal role in influencing political policy in the country.

An informal role would be about the only one women would be allowed in politics in the early part of the century. Most state constitutions defined voters as male property owners. Only in New Jersey did women vote, a few as early as 1776. The state's 1790 election law referred to eligible voters as "he or she." In 1807, however, the legislature restricted the vote to free, white adult men, after reports that young men dressed as women cast fraudulent votes in a hotly contested election. Aside from some states that allowed women to vote in local school board elections, women were thus disenfranchised and their participation in politics would revolve around the informal use of "influence" to affect male voters and officials. At the same time, the franchise expanded for men, as nearly every state reduced property requirements over the next thirty years, and most did away with them entirely.

As the vote became more widespread for men, voting and politics became male rituals, increasingly seen as an activity that no women should even want to participate in. Catherine Maria Sedgwick, a noted novelist of the early nineteenth century and daughter of a Federalist congressman, reminisced in 1835 about the early days of the nation when Federalist women had displayed party symbols on their clothes and might even refuse to marry men of the opposing political persuasion. Her novels portrayed women of the post-Revolutionary era "so imbued with the independent spirit of the times" that they could never agree to the surrender of rights that constituted marriage and chose instead to remain single. Alas, Sedgwick lamented, no such interest in politics occupied women in 1835.

This was not exactly true. The revolutionary generation was dying, and a new generation of political leaders emerged to redefine the nation and carve out roles for themselves within it. Violent disagreements in the realm of politics, especially over the role of federal versus state governments, threatened to undo the country. Women often appear at events related to the political wrangling, constant during the first third of the nineteenth century, in part because such turmoil always had economic and social consequences that affected women's lives. Federal policies in 1807 and 1808, for example, had restricted trade between America, Great Britain, and France, as Presidents Jefferson and Madison both used economic weapons in an international struggle America was trying to stay out of. The policies failed, ruining New England's shipping economy, and many merchants turned to illegal smuggling to survive. In 1808, a group of women in Augusta, Maine, marched on the local jail to free prisoners who had disobeyed the Embargo laws. Federalists and Republicans also disagreed over the second war with Great Britain—the War of 1812. That disagreement spilled over into the schoolyard. Julia Hieronymus Tevis recalled that the political animosity between supporters and opponents was so great that she saw "girls of our school in battle array on the green common . . . fighting like furies." By 1814, Federalist politicians in New England were so angry at the wreckage of their economy, as well as the war, that they met in Hartford, Connecticut, and voted to secede from the nation. They argued that since the Constitution did not explicitly give the power to Congress to limit American exports to Europe, then the federal government had no constitutional right to do so.

The Hartford Convention failed in its call for secession, largely because a few weeks later the Americans defeated the British at the Battle of New Orleans, two weeks after the formal end of the war. By then, women were so involved in the partisanship created by the War of 1812 that one historian Rosemarie Zagarri has suggested that many Americans began to fear for the stability of the domestic sphere. If women could be as passionate about politics as men were, something had to be done to prevent disruption over political issues at home. Much of the postwar literature—sermons, articles, novels, and the like—instructing women on how to behave in society thus focused on turning women's attention to domestic matters and leaving politics to men.

The partisanship that had led to the Hartford Convention—the relationship between the federal government and the states—did not disappear, however. In 1832, those issues came to a head in the *Nullification Crisis.* President Andrew Jackson, elected in 1828, became enraged at his vice president, South Carolinian John C. Calhoun, because Calhoun opposed the president's effort to increase the tariff (the federal tax on imports and, along with land sales, the major source of government income). Jackson threatened to march down to South Carolina and hang Calhoun from the highest palmetto tree in the state. Furious at the federal government for imposing an onerous tariff, South Carolinians held a convention to declare that the federal tariff law would be "null and void" within the state, triggering the Nullification Crisis. The struggle was epic, pitting the president against the vice president and the federal government against a leading state. In this crisis, states rights' supporters argued that the Constitution should be interpreted strictly and that a protective tariff was unconstitutional since it was not mentioned anywhere in the document. They nearly came to blows with loose constructionists, who argued that as long as the means to constitutionally mandated ends—in this case, raising revenue to pay for operating the government—were legal, they were acceptable. The Nullification Crisis ended peaceably, thanks to the intervention of Sen. Henry Clay of Kentucky, whose skills at political compromise crafted a compromise tariff to lower the tax rates gradually. It had reached such a fevered pitch, however, partly because of disagreement over the correct interpretation of the

Constitution, but partly because of bad blood between President Jackson and Vice President Calhoun over Margaret "Peggy" Eaton.

The so-called Eaton Affair provided the nation with another example of the risks that came when women meddled in government, as well as displaying the power of the female sphere of social networking in the capitol city. Margaret Eaton, daughter of a Washington innkeeper and widow of navy purser John Timberlake, married Sen. John Eaton, Jackson's secretary of war. Rumors flew that Timberlake had killed himself over his wife's alleged dalliances, and the wives of cabinet officers, led by Vice President John Calhoun's wife Floride, refused to accept Margaret Eaton as part of the social circle of Washington. They viewed her hasty remarriage as proof of her loose morals and ostracized her, refusing to call upon her and refusing to accept her social calls on them. Eaton and Jackson both were outraged by Margaret's treatment, Jackson not only because he liked Margaret, a vivacious and attractive young woman, but also because the attack on Margaret reminded him of the scurrilous attacks on his wife Rachel, who had died just prior to Jackson's first term. Apparently unknowingly, Rachel had first married Jackson prior to the finalization of her divorce from her first husband, and the opposition political party seized upon that scandalous behavior and trumpeted it about in the election of 1828. Jackson blamed the attacks for Rachel's death, so when similar attacks came out against Margaret Eaton, he had little patience for the cabinet wives and their campaign against her.

The Eaton affair ended when Jackson's cabinet resigned. Calhoun's place on the 1832 ticket ended as Jackson replaced him with Martin Van Buren, a widower quite happy to please the president by being nice to Mrs. Eaton. The intrigue and scandal wrought by women gossiping and using their influence in the male political realm, it seemed to many, proved that politics could be damaged only by including women. Jackson had defeated the "phalanx of ladies," as he termed the cabinet wives, but had to destroy his cabinet to do so. Surely such interference in the affairs of state could not be good for the country. The ladies never resumed their powerful public roles as wives of cabinet officers, and returned instead to their homes. There, they resumed their roles as Republican women and Republican mothers, shifted to the margins of political activity by those opposed to women's involvement in politics. Women's politicization became a liability to Americans by the end of the first third of the nineteenth century, rather than a strength. Women's place was in the home, in separate spheres of activity in which women worked apart from men. Those separate spheres of men and women were necessary, most Americans believed, because men and women were so different. The public sphere of politics, warfare, factories, alehouses, or other public institutions was so rough and tumble that no woman should be interested in activities within that sphere. If she were, not only was her behavior deemed inappropriate, but she herself was suspected of being "unwomanly."

In truth, as important as politics were in the consolidation of the country's power and in the construction of roles for its citizens, another event had a far greater impact on women's daily lives: the industrialization of America and the resulting changes to the market economy.

THE INDUSTRIAL REVOLUTION

The United States in 1800 was an agricultural and commercial society, manufacturing few goods. The Louisiana Purchase of 1803 doubled the physical size of the country in 1803, and between 1800 and 1840 the population grew dramatically: from 5.3 to 17 million. Towns and cities grew exponentially: by 1820, New York had over 100,000 people; Boston, Philadelphia, Baltimore, and New Orleans had populations ranging from 35,000 to 100,000. Unable to cope with the influx of settlers and immigrants, crowded urban living spawned innumerable problems, as people searched for jobs, food, clothing, and shelter in an unforgiving economy that cycled from boom times to market collapses. Laborers in the mixed economy included skilled artisans who fashioned specialty goods, such as fine furniture, by hand. Other specialty manufactured items, such as china, wine, or fine fabrics, were imported from Europe. More common manufactured items, such as hats or shoes, were made in America in what was called a *putting-out system*. Under this system, an entrepreneur distributed raw materials to farm families, who then made the goods at home. Most of the family members doing the actual labor were women and girls, since their domestic duties allowed them to be sedentary long enough to produce an item, while men and boys more often labored in the fields tending crops, chasing cattle, or logging lumber. In the putting-out system, once women and girls had completed the goods, the entrepreneur picked them up and distributed them for sale. Two of the most important items manufactured in New England, the region with the most home manufacturing, were rough leather shoes, worn by working people throughout America, and palm leaf hats, worn by Southern slaves as they toiled in the fields.

For a while, manufacturers found the putting-out system quite profitable for small items, but entrepreneurs turned increasingly to the factory method for manufacturing larger items, for which there was even greater demand. Factories concentrated production and labor into one place that could hold all the machinery needed to produce the goods, and where workers could be closely supervised to achieve maximum efficiency. Greater efficiency netted higher profits. It also meant faster production of goods, because transportation costs declined. By centralizing production and using new sources of power such as the steam engine, entrepreneurs produced goods faster, cheaper, and more reliably. The factory workers who actually made these goods were paid either wages for the hours they worked or by the piece—*piecework*—for the pieces they produced.

In the United States, as in England where the Industrial Revolution started, large-scale manufacturing began in the textile industry. Given how time-consuming the labor of producing cloth was, it is little wonder. Consider cotton. The simplest fabric available took enormous amounts of time and labor to produce. The cotton boll, when harvested, had to be cleaned of seeds (ginned), combed (carded) until the fibers were smooth and straight, and then spun into thread. The thread had to be dyed the desired color, then strung (warped) on a loom. Then another thread (the weft) had to be woven back and forth. The cloth produced then had to be cut and sewn by hand to make a single garment. The labor needed to produce cloth, a product used by everyone, cried out for a more efficient method of production. In England, where the mechanization of textile production first took place, the process began with the development of a spinning jenny in 1720 that produced mechanically spun thread, then a carding machine (1748), then a power loom (1785).

The United States, however, unlike England, at first lacked the technology to mechanize the textile industry. British laws forbade any exportation of the technology that had made it the world's first industrial power. Like most attempts to keep technology from spreading, this effort was doomed. By 1793, only ten years after the American Revolution, Samuel Slater built the first U.S. textile mills in Pawtucket, Rhode Island. Slater, a former millworker and superintendent of one of England's first mills, brought the plans for the spinning jenny out in his head when he emigrated to America in 1789.

Slater hired whole families, including women and children, to work in his mills under annual contracts. He also provided company housing, paying wages to the father, often as a credit at the company-owned store, thus reinforcing the patriarchal family structure by controlling the access women had to their own wages. Slater feared that if women and children controlled their own pay, the stability of not only his workforce but also of the patriarchal family would be disrupted. By hiring women who worked as part of a family, he thought his female workforce would be more docile and dependent than single women might be. He thus tried to guarantee a dependent and pliable workforce, a pattern later manufacturers would also follow.

Slater's success at mechanizing spinning prompted male employees to leave, taking the knowledge they gained in the mill to build their own spinning jennies. By 1809, sixty-two spinning mills, employing hundreds of families, operated around the country but primarily in New England. Another entrepreneur, Francis Cabot Lowell, sought to take advantage of the increased supply of yarn by building a power loom to speed the weaving of yarn into fabric. The great cycle of industrial innovation known as the Industrial Revolution had begun.

Founder of the textile industry in the United States, Lowell toured English factories and, upon his return designed and built a model power loom. In 1814, he opened a factory in Chelmsford, Massachusetts (later renamed Lowell in his honor). Lowell's first factory, the Boston Manufacturing Company of Waltham, Massachusetts, succeeded so well that later factories in the area adopted what was called the Waltham Plan to run their textile mills in the most efficient manner possible. This plan integrated all parts of production under one roof. From cotton boll to finished bolt, from sheep's wool to woolen goods, from raw silk to finished fabric, all the raw materials, machinery, and workers were located on one site. In this way, manufacturers hoped to gain maximum profit by ensuring maximum efficiency.

Rather than hiring entire families, mills employed large numbers of single women, since they were tall enough to work new machinery, such as power looms, that children could not operate. Less costly than men to hire and thought to be "tractable," or easier than men to control, these young women were recruited from farms throughout New England. To attract and keep loyal employees, the companies paid wages that were high—$3.00 to $3.50 a week—far higher than wages they might earn at home. More importantly, though, mill owners assured parents that their daughters would be safe by promising to provide moral guidance and to watch over them. The factory system would act *in loco parentis*, a Latin term meaning "in place of a parent." To do so, the company built dormitories for the so-called operatives, factory girls, or *mill girls* to live in. In this textile village, they slept, ate, and worked.

New England Mill Girls

Mill girls became famous throughout America. Early manufacturers assumed that men would do millwork and other industrial jobs, not women. Journalists worried about the mill girls' morals, concerned that they might corrupt themselves or others, living as they did on their own, away from the patriarchal household. Others fretted that the country was heading down the wrong road by allowing its flowers of young womanhood to work at such jobs. Women, thought many, should be home raising children, caring for their husbands, and staying firmly within their separate sphere of activity, not working out in the world. Many Americans opposed industrialization because they looked at its terrible physical, human, and environmental costs in Europe, particularly in England, and did not want the same slums, corruption, poverty, and displacement here.

Employers had to overcome that opposition, in part because women's labor was so much cheaper than men's. Each textile company faced the task of convincing parents to let their daughters go into the mills. Eventually, recruiters from mills drove long black wagons, called *slavers*, across Vermont and Rhode Island and other New England states, canvassing the countryside for women workers. Some girls or women decided to go on their own; sometimes parents decided daughters needed to work to support the family; sometimes towns packed off orphan girls to the factories. Many mill girls sent money home to needy families. Like most farmers throughout history, those in New England were land rich and cash poor, so it boosted the family income to have children earning cash. Other mill girls kept their earnings for a dowry, working until they married. Some wed sweethearts from their villages but many others married mechanics, shopkeepers, and other men they met in mill towns, then settled there. Factory owners made sure that the girls were strictly supervised in company boardinghouses, while providing them with some educational, cultural, and religious activities, including music classes and lectures. Mill girls in Lowell, Massachusetts, even had their own publication, the *Lowell Mill Offering*, which published their contributions of stories, poetry, and letters to the editor, recording their factory experiences and their reactions to the popular perception that mill girls had loose morals and bad habits.

Supervising mill girls and providing these activities proved expensive for the mill owners and unpopular among many workers. Grouped together, the young women learned from one another in discussions in the boardinghouses and conversations during their long workdays. Many did not like having to attend functions at night when they wanted to enjoy what little free time they had. The mill timetables that have survived from the 1830s and 1840s indicate that most girls worked ten to fourteen hours a day and averaged seventy-three hours of work per week. When the economy went into periodic slumps, the management tried to improve profits by *speed-ups* (making the machines go faster and forcing the girls to work faster to keep up with them) or *stretch-outs* (making girls work more machines for the same wages). When that happened, some mill girls left for other jobs. But other young women went on strike, staging what were called *turnouts*. In 1834 and 1836, women turned out against the management when their wages were cut 10 to 15 percent at the same time that boardinghouse rates rose. Such actions ended when a financial depression, the Panic of 1837, hit. Hard times stayed with the country for years, and factories throughout America instituted speed-ups and stretch-outs, much to the dismay of the workers.

Women textile workers in Massachusetts were so angered by these actions that they eventually petitioned the state legislature to investigate working conditions in the mills and called for the state to impose a ten-hour day. The language that mill girls used to protest their working conditions was literally revolutionary in nature, borrowing from the rhetoric of the American Revolution. Lowell mill girls declared in signs they carried, letters they published, and petitions they circulated that they would not be made into "slaves" by the mill owners. They pointed out that they were, after all, the daughters of patriots. "As our fathers resisted unto blood the lordly avarice of the British ministry, so we their daughters never will wear the yoke which has been prepared for us," one declared in an 1836 turnout. Ironically, an antislavery speaker who had arrived in Lowell in 1834 to rail against slavery had been met by a stone-throwing mob. New England textile mills depended on Southern slaves to pick cotton to supply them with raw materials and on Southern slaveowners to buy much of the cloth that they produced. Yankee girls, concerned with their own rights, did not make the connection between the enslavement they wished to avoid themselves and those Americans already enslaved in part because of the mills they struck against. Instead, the mill girls stated boldly that, as workers, they should be free.

While factories provided some real opportunities for women as wage earners, they also helped change the face of American rural life, leading to a breakdown in the rural community as young women left the farms for the cities and towns. For some women, employment in mills led to disaster. Most of the mill girls were just that: young girls and women, ages fifteen to twenty-five, running all the machines on the premises. Some male supervisors took advantage of the sexual vulnerability of the women

HARRIET HANSON ROBINSON DESCRIBES LIFE AT THE LOWELL MILLS

Harriet Robinson worked in the Lowell Mills from 1834 to 1848, far longer than the average mill girl. In her autobiography, published in the 1880s, she commented on the transformative power millwork had for women, who had so few choices in their lives to earn their keep.

"In 1832, Lowell was little more than a factory village. . . . Help was in great demand and stories were told all over the country of the new factory place, and the high wages that were offered to all classes of work-people; stories that reached the ears of mechanics' and farmers' sons and gave new life to lonely and dependent women in distant towns and farm-houses. . . . At the time the Lowell cotton mills were started the caste of the factory girl was the lowest among the employments of women. In England and in France, particularly, great injustice had been done to her real character. She was represented as subjected to influences that must destroy her purity and self-respect. In the eyes of her overseer she was but a brute, a slave, to be beaten, pinched and pushed about. It was to overcome this prejudice that such high wages had been offered to women that they might be induced to become mill-girls. . . .

who worked for them. Premarital sex resulting in pregnancy was not uncommon in New England or elsewhere in America, but it was becoming less acceptable. *Premarital* sex in the colonial period had meant just that: sexual relations between people who planned to marry when their economic circumstances allowed. This pattern changed with industrialization and the urbanization that accompanied it. Mill towns provided more anonymity and less social pressure for a man to marry a woman whom he had impregnated, and women deserted by the fathers of their children became more common after 1800. Most unmarried mothers suffered severe social and economic distress and had few options: they could give up their babies for adoption, abandon them to an orphanage or church in hopes that someone would care for them, or keep them and try to raise them alone or with help from kin or friends. But without a social welfare system to provide services such as daycare or health insurance, women with babies had to find employment that would enable them to care for both themselves and their children. Prostitution was one such "profession," and many young women, deserted by the men who had seduced or abused them, took this option.

Mill life offered many young women their first taste of life in association with other girls their age. Some found the educational and cultural events enlightening and took advantage of the opportunity to become more literate and express their creativity. Others learned the joys of solidarity at the workplace. Whether they returned to family farms, married and set up their own households, or moved on to other jobs, women often found that their years at the mill changed their perspective. (See Primary Source 4-1.)

"It is well to digress here a little, and speak of the influence the possession of money had on the characters of some of these women. We can hardly realize what a change the cotton factory made in the status of the working women. Hitherto woman had always been a money saving rather than a money earning, member of the community. Her labor could command but small return. If she worked out as servant, or 'help,' her wages were from 50 cents to $1.00 a week; or, if she went from house to house by the day to spin and weave . . . she could get but 75 cents a week and her meals. As teacher, her services were not in demand, and the arts, the professions, and even the trades and industries, were nearly all closed to her.

"As late as 1840 there were only seven vocations outside the home into which the women of New England had entered. At this time woman had no property rights. . . . The law took no cognizance of woman as a money-spender. She was a ward, an appendage, a relict. Thus it happened that if a woman did not choose to marry, or, when left a widow, to re-marry, she had no choice but to enter one of the few employments open to her, or to become a burden on the charity of some relative."

Source: Harriet H. Robinson, "Early Factory Labor in New England," in *Fourteenth Annual Report,* Massachusetts Bureau of Statistics of Labor (Boston: Wright & Potter, 1883), 380–382, 387–388, 391–392.

Symbols of the new age, the mill girls embodied an expansiveness in American women that would find expression in other arenas throughout the first half of the nineteenth century.

Industrialization in the South

Industrialization in the American South took a slightly different turn. Southern states were largely agricultural and remained so throughout the first half of the nineteenth century. The river system of the South lent itself to easy transportation of goods to market via water to the Atlantic and Gulf coasts. The longer growing season and rich soil made crop production and raising livestock easier and more profitable, and the use of slave labor allowed even small farmers to reap profits. But the international trade that the South relied upon for much of its wealth was hurt by the 1807 embargo on exports to Europe, and was further damaged by the War of 1812. When the dust settled, the success of new industries in the Northeast and Middle Atlantic states convinced some Southerners that industrialization, not agriculture, was the key to the region's survival. Embargoes and wars prevented cotton, which after 1800 was the South's primary crop, from being shipped to Europe. With the loss of those markets, cotton prices fell. Southerners favoring industrialization believed that they should build local mills to buy the cotton Europe could not. These new Southern mills would compete with mills in New England to keep cotton prices high. After 1820, Southern entrepreneurs built dozens of cotton mills, borrowing the North's technology, factory supervisors, and occasionally even importing some of its workers. Georgia, the most heavily industrialized state, built its first mill in 1811, and by 1828 had forty more, along with railroads and canals built to move the cotton and textiles to market.

Patriarchal culture, stronger in the South, influenced staffing at the mills. "There is nothing in tending a loom to harden a lady's hand," said one promoter of manufacturing, trying to convince Southern men in a culture that valued women for their femininity that millwork would not affect the "ladylike" appearance of Southern women. But despite such reassurances, many Southerners opposed letting their daughters go off alone to work in the mills. Many of the Yankee mill girls who were hired instead soon left, unhappy with low wages and uncomfortable working conditions, and Southern mill owners found fewer independent women to hire. Consequently, mill owners tended to hire family members together. Some 75 percent of the workers at the Cedar Falls Manufacturing Company in Randolph County, North Carolina, for example, were single women, but four-fifths of them lived with at least one parent and worked with a sibling, rather than residing in the boardinghouses that factory owners built in the style of the New England mills. Only a minority of Southern mill workers lived in factory towns.

Mill owners considered single or widowed white women best suited for factory work, preferring not to rely on slave labor. Slaveowners believed slaves were too valuable in the fields to send them to factory jobs and factory owners found slaves too expensive to buy and too pricey to rent, since they would not be available during planting and harvest seasons. Few white men worked in mills either. Most white Southern men viewed wage labor as beneath them, viewing it as a form of industrial slavery. They held fast to the traditional role of yeoman farmer—the industrious, honest, virtuous tiller of the soil—which they viewed as the backbone of the nation. In addition, mill owners feared white male workers would be less tractable than women and more likely to strike. Single and widowed women were also much cheaper to hire than men. The average wage for a woman millworker in the South was ten dollars per month; for a man it was twenty dollars.

In other industries in the South, particularly in mining, which required an enormous number of workers hired for a relatively short period of time, women workers were often paid on a task basis, and wages were more likely to vary according to the degree of skill a woman worker needed for her job. Company files record scores of names of women workers performing myriad jobs: hauling wood, loading charcoal, hand-picking slugs of iron to send to the blast furnace. In east Tennessee in 1846, Nancy Ann Butter hauled two loads of coal, fifty bushels each, for one dollar at the same mine where her father and mother both worked. In 1849, Allison Viols, a worker at Gaston County High Shoals Gold Mine in North Carolina, earned one dollar for hauling a load of ore, a "task" job; Mary Carr from Hamilton County, Tennessee, who stoked the locomotive's engine with wood, was listed in the records as a railroad "fireman." Women would eventually make up 3 percent of the workforce in the mining industry in the United States, which included the South, despite its cultural bias against white women working for wages in male-dominated occupations.

Industrialization and the Market Economy in the Midwest

In the Midwest, industrial production proceeded much faster and extended much farther than it did in the South. Here manufacturing tended to cluster in growing towns and cities along transportation routes such as rivers (Pittsburgh, Pennsylvania, and Cincinnati, Ohio, on the Ohio River); lakes (Toledo, Ohio, and Detroit, Michigan, on the Great Lakes); and canals (Rochester and Buffalo, New York, along the Erie Canal). These cities served as commercial centers for the far-flung regions they served. Women living in communities nearby participated easily in the expanding market economy that developed alongside these improvements in transportation, sending the crops they raised and the goods they fashioned to market and receiving, in return, cloth, shoes, and other manufactured products other women made and city shopkeepers sold. Such access to markets created wealthy cities that supported some unheard-of civic luxuries such as free public education, begun in Buffalo in 1838. With public education, common people, including women, could be taught to be responsible citizens, thus bringing full circle the notions of Republican Motherhood and civic virtue from the days of the founding of the republic to the "modern" era of 1840.

As industrialization followed the rivers, cities such as Cincinnati, the "Queen City of the West," enjoyed boom times. By 1830, it was the central market town for a million people who lived along the Ohio River and in the surrounding states, connected to the city by turnpikes, canals, and railroads. By 1850, it was the sixth largest city in America and third in manufacturing. Immigrants from Germany and Ireland flooded into the city, working in construction industries as well as flour and lumber mills. In addition, the city had distilleries, breweries, tanneries, and heavier industry: metalworking, machinery, and steamboat production.

Of particular importance to women wage earners was the Midwest's garment industry, along with the shoe and boot-making industries. Although most women worked in domestic service in midwestern cities, others found work in the clothing industry as seamstresses and milliners, either in the home or in the factories. They worked for less pay than men and often combined wage work with caring for their families by taking in boarders and laundry. When working conditions grew unbearable, some women responded by forming protective associations. The Cleveland Female Protective Union, founded in 1850, sought to improve the pay (two dollars a week) and lessen the hours (six sixteen-hour days) their members worked. The group opened its own store to sell its merchandise, paying its workers higher wages than they could earn in the rest of the city. Other garment factories undercut their prices and drove them out of business in less than a year.

Women's Inventions

Industrial development and expansion demanded new inventions by both men and by women. Inventors abounded in the United States, in part because of the way that science was practiced in the first part of the nineteenth century. While a college education or advanced degree are needed to participate in the professional scientific world today, without the institutions, bureaucracies, and agencies that sponsor scientific research and with scientific knowledge less specialized, invention was the domain of the amateur. This domain included women, many of whom invented products that stemmed not only from their own interests, but also from a desire to help support their families. Most of the women scientists and inventors in the early years of the Industrial Revolution created practical devices that helped them and their families in their everyday lives, rather than authoring the theoretical studies that became part of institutionalized science during the second half of the nineteenth century.

The first patent granted to an American woman went to Mary Kies's in 1809 for a weaving process she invented that combined straw and silk. The earliest should have gone to Sybilla Masters, a Pennsylvania colonist who invented a new mill to process Indian corn in 1715, but as a British colonist she was under the law of coverture, which meant the patent was issued instead to her husband. After the American Revolution, one of the many new laws passed to organize the United States was the Patent Act of 1790, which allowed the federal government instead of individual states to issue patents. This encouraged inventors to patent their works because they no longer feared losing the rights to their inventions to a competitor from a different state. By 1802, so many applications flooded into the government that a separate Patent Office was created to handle the workload. Since the Patent Act contained no reference to gender in its language, either in applying for or in granting patents, women inventors felt free to use the system as it existed.

In this context Mary Kies patented her weaving process. Kies' work was an offshoot of Betsey Metcalf's bonnet, invented in 1798. Metcalf's new way of braiding straw to make the straw bonnets all women wore soon generated "braiding bees" instead of sewing ones, and led to the bonnet's widespread manufacture by women and children who sold them for cash or used them for barter. Despite the bonnet's popularity, Metcalf said she never applied for a patent because she was satisfied with her earnings of more than $1 a day, at a time when the estimated per capita income was $131 per year. Historian Anne MacDonald quoted Metcalf as saying, "Many said I ought to get a patent; but I told them I did not wish to have my name sent to Congress." A similar sentiment against public notice may have stopped other women inventors from drawing attention to themselves.

Early patents for inventions by women revolved around the domestic world and reflected the assumptions of that world. Elizabeth Adams, for instance, invented a pregnancy corset that afforded "looseness above the abdomen [to allow] the parts to rise upward, in case the patient is in a sitting or stooping posture." Her corset reflects the fashion expectations of the day—that middle-class ladies would always be corseted under their clothes—with the reality of pregnancy's effects on women's bodies. Mary Ann Woodward invented a fan activated by a rocking chair, so that a woman could rock a baby and cool herself at the same time. Nancy Johnson

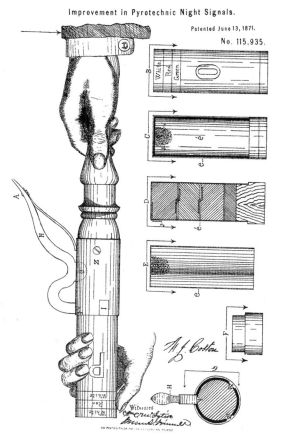

MARTHA J. COSTON.

Improvement in Pyrotechnic Night Signals.

Patented June 13, 1871.

No. 115,935.

MARTHA COSTON'S SIGNALING FLARES   While most women inventors focused on domestic inventions, Martha Coston patented a signaling device used by ships to communicate at night in 1859. It was used by the U.S. Navy until the mid-twentieth century.

invented a hand-cranked ice-cream maker. Catharine Beecher, probably the most widely read domestic advice author of the nineteenth century, designed the "perfect" stove with a reservoir at one side for a constant supply of hot water. Ellen Curtis Demorest patented an inexpensive hoop skirt and an Imperial Dress Elevator, a device to hoist long, flowing skirts out of the mud, which came in handy during this era of unpaved streets and roads. An astute businesswoman who produced a best-selling woman's fashion magazine with her husband, Demorest uncharacteristically failed to patent the paper dress patterns that she and her designers invented and that her husband included in the midcentury issues of *Mme. Demorest's Quarterly Mirror of Fashions*. Several years later a man, Ebenezer Butterick, did. These dress patterns revolutionized home sewing in the second half of the century.

One of the most prolific nineteenth-century inventors was Clarissa Britain, of St. Joseph, Michigan, who held nine patents. She invented a simple device, the potato boiler, that made cooking safer. It vented steam from the pot so that the cook could lift a basket with the potatoes in it out of the boiling water without scalding herself. She also invented a dinner pail with a lantern on it so that miners working far underground could see to carry in and eat the food their wives made for their dinners. Other women patented pulleys and slings to lift and turn patients; sanitary napkins; pessaries (similar to diaphragms) that could prevent pregnancy; and hexagonal houses with a third more square footage than a four-sided house having the same length walls.

These inventions illustrate the creativity women brought to the mundane, arduous, and vital tasks of running a home and caring for others. Still, success as a woman inventor was difficult. Even seemingly simple inventions often required that their designers be literate and know basic mathematics, but education for women remained limited and expensive, especially beyond the primary level. Registering a patent was also costly, requiring that the applicant supply two sets of professional drawings and a scale model of the invention. Usually inventors needed a patent attorney's help. Then again, a patent did not a product make. Thousands of patents were issued for items never produced and sold. Only when inventors sold the rights to their inventions to a manufacturer could they hope to make money. Even then, without adequate capitalization, production might be impossible, and borrowing money for setting up a business meant entering a contract. Married women still fell under the restrictions of coverture. While a woman could, with her husband's help and permission, borrow money or apply for status to do business as a *feme sole* trader, marital laws transferred the ownership of a patent to that same husband. Once again, women's lack of legal rights hampered them from tasks men could accomplish more easily.

Popular disapproval of women doing anything in the public sphere, including registering a patent, further limited women's work as inventors. Would-be women inventors heard advice such as that offered by George Washington Burnap, a leading clergyman and lecturer: "The God who made them [women] knew the sphere in which each of them was designed to act, and he fitted them for it by their physical frames, by their intellectual susceptibilities, by their tastes and affections." Many men and women both agreed with Burnap that women's roles in society should be separate and apart from men. In particular, most felt that women and men were so different that the separate spheres of men and women were God-given and ought not be tampered with nor argued against. Certainly public participation in the masculine field of science and the market economy pushed the boundaries of the separate spheres.

NATIVE AMERICAN WOMEN AND THE MARKET ECONOMY

The market economy's expansion had consequences for the interaction between Natives and whites that few could have foreseen. In the Northeast, John Adams wrote to Thomas Jefferson in 1812 that he had seen Indian women, native to the area of Quincy, Massachusetts, walking from town to town, literally covered from head to foot with handmade baskets for sale. The few Indians who survived in the area that had once been home to thousands lived under guardianship systems that prevented them from moving about seasonally, as their ancestors had done, to hunt game. Many Native men adjusted by going off to sea on whaling voyages, while the women made and sold baskets, went into domestic services, and married non-Indians and free blacks, so that eventually the groups that had lived in the area for hundreds of years became nearly extinct.

In the Southeast, the five so-called civilized tribes—the Cherokee, Creek, Chickasaw, Choctaw, and Seminole—faced attacks on their lands and their ways of life as whites poured into the region after the American Revolution. Among these groups, the fate of the Cherokee is the best documented as it tried to accommodate white demands with its own desire to survive as a culture. In an attempt to ease tensions by acculturating the Indians into the mainstream of American life, the government sent Cherokee women cotton seed and spinning wheels. Within six months after their first harvest, the women were able to weave cloth worth more than the pelts their men brought home from the hunt. Their weaving placed the women within the market economy, as did their work in the group's production of salt, saltpeter, beef, swine, corn, wheat, turpentine, pitch, tar, potash, maple sugar, silver, and gold.

Cherokee women continued to exercise considerable political power, even as the question of the group's continued residence in Georgia came to the fore. Cherokee matrons had always been able to speak in council and to help decide the fate of captives. They could grant pardons to prisoners condemned to die, as well as serve as negotiators. Because women were used to having a voice in political matters, they seldom hesitated to tell male councils their opinions, as well as to explain why the men should pay attention to them. As one Cherokee woman put it to the all-male council: "I am in hopes that if you Rightly consider that woman is the mother of All—and the Woman does not pull Children out of Trees or Stumps nor out of old Logs, but out of their Bodies, so that they ought to mind what a woman says." Cherokee women political leaders—Beloved Women—continued to include speakers representing the voice of the Women's Council and voting in the Cherokee governing council. Cherokee Beloved Woman Nancy Ward fought against giving up traditional lands to whites, but her advice not to cede any lands went unheeded, and after her death in the early 1820s, pressure to remove the Cherokee to lands west of the Mississippi intensified. The political leadership of both women and men could not protect the Cherokee from a cruel fate, especially after the discovery of gold on Cherokee lands in 1829 (see Chapter 5).

Farther west, entrepreneurs moved into the Louisiana Territory to trade and settle. From 1804 to 1806, Meriwether Lewis and William Clark followed the Missouri River in an attempt to find a river passage to the Pacific. On their long and difficult journey through the northwestern territory of the United States into present-day Oregon, they received crucial help from a Shoshone woman, Sacajawea. Her life exemplifies many of the characteristics of Indian–white interaction of the period. Probably born in eastern Idaho, Sacajawea, like many Indian women before her, married a French Canadian fur trader. Her husband, Toussaint Charbonneau, was a *voyageur,* traveling the group's hunting grounds to obtain furs. When Lewis and Clark arrived with the Corps of Discovery, commissioned by President Jefferson to explore the territory, they hired Charbonneau as guide. He agreed to take the job only if Sacajawea, then pregnant, came along, believing the presence of a woman and her baby would convince any Native Americans that the Corps encountered that their intentions were peaceful. Soon, however, Sacajawea's skills as diplomat and translator and her knowledge of the inhabitants and geography of the lands that the Corps traversed became evident. William Clark's journal indicates that her aid proved critical to the survival of the Corps, again and again. She provided food from plants native to the region, saved the Corps' records when a canoe overturned, negotiated with Indians they encountered, and prevented bloodshed through the use of her diplomatic skills. She also guided the Corps to the Pacific Ocean through mountain passes that shortened their journey to the sea by days, if not weeks.

The land they reached, the Northwest, was prime territory for exploration and expansion. The rich valleys of Oregon, the fur-bearing animals of the hinterlands, the millions of acres of timber, all served as magnets to attract settlers and entrepreneurs to the region. In 1808, John Jacob Astor founded the American Fur Company, which held a monopoly on furs from the region. Astor's phenomenal success made him the richest man in America. His wife, Sarah Todd Breevort Astor, was also his business partner. She advised her husband on the quality of furs, evaluating the pelts as they arrived from the west, and John paid her for her evaluations, declaring her fees "well worth it." Sarah donated the money to charity.

As had been the case in the Great Lakes region in the eighteenth century, in the Northwest traders continued to depend on Native American women for their success as they continued to develop the market economy

SACAJAWEA COIN In 2000, the U.S. government honored Sacajawea's role in Lewis and Clark's successful expedition by issuing a dollar coin. The coin depicts Sacajawea carrying her child on her back in traditional fashion.

in the region. In the Puget Sound area (present-day Washington State) and throughout the central coast of Oregon country, Indian women exercised their traditional political authority within the trade-based economy. Among the Coast Salish tribes, where the fur trade had a firm foothold by the 1810s, women acted as political leaders, shamans, and traders. They also served as intermediaries in conducting diplomacy with Anglo traders; by the 1830s, many had intermarried with whites, establishing new trade ties and alliances. Indian women throughout the region served as mediators between traders and Indian men, preparing pelts to travel to market, supplying food, and fashioning the canoes, snowshoes, packs, and clothes the traders used. Many *voyageurs* continued to marry Indian women or, more commonly, *metís* women, the daughters of earlier explorers and trappers. Like Sacajawea's marriage, many of those relationships (some 70 percent by one count) were long-lived, but some lasted only for the length of a fur season, after which a trapper would abandon his Indian wife.

As Native American women married into the white communities, whites expected them to assume European-style clothing, dress, and often behavior, including occupying the separate sphere white women were supposed to inhabit. One Spokane woman was no sooner married to a clerk from the Pacific Fur Company in 1814 than she was handed over to the local dressmaker who outfitted her by getting rid of her "leathern chemise" and supplying more "appropriate" European clothing. Some Native women resisted such assimilation by keeping their own clothing, faith, or notions regarding acceptable behavior. Qanqon-kamek-klaula, a Kootenai woman from the Columbia River region, married a white trader who sent her back to her people when he found her sexual behavior too liberated for his standards. Perhaps as a way to save face with her kin, she announced to them that her ex-husband had transformed her into a man and left her with magical powers. She lived life as a man—a berdache—thereafter, dressing as a man, healing others, and courting women. Most Indian women, however, unlike Qanqon, retained their sexual identity, even while they subsumed their Native one to remain in white society.

Increasing Anglo–Native interaction continued in similar fashion in the Southwest, beginning with Zebulon Pike's exploration in 1806 to 1807, as Anglos expanded into the region for trade and then settlement. Lt. Pike, sent to spy on Spanish activities along the new American border at the southwestern edge of the Louisiana Territory, traversed the Great Plains and eventually wound up in modern-day Colorado. He made notes of the various Native Americans he encountered and eventually published a record of his travels in the region describing both the landscape and the trade possibilities with Indians and Mexicans, especially along the Santa Fe trail. The Navajo were particularly active in trade throughout the area. The market for Navajo women weavers' blankets and their rugs, the first native tapestries in the United States, were so prized and so expensive that only the most important Native Americans of other groups were likely to own them. Trade in Navajo women's woven goods expanded beyond other Indian groups in the Great Plains and the Great Basin to wealthy white Americans. White travelers to the deserts the Navajo called home purchased the weavings, or made paintings, drawings, and, later, photographs of Utes, Blackfeet, and members of other groups proudly displaying their beautiful Navajo cloth. Navajo women's woven goods thus became a commodity that brought the Navajo into the U.S. market economy during the first half of the nineteenth century.

In the Great Plains, white interaction with Native Americans took a deadly toll. Traders and merchants followed the trail blazed by Lewis and Clark from 1804 to 1806. The battles of the 1700s over guns, horses, and control over trade became battles to survive against the smallpox and cholera epidemics that followed the Americans along trade routes and struck Native villages in the 1800s. Widespread epidemics hit the region in 1816 and 1819, but the worst struck in June 1837. The effect was devastating. Mandan Indians, for example, lived in the region of present-day North Dakota, where French fur traders estimated their population to be about 15,000 in 1738. By June 1837, after an American steamboat with smallpox aboard landed, their population had fallen to 2,000. By October of the same year, the resulting smallpox epidemic had left only 138. Between 1837 and 1840 the Great Plains were depopulated by such epidemics, killing thousands upon thousands, and displacing the hundreds left behind. Smallpox killed the caretakers and healers as fast as the sick. Women followed their husbands and children to the grave.

Changes in Native American societies, including the roles of women, came about because of the expansion of the market economy, land dispossession, westward exploration and expansion, intermarriage with whites, and depopulation, particularly in the Great Plains. The disadvantages wrought by these changes to the women and men who lived in the regions were often hidden by white Americans' preference to declare and promote the advantages.

THE PLIGHT OF ENSLAVED SOUTHERN BLACK WOMEN

The 1830 U.S. Census listed 2,003,800 slaves and 326,200 free blacks in the United States. The Constitution embedded slavery in the nation with its Three-Fifths Compromise, which allowed states to count three-fifths of their slaves when determining their population for representation in the House of Representatives. Despite the Constitution's 1808 ban on the importation of slaves from Africa, the potent combination of Eli Whitney's cotton gin and the rise of industrialized textile production had guaranteed not only the survival but also the growth of slavery. Slaveowners believed that slave labor was essential to produce cotton, and cotton became America's major export, both to the outside world and also to the northern states. Slave imports rose in the first part of the nineteenth century and many slave women feared sexual exploitation, along with unremitting labor, as part of their daily lives. The momentary hope after the Revolution that the words "all men are created equal" would lead to the end of slavery—even after the widespread disruption of Southern planters' control over their slaves during the war, even after the Northern states abolished slavery, even as slaves continued to resist and rebel against the dreadful institution—that hope faded in the light of industrial production's demands for cheap labor to produce raw materials.

The vast majority of African Americans were slaves living in the American South. Much of slave women's lives revolved around the agricultural world, particularly the production of cotton, tobacco, rice, and sugar. Short staple cotton, grown in Southern lands away from the coast, quickly became the most lucrative crop. So profitable was cotton that soon cotton farms became plantations with dozens, sometimes hundreds of slaves to work the labor-intensive crop. As the United States added land, first with the Peace of Paris in 1783 and then with the purchase of the Louisiana Territory in 1803, cotton plantations pushed ever westward. New states formed in the South— Kentucky (1792) and Tennessee (1796) saw the first influx of slaves accompanying their owners eager to take advantage of lands west of the Appalachians after the Revolution. In the Lower South, Louisiana (1812), Mississippi (1817), and Alabama (1819) all used plantation agriculture that employed slaves, many of them women, in fields of cotton and sugar.

In both the Lower and Upper South tobacco farming declined in the nineteenth century, although tobacco growing continued and tobacco factories hired black women to process the leaf. In the states of the Upper South, including the Chesapeake, farmers shifted to mixed farming: corn, wheat, dairy, and produce. Such staples required more skilled workers. Owners made male field hands into herdsmen, stockmen, and plowmen and transferred them from the fields. Women made up the difference as field hands, continuing the work men had done before, as well as adding new tasks needed for mixed agriculture: collecting manure to fertilize the crops, grubbing stumps out of the fields, breaking ground if plows could not. Overall, the new mixed-crop agriculture took fewer slaves to accomplish, so owners hired out or sold excess slaves to the Lower South. There, imports of slaves rose to replace those who had died, escaped, or been stolen by British troops during the Revolution. By 1800, the disruption to slave-owners, slave society, and slave-produced crops had eased. Georgia had restored its population of slaves, which had dropped from 15,000 to 5,000 between 1775 and 1783. South Carolina had replaced the 25 percent of its slave population it had lost during the War for Independence and brought rice production back by the 1790s. The state then added cotton as a major crop, producing only 10,000 pounds in 1790 but 6 million pounds by 1800—a 600 percent increase. Such labor-intensive agriculture demanded more slaves, and in 1803, the state reopened the Atlantic slave trade it had banned in 1787, importing 90,000 new slaves by 1808, when the federal government closed down the trade. After that, slaves were imported into the region from the Upper South.

Slaves continued to work by the task system of labor with the restoration of rice production, in part because it demanded more skilled tasks, performed mostly by men. Cotton production, on the other hand, required

HARRIET JACOBS, *INCIDENTS IN THE LIFE OF A SLAVE GIRL*

Harriet Jacobs published her memoir in 1861. Lydia Maria Child, a noted author and abolitionist, edited Jacobs' work and became a friend and supporter. The narrative seeks to attract white middle-class Americans to the abolitionist movement, but many readers were shocked and offended by scenes of sexual harassment. In this passage, Jacobs recounts falling in love with a young man in the neighborhood, as well as the reactions of her owner and his wife. "Dr. Flint" refers to James Norcom, Jacobs' owner.

"Why does the slave ever love? Why allow the tendrils of the heart to twine around objects which may at any moment be wrenched away by the hand of violence? When separations come by the hand of death, the pious soul can bow in resignation, and say, "Not my will, but thine be done, O Lord!" But when the ruthless hand of man strikes the blow, regardless of the misery he causes, it is hard to be submissive. I did not reason thus when I was a young girl. Youth will be youth. I loved, and I indulged the hope that the dark clouds around me would turn out a bright lining. I forgot that in the land of my birth the shadows are too dense for light to penetrate....

"There was in the neighborhood a young colored carpenter; a free born man. We had been well acquainted in childhood, and frequently met together

less skill and used the more regimented gang labor. What skilled jobs the crop required were filled by men, so disproportionately more women were in the fields planting, hoeing, and picking the crop. Gang labor, closely supervised by male overseers and drivers—both black and white—provided fewer opportunities for slave women to continue to produce items for their own sustenance, such as garden crops and homemade cloth. Consequently, fewer women from cotton plantations were able to participate in the urban markets in which slave women had sold goods since before the Revolution, and that enabled slaves under less regimented conditions to take advantage of the social life the slave and free black communities had surrounding those market communities.

Increased numbers of slaves came not only from Africa, but also from Northern states who were abolishing slavery and from Upper South slaveowners selling slaves—a practice that became more lucrative than growing tobacco. Owners also relied on the *natural increase* of slave women giving birth. Some owners ensured continued increase in the number of slaves by keeping slave families together and promoting slave "marriages" (that were unrecognized by state laws); some bred slaves from their own or other plantations; some impregnated their slaves themselves resulting in children with white plantation owner fathers and slave mothers. Economically valued for their work ability and their fertility, slave women were constantly subject to sexual attacks. One of the most telling portraits of the cost of this exploitation to the souls of black women comes from Harriet Jacobs' *Incidents in the Life of a Slave Girl*, a memoir written by a North afterwards. We became mutually attached, and he proposed to marry me. I loved him with all the ardor of a young girl's first love. But when I reflected that I was, a slave, and that the laws gave no sanction to the marriage of such, my heart sank within me. My lover wanted to buy me; but I knew that Dr. Flint was too wilful and arbitrary a man to consent to that arrangement. From him, I was sure of experiencing all sorts of opposition, and I had nothing to hope from my mistress. She would have been delighted to have got rid of me, but not in that way. It would have relieved her mind of a burden if she could have seen me sold to some distant state, but if I was married near home I should be just as much in her husband's power as I had previously been, —for the husband of a slave has no power to protect her. Moreover, my mistress, like many others, seemed to think that slaves had no right to any family ties of their own; that they were created merely to wait upon the family of the mistress. I once heard her abuse a young slave girl, who told her that a colored man wanted to make her his wife. "I will have you peeled and pickled, my lady," said she, "if I ever hear you mention that subject again. Do you suppose that I will have you tending *my* children with the children of that nigger?" The girl to whom she said this had a mulatto child, of course not acknowledged by its father. The poor black man who loved her would have been proud to acknowledge his helpless offspring."

Source: Harriet Jacobs, *Incidents in the Life of a Slave Girl, Written by Herself* ed. L. Maria Child (Boston: [published for the author]) 1861), 58–59.

Carolina slave who was sexually abused by her owner before her escape in 1835. (See Primary Source 4-2.) She hid in a crawlspace above a porch attached to her grandmother's quarters for the next seven years, coming out only at night to exercise. She nearly went mad in the space: no light, no ventilation, rats and mice crawling over her bedding, so hot in the sweltering Carolina summers that mosquitoes, she wrote, would not deign to occupy the space. Finally, in 1842, she escaped to Philadelphia where members of the Underground Railroad aided her to move farther north.

Amy Kirby Post, an abolitionist and woman's rights advocate from Rochester, New York, met Jacobs and encouraged her to tell her story. Jacobs' book, edited by another leading white abolitionist, Lydia Maria Child, became a best-seller despite its sexually explicit content. Jacobs insisted on keeping what were, for the era, graphic details in the text, pointing out that "This peculiar phase of slavery has generally been kept veiled; but the public ought to be made acquainted with its monstrous features. . . . I do this for the sake of my sisters in bondage." With sexual assault a constant possibility, in a society that did not protect women from assault because of their race, black women found themselves mired in the racist assumptions of white society about their nature and being: that they were sexually available, lewd, licentious, and promiscuous; that they deserved no better, a stereotype historian Deborah Gray White labeled the "Jezebel." That the law regarded them as property eased any discomfort their abusers might have felt. Slave women, one ex-slave explained, were seen as "nothing but cattle."

This emphasis on slave women as "breeders" not only oppressed and exploited them, but they also had to face the pain of seeing their children raised as slaves and the knowledge that their children might be sold away to another owner. The birthrate remained higher among blacks than whites at midcentury, with the average African American woman having eight children, at a time when the birthrate among white women had dropped substantially from the average of seven children in 1800 to about five by midcentury. In addition, infant mortality and maternal mortality rates among slaves were quite high compared to the rates of whites. Slave women who had given birth were not given enough recovery time, enough food, enough nursing time. If slave women needed to nurse their babies, they had to take their children to fields, put them at the end of the row and then work their way down and back, and hope their children did not get bitten by a varmint or carried off by an alligator in the interim. Many African American babies died because their mothers were forced to neglect them to care for their white owners' children and crops.

The majority of enslaved women, about 95 percent, worked in the fields alongside slave men. They shared in the backbreaking work of chopping cotton, to thin out the plants and destroy the weeds. Rows were then hoed and plowed; cotton was harvested eventually by hand and placed in sacks, then dumped into bales that weighed 1,000 pounds each. In the hot Southern sun, the work was brutally hard, and women slaves were not excused from the labor because of their gender. All of the major Southern commodities produced for profit—tobacco, sugar, rice, indigo, lumber, iron, gold—relied on southern black slave women laboring beside slave men.

Working in factories, in the few areas that had industrial production, or doing domestic work were two of the ways out of the fields. Slaveowners hired out slaves to some factories, mostly sugar refineries and tobacco processing plants. Some slave women were employed in the mining industries at various tasks, particularly domestic ones. Domestic service in private homes was more common. Large plantations required house "servants," as slaves were usually called by their owners. Cooking, nursing, cleaning, sewing, caring for children, and other domestic chores continued to be the province of slave women, as was the production of household goods, such as soap, candles, bed linens, and foodstuffs. Unlike male slaves, few female slaves were trained in skilled work beyond sewing, but some were hired out for those skills. Some owners allowed slaves to keep some or all of the small wages that they earned in hopes of purchasing freedom for themselves or others. Others made promises and kept the wages, or raised the purchase prices of slaves as slaves earned more income so that freedom never came.

As was true for other women who worked for wages, slave women faced a "second shift" of responsibilities when they returned to their quarters after field work. Families must be fed and tended to, and while some women were so beaten down by the work they did that they could barely care for themselves, most slave women cared for their families, tended a small garden plot to supplement whatever food was provided by the owners, and constructed garments and quilts to protect against chilly winter

SLAVE WOMAN WITH OWNER'S CHILD   Slave women often had to neglect their own children to care for their owners' children. The death rate for slave children was much higher than for white children.

nights. Slave quilts that have survived are beautifully pieced and embroidered with family stories and names, with biblical allusions to freedom and with images of the North Star that led runaway slaves toward the Northern states and freedom. At the same time that women produced these objects that kept their children warm, they also expressed themselves politically and creatively.

As agricultural production grew on a massive scale in the South, slaves became more valuable and greater in number, and the internal slave trade increased. Some slaveowners, particularly those in the Upper South with excess slaves to care for, changed their strategies. Instead of promoting slave families for stability, they broke more families apart for sale, with slaves being sold "down river" to the huge plantations of the Lower South that had developed along the Mississippi River. From 1820 onward, about 34 percent of all slave families were broken by sale. At the same time, slave ownership was coming under increasing attack from the outside, from northern states that objected to slavery on economic grounds and disliked competing with unpaid labor, and from abolitionists and others who objected to slavery on moral grounds. White Southerners became increasingly defensive about their "peculiar institution," as they now called slavery, and feared resistance and rebellion. They cracked down on slaves' autonomy, not allowing them to meet even for religious services, not allowing them to be taught to read lest they communicate too easily with others to plot a rebellion against their owners.

Resistance to slavery, however, continued as it had in the eighteenth century, and was a constant in the lives of slaveowners and slaves. Many slaves practiced passive resistance at every opportunity. They worked as little as possible for as long as possible. They pretended that they found simple instructions hard to understand, stalled, or became distracted. Some enslaved women resisted by using menstruation, pregnancy, childbirth troubles, or other physical complaints to avoid work. Passive forms of resistance exasperated slaveowners and led them to the false conclusion that slaves were lazy or stupid, rather than cleverly keeping their labor for themselves.

Active resistance proved far more dangerous. Some slaves sabotaged their owners by breaking tools or stealing food. They poisoned their owners, a choice particularly popular with women who were cooks for the white families they served, and some even "stole themselves" by escaping. Active resistance was risky and the success rate was low. Slaveowners believed that disobedience required physical punishment. Indeed, the laws of the South, made largely by elite white men who owned slaves themselves, required slaveowners to punish slaves who resisted openly, lest the slave society be threatened by others of the same mind. Owners or their overseers whipped, flogged, beat, raped, branded, and imprisoned slaves or sold them or their relatives away. Women slaves were not immune to such physical punishment, and women slaveowners did not let the victim's gender stop the punishment. Harriet Jacobs reported that her owner, while bereft of energy most of the time, had enough to sit in a chair and watch a slave woman be whipped "till the blood trickled from every stroke of the lash."

The plight of enslaved Southern black women worsened in the first part of the nineteenth century as slavery grew more entrenched in the United States. Changes in agriculture put more women in the fields and brought more enslaved women from Africa. While work patterns among rice planters continued to provide slave women with time to care for their own gardens and products that they could market, the gang labor demanded of cotton production greatly limited their freedom to participate in the slave market economy. Greater demands for labor also led to sexual abuse that increased natural reproduction rates. Despite attempts to resist, slave women's daily lives, filled with backbreaking labor, faced such control by owners and the law that few had any opportunities to rebel.

THE REFORMING IMPULSE

Politics, industrialization, expansion, and slavery all created problems in American society that many sought to ameliorate. While politics was one avenue to relief, the reforming impulse acted upon by Americans in the first half of the nineteenth century owed a great deal to religion. One of the great religious revivals in American history, the Second Great Awakening, linked the religious actions of the individual to the larger secular world. The Second Great Awakening's theology emphasized individual responsibility and human perfectibility. Accordingly, individual Americans thought that they had the opportunity to make America a better place by reforming the individuals that made up society. For women interested in making the world a better place, while denied the vote and the opportunity to serve in political office, the religious links provided by the Second Great Awakening meant that women could start from within their designated separate sphere of heart and home, family and morality, to go forth into the world in reform movements. These movements helped people cope with the chaos generated by political dissension, economic dislocation, and the greatest scourge of the nation, slavery.

The Second Great Awakening

The Second Great Awakening was a period of evangelical Christian religious revival that swept the country beginning about 1800. This Second Great Awakening, like the first that had preceded it in the 1730s through the 1770s, was based on a personal appeal to the emotions. Its converts experienced a moment of conversion, rather than merely an intellectual acceptance of the presence of God. The Second Great Awakening also reestablished the orthodoxy of free will. Free will argued that humans have the power to choose—or not—their salvation from eternal damnation. In this view, sin was the equivalent of selfishness, and virtue was disinterested benevolence: doing good with no thought of personal reward or glory. Humans were regarded as perfectible through religious means and personal action. Moreover, because social evils stemmed from the personal evil of the individual, if one could cure the person of personal evil, one could cure society of its ills.

As was true of the first Great Awakening, the emphasis was on the hearts and emotions of converts, rather than intellectual rationalism. This evangelical religious revival appealed to women in particular because it emphasized the confession of sins and the redemption that follows that act. Brought up as daughters of Eve, most women viewed themselves as sinful creatures. The conversion from sin to proper behavior through the public confession of sins was personal and emotional, both qualities thought to be part of the woman's sphere. Many women thus preferred the emotionality of the religious sects that took part in the Second Great Awakening's religious revival, particularly the Baptists and Methodists. Sermons became theatrical events, where preachers and parishioners alike, in the throes of emotion, shouted, wept, and sometimes threw themselves to the ground. Such emotional display attracted many and repelled others. Many who attended were appalled not only at the raw emotion exhibited, but particularly by the women who took part in the services, who exhorted fellow congregants to repent, shouting, crying, at times fainting away due to excess emotions. Historian Cynthia Lyerly tells of Dr. Thomas Hinde of Hanover County, Virginia, who was so outraged when the women of his family embraced Methodism, for example, that he sent his daughter Susanna forty miles off to live with her aunt, telling her to give up the religion or she would never come home again. The aunt proved a poor choice, since she had secretly become a Methodist and actually held services in her home. Hinde's wife Mary also began attending services, and Hinde attempted to treat her for her religious derangement by applying "a blister to her neck to bring her to her senses." The treatment, otherwise unexplained, failed. Mary Hinde continued to go to church; eventually Thomas Hinde also converted to Methodism.

Dr. Hinde perceived Mary and Susanna's involvement in Methodism as a direct threat to his authority over his family. He was correct. Methodism and other evangelical sects such as Separate Baptists, New Light Presbyterians, and Congregationalists allowed women to speak aloud about their experiences and to encourage others to do the same. Women participants caught up in religious fervor might shout, cry, or even become unconscious. An individual's direct communication with God, part of the evangelical belief, not only made women "uncommonly happy," as a participant described one North Carolina woman, but also gave women a degree of power male leaders found disconcerting.

Churches that had fully embraced the notion offered by St. Paul that "women should keep silent in the churches" had no use for religious revivals that not only permitted but encouraged public participation by women and even by African Americans. Men who were part of this reform effort, such as the famous preacher Charles Grandison Finney, encouraged men to look to women in their personal lives for guidance in moral issues. That guidance, however, given beliefs regarding women, meant women should use gentle persuasion to teach their men, not preach in churches or take political action. Those methods, after all, involved women participating in the public sphere, and most people accepted the popular culture's notion that women were not suited for the public sphere. Public speaking and public action were not roles many men desired for the women in their lives to assume, and some women were actually committed to insane asylums because of their embrace of religious enthusiasm.

Ironically, despite the belief many held that women's God-given role was within the domestic sphere, few regarded women as invading men's sphere by providing help for the poor and destitute. There were so few social services provided, and so great was the need for them, that women simply had to work within that male sphere of the public, political world to care for others. The primacy of women's roles as caretakers thus trumped the separate sphere they were to occupy. Such was the rationale for women justifying their work in the reform movements that began in the early part of the nineteenth century.

Fields of Reform

The need for reform could not be gainsaid. The nineteenth century spawned a host of problems that often seemed to have few solutions. Many women, prompted by the religious enthusiasm of the Second Great Awakening, formed voluntary associations to practice *voluntary benevolence*, where women volunteered to do good with no thought of reward. Others participated in male-led organizations as women's auxiliaries formed to support men in their drive to reform the country.

One of the ways women got involved in reform was through Bible and tract societies designed to help spread the Christian Gospel, the teachings of Jesus Christ. Women were particularly interested in establishing Sunday schools to provide spiritual training for the young. By the 1820s, hundreds of Sunday schools existed throughout New England with some 50,000 children enrolled. For many children, this was their only means to an education, since Sunday schools also taught them how to read and write. Required public schooling was not the norm in the 1820s, nor was it available in most states, especially in the southern part of the United States. If children were going to learn how to read and write, Sunday schools might be their sole opportunity. All to the good, the reformers thought, since children were then learning a skill and a religion at the same time.

In addition to setting up Sunday schools, women also raised money for various causes by sewing and knitting goods, and then holding a craft show or fair to sell them to the public. The proceeds were used for various causes: to educate ministers, to fund missionaries, to assist the local poor, or to support churches. Some groups combined their endeavors, leaving Bible tracts when visiting the poor to give them food. What these women saw on their visits opened some middle-class eyes to the problems that the poor faced with so little social support from their communities. Women developed new institutions to deal with the social problems they encountered. Orphan asylums, for example, provided housing for hundreds of orphans, especially young girls, to protect them from economic need. By ensuring that these young children had food and a place to live, reformers hoped to keep them from poverty and the sexual exploitation that often went with it, as young girls might sell their bodies to avoid starvation. Other orphan asylums, such as the Cincinnati Orphan Asylum founded in 1832, focused on caring for poor, white children given to the asylum or temporarily taken from parents who could not provide for them after losing their jobs or because they were ill, as well as children bereft of parents who died. A cholera epidemic in the city in 1849 filled the asylum, and the benevolent women who ran the orphanage eventually placed many such children as servants or as adoptees.

Women formed numerous associations to help the poor and indigent. In Cincinnati, additional orphanages directed their efforts at specific ethnic groups: St. Joseph's served Irish Catholics; St. Aloysius Orphan Asylum, the German Catholics; the New Orphan Asylum for Colored Youth cared for African Americans; the Children's Home for white Protestants, and the German Protestant Orphan Asylum, for children of that ethnic and religious background. In New York City, the Society for the Relief of Poor Widows with Small Children began in 1797 with fifteen women led by Isabella Graham. By 1816 the Society supported over 200 widows with some 500 children among them. A board of managers ran the Society, each watching over a district to ensure that the widows they helped behaved in a morally upright fashion, as defined by their middle- and upper-class patrons. That meant they were not to beg, to sell liquor, or to have sexual relationships outside of marriage. In addition, they were not to own property or have a living husband.

Over time, the Society became interested in going beyond relief to real reform to teach women marketable skills so that they could support themselves without the Society's help. Teaching women to spin was one way that the Society's goals expanded. The Society set up and ran a tailoring and spinning shop to teach widows a craft that they were bound to succeed in, given the demand for clothes. They also began fund-raising so that they could educate not only children, but also adults in Sunday schools. Graham's daughter, Joanna Graham Bethune, followed in her reforming mother's footsteps. She founded the Orphan Asylum Society, the Female Sabbath School Union, the Infant School Society, and the Society for the Promotion of Industry, which employed 500 women.

As did most of the women's benevolent associations in the nation, these organizations started as small and personal enterprises, but as the number of people they aided grew larger, the organizations evolved into bureaucratic structures. Members drew up constitutions, elected officers, and held formal meetings. They wrote minutes, filed reports, and printed tracts describing their work. They solicited funds, managed and invested them, and distributed them. Lydia Maria Child, an author of historical romances and household advice books, praised such women and recognized the power of

THE NEED FOR TEMPERANCE Popular mid-nineteenth-century illustrators Currier & Ives portrayed a husband sleeping off his overindulgence while his wife and children listened to the local minister read the Bible in this print supporting the temperance movement. Prayer and suffering until men came to their senses were sometimes the only options for women as dependents under coverture.

such activity to transform not only the needy, but also the lives of the women participants: "They have changed the household utensil into a living energetic being," she wrote.

Reform efforts tried to save people spiritually as well as care for their material needs. They also tried to change human, particularly male, behavior. One such arena for reform was the *temperance movement*. Temperance, which called for limiting or abolishing alcohol consumption, began by establishing temperance societies in New York in 1808 and in Massachusetts in 1813. By 1836, there were 6,000 temperance societies in America, most calling for their members to quit consuming alcohol completely. The drinking rate in early-nineteenth-century America was extremely high compared to modern times. The average consumption of absolute alcohol, which is the amount of actual alcohol in a drink (still about 6 percent for most beers and 10 percent for most wines) was close to seven gallons per year per person, as compared to about two gallons in America today. A dram at breakfast and liquor at lunch seemed to be the norm, and overconsumption of drink led to incompetence and accidents in shops and industries, along with high rates of poverty, crime, violence, and civil disorder.

Women were particularly vulnerable to the effects of alcohol abuse because of the laws of coverture. Under coverture, a husband so inclined could not only drink through his own wages, but also those of his wife, and she had no recourse and few resources if she decided to leave the marriage. Another problem women faced was that child custody laws awarded children to husbands in cases of divorce, assuming even a drunken patriarch was a better parent. Many women suffered spousal abuse rather than leave their children. Temperance societies responded to such issues by calling first for drinkers to moderate their consumption. When that did not succeed, reformers pushed for total abstinence and, by 1834, women members and auxiliaries joined male temperance societies to sign up individuals as *teetotalers* who promised never to drink again.

Another reform movement that sought to improve the country by changing human behavior was *moral reform* or the antiprostitution movement. Prostitution was a major problem in all urban areas of America. Moral reformers attacked the problem in different ways, determined to end the double standard of sexuality that flourished in the nineteenth century, as it had for years. This standard presumed that men were allowed to behave with a sexual freedom that was nearly license, while women were expected to be pure—virgins until marriage and faithful thereafter. Moral reformers believed that all Americans should strive to be chaste. They began with childhood education, proclaiming that children should receive a pious and moral upbringing and education. They also sought to end prostitution by calling for laws against seduction (enticing young women to unlawful sexual intercourse without the use of force), adultery (sexual intercourse where one party was married—usually the man), and lechery (the inordinate indulgence by an individual in sexual activity). None of this was behavior easy to legislate against. So, moral reformers also sought to reform prostitutes, whom they called "fallen" or "disorderly" women, by providing them with emotional support, employment opportunities, and moral education. Reformers wanted to prevent women from falling into prostitution in the first place. Prostitution was not new, but industrialization had exacerbated the problem, and once a child was born to an unmarried young woman, prostitution was a profession where unwed mothers could keep their children with them. Some brothel madams actually promoted themselves as employers by pointing out their "daycare" arrangements to prospective employees.

Moral reformers, as historian Nancy Woloch put it, wished to "obliterate licentiousness from the minds of men and drive vice from the face of the earth." Their most powerful drive began with the New York Female Moral Reform Society (NYFMRS), founded in New York City in 1834. Lydia Root Finney founded the group. As the wife of Charles Grandison Finney, who remained a key minister in the Second Great Awakening, she exemplified the strong link between the religious revival sweeping America and the reform efforts of women. By 1837, the NYFMRS had 250 auxiliaries in numerous cities, with over 15,000 members. It held annual conventions, published its own newspaper as well as its own journal, the *Advocate of Moral Reform*, which had 20,000 subscribers only a few years after its 1835 beginnings. Eventually, the NYFMRS would become the American Female Reform Society with over 500 auxiliaries nationwide.

Along the way to becoming a national organization, the group changed its focus from saving young men from prostitutes to saving the prostitutes from men. It discovered that both industrialization and immigration, which increased greatly in the second quarter of the century (see Chapter 5), led to the development of a large migrant population, particularly of young girls who lived in cities beyond the influence of mothers, ministers, and their community's traditional values. These young women were vulnerable not only to men generally, but also to prostitution specifically. Reformers proved determined to rescue these women, even though some of their group efforts wound up costing them supporters when they created public spectacles of themselves. For instance, women sometimes visited brothels and searched for runaways. They stood outside the doors, singing hymns and praying publicly. They also made note of who entered the brothels and threatened to publish the names of their customers. Such acts offended many who believed women ought not to even know about brothels, much less stand in front of them. The reformers were not dissuaded, however. They continued their public political actions by petitioning and lobbying for laws to make seduction a crime, gathering thousands of signatures on petitions sent to legislatures. As a result, antiseduction laws were passed in Massachusetts in 1846 and in New York in 1848.

Moral reformers also founded and funded homes as refuges for former prostitutes. Named after Mary Magdalene, the prostitute Jesus befriended in the Bible, Magdalene Societies included employment services to provide jobs for women who gave up prostitution. The groups were initially successful, but began to fall apart because of public discomfort with the mixed-sex audiences who attended their meetings, as well as the overall topic of moral reform. Men and women in the audience listened together to anti-prostitution speakers. Opponents to this mixed-sex practice referred to the groups as "promiscuous audiences." Such activity seemed morally suspect, given the graphic nature of the very public discussions of sexuality and exploitation. Many Americans began to view moral reform as too far outside the woman's sphere for public action on what was ordinarily such a private part of life, and the opposition eventually drove many of the reformers on to other areas of interest.

Some reformers turned to work for education, such as Prudence Crandall, who allowed a young black woman, Sarah Harris, to enroll in her school in Canterbury, Connecticut, in 1832. When townspeople protested, she turned her academy into a school advertised as being for "young ladies and little misses of color." She was arrested for her pains. Other reformers focused primarily on white women's education. Higher education proponents included Emma Willard, who founded the first female seminary in Troy, New York, in 1821 and Mary Lyon, who did the same in Mount Holyoke, Massachusetts, in 1837. Southerners founded the world's first real women's college, Georgia Female College (known today as Wesleyan College), in 1836. The first coeducational institution, Oberlin College in Ohio, opened its doors to both women and men, black and white, in 1833.

Other reform movements abounded, all desirous of improving Americans' lives. In the 1830s, Sylvester Graham called for dietary reform by asking men and women to limit their sexual appetites and to eat a vegetarian diet to improve their health, along with his "Graham" crackers. The former directive may well have been particularly popular with women trying to control the number of pregnancies they had. Another physical reform effort promoted healthful outdoor exercise and sporting activities to strengthen the bodies of women, particularly rural women, worn down by hard work. Historian Linda Borish found that magazines and journals seeking to improve women's health all suggested physical exercise: walking, "berrying," collecting flowers, horseback riding, skating, and other activities. Publications often promoted various reform issues: Sabbatarianism called for closing down businesses on Sunday; antidueling groups sought a ban on dueling, still common in Southern states; women's groups dedicated themselves to taking better care of the handicapped, the insane, and the mentally ill; religious auxiliaries sent Christian missionaries to foreign lands to spread Christianity. Others supported ending tobacco use or building libraries. Public lecturers such as Lucretia Coffin Mott, a Quaker preacher from Philadelphia, argued for a shorter workday and better working conditions, preventing war, and, particularly, abolishing the institution of slavery.

Free Black Women and Reform

One of the most radical reform movements was the one to end slavery, the *abolition movement*. All black Americans, slave and free, faced harsh discrimination. Each time there was a rebellion by slaves in a Southern community, or even a rumor of a rebellion, attacks against free blacks increased nationwide and new restrictions were placed upon the free black and slave communities. After Prosser's Gabriel led a slave rebellion in Virginia in 1800, state legislators passed laws that made freed blacks leave the state within a year, leaving their still-enslaved families behind. In July 1822, following rumors of an alleged plot by free black carpenter Denmark Vesey to lead a rebellion in Charleston, South Carolina, the state legislature passed a law forbidding owners from freeing their slaves without legislative approval. After Nat Turner led a small army of rebellious slaves, including one woman, across the Virginia countryside in an 1831 rampage that left fifty whites and many of Turner's followers dead, it became illegal to teach slaves to read or to write (the two skills were taught separately). The latter restriction did not stop the practice: Mary Peake, a black woman in Hampton, Virginia, continued to teach despite the law; Emily Howe, a white northern teacher at a plantation in Prince Edward County, Virginia, did the same, writing to her mother that "We have several men who can read & one named Aaron a blacksmith who can not only read but write also, & who reads & prays regularly in his family."

Not all African Americans in the country were slaves, but all suffered because of slavery. While some free blacks lived in the South, most lived north of the Mason-Dixon Line that first divided Pennsylvania from Maryland and eventually the free states from most of those allowing slavery. Slavery was technically forbidden in the Old Northwest Territory, from which the states of Ohio (1803), Indiana (1816), Illinois (1818), and Michigan (1837) were formed. Further south and still below the Mason-Dixon Line, Missouri applied for statehood in 1818. As a result, contentious debate arose regarding the expansion of slavery into the new lands west of the Mississippi. When it was over, Congress had agreed to the Missouri Compromise, which drew a line along the southern border of the state. In the Louisiana Territory, north of that line, slavery was disallowed, except for the state of Missouri. Such a line, wrote Thomas Jefferson in 1820, nearing the end of his life, was asking for trouble: "A geographical line, coinciding with a marked principle, moral and political, once conceived and held up to the angry passions of men, will never be obliterated; and every new irritation will mark it deeper and deeper." Slavery would become the issue that nearly tore apart the country, as people sought to extend slavery or prevent the institution from expanding.

Wherever they lived, all free blacks faced widespread discrimination and sometimes vicious racism. Even in the free North, blacks had to prove they were free by carrying identification papers. They could not carry guns; they had limits on where they could go, where they could live, and what kind of jobs they could hold. The racist attitudes prevailing in America that measured people's character by the color of their skin affected even the elites among the free black society that developed in the first part of the nineteenth century. Among free blacks, wealth and connections determined status, but they also made distinctions based on skin color, with lighter-skinned blacks holding higher status than those with darker skin. Those with lighter skin were mixed-race children, offspring of slave women and their masters. Among free blacks, more women than men were free, in part because when masters manumitted their slaves, they tended to free the mothers of their children first.

More free blacks lived in urban areas, and throughout the South, free black women constituted a small but distinct population in all the major cities. Much likelier to have jobs outside the home than white women, they owned small businesses; worked as cooks, midwives, seamstresses, laundresses, and peddlers; labored in tobacco and other factories. More than half of the free black women in Petersburg, Virginia, for instance, were wage earners; only 10 percent of white women were. Marketplaces in many cities were filled with goods sold by free black women, although in other cities, such as Memphis, Tennessee, free blacks were forbidden by law from operating market stalls and competing with poor whites. Free black women who were able to sell goods in the markets not only supported themselves, but also used their earnings to support their families and even to buy family members who were enslaved. Alethia Tanner of Washington, DC, for instance, not only bought her own freedom in 1810 for some $1,400, but then also purchased her sister, ten nieces and nephews, and her sister's grandchildren, along with seven other slaves over the next two decades.

Free black women also formed *voluntary associations* to improve their communities. The Female Benevolent Society of St. Thomas had been formed in Philadelphia as early as 1793 as a mutual aid society, and in 1818 the Colored Female Religious and Moral Society was organized in Salem, Massachusetts. By 1830, Philadelphia had more than twenty-seven such mutual aid societies, formed by women drawn from the city's working class as well as the small middle class and the even smaller black elite. In addition to the aid societies, free blacks formed literary societies, schools, and churches. The African Methodist Episcopal Church, established in 1816, even allowed women preachers such as Juliann Jane Tillman to speak.

Black voluntary associations began in the North, where there were more opportunities for free blacks to gather, and developed only slowly in the South. Their chief concern was the welfare of the black communities in which they lived. In the days before unemployment insurance, workers' compensation, and Social Security, all workers had few resources if they were fired, laid off, hurt, or widowed, but this was especially true for African Americans. Most private and public charities favored white applicants for relief, so free black women organized to help their own. In Philadelphia, for instance, one group of 200 working-class women pooled their savings to help their members during sickness and unemployment. In Memphis, the Daughters of Zion of Avery Chapel hired a physician for all their members as a way of ensuring health care.

One of the most pressing concerns for black women was education. As early as 1827, a free black woman signing her letter "Matilda" published her thoughts in *Freedom's Journal*, the first African American–owned paper in the United States, pleading for education for women. "Ignorant ourselves," she wrote, "how can we be expected to form the minds of our youth, and conduct them in the paths of knowledge?" All mothers should

MARIA STEWART CHALLENGES FELLOW AFRICAN AMERICAN WOMEN

Between 1831 and 1832, Maria W. Stewart delivered four speeches in Boston. She broke new ground as one of the first African American woman to speak in public. Her lectures condemned slavery and promoted education. This speech, given to the women of the African American Female Intelligence Society, called on black women to educate themselves so that they could move beyond the poverty and prejudice that affected so many.

"Oh, do not say you cannot make anything of your children; but say, with the help and assistance of God, we will try.

Perhaps you will say that you cannot send them to high schools and academies. You can have them taught in the first rudiments of useful knowledge, and then you can have private teachers, who will instruct them in the higher branches.

"It is of no use for us to sit with our hands folded, hanging our heads like bulrushes lamenting our wretched condition; but let us make a mighty effort and arise. Let every female heart become united, and let us raise a fund ourselves; and at the end of one year and a half, we might be able to lay the cornerstone for

read, she argued, to learn that "which could never be taken from them." The first Catholic community of black nuns, the Oblate Sisters of Providence in Baltimore, ran a school to teach the children of free blacks in Maryland, and Quakers continued to educate black children as part of their ministry.

As participants in voluntary associations, black women informed themselves and others about the issues of the day, meeting weekly to discuss literature or contribute letters and articles to black newspapers. They also participated in politics, to the extent that they were able, throwing their energies into the cause of abolishing slavery. In 1832, free black women in Salem, Massachusetts, formed the first female abolition society. Charlotte Forten, the wife of leading Philadelphian James Forten, began another such group the next year in that Quaker stronghold. In 1832 and 1833, Maria W. Stewart, a widow from Boston, addressed the African American Female Intelligence Society, a group that raised funds to help the sick and to buy books for the group to read and discuss. (See Primary Source 4-3.) Already the published author of a pamphlet, *Religion and Pure Principles of Morality*, calling for the abolition of slavery, Stewart spoke in public about the need for African American women to use their influence over their families to push them toward economic and educational advancement. A later speech, when she criticized African American men for not doing enough to meet those goals, proved so unpopular she stopped speaking in public, but her message remained. Even for free blacks in the North, freedom was not enough.

the building of a high school, that the higher branches of knowledge might be enjoyed by us....

"O ye fairer sisters, whose hands are never soiled, whose nerves and muscles are never strained, go learn by experience! Had we had the opportunity that you have had to improve our moral and mental faculties, what would have hindered our intellects from being as bright, and our manners from being as dignified, as yours? Had it been our lot to have been nursed in the lap of affluence and ease, and to have basked beneath the smiles and sunshine of fortune, should we not have naturally supposed that we were never made to toil?... Did the pilgrims, when they first landed on these shores, quietly compose themselves, and say, 'The Britons have all the money and all the power, and we must continue their servants forever?' Did they sigh and say, 'Our lot is hard; the Indians own the soil, and we cannot cultivate it?' No, they first made powerful efforts to raise themselves. And, my brethren have you made a powerful effort? Have you prayed the legislature for mercy's sake to grant you all the rights and privileges of free citizens, that your daughters may rise to that degree of respectability which true merit deserves, and your sons above the servile situations which most of them fill?"

Source: William Safire, *Lend Me Your Ears: Great Speeches in History* (New York: Norton, 1992), 564.

Women and Abolition

Black and white abolitionists sought to ameliorate the terrible conditions under which slaves labored. The abolition of slavery took several forms: colonization, gradual emancipation, and immediate emancipation. Colonization attempts, which were designed to return freed slaves to Africa, flourished after 1816 with the founding of the American Colonization Society (ACS). The ACS established a colony named Liberia on the west coast of Africa in 1821. Recommending gradual emancipation that paid or otherwise compensated slaveowners for the loss of their property, the ACS then proposed to send the freed slaves to Africa, where they not only would be free but could also serve as missionaries for Christianity, an aspect of colonization that drew both white and black supporters, particularly from states in the Upper South: Maryland, Kentucky, and Virginia.

More black Americans opposed colonization than supported it, however. African Americans saw themselves primarily as American, not African, since many of their families had been in the country for over 150 years. Instead of colonization, most favored emancipation, either gradually as had been done in the northern states after the Revolution, or immediately, as proposed by David Walker, a black activist who called for slavery's violent overthrow, and William Lloyd Garrison, publisher of the abolitionist newspaper *The Liberator*.

Both black and white women were active in the abolitionist movement. Maria Stewart, the first American woman to speak publicly against slavery, was unusual—an educated black woman, a public speaker, and a published writer. The tiny black middle class who supported her and formed antislavery societies were few in number, but did make their presence known, particularly in Philadelphia and Boston, two centers of black antislavery work. Since most black women in America were illiterate, poor, and employed as wage labor or slaves, most women in the abolitionist movement were white, middle class, and coming from the same reform movements that supported temperance, moral reform, and education. While most abolitionists were Northerners, ironically, two of the greatest women abolitionists of the early history of the movement were white Southerners: Angelina and Sarah Grimké of South Carolina.

The Grimké sisters grew up on a large plantation near Charleston, South Carolina. Their father was an attorney and later a state supreme court justice. Sarah, born in 1792 and the elder of the two, exhibited abolitionist tendencies early on. After seeing a slave whipped at age 5, the story goes, she ran away to a steamboat to see if she could travel to live in a place without slavery. She learned to read and longed to be an attorney, but her father did not believe in women working outside the domestic sphere. He forbade her to study anymore, but she turned her attention to educating the youngest girl in the family, Angelina, and to teaching her personal slave to read, writing later, "The light was put out, the keyhole screened, and flat on our stomachs, before the fire, with the spelling-book under our eyes, we defied the laws of South Carolina."

When Sarah's father needed medical care in 1818, Sarah took him to Philadelphia, where she discovered the Quaker faith. In 1821, she moved to Philadelphia permanently. Angelina, whom Sarah had converted to Quakerism on a visit back home, came to live with her sister in 1829, and it was she who wound up speaking in public about abolition first. In 1835, she wrote a letter to Garrison, who published it in *The Liberator* without her permission. Angelina was rebuked by her Quaker meeting, less for the content of her letter than her failure to ask the meeting for permission to publish it. Stung by the criticism, she and Sarah turned from the Quakers to focus on abolition. Angelina's letter, reprinted in all the major abolitionist publications of the day, attracted attention and support for the sisters, who left Philadelphia for Providence, Rhode Island, and a less conservative meeting of Quakers.

The sisters began publishing antislavery pamphlets: Angelina, *An Appeal to the Christian Women of the South*, Sarah, *An Epistle to the Clergy of the Southern States*, both published in 1836. In 1837, Sarah published *An Address to Free Colored Americans*, and Angelina brought out *An Appeal to the Women of the Nominally Free States*. The sisters began to tour the Northeast, visiting sixty-seven cities to speak out against slavery. Their actions were unheard of. While Frances Wright, a British citizen, had spoken out in public against slavery as early as 1828, and Maria Stewart had given three abolitionist speeches in 1832 and 1833, no women had ever gone on such a substantial lecture tour as did the Grimké sisters. The clergy of the many churches where the sisters found their audiences were often appalled at the spectacle of women speaking in public. In Massachusetts, the clergy of

Boston issued a Pastoral Letter condemning the sisters' public reform efforts. The ministers argued that while it was commendable for women to exercise their influence on society through "unostentatious prayer" and other efforts, public speaking was immodest and inappropriate. When any woman "assumes the place and tone of a man as a public reformer," they wrote, "she yields the power which God has given her for protection, and her character becomes unnatural." Such a criticism of their efforts on such grounds convinced the Grimkés that the slaves were not the only ones chained by oppression. Women were as well. In 1838, Sarah replied to the criticism of their efforts with a series of letters to abolitionists, later published as a pamphlet: *Letters on Equality of the Sexes and the Condition of Women.*

In fifteen letters, Sarah traced the history of women from creation to the present day, and examined their status throughout the world. She argued that God had created women equal to men and had never made them unequal. In another letter, in response to the clergy's complaint, she argued that women had the same moral duties and responsibilities to act against an immoral world as men. Free women, white and black, faced many of the same limitations as did slave women. Women were limited in their educational opportunities, she wrote, sometimes in subtle ways: "In most families, it is considered a matter of far more consequence to call a girl off from making a pie, or a pudding, than to interrupt her whilst engaged in her studies." But there had also been women in history who had done great things, despite men, and even, occasionally, with their help. Yet under the legal systems of the United States, those women would remain the exception, because the laws meant that for a married woman (which was the case for nearly every free woman of the time), "the very being of a woman, like that of a slave, is absorbed in her master." Under *feme covert* status, women's individuality disappeared. Under slavery, the same occurred. What she wanted, wrote Sarah Grimké, was not to ask for her rights as a favor from men. "I surrender not our claim to equality. All I ask of our brethren, is that they will take their feet from off our necks, and permit us to stand upright on that ground which God designed us to occupy."

This magnificent set of letters not only linked the status of free white and black women with the status of those enslaved, it also linked the abolitionist movement with the beginnings of another reform, the woman's rights movement, which called for equality between women and men. It was not enough to free the slave, argued woman's rights reformers, for then slave women would still be free in name only. Women must also be freed from the discriminatory bonds of womanhood they shared. The linkage of these two radical causes split the abolitionist movement in two. The Garrisonians followed the Grimkés, at least as far as demanding that women abolitionists be able to participate equally in antislavery organizations. Other abolitionists could not stomach the radical nature of the Grimkés' views and broke away, worried that adding woman's rights to their reform efforts would drive so many people away that abolition would fail.

It would not fail. In the decades to come, as slavery hardened as an institution, as abolition became a more popular cause, and as political compromise gave way to political absolutism, slavery would be banished. But it would take a civil war to do so, and women's roles in such an event would move them far outside their separate sphere.

THINK MORE ABOUT IT

1. Return to the opening vignette about Abigail Adams pondering the fate of the new republic in 1800. In the decades to come, the nation and its people would reinvent themselves, but the degree to which people could do so reflected their position in society. Reflecting broadly on what you have read in this chapter, which groups of women were most successful in reinventing themselves in the early decades of the nineteenth century? Which women were most constrained, and why?

2. Women became involved in politics in a variety of ways during the early nineteenth century, but this involvement was controversial. What informal roles did some women play? Which formal rights did some women have? What examples illustrate the growing concern over women acting in the realm of politics? How does this issue demonstrate one of the themes of this book: that women have not experienced steady progress toward greater rights?

3. The image of the New England mill girl is important in understanding how Americans understood the early years of industrialization. Discuss the backgrounds, the work lives, and the social and political experiences of the mill girls. What do you make of the challenges and opportunities this work represented for those who pursued it? How did the experience of Southern women textile workers contrast with that of the Northern and midwestern mill girls?

4. Women inventors demonstrated their creativity and ingenuity, especially with regard to many domestic tasks. Discuss several of these inventors and their inventions. What obstacles did women inventors face?

5. Discuss how three of the following processes affected diverse Native American women in the early nineteenth century: the expansion of the market economy; land dispossession; westward exploration and expansion; intermarriage with whites; and depopulation. Be sure to assess the range of Native women's responses to these processes.

6. Why and in what ways did the lives of enslaved women worsen during the first part of the nineteenth century? Pay attention to such issues as the expansion of the cotton economy and how patterns of labor changed as a result, the growth of slave trading between states in the Upper and Lower South, sexual abuse, and white fears of slave resistance.

7. Define the reforming impulse of the first half of the nineteenth century and the array of reform activities that resulted from it. How did women active in new religious movements and various reform movements express their autonomy and justify their participation in the public sphere? What obstacles did they face? What were their accomplishments? Which areas of reform do you think were most important?

8. What did you learn in this chapter that you did not know before? How does this new information help you understand the overall story of women in American history? What topics would you like to explore further?

READ MORE ABOUT IT

Catherine Allgor, *Parlor Politics: In Which the Ladies of Washington Help Build a City and a Government*

Susanna Delfino and Michele Gillespie, *Neither Lady Nor Slave: Working Women of the Old South*

Thomas Dublin, *Women at Work: The Transformation of Work and Community in Lowell, Massachusetts, 1826–1860*

Julie Roy Jeffrey, *The Great Silent Army of Abolitionism: Ordinary Women in the Antislavery Movement*

Gerda Lerner, *The Grimké Sisters of South Carolina*

Anne L. Macdonald, *Feminine Ingenuity: How Women Inventors Changed America*

Rosemarie Zagarri, *Revolutionary Backlash: Women and Politics in the Early American Republic*

KEY CONCEPTS

Revolution of 1800

Nullification Crisis

Eaton affair

putting-out system

mill girls

Patent Act of 1790

civilized tribes

natural increase

peculiar institution

Second Great Awakening

voluntary benevolence

temperance

moral reform

abolition movement

Missouri Compromise

voluntary associations

woman's rights movement

Chapter 5

RIGHTS CONTESTED

Rebecca Neugin of the Cherokee Nation, Georgia

THE CULT OF TRUE WOMANHOOD
Primary Source 5-1: Advice to Young Ladies on Their Duty and Conduct in Life

WESTWARD MIGRATION
Life in the West
The Mexican-American War
Chicana Women
The Gold Rush
Primary Source 5-2: Julia Anna Archibald on the Way to Pikes Peak

THE WOMAN'S RIGHTS MOVEMENT
The Road to Seneca Falls
Seneca Falls and Woman's Rights Conventions
Transcendentalism and Woman's Rights
Primary Source 5-3: Margaret Fuller, *Woman in the Nineteenth Century*
Women Politicos and Domestic Feminists

THE ANTEBELLUM SOUTH
The Southern Lady
Yeoman Women of the South

THE CIVIL WAR
The Road to War
Women in the War
Primary Source 5-4: Marie Ravenel de la Coste of Savannah
Primary Source 5-5: Ellen Morgan Writes to Her Confederate Soldier Husband

THINK MORE ABOUT IT

READ MORE ABOUT IT

KEY CONCEPTS

n 1838, three-year-old Rebecca Neugin, a Cherokee woman living in Georgia, unwillingly participated in one of the most shameful episodes in American history. She and her family were driven out of their home into stockades, imprisoned with few supplies and less food, and marched to Indian Territory, where they would be resettled after a horrific journey known as the Trail of Tears. "When the soldiers came to our house," Neugin remembered in an oral history in 1932, "my father wanted to fight, but my mother told him the soldiers would kill him if he did and we surrendered without a fight. They drove us out of our house to join other prisoners in a stockade. After they took us away, my mother begged them to let her go back and get some bedding. So they let her go back and she brought what bedding and a few cooking utensils she could carry and had to leave behind all of our household possessions." White settlers immediately seized the houses, possessions, and lands of the departing Cherokees, occupying their farms where crops were already sown and growing.

The U.S. Army drove the Cherokees away from their ancestral lands following a directive from President Martin Van Buren. Handpicked successor to Andrew Jackson, Van Buren continued Jackson's policy responding to pressure from white Americans eager to mine the gold that had been discovered on Cherokee lands in 1828. That same year, Georgia extended its state laws to

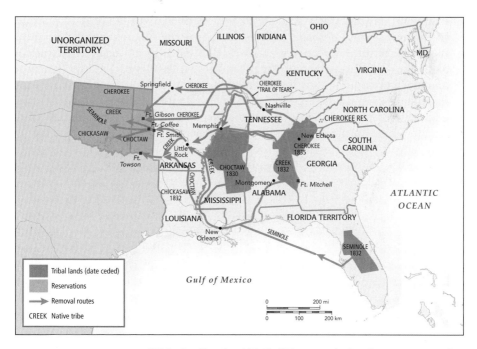

MAP OF TRAIL OF TEARS While the Cherokees' Trail of Tears was the best-known instance of the government's removal of Indians, this map shows the other groups in the Southeast forced to leave their homes. By land and sea, thousands of Indian women, men, and children traveled to new settlements in what would become known as Indian Territory. Thousands more died along the way.

the Cherokee Nation and prohibited Cherokees from testifying against whites in court. Harassed continually, the Cherokees contested the law by filing two lawsuits, both of which were decided in the tribe's favor: *Cherokee Nation v. Georgia* (1831) and *Worcester v. Georgia* (1832). President Jackson, however, refused to enforce the Supreme Court's rulings in favor of the tribe. Instead, he pushed for their removal west, where, he argued, they would be protected from the annihilation sure to follow if they continued to occupy lands that white Americans wanted.

In July 1838, the Cherokees were finally rounded up and the Trail Where They Cried, known to whites as the Trail of Tears, began. Four thousand Cherokees lost their lives along the route, including women forced to march while in labor and to give birth as best they could along the side of the road. They arrived in Indian Territory, present-day northeastern Oklahoma, in the spring of 1839. There they built sod or log houses and reestablished their farms in a land colder in the winter and drier in the summers than their traditional lands they had occupied for centuries. They came into conflict with other Cherokee groups from Texas and Arkansas who already occupied the lands to which the eastern Cherokees had been sent. The changes the group underwent were profound, but for Rebecca Neugin and the women of her tribe, the greater changes in their lives had actually come in the years before removal.

When Neugin's mother insisted she be allowed to return to their confiscated house to retrieve things that she needed to run the household, her focus on domestic items symbolized the decline in the traditional political roles enjoyed by Cherokee women. By 1838, the Cherokee had become a nation patterning not only its political life but also its social organizations along the same lines as white Americans. It had developed a written language and had drawn up a constitution modeled on the U.S. Constitution. Many Cherokees were Christian and, after 1817, Cherokee elites had wholeheartedly adopted white notions of women's place in society, notions promulgated by the Christian missionaries whose numbers had increased dramatically as the Second Great Awakening took hold in the South. The public and political roles that Cherokee women had enjoyed for centuries—in the Woman's Council, in the National Council, and because they owned the tribal land—declined precipitously. By 1827, the Cherokees had declared that only free men would be allowed to vote and serve on the General Council, writing a constitution that specifically excluded women. With the decline in their traditional political roles, women found their power confined to domestic roles, the same roles expected of white women. Missionaries instructed them in these roles in the east before removal, and Cherokees enforced them through education in the Cherokee Female Seminary, a boarding school the Cherokee Nation began in 1851 in Tahlequah, Oklahoma, where they lived after removal.

What happened to Cherokee women—the decline in their traditional political roles and the corresponding emphasis by their leaders on women's value as domestic workers—exemplified the contest between powerful political, social, and cultural forces, and the rights that many Americans struggled to maintain. As the U.S. government drove Native people from their traditional lands in an attempt to assuage white Americans' never-ending thirst for new lands, they expected uprooted Native women to assume the roles of white women. Governmental laws, rules, and regulations rewarded Native compliance not just with the political demand that Native Americans leave their lands, but also with their adoption of white standards of proper behavior. Government land grants to Native families, for instance, not only placed Native peoples in new geographic areas, but also demanded personal ownership of small plots of land by the father as patriarch of the family. Seasonal migration from hunting grounds to summer grounds, communal living, and communal property, long the way of life for many Native Americans, were deemed unacceptable by the government and the white society that surrounded them. Many Cherokee women assumed white ways of dress and behavior and attempted to acculturate to white ways to avoid displacement or destruction. Small wonder that Rebecca Neugin's mother was willing to stand up to American soldiers to retrieve the domestic goods that enabled her to care for her family. By the time of the Trail of Tears, domesticity had become her world, as it would be for most American women during the nineteenth century, in a cultural phenomenon called the Cult of True Womanhood.

At the same time, however, many women contested society's right to limit their behavior by defining propriety. As Neugin's mother fought the soldiers' definition of her as an uncivilized woman who would not value domestic items, so other women acted in ways designed to keep, enhance, or restore their autonomy. The westward migration of Americans enabled many women unaccustomed levels freedom of action as they moved from more urban regions to the ever-receding frontier. Other women sought to expand their legal and political rights, participating in political conventions and reform movements. Still others sought to limit the lives of enslaved women to maintain white elite control of the South. Nationwide, the struggle over rights in this era was profound—a contest that eventually led to a civil war.

THE CULT OF TRUE WOMANHOOD

The notion that women belonged in a separate sphere of activities from men has been a constant ideal in history that has seldom reflected the realities of women's lives. By the mid-nineteenth century in America, however, that notion had become so entrenched and so powerful that historians have deemed it the *Cult of True Womanhood*. In a quest for social stability at a time of political and economic upheaval, Americans made the white, middle-class, Anglo-Saxon Protestant family the ideal American family that everyone in America should aspire to. Thus, a "True" American family consisted of a white, native-born, Protestant father at work, paid well enough so that a mother could stay at home, caring for children who were to be as little flowers around the garden. Each family member had a separate sphere to occupy, a distinct role to play. Popular culture helped define these roles and instructed people about how to behave in them.

ADVICE TO YOUNG LADIES ON THEIR DUTY AND CONDUCT IN LIFE

Timothy Shay Arthur wrote popular nineteenth-century advice articles and books that disseminated the values of True Womanhood. He published often in the pages of Godey's Lady's Book, the most popular women's magazine of the day. Here, he instructs young women regarding proper behavior when invited out by young men.

"In regard to invitations from young men to go with them to places of public amusement we think as a general rule they should be declined. And this for several reasons. We do not believe any young lady should appear at a ball, the theatre, or a concert except in company with her parents, brother, cousin, or some very intimate friend of the family, unless she be under engagement of marriage and then her [fiancé] becomes her legitimate protector and companion.

For women, their model role was True Womanhood. As historian Barbara Welter describes the role, True Women possessed four distinct characteristics. They were pious, which meant that they were naturally more moral and more interested in religion than men. True Women were also sexually pure, expressing no interest in sex until after marriage, and then only for procreation and to satisfy the lustful yearnings of their husbands. True Women submitted to authority figures within their families and in society. Finally, True Women focused on the domestic in their interests and activities. Their God-given role in life was to make their homes into warm havens from the cold and heartless world where their husbands and fathers labored: the world of politics, business, and growing industry.

Social and cultural institutions such as the law and the church provided powerful support for maintaining the patriarchal family structure that provided the roles that True Women were supposed to pursue. According to the law, as had been true during the colonial era, the husband owned all personal property, the wife gave up control over all real property to her husband at marriage, the children were controlled by the father, and enslaved women continued to be defined as property. While some changes took place in individual states, including laws passed that allowed married women to own property (in 1839 in Mississippi and 1848 in New York), most married women's legal rights were limited by state laws to those that legislators—and their husbands—wished them to enjoy.

Organized religion also promoted notions of True Womanhood. Particularly powerful and popular in the days of the Second Great Awakening, churches were not only religious centers, but social and cultural bulwarks as well. Here, women, men, and children learned what God expected of them. Preachers promoted the notion of True Womanhood in their sermons, declaring that while women were morally superior to men, they should remain subservient to men in other ways. For example, although Quakers had long allowed women to speak in meetings and the African

In the first place to accept of such attentions would be for a young lady to lay herself under an obligation that might at some after period be very embarrassing or so interfere with her feelings of independence as to make it difficult for her to act towards an individual who had thus sought to gratify her as both feeling and judgment dictated, and in the second place, her thus appearing in public with a young man known not to be an intimate friend of the family would naturally give rise to the belief that she entertained for him a preference that did not exist and thus place her in a false light in the eyes of her acquaintances and this would more certainly be the case if some other friend whose invitation she felt compelled to decline were to offer a like attention."

Source: T. S. Arthur, *Advice to Young Ladies on Their Duty and Conduct in Life* (Boston: Phillips, Sampson & Co., 1849), 155–156.

Methodist Episcopal Church even officially recognized African American Jarena Lee as an itinerant evangelist, the majority of churches strictly limited women's public roles. Instead, preached most ministers, True Women's God-given task was to guide men and children toward a moral life. They should neither hold authority over men, nor preach to them, nor teach them, nor contradict them—in public or at home. Instead, women should influence men to behave properly by setting the right example through their religious devotion.

The practical component of being a True Woman was called the *Cult of Domesticity*. Popular culture promoted these beliefs through what was called "prescriptive" literature: sermons, speeches, magazines, novels, plays, short stories, advertisements, school lessons, and dozens of advice books that told women what to do. (See Primary Source 5-1.) To make sure that True Women had the proper skills needed for their appointed station in life, one leading advice book admonished: "All ornamental branches of education are to be encouraged [for women]; but they will not make amends for the want of skill to cook a meal of victuals, make a plain garment or darn a stocking. There is more science in boiling a potato, or raising bread, and more judgment required, than there is in executing the finest piece of embroidery . . . your ornamental work will please the sight, but it will never set off against heavy bread and hard, watery potatoes." This kind of advice became widely available as new inventions such as mechanized printing presses lowered the cost of prescriptive literature.

Domesticity went hand-in-hand with True Womanhood. Both dictated that all women should be satisfied by the intertwined goals of raising children, practicing good housewifery, and undertaking the elaboration of the interior. A woman's first duty was to have children and to rear them to become good, moral citizens of the nation, a task similar to that proposed in the late eighteenth century for Republican Mothers. A good housewife met an increasing standard of cleanliness. Dirt floors of the colonial era vanished, replaced by carpets or painted or tiled floors. A dirty floor meant the keeper of the house was lazy or slovenly or a poor supervisor of household labor, and thus not a True Woman. A True Woman also made a house a home by decorating it with all manner of embellishments, knickknacks, statuary, paintings, and objets d'art, all of which made the home's interior more elaborate, cost money that husbands should be supplying, and made dusting and cleaning more time-consuming and complicated. Adding rugs to floors, for example, made the interior of a home more elaborate and attractive, as well as warmer in winter, but required laborious cleaning. Instead of sweeping, women—whether wives, servants, or slaves—had to pull up carpets every spring, carry the heavy rugs outdoors, hang them over a clothesline, beat them with a heavy metal rug-beater, roll them up to store for the summer, then put them down again in the fall. Similarly, more pots and pans, dishes and clothes, wall hangings and furniture, knickknacks and memorabilia kept in bigger homes with more rooms, all meant much more work for women.

A corollary of household elaboration was a growing use of servants, whom True Women were expected to properly supervise, and to the ranks of which immigrant women were expected to aspire. Immigration to the United States rose exponentially in the 1830s through the 1850s, particularly from Ireland, where a potato famine in the 1840s meant starvation for many who stayed. A great many immigrants came as well from Germany, where crop failures and political unrest displaced thousands, and from Sweden, where overpopulation and unemployment convinced thousands to leave in search of new economic opportunities. Many of the young women who emigrated worked as domestic servants in middle-class homes. Women servants faced hard, tedious labor with little chance for advancement and little time to form their own families. Sexual exploitation by employers was also a threat, along with the financial insecurity that came with low wages. The jobs were often unpleasant, but for many immigrant women they could also represent the hope of a first step on their way up the American economic ladder.

For middle-class women, domesticity became a career and one that required instruction. Published advice books covered every imaginable contingency and were geared to appeal to those wishing to rise to middle-class status as well as those already there. Lydia Maria Child, a novelist and children's author (with a distressingly improvident husband), published one titled *The Frugal Housewife: Dedicated to Those Who Are Not Ashamed of Economy*. Catharine Beecher, founder of five academies for young women, published *A Treatise on Domestic Economy for the Use of Young Ladies at Home and at School* in 1841. With her sister, the best-selling novelist Harriet Beecher Stowe, she later wrote a best-seller: *The American Woman's Home, or Principles of Domestic Science*.

Beecher, who ironically was unmarried and without children, was the daughter of the Reverend Lyman Beecher, one of the most famous clergymen of his day. She promoted the ideals of True Womanhood with religious fervor, arguing that women should practice what one historian has called "female-led domestic government." Since women were naturally more moral than men and more capable of organizing and running the household, proclaimed Beecher, they should serve as the moral leaders of the family and the caretakers of the home. Throughout her life, Beecher stressed the great national importance of domesticity: "The success of democratic institutions, as conceded by all, depends upon the intelligent and moral character of the mass of the people. . . . It is equally conceded, that the formation of the moral and intelligent character of the young is committed mainly to the female hand." Thus, by adhering to the Cult of Domesticity and the tenets of True Womanhood, women not only followed their natural inclinations, they became patriots.

Women deviated from the model at their peril. Actress and playwright Anna Cora Mowatt, for instance, was excoriated in the New York press for her performances in public in the 1840s, when she read the works of Shakespeare and others to audiences to help support her family. Mowatt, daughter of a New York merchant and wife of a lawyer, was expected to be a True Woman because of her husband's rank in the social hierarchy of the times, even though she could not afford the role after her husband developed health problems and could not work. Such realities did not matter to proponents of the Cult of True Womanhood. Others in society were more forgiving: Mrs. Frances Sargent Osgood, a poet and writer who published in the New York press and in ladies' magazines, wrote in praise of Mowatt's performances: "Ne'er heed them, Cora, dear,/The carping few, who say/Thou leavest woman's holier sphere/For light and vain display."

In fact, "Cora" had left her "holier sphere" to make a living. Life circumstances drastically restricted the ability of women to achieve the status of True Women. Only those middle- or upper-class women supported by men with incomes large enough to allow them to stay at home could be True Women. In addition, the True Woman was white, native-born rather than an immigrant, Protestant instead of Catholic or Jewish or a nonbeliever. The power of this model in mid-nineteenth-century life was such that it served as a cultural touchstone for Americans, who measured—and criticized—all women, based on their abilities to exhibit its characteristics. Despite women's actual circumstances, every American woman, whether she believed in or cared about the idea, tended to be measured by the standard of True Womanhood, and many sought to achieve the ideal, despite their ethnic or economic background.

The continuing Industrial Revolution made promulgating the Cult of True Womanhood easier and, for critics of industrialization, more urgent. Industrial production of newspapers and other documents increased Americans' awareness of the tenets of True Womanhood. At the same time, factories increased in number and kind, further separating wage-earning labor from home. Women who worked in factories were often seen as morally suspect. Social critic and intellectual Orestes Brownson criticized the Lowell mill girls, for instance, claiming that factory girls would never marry, nor return home with their moral reputations intact. Indeed, he wrote, the fact that a woman "'had worked in a Factory' is almost enough to damn to infamy the most worthy and virtuous girl." Small wonder that parents demanded oversight of their daughters who worked there.

The factories did provide young women with role models far outside the ideal of True Womanhood, that was certain. Sarah Bagley, who arrived at the Lowell mills in 1836, soon took issue with the *Lowell Offering* for promoting the cultural norms of True Womanhood. Instead, Bagley pushed for labor reform as the mills demanded increased output for the same wages after the Panic of 1837. By 1844, Bagley had organized the Lowell Female Labor Reform Association to demand the state legislature mandate ten-hour workdays. In 1845, Bagley left her job at the mills and spent her time organizing branches of the labor association in other towns. She worked as the corresponding secretary for the New England Working Men's Association, another labor group, and eventually became the nation's first female telegraph operator, scarcely the acts of a woman who accepted the dictates of True Womanhood.

Bagley's life choices show that while True Womanhood and the Cult of Domesticity had their adherents, many women found that their lives, especially when they changed dramatically, could no longer sustain the demands of True Womanhood. In particular, the movement of Americans into the trans-Mississippi West challenged the tenets of the Cult of Domesticity and True Womanhood.

WESTWARD MIGRATION

Since arriving on the continent during the colonial era, whites had always sought more land. The emigrants to the country had displaced Indians, put acres to the axe, farmed and settled, developed towns and cities. Many then moved on again, marching over land and traveling by water, displacing more Native Americans, and resettling again. Decade after decade, white Americans moved west. By the mid-nineteenth century, it was their "Manifest Destiny" to "overspread the continent," wrote John Louis O'Sullivan in *U.S. Magazine & Democratic Review*, whatever the toll on the Native inhabitants or the environment. It was their God-given right and duty, thought many expansion-minded Americans, to occupy and settle lands that others had left "unimproved."

Manifest Destiny's religious fervor included converting the lands west of the Mississippi not only to American-style farms and settlements, but to Protestant Christianity as well. The movement west followed the same pattern as had occurred when Europeans first came to the North American continent, beginning with a biological exchange that decimated Native American groups in the region. American traders arrived in 1832 in the Pacific Northwest region, for example, and inadvertently brought malaria with them, a new disease that reached epidemic proportions. Sicknesses also followed the fur trade routes American traders used, and Indian losses and displacement soon followed.

After the traders came missionaries. Narcissa Whitman, the first white woman to cross the continent, came with her husband Marcus in 1836 to the Walla Walla River in present-day Oregon, where they planned to convert the Cayuse Indians to Christianity. Setting up both a church and a mission school, the Whitmans were determined to win over the Native Americans in the area. But they failed to use methods that respected the Indians' social and political expectations, such as gift-giving, and the couple soon spent more time helping the Americans who traveled along the path the Whitmans had blazed, called the "Oregon Trail," than working with the Indians they had originally come to help. The travelers brought diseases with them, and after a measles epidemic in 1847 killed nearly all the Cayuse children yet only a few of the white children, the Cayuse attacked the mission, killing the Whitmans and twelve others and burning the mission to the ground. A war against the white militia two years later ended with the capture of the Cayuse leaders and, as was the case for many Native Americans following the cycle of death wrought by the contact with white Americans, the remaining Cayuse joined with other groups in the region to survive. American expansion into Oregon Territory was scarcely slowed.

Americans' pattern of settlement began with trade, first with Indians who supplied deer hides, beaver furs, or other pelts to trappers and hunters. Explorers, missionaries, land speculators, and government agents followed, all of whom interacted with Indians. When the treaties that either bought or stole the Indians' lands were completed (and often before they were finished), settlers moved in, displacing the squatters who had come when settlement was still illegal. Slowly and unevenly, trading centers, small farms, then towns developed in the immense territory stretching from the Mississippi River to the Rocky Mountains, known as the Great Plains. Here an agricultural revolution would proceed apace, as settlers shot buffalo, deer, and elk; reaped rich harvests of corn, wheat, and cotton; and raised hefty beef and hogs, benefiting from improved technology that increased yields. A revolution in transportation methods, including canals and railroads, made it both easier and cheaper for these settlers to sell their products via water and overland to an ever-expanding market. The continuing cycle of Indian displacement, migration from the East and from abroad, the expansion of towns, and the resulting population growth resulted in a demographic revolution as well, as the Indian population continued to decline, while white and black populations increased exponentially.

The majority of northern and midwestern women who moved to the trans-Mississippi West were white women from the East, who usually migrated as part of a whole family. The largest number traveled beginning around 1840 as part of the nineteenth-century *Great Migration* to what would become the Oregon and California Territories. Migrants jumped off from cities lying along the Missouri River, such as St. Joseph and Independence in Missouri, or Nauvoo in Illinois, to start the trek west. Most journeyed in search of farmland; some searched for converts; others, such as the members of the Church of Jesus Christ of Latter-day Saints (the Mormons) under the leadership of Brigham Young, searched for asylum from persecution for their religious beliefs and practices, which included polygamy.

Emigrants headed for the rich lands of Oregon, jointly occupied by the United States and Great Britain until 1846, when the Buchanan-Pakenham Treaty assigned the land south of the 49th parallel to the United States.

Earlier travelers told stories describing the wonders of the territory's fertile valleys, rushing rivers, and bountiful wildlife. To reach this fabulous land, settlers had to journey 2,000 miles, crossing the Great Plains and the Rocky Mountains, trudging through areas that became the modern states of Kansas, Nebraska, Colorado, Utah, Wyoming, and Idaho, then making their way along the mighty Columbia River. On this long and hazardous route they beheld flora, fauna, and landscapes that most had never seen before and encountered Indians, some hostile and some friendly, whose reactions they could not predict. Along with the household goods and farm implements jammed into their prairie schooners, the covered wagons that carried their supplies, these westward migrants carried with them cultural assumptions about how they should live, including notions about proper activities for women and the concept of women's separate sphere.

Life for women on these trips proved difficult because they had many of the same chores as they did when living at home, but their "houses" were now on wheels and they had no general stores nearby. Families began their trips maintaining a gendered division of labor. Men drove livestock and hunted for food; women cared for children, cooked meals, mended clothes, and carried on the familiar range of domestic duties. But life on the trail and in early settlements soon precluded such division of roles. The trip demanded more work from everyone. Children tended livestock,

Camp 100 ~ Humbolt ~ River

COVERED WAGONS ON THE WAY WEST, 1859 Most white women who moved West did so in covered wagons as parts of large groups. This drawing shows an encampment on the banks of the Humboldt River in western Nevada in July 1859. Women and men share cooking chores and haul water. In the right side of the drawing, a couple takes advantage of the privacy offered by the wagon's cover to do a little courting.

fetching feed and water, while men took care of the wagons, clumsy and rickety vehicles requiring frequent repair. Women gathered buffalo chips— dried buffalo droppings that burned rather nicely to feed the fires—essential fuel on the wide prairies that offered no trees for firewood. Women also cared for children and prepared food for the day's drive. At the end of day, while men rested and children played, women began what scholars now call the "second shift," the many chores that had to be completed after they finished all their other work.

The second shift began as soon as the wagons stopped. Then it was time to gather fuel and prepare the fire; milk the cows, fix and cook dinner, then clean up; wash and mend clothing; nurse the sick, help deliver the babies of women in childbirth, and take care of any other medical needs of the family or of others in the wagon train. If women were ailing, or if they died along the route, men in the family performed these jobs, but those on the wagon train saw this as men temporarily helping out, rather than men shifting to women's roles. Along the road, work still remained gendered; domestic labor, now more arduous, remained women's work.

Life in the West

Emily Dickinson, the brilliant and reclusive poet of the mid-nineteenth century captured the beauty, the solitude, and the vastness of the Great Plains, despite never having seen the region:

To make a prairie it takes a clover and one bee,

One clover, and a bee,

And revery.

The revery alone will do,

If bees are few.

The spareness of Dickinson's poem echoed the spareness of the amenities that many women found in the West. While the reality of the harshness of frontier life meant all must pitch in, regardless of the task, any suspension of gendered work roles was viewed as temporary, as it had been on the trail. Once settled at a homestead, the prevailing assumptions most people held about women's roles and societal structures continued. Most men and probably most women wanted to return to their separate spheres as soon as possible. For many women the cultural rewards of being thought a True Woman and the importance they had in the domestic arena outweighed the desirability of having work loads more equitably distributed.

On the Great Plains, some travelers settled instead of continuing on to Oregon. Farms there were large, homesteads spread out, and life was hard. On frontier farms, women's duties never ceased. Men could take a day off from clearing or plowing land, but children had to be fed, cows milked, and chickens cared for every single day. During the first two or three years of settlement, many women had few nearby neighbors and neither schools nor churches, all of which had been central to women's sense of community in the East. One woman wrote in her journal that she would paddle slowly upstream a local river against the current for twenty or thirty miles to visit a neighbor; on her return trip, to her sorrow, the current carried her back four times faster. Such isolation made women lonely. Mollie Sanford in Nebraska wrote in her diary wistfully that "If the country would only fill up.... We do not see a woman at all. All men, single or bachelors, and one gets tired of them." The imbalance in the sex ratio of men to women was not Sanford's imagination. In Oregon in 1850, for instance, there were 137 men to every 100 women. Such isolation and imbalance could actually endanger families, because when accidents happened or illnesses struck they had no one to help them, and women used to the help and companionship of other women in childbirth often desperately sought neighbor women's company when the time came, providing food and lodging for those who attended the childbirth, as part of a ritual shared by all women on the frontier.

As the number of women immigrants to the West increased, farms became less scattered, and tiny settlements became towns. In towns, frontier women organized churches and schools, trying to meet the ideal of True Womanhood. Among the settlers were German-speaking immigrants from Europe, who had come to America after famines, poor harvests, and depressions in the weaving industries at home. Germans had first moved into Missouri and Illinois in the 1830s and 1840s; more came and settled on the prairies—Iowa in the 1840s and 1850s, and Nebraska and Kansas in the 1850s and 1860s. Scandinavia immigrants came too, with many taking up farmland in Minnesota and Wisconsin.

Immigrants often settled with others from their homeland, establishing communities that maintained familiar class divisions, religious affiliations, and ways of life. As did other women on the frontier, they moved from primitive living conditions, requiring them to clear land or even quarry rock for their houses, to more orderly and familiar work in the fields after settlement. They sold their homespun cloth, milk, butter, and eggs to earn cash for their families, and prized education for their children. Selling continued to be the primary sources of income for women and families, providing women with substantial rewards and occasional independence from the grind of farming. But reaching the point of making money through these means took a great deal of labor. Advertisements to attract immigrants to the frontier alerted them to qualities they would need to get along in their new land. Not only should an immigrant woman possess a strong body and nerves, along with "robust health," and a "resilient soul," proclaimed one promotional flyer, but also a "great lack of consideration for herself" and "friendly obligingness to others," qualities any True Woman would gladly claim she possessed.

Another group of migrants to the West were African American women, but if they sought to be viewed as True Women, the nineteenth-century racism that whites extended to the frontier limited that perception. Most African American women on the frontier in southern territories such as Arkansas came as slaves, brought by their owners in the early days of settlement. The small number of free black women who emigrated to free areas in the West suffered from the same racist laws that they faced in the

East. Some states, notably Indiana and Illinois, had forbidden any more free blacks from even entering to settle, a pattern of discrimination true of Oregon Country as well. In 1844, before that area became a U.S. territory, settlers there banned slavery and also passed a *Lash Law* ordering all blacks, free or enslaved, to be whipped twice a year until they left the region. Some companies in charge of organizing wagon trains to Oregon during the Great Migration would not even allow African American settlers to join them. In 1850, Oregon Territory's Donation Land Act allowed only whites and "half-breed Indians" to claim lands to settle, excluding all free blacks, and the 1857 state constitution forbade any further admission of free blacks. California, a territory in 1847 and a state by 1850, required free blacks to carry certificates documenting their free status, and other western states required that they post bonds, often as high as $1,000, for good behavior.

Aside from the black towns in Kansas and Oklahoma that ex-slaves established after the Civil War, African American women did not emigrate in large numbers to the West, a pattern that lasted for decades. (As late as 1920, less than 1 percent of the female population in the Mountain and Pacific states were African American.) Isolation compounded free black women's problems in these regions, as racism had always affected their lives back east. Charlotte Forten, for instance, daughter of a wealthy and prominent Philadelphian and granddaughter of James Forten, an inventor and one of the richest African American men in the late eighteenth century, was a teacher, a poet, an essayist, an organizer of a missionary group, and an abolitionist. Despite her education, grace, and sophistication, she still suffered from racial slurs and prejudices, and was once refused service at an ice-cream parlor because of her skin color. "I wonder that every colored person is not a misanthrope," she wrote in 1853. "Surely we have everything to make us hate mankind." African American women, free and enslaved, had to create for themselves a different kind of womanhood—self-reliant and self-protective. A True Woman might be a westerner, even might be a foreigner, but never could she be black.

Nor, it seemed, could True Women be Hispanic. When Mexico became independent of Spain in 1821, it lifted a trade embargo, opening the area to commerce. Soon Americans began following the Santa Fe Trail from Missouri to Mexico. First came merchants trading goods, then trappers, who sought the pelts of animals in the New Mexican mountains. Pioneers soon followed, intermarrying with the region's Hispanics (Spanish-speakers), Mexicans, Chicanas (Mexican Americans), *mestizas* (mixed-race women), and Indians, buying or simply taking land for settlement. Beyond these economic forces, which displaced many Native women, the lives of women in this area were also affected by changes in religion. The Mexican government, now a republic, began secularizing their society, taking over the lands and missions of the Roman Catholic Church. Women who had made tiles for the church lost their jobs; older workers on former church lands became tenant farmers. In addition, Hispanic and Indian women's traditional textile production was undercut by products now imported from New England's mills. Money-making operations in the Southwest region shifted to large-scale agriculture and sheep-raising, fields of endeavor dominated by men.

Women were forced into less powerful, more economically subservient roles. While such submission to authority and focus on domestic roles might indicate Hispanic women had become True Women, white racism and religious prejudice precluded recognizing them as such. They were not white, nor Protestant; thus, they were not True Women.

The Mexican-American War

The continued influx of Anglo settlers into the area of Mexico known as Texas eventually resulted in a drive for independence by the American population who had emigrated there in the first third of the nineteenth century. They successfully revolted against the Mexican government in 1835, establishing the Lone Star Republic, then gained admission to the United States as the state of Texas in 1845. Mexico sought to reestablish its control over the region, leading to the Mexican-American War from 1846 to 1848. The war pitted a Mexican government convinced that Texas was still legally a part of the Mexican Republic against an American government determined not only to support the Americans living in Texas but also to seize as much Mexican land as possible.

Unlike the American Revolution, where guerilla warfare and the defense of their homes and farms led numbers of women to take up arms against the enemy, albeit temporarily, the Mexican-American War was fought largely by men on foreign soil, far from the homes of most of the American combatants. Consequently, the war did not disrupt American lives to the degree earlier wars had—for Americans it was a small war. Despite its geographic distance from most Americans and its limited size, the war did attract a few women participants, as other wars had. Jane McManus Storms Cazneau, a Texas landowner and promoter of Texas annexation, joined a secret U.S. mission to Mexico before the war to attempt a peaceful settlement. She was also the only person allowed behind enemy lines, reporting on the action for the *Baltimore Sun*. She then returned to Washington and reported to President James K. Polk, quite an accomplishment during a time when women were valued primarily for their domestic skills.

Camp followers in the war included women such as Sarah Borginis, who served first as a cook until the 8th Cavalry unit she cooked for moved to Fort Texas. When the Mexican army commenced bombarding the fort, Borginis received a musket and, according to the story, never missed a target nor preparations for a meal. General Zachary Taylor breveted her, an honorary promotion that made her the first woman colonel in the U.S. Army, a ranking she kept until her death, when she was buried at Fort Yuma, Arizona Territory, with full military honors. Other women disguised themselves to fight as men. Eliza Allen, known as George Mead, fought at the battle of Monterrey in 1846, and was wounded at the Battle of Cerro Gordo. While recuperating, she met up with William Billings, the man she loved, had followed into action, and would marry after the war. According to her autobiography, *The Female Volunteer; or, The Life and Wonderful Adventures of Miss Eliza Allen, a Young Lady of Eastport, Maine*, published in

1851, Allen recovered from her wounds, continued to disguise herself, continued to fight, and was never discovered. She continued to dress as a man even after the war was over.

Chicana Women

The Mexican-American War ended with the Treaty of Guadalupe Hidalgo in 1848, ceding the United States the territories of New Mexico, Utah, Arizona, Nevada, and inarguable titles to Texas and California. But the agreement did not end bitter disputes over landownership and taxation between Anglos and Mexicans living in those lands. In 1851, Congress passed the Gwin Land Act to resolve these property disputes, but the act only served to further consolidate landownership in the hands of Anglos. As a consequence, more and more Mexican American men (Chicanos) left the area to seek wage work elsewhere, often traveling long distances and leaving behind the women who had become economically dependent on them to head their households.

When investors and speculators began building railroads in the area, such as the Atchison, Topeka, and the Santa Fe rail line that opened in 1859, more and more Chicanos left farms and ranches to build railroads that were hundreds of miles away. Without their men at home to labor on the farms, and without men to file claims in court to recover what had been their traditional lands, many Chicanas lost possession of their families' self-sufficient farms. Because most women in the new U.S. territories now lived under the traditional American legal restrictions of *feme covert* that prevented married women from suing in court, they lost as well what had become their center of power, the farm, and became marginalized in both politics and the economy. Their husbands gone for jobs, their farms taken from them by unfair judges or in payment for legal debts incurred in their fight to retain their property, many Chicano and Hispanic households became woman-centered and isolated, as women and their families were driven off their lands into small towns where they struggled to survive.

In these households, women banded together to share tasks and knowledge. The isolation of settlements in the Southwest, a vast territory where people clustered near scarce water sources, increased the value of women to the community as a whole because of their crucial roles as caretakers. But the isolation also reinforced women's dependence on male-controlled systems of property, of the law, and of the church. With men absent in search of work, Hispanic women became more likely to hold wage-earning jobs than white women, and to support their families until their husbands could send money home if and when they found work. Hispanic women were also more likely to live in female-headed household than were whites, and more likely to live with extended families, referred to as *la familia*, that included close friends.

Most Anglo settlers regarded Chicanas as inferior to them, and tried to impose their ethnocentric standard of True Womanhood on women who lived in a very different place and had different cultures and ways of life.

JULIA ANNA ARCHIBALD ON
THE WAY TO PIKES PEAK

Julia Archibald, a woman's rights advocate and fan of bloomers (see page 202), headed for the Pikes Peak gold rush in June 1858. She wrote letters about her adventures to Lydia Sayer Hasbrouck, the editor of The Sibyl, *a woman's rights paper published in Middletown, New York. Archibald wore her bloomers throughout the trip to the top of Pikes Peak, an act so daring that a children's book about* her, A Bloomer Girl on Pike's Peak, *was published in the 1940s. Archibald and her husband did not find gold; they moved on to New Mexico Territory where her husband, James Holmes, served as territorial secretary.*

"Believing, as I do, in the right of woman to equal privileges with man, I think that when it is in our power we should, in order to promote our own

The observations made by Kentuckian Susan Shelby Magoffin in 1846 are typical. When Magoffin, one of the earliest white women to travel on the Santa Fe Trail, first encountered Hispanic women, she was appalled by how they looked and behaved. Their arms and necks were bare, she complained, and their bosoms exposed. They smoked cigarettes, they nursed babies in public, and they insisted on hiking their already too-short skirts clear up to their knees when they crossed a river. Instead, presumably, they should have used a new invention promoted in Sarah Josepha Hale's *Godey's Lady's Book*, a veritable instruction book for True Womanhood. Hale's book showed an "Imperial Dress Elevator" that would lift one's dress up from the ground without showing too much ankle.

Yet after Magoffin began to talk to the women, to attend meals with them, and to share recipes and stories of homes and families, she began to see beyond her superficial impressions and to appreciate their similarities, as well as their humanity. The adjustment may have been mutual. There are few records of what the women whom Magoffin dismissed so imperiously at first thought of her, but in Fanny Calderón de la Barca's memoir, *Life in Mexico* (1840), she wrote that Chicana and Hispanic women faced a trial unknown to American women who embraced the strictures and fashions of True Womanhood: the stifling heat of the American Southwest. The reality of their lives led them to choose more practical clothing than the layers of petticoats and crinolines Magoffin expected True Women to wear, regardless of circumstance. Despite such regional, ethnic, racial, class, and other variations in women's experiences and aspirations in the first half of the nineteenth century, all women tended to be measured by the image of True Womanhood when they came into contact with the dominant Anglo culture. Although True Womanhood was just an image, it was a cultural image so powerful and pervasive that it was imposed on women even when their lives deemed it impractical and irrelevant. When women fell short of the image, for whatever reason, they were criticized.

independence, at least, be willing to share the hardships which commonly fall to the lot of man. Accordingly, I signified to the Guardmaster that I desired to take my turn with the others in the duty of guarding the camp, and requested to have my watch assigned with my husband. The captain of the guard was a gentleman formerly from Virginia, who prided himself much upon his chivalry, (and to use his own expression, was 'conservative up to the eyes,') was of the opinion that it would be a disgrace to the gentlemen of the company for them to permit a woman to stand on guard.... He believes that woman is an angel, (without any sense,) needing the legislation of her brothers to keep her in her place; that restraint removed, she would immediately usurp his position, and then not only be no longer an angel but unwomanly."

Source: From Julia Anna Archibald, letter to the editor "Sister Sayer," *The Sybil* (Middletown, NY), March 15 and April 1, 1859.

The Gold Rush

Another group of women in the west who found little reason to embrace the strictures of that image were those who ventured there on their own, searching for independence, freedom, opportunity, and adventure. Although the vast majority of women who traveled to the West did so as members of family groups—some glad to go, some under husbandly duress—these single women went alone or in small groups, and seem to have had the same motivations as single men. Late in 1848, gold was discovered in California, and the mad rush west to find the precious metal soon began. (See Primary Source 5-2.) Although 95 percent of those who set off to make their fortunes panning gold were men, the women who also traveled to California to work as miners relished the adventure.

In his farewell address in December 1848, President James K. Polk announced that gold had been discovered in the hills of California. Within two years, more than 90,000 Americans rushed to the territory and California had become a state; 300,000 people lived there by 1854. The Gold Rush was a free-for-all with thousands looking for easy riches, hundreds looking to supply miners' needs, and state and local governments too small to keep the peace. Along with lawlessness came a building boom. San Francisco, it was estimated, had thirty new houses and two murders per day. Gold miners' wages averaged eight dollars per day, compared with a coal-miner's wage of a dollar a day back east. The cost of living was correspondingly high: a four-cent loaf of bread in New York sold for seventy-five cents or more in the gold camps.

The lack of social order, churches, and other civic institutions, including stable families, led to massive social problems, notably drinking, prostitution, gambling, and violence. Most miners were single men living on their own. When they returned from their claims, many sought the saloons first and sexual partners second; prostitution proliferated. As many as 20 percent of the women in the gold fields worked as prostitutes, and in some places, prostitutes outnumbered nonprostitutes by a ratio of 25:1. For women in California and elsewhere in the West, prostitution was the single most lucrative job available. Some women also found other ways to make money in the largely male world of the mining camp, once again doing work that men did not want to do for themselves, or that less-fortunate failed miners had taken on because of the lack of women. They ran boardinghouses, where beds were in such demand that they were rented to several men each day for eight hours at a time; they did laundry and sewed; they worked as nurses and cooks; they made and sold bread and pastry.

One such entrepreneur, Mary Jane Caples, wrote that she had "concluded to make some pies and see if I could sell them to the miners for their lunches, as there were about one hundred men on the creek, doing their own cooking—there were plenty of dried apples and dried pealed peaches from Chili, pressed in the shape of a cheese, to be had, so I bought fat salt pork and made lard, and my venture was a success. I sold fruit pies for one dollar and a quarter a piece, and mince pies for one dollar and fifty cents. I sometimes made and sold, a hundred in a day, and not even a stove to bake them in, but had two small dutch ovens." One anonymous settler wrote to a San Francisco newspaper in 1850 that smart women could do well in Gold Rush country: "It is the only country I ever was where a woman ever received anything like just compensation for work."

Of the women who worked as miners themselves, little is known. As was true for most ordinary working-class Americans, few written documents survive. Even before the California Gold Rush, census reports listed women in the New Mexico region in the 1840s who earned money holding the job of "gold panner," a task that involved slowly swirling water in a pan to see if there was any gold in it. Hispanic and Native American women also panned for gold in California, as did daughters and wives of Anglo miners. Mining was not an approved activity for True Women, however. "Mountain Charley," Elsa Jane Guerin, for instance, disguised herself so she could prospect for gold. She succeeded not only at her prospecting, but also at her subterfuge. She even served as a soldier in the Civil War, before eventually resuming her life as a woman and a mother in St. Louis. Parisian emigrant Marie Suise arrived in California in 1850, cut off her hair, assumed male clothing, and finally got enough gold to buy land that held more, a fact that she disguised by planting grapes and pretending the land was only good for vineyards.

Other women miners did not bother to disguise themselves. They occasionally appear in photographs of mid-nineteenth-century miners, standing alongside men; traces of them show up in diaries, journals, newspapers, and court records. Whether they worked alongside their husbands or by themselves, women miners always labored under the threat of violence from those greedy for whatever they could grab. If women miners were single, they had only to worry about claim jumpers or thieves who might steal all they had wrested from the earth. If women miners were married, however, they labored as well under the restrictions of *feme covert* status, a stumbling block here as elsewhere. Failing to acknowledge a husband's rights to property could be dangerous. One miner's wife refused to give her husband the gold that she had found after he had drunk away his own share. He picked up his gun and shot her dead. While the long journey overland or by sea to California could become a highly lucrative enterprise for women, that fortune was always tempered with the knowledge that there was little they could do to protect their property from their husbands. Even on the frontier, True Women lived under unjust laws. Reforming those laws was not a contest undertaken by True Women, but required instead women willing to fight on the male turf of politics.

THE WOMAN'S RIGHTS MOVEMENT

Often after school in the 1820s, Elizabeth Cady went to the office of her father Daniel Cady, a judge and lawyer in the small town of Johnstown, New York. There she observed Judge Cady listen sympathetically and politely to women seeking his aid and advice. In her town, Elizabeth wrote in her autobiography years later, "many men still retained the old feudal ideas of women and property. Fathers, at their death, would will the bulk of their property to the eldest son, with the proviso that the mother was to have a home with him. Hence it was not unusual for the mother, who had brought all the property into the family, to be made an unhappy dependent on the bounty of an uncongenial daughter-in-law and a dissipated son. The tears and complaints of the women who came to my father for legal advice touched my heart and early drew my attention to the injustice and cruelty of the laws." The tenderhearted girl could not understand why her father could not help these women until, as she wrote, "he would take down his books and show me the inexorable statutes." Those laws limiting women's ownership of property seemed patently unfair to Elizabeth. The law students her father taught, amused by the girl's interest, teased her by reading out from the statute books the worst of the laws. One Christmas morning, after Elizabeth showed off her new coral necklace and bracelet, one student tormented her by telling her, "if in due time you should be my wife, those ornaments would be mine; I could take them and lock them up, and you could never wear them except with my permission. I could even exchange them for a box of cigars, and you could watch them evaporate in smoke."

Appalled at the prospect and determined to do something about the injustice she was witness to, Elizabeth Cady decided to cut all the offending statutes out of her father's law books, to ameliorate, she wrote, "the wrongs of my unhappy sex." Her father, catching wind of her plan, explained that laws were made by legislatures, and law books were found in libraries everywhere, so destroying his law books would not change those laws. "'When you are grown up, and able to prepare a speech,' said he, 'you must go down to Albany and talk to the legislators; tell them all you have seen in this office—the sufferings of these . . . women, robbed of their inheritance and left dependent on their unworthy sons, and, if you can persuade them to pass new laws, the old ones will be a dead letter.' Thus was the future object of my life foreshadowed," she wrote, "and my duty plainly outlined by him who was most opposed to my public career when, in due time, I entered upon it."

Elizabeth Cady would grow up to give that speech in Albany and elsewhere, even as her father objected to her public career. She would marry Henry Stanton, raise seven children, and become one of the leaders of the woman's rights movement of the nineteenth century. Spurred by a sense of injustice based on the ideology of equal rights, her lifelong passion would be to reform American social, political, and cultural institutions so that women's lives might be fairer. Unlike women reformers who used the Second Great Awakening and notions regarding True Womanhood to help make the world a better place (since the world was just a larger bit of home), Stanton's ideology rested on the Declaration of Independence and the argument that all men—and women—were created equal.

The Road to Seneca Falls

Reform efforts in the first part of the nineteenth century had taught women how to speak before an audience. When women moved into public speaking, most of them were terrified—and with good reason. Aside from the widespread human fear of public speaking, women who spoke in public in the nineteenth century were noticeably outside the private sphere, and there was little room to retreat. Many women began anyway, first with what were called *parlor talks*. A woman would invite a woman speaker into her house to speak in her parlor, with tea and cookies and an audience of women only. As the speaker's popularity grew, she might speak in a parlor with an audience of both men and women.

Women speaking in parlors eventually led to women speaking on the public stage, and once women spoke in public, the door to public activity opened a bit wider, although still not without harsh criticism of the speakers. By the 1840s, not only were women speaking in public, but some women were even testifying before legislative bodies, just as Elizabeth Cady Stanton's father had suggested. In 1848, for instance, Ernestine Rose spoke in front of the New York state legislature. Rose, a Jewish emigrant from Poland, had studied Hebrew scriptures and the Jewish Talmud, intellectual exercises ordinarily forbidden to women, but her father, a rabbi, indulged her desire for knowledge. Intellectually precocious, Rose protested the Orthodox Jewish prayer that began "I thank thee, Lord, that Thou has not created me a woman." She was, she said, "a rebel since the age of five." Forced into an engagement against her will by her father, she asked court authorities to release her from the betrothal and succeeded. She eventually came to America, where she lectured against slavery and for religious toleration. When the New York state legislature took up the question of whether married women should be allowed to keep their property, Rose gathered signatures on petitions, crisscrossed the state to speak on the issue, and then testified in favor of the Married Women's Property Act. This act, the second in the country after Mississippi's in 1839, allowed women to keep control over their property even if they married. Women could also keep any income, such as rent, that their property produced. They could sell property, they could pass property on to their daughters or sons, and, perhaps most important in the boom–bust economy, their property would no longer be taken automatically to pay their husbands' debts.

The passage of the property law in New York, for which Stanton had also worked, presaged a continuing push by Rose, Stanton, and many other reformers from the state for more equality and justice for women. In the summer of 1848, Stanton and Lucretia Mott, an old friend and fellow abolitionist, found themselves in Seneca Falls, a small town in upstate New York where Stanton and her husband Henry had moved the year before. Mott and Stanton had met eight years previously when both had attended the World Anti-Slavery Convention in London, England. There, the two women, elected delegates to the convention from their antislavery societies, were denied seats because they were women. Outraged, they agreed that something should be done about discrimination against women. Meeting again, comparing notes on all that was wrong in America for women, Stanton and Mott called for a convention to be held a week later, on July 19 and 20, 1848. At first, they were afraid no one would come. But come they did, some 300 women and men, including Frederick Douglass, who recorded and published the only surviving report of the convention.

Seneca Falls and Woman's Rights Conventions

During the first day of the convention, only the women were allowed to speak; on the second day, men could join in. Thirty-two-year-old Elizabeth Stanton rose and stated the purpose of the convention: "We have met here today to discuss our rights and wrongs, civil and political." After Lucretia Mott urged all to participate in debating the issues, Stanton took the floor again and read aloud a Declaration of Sentiments, eleven resolutions she and others had crafted, stating those "rights and wrongs." Beginning with the phrase "all men and women are created equal," and deliberately patterned after the Declaration of Independence, the Declaration of Sentiments listed the difficulties women faced when trying to act upon their rights as individuals. The most controversial resolution was the ninth, which called for *woman suffrage*—giving women the right to vote. Stanton complained that it was "grossly insulting" that "drunkards, idiots, horseracing rumselling rowdies, ignorant foreigners, and silly boys" had the vote while women did not. "The right is ours," she declared. "Have it we must. Use it we will." Frederick Douglass joined Stanton in her quest. "The power to choose rulers and make laws," he pointed out, "was the right by which all others could be secured." Despite opposition from those who feared the notion of women voting was too radical for the times, and despite Stanton's anti-male rhetoric, the convention voted in favor of the Declaration on July 20.

The Declaration met with scorn and ridicule when it was published in the newspapers during the next few weeks. Most Americans thought any calls to extend suffrage to women seemed absurd, and the press had a field day making fun of the women and generally carrying on about the collection

Elizabeth Cady Stanton and her daughter, Harriot. from a daguerreotype 1856.

ELIZABETH CADY STANTON AND DAUGHTER HARRIOT, 1856 Elizabeth Cady Stanton with her daughter Harriot, her sixth of seven children, in 1856. As was the case for most nineteenth-century woman's rights advocates, Stanton pursued her vision despite her domestic duties. She hoped to create a nation where all men and women could pursue their happiness, as the Declaration of Independence promised. That promise could be fulfilled, she wrote in the Declaration of Sentiments, only if women were given the inalienable right to govern themselves.

of "hens" and their lunatic ideas. But woman's rights advocates met again. In 1850, they held the first National Woman's Rights Convention, in Worcester, Massachusetts. In 1851, they held another, where Ernestine Rose spoke out in favor of women's rights. Many of the women who heard her brilliant and forceful speech would be the leaders in the fight for the vote over the next half-century. Rose argued against existing laws that enforced coverture. Those laws, she reasoned, assumed the existence of an ideal woman, as well as an ideal man, concepts supported by state legislators who argued that women were "protected" by their husbands under coverture. Such laws assumed, she said, that "the husband provides for the wife, or in other words, he feeds, clothes, and shelters her! I wish I had the power to make every one before me fully realize the degradation contained in that idea. Yes! he keeps her, and so he does a favorite horse; by the law they are both considered his property." Legislators needed to understand the humiliation inherent in such a status for women, argued Rose. While some might try to "throw the mantle of romance over the subject and treat woman like some ideal existence, not liable to the ills of life," Rose preferred to deal with "sober, sad realities, with stubborn facts." For legislators who protested she painted too gloomy a picture of the relationships between men and women, Rose explained, "I shall be told that the law presumes the husband to be kind, affectionate, and ready to provide and protect his wife. But what right, I ask, has the law to presume at all on the subject? What right has the law to intrust the interest and happiness of one being into the hands of another?"

What right indeed? What was apparent from Rose's articulate and impassioned speech is that she and other activists supporting women's rights had benefited from nineteenth-century increases in women's literacy, from the publication of well-argued philosophical discourses regarding the nature of women and their abilities, and from the increasing number of writings that supported the education of women as rational beings. Those writings represented the first step in solving the problems women faced by articulating exactly what the problems were.

Transcendentalism and Woman's Rights

One such work came from the pen of Margaret Fuller. Fuller, whom America's foremost man of letters, Ralph Waldo Emerson, considered "brilliant," argued in her book *Woman in the Nineteenth Century* that women needed "not as a woman to act or rule, but as a nature to grow, as an intellect to discern, as a soul to live freely and unimpeded, to unfold such powers as were given her." (See Primary Source 5-3.) Such philosophical discourse came out of the reform movements that Stanton and Mott participated in, but also from an intellectual and philosophical movement called *Transcendentalism*, centered in Boston and participated in by many of the major American intellectuals of the time. Transcendentalists argued that the rationalism of the eighteenth century needed to be replaced by a more intuitive understanding of humans and nature, and believed that the soul was more important than reason in helping people divine universal truths. They also believed that those souls included those of women, so they included women in their meetings and discussions, and regarded women's writings with respect. Fuller, Louisa May Alcott, Emily Dickinson, Julia Ward Howe, Elizabeth Palmer Peabody and her sisters, Mary Tyler Peabody Mann, and Sophia Amelia Peabody Hawthorne, were only a few of the circle of women Transcendentalists. Male writers such as Emerson, Henry David Thoreau, and Nathaniel Hawthorne focused their work on examining a distinctively American culture. Emerson, in particular, used the ideas of Transcendentalism to promote his belief that Americans could and should have their own culture, separate from Europe. Women Transcendentalists often focused more on suggesting women should develop their own culture, separate from men, or at least less dependent upon male approval. These writings and the ideas they expressed provided the intellectual underpinnings necessary for a woman's rights movement.

By 1848, then, there existed reform-minded women with organizational skills and abilities gained from their experiences in reform movements; networks of individuals in touch with one another, communicating ideas regarding women's rights; philosophical and popular writings that supported the idea of women's rights by articulating the problems and solutions;

MARGARET FULLER, WOMAN IN THE NINETEENTH CENTURY

Margaret Fuller, wrote Lydia Maria Child, sought to answer questions about women: "What is woman's true mission? What is the harmonious relation of the sexes?" She envisioned a world where men were not masters, but friends; a place where women could do as they wished, unimpeded by barriers to occupations or tasks. One reviewer called her work "vigorous and significant." If her meaning was not always clear, said the reviewer, it was "the defect of a mind that has too many thoughts for its words."

"We would have every arbitrary barrier thrown down. We would have every path laid open to Woman as freely as to Man. Were this done, and a slight temporary fermentation allowed to subside, we should see crystallizations more pure and of more various beauty. We believe the divine energy would pervade nature to a degree unknown in the history of former ages, and that no discordant collision, but a ravishing harmony of the spheres would ensue.

"Yet, then and only then, will mankind be ripe for this, when inward and outward freedom for Woman as much as for Man shall be acknowledged as a

and the dynamic and radical Elizabeth Cady Stanton, determined to do something about women's status in America. The Seneca Falls Convention's Declaration of Sentiments was too radical to be accepted by the majority of Americans, however. It was not the political action that the Declaration represented that seemed to be the problem, but the demand for the vote. After all, women had been participating in partisan politics and in the political world since the country's founding. The "fiery frenchified dames" had supported the French Revolution; the ladies of Washington had created the social underpinnings of the new government; women had voted in New Jersey elections until 1807, and taken partisan politics to heart. The political power that the actions of those women represented, however, had been diminished by the public expectation—nay, demand—that women would choose, instead of partisan political activity, the role of the Republican Mother or the role of the True Woman. Demanding the franchise in such a cultural milieu was doomed to failure. On the rare occasions in the nineteenth century when women did vote, they did so as mothers, not as part of the body politic. Kentucky widows with children, for instance, gained the right to vote in school board elections in 1838, exercising the franchise because of their culture's view of motherhood, not because of women's inalienable rights to self-government.

Women Politicos and Domestic Feminists

The lack of the franchise, however, never precluded interested women from participating in partisan politics. *Women politicos*, actively engaged in politics and the affairs of government, and concerned more with partisan political activity than the actual business of government, supported the Whigs, the *right*, not yielded as a *concession*. As the friend of the negro assumes that one man cannot by right hold another in bondage, so should the friend of woman assume that man cannot, by right, lay even well-meant restrictions on woman. If the negro be a soul, if the woman be a soul, apparelled in flesh, to one Master only are they accountable. There is but one law for souls, and, if there is to be an interpreter of it, he must come not as man, or son of man, but as son of God.

"Were thought and feeling once so far elevated, that man should esteem himself the brother and friend, but nowise the lord and tutor, of woman,—were he really bound with her in equal worship,—arrangements as to function and employment would be of no consequence. What woman needs is not as a woman to act or rule, but as a nature to grow, as an intellect to discern, as a soul to live freely and unimpeded, to unfold such powers as were given her when we left our common home. If fewer talents were given her, yet if allowed the free and full employment of these, so that she may render back to the giver his own with usury, she will not complain; nay, I dare to say she will bless and rejoice in her earthly birthplace, her earthly lot."

Source: From L.M.C., "Review," *The Broadway Journal* 1, no. 7 (1845); Margaret Fuller, *Woman in the Nineteenth Century* (New York: Greeley & McElrath, 1845), 26–27.

Jacksonian Democrats, the Americans or "Know-Nothings," the Republicans, and other formal political parties of the period. By the 1840s and 1850s, these women politicos sought to continue earlier traditions of participation, but they did not necessarily seek the vote, since that raised the hackles of so many. Instead, they marched in parades for candidates and made and presented banners at Fourth of July celebrations, held for presumptive officeholders. They attended Southern barbeques, where rowdy crowds ate and drank at the expense of the candidates, current and potential. Women politicos wrote letters to newspapers on the issues of the day and published pamphlets and books promoting candidates and their ideas. One such writer, Anna Ella Carroll of Maryland, wrote campaign biographies of Millard Fillmore, who ran for president in 1856, and for John Minor Botts, an unsuccessful candidate for the Republican presidential nomination in 1860. Before and after her Mexican War adventures, Jane Cazneau lobbied for the annexation of Cuba, and edited a newspaper, *La Verdad* (the Truth), for Cuban exiles in New York, discussing the island's strategic location and its economic importance to the United States.

Other women politicos included Louisa S. C. McCord, who published her work under her initials only (L. S. C.) in Southern newspaper and journal columns. In 1848, McCord published a translated essay by a French economist deploring the protective tariff, and editors soon solicited her to write essays supporting slavery and opposing women's rights. Despite her own activities, she argued that women were "made for *duty*, not for *fame*." Another woman politico was Mary B. Davis, a resident of Peoria, Illinois, who attended and then reported on the political conventions of the Whig and Liberty Parties. Anne Charlotte Lynch Botta, a poet, ran a salon for both literary and political figures in New York City beginning about 1855.

Emily Pomona Edson Briggs wrote about women employed by the government as well as political trends in Washington and Philadelphia newspapers, and eventually became the first woman to report directly from the White House. Eliza Farnham wrote about the customs and institutions of frontier democracy that she witnessed in California. Mary S. C. Logan of Illinois wrote on behalf of her husband John, a successful candidate for the U.S. House in the 1850s; she later became a magazine editor. Immigrant women expressed their political leanings as well. Anna Uhl Ottendorfer was by 1849 a publisher of *New Yorker Staats-Zeitung*, a daily newspaper that served as the voice of the liberal German community. In March 1852, Milwaukee resident Mathilde Franziska Anneke, a refugee from the German Revolution of 1848, founded *Deutsche Frauen-Zeitung (German Women's Paper)*, which brought her advocacy of woman's rights to the large German population of the Upper Midwest. She commented not only on political questions of the day, but also on woman suffrage and abolition.

For many of these women, their involvement in politics was part and parcel of the other activities that they pursued: Eliza Farnham, after her return from California, became interested in prison reform, working with Georgiana Bruce Kirby, a Transcendentalist, to make life better for female inmates at Sing-Sing, the notorious prison in upstate New York. Kirby, an active antislavery crusader, also worked for the temperance movement and eventually supported woman suffrage. Unlike Kirby, Dorothea Dix, a better known advocate for prison reform, did not favor woman suffrage. She was instead a *domestic feminist*, one of many women who found their rationale for public actions in the True Womanhood's designation of women as the moral force of the family and, by extension, moral arbiters for the nation. Domestic feminists used this idea, justifying their reform actions in the wider world because they were ameliorating social ills. Dix, for example, worked tirelessly, first to get mentally ill individuals out of prisons, then for prison reform. Despite testifying before state legislatures in pursuit of her goals, Dix did not support woman suffrage as a method to end suffering. Instead, by defining her activities as a method to reform the world by doing good, as True Women should, Dix, along with countless others, could change the world without the criticism and resistance that would follow an attempt to enter the world of partisan politics. That world had become increasingly male by the 1850s, as the franchise was extended even to men who had no property. Local political issues sparked heated rhetoric and even violence. One group of "politicians" in Baltimore, for instance, were called the Blood Tubs because they convinced voters to support candidates by grabbing a voter, holding him upside down over a tub of blood collected from the butcher, and dunking his head in it until he understood who it was he was supposed to vote for. Politics in the nineteenth century was not for the faint hearted, and most Americans believed it was certainly not for women.

Some Americans believed that true reform demanded a retreat from existing society, politics and all. The number of communal societies grew during the middle nineteenth century, and reform groups such as the Shakers withdrew from American culture, forming small self-sufficient groups separate from the larger society, and living on large farms or other communities closed to outsiders. The Shakers were "shaking Quakers," so named for the religious fervor that led members to dance as a physical expression of their faith during services. Led in the mid-nineteenth century by Lucy Wright, Shakers practiced faith healing and the open confession of sins to the members of the church. In settlements such as Pleasant Hill, Kentucky, the largest Shaker community by 1850, Shakers held property in common, worked for their common good, segregated themselves by sex, and practiced celibacy. The houses they shared even had separate staircases for men and women members. The communal life Shakers lived included a hierarchy in which both sexes participated: a female eldress and a male elder headed the "family" of converts. While their government was egalitarian, chores were gendered. All Shakers were required to work with their hands, and the goods they produced for sale kept the society going. Each brother, however, was assigned a sister to mend and wash his clothing, to tell him when to get new clothes, and to reprove him if he was not orderly. Even within an egalitarian reform community, the need for a True Woman to watch over the family seemed inescapable.

Many other reform movements in the mid-nineteenth century incorporated the ideals of True Womanhood and the belief that women and men should operate in separate spheres as a part of their efforts. Beginning in 1841, for example, temperance reformers formed Martha Washington societies to treat women alcoholics separately from men. By separating women from men, the Martha Washingtonians sought to recognize and protect women's higher moral sensibilities, despite the degradation those women had suffered when they fell victim to alcohol abuse. Such groups as Rebecca Cromwell Rouse's Martha Washington Society in Cleveland went beyond temperance and extended reform efforts to prostitutes and to the care of orphans. The most widespread reform group of all, missionary societies, sent missionary couples not only to work with Native American groups in the West, but also to foreign lands such as Burma. Before leaving, women missionaries were counseled that they would be able to spread the Gospel to foreign women that their missionary husbands would never be able to reach. The domestic feminism that had provided a foundation for earlier reform movements continued to undergird reform in the mid-nineteenth century.

Reforming women who confronted sexual discrimination in their work occasionally moved to the more radical camp of women's rights because of that discrimination. The Sons of Temperance group, which by 1850 had thousands of members nationwide, excluded women from their ranks, but did recognize their counterpart, the Daughters of Temperance. When the Sons of Temperance called a meeting in Albany in 1852, Susan B. Anthony, a temperance advocate from Rochester, attended as a certified Daughter's delegate. When she arose to speak, however, the presiding officer of the convention told her that "sisters were not invited there to speak, but to listen and learn." She and other women delegates, including Elizabeth Cady Stanton, walked out of the convention and held a meeting of their own, where they planned a Woman's State Temperance Convention for the spring. Anthony, a Quaker schoolteacher who had been fired for demanding the same wage that was paid to male teachers at her school, had met Stanton in 1851 when on her way to a temperance meeting. Stanton had spent the years since the Seneca Falls convention publishing articles and letters on temperance, women's issues, antislavery reform efforts, even on dress reform. Dress reform favored Amelia Bloomer's costume called *bloomers* (full trousers worn underneath a short skirt). Stanton, Bloomer, and others argued against the "tight lacing" of corsets that restricted women's breathing and affected their health, but which most women put on to fit into the fashionable clothing of the day—five yards of material, hoops, and petticoats that weighed upward of twelve pounds. Stanton, who wore bloomers for several years until she bowed to public criticism and stopped, became fast friends with Anthony, her coworker in the cause of women's rights for the next fifty years. Anthony, who remained unmarried, rented the halls and gave the speeches. Stanton, married with seven children born between 1842 and 1859, shared her substantial intellect as she could. "How much do I long to be free from housekeeping and children," she wrote to Anthony in April of 1852, "so as to have some time to read and think and write. But it may be well for me to understand all the trials of woman's lot, that I may more eloquently proclaim them when the time comes."

THE ANTEBELLUM SOUTH

Women who wanted to be involved in political life or reform efforts in the antebellum South found themselves without as many of the public forums Northern women activists enjoyed. Fewer cities, fewer churches, and fewer factories meant fewer places women could gather together, learn from each other, or act in concert. The ideal of True Womanhood that helped direct the work of women reformers was different in the South as well. There, the Cult of True Womanhood was a *Cult of White Womanhood*, manifested as the "Southern Lady." The Southern Lady had all the qualities of the American True Woman—piety, purity, domesticity, and submissiveness, with a critical additional quality that was always emphasized: she was white. This stress on racial purity had a sexual component that had consequences throughout Southern society.

The Southern Lady

From the 1840s on, Southerners faced increasing attacks on their "peculiar institution," as they called slavery, and they hunkered down for a fight. To control slaves, Southerners had long instituted a rigid and racist patriarchal society, allowing little criticism and less freedom. Despite the fears that slaveowners had regarding liberties that slaves might take if not strictly controlled by male overseers and owners, the Southern economy demanded a degree of autonomy for women. When the master of a plantation was away, his wife was in charge. Deemed the "plantation mistress," she was responsible for the care of her own family, of slaves and their families, and for the complicated management of daily life on the plantation, while at the same time maintaining the racial separation and moral superiority required of the Southern Lady. The task was not easy. As historian Anne Firor Scott pointed out, ideal Southern ladies lived on pedestals, while plantation mistresses worked hard. Plantations were large farms producing crops, livestock, and goods for sale, and had many "hands" at work, and these elite white women supervised major enterprises. Depending on the size of the plantation, for instance, clothing manufacture alone could reach near-industrial proportions. In addition, because many plantation owners ran businesses in town to help fund their farms, and men's trips to conduct business often lasted weeks or months, their wives often found themselves running plantations alone. Under these circumstances, *feme covert* status was a tremendous hindrance to operating plantations. Nevertheless, wives rarely gained their husbands' support to plead for *feme sole* trader status, since part of the Southern ideal was that men took care of their wives. Southern Ladies were not independent women.

THE SOUTHERN LADY Anna Calhoun Clemson, daughter of Sen. John C. Calhoun of South Carolina, epitomized both True Womanhood and the Southern Lady. Beautiful and accomplished, she graduated from a women's academy in Columbia, South Carolina. Her father valued her education, but cautioned her to remain in the private sphere, writing to her in March 1832 that he was "not one of those who think your sex ought to have nothing to do with politicks. They have as much interest in the good condition of their country, as the other sex, tho' it would be unbecoming them to take an active part in political struggles."

Regardless of the work they did, plantation mistresses were part of a strict hierarchical system, under the control and supervision of their husbands, fathers, or brothers. Only God stood above these white men, but it was a God used by white men to support their ideas regarding the proper roles for women and African Americans. Plantation mistresses were expected to be True Women of spotless reputations. Despite the close daily interactions that occurred between slaveowners and the enslaved, plantation mistresses were expected to maintain an absolute racial divide, treating all blacks as inferiors and regarding black men as sexual predators. Thus, day in and day out, plantation mistresses maintained the slave system.

Some embraced this role and reinforced slavery throughout their lives. When Harriet Beecher Stowe, a Northern abolitionist, published the antislavery novel *Uncle Tom's Cabin* in 1852, Southern Lady Louisa S. C. McCord took exception. Not only were there pious Christian slaveholders, argued McCord, but they thought it was "not expedient only, but right, holy and just" to be so, "for the good of the slave." The absolute power plantation mistresses exercised over slaves, however, could lead to scenes of unimaginable cruelty. One slave recalled a mistress who had preferred "instruments of torture" such as an oak club she used on slaves' hands and feet. When she could not lay her hands on it, "she could relish a beating with a chair, the broom, tongs, shovel, shears, knife-handle, the heavy heel of her slipper, or a bunch of keys." Another slave recalled that her mistress wanted to whip a slave late in her pregnancy, and had a hole dug out in the ground to accommodate the slave's swollen belly so she could lie face down on the ground for her whipping. Determined to exercise control, many plantation mistresses did not hesitate to use physical force against their slaves.

For others, slaveholding was not always easy. Some women, whose slaves waited on them when they were sick, nursed their babies, took care of their children, and tended to their intimate physical needs, found treating these slaves as inferiors more contradictory. "Slavery is indeed a fearful evil; a canker in the bud of our national prosperity; a bitter drop in the cup of domestic felicity," Mrs. Virginia Randolph Cary had written in her book, *Letters on Female Character*, published in 1828 in Richmond. Later writers grew more cautious about criticizing slavery amid growing fears regarding abolition and slave rebellions in the South. Some Southern women, for instance, promoted not abolition but colonization, and advocated sending freed slaves to Africa. By the 1850s, Virginian Anne Rice had sent a number of her slaves to Liberia, the colony founded by the American Colonization Society. At the same time, she apologized to a friend for her antislavery views since they were so at odds with the rest of her culture. Most plantation mistresses probably accepted a situation that they had little power to change and that brought them privilege and their husbands and sons wealth.

The proximity of elite white Southern Ladies to black male slaves disturbed white men, terrified that "their" white women might be attacked by or attracted to black men. The sexual double standard that presumed it was acceptable for men to have sex outside of marriage held true in the South, as did the belief that enslaved women had no right to refuse their masters' sexual advances. Southern white men regarded black women as their property and maintained they had the right to sexually abuse and rape their slaves—and they did so. Nonslaveholding white men also forced themselves on black women. At the same time, white men were convinced enslaved men could not be trusted anywhere near Southern Ladies or any white woman. Southern white men believed that black men had great sexual potency and were overwhelmingly and uncontrollably attracted to white women. Most of this irrational fear stemmed from white men's own behavior since, as South Carolinian Mary Chesnut, a famous diarist, pointed out in 1861, "This is *only* what I see: like the patriarchs of old, our men live all in one house with their wives & their concubines, & the Mulattos one sees in every family exactly resemble the white children—& every lady tells you who is the father of all the Mulatto children in everybody's household, but those in her own, she seems to think drop from the clouds or pretends so to think—. . . . Thank God for my countrywomen—alas for the men! No worse than men everywhere, but the lower their mistresses, the more degraded they must be." More was at work here than just the sexual double standard that allowed men sexual freedom but viewed such behavior by white women as indecent and unnatural (and certainly not "ladylike"). Racial slavery made Southern society a powder keg regarding sexual issues at the same time that it reinforced the power of whites who owned slaves. Enslaved women, in particular, had few resources to aid them and paid a terrible price for this system.

The well-to-do white woman who became a Southern Lady derived considerable benefits from the system, but there were costs for her as well. Life for elite white women in the South was complicated by racial slavery, by men fearing interracial relationships between white women and black men; by men determined to control uprisings by inferiors, be they slaves or women; by men opposed to women exhibiting any signs of independence. Consequently, white women in the South faced a more rigid and patriarchal society than did Northern or Western women. To be a "lady" in Southern society was to be part of a rigid, sexist, patriarchal, racist Cult of White Womanhood, separated from both white male society and from black society, including black women.

Yeoman Women of the South

Plantation mistresses represented only a tiny part of Southern white womanhood, as statistics make clear. In 1860, there were nearly 1.5 million white families in the South. Of these, fewer than 400,000, or one in four, owned slaves, and only one in eight owned more than five slaves. In a largely agricultural society where wealth depended on the ownership of land and slave labor, most white women occupied low rungs on the economic ladder. Always higher in the social order than slaves or free blacks, these white women were the wives of small or *yeoman* farmers, and many were poor. Their poverty did not make them oppose slavery, however. Instead, poor whites supported this racial system, believing themselves superior to any black person. Even the poorest whites, who were looked down upon as white trash or "crackers" by their social betters and were usually unable to improve their lot in life, could still feel superior to—and oppress—black people.

Poor whites and those with a bit of property might make enough money to raise their social and economic status someday. In the South this translated into buying or hiring slave labor so that the farm wife could stay in the house, just like a lady, instead of going into the fields to work. Many yeoman farm families worked toward the day when they could enter the ranks of slaveowners. But simply owning a slave did not make a woman a Southern Lady. The rigidity of Southern culture and its traditions tended to exclude nearly anyone who was not born into ladyhood from ever gaining this exalted status. The circle of elite Southern society was small, and kept that way, often through marriages among neighbors and kin. These marriages created dynasties, further concentrating wealth and power in the hands of a few.

The reality of Southern women's lives, even among the elite, was hard. White women married younger in the South, on average at age 20, compared to 24 in the North, and elite women usually married even earlier. Marriage was more important for Southern white women than elsewhere in the nation because there were fewer options for unmarried women to care for themselves. There were fewer jobs in factories, domestic servants were black, not white, and, by definition, Southern Ladies did not work outside their homes. White women who remained single in their twenties and thirties served their families by doing the tasks too onerous or unpleasant to be done by other family members, such as caring for sick kin, doing the household sewing, attending to children. These women often lived a peripatetic life with no homes of their own and were usually pitied. "Alas," wrote one Southern lady in a family letter, "Cousin Sarah is well, but not married."

Life in the South for white women and men both generally was more unhealthy than in the North, and women, as the primary health care providers for families, suffered proportionately. Death rates were higher because of the hot and humid climate that bred hosts of mosquitoes carrying malaria and yellow fever. In 1819 in New Orleans, more than 2,000 people died from yellow fever; in 1853, nearly 8,000 died. A combination of factors led to higher maternal and infant mortality rates in the South than in the North. Southern white women had less information about and less access to effective birth control (withdrawal, douches, and condoms were the most common methods), and had higher rates of childbirth. Infant mortality rates were higher because the climate was so unhealthy and because so many women gave birth to too many children at an early age or bore too many children within in a short span of years. Men whose wives died in childbirth usually remarried, and the cycle of high infant and maternal mortality continued. Having children was critical for a rural society, where more hands meant more labor. It was also crucial in a patriarchal society, since property owners wanted children, preferably sons, to inherit their land and slaves.

Southern white women also tended to have less education than Northern women, who in turn were less educated than Northern men. Daughters of plantation owners attended "dame schools" on the plantation, and girlfriends from neighboring plantations might join them by day or attend as boarders. Older girls might go to one of the female academies located throughout the South. There were a surprisingly high number of academies for young ladies, even in the Deep South. Historian Loyce Miles found hundreds of secondary schools for young women in the three states of Louisiana, Mississippi, and Alabama. The curricula of these schools ranged from little more than needlepoint and watercolors to that of schools such as Milton Academy in Alabama, where young girls received the same classical education studied by boys the same age. Fears that educating young women might be unsettling to the patriarchy were assuaged by comments such as those of Sallie Reneau, who testified before the Mississippi state legislature in favor of women's education. In 1856, emphasizing the True Woman ideal, she said, "We are not teaching women to demand the rights of men nor to invade the place of men. The conditions are supplied here for the higher training of the mind, of the sensibilities of her aesthetic faculties, and of the moral and religious parts of her being." Despite the fact that all young women could benefit from such training, the social hierarchy maintained itself in terms of education, too. Elites and daughters of yeoman farmers were educated, poor whites and slaves generally were denied any education beyond the basics required to perform their assigned labor. Slaves were expressly forbidden from learning to read.

Religion was more important than education for women in the South, and Southern women of all classes were encouraged to express their piety through service to the church. By 1850, however, some powerful Southern men had become concerned that women's religious devotion might lead to problems. In the North, churches were becoming hotbeds of abolitionism and other reform activities, and planters feared the same might happen in the South. Consequently, they began restricting their wives' activities by encouraging them to limit their church attendance to Sundays and urging them to make their religious observances more private. They also passed laws forbidding slave women from attending church—or any other meeting where slaves might plan an insurrection. Restricting the ways that women gathered and exchanged information and ideas was only one of the ways that Southern planters used to make sure that the society they dominated stayed just the way it was—with them entrenched at the top and in control.

THE CIVIL WAR

Southern slavery contributed greatly to the rise in sectional tensions in the 1840s and 1850s, as did increasingly strident political partisanship. Many Americans began to oppose extending slavery into the western lands as they organized into territories. The Liberty Party ran an antislavery candidate, James Birney, for president in 1840 and again in 1844. After the

Mexican-American War ended and millions of acres were added to the Union, the Free-Soil Party took up the cause in 1848, nominating former president Martin Van Buren on a platform that called for prohibiting any slavery in any new territories, confining the practice instead to the Southern states where it already existed. Van Buren lost to President Zachary Taylor, but the Free-Soil Party continued its drive to limit slavery, fighting for the cause throughout the congressional debates that produced the Compromise of 1850.

The Compromise of 1850 organized the lands gained from Mexico and passed a new stricter *Fugitive Slave Act* to return escaped slaves to their owners, a measure excoriated by Northerners but demanded by Southerners who were increasingly fearful that slavery would be banned by the federal government. The political din quieted only momentarily. Free-Soilers continued to protest any extension of slavery, nominating John P. Hale for president in 1852. Hale lost, as did Whig Party candidate Winfield Scott to Democrat Franklin Piere, but the election also destroyed the Whig Party, the major political party that had opposed the Jacksonian Democrats since the 1830s. Such a loss marked the end as well of the period when politicians could compromise over the issue of slavery in the territories. A new, more sectional party replaced the Whigs, and in 1856 the Republican Party took its place in the race for the presidency. Republicans represented Northerners who opposed the extension of slavery. Politicians who had always managed to resolve questions over slavery extension with political means now faced partisanship far more sectional and far more unyielding. Their ability to compromise also fell before the deaths of the great statesmen of the past—John. C. Calhoun, Henry Clay, and Daniel Webster—as well as a series of weak presidents—Millard Fillmore, Franklin Pierce, and James Buchanan. By the end of the decade, the country's political system, facing critical questions regarding the government's right to interfere with the institution of slavery, would collapse into civil war.

The Road to War

As the country struggled with the effects of the Compromise of 1850, Southern and Northern women increasingly divided over the issue of slavery. The Compromise had come about when lands added to the United States after the Mexican-American War had to be organized. The South, desperate to preserve slavery and hoping for new slave states, agreed to allow the new territories to use popular sovereignty to decide for themselves to be free or slave, but insisted on a stronger Fugitive Slave Act in return. The government's first Fugitive Slave Act, passed in 1793, had long been ignored by slavery opponents in Northern states. Some states had even passed "personal liberty laws," forbidding local officials to capture and return escaped slaves. The new Fugitive Slave Act, in contrast, required citizens to help capture and return slaves or face fines and jail time. In addition, anyone could accuse any African American of being a slave, and the new act provided no way for the accused to defend themselves. There was no right to a lawyer, no right to a jury, no way to prove one was free. For escaped slave women living in the North, the act had even more sinister effects than for men. Because children inherited the legal status of their mothers, rather than their fathers, enslaved women's children were as much at risk of reenslavement as the women themselves. Often people were surprised by the revelation that their spouses were escaped slaves. Men and women both left for Canada, where slavery was illegal, and some families even broke apart as women fled with their children and left their husbands behind.

Opposition to the Fugitive Slave Act in the North was vociferous, and arguments over abolition, colonization, the nonextension of slavery into the new territories, and the role of Congress in these matters soon took precedence over all other reform issues. In Virginia, for example, those who worked for temperance, moral reform, and colonization found their efforts dismissed by Northern reformers who could not accept reform efforts from people they regarded as slaveholders. Just as Southern politicians became increasingly isolated in the halls of government, so Southern women reformers found themselves frustrated in their attempts to explain the South as it really was, particularly after the publication of Harriet Beecher Stowe's *Uncle Tom's Cabin*. The best-selling novel, published in 1852, painted a portrait of slavery so distasteful and so compelling that the South's sectional identity became further solidified as racist, sexist, and unyielding to morality or reason.

In the North, reformers continued other efforts, but public attention began to focus on abolitionists. Great orators appeared on the lecture circuit, of whom Sojourner Truth was perhaps the best known. A former slave from New York State who had been born Isabella Baumfree, she became an itinerant preacher in 1843, and tied women's rights and antislavery issues together in her speeches during the 1850s. Legend credits her with giving a speech that vividly illustrated the link between the two causes. In it, Truth was said to have declared,

> That man over there [a preacher arguing against women speaking against slavery and for woman's rights] says that women need to be helped into carriages and lifted over ditches and to have the best place everywhere. Nobody ever helps me into carriages, or over mud-puddles, or gives me any best place! And ain't I a woman? I have ploughed and planted and gathered into barns and no man could head me! And ain't I a woman? I have borne thirteen children, and seen them almost all sold off to slavery, and when I cried out with my mother's grief, none but Jesus heard—and ain't I a woman? . . . That little man in black there, he says women can't have as much rights as men, 'cause Christ wasn't a woman! Where did your Christ come from? . . . From God and a woman! Man had nothing to do with Him.

The speech was, in fact, a later creation by a woman's rights advocate Frances Dana Gage, but the ideas expressed in it were ones that Truth used in speeches throughout the 1850s as she traveled the antislavery circuit. By the mid-1850s, Truth became a symbol used by antislavery activists to support the abolition of slavery as she continued to speak out in favor of the emancipation of slaves and women's rights.

Truth was but one of many African American abolitionists growing more active during the 1850s. Marylander Harriet Tubman had escaped slavery herself and then led over 300 other slaves to freedom along the Underground Railroad. When the Fugitive Slave Act passed, Tubman moved her family from Philadelphia to Canada to avoid recapture, but she continued to return to the South to lead others to freedom. By 1856, Southern planters had a price on her head of $40,000 (comparable to $750,000 today) for her capture, dead or alive. Free black women also played an important role in promoting abolition. Mary Ann Shadd Cary, a free Delaware resident who had worked for the Underground Railroad, moved with her brother Isaac to Canada after the Fugitive Slave Act was passed. She wrote a tract, *Notes of Canada West*, urging other free blacks and fugitive slaves to come to safety there. In 1856, she married Thomas F. Cary and had two children but continued her activism. She opened a racially integrated school, relying in part on the American Missionary Association, one of the many religious reform groups at the time, for support. She founded a newspaper, *The Provincial Freeman*, to provide information to expatriate black Americans. She traveled back to the United States to deliver lectures and to gather information to counter rumors spread by opponents that black emigrants to Canada were starving. Another free black, Frances Harper, a poet, writer and lecturer, published many of the stories of escaped slaves to publicize the distress of the enslaved and to garner support for the cause of abolition.

Much of politics in the 1850s narrowed in purpose, focusing on slavery and whether it should be abolished or preserved, and American women had plenty to say on both sides of the issue. But other issues continued attracting women's interest and moving them to public actions. Ten annual woman's rights conventions, held between 1850 and 1860, provided platforms for continuing discussion of civil and political rights for women. The passage of the Maine Law in 1851 prohibited any consumption or sale of alcohol in the state, and gave hope to women temperance advocates. Five other states followed Maine's lead in the 1850s, and thousands of American women joined temperance groups. Education reformers continued to promote women's education, building "normal" schools to train women to be teachers in tax-supported public schools, designed in part to Americanize immigrants. By 1852, public schooling was mandatory in Massachusetts, providing teaching opportunities for women graduates of normal schools. Better treatment for people imprisoned or mentally ill became an international crusade for Dorothea Dix and her supporters when she traveled to England, Scotland, France, Russia, Turkey, and other nations to inspect their jails and almshouses and to suggest new techniques. Women's participation in national politics continued as "Whig women," who had marched and campaigned for candidates in the 1840s, searched for a new partisan political home after the decline and end of the Whig Party in the 1850s. The Know-Nothing Party, an anti-immigrant, anti-Catholic group, for example, accepted women's participation in their mass meetings, and the Republican Party also attracted many women. Jessie Benton Frémont, wife of the 1856 Republican candidate for president, John C. Frémont, worked as his campaign manager and was so popular with crowds that the cry was for "Frémont and Jessie, too!" After her husband lost the election to Democrat James Buchanan, Jessie and John moved to California where he lost the family fortune and she supported the family, writing a best-selling history of his adventures under his name. Women in another far-western region, Utah Territory, dealt with armed conflict. In 1857, Mormon women in Utah faced the unpleasant prospect of war over their church's stance on polygamy as U.S. troops arrived to put a new non-Mormon territorial governor in place. Over 30,000 people left their homes and were relocated by church leaders as part of the "Utah War," when, as the platform of the 1856 Republican Party put it, U.S. troops fought to rid America of "the twin relics of barbarism—polygamy and slavery."

The issue of slavery, however, remained central to American political and social life, and it was not going to go away. The South feared abolition of the institution would follow the election of Republican Abraham Lincoln

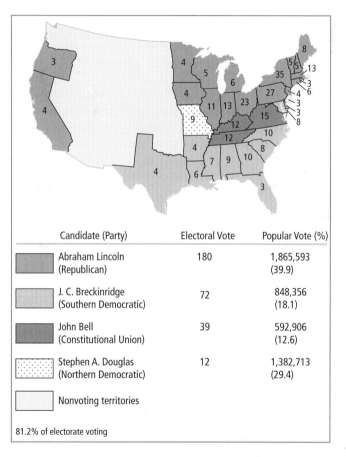

Candidate (Party)	Electoral Vote	Popular Vote (%)
Abraham Lincoln (Republican)	180	1,865,593 (39.9)
J. C. Breckinridge (Southern Democratic)	72	848,356 (18.1)
John Bell (Constitutional Union)	39	592,906 (12.6)
Stephen A. Douglas (Northern Democratic)	12	1,382,713 (29.4)
Nonvoting territories		

81.2% of electorate voting

MAP OF THE ELECTION OF 1860 The election of 1860 foreshadowed the division of the country in 1861. The Confederacy included Tennessee and Virginia; the Border States—Kentucky, Missouri, Maryland, and Delaware—remained with the Union. Woman politico Anna Ella Carroll had no doubt, she wrote to Maryland governor. Thomas Hicks, that Lincoln's election would "lead to an attempt on the part of the Southern leaders to dissolve this Union."

in November 1860. Lincoln, a purely sectional candidate, won with less than 40 percent of the popular vote, an amount less than the percentage won by losing major-party candidates in previous elections. Lincoln had campaigned on the Republicans' platform of opposing the extension of slavery into the territories. Southerners viewed such limits on their property as an unconstitutional attack on their property rights and argued that the North should desist, or the federal union should be dissolved. Ever hasty, South Carolinians voted to secede from the Union on December 20, 1860. Ten other states followed them and declared themselves to be the Confederate States of America. The Civil War began in April 1861, as Lincoln tried to bring the rebellious states back into the Union and the Confederacy tried to make itself into an independent nation.

Women in the War

As in other American wars, women played different roles in the Civil War depending on their geographic location and proximity to battles, their economic and social class, and their political and philosophical views. White women in the far western territories, for example, were not much affected by the great battles that raged in the East, but as Union troops were recalled from the far West to serve in the armies in the East, the transfer of troops threatened the security of those white families remaining in the region. A Sioux uprising in 1862 in Minnesota Territory, for example, took place when it did because so many young white men had left the area to fight the Civil War. Angered by treaty violations that included the government's failure to pay them their promised annuities and facing starvation as a result, the Dakota Sioux went to war against the remaining Americans in the region. Forty thousand settlers fled, and 107 captives were taken, mostly women and children, before the Sioux were defeated and 38 Indians were hanged. In 1864, fearful of Indian resistance in Colorado, sparked in part by troop withdrawals to fight the Civil War, a small U.S. cavalry unit led by a confirmed Indian-hater, Colonel John Chivington, attacked the Arapaho and Cheyenne Indians camping on protected land at Sand Creek. The Native men were away hunting; Chivington and his troops killed mostly women and their children. These atrocities and others affected both white and Native women in the western territories, while in the East, the Civil War and its battles tore apart the lives of women there.

The geographic proximity of eastern women to the fighting often affected their daily activities. When the Union instituted a blockade of Southern ports, imported goods that Southern women had relied on for years became unavailable. As battles raged in towns across the Southern states, women faced destruction of their property and attacks on both themselves and their slaves. Women on both sides who had relatives in the war suffered the anguish of the loss of their men, or of not knowing their fates. Regardless of geography, however, women everywhere became involved in the war in various ways: through their opposition to or support for slavery; through "sanitary" and nursing work; through paid labor; through service in the military; and in the role women have always held in wartime—through managing house and home while waiting for men to return.

Leading women of the American antislavery societies continued their work during the war. President Lincoln had declared the war to be one to preserve the Union, but when he met Harriet Beecher Stowe, author of the antislavery novel *Uncle Tom's Cabin*, he shook her hand and said, "so you're the little lady who wrote the book that started this great war." The war might have been to save the Union at first, but abolitionists saw it as the perfect opportunity to rid the United States of slavery. Matilda Joslyn Gage, a woman's rights advocate and abolitionist whose home near Syracuse, New York, was a stop on the Underground Railroad, continued to hide escaped slaves until the end of the war. Julia Ward Howe, another abolitionist, wrote a poem later put to music as the popular "Battle Hymn of the Republic," a song replete with religious imagery that declared the Union's role was to fight to free the slave: "As Christ died to make men holy, let us die to make men free." Others worked teaching freed blacks and escaped slaves. Emily Howland in upstate New York educated African Americans who came through her community on the Underground Railroad. Susie King Taylor, a former slave, escaped to St. Simon's Island off the coast of Georgia as soon as it was under Union occupancy and worked not only as a nurse and laundress for the 33rd United States Colored Troops of the Union Army, but also as a teacher of the unit's soldiers. Charlotte Forten, the Philadelphia writer and abolitionist, was another African American who served her people as a teacher in areas occupied by Union troops and filled with escaped slaves. Union authorities deemed these refugees "contraband of war" so that they would not have to be returned to their owners, and Lincoln proclaimed the end of slavery in the areas rebelling against the Union with the Emancipation Proclamation of January 1, 1863.

This proclamation changed the nature and *raison d'etre* of the war from one to preserve the Union to a war to end slavery. Abolitionists who were also woman's rights advocates postponed much of their work on women's rights in favor of working for emancipation until the war's end. Susan B. Anthony and Elizabeth Cady Stanton, who had joined forces in 1850, focused their efforts on passing a Thirteenth Amendment to the Constitution that would ban slavery completely. They formed the National Women's Loyal League in 1863 to further that goal. Five thousand members collected 400,000 signatures, gaining valuable experience that they would use in the suffrage movement after the war. The amendment passed in January 1865, and was ratified by the end of the year.

Northern women also undertook what was termed "sanitary" work in their wartime activities. The massive amounts of materiel needed to pursue the war strained the resources of the U.S. Army, and the U.S. Sanitary Commission was formed in 1861 to provide volunteer services to supplement the army. Along with the Woman's Central Relief Association, the commission raised funds and collected supplies to ship to armies in the field by holding giant "sanitary fairs" in major cities, where they sold goods, held raffles and auctions, and collected items for the soldiers. The Sanitary

MARIE RAVENEL DE LA COSTE
OF SAVANNAH

One of the saddest duties nurses faced was writing to families whose sons and husbands had died. One Civil War song, written by Marie Revenal de la Coste of Savannah after her service in a Georgia hospital, titled "Somebody's Darling," expresses with pathos the sorrow felt by women nursing wounded men who often died far from home.

"Into the ward of the clean white-washed halls,
Where the dead slept and the dying lay;

Commission also sold and provided medical supplies to armies, provided hospitals, inspected camp sites for proper hygiene, and nursed the wounded. All this was necessary because the army was far too small to do these duties by itself at the beginning of the war. With nearly 3 million men, North and South, mobilized over the course of the war, civilian participation, particularly by women, was absolutely essential.

Soldiers' Aid Societies in the North and Ladies' Aid Societies (and, later, the Women's Relief Society of the Confederate States, organized in 1864) in the South also sprang up to assist the soldiers of their respective sides. Ladies might gather for tea and cookies and a sewing bee at first, but soon they gathered to roll bandages, prepare slings, and fashion wound dressings to ship to the front. Women also shipped food supplies to supplement the army rations of hard tack (a dried cracker), dried beef, dessicated (dried) vegetables, and coffee. The experiences women had prior to the war in voluntary organizations, more often in the North than in the South, benefited them as they organized to supply soldiers the delicacies and necessities from home that reminded them what they were fighting for.

Nursing attracted numerous women during the war as well. While women's roles at home had long included nursing family members, no nursing profession existed for women in the 1800s until the Civil War. A British role model existed for women who wanted to help: the British nurse, Florence Nightingale, who had served in the Crimean War from 1854 to 1856 in Turkey. Deemed the "Lady with the Lamp" by the British press, Nightingale practically single-handedly cleaned up the medical system for wounded soldiers in the British troop hospitals, and returned to England where she used applied statistics to reform medical care there. In the United States, President Lincoln appointed Dorothea Dix as Superintendent of Army Nurses on April 20, 1861, and she became head of the first official nursing group in the U.S. Army Medical Department. Dix was eager to help, but had to proceed carefully. The Cult of True Womanhood could scarcely allow women to see wounded, naked, and bleeding men, much less care for them in the forced intimacy that nursing required. Male doctors also resisted, preferring the traditional army stewards who had served the army as nurses for years, despite their lack of training.

Wounded by bayonets, sabers and balls,
Somebody's darling was borne one day.
Somebody's darling, so young and so
  brave,
Wearing still on his sweet yet pale face,
Soon to be hid in the dust of the grave,
The lingering light of his boyhood's
  grace.

Chorus:
Somebody's darling, somebody's pride,
Who'll tell his mother where her boy
  died?"

Source: Adapted from *Library of Southern Literature,* ed. Charles Alphonso Smith, vol. 14 (Atlanta: Martin and Hoyt Company, 1907), 6119.

The doctors could order stewards about, since they outranked them, but civilian women caused problems. Practical experience meant that women argued with male doctors and refused to administer treatment they knew would cause greater trouble. Dix also worried that some young women would volunteer to serve as nurses while in search of potential husbands. Consequently, she would not take on anyone under thirty-five, and only women who were "matronly persons of experience, good conduct, or superior education and serious disposition."

She should have listed "white" as another prerequisite. African American women seeking to volunteer, as well as white women Dix had refused to hire, worked as individuals volunteering their time and efforts, rather than being employed—and paid—by the Union. Numbers of free black women did find paid employment as laundresses and cooks in army hospitals, however. Over the course of the war, some 21,208 Union women served with pay in military hospitals; unknown numbers of free black and white women volunteers served troops in the field as well as in hospitals without pay. Many Confederate records did not survive the war, but references to women's service for the Southern cause include Phoebe Pember of South Carolina, who served as the matron of Chimborazo Hospital in Richmond, Virginia. Sally Louisa Tompkins ran a friend's Richmond house as a hospital at the request of the Confederate government after the First Battle of Bull Run in 1861. When the Confederate government shifted from privately run to government-run hospitals, Confederate president Jefferson Davis made Tompkins a captain in the army so that she could continue to run her hospital. It boasted the highest proportion of injured men returned to the ranks of any other Confederate hospital. "Captain Sally" was paid by the government, which helped offset some of the personal expenses she incurred in running the hospital. Most women who worked as volunteers were never reimbursed for their contributions to the war effort, nor compensated for the hours spent tending the wounded and dying (see Primary Source 5-4).

The most famous Civil War nurse was Clara Barton. Rejected by Dix and determined to serve, Barton gathered supplies and occasionally a helper, and traveled to battle sites on her own. She was often in harm's way as she tried to care for men on the field. At the battle of Antietam in

September 1862, for instance, a bullet tore through her dress and killed the soldier she was holding. Her work in the field lasted for most of the war, and afterward, she set up an office in Washington to try to determine the fates of soldiers missing in action and to notify their families.

Barton had been a clerk in the Patent Office in Washington when the war broke out. A number of women were similarly employed in the nation's capitol, and as men first volunteered and later were drafted for service, women moved into their jobs with alacrity. The pay was far better than in traditional women's jobs—fifty dollars a month—but room and board in a city at war ate up most of it. Women were essential in the labor force during the war, no matter the pay. "Treasury girls," as they were known in both the Union and Confederacy, ran the printing presses, kept government records, and clerked in government offices. Women replaced men in other industries as well. Ninety-five percent of the millworkers in the New England factories were women by 1862. Teaching became a woman's profession as well, as 1 in every 12 adult males in the nation went to war. Even in the South, where women factory workers were uncommon, the war changed things. In Richmond, for example, white working-class women found jobs making cartridges at the Brown's Island Ordnance Plant. Nearly 300 girls and women worked there, turning out 74 million percussion caps and 72 million small-arms cartridges between 1861 and 1865. The work was dangerous: on March 13, 1863, an explosion killed 43 girls and women—the youngest only 10, and the oldest 67. The event did not dissuade others from seeking a job during the hard economic times caused by the war. As the factory reopened after burying the dead, 53 women stood outside hoping to be hired.

The most unusual profession that women assumed during the war was that of military service. Some women served as *vivandieres* (a French term meaning "hospitality giver"). They wore feminized versions of the regimental uniforms and became sort of mascots for various units of Louisiana Zouaves, named after the flashy North African/French-style uniforms they wore. *Vivandieres* might work as sutlers, providing a commissary for soldiers to purchase creature comforts; some served as nurses; all carried trademark flasks of brandy or wine to use as needed. A few may have fought in battles, but most seem to have left before the battles started and few appeared after 1861.

More commonly, women fighting in military units disguised themselves as men and served as soldiers. They relied on Victorian modesty and their resemblance to their underage male compatriots to help them pass for men. Mary Livermore, a nurse and member of the U.S. Sanitary Commission, wrote about numerous women soldiers she had heard of. Historians DeAnne Blanton and Lauren Cook have discovered hundreds who disguised themselves as men to join the army, usually following their husbands or sweethearts, but oftentimes joining up just for the adventure of it. Sarah Rosetta Wakeman, a New Yorker who had disguised herself in 1862 to earn a better living than she could as a woman, joined the service as Lyons Wakeman. In February 1864, she marched with her unit to the Red River campaign in Arkansas, but died on the way of dysentery and was buried in Louisiana. Her identity remained unknown until 1994, when Cook discovered and published her letters to her family. Southerner Loreta Velazquez served the Confederacy as Lt. Harry Buford, and went on the lecture circuit to tell of her adventures to an admiring public after the war. Mrs. S. M. R. Blaylock, having served for two weeks beside her husband in the 26th North Carolina Infantry, revealed her identity after her husband was discharged so that she too could return home. Mary Scaberry, alias Charles Freeman, of the 52nd Ohio Infantry was found, upon admission to the hospital for a fever, to suffer from a sexual "incompatibility"—her gender. Albert D. J. Cashier, on the other hand, was never found out to be Jennie Hodgers, and served the entire war from 1862 until 1865. She continued the charade after the war; not until her leg was fractured in 1911 did doctors discover that she was a woman.

Women served not only in disguise as soldiers, but also as spies. Belle Boyd, a teenager, served General Thomas "Stonewall" Jackson in the Shenandoah Valley as a courier between Confederate troops and generals. Arrested six times and imprisoned twice, she persuaded her last Union captor to marry her and defect from the Union. She escaped to England, wrote her memoirs, and like Velazquez, related her thrilling adventures on stage

HARRIET TUBMAN Despite lifelong seizures caused by a head wound inflicted on her by an overseer, Harriet Tubman served her country as a nurse, a spy, and a scout during the Civil War. In 1863, she helped lead an armed assault against South Carolina river plantations by black Union soldiers, rescuing over 700 slaves.

ELLEN MORGAN WRITES TO HER CONFEDERATE SOLDIER HUSBAND

Ellen and Henry Morgan lived in Claiborne Parish, Louisiana. Henry served with the Confederate Army from 1862 until 1865. Ellen spoke of trying to send him food in her letters—the Confederacy was short of everything by the spring of 1865. She missed her husband and longed for him to return to their farm. He came back after the war was over, but she and their son Charley had died of typhoid fever a week before his return.

Dear Henry,

I seat myself this evening to let you know that wee ar well and i hope this will find you enjoying the same blessing. Henry i got the letter you sent. . . . i have nothing to write only wee hear pease talk on every side. I hope and pray to God that it may bee so. Henry I have no idey of coming down thair now. Henry our corn is as clean as it can be. Henry you [don't] need to think that i don't think of you when i am eating for you are never off my mind. Henry i am glad to send you soemthing to eat. . . . Henry i wish you was hear to knight. I have a churn of butter milk and a fine chance buter and too hundrad eggs. . . . I intend you shall have some of them. Henry if it had been in my pour [power] you wood have had something to eat long ago. I think of you all day and dream of you at knight. Henry your wheat is find. Your oates is tolerbel. . . . Henry you

after the war. Rose O'Neal Greenhow, another spy for the Confederates, lived in Washington, DC. Her parlor was popular with politicians and served as a central locale for military information and political gossip that Greenhow then transmitted south. Arrested and deported to Richmond, she was eventually dispatched to England by Confederate President Davis. She came back to the United States in 1864, bearing information for Davis, but her ship ran aground and her lifeboat swamped in heavy seas. The gold she had hidden in her skirts for the Confederacy dragged her down to her death.

Noted actress and Union spy Pauline Cushman publicly declared her Southern sympathies, but actually served as a double agent for the Union. She was on the way to being hanged after she having been found out, when Union forces rescued her in the nick of time. Cushman's information was so valuable that she was commissioned a major in the U.S. Army to ensure she would continue her work. Harriet Tubman also worked, not only as a spy, but also as a nurse, a scout, and a recruiter for the Union Army. She received an official commendation, but no pay for her services. Elizabeth Van Lew was another double agent for the Union. A local resident, she visited Union prisoners in Richmond's Libby Prison. There she helped some prisoners escape, and assisted others who had been newly captured and still had valuable information regarding troop numbers, strengths, and locations they wanted to transmit to the Union. Van Lew also gathered information from Jefferson Davis's home by infiltrating it with one of her former servants, and she hid messages to Union General Ulysses Grant in eggs that she sent to him in baskets of farm produce.

ought to see Charley walking. He lockes so sweet a-walking. Henry thar is a heap of sickness here . . . the tiford [typhoid] fever. . . . Henry i have an idey of having the potatoe patch whear wee had it year bee fore last. . . . Henry i wish you was hear today. It is a-Sunday and i am at home by myself. May the God of Pease be with you is my prayer. Right soon and often. No more at present onely i remain your trew and affectionate wife untill death. E.P. Morgan

April 16, 1865

Dear Henry

I seat myself to let you know that i am not well at this time. I am afraid that i am going to have the fever. I feel so bad i haven't been abel to do much this week. I am abel to be up. Charley fell out doars yesterday and like to kild him. He has bin frentful ever sens. . . . I hope this will find you well. Henry I hante got much to right. . . . Henry i wish that all of the men that dont try to git you boys eney things to eat was thair and had to stay thair till the war ended, that dont care nothing for you all nore your familys. Henry i have no idey you can git anything to eat without i bring it to you. Henry you don't know how bad it hurts me to think you are thar and cant git anuff to eat when you have got plenty at home. . . . henry i will tell you one thing sartin. I want you to come home without fail. . . . i cant send you nothing to eat. I feald mad anuff about not being abel to sen you something to eat that i could whip every man in the Confederacy. Henry I will sen you 5 twists of tobacco. Good by dear man. I hope wee meat again soon. E. Morgan.

Source: *Historic Claiborne*, published by Claiborne Parish [La.] Historical Association, 1962.

A number of Confederate women, particularly in the Border States where many of the Civil War's battles took place, committed sabotage as their contribution to the war effort. Over 120 women were tried by Union military courts for crimes committed in their guerilla campaign against the Union. These women cut telegraph wires and smuggled quinine, opium, blankets, civilian clothing, boots, thread, and all manner of contraband. They informed Confederates of Union troop movements, shot at Union troops, helped Union soldiers desert, smuggled in morale-boosting mail hidden in voluminous petticoats, and worked in bordellos, enticing men to desert or infecting them with sexually transmitted diseases that prevented them from serving out their time.

Women involving themselves in the public sphere during the war were not typical. The vast majority of women, though affected in some way by the war, remained in their homes and kept them going until the men came back. They endured considerable privation. Women in the capital city of Richmond, for example, faced skyrocketing inflation. Bacon that cost $1.25 for ten pounds in 1860 sold for $10 in 1863—an inflation rate of 700 percent. Four pounds of coffee went from 50¢ to $20, a 3,900 percent increase, in the same period. Irate at price-gouging by merchants who took advantage of the shortages caused by the Union blockade, and desperate for supplies to feed and care for their families, women rioted in the streets in March and April of 1863. In seven other communities across the South that spring, women marched on shops, broke down doors, and seized bacon, flour, and coffee, often at gunpoint. Such behavior was incomprehensible to men used to seeing women as Southern Ladies. Richmond city council members, shocked by the violence, complained that the perpetrators were "base and unworthy women" whose actions were "instigated by worthless men," but, two days later, approved a relief program to ease some of their constituents' suffering.

Letters from wives left at home during the war often begged men—husbands, sons, and brothers—to come home just long enough to get the crops in or sown. (See Primary Source 5-5.) Many men deserted to do just that, sometimes returning to their units and sometimes not. In the South, in particular, women who were left behind had to cope with laws that set all slaves, including house-slaves, to work in the fields and that provided only one white man to control every twenty slaves in the population. Since most southern farms had no slaves or fewer than ten slaves, few white men were around, meaning women had not only to get the farm work done, but also had to supervise field hands as well. When the Union Army came close, slaves fled for the Union lines, where they would be immediately freed. White Southern women were often aghast when the slaves left them so abruptly, little understanding the aspirations of enslaved women and men.

White women left behind, North and South, often had to act on their own, and married women continued to suffer from the restrictions of *feme covert* legal status. In some areas, the legal restrictions that bound women were loosened for the course of the war. In one county in Texas, for instance, historian Angela Boswell found court records showing that contracts women signed when acting as *feme sole* during the course of the war were deemed valid but, once the war was over, those same women were restored to *feme covert* status whether or not they wished to be and any independent contracts they tried to sign were declared invalid. As was the case for earlier exceptional circumstances, once the crisis was over, women were expected to return to their appropriate sphere.

The Civil War in America was a time of great trial for American women as well as men. It settled the questions of secession and slavery, but it cost more than 620,000 lives, a number of war deaths greater than all of America's other wars combined. The Civil War also skewed the sex ratio for an entire generation of women, particularly white women in the South; they grew up with fewer men, fewer chances to marry, and fewer opportunities to start their own families. For most African American women, however, the war gave them the single most important right that they had longed for: freedom. Delia Garlic, an Alabama slave during the war, was interviewed years later, her voice recorded in the dialect of the Deep South. "Slavery days was hell," she remembered. "I was growed up when de War come, and I was a mother before it closed. Babies was snatched from deir mother's breast and sold to speculators. Chillens was separated from sisters and brothers and never saw each other again. 'Course dey cry. You think dey not cry when dey was sold like cattle? I could tell you about it all day, but even den you couldn't guess de awfulness of it." Freedom was better, reminisced an ex-slave from Texas, Margrett Nillin. "What I likes bes', to be slave or free? Well, it's dis way. In slavery I owns nothin' and never owns nothin'. In freedom I's own de home and raise de family. All dat causes me worryment and in slavery I has no worryment, but I takes de freedom."

THINK MORE ABOUT IT

1. Return to the opening vignette about Rebecca Neugin, her mother, and others forced to march on the Trail of Tears. How does the story of these Cherokee women exemplify this chapter's themes of the contest over rights that took place during the antebellum era?

2. Define True Womanhood and the Cult of Domesticity. How were these ideals promulgated? How did they affect diverse groups of American women in the mid-nineteenth century? Examine in detail at least three situations for women that challenged the tenets of these ideals.

3. What effects did westward expansion have on diverse groups of women? In addition to the long-term process of increased settlement in the formerly Native lands in the trans-Mississippi West, make reference to such events as the Mexican-American War and the Gold Rush.

4. Trace the rise of the mid-nineteenth-century woman's rights movement, including its key events and the major figures in its development. What were its main aims and principle ideas? Why did the demand for woman suffrage encounter such stiff resistance? In addition to advocating for expanded rights, how else did women participate in the public arena during this era?

5. Compare and contrast the lives of Southern women to those elsewhere in the nation. How did the rigid racial hierarchy of the South, including the institution of chattel slavery, shape the lives of all Southern women and with what consequences?

6. Discuss the following statement: "Although few women in the North or South participated actively in the Civil War, the war had profound effects on most American women, whatever their background and geography." In your discussion, be sure to focus on a range of women, detailing their involvement in wartime activities and the ways that their lives changed as a consequence of this long, deadly, and consequential conflict.

7. What did you learn in this chapter that you did not know before? How does this new information help you understand the overall story of women in American history? What topics would you like to explore further?

READ MORE ABOUT IT

DeAnne Blanton and Lauren M. Cook, *They Fought Like Demons: Women Soldiers in the American Civil War*

Joan E. Cashin, *A Family Venture: Men and Women on the Southern Frontier*

Drew Gilpin Faust, *Mothers of Invention: Women of the Slaveholding South in the American Civil War*

Thavolia Glymph, *Out of the House of Bondage: The Transformation of the Plantation Household*

JoAnn Levy, *They Saw the Elephant: Women in the California Gold Rush*

Megan Marshall, *The Peabody Sisters: Three Women Who Ignited American Romanticism*

Sally McMillen, *Seneca Falls and the Origin of the Women's Rights Movement*

Nell Irvin Painter, *Sojourner Truth: A Life, a Symbol*

Glenda Riley, *Women and Indians on the Frontier, 1825–1915*

Anne Firor Scott, *The Southern Lady: From Pedestal to Politics*

KEY CONCEPTS

Trail Where They Cried/Trail of Tears

True Womanhood

Cult of Domesticity

Manifest Destiny

Godey's Lady's Book

Gold Rush

parlor talks

Married Women's Property Act

Seneca Falls

woman suffrage

Transcendentalism

Declaration of Sentiments

women politicos

domestic feminists

Cult of White Womanhood

Uncle Tom's Cabin

Maine Law

Vivandiere

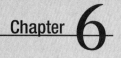

RECONSTRUCTION, RESISTANCE, AND REFORM

Eda Hickam of Missouri

RECONSTRUCTION AND RESISTANCE

Southern Women During Reconstruction
    Primary Source 6-1: Freedman Eliza Files a Claim
Northern Women During Reconstruction
Native American Women in the West
    The Indian Wars
    The Dawes Act

REFORM RETURNS

Women's Education and the Professions
The Woman's Rights Movement
Prohibition and the Woman's Christian Temperance Union
    Primary Source 6-2: Frances Willard Urges Her Followers
        to "Do Everything"
Labor Reform and Resistance
The National Economy and Domesticity
Birth Control and Voluntary Motherhood
    Primary Source 6-3: Harriot Stanton Blatch on
        Voluntary Motherhood
Agrarian Reformers
The Women's Club Movement
African American Women in the Club Movement

THE PANIC OF 1893

THINK MORE ABOUT IT

READ MORE ABOUT IT

KEY CONCEPTS

I n 1890, forty-two-year-old former slave Eda Hickam filed a lawsuit against a white family in Cooper County, Missouri, claiming they had never told her that she had been freed by the Civil War. For twenty-five years, she had lived on an isolated farm in the middle of the state, the only slave of Joseph Hickam. She worked in the house as a domestic and had little contact with the free black community in the area, including her stepfather, her only kin. After the Civil War ended, her owner would not allow her to speak to other African Americans. Once, according to a deposition, an African American named Mr. Cosgrove was passing by the farm, and said hello to Eda as she worked near the woodpile. Her "owner's" son James struck her in the face and warned her against conversing with "no dam free negro." When Eda's stepfather Sam Davis asked after her, not having seen her for many years, Joseph Hickam told him she was fine, but that Davis could not visit her since that would "disturb her."

After Joseph Hickam died in 1889, his family divided his inheritance, a substantial estate of some $7,000, and told Eda she was on her own. She would receive nothing from Joseph Hickam's estate since, the white Hickams

LEADERS IN THE WOMAN'S RIGHTS MOVEMENT   By 1870, woman's rights activists had achieved national notice. This poster portrays seven of the leaders of the movement: orator Anna Dickinson is in the center. Clockwise from the top are abolitionist Lucretia Mott, Elizabeth Cady Stanton, Civil War nurse Mary Livermore, abolitionist Lydia Maria Child, Susan B. Anthony, and writer and peace proponent Grace Greenwood. These women participated in all the major reforms of the era: against capital punishment, for prison reform, against slavery, for woman suffrage, equality in marriage, black suffrage, and more.

argued, Eda had been told of her freedom but had decided to stay with them as unpaid labor, where she was treated like "family." She had received, according to their testimony, "the same kind of grub, and the same kind of clothing." Eda Hickam denied she had ever been told she was free. Instead, she claimed she had been forced to work illegally as a slave for twenty-five years. She wanted to be paid—$5 a month for twenty-five years of labor, plus interest. On January 9, 1890, the probate court awarded Hickam $785, half of what she asked for; after the family appealed, the amount was reduced to zero.

That same year, in Washington, DC, the National Woman Suffrage Association (NWSA), founded by Elizabeth Cady Stanton and Susan B. Anthony, and the American Woman Suffrage Association (AWSA), founded by Lucy Stone and Henry Blackwell, joined forces to form the National American Woman Suffrage Association (NAWSA). The two organizations had spent the preceding twenty-five years pursuing the same goal of woman suffrage by different paths. The NWSA sought a federal amendment to the Constitution to guarantee women's right to vote. The AWSA preferred to amend state constitutions, working state-by-state. Twenty-five years of struggle, however, had netted the groups only one state where women voted. Wyoming, which had granted women the right to vote in 1869 while still a territory, kept woman suffrage in its state constitution when admitted to the Union in 1890. Reporters often traveled to Wyoming to determine the effect of the vote on its men, women, and government. They found no evidence of feminized men, masculinized women, nor of practitioners of the "pestiferous free love doctrine" that many Americans feared would follow woman suffrage. Instead, they found white, middle-class women in their Sunday best determinedly registering voters, believing, as one suffrage convention banner put it, that "the vote of women transformed Wyoming from barbarism to civilization." The limits of their strategies apparent to leaders in both the NWSA and the AWSA, the groups decided to join forces to concentrate their efforts. Thirty years later, that organization would achieve the vote for all women in America, including Eda Hickam.

These two events, juxtaposed in time, illustrate the differences in opportunities afforded to American women of different classes and races in the decades that followed the Civil War. Between 1865 and 1890, poverty, a lack of education, isolation, and segregation meant that for many African Americans, emancipation had limits. On the other hand, increasing opportunities for middle- and upper-class women of both races to act through local, state, and national organizations would bring about reforms that one day might benefit all women in America. In the chaotic aftermath of the Civil War, women and men worked to reconstruct and reunify the country. Along with those efforts came continued attempts to reform America into a different nation than had existed before the war, an impulse that met resistance from those with vested interests in maintaining the status quo. In every realm, women's lives reflected these conflicts and women worked to resolve them, meeting with some success, but often defeated by the forces of industrialization and economic upheaval.

RECONSTRUCTION AND RESISTANCE

Reconstruction refers to the period of time immediately after the Civil War when the country repaired the damage that four years of unremitting warfare had caused. It literally offered a chance to reconstruct the country, and different Americans provided competing visions of what a reconstructed country might look like. Since the North had won the war, many Northern reformers saw an opportunity to remake the South into a society that, ideally, resembled the North. White Southerners, on the other hand, wanted a reconstructed South that looked as much like the one of the 1850s as possible. African Americans, north and south, saw an opportunity to build a society where four million ex-slaves and free blacks had the same opportunities as white Americans. There was plenty of work to do.

Before his assassination in April 1865, Abraham Lincoln had called upon the nation to care not only for the soldier who had fought the battles, but also "for his widow and for his orphan." Over four years of warfare, 620,000 Northern and Southern men had died, including more than 20 percent of white male Southerners. Many more men had been left wounded or maimed. The number of veterans to care for was staggering: there were two million Union veterans alone, and over a million Confederate. There were not enough private or state organizations to care for such massive numbers of people displaced or made destitute, however, and the government soon stepped in. Immediately after the war, the Union Army distributed millions of rations to feed the Southern population, and provided medical care in U.S. Army hospitals. The federal government also established hospitals, convalescent homes for soldiers who had no one to care for them, and monthly cash pensions. The Pension Act of 1862 provided pensions to Union Army veterans, as well as their surviving widows, dependents, and even "orphan sisters," providing sustenance for not only Northern soldiers but, more often, for their widows and children. Widows and orphans of the "gallant dead," said one Republican Party leader in 1868, are "a sacred legacy bequeathed to the nation's protecting care." For white women in the South, however, the federal government offered little help. They were relatives of men who had, after all, rebelled against the U.S. government. Instead, Southern states tried to assist their needy citizens.

Southern Women During Reconstruction

The Civil War, fought mainly in Southern states, led to the widespread physical destruction of not only land, buildings, roads, bridges, and railroad lines, but also men. Nearly half of the 1866 budget of the state of Mississippi went to purchase crutches or artificial limbs for returning soldiers. Southern white women had to readjust to life as widows or wives of injured veterans, as orphans, or as single women who would never marry because most of the eligible men in their towns had died. The federal census of 1870 revealed the change in Southern demographics: 84,000 more women than men lived in the four states of Virginia, Georgia, North Carolina, and

South Carolina where much of the fighting had taken place. The effects of the skewed sex ratio continued for years, costing many women the opportunities to marry and raise children.

In addition to the physical costs of the war, its psychic costs were also very high. Virginia women were the first to form Ladies' Memorial Associations, populated by women who had worked on benevolent causes before the war. These groups gathered and reinterred the Confederate dead—the thousands of soldiers buried on farms and accidentally dug up as farmers returned to plow the land again. The women memorialized them with ceremonies and monuments, lest any Southerner forget the "Lost Cause." Such activities gave comfort not only to the widows and orphans soldiers left behind, but to the others who sought a way to understand the death of their antebellum world. Historian Lee Ann Whites has called the war a "crisis in gender," because afterward Southern white men's positions as authoritative patriarchs diminished due to their physical disabilities, their loss of property and slaves, and the political changes taking place that limited their power. White women reared to be Southern Ladies experienced the crisis as well: protecting farms or plantations from invading Yankees, working in a gunpowder factory, caring for men disabled by shell-shock or amputation required white women to adjust their expectations of what life would hold for them.

With fewer menfolk around, white women had to care for themselves. "Those once gifted with wealth," declared the Columbus, Georgia, *Enquirer,* "have accepted poverty and labor cheerfully." Cheerfully or not, women farmed, doing the work themselves. Sallie Elmore Taylor of South Carolina hated the country, but had to return to farm the family plantation after the war. She also earned money by giving music and French lessons. So many women in Alabama took over the work of farming that in 1871 the trustees of the University of Alabama thought women should be admitted to horticultural classes at the school. White women in towns undertook all kinds of jobs as well, laboring as teachers, laundresses, seamstresses, and, eventually, cotton millworkers. They also kept boardinghouses and opened schools. Women sold produce from their gardens, learned to set type, and became postmistresses for the hated but lucrative federal government. Elizabeth Van Lew, the Richmond Unionist who spied for the Union during the war, was rewarded for her loyalty with the position of postmistress in Richmond, a job that required she take a loyalty oath to the Union. While not a problem for Van Lew, that oath gave many Confederate sympathizers pause, but women desperate to feed their families did not always have the luxury of maintaining political principals.

Political principals of the past ran headlong into political changes wrought by the war. The Thirteenth Amendment to the Constitution answered the question of whether the federal government could interfere with the institution of slavery by abolishing it. When the amendment was ratified in 1865, the issue that had polarized national politics for years was resolved in a way that many Southerners resisted. Many Northerners who supported the end of slavery presumed that white Southerners would deal with former slaves, called *freedmen* (a gender-inclusive term), on an equal

FREEDMAN ELIZA FILES A CLAIM

Freedmen frequently came into conflict with whites over labor contracts. Whites wanted to limit black workers' freedom of movement; blacks wanted the freedom to move on when they disliked working conditions. In 1867, one such dispute was recorded in the Freedman's Bureau records. Note that here, a mother feared her son would be sold into slavery; the story that Eda Hickam told in her lawsuit against her former owners may have happened elsewhere.

Case between Jas. T. Bean and E. A. Raborn about Freedwoman Eliza, both claiming to have a contract: Magistrate Court Held at Union Church, Pike County, Ala., Feb. 25th, 1867.

Eliza says that she has never signed her hand on a written contract. . . . Abraham (her husband) made a contract for himself and not for her. He (Abe) told Mr. Bean that he intended for his wife to stay in the house and spin.

W. B. Salter, witness for plaintiff says that sometime about the last of January he went to Mr. Bean's to hire Eliza's son, Mr. Bean told her that he was still willing to feed her and one child, Eliza made no reply to this, she told Mr. Salter that she was to get fifty cents a day for every day she worked in the field. Second time he went also. She would send the boy but if I (Eliza) want him to go to my son's anytime in the Fall will you give him up? That she would stay there—Mr. Bean has weighed us out two weeks rations. Eliza called, on oath, again says that she told Mrs. Mary Ann and Mrs. M. A. Raborn that she had become dissatisfied and was going to Barbour to her son's to stay with him. That Mas Jim

footing with whites. This did not happen. The hostility many Southerners felt toward freed slaves was expressed not only by keeping word of their emancipation from them, as happened to Eda Hickam, but also by overt acts of violence. Black women were attacked for acting "uppity," for refusing to work for their former owners, or for wearing clothes deemed appropriate only for whites. Black men were beaten or even killed when they behaved in ways that did not defer to whites, such as not stepping off the sidewalk when a white person passed, or not removing their hats for a white man. One black veteran was beaten for declaring that he was proud to have been a Union soldier. Many black men were lynched after being falsely accused of raping white women; many black women were attacked, beaten, and raped by white men attempting to terrorize black communities. Groups dedicated to white supremacy included the Ku Klux Klan, founded in Tennessee in 1866, and the Knights of the White Camellia, founded in Louisiana in 1867. Both groups roamed the countryside with hooded and masked riders who used beatings, lynchings, arson, and torture to control blacks, and also whites who cooperated with Union forces occupying the South. In addition to violence, white efforts to limit the freedmen included laws designed to keep ex-slaves in subservient positions. States such as South Carolina and Mississippi instituted *black codes* as early as 1865.

had told her she could go to her son's if she wanted to, and she thought if she could go away when Mr. Bean was at home she could go when he was absent and she told Mrs. E. A. Raborn she had quit and was going off and Mrs. E. A. Raborn told her if she was going or quit, she wanted her and would feed and clothe her and her two children which she agreed to. Says that her reasons for being dissatisfied was that she heard Mr. James Bean, Mr. W. B. Salter, and Mr. E. A. Raborn were going to take her son off and sell him; also that she and the freedmen did not get along well together, the reason was that the black women would not help her bring wood or water when her child was not a week and two or three days old.

Witness Henry (a freedman) says that Eliza said she was going to stay all the year—said she was satisfied there—that "Mas James" would give her victuals and clothes and that was as well as she could do anywhere. . . .

Cross Examination

Philip says Eliza told him that she went in the house and asked "Mas James" what he was willing to give her—he told her he was not willing to give her more than what she would eat and milk extra. Defendant's witness, Mrs. E. A. Raborn says that Eliza said to Mr. Bean "Mas Jim" you told me that I could go to my son or get me a home anywhere else and Mr. Bean said "Eliza, I told you you could go to your son's after a while," also that Eliza told her (Mrs. R.) that she had left Mr. Bean's and if she did not take her she was going to start to her son's in Barbour County the next day, and she hired her from Mr. Bean's statement at his house. She thought Eliza was at liberty to get her another home when she became dissatisfied.

Source: Records of the Assistant Commissioner for the State of Alabama, Bureau of Refugees, Freedmen and Abandoned Lands, 1865–1870; National Archives Publication M809 Roll 23; "Miscellaneous Papers," http://freedmensbureau. com/alabama/unionchurch.htm.

These laws limited blacks' freedom of action, insisting that annual labor contracts between "masters" and "servants" be signed, instead of allowing employees to seek out and work for employers. Such laws destroyed one of the most important rights workers had, that separated freedmen from slaves: the right to quit a job they did not want to do.

The new president, Andrew Johnson, did little to rectify the situation. By December 1865, Congress, under the leadership of the Radical Republicans who believed the South had to be punished as well as restructured, took charge of the reconstruction effort. Federal assistance for ex-slaves had first come from the federal government just before the end of the war. On March 3, 1865, Congress established the Bureau of Refugees, Freedmen, and Abandoned Lands, known as the Freedmen's Bureau. The bureau assisted former slaves with everything from food, transportation, and medicine to jobs, land, and housing to settling legal and criminal disputes between ex-slaves and ex-masters. As the South began to recover and turned to restoring its agricultural production, the Freedmen's Bureau helped, but also sometimes forced, ex-slaves to enter labor contracts with employers. It resolved disputes between them, often to the benefit of employers. (See Primary Source 6-1.) Newly freed families resisted being put in work gangs as they had been during slavery. Instead, they preferred contracts that allowed individual families to work land by themselves, sharing a part of the crop with the owner as payment, a practice called *sharecropping*. This arrangement allowed many black women to work in the field or in the house, as they chose, rather than being forced into field labor. White men used to ordering black women about during slavery times seemed particularly annoyed by this. David Dickon, a Georgia planter, complained that "one-half of the women and children are absent, housekeeping, idling, and other things . . . each family must have its housekeeper and washer." Dickon resented the loss of his labor, while the former slave women enjoyed their ability to take care of their families in relative safety.

Of primary importance to ex-slaves was reconstructing their families, and the Freedmen's Bureau helped with family reunions and even marriages. After the war, women and men searched for family members who had been "sold away," attempting to reunite with them. Because state laws in the South did not recognize slave marriages, thousands of African American couples also legally tied the knot during Reconstruction, married in some cases by bureau officials. Such an act not only reaffirmed the couple's commitment to each other, but also placed black women at least nominally under the protection of their husbands in an increasingly hostile Southern environment. Proof of marriage was also essential to claim army pensions for deceased or wounded soldiers. Marrying again provided black women and men the paperwork necessary to receive the pensions they were due.

As Radical Reconstruction replaced President Johnson's more lenient attempts to reconcile with the South, African American men and women took full advantage of their opportunities to participate in the more inclusive political systems being developed. Each former Confederate state had to draw up a new state constitution. Women could not vote, but they attended political meetings, rallies, parades, and churches, where political questions were debated and leaders were made. They also participated in public celebrations of Emancipation Day, marking an annual celebration of the Emancipation Proclamation. In one Norfolk, Virginia, celebration, black women marched in parades, served on committees that decorated and illuminated the celebrations, and rode in the Liberty Car, at the pinnacle of which sat a young woman representing the Goddess of Liberty. African American women also participated in the discussion of civil rights taking place in the southern states during Reconstruction. The Rollins sisters, Frances and Charlotte, members of an elite free black family in Charleston, South Carolina, used their educations and their interest in woman suffrage and women's rights to organize the South Carolina Branch of the American Woman Suffrage Association to push for a state constitutional amendment to allow women to vote.

By far the most important public action taken by black women after the war was to educate freedmen. Forbidden by law to learn to read and write before the war, ex-slaves craved knowledge, especially literacy. Charlotte Forten, of the elite black Philadelphia family, arrived at the Sea Islands of South Carolina as early as 1862 to conduct school for some of the 10,000 slaves living there when the Union Army captured the islands. She and her white friend, Laura Towne, were so successful that within a year, 1,700 students enrolled in 30 schools with 45 teachers. After the war the pace quickened, as the federal government provided funds through the Freedmen's Bureau, and northern religious organizations sent teachers south. Black and white women and men taught hundreds of thousands to read and write. Many Yankee teachers who went south tried to inculcate white, middle-class cultural values in their students along with book learning, but failed to respect much of the existing Southern black culture. Freedman grew to prefer teachers of their own race, who understood that ex-slaves who had been whipped would view corporal punishment, commonly used in Northern schools, differently than did misbehaving Yankee children. Black colleges were established to train teachers, and the first African American woman lawyer, Charlotte E. Ray, graduated in 1872 from the law school at Howard University, named after Oliver Otis Howard, head of the Freedmen's Bureau.

Attempts to educate former slaves did not pass unnoticed by white Southern men and women who protested, often violently, by beating students, burning schools, and killing teachers. Whites also abandoned public schools when black students tried to attend. Violence against black women and girls always carried the threat of rape, and few white men were arrested, much less successfully prosecuted, for the crimes they committed against African American women. Many black women in the South found participation in the public world of school and work so risky that they preferred to remain in the private sphere, caring for their families, and embracing the tenets of True Womanhood popularized before the war. Other black women assumed, as reformers had done before the war, that they too could undertake reform in the wider world, becoming part of the movement to "uplift" the race—in other words, to improve the lot of all African Americans. "In the civilization and enlightenment of the Negro race," argued one North Carolinian woman, "its educated women must be the potent factors."

Southern race relations were in flux during the period of Reconstruction, and many black Americans believed that both racial and gender discrimination would end in the new South. Skilled artisans, successful merchants, and professionals took advantage of a society that was going to have to redefine the rules of social interaction, now that slavery was dead. They created urban African American communities of affluence, and marked their entrance into such communities with conspicuous consumption. In New Bern, North Carolina, for example, well-to-do African Americans purchased elegant carriages and served lobster at their tables. They lived in substantial houses with the trappings of middle-class wealth: pianos, lace curtains, and servants to wait upon them. Black fathers who had been slaves sent their daughters to colleges, such as Oberlin and Scotia Seminary, instead of watching the young women earn wages. Such social mobility was apparent in North Carolinian Mary McLeod's life. She came to Scotia Seminary, a Presbyterian women's school modeled after Mount Holyoke and possessed of a biracial faculty, in 1887. One of fifteen children, McLeod was so poor that she had never used a knife or fork, never even climbed a flight of stairs. She used her education so well that eventually she would reach the national political stage as a member of President Franklin Roosevelt's "Black Cabinet" (see Chapter 8).

Such changes in the lives of African Americans appalled white Southerners who dismissed blacks' achievement of material wealth as "colored swelldom." It was difficult for whites to maintain their prewar assumptions that excused slavery by arguing that blacks were inherently lazy and unreliable when they saw residents in Southern towns and cities whose daily lives put the lie to such ideas. In the generation after the war, as historian Glenda Gilmore has shown, African Americans moved from being field hands to being teachers, from being carpenters to being builders, from being farmers to being politicians. Southern whites struggled mightily to contain the black community and prevent further disruption of their white supremacy. When black codes failed to limit black success, whites used violence and racial segregation and discrimination embedded in law. They also held onto the notion that only white women could exhibit proper "womanly" behavior, forever excluding black women from acceptable society except as maids and domestic workers.

Emigration and migration offered black women still another way to cope with the difficulties of Southern life during Reconstruction. A few emigrated to Liberia, the American colony in Africa founded as the destination for freed slaves earlier in the century. Many more migrated to cities, particularly to Atlanta, where domestic work such as housekeeping and laundry was plentiful. Numbers of women also left with their families or on their own to head west taking advantage of the 1862 Homestead Act, which granted 160 acres of land free to those who would settle and farm it for five years. Between 1865 and 1890, some 40,000 black citizens, called the *Exodusters*, moved West. Some settled in the all-black town of Nicodemus, Kansas, while others moved on to Oklahoma, Nebraska, the Dakotas, Colorado, and Montana. Charles and Lula Pettey of North Carolina led a group of freedmen to California in 1881, where they founded the town of Petteyville and Charles became pastor of the downtown church. By 1889, Yankton, South Dakota, had fifty-nine African Americans, including a woman journalist, Kate D. Chapman, and a twenty-member African Methodist Episcopal church. "The schools, churches and hotels are thrown open to all regardless to color," wrote Chapman in an article celebrating her town, and "the feeling that exists between the two races is friendly in the extreme." The number of blacks who left the South remained small, however, and according to the 1910 federal census, 90 percent of all American blacks still lived in the South.

Northern Women During Reconstruction

Because much of the Northern landscape remained unscathed by the Civil War, reconstruction in the North did not entail rebuilding and repairs. Instead, the Northern economy grew rapidly, led by war industries, but soon including the expansion of all major industries as well as the financial sectors. The boom–bust cycle that characterized the nineteenth-century economy continued on an ever-larger scale, as the population increased and cities grew.

New professions opened for women in the North's booming economy, thanks in part to their activities during the war. Practicing medicine, either as a doctor or nurse, became more respectable professions for women as a result of the countless thousands of women who had volunteered their medical services on the battlefields and in the hospitals. Dr. Elizabeth Blackwell, who received the first medical college degree given to a woman in 1849, had opened the New York Infirmary for Women and Children in 1857. Dr. Marie Zakrzewska, a German immigrant and one of the women Blackwell took under her wing, opened the New England Hospital for Women and Children in 1862, where she mentored hundreds of women physicians, including Dr. Anita Tyng, the first woman surgeon in the country. By 1880, more than 2,000 women doctors practiced medicine in the North, and a few medical colleges accepted both black and white women for training. Although many women doctors suffered from unreasonable prejudices that prevented them from succeeding in private practice, they worked successfully in charity hospitals, clinics, and settlement houses where their services were highly valued.

More common than doctors were nurses. The Woman's Hospital in Philadelphia opened in 1861 and served as one of the first places to train women as professional nurses. Other nursing schools opened after the war in Boston, New York, and New Haven. Jane Woolsey, a New Yorker who had served as a nurse during the war and at an army convalescent hospital afterward, turned to hospital reform and nurse training after the war. Jane's sister Georgeanna Woolsey, who had served as a nurse aboard a Union hospital transport vessel, helped found the Connecticut Training School for Nurses. Other women who had served during the war with civilian relief groups, such as the U.S. Sanitary Commission or the U.S. Christian Commission, worked at hospitals and charities afterward, caring for the sick and the destitute. Louisa Lee Schuyler, for instance, organized the New York State Charities Aid Association to inspect poor houses, work houses, and other public institutions that provided relief.

Charity organizers focused their efforts on those they termed the "worthy" poor, basing their standards of worthiness on white, middle-class notions of propriety. The worthy poor were those who were poor through no fault of their own. They were not drunkards, prostitutes, or street beggars, but instead were orphans, elderly people, widows with small children, unemployed men who would work if they could. The worthy poor accepted charity with gratitude, and maintained their moral standards in the face of destitution. These ideas about who would benefit from assistance guided the *settlement house movement* that began in the mid-1880s, providing safe havens and schoolrooms for the massive numbers of poor immigrants moving into northern cities. The most famous was Chicago's Hull House, founded in 1889 by Jane Addams and Ellen Gates Starr. These women and their followers taught the poor and immigrants not only how to read but also how to behave like middle-class Americans. The settlement house movement expanded greatly after 1890 as European immigrants continued to flood into the cities of America.

For other native-born and immigrant women who sought new opportunities, migrating west provided new possibilities. Homesteading in the territories beyond the Mississippi, women could settle in nine states carved out of the region between 1864 and 1890: Nevada (1864); Nebraska (1867); Colorado (1876); North and South Dakota, Montana, and Washington (1889); and Idaho and Wyoming (1890). As federal land was sold to railroads or claimed by homesteaders, the Great Plains provided the customary opportunities and hardships of frontier life. Women immigrants coped with sod houses, blizzards, silver strikes, and gold rushes that garnered great wealth or left behind ghost towns; Native women coped with invasions, warfare, and removal. Wars for control of the Great Plains followed the American Civil War.

Native American Women in the West

The Civil War had drawn federal troops away from western posts to fight back East. Native Americans took full advantage of the situation, increasing raids against settlers in the region, and trying to drive them back and off their traditional Native lands. When the Civil War ended, the federal armies returned in greater force than before and conflicts between Native Americans and whites escalated. Outgunned and outmanned, Native Americans nevertheless continued to fight to preserve their ways of life and protect their futures as best they could.

During the Civil War, Colonel Christopher "Kit" Carson had rounded up and driven the Diné, known to white Americans as the Navajos, to the Bosque Redondo reservation at Fort Sumner, New Mexico Territory, in 1864. Reservations had long been used by the federal government to house Native Americans whose lands the government had taken or purchased, as well as to protect Indians from white settlers. In the West as elsewhere, reservations usually contained far fewer resources, such as water and arable lands, than did Indians' traditional lands. As a result, many, such as the Cherokee in the 1830s, resisted moving to reservations (see Chapter 5). As difficult a trek as the Trail of Tears had been for the Cherokees, the "Long Walk"of the Navajos to their reservation left the people traumatized, suffering from malnutrition, disease, and the utter destruction of their way of life. The U.S. government burned their houses, slaughtered their livestock, and tried to force them to adopt the white style of farming. The Diné resisted and finally, in 1868, the United States and the Navajo nation signed a treaty. Navajos could return to their traditional lands, have 15,000 sheep to replenish their herds, and could rebuild, if they stayed on their reservation and became farmers and ranchers.

While white Americans no doubt understood this as an act of restoration, it forced the Navajo people to adapt traditional ways to make up for their losses. For Navajo women weavers, for instance, who were renowned for their skill in creating blankets of both beauty and utility, the Long Walk had destroyed their sheep and taken the women away from the natural materials they used as dyes. On the reservation, their products transformed. Women used more cotton thread and synthetic dyes to weave both blankets and rugs, resulting in brightly colored products that appealed to a different market than before. When the railroad arrived in the early 1880s, the

Navajo economy shifted to producing goods for trade with the rest of the country, and women sold wool instead of weaving it into their traditional blankets. By the 1890s, Navajo women weavers had become part of the larger American economy, producing goods for sale to tourists, using cash instead of barter systems, and modifying their means of production to survive in the growing industrial economy.

Farther north in the Great Plains, Native American women coped with changes in their lives brought by the arrival of the transcontinental railroad and the simultaneous slaughter of the buffalo. Groups such as the Crow, the Cheyenne, the Arapaho and many others relied on the buffalo for sustenance, both physical and spiritual. Indians used every part of the animal: skins for clothing and shelter, bones for weapons and tools, even muscle sinews for stringing their bows. Buffalo migrated in a path that ran from the Great Slave Lake in northwestern Canada to Mexico. The transcontinental railroad between Nebraska and California, completed in 1869, split the migration path of the buffalo in two, and Americans, traveling in railroad coaches, killed millions of buffalo by shooting at them out of the train windows, while others hunted on horseback. The destruction was unparalleled, the buffalo population diminishing from perhaps 40 million in the early part of the century to near extinction by the end.

Pretty Shield, a Crow medicine woman interviewed by Frank Linderman, a white writer who lived among numerous nineteenth-century Indians, spoke of the effect of the buffalo's demise on the Indians. It did not seem possible, she said, for the buffalo to disappear. There had always been so many. She could think of no other Indians who would destroy the buffalo, "yet the white men did this, even when he did not want the meat." The result was hunger, sickness, and fear among the Indians. "After this, their hearts were no good anymore," she said, and had it not been for federal shipments of food, the Indians would have starved. Increased dependency on whites for sustenance was not all the Indians suffered. Pretty Shield also described what the warfare against the Plains Indians and their displacement cost Native American women: "We women sometimes tried to keep our men from going to war, but this was like talking to winter-winds; and of course there was always some woman, sometimes many women, mourning for men who had been killed in war. These women had to be taken care of. Somebody had to kill meat for them. Their fathers or uncles or brothers did this until the women married again, which they did not always do, so that war made more work for everybody. There were few lazy ones among us in those days."

The Indian Wars

The Indians fought white encroachment on their lands throughout the 1880s before they were overwhelmed militarily. One of the most powerful Indian groups were the Apaches, a migratory group in the Great Plains who raided others for supplies when food was scarce. Their raids on white settlements frightened Americans and brought the U.S. Cavalry in to retaliate. In 1875, the Apaches were ordered to a reservation; one of their best-known warriors, Geronimo, successfully evaded capture by American forces for the next eleven years. Another leading Apache warrior and medicine woman, Lozen, successfully led her warriors into repeated battles against both Mexican and U.S. cavalries. Lozen and Geronimo joined forces, but the two finally surrendered to superior numbers in 1886.

The last massive battle between Indians and American troops came in 1890 at Wounded Knee, when the government attempted to bring Sioux supporters of a messianic group, the Ghost Dancers, under control. In Wounded Knee, South Dakota, the army separated Sioux men from their guns and their families. According to eyewitnesses testifying at a council meeting between the Sioux and the U.S. Commissioner of Indian Affairs afterward, a shot was fired, the Sioux drew their knives (their only remaining weapons), and the army opened fire. It was a bloodbath and the deaths of the Sioux women and children made it worse. A Lakota Sioux named American Horse, who supported the government's attempt to control the Ghost Dance movement, testified in a meeting with the Commissioner of Indian Affairs that "it would have been all right if only the men were killed; we would feel almost grateful for it. But the fact of the killing of the women, and more especially the killing of the young boys and girls who are to go to make up the future strength of the Indian people, is the saddest part of the whole affair and we feel it very sorely."

Native Americans were not entirely alone in their dismay. Protests against their treatment came with the remarkable work of two women: Helen Hunt Jackson and Sarah Winnemuca. Jackson, a successful author of children's books, attended a public lecture in Boston in 1879, where she heard Chief Standing Bear, a Ponca Indian, describe the miseries of the Poncas' forced removal to a reservation. Outraged by what she had learned, Jackson circulated petitions, raised funds, and wrote letters protesting the treatment of the Poncas. She also wrote *A Century of Dishonor: A Sketch of the United States Government's Dealings with Some of the Indian Tribes*, and distributed it to members of Congress in 1881. "Look upon your hands," read a red-lettered warning on the cover, "they are stained with the blood of your relations." The book had little apparent impact on Congress, but after Jackson traveled to California and reported on abuses against Indians there, the U.S. Commissioner of Indian Affairs, Hiram Price, appointed her an agent of the Department of the Interior to investigate conditions. Her 1883 report detailing the dishonesty of Indian agents and their outright thievery, as well as the miserable conditions of the California Indians on reservations, convinced the House of Representatives to pass a bill that called for more lands and schools to help the Indians in the region. The bill passed the House but died in the Senate. In 1884, Jackson tried to wake up the country yet again, this time through a novel, *Ramona*. She hoped to use literature to publicize the plight of the Indians in the same way Harriet Beecher Stowe used it to illuminate the plight of the slaves in *Uncle Tom's Cabin*. Jackson died less than a year after the publication of *Ramona*, hoping her work would live on and help Native Americans.

Sarah Winnemucca, a Northern Paiute from western Nevada, wrote as well. Her autobiography, *Life Among the Piutes: Their Wrongs and Claims*, is

Bradley & Rulofson.   *Sarah Winnemucca*   San Francisco, Cal.

SARAH WINNEMUCCA   Sarah Winnemucca, shown here in native Paiute dress, has a statue in the U.S. Capitol in Emancipation Hall. She stands holding a book to symbolize her career as a teacher, as well as the first published Native American woman author. She also carries a shell flower, her name in Paiute. That bronze statue, cast by artist Benjamin Victor in 2005, is one of two that represent the state of Nevada in the Capitol, and one of only three Native American women mentioned in the U.S. Capitol, along with Pocahontas and Sacajawea.

most certainly the first published work by a Native American woman. Winnemucca also went on the lecture circuit, giving some 300 to 400 speeches in the East to plead for Indian lands to be restored and Indian prisoners released. Unlike other Indian women activists or fighters, such as Lozen, or Other Magpie, a Crow woman who fought to avenge her brother's death, Winnemucca fought with words and sought accommodation with the Anglos who had invaded the west. Accepting that reservation life was probably inevitable, she demanded honest Indian agents, instead of those being sent by the government who did little but line their pockets, she wrote, "and the pockets of their wives and sisters, who are always put in as teachers . . . and yet they do not teach." After she finished her tour, Winnemucca returned to Lovelock, Nevada, to open a school. Despite concerted lobbying by white Americans who supported her ideas, the school failed when the federal government refused to fund it.

The Dawes Act

The reservation system that the U.S. government used to subdue and control the Native Americans in the West had long-reaching effects on Native populations. Throughout the Great Plains, the Southwest, and the Pacific region, Natives who had been able to sustain themselves through their own efforts—harvesting all that the land or sea had to offer them, trading over networks eons old, warring against each other, enslaving each other, allying with others against enemies—much was changed when the Native Americans were rounded up and restricted to reservations. The system failed to convince Indians to change their cultures, however, and many continued to resist attempts that white Americans made to reconstruct their lives so they would live more as whites did.

In 1887, the federal government, displeased with continued Indian resistance to the reservation system, passed a bill known as the Dawes Act. This law, also known as the Allotment Act, modified the reservation system, dividing reservation lands into allotments to farm or use for grazing in the Anglo fashion. The act gave heads of households 160 acres each; single people got half as much. Once Indians had, according to the act, "adopted the habits of civilized life," which meant giving up their dress, their hair, their language, their marriage customs (such as extra spouses), and their communal landownership, then they would be given title to the lands and would be declared citizens of the United States. Native adults chose their allotments from the reservation lands the Indians occupied, while American Indian agents chose allotments for orphan children. Some groups, such as the Nez Percés in Idaho Territory, chose allotment, but then used the lands to shore up their traditional ways, rather than farming lands as the federal government wanted them to. For others, reservation lands they were assigned to were often so poor that they could not be farmed, or so rich that whites soon took those lands back. The government also insisted that Native Americans hold the land in allotment for twenty-five years before they would issue title, and included a provision allowing the government to change the rules of the act, if it was "in the best interests of the tribe."

Native Americans who tried to assimilate under the Dawes Act found that their traditional ways soon disappeared or were devalued, even by themselves. The change from communal to individual property ownership by male "heads" of families meant that women, even those in matrilineal groups, were forced out of positions of power and relegated to the role of Anglo-American women: dependent. Hopi women, for example, who had owned and distributed the crops and goods their households produced, protested the allotment system to the Bureau of Indian Affairs. The house, the lands, and the family itself could not be separated and placed under the government, they said, nor under the rule of men. These things were inseparable from women because the woman "is the heart of these, and they rest with her." The resistance of these women and countless others to the annihilation of their communal culture frustrated Massachusetts Senator Henry Dawes, author of the Allotment Act. He did not understand Native Americans' preference for communal property over individual landholding, since then "there is no enterprise to make your home any better than that of your neighbors." "There is no selfishness," among the Indians, he puzzled, who were "at the bottom of civilization." Without that selfishness, Dawes saw no hope for progress. Indians would simply have to learn to act as individuals and to support themselves as wage laborers within American society, whites believed, rather than ask American society to give up its civilized selfishness.

REFORM RETURNS

Various groups sought to achieve the "progress" that Dawes favored by continuing the reform efforts that had preceded the Civil War. Now that the war was over, reformers returned to earlier activities. As the economy expanded, so did women's ability to educate themselves and enter new professions. The woman's rights movement, temperance, labor reform, and economic reforms attracted new supporters and made additional progress toward their goals. Other reform movements appeared on the national stage: birth control and voluntary motherhood, agrarian reform, and the women's club movement. Spurred by the sentiment of reconstruction and the desire to ameliorate social ills, a bewildering array of reform efforts sought to change how America functioned.

Women's Education and the Professions

Education for women after the Civil War reached new levels. The Morrill Land Act of 1861 provided each state in the country with at least 30,000 acres of federal land that could be sold to raise funds for a coeducational land-grant college. These colleges were to teach the "agricultural and the mechanic arts," read the legislation, "in order to promote the liberal and practical education of the industrial classes in the several pursuits and professions in life." Over seventy land-grant colleges were founded under the

Morrill Act, including such schools as Cornell, Pennsylvania State University, Ohio State University, Kansas State University, and others. These land-grant colleges benefited farmers of both sexes and both races: because the colleges were required to be coeducational, women flocked to them to learn subjects such as horticulture and home economics. In 1890, the act was amended to allow former states of the Confederacy to participate. While schools such as Clemson University in South Carolina, Auburn University in Alabama, and other southern land-grant colleges were coeducational, they all discriminated against African Americans. Southern states built parallel black land-grant institutions so they could still receive federal money.

Private women's colleges also grew in size, scope and number. In the Northeast, seven small liberal arts institutions opened, most of them between 1865 and 1889. Vassar College in Poughkeepsie, New York, began classes for women in September 1865 with 353 students and 30 faculty, of whom 22 were women. Bryn Mawr, another of the so-called Seven Sisters colleges, opened in Pennsylvania in 1885, and Barnard College opened in New York City in 1889. The other "sisters" included Mount Holyoke, originally founded by educational reformer Mary Lyon in 1837; Wellesley, chartered in 1870; Smith College, founded by philanthropist Sophia Smith in 1871; and Radcliffe, begun as the Harvard Annex in 1879. The schools were linked socially and politically to the Ivy League schools of the Northeast, such as Harvard, Brown, and Princeton, attracting students from similar backgrounds. Women's colleges also attracted women administrators as well as women faculty, who were not allowed to teach in men's colleges or most coeducational colleges.

In the South, private women's colleges, where higher education continued to be valued for its ability to reinforce Southern ideals of piety and femininity, were segregated by race. White women could receive a liberal arts education in the seminaries that continued their antebellum practices, and in new schools such as H. Sophie Newcomb Memorial College for Women in New Orleans, founded in 1886. Black women could attend Barber-Scotia College in Concord, North Carolina, by 1867; and Huston-Tillotson College in Austin, Texas, founded in 1876. Sophie B. Packard and Harriet Giles, two former abolitionists, founded perhaps the best known and most rigorous academic institution for African American women: Spelman College in Atlanta, Georgia, in 1881. By the turn of the century, black educators resolved a long-standing argument about whether African American women should pursue vocational or liberal arts education by providing opportunities to pursue both.

Higher education opened new professions, such as law, to women. Before the Civil War, lawyers trained by "reading the law," or apprenticing with licensed lawyers. Lawyers' training changed after the Civil War and many states required formal schooling. The first woman licensed to practice law, Arabella Babb Mansfield, was admitted to the Iowa bar exam in 1869, after a judge ruled that while Iowa statutes restricted women from taking the bar exam, the court was justified in interpreting laws in ways that would prevent such a "manifest injustice." Myra Bradwell in Illinois did not achieve her goal so easily. She passed her licensing exam in 1869 as well, but had to appeal to the state courts and then to the U.S. Supreme Court before receiving her license in 1890. In 1871, Phoebe Couzins was the first woman to graduate from law school, receiving her degree from Washington University in St. Louis. In 1872, Charlotte E. Ray became the first black woman lawyer in the United States after graduating from Howard University. None of these women were able to practice law, however, as prejudice against women lawyers was too great.

One of the first women to have both a law license and a career as a lawyer was Clara Shortridge Foltz of California. Married to an unsuccessful man who first deserted her, then eventually divorced her for another woman, Foltz had tried to earn a living through the traditional women's occupations of taking in boarders and sewing. She even went on the lecture circuit, but could not make enough money to support her family. Foltz eventually read the law and then lobbied the California state legislature to remove the restriction that allowed only white men to practice law. In 1878, California's Woman Lawyer bill passed and Foltz became the first practicing woman lawyer in the United States. In a career that spanned fifty years, Foltz also published a magazine and spoke out for woman suffrage, living long enough to cast a ballot herself. Another suffragist, Belva Ann Lockwood, successfully lobbied the Supreme Court to admit her to practice in 1879, before using her law career to launch a run for the presidency in 1884.

Women lawyers were uncommon; women clerical workers were not. This new profession resulted from the vast expansion of the federal government's bureaucracy during the Civil War and the successful influx of "Treasury girls" into that bureaucracy, as well as from the creation of new office machinery, especially the typewriter. Clerks and stenographers embraced the machine, which not only produced letters more quickly but also, with the use of "carbon paper," which, when inserted in front of a second sheet, transferred what was typed, reducing the onerous task of copying. Advertisers recognized the influx of women into the clerical profession. They used the female figure of Columbia in advertisements to promote the typewriter as a mechanical marvel that not only replaced the quill, but also was a machine, one advertiser claimed, "so simple a woman could use it." A portrait of the typewriter's inventor, Christopher Sholes, showed him seated with a procession of angelic-looking young women typewriters (the noun then described both the machine and the operator) gratefully proceeding to their offices nearby.

All of the more lucrative opportunities for women were found in urban areas, north and south. Southern rural women, however, benefited from a shift in cotton cloth production to the South, beginning in the 1880s. Determined to recover from the war, Southern landowners shifted from sharecropping with those who worked their fields to tenantry, asking for cash as payment for using the land instead. They invested their capital in cotton mills. Mill villages sprang up and poor whites, particularly women—widowed, single, female heads of households—who had little access to agricultural jobs flocked to the mills. Older women could also make a living running the boardinghouses that companies provided for workers. Southern mill villages provided communities for working women, as the Lowell mill towns had done, with all the benefits and drawbacks of those in New England.

All of the 338 occupations listed in the 1870 federal census included at least one woman, but despite the fact that women were entering new professions and fields after the Civil War, some 93 percent of women who earned wages in America did so in one of nine jobs: domestic service, agricultural labor, seamstress, milliner, teacher, textile mill worker, or laundress. For the vast majority of wage-earning women, the same domestically oriented tasks that had defined their labor before the Civil War defined it afterward as well.

The Woman's Rights Movement

Women's formal and informal political activities had not ceased during the Civil War, but most activists had shifted their focus to the emancipation of slaves and the passage of the Thirteenth Amendment banning slavery. A few kept alive the broader issues of reform. Activist Anna Dickinson, for instance, campaigned for Republican Party candidates during and after the war, and gave speeches not only in favor of emancipation, but also supporting prison and moral reform, as well as labor reform. Her work as a hired spokesperson for the Republican Party was unusual not just because of her gender, but also because she continued to speak out on issues other than emancipation. Suffragist Susan B. Anthony, never asleep in the cause of women's rights, despaired when the New York state legislature gutted part of the state's Married Women's Property Act, depriving widows of control over property left to them at their husbands' deaths. No one seemed to notice, and all the other activists she talked to counseled patience until the war ended. Martha Wright, a friend, fellow suffragist, Underground Railroad participant, and mother of a son at war, pointed out to Anthony the folly of pursuing women's rights when "the nation's whole heart and soul are engrossed with this momentous crisis . . . nobody will listen." Even Elizabeth Cady Stanton, Anthony's long-time partner in the pursuit of the vote for women, urged Anthony to put aside their demands for the course of the war.

Anthony and Stanton worked instead for the Thirteenth Amendment through the National Women's Loyal League, but after the amendment passed, they thought that Reconstruction provided an ideal opportunity to gain equal rights for women. Along with abolitionist leaders such as Wendell Phillips and Frederick Douglass, they knew that the Thirteenth Amendment was incomplete because it did not make former slaves citizens of their country nor guarantee them the right to vote. So in the summer of 1865, former abolitionists and Republicans in Congress began circulating drafts of a Fourteenth amendment that would achieve these goals of citizenship and suffrage.

Passed in 1866, but not ratified until 1868, the Fourteenth Amendment made citizens of everyone born or naturalized in the United States. It also prohibited states from abridging "privileges and immunities" any U.S. citizen enjoyed. If any state denied the right to vote in federal elections to any male citizen, aged twenty-one or older, that state's representation to Congress would be reduced. The amendment also forbade states from sending ex-Confederates to Congress and repudiated the Confederate debt, thus guaranteeing poverty for thousands of former Confederates who had purchased Confederate bonds during the war.

By guaranteeing equal citizenship rights to all, the amendment provided an opportunity to give the vote to both blacks and women. But because the amendment punished states only if they restricted male voting rights, it meant that states could keep women from voting. In other words, the amendment did not say women or black men could not vote. It did not say that voting was a right of citizenship. It said only that no state could deprive Americans of the rights of citizenship without due process, and that only male citizens' rights to vote were protected by this amendment. If their rights were limited—if a state restricted men, white or black, from voting—then the state would be punished by limiting its proportional representation in the House of Representatives. It meant black men might be able to vote, but no women were likely to be allowed to vote.

The problem with the Fourteenth Amendment's wording came from the insertion of the word *male* into the amendment and thus into the Constitution. Woman's rights advocates opposed the amendment because, they argued, it would take another specific amendment to give women the right to vote. Stanton and Anthony in particular were fearful—and furious. They appealed to former abolitionists such as Frederick Douglass and Wendell Phillips to pull their support for the amendment until it was rewritten to guarantee the protection of women citizens, too. But Douglass, who had supported the woman's rights advocates through thick and thin, could not bring himself to deny the right to vote to the millions of freedmen. Phillips refused as well, saying succinctly, "This is the Negro's hour." America was still a patriarchy and that fact meant black men had to have the same powers as white men in order to be part of the rulers instead of the ruled. Douglass had to think of black men, not just women's rights, and he wanted those men to have power.

Douglass also knew that the Republican Party would not risk losing elections by supporting such an unpopular cause as women's right to vote. The notion remained too radical for most nineteenth-century Americans—men or women—to accept. Republicans also wanted black support in Congress and a Republican for president. By supporting protection for black male voters, they could achieve those goals. If they supported votes for women, they might lose every election. Wendell Phillip laid out the platform for reforming America in this order: "Negro suffrage, then temperance, then the eight-hour [workday] movement, then woman suffrage." Stung by Douglass's refusal to support them, but determined not to give up, Anthony and Stanton attacked the text of the Fourteenth Amendment with letters, speeches, articles, and an Eleventh National Woman's Rights Convention. Anthony, Stanton, and Lucretia Mott also formed the American Equal Rights Association (AERA) to fight against the Fourteenth Amendment and for including woman suffrage as a part of a Fifteenth Amendment.

In 1867, the question of extending the vote to black men and all women came up for consideration as both New York and Kansas revised their state constitutions. The two states served as testing grounds for the arguments supporting these two issues. In New York, Horace Greeley, chair of the committee in the state legislature that was considering whether to let women vote, told the supporters that "the best women I know do not want to vote." He asked Stanton, testifying in front of the suffrage subcommittee why women should get the ballot when they were not ready to defend it with a bullet. Stanton replied, "We are ready to fight, Sir, just as you did in the late war, by sending our substitutes," referring to the Civil War practice where wealthy men bought their way out of service in the army. It was a fierce insult, made worse when Stanton read aloud the signatures on a petition supporting woman suffrage; the signers included "Mrs. Horace Greeley." Greeley, who had been an old friend and supporter of Stanton for years, took his revenge by issuing a committee report recommending only universal (white and black) manhood suffrage.

In the spring of 1867, Lucy Stone and her husband Henry Blackwell traveled to Kansas to speak in favor of universal manhood suffrage and woman suffrage. Anthony and Stanton followed in September, after the failure in New York. The four spoke frequently throughout the state—two or three times a day and once on Sundays. Stanton and Anthony joined forces with George Train, a tall, handsome, wealthy, eloquent racist with Democratic presidential ambitions. Stanton's alliance with Train and her promotion of his ideas that only educated whites should vote, rather than all men and women regardless of race, split the American Equal Rights Association in two. Both woman suffrage and black suffrage were defeated. Lucy Stone denied any connection between the distasteful Train and the AERA, and William Lloyd Garrison wrote to Anthony that he was astounded that "you and Mrs. Stanton should have taken such leave of good sense as to be traveling companions and associate lecturers with that crack-brained harlequin and semi-lunatic, George Francis Train."

Train appealed to Stanton in particular because she had come to believe that the vote should be limited to the educated, rather than everyone. Train also supported woman suffrage and was willing to put his money behind the cause. He financed the newspaper, *The Revolution*, that published Anthony's and Stanton's ideas for political reform for women and the nation. The newspaper eventually failed, in part because of its association with Train as well as its attacks on former abolitionists now working for black male suffrage instead of woman suffrage. Arguments over where people should put their suffrage support were cataloged in its pages. Disagreements were made worse when the Fifteenth Amendment passed in 1869. That amendment said that suffrage could not be denied to U.S. citizens because of "race, color, or previous condition of servitude." The word *sex* was not there. Black male suffrage came first: male ex-slaves could vote, but women who wanted to vote were not protected by the Constitution.

In 1869, woman's rights advocates finally split into two groups, each with a differing vision of what to do next. The National Woman Suffrage Association, founded in May of 1869 and led by Susan B. Anthony and

Elizabeth Cady Stanton, would work for a constitutional amendment to give women the vote. The NWSA allowed only women to be members and officers because Elizabeth's husband Henry Stanton suggested "women could do it better alone" in their fight for the franchise. The NWSA was also concerned with social issues such as equal rights, equal pay, an eight-hour day, divorce and child custody rights, birth control, property rights, and labor unions. But first and foremost the NWSA focused on gaining woman suffrage, since it believed that the other reforms could be accomplished only by women who voted.

Members of the NWSA included former abolitionists as well as participants in and supporters of the Seneca Falls Convention—Lucretia Mott, Martha Wright, Ernestine Rose, Anna Dickinson, and "Mrs. Horace" Mary Greeley. The NWSA was the most successful of woman suffrage groups at raising money and at attracting support. Anthony, in particular, traveled ceaselessly. As a single woman, she had few domestic responsibilities to tie her down. Stanton, on the other hand, was at times overwhelmed with her seven children and the demands of her household. But when Stanton could get to a meeting, what a picture she presented—a sweet-faced, round little woman, whom nobody would suspect of thinking of anything beyond the next day's meals, instead proposing nothing less than a radical reworking of the entire structure of American society! Stanton was the theoretician of the two; Anthony the organizer and promoter. They were a brilliant team, and worked together from 1851 until Stanton's death in 1902.

A second group formed to fight for suffrage was the American Woman Suffrage Association, founded in November 1869. Led by Lucy Stone and Henry Blackwell, it included many leading former abolitionists since the AWSA focused on achieving black suffrage first, then woman suffrage. The group published *The Women's Journal* to counteract Stanton and Anthony's *Revolution*, outlasting the latter publication and eventually serving as the official organ for the woman's rights movement. The AWSA fought for the vote primarily at the state and local level. While it did petition Congress to pass laws granting woman suffrage in the territories and in the District of Columbia, and it did ask for a federal amendment, the vast majority of its work focused on changing each state's constitution to allow woman suffrage, and it included no economic and social issues in its campaign for the vote.

Having two organizations competing to support the same goal meant the woman suffrage movement was in danger of losing its power by dividing its interests. In 1870, a first-rate scandal further diluted its power. Victoria Woodhull, a new voice on the stage, published her theories regarding women's rights. Her ideas attracted new supporters, including Stanton and Anthony, but her conduct sensationalized and undercut the woman's rights movement. Woodhull, speaking before the House of Representatives Judiciary Committee in 1871, argued that the Fourteenth Amendment allowed women to vote. Her idea was not unique—Susan B. Anthony would use it in 1872 to vote in the election—but Woodhull's attractive and vivacious personality and important friends brought her and the woman's rights movement considerable notice. Woodhull then went on to announce that she would run for president of the United States in the 1872 election, not mentioning the fact she did not meet the minimum age requirement of thirty-five. Using the race as publicity for the cause of woman's rights, Woodhull put Frederick Douglass on her ticket as her vice presidential running mate without his agreement and began her campaign.

Daughter of a traveling medicine show quack, Woodhull had arrived in New York City in 1868 and met Cornelius Vanderbilt, a wealthy railroad magnate. In gratitude, after Woodhull and her sister, Tennie C. (called Tennessee) Claflin convinced him they had contacted the spirit of his dead wife, Vanderbilt set the two up as brokers on Wall Street, where the attractive sisters became known as the "Bewitching Brokers." He also backed the sisters' publication, *Woodhull and Claflin's Weekly*. It contained articles on women's rights but also on far more radical reform issues such as free love, liberalized divorce, short skirts, legalized prostitution, tax reform, public housing, and dietary reform. The contents of the *Weekly* scandalized Americans, and as Woodhull began campaigning for president, her first husband appeared and moved in with Woodhull and her second husband. The press suggested Woodhall was a bigamist. Woodhull complained about the story, then exposed an affair she said the press was ignoring: the ongoing liaison between the Reverend Henry Ward Beecher, the married brother of Harriet Beecher Stowe and member of the famed Beecher family of preachers, and one of his parishioners, Elizabeth Tilton, wife of Theodore Tilton, a leading publisher. Tilton sued Beecher for the alienation of affections of his wife; Woodhull published the lurid accusations in her *Weekly* and was arrested for disseminating obscenities through the mails. She was acquitted, and Beecher and Tilton went through a six-month trial that was a national scandal before Beecher was acquitted. Woodhull, having lost the election in the midst of the scandal, moved to England to lecture and settle down with her sister and a third husband.

Woodhull's fame as a woman's rights supporter and her infamy as a proponent of what many Americans saw as radical, if not downright immoral, causes gave opponents considerable ammunition against woman suffrage. The movement suffered further in 1872, when Anthony called for women nationwide to vote in the election, arguing that the Fourteenth Amendment provided that right for women citizens. She was arrested, and other women began court challenges to secure their right to suffrage. In 1875, the Supreme Court unanimously ruled in *Minor v. Happersett* that the Fourteenth Amendment did not guarantee woman suffrage. In 1878, activists turned to Congress, proposing a constitutional amendment for woman suffrage that would be introduced in Congress every session for the next forty-one years, although seldom voted upon. By the late 1870s, the woman's rights movement entered a period when they seemed unable to garner any favorable press. Despite activists keeping the issue of woman suffrage alive, and women winning the right to vote in Wyoming Territory and keeping it as Wyoming entered the Union in 1890, progress toward national woman suffrage was slow.

In 1890, the split between the NWSA and the AWSA was mended when they formed the National American Woman Suffrage Association—the NAWSA, also called the "National." Led by Carrie Chapman Catt of

Iowa, and Dr. Anna Howard Shaw of Big Rapids, Michigan, the united group put far less emphasis on social reforms and far more emphasis on winning the right to vote. The new leaders also focused their rhetoric less on the rights that women possessed and more on the special qualities women would bring to the polls. Women's superior moral abilities, the group argued, meant that voting women would help clean up politics.

In addition to the causes of suffrage and women's rights, politically active women during Reconstruction formed coalitions with other women and men to achieve various political goals: prohibiting the production of alcohol; enfranchising or disenfranchising black men; preserving Catholic schools or promoting Protestant ones; and promoting a protective tariff or fighting against higher taxes of any kind. Women's political views and actions were as varied as men's. There was no single "woman's point of view" that politicians could use to determine what to do to help women. Women's politics were affected by their economic and social class, the political stances that partisan groups took, by their religion, their region, their race, in short, by all the factors that made men's political actions and views different.

As Democrats, Republicans, or supporters of third parties, women continued to participate in formal politics during Reconstruction and beyond, just as they had done prior to the Civil War. More women were included in party rallies as speakers as well as in their traditional roles as supporters. They sang in glee clubs, marched in parades, and gave so-called stump speeches, named after the tree stumps that originally served as platforms. Smaller third parties attracted women's supporters. Mary Todd was on the platform committee for the California Greenback-Labor Party in 1882; the party also nominated her for state attorney general.

African American women joined black men in political activities as well, marching with them in Republican campaign parades. Freedwomen in Georgia donated funds to help pay male speakers, and wore Ulysses Grant buttons during his campaign for the presidency. Political conventions in the South were often held in churches, and black women voted along with the men. Not until after the Fifteenth Amendment failed to guarantee black women any right to vote, did men exclude women from voting at these kinds of conventions. Black codes were replaced by *Jim Crow* laws, which codified segregation between the races, beginning about 1877, after Union forces withdrew from the South and returned the state governments to conservative white southerners. Denied the vote both because of their race and their gender, African American women lived in a world of double discrimination and oppression.

Prohibition and the Woman's Christian Temperance Union

As it became clear that women were not going to be allowed to vote under the Fourteenth Amendment, activist women looked to new political parties to promote their causes. The Fourteenth and Fifteenth Amendments widened the franchise to include all men as voters, thus increasing the

FRANCES WILLARD URGES HER FOLLOWERS TO "DO EVERYTHING"

Frances Willard, president of the Woman's Christian Temperance Union, began her address before the Second Biennial Convention of the World's Woman's Christian Temperance Union in October 1893. She addressed the "White Ribbon Army," referring to the ribbons members wore, and proclaimed the necessity of including other reforms as part of the temperance movement and a part of her "Do-Everything Policy."

"Beloved Comrades of the White Ribbon Army:

"WHEN we began the delicate, difficult, and dangerous operation of dissecting out the alcohol nerve from the body politic, we did not realize the intricacy of the undertaking nor the distances that must be traversed by the scalpel of investigation and research. In about seventy days from now, twenty years will have elapsed since the call of battle sounded its bugle note among the homes and hearts of Hillsboro, Ohio. . . . [W]e know that but one thought, sentiment and purpose animated those saintly 'Praying Bands' whose name will never die out from human history. 'Brothers, we beg you not to drink and not to sell!' . . . The 'Do Everything Policy' was not of our choosing, but is an evolution as inevitable as any traced by the naturalist or described by the

importance of political parties as agents of change. Prohibition, for example, benefited not only from women's participation in the Woman's Christian Temperance Union (WCTU), founded in 1874 by women in the Midwest, but also from the support of the Prohibition Party, originally founded in 1869. The WCTU was the largest organization of its kind. Its first president, Annie Wittenmeyer, a former Civil War nurse, led the group in founding 1,000 chapters in 23 states. Frances Willard, a former college president and successor to Wittenmeyer, visited every town and city in America with a population of 10,000 or more to set up chapters and promote temperance, physical fitness, and her "Do Everything" philosophy. That philosophy argued that women should learn about and speak out on every social issue that concerned them, should own their own businesses, and should get involved in the public sphere not only of the nation, but also of the world. Willard practiced what she preached, learning to ride a bicycle at the age of sixty and forming the World WCTU (1883) as she guided the national organization between 1879 and 1898. (See Primary Source 6-2.)

The link between the WCTU and the Prohibition Party was particularly strong. The party hired four WCTU women as paid campaign lecturers, and at one point, women were more than 30 percent of the delegates to the national party conventions. Frances Willard served on the executive committee, and the national platform endorsed woman suffrage as a way for the party to achieve prohibition. Members of the WCTU who were too retiring for such public activities helped the cause by collecting names historian. Woman's genius for details, and her patient steadfastness in following the enemies of those she loves 'through every lane of life,' have led her to antagonise the alcohol habit and the liquor traffic just where they are, wherever that may be. If she does this, since they are everywhere, her policy will be 'Do Everything.'

"A one-sided movement makes one-sided advocates. . . . An all-round movement can only be carried forward by all-round advocates; a scientific age requires the study of every subject in its correlations. It was once supposed that light, heat, and electricity were wholly separate entities; it is now believed and practically proved that they are but different modes of motion. . . . Some bright women who have opposed the 'Do-Everything Policy' used as their favourite illustration a flowing river, and expatiated on the ruin that would follow if that river (which represents their do-one-thing policy) were diverted into many channels, but it should be remembered that the most useful of all rivers is the Nile, and that the agricultural economy of Egypt consists in the effort to spread its waters upon as many fields as possible. It is not for the river's sake that it flows through the country but for the sake of the fertility it can bring upon adjoining fields, and this is pre-eminently true of the Temperance Reform. . . .

"Let us not be disconcerted, but stand bravely by that blessed trinity of movements, Prohibition, Woman's Liberation and Labour's uplift."

Source: "President's Address," in the Minutes of the Second Biennial Convention of the World's Woman's Christian Temperance Union (Chicago: 1893), 37–38.

and addresses of potential voters and sending them to headquarters, along with enough money to pay the postage for the WCTU mailings. Other women, less shy, attended or participated in parades or gave stump speeches. Sallie Chapin, a South Carolinian, successfully spoke in Allendale, Mississippi, in part because the town's liquor dealers prevented men, not women, from lecturing on temperance. Still others carried out saloon raids, singing hymns outside their doors to shame the imbibers within.

The Prohibition Party ran candidates for president against Republicans and Democrats. Prohibitionists hoped to use the nonsectional issue of temperance to win support from Southerners, since the white South was ferociously Democratic after the war, and busily preventing black Republicans from voting. Southern women temperance supporters, however, preferred to appeal to the Democrats to add prohibition to their party's platform rather than desert their party for the Prohibition Party. Southern WCTU members also used less public means of political action than their Northern counterparts: petitions instead of parades, for example, to raise the same points, but their pleas to the Democrats were largely ignored and, in the end, neither major party embraced prohibition or woman suffrage.

Labor Reform and Resistance

Working-class women's involvement in labor movements had a long history, since women numbered among the first factory workers in the country. When the textile industry required women operatives to speed-up or stretch-out their production, working faster or doing more work for the same wage, women workers had protested and turned-out, trying to force owners to restore their wages. Economic growth after the Civil War brought far more women into the paid labor force than ever before, and they were paid less than men were for doing the same work. Male laborers, underpaid and overworked as well, tried to form labor unions to protest working conditions and wages. The Supreme Court had ruled in *Commonwealth v. Hunt* (1842) that unions were legal, but economic hard times in the first half of the century limited their numbers. Not until after the Civil War did union formation increase.

Unions asked for reforms such as an eight-hour day, replacing the ten- to twelve-hour day that was common; the abolition of child and convict labor, both so cheap that regular wage workers could not compete; the institution of a graduated income tax, so the rich would pay more than the poor; equal pay for equal work; and the development of a federal bureau of labor statistics to provide information labor groups could use to challenge owners during any negotiations. Among the many groups that demanded higher wages and better treatment from their employers were craft unions, which were groups organized around a specific trade. These included the first women's union, the Collar Laundry Union of Troy, New York (1864), as well as the mixed-sex Cigarmakers International Union (1867), and the Women's Typographical Union (1869). Most labor groups negotiated by presenting a united front, but would strike if necessary. The laundresses of Jackson, Mississippi, for example, struck in 1866 after the mayor ignored their petition for higher wages. Their plea explained the need for higher wages to offset higher prices that made it "impossible" for them to "live uprightly and honestly." In declaring that they would set uniform rates for the laundry they did, they carefully explained that they did so not to exploit their employers, but to "live comfortably if possible from the fruits of our labor." In Galveston, Texas, in 1877, washerwomen and domestic servants did the same. In 1881, Atlanta laundresses formed a 3,000-member Washing Society, canvassed door-to-door, met in churches to plan, and struck to raise their rates and protect their independence from the white community. Despite arrests of activists and threats to build a competing laundry or to lay high taxes on Washing Society members, the women held fast and openly informed the public of their desire for respect and decent wages, quite an accomplishment in the racist South, which preferred more docile workers.

In 1869, the first national women's labor union, the Daughters of St. Crispin (patron saint of shoemakers), was founded in Lynn, Massachusetts, to organize workers in the shoe industry. It proved short-lived, however, ending in 1873 during a national economic depression. Women looking for union support had more luck with the Knights of Labor, which began admitting women as well as African Americans to its organization in 1881. Within four years, the Knights had a Women's Department with a full-time organizer, Lenora M. Barry, who inspected factories and working conditions. She found factories where women stood in bare feet on water-covered stone floors in the dead of winter and were not allowed to change into dry clothes to walk home; other factories where corset makers were fined ten cents for "eating, laughing, singing or talking," and were subject of rules "equally slavish and unjust." Elizabeth Rodgers of Chicago, one of many women leaders in the Knights, served as a "Master Workman" at the District Assembly, where 600 delegates represented 40,000 women workers. By 1887, the union had 65,000 women active in a membership of 700,000, and combined their support for equal pay and decent working conditions with support for woman suffrage and temperance.

The Knights of Labor preferred negotiations to strikes at first, but they were gradually thrust into militant action as members saw negotiations against powerful employers—Big Business—fail. As the group became more militant, the public grew more distrustful of their goals. In May of 1886 in Chicago, after a series of strikes citywide calling for an eight-hour day, the Knights of Labor went on strike at McCormick Harvesting Company, trying to gain the shorter workday. The company used nonunion workers, called *scabs*, as strikebreakers, and protected them with police. A fight broke out with the strikers, four were killed and many others injured. The next day, a rally at Haymarket Square held in support of the strikers degenerated into a riot after police were sent in. Someone threw a bomb; seven police officers and four strikers died. Scores of men and women were detained, arrested, beaten, or coerced into confessions. Along with union members, many anarchists (who opposed both capitalism as an economic system and most forms of government) were rounded up. Eight men were convicted of conspiracy to commit murder, and sentenced to be hanged.

Lucy Parsons, a mixed-race former slave from Texas who had emigrated to Chicago in 1873, was arrested after the Haymarket Riot. She went to jail but was eventually released. A leader of the Working Women's Union, she had long joined with labor agitators fighting for decent working conditions. Her husband, Albert, one of the alleged conspirators, was convicted and sentenced to death, despite the fact he was at home during the bombing. Lucy organized petitions and went on a national tour to give speeches against the wrongful convictions of her husband and other activists, achieving international notice for her eloquence. Thousands came to hear her speeches, and the Chicago police regarded her as "more dangerous than a thousand rioters." Her appeals failed. Her husband and the other agitators were executed on November 11, 1887, while she and her children, who had come to try to visit him prior to the execution, were locked in a jail cell until it was over. Parsons' radical beliefs, support for anarchists, and agitation on behalf of militant labor made her the enemy of big business and a hero to thousands of laborers.

Most Americans blamed the Knights of Labor for the Haymarket Riot, despite the Knights divorcing themselves from the Parsons and the other convicted men in an attempt to save their organization. Union men and women fled to join the more male-oriented American Federation of Labor (AFL), founded in 1886. The AFL allowed women as members and sometimes actively recruited them, but were not as inclusive as the Knights of Labor. As a confederation of craft unions, they accepted only skilled laborers rather than unskilled workers, of which women were the majority.

Women did organize some locals, the smallest units in unions where members participated directly, electing leaders and collecting dues. Elizabeth Morgan joined with other Chicago women and organized the Ladies Federal Labor Union No. 2703, representing twenty-two different trade groups of women, including clerks, typists, music teachers, gum makers, candy makers, bookbinders, dressmakers, and even housewives. No. 2703 allied with other reformers to tackle social issues that affected women, including suffrage, factory inspections for safety, and compulsory public education.

Despite these efforts, women's unions were limited in number and scope within the AFL, soon the largest and most powerfull union in the country. Led by Samuel Gompers, the AFL in general upheld the ideal of the "family wage" for male breadwinners and believed that women were unfair competitors in the labor market. Even the atmosphere in their meetings, held in saloons at night, discouraged female participation. As Alice Henry, a member of the Chicago Employees' Association and early historian of the union put it in her 1915 history of trade women: "the inferior position held by women in the industrial world was therefore inevitably reflected in the Federation." The organizational structure that had provided working-class women with real opportunities in the Knights of Labor went missing in the AFL, which focused its concerns on male-dominated trades such as iron and steel production, building trades, mining, and other skilled crafts. So few women worked in heavy industry and so many women worked in domestic service (2.76 vs. 30.83 percent) that organizing women into any sort of union was difficult. Nevertheless, by 1890 nearly 19 percent of working women were unionized.

While there were fewer women than men in unions, women whose husbands, fathers, brothers, and sons belonged to unions often joined them in strikes. Near Pittsburgh in 1892, the Amalgamated Association of Iron and Steel Workers, the leading craft union at Andrew Carnegie's Homestead steel mill, wanted to negotiate for better pay as management tried to save money by installing labor-saving devices and cutting wages. Henry Clay Frick, Carnegie's partner, locked out the workers and brought in 300 private detectives from the Pinkerton Detective Agency to break the union and control the mill. The Pinkertons, as they were called, marched into town and were met by a mob of women as well as men. The crowd assaulted them. "The women pulled us down, spat in our faces, kicked us, and tore our clothing off while the crowd jeered and cheered," said one Pinkerton. Many of the workers in the mill were not union members, but the community as a whole understood that if Carnegie and Frick succeeded in breaking the union, it threatened the livelihood of all workers. They rallied against the Pinkertons to keep these paid thugs out of their town, but the strikers met defeat when the state militia arrived in force to rescue the Pinkertons and end the lockout.

The National Economy and Domesticity

Working women's participation in union activities and their need for a living wage and decent working conditions reflected not only their own concerns but also society's gendered expectations of what was appropriate work for women. The notion of True Womanhood had been disrupted, but not destroyed by the Civil War. The definition of the American middle-class family remained one that included a non-wage-earning wife and children, and membership in the middle class remained the goal for millions of Americans, including new immigrants. To achieve that goal, men had to earn more so that their wives could stay at home. Earning more meant continuing struggles between labor and management in a rapidly changing economy.

As the American economy became more complicated, women understood the relationship between larger public economic policies and their lives. One example of this is found in the links women and politicians drew in the fight over the tariff in the 1880s. The tariff remained one of the biggest sources of income for the federal government. In 1861, the Morrill Tariff raised rates drastically on imports of finished goods, which would protect American industries trying to compete with foreign imports, but more important, would raise revenue for a government embarking on a Civil War. Later amendments raised rates even higher so that the Union could pay for the war, as well as pay for pensions after the war. After the war, Congress never lowered the rates. The tariff raised so much money that by the 1880s the government had a substantial surplus.

Many women and men in the largely Northern industrializing economy continued to support a high tariff. They argued that protecting American industries helped employers increase industrial production. That led them to hire more workers and pay workers better wages. These higher wages meant that male workers might earn enough money so that women dependent on them—their wives and daughters—would not necessarily have to work for wages at all. Women could return to or stay at home, which was where American society believed they ought to be. Still others believed that the higher pay for workers might achieve moral reform. High wages, for example, would prevent poor women from resorting to prostitution because women would have an adequate income from their own labor or from their husbands' labor.

Rural Americans, by and large, did not see the same link between a high tariff and the return of women to the home. They fought against the tariff. Desperate for relief from high prices for goods they needed to purchase and could not produce themselves, they saw the federal surplus as evidence that the tariff needed to be lowered. In 1887, President Grover Cleveland, elected in 1884 as the first Democratic president since before the Civil War, took on the task of convincing Congress to lower the tariff. He believed that a high tariff pushed up prices for everyone while protecting the jobs of only about 15 percent of American workers. Higher prices for manufactured goods meant less disposable income. That meant that men's wives, sisters, mothers, and children would have to work for wages too. In such circumstances, women might be forced to degrade themselves with labor that society thought they should not do, working in coal mines or other heavy industries, or more likely, as reformers suggested, becoming prostitutes. President Cleveland proposed readjusting the tariff rates downward. He made the issue a key part of the election campaign of 1888, when he ran against Republican Benjamin Harrison.

Cleveland's new wife, Frances Folsom Cleveland, whom he had married in 1886, assisted him in his 1888 campaign. Her actions showed not only the link that Americans perceived between larger economic issues and personal lives, but also reflected the balancing act required of women who sought to contribute to society within the continuing strictures regarding women's proper behavior. An attractive twenty-one-year-old, Frances repaired much of the president's reputation that had suffered from the disclosure during his first campaign for president that he had fathered a child born out of wedlock many years before. She also provided the country with a first lady for the first time since 1881, since the previous president, Chester Arthur, was a widower. In addition, she offered the country an acceptable role model of an educated woman. The first lady had graduated from Wells College, a woman's college founded in 1868 in Aurora, New York, and was the only first lady to date to have earned a college degree. Instead of a career, however, she chose marriage and embraced domestic life, thus easing the American public's fears about the dangers of educated women.

The popular press constantly reminded women who wanted an education that the general public clung to the notion that women should be educated to be better wives and mothers, not lawyers and doctors. Apparently agreeing with her husband's assertion that "a woman should not bother her head about political parties and public questions, and . . . should be content to rule in the domain of the house," Frances pursued the traditional domestic concerns of the first lady, yet sought to expand those social duties to include opportunities for women of other classes. She held Saturday afternoon receptions at the White House for working women; she distributed gifts to the poor children of Washington as part of the Colored Christmas Club; she helped found the University Women's Club; she was instrumental in pushing for educational opportunities for young women, including the New Jersey College for Women. The public took notice of her kind of activism and approved. In January 1888, students at Leveret College in Georgia named a literary society after her. She received so many fan letters that, for the first time, the first lady had to have a professional social secretary. Her hairstyle was copied, her fashion sense imitated, and her interests duplicated by thousands of American women, fascinated with the new first lady.

Frances Cleveland represented an acceptable image of a modern yet conventional woman in a changing era. In failing to support the cause of woman suffrage or speak out on political issues, despite her college degree, she mirrored the position many upper-class educated white women took near the end of the century. Education and wealth proved no match for the demand that women remain in a private sphere. Cleveland's public reticence, however, did not keep politically active women from using her image and name to push their own agendas, just as commercial advertisers, without her permission, used her image to sell almost everything. Democratic partisan women started Frances Cleveland Influence Clubs in 1888.

FIRST LADY FRANCES CLEVELAND In the White House about 1888. The ornate window, furnishings, plants, and accessories show the increasing elaboration of the interior characteristic of the era of expansion and growth after the Civil War, deemed the "Gilded Age."

Young women marched in parades, rode on horseback, and gave stump speeches denouncing high tariffs under the banner of the clubs. Cleveland's face appeared on badges, banners, and milk pitchers, and on campaign posters between her husband and Allen Thurman, the vice presidential candidate. In the Midwest in particular, Democratic women used the overwhelming popularity of Frances Cleveland to justify their own participation in politics as members of Frankie Cleveland clubs.

Americans' enthusiasm for the first lady did not translate to the ballot box; Cleveland won the popular vote, but lost the electoral vote. The tariff was not lowered until the early part of the next century. Cleveland ran again for president in 1892 and won. The enthusiasm women had for his wife had not abated. Still, he protested when Mary Frost Ormsby, a Democratic activist in New York, wanted to form a national Frances Cleveland Influence Club. Using Mrs. Cleveland's image on party ephemera and linking her name to small clubs were allowed, but the president would not permit a national organization to use his wife's image in such a manner, too far outside presidential and husbandly control to be tolerated. In President

Cleveland's view, educated women from the first lady on down still needed to respect the limits of domesticity.

Birth Control and Voluntary Motherhood

Despite the desire of Americans from the president on down to control women and channel their behavior into acceptable patterns, women often resisted attempts by society designed to limit their personal freedom. That resistance took many forms. One was controlling fertility by limiting the number of children they had. In the era after the Civil War, as the country gradually became more urban, families needed fewer children to work the farms. Fertility rates declined after the Civil War, in part because of the loss of young marriageable men to the war, but also because more women were learning about, gaining access to, and using ways to achieve *voluntary motherhood.*

Limiting fertility, or voluntary motherhood, took many forms, and documents that record women's use of birth control are scarce; such private matters were seldom discussed even in women's diaries. Women had long used abortions and abortifacients (drugs inducing miscarriage); such methods were legal under British and American law and ended about 20 percent of all pregnancies. From the late 1840s, however, and particularly after the Civil War, legislators passed laws to limit the availability and use of many birth control methods. Many feared a decline in the birthrate would mean a corresponding decline in the strength of America. Some feared a decline in the number of white, native-born babies would mean that control of the country would fall to immigrants. Some objected to the advertising of abortifacients and abortionists, both explicit and omnipresent in the larger cities, and some feared for the health of the women who used such treatments.

Limiting access to information about birth control began with physicians. Over the course of the nineteenth century, medical schools trained mostly male physicians and sought to control medical licensing to limit the practice of medicine to those who had gone through formal training. This movement to professionalize medicine, supported by the American Medical Association (founded in 1847), defined anyone not trained in an AMA-approved medical schools as an "irregular" physician. Many Americans preferred irregular physicians—midwives, homeopaths, osteopaths, and other traditional practitioners—as alternative sources of health care, including information on birth control. Yet, despite regular physicians' dismal rate of patient deaths, they largely succeeded in replacing irregular medicine with the more scientific and formal medicine that they practiced. Physicians replaced midwives for prenatal care and childbirth, and abortion, legal everywhere before 1830, was gradually limited by state laws so that it had become largely illegal by 1880, practiced only by proponents of irregular medicine.

Whether women went to regular or irregular physicians, many wanted information so they could limit the number of children they had. Finding and using information about fertility was closely linked to social and economic class: the wealthy had fewer children than the poor. Condoms made of sheepskin had been available for years, but only to the wealthy. Charles Goodyear's 1846 discovery of how to vulcanize rubber so that it remained pliable and stable led to the invention of cheaper condoms and of diaphragms, imported from Europe to America later in the century, for use by the middle class. Doctors and priests recommended abstinence to the poor, along with instructions to accept their lot in life. Male continence, where men refrained from ejaculation completely, was recommended by the voluntary motherhood supporters, who believed no woman should be forced against her will to bear a child. Withdrawal before ejaculation (*coitus interruptus*) continued to be the most popular form of birth control, along with douching after intercourse and abortion.

In 1873, birth control information went even further underground when Congress passed the Comstock Act. Named after Anthony Comstock, founder and secretary of New York state's Society for the Suppression of Vice, the law gave Comstock nearly dictatorial powers to declare material "obscene" and remove it from the U.S. mails. Offended by both the prostitutes and the explicit advertisements for birth control that he saw while a salesman in New York City, Comstock decided that the availability of birth control promoted promiscuity. After only an hour's debate by Congress, male representatives deemed birth control information obscene and illicit under the provisions of the Comstock Law. Such information could no longer be sent through the mails, which meant that women too shy or unable to ask their physicians for it had little access to it. Comstock became a U.S. Postal Service inspector and personally went after those he deemed violators of his standards of decency. State after state adopted versions of the Comstock Law, opposing most uses of contraception.

Despite the fact that contraceptives limited pregnancies, most activists supporting voluntary motherhood opposed their use. They viewed most birth control methods as unnatural and feared men would demand sexual submission more often if the fear of pregnancy was removed. Supporters of voluntary motherhood supported voluntary sex instead, so that women could control not only their fertility, but their sexuality as well. Consequently, the majority of those who promoted voluntary motherhood did so by recommending periodic abstinence, where couples used the so-called rhythm method and had sexual intercourse on days when the woman was least fertile, or permanent abstinence—celibacy. This, argued proponents, could be enforced by the woman. A woman's right to refuse her husband's request to have sex was a radical notion at a time when both law and custom made having sex with her husband her duty. For reformers, however, a woman's right to refuse provided evidence of her independence and of her rights. (See Primary Source 6-3.) Elizabeth Cady Stanton was so convinced of the necessity of women being able to control their fertility that she held women-only sessions during her 1871 lecture tour, where she spoke "the gospel of fewer children & a healthy, happy maternity." Stanton and other reformers were not interested in promoting sexual freedom for women, but rather freedom from sex that produced the risk of unwanted motherhood.

HARRIOT STANTON BLATCH ON VOLUNTARY MOTHERHOOD

Harriot Stanton Blatch, Elizabeth Cady Stanton's daughter, followed in the footsteps of both her famous mother and her colleague Susan B. Anthony. Prompted by Stanton, Anthony founded the National Council of Women of the United States in 1888. The group held its first meeting in 1891, with a program of speeches on temperance, education, women's political status, and women's associations. An extra session was added that allowed speakers on topics such as dress reform, literature, and legal disabilities. The last speaker that evening was Harriot Stanton Blatch, who addressed the issue of voluntary motherhood. Throughout her talk, she linked the ideas of planned maternity to progress, using the language of Charles Darwin's theories on evolution, an ideological development of the late nineteenth century called Social Darwinism.

"Men talk of the sacredness of motherhood, but judging from their acts it is the last thing that is held sacred in the human species. Poets sing and philosophers reason about the holiness of the mother's sphere, but men in laws and customs have degraded the woman in her maternity. Motherhood is sacred,—that is, voluntary motherhood; but the woman who bears unwelcome children is outraging every duty she owes the race. The mothers of the human species should turn to the animals, and from the busy caretakers, who are below them in most things, learn the simple truths of procreation. Let women but understand the part unenforced maternity has played in the evolution of animal life, and their reason will guide them to the true path of race development. Let them

Agrarian Reformers

The hard times after the Civil War that drove so many activists into new areas of reform were particularly noticeable in the rural sections of the country. Not only did the manufacturing sector expand after the Civil War, so did agriculture. New areas opened for white and black settlement, and new inventions and machinery increased agricultural production. Huge numbers of immigrants from Europe and migrants from the South and the East headed to the Great Plains to grow wheat and raise cattle on land that until recently had been populated by Indians, who were quickly being limited to reservations. Free blacks migrated to own their own farms or share-cropped on lands where they had once been slaves. While agricultural production increased, the changes in the ways farmers did business were costly. It took more money to buy land, and the machinery to farm it was expensive. In the South, sharecropping was a ticket to constant debt, since the landowners provided the seed on credit and sharecroppers seldom made enough to pay back what they had borrowed after their crops came in. When landowners began to demand cash from tenants instead of a proportion of the crop, farmers suffered even more. Even if they produced more crops, the increased production led to a decrease in price, as supply outstripped demand. Even shipping crops to market cost more money than it had before. Crops were note that natural selection has carefully fostered the maternal instinct. The offspring of the fondest females in each animal species, having of course the most secure and prolonged infancy, are 'naturally selected' to continue their kind. The female offspring gains by inheritance in philoprogenitiveness, and thus is built up the instinct which prepares the females of a higher species for a more developed altruism. Through countless ages mother-love has been evolved and been working out its mission; surely women should recognize the meaning of the instinct, and should refuse to prostitute their creative powers, and so jeopardize the progress of the human race. Upon the mothers must rest in the last instance the development of any species.

"In this work women need not hope for help from men. The sense of obligation to offspring, men possess but feebly; there has not been developed by animal evolution an instinct of paternity. They are not disinherited fathers; they are simply unevolved parents. There is no ground for wonder that this is so; for in but a few species among the lower animals is even a suggestion of paternal instinct found.... Men like to accumulate, and hand down their accumulations with their name. This is a method of securing some sort of immortality, and gives rise to the neglect of illegitimate children, the preference of male to female offspring, the law of primogeniture.... A woman does not discriminate between her legitimate and illegitimate child; [but] mothers [were not] instrumental in making legal codes.... Ever since the patriarchate was established there has been a tendency to cramp the mother in her maternal rights; so we see no race improvement comparable with our advance in material science. Those who could improve humanity have been hindered by those who prefer to improve steam-engines."

Source: From Harriot Stanton Blatch, "Voluntary Motherhood," in *Transactions of the National Council of Women of the United States, Assembled in Washington, DC, February 22 to 25, 1891*, ed. Rachel Foster Avery (Philadelphia: 1891), 280–281.

now stored in grain elevators, whose operators took a percentage of the value of the crop as payment. Crops were then shipped to markets by railroad. The railroads were monopolies, able to set any price they pleased. As the railroads crisscrossed the country, the cost of moving goods lessened, but railroads often kept the difference, racking up huge profits. The agricultural sector of the U.S. economy suffered a financial panic and depression from the 1870s on, made worse by droughts and bad harvests.

Farmers organized to meet the challenges. In 1867, Oliver Kelly of Minnesota founded the National Grange of the Patrons of Husbandry, the *Grange*. Begun as a social and educational organization, by 1875 some 875,000 farmers belonged to the Grange and turned their interest to a fight against monopolies and middlemen—the railroads, banks, and merchants more interested in profit than fair treatment. Members of the Grange formed cooperatives to buy in bulk to save members money. They also formed banks to loan money to farmers at lower rates of interest, built cooperative grain elevators to store members' crops until market prices increased, and even attempted to manufacture farm equipment for sale to members. "Grangers" lobbied state legislatures, pushing them to regulate grain elevators as well as the railroads that transported products to market.

Women in the Grange were equal members of the organization, rather than being shunted off into women's auxiliaries. They published articles in

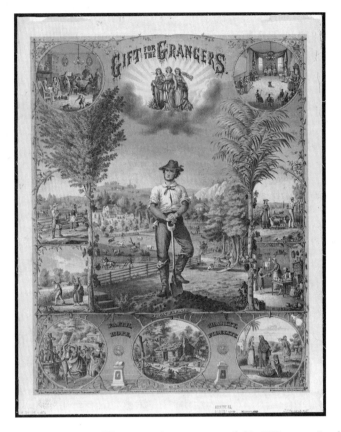

"GIFT FOR THE GRANGERS"   Women are in every scene of this 1873 promotional poster for the Grange that celebrated the work of farmers, from the lower right's portrait of women in biblical times to the women of the "modern" era, herding sheep, dancing, listening to a speaker, playing the piano, sowing crops, and feeding a child.

the periodical *The Grange Visitor* and lobbied state and local organizations to support farmers' interests. At social gatherings, they put on pageants that illustrated the plight of the farmer. Grange women had full voting rights in the group, and the Grange supported woman suffrage. An upturn in the agricultural economy in the 1880s and the failure to achieve many of their goals, however, cost the Grange much of their membership. The group eventually returned to its social and educational roots, surviving into the twenty-first century.

Other groups arose with interests similar to those of the Grange. One of the most powerful, the Farmers Alliance, formed in 1877 in Lampasas County, Texas. Thirteen years later, the group had spread throughout the South, then the Midwest, and spawned a separate Colored Farmers Alliance in Southern states. Cooperative purchasing and marketing, as well as a federal farm credit plan characterized the Farmers Alliance, and the groups had social and political activities as well. Alliance Glee Clubs performed songs supporting farmers' issues, while Alliance publications supported equality for women, declaring that the Alliance had come "to redeem woman from her enslaved condition, and place her in her proper sphere." That proper sphere was apparently outside the domestic circle, and as one North Carolina woman put it, "Drudgery, fashion and gossip are no longer the bounds of woman's sphere." Instead women took political action. Alliance women traveled the circuit promoting the group's ideas. The Alliance's best-known orator was Mary Elizabeth Lease, a tall, imposing mother of four from Kansas, long involved with prohibition and woman suffrage. She stumped the Great Plains states, instructing farmers appalled by high rates for mortgages and railroad shipping to "raise less corn and more hell!" Her oratory was stirring, causing newspaper editor William Allen White of Emporia to remark, "she could recite the multiplication table and set a crowd hooting and harrahing at her will."

In 1890, Lease joined other Farmers Alliance members in founding the Populist Party, a third party that would compete with the Democrats, seen as too Southern and too conservative, and the Republicans, deemed to be in the pocket of big business. For a third-party, newly formed political organization, the Populists were surprisingly successful in the 1890 elections. They won the governor's seat and took control of one legislative house in Kansas, and won both houses in the Nebraska legislature. Both states sent senators from the Populist Party to Washington. The party also did well in South Dakota and Minnesota, and by 1892, the Populists ran a national candidate for president, James Weaver of Iowa. Lease, a voting member of the party like other women delegates to the convention, gave the speech seconding Weaver's nomination for the presidency.

A drought in the 1880s, low prices for cotton by 1890, and an influx of reformers—the Knights of Labor, the Greenbackers (who supported paper money, making cash easier to come by for farmers), the WCTU, the "Christian Socialist" German immigrants, along with farmers, North, West, and South—all contributed to the success of the Populists. Supportive of both woman suffrage and temperance, the Populist Party also wanted agrarian reform. It wanted the government to help end the foreclosures of farms. It also called for a progressive income tax, as well as government regulation and public ownership of railroads and telegraph lines. Lease and other women speakers lectured and wrote and toured the country, many borrowing imagery from the abolitionist movement to use in their political rhetoric. One pamphleteer, Mary Hobart, wrote that those suffering the "bondage of class legislation" needed "emancipation," words that drew parallels between farmers and former slaves to illuminate how dire was the fate of farmers. Her words were somewhat ironic; the issue of race beleaguered the Populists as politicians such as Tom Watson of Georgia attempted to attract black supporters but refused to consider them social equals.

Other Populist speakers emphasized the moral consequences of the country's current economic policy, arguing that economic distress led women to prostitution and that the next "abolition" movement should be the abolition of the sex trade. Still others pointed to the work of labor unions and successful strikes, suggesting possible actions Populists could adopt to achieve their goals. Populists focused attention on the damage done to rural families, still the majority of Americans in the 1890s, and urged men to vote for "Sallie and the babies"—in other words, their wives and children—to protect the family from the corruption of Republicans and Democrats alike by voting Populist. The Populist Party would continue to attract followers in the 1890s, fighting against what they called the "moral, political, and material ruin" they feared would destroy America.

The Women's Club Movement

Rural women who joined the Grange or the Farmers Alliance, or who worked for the Populist Party, recognized the power of collective action to help reshape America, as did the suffragists who had united to form the NAWSA. Other women established clubs throughout the country to use the power of community to attempt change. Having worked together in voluntary benevolent organizations before the Civil War and in relief organizations during the war, women sought to continue their efforts to improve American life through women's clubs after the war.

In 1868, Jane Cunningham Croly, a New York journalist, founded the Sorosis Club of New York. In 1890, she called for a national women's club organization, the General Federation of Women's Clubs. In the intervening years, the *women's club movement* blossomed. Whether for social gatherings, civic or educational purposes, self-improvement or community outreach, women's clubs enrolled thousands of members during this time. Members were mostly middle class and middle-aged, with time and wealth enough for leisure pursuits. The Sorosis Club of New York City, established by women who had been barred from a celebration with famed author Charles Dickens, provided a place for women to socialize, learn, and improve themselves and their worlds. Woman suffrage and religions were the only two topics banned from discussion. Invited members might listen to a lecture on the ways that women were portrayed in art, or might sponsor a scholarship for a young woman artist. Literature, science, the home, business, philanthropy, drama—all were topics for discussion, and meetings provided occasions for networking and education. Soon Sorosis groups sprang up all over America.

In Boston, Julia Ward Howe founded the New England Women's Club in February 1868. It met every Monday, alternating discussions of art and literature with lectures by experts in other fields of interest. Important community questions, wrote Howe in an early history of the club, as well as "reforms which have proved very valuable, were sometimes started at these meetings, and have been much forwarded by the action of the club." These two organizations, Sorosis and the New England Women's Club, promoted the notion of women allying with each other locally and then reaching out to regional and national groups to network with each other. There was an astounding variety of women's clubs: the Society for the Encouragement of Studies at Home; the Zenana Missions in India; Women's Press Clubs in major cities; the Promotion of Physical Culture Club; the Woman's Army Relief Corps; Ladies' Catholic Benevolent Association; the Woman's Club of Indianapolis; the Emma Willard Association; the

Non-Partisan WCTU; the Shut-In Society; the Century Club of San Francisco; the Columbian Association of Housekeepers; the New York Association of Working Girls; the Eastern Star organization; the Nebraska Ceramic Club; the Girls' Mutual Benefit Club; the Girls' Friendly Society. Church women organized and funded groups such as the Woman's American Baptist Home Missionary Society to support their churches' missionary outreach. Beginning in 1873, the Association for the Advancement of Women held annual three-day conferences in American cities, lecturing on women's roles and capabilities to all who were interested, and inspiring many listeners to form their own women's clubs at home. The interests represented by women's clubs truly ran the gamut.

In the South, where there was not as substantial a tradition of women's benevolent associations, the women's club movement began a decade later than in the Northeast and the West. Many Southern women found their way to the club movement through the WCTU, while others formed clubs to satisfy their desires for more education. The Atlanta History Club in Georgia studied nineteenth-century history, the Quid Nunc club in Little Rock, Arkansas, pondered Greek and Roman history. Ladies' literary clubs in the South built free libraries, studied Shakespeare, read poetry, and, not incidentally, kept the image of the Southern Lady alive. The Nineteenth Century Club of Memphis, for example, proposed not only to widen women's intellectual horizon, but also "to better fit them to direct the education and training of their children, and bring them nearer a true place in their husband's life and interests."

African American Women in the Club Movement

Excluded from most white women's clubs, African American women formed their own clubs not only to educate themselves but also to promote the "uplift" of the race. Many black women embraced some of the tenets of True Womanhood after the Civil War, but not all. Although black women were encouraged to marry, raise children, and keep a home, they were also encouraged to be activists. Marriage was not seen as an impediment to black activism, as it was for white "True Women." Because enslaved and free black women had long worked outside the household, the African American community valued women's self-sufficiency. As African American historian William T. Alexander declared in *The History of the Colored Race in America* in 1888, "We want men and women who will think for themselves." Black women doctors, editors, and activists were praised by the black press and women who pursued careers outside the home were still seen as beautiful and feminine.

Mary Ann Shadd Cary's career exemplifies not only the activism expected of educated free black women, but also the interweaving strands of reform efforts by many women that preceded the Civil War and continued in the decades after. After the Emancipation Proclamation took effect in 1863, Cary suspended her work for the colonization of escaped slaves in Canada. Martin Delany, a leading black activist, hired Cary to recruit African American troops for the Union Army. As had thousands of other women during the war, Cary ignored social conventions to serve her country, and spent months recruiting, persisting in the face of harassment by opponents of black soldiers as well as opponents of black people. After the war, Cary moved to Washington, DC, where she addressed the Colored National Labor Union, giving a speech on women's rights and demanding that black women have a place in black labor unions. She found a job as a teacher and soon became a principal of the Lincoln School, while attending the law school of the newly created Howard University, the first African American woman to do so.

Cary became active in the black temperance movement, giving lectures linking temperance with women's rights, education, and moral reform. In 1880, she formed the Colored Women's Progressive Franchise Association, promoting black women's rights and entrepreneurship. Refusing to accept the limits of True Womanhood imposed on "proper" ladies, Cary argued that black men needed to share power with black women to benefit both. She received her law degree from Howard University in 1883, but because the bar association for the District of Columbia would not certify her—nor any black lawyer—she never made a living as a lawyer. She had instead worked as an educator, a newspaper publisher, a writer, an abolitionist, an emigrationist, and an army recruiter, building a life that served innumerable reform efforts in the nineteenth century. Yet when she died in 1893, she felt stymied by discrimination against her both as a black person and as a woman.

THE PANIC OF 1893

The same year Cary died, in February 1893, just days before newly elected President Cleveland took office for his second term, the Philadelphia & Reading Railroad, one of the most important and powerful railroads in the eastern part of the country, went bankrupt. Collateral businesses and banks, dependent on the railroad, went under. The stock market crashed, and European investors withdrew from the American market. The agricultural sector, already depressed, sank further. Four million Americans lost their jobs and the unemployment rate reached 25 percent. Credit tightened. Interest rates soared. Fifteen thousand businesses and 500 banks failed in the Panic of 1893. President Cleveland, a fiscal conservative, did little, believing the economy would best right itself without intervention.

Activists were horrified by the impact of the Panic of 1893 on the lives of the disadvantaged in American society. Once again, women without property laws to protect them were at the mercy of their husbands' creditors. Once again, the failure of society to provide for the unemployed resulted in homelessness and starvation. Once again, the poor got poorer, while the rich seemed little affected by the calamity. So once again, the call went out for women to be allowed to participate in public action in order to help solve the country's problems. Caroline Nichols Churchill, publisher of a Colorado woman's rights newspaper, *The Queen Bee*, made clear the absolute necessity of women winning the right to vote. In an 1893 editorial written in support of that western state's successful vote on woman suffrage, she pointed out the benefits of involving women in government. Give women the vote, she argued, and "the women of this nation can arrest the development of rascality sufficient to prevent history from repeating itself. . . . The emancipation of the women of the country simply means the dawn of a golden era." After 1893, the fight for that "golden era" began in earnest.

THINK MORE ABOUT IT

1. Return to the opening vignette about Eda Hickam. How does her effort to gain payment for work she did for a white family exemplify the tenacity of African Americans and other women to assert their rights in the last half of the nineteenth century? Juxtaposed with the growing suffrage movement of the era, how does Hickam's struggle illustrate the differences in opportunities afforded American women of different backgrounds?

2. Compare and contrast the lives of Southern, Northern, and Native American women during the period termed *Reconstruction*. What common problems did they face? What particular issues confronted each? How did gender shape their similar and different experiences?

3. As in earlier periods, both violence perpetrated by whites and laws passed by the federal government shaped Native American lives during the late nineteenth century. With reference to at least three concrete examples, discuss how these two forces dramatically altered the lives of Native American women in the years following the Civil War.

4. While most women workers continued to be employed in the jobs that had a predominantly female labor force, some areas of paid work expanded and others opened up for women after the Civil War. How did these developments connect to the rise of reform movements during this era?

5. The disputes within and fracturing of the women's rights movement following the Civil War demonstrate how difficult it is to change deeply entrenched attitudes and ideas. What were the major issues that divided supporters of women's rights during these years? How were the categories of race and gender intertwined in these debates?

6. The movement to reform American society absorbed the energies of many women in the late nineteenth century, building on and expanding beyond the efforts of antebellum women. Examine in detail the activities of the WCTU and at least two other reform and club movements that blossomed after the Civil War. Which groups of women did each of these movements attract? How did they seek to address the problems of an industrializing, urbanizing society where inequalities persisted? Taken together, what vision of America did these movements put forward?

7. Laws continued to constrain women's lives in important ways in the late nineteenth century. Thinking broadly about diverse women, discuss how various laws and the American legal system's conception of gender and race hampered women's activities and rights in a variety of arenas.

8. What did you learn in this chapter that you did not know before? How does this new information help you understand the overall story of women in American history? What topics would you like to explore further?

READ MORE ABOUT IT

Ellen DuBois, *Feminism and Suffrage: The Emergence of an Independent Women's Movement in America, 1848–1869*

Rebecca Edwards, *Angels in the Machinery: Gender in American Party Politics from the Civil War to the Progressive Era*

Carol Faulkner, *Women's Radical Reconstruction: The Freedmen's Aid Movement*

Tera W. Hunter, *To 'Joy My Freedom: Southern Black Women's Lives and Labors After the Civil War*

Caroline E. Janney, *Burying the Dead but Not the Past: Ladies' Memorial Associations and the Lost Cause*

Donald B. Marti, *Women of the Grange: Mutuality and Sisterhood in Rural America, 1866–1920*

Catherine Gilbert Murdock, *Domesticating Drink: Women, Men, and Alcohol in America, 1870–1940*

Barbara Miller Solomon, *In the Company of Educated Women: A History of Women and Higher Education in America*

Robert E. Weir, *Beyond Labor's Veil: The Culture of the Knights of Labor*

KEY CONCEPTS

National Woman Suffrage Association
American Woman Suffrage Association
Reconstruction
freedmen
black codes
Exodusters
Dawes Act
Seven Sisters Colleges
Thirteenth Amendment

Fourteenth Amendment
Fifteenth Amendment
Minor v. Happersett
Woman's Christian Temperance Union (WCTU)
Knights of Labor
voluntary motherhood
Comstock Act
Grange
Populist Party
women's club movement

Chapter 7

NEW CENTURY, NEW WOMAN

The Women's Pavilion of the Chicago Columbian Exposition of 1893

PUBLIC POWER AND PUBLIC VOICES

I n 1893, the United States held a celebration in Chicago to show the world that the country had overcome civil war and its attendant troubles. The great *Columbian Exposition*, celebrating the 400th anniversary of Columbus's arrival (a year late), showcased changes that had occurred in the country since 1865. Vast halls filled with machinery occupied a temporary city constructed on Chicago's South Side. The World's Fair, as it was called, allowed America to show off new developments in industry and the sciences, as well as women's accomplishments. This was not the first time the country had highlighted women's achievements. The nation's Centennial Exposition in Philadelphia in 1876 had included, at the last minute, a separate women's building, allowing visitors to glimpse a woman running a steam engine to signify women's entry into traditionally masculine spheres. It had also included exhibits on dress reform, women inventors, and labor-saving devices. Officials held the Centennial Exhibit's Women's Day on election day, when men would be at the polls and absent from the fair, thus preserving the separate spheres of men and women. Nevertheless, suffragists Elizabeth Cady Stanton and Susan B. Anthony had taken the opportunity to present a very political Declaration of Women's Rights at a July 4 ceremony.

The 1893 Columbian Exposition Women's Pavilion was different. Designed by a woman architect, Sophia Hayden, and overseen by a Board of Lady Managers, the Women's Pavilion was organized by a committee of women delegates from each state, the city of Chicago, and innumerable countries. Exhibits included two of the settings in which women worked: a hospital and a kindergarten. Ten-foot-tall statues of winged figures served as a focal point, surrounded by smaller figures representing the womanly virtues of love, charity, maternity, and sacrifice. Well-known Impressionist Mary Cassatt installed a triptych mural at one end of the building. Titled *Modern Woman*, its central panel, called "Young Women Plucking the Fruits of Knowledge or Science," depicted young women picking fruit from a "tree of knowledge," while at the other end of the building, *Primitive Woman* by Mary Fairchild MacMonnies, reflected women's previous place in the world by showing primitive women

WOMEN'S PAVILION, COLUMBIAN EXPOSITION   The Women's Pavilion at Chicago's 1893 Columbian Exposition was designed by Sophia Hayden, who had just graduated from the Massachusetts Institute of Technology. The Pavilion, measuring 388 by 199 feet and costing over $150,000, showcased American women's accomplishments in spectacular ways. This photograph shows the artificial lagoon that fronted the building.

carrying jars of water on their heads. The pavilion's library exhibited 7,000 books by women authors and statistics gathered on women's status around the world. The Spanish display included the sword and jewels of Queen Isabella, who had funded Columbus's voyage. Another showcased women's inventions and discoveries, another cooking schools. The Seven Sisters promoted women's education. While the exhibits ignored the wage-earning women at the fair who sold tickets, operated booths, and swept the streets, the exhibits did celebrate the accomplishments of the elite and middle-class women who had worked so hard to reconstruct and reform the country after the Civil War, and who had accomplished so much to benefit American society.

After all the celebration, however, came catastrophe. In July 1894, a fire leveled the remaining buildings of the Chicago World's Fair. It seemed symbolic, somehow—the gleaming white buildings representing so much progress and wealth charred into blackened rubble. America was in trouble. Despite the palatial homes of the super-wealthy, the so-called robber barons of the late nineteenth century, many city dwellers seemed mired in irremediable poverty. The wage-earning women swept up at the fair and then went home, unemployed when the fair ended, while the elites who planned the exhibitions returned to mansions and lives of plenty. Farmers were drowning in debt and losing their farms, dumping milk while children in cities starved. The economic upheaval called the Panic of 1893 and the resulting depression made the lives of average Americans and many immigrants so difficult that their daily survival was often in doubt. To respond to the national crisis, the disparate strands of reform efforts coalesced into powerful national organizations between 1893 and 1913, in the period historians call the Progressive Era.

Progressives continued the reform efforts that characterized American society earlier in the nineteenth century, but defined progress in many different ways. Some, such as three-time presidential candidate Democrat William Jennings Bryan, defined it as an idyllic return to a past populated by yeoman-farmers, filled with moral rectitude and Protestant religious fervor. Others, such as revolutionary Emma Goldman, saw progress in the destruction of middle-class culture and its coercive rule of law. Its replacement instead would embrace socialism, sexual freedom, women's liberation, and anarchism, and would reject government to achieve social and political liberty. A Russian emigrant moved to action following the executions after the Haymarket riot, Goldman lectured throughout the United States in the 1890s and early 1900s, rejecting existing American culture because it prevented real freedom. Goldman's pessimistic view that modern culture must be destroyed to make progress contrasted with the ideas of Jane Addams, whose Hull House workers sought to transform immigrants into Americans through education, assistance, and social reform, as well as with the ideas of Ida Tarbell, one of many journalists dedicated to exposing corruption so that existing institutions might be forced to live up to American ideals.

Progressives included many women, all determined to better America at the turn of the century. The new century—the twentieth—called for a *New Woman*, which historian Catherine Lavender has defined as women who represented the "vanguard of social usefulness and personal autonomy—independent womanhood." For many Americans, the New Woman ideal eventually replaced the ideal of True Womanhood. New Women, often college educated, often employed outside the home, took pride in being self-supporting and independent. They included feminists, who fought against America's traditional patriarchal dominance and its assumptions about women and were determined to act independently and to help the world. According to writer Charlotte Perkins Gilman in her 1914 article "Is Feminism Really So Dreadful?" a feminist was one who came "running, out of prison and off the pedestal; chains off, crown off, halo off, just a live woman." American women, Progressives and feminists both, laid claim to a greater share of public power and public voice at the dawn of the twentieth century, responding to economic and labor concerns, immigration issues, social and political changes, and achieving at long last the right to vote.

ECONOMICS, POLITICS, AND THE ELECTION OF 1896

The pace of economic change accelerated in the last decade of the nineteenth century. The catastrophic effects of the Panic of 1893 stemmed from the nature of the American economy, as the boom–bust nineteenth-century economic cycle was exacerbated by a huge growth in population and urban living. An unstable banking system, arguments over the basis for American currency, unparalleled increases in gold and silver flowing from new western mines all unsettled the economy. The tariff remained a major political issue. The rise of big business, of mass production and mass consumerism, unfettered by regulation, affected all Americans, as the government allowed market forces to operate largely uncontrolled, and the law of supply and demand prevailed.

The exponential growth in immigration and urbanization in the 1880s and 1890s led to abysmally low wages for a huge population of pieceworkers, made up mostly of women and children, laboring under appalling working conditions, trying to eke out a living. Few women had the means to change the system through the vote, and few women enjoyed the power that came from owning property. Excluded from these methods to exercise influence on the nation's political and economic systems, women disproportionately experienced the hard blows of these hard times. Many Americans believed that the blame for hard times could be laid at the feet of those who controlled the money supply, those banks that refused them credit, and the tariff, which kept prices higher on manufactured goods. Economic institutions became targets for the rage of rural women, unionists, anarchists, and miners, and of shoppers as well. Except for the very wealthy living in splendor, to many Americans, money seemed to be, if not the root of all evil, at least at the root of the economic troubles they faced. Economic concerns came to the fore in the elections of the late nineteenth century, and women involved in partisan politics had much to say on the topic.

The presidential election of 1896 revolved around economic issues. Republican William McKinley supported a high protective tariff and the gold standard. William Jennings Bryan, nominee of both the Democratic and the Populist parties, supported a lower tariff and "bimetallism," arguing that the government should redeem paper money in silver as well as gold specie. Tariff rates affected everyone. This tax on imports, designed partly to raise revenue and partly to protect American industry, continued to serve in the late nineteenth century as one of the government's most important sources of money. Producers of American goods preferred a high tariff to restrict foreign competition. Consumers of goods, American and otherwise, preferred a low tariff to ensure low prices. After Congress steadily increased tariff rates during the Civil War to help raise money for the war effort, reformers passed some slight reductions until 1890. The McKinley Tariff of 1890 raised rates to an average of 48 percent, resulting in much higher prices for many goods. As the most noticeable tax Americans paid, the issue of the tariff often arose in political campaigns.

Bimetallism, on the other hand, was a relatively new issue. The nation's money supply took the form of hard money—gold and silver specie—and soft money—banknotes and other kinds of paper that represented specie. Governments wanted to have as much specie in their "reserves," or storage, as possible since specie had more value in the international economy than did paper money. During the Civil War, both sides had depended on the use of soft money, a flexible supply of money called "greenbacks" in the North, and Confederate paper money and war bonds in the South. These last two became worthless when the Confederacy lost, throwing the Southern economy, already suffering the loss of slave property, slave labor, and property damage, into complete disarray. The federal government would still redeem Northern greenbacks for gold, although by the mid-1870s, it cost only seventy-five cents in gold to redeem one dollar in greenbacks. This decline in the value of the paper money meant trouble for rural Americans, North and South, who had come to rely on the greenbacks as a way to pay their debts.

As gold and then silver continued to appear in rich veins in Nevada, Colorado, Utah, and other western states, many people called for the government to redeem greenbacks in silver as well as gold. As lucrative as gold mining was, great silver strikes in the West in the late 1870s made silver more readily available. It would be worth even more if it could be used to redeem paper money rather than just for commercial trade. Those who opposed redeeming paper money in silver as well as gold feared inflation. If paper money were worth more because it could be redeemed more easily, the value of the paper money would rise, and so could prices. Southern and western farmers and others who relied on paper money, however, would benefit because paper money would be worth more, so they could pay their debts more easily.

The federal government eventually responded to the clamor for silver redemption with the Sherman Silver Purchase Act of 1890, allowing silver to be used as specie. The act backfired: so much silver flooded the market that prices for the commodity dropped, and in western silver mines, owners cut miners' wages as the value of silver declined. Workers protested, sometimes violently. The act also affected those who held banknotes. They wanted to redeem banknotes for gold, since silver was worth so much less. As the demand for gold to redeem banknotes increased, the country's gold reserves dropped so much that financiers panicked. They called in their loans, tightened the nation's credit, and contributed greatly to the Panic of 1893. Congress revoked the Silver Purchase Act, and a four-year financial depression followed, with high unemployment, low wages, and considerable unrest, leading many Americans to support free silver in a renewed call for bimetallism.

By this time, adult women in the western states of Wyoming, Utah, Colorado, and Idaho—all states supporting free silver—could vote in the national election between McKinley and Bryan. While McKinley campaigned quietly from his front porch in Ohio, thirty-six-year-old Nebraska Congressman Bryan ringingly declared his support for what was termed *free silver* in a stirring speech in which he declared, "You shall not crucify mankind upon a cross of gold!" The silver question garnered enormous amounts of press and opponents of free silver were quick to point out the presumed effect it would have on women. Republican newspapers, such as the *National Register*, argued that free silver would lower working women's wages, with little chance for them to "remedy their condition" because most women did not work in industries with unions. The Populist *People's Party Paper* portrayed a pyramid of steadily increasing burdens if the gold standard were allowed to continue, with "Ruin" at the top; "Business Failures," "Uneducated Children," and a "Dearth of Marriages" in the middle; and

"Hungry Women and Children" near the bottom—all blamed on the lack of free silver.

As usual, women participated all over the country in the election even if they could not vote. At Vassar College in Poughkeepsie, New York, for instance, where supporting woman suffrage was against school policy, young women dressed up as the candidates, held parades and rallies, gave speeches, and even held a mock election. The *New York Times* covered the Vassar women's activities, as did the suffragist magazine the *Woman's Journal*, pleased at the progress made, the reporter wrote, "from the time when no woman suffrage speech might even be whispered at Vassar College!" In North Carolina, Republican Sarah Dudley Pettey described fellow black women campaigning for McKinley by canvassing tenements "where the laboring classes dwell" to share their views and urge "wives, sisters, and mothers . . . to influence their husbands, brothers, and sons." Women also showed up as characters in political cartoons. One anti-silver cartoon in the *Los Angeles Times* portrayed women as witches, labeled "Anarchy" and "Populism" and dancing around a cauldron fueled by "Discontent" and "Doubt." One Denver paper had pro-silver beauties, labeled "South" and "West," trying to woo the president away from anti-silver hags, labeled "New England" as well as "Old England."

In the largest voter turnout in American history, McKinley and the Republicans won the election of 1896. The Populist movement, supported by so many women voters and activists in the West, Midwest, and South, declined precipitously, and, as is often the case with groups involved in losing political causes, women's participation in partisan politics shrank over the course of the next decade, as they turned to nonpartisan political strategies, public nonpartisan reform, and a nonpartisan drive for the vote.

WOMEN WORKERS AND LABOR REFORM

In 1896, a Seattle paper discussed women's importance to the country's economy, saying, "What have women to do with political economy? it may be asked. They are at the bottom of all economy. . . . Women are the savers. . . . The money a woman wants—and the Lord knows she needs more than she gets, usually—is the best money that can be had. The best is the cheapest with her—always." Although this sentiment did not necessarily apply to all women, in truth, women were critical to the U.S. economy. By 1890, there were 3,712,000 women in the labor force, 18.9 percent of all working-age women in the country. By 1920, there were 8,347,000, or nearly 25 percent of the working-age women in the United States. Problems associated with the growing economy affected women, whether as workers themselves, or as wives and mothers of workers.

Changes in the industrial sector and the rise of big business that began during Reconstruction and the Gilded Age continued during the Progressive

Era. Mechanizing tasks and standardizing parts eventually led to large-scale manufacturing on assembly lines, where the product moved from worker to worker until fully assembled. Economies afforded by the scale of manufacturing contributed to massive increases in production by American workers. The government exercised little control over the powerful corporations, monopolies, and trusts that controlled major sectors of the American economy: steel-making, railroads, oil production, banking, and manufacturing. While these companies helped make American industry productive and prosperous, reformers claimed that the unimaginable wealth corporations generated came from exploiting workers, fixing prices, and polluting the environment, as well as buying corrupt politicians to ensure their companies' continued profitability. Standard Oil Company, for example, was a trust that fixed the price of oil, as well as the pay levels of the workers who drilled for the commodity. The hundreds of companies turning out newfangled automobiles in 1900 plummeted to only a few dozen by 1920, as large companies like Ford and General Motors began dominating the marketplace and fixing the prices of cars and wages.

The dynamic economy, exploiting the tremendous natural resources available in America, took full advantage of the lack of oversight from government. Advertisements for goods increased consumers' wants and needs. Producers relied heavily not only on a cheap labor force, with a large component of recent immigrants paid next to nothing, but also on an expanding world economy in which America played an increasing role. Large manufacturing concerns pumped out goods, using the railroads to ship them, a large-scale distribution mechanism that meant those goods could travel cheaply, far and wide. A growing market usually meant more goods for more Americans. However, workers, particularly women workers, were so poorly paid that the American economy suffered from a crisis of overproduction.

American workers and their immigrant colaborers did not go meekly into the night of exploitation and poverty. Critics of capitalism's excesses complained loudly and vociferously about common labor practices: ten- to fourteen-hour workdays, six days a week; piecework; women and children laboring instead of men for half the pay or less; cuts in wages for working the same hours when the market took a downturn; lockouts to close down a workplace when workers protested conditions; hiring cheap immigrant labor to break unions and replace striking workers. Women formed unions and filed lawsuits to fight for their rights to be treated fairly and equally throughout the Progressive Era.

The Women's Trade Union League

The earliest unions had been formed by women before the Civil War and more came into being during the Reconstruction Era (see Chapter 6). Most large labor unions remained committed to improving the lot of male workers, however, and either forbade women from joining or paid little attention to their interests. Mary Kenney O'Sullivan, despite her role as the first woman general organizer for the American Federation of Labor (AFL), grew frustrated with the AFL's refusal to pay much attention to the concerns women had. In 1903, O'Sullivan joined Jane Addams of Hull House and other leading social reformers, including Florence Kelley, Alice Hamilton, Sophonisba Breckinridge, and Lillian Wald, to form the *Women's Trade Union League* (WTUL), an organization made up of trade unionists and their sympathizers, promoting fairer labor standards for all. While the WTUL wanted first to organize wage-earning women into trade unions, it also sought to integrate working women's concerns with the woman's rights movement. Linking working-class interests to middle-class reformers with disposable income meant larger contributions from well-organized activists. The WTUL fought for equal pay, an eight-hour day, a minimum wage, the abolition of child labor, and health benefits, as well as protective legislation, designed to protect women workers from having to work the same way that men did even when they were physically weaker. These laws were particularly important given the number of women who worked while pregnant.

Since the greatest proportion of women working outside domestic service were garment workers, the unions found ready converts in that field. The International Ladies' Garment Workers Union, founded in 1900, was made up largely of Jewish women garment workers. The International Glove Workers' Union of America, led by Agnes Nestor in 1902, unified young women glove makers in Chicago. Both unions went on to join forces with the WTUL. The collective power exercised by the WTUL convinced Illinois lawmakers to pass a 1909 law limiting women's workdays to ten hours. Other victories by the WTUL included higher pay rates, an accomplishment the group promoted in pamphlets they distributed to workers in major cities. Jane Addams wrote one such pamphlet for the WTUL in 1909, decrying the working conditions for laundresses and promoting the success of the unions: "How would you like to iron a shirt a minute? Think of standing at a mangle just above the washroom with the hot steam pouring up through the floor for 10, 12, 14 and sometimes 17 hours a day! Sometimes the floors are made of cement and then it seems as though one were standing on hot coals, and the workers are dripping with perspiration. They are breathing air laden with particles of soda, ammonia, and other chemicals! The Laundry Workers Union in one city reduced this long day to 9 hours, and has increased the wages 50 percent."

Union success depended on strikes, and the WTUL joined forces with unions in several cities in the early twentieth century as they struck for better conditions. Miners' strikes, railroad workers' strikes, steel workers' strikes—even after the 1908 Supreme Court rulings allowing employers to fire union members and forbidding boycotts by union workers because such actions were a conspiracy to commit restraint of trade—strikes continued. In New York City in 1909, Rose Schneiderman, a WTUL member, led garment workers in a strike against the manufacturers of the popular ready-made blouse called a shirtwaist. The garment was inexpensive enough for even working-class women to buy, but its low price meant factory owners cut wages to continue making a profit on the garment. The strike demanded owners recognize the union, after many women had been fired for joining it, then demanded a fifty-two-hour workweek. So many women garment workers participated that the press deemed the strike "the Uprising of the 20,000." Not only did the WTUL help fund and publicize the workers' concerns, but their cause was also taken up by the upper-class women of New York who supported other reform efforts, such as woman suffrage. Alva Belmont, a suffrage supporter and one of the richest women in the city, watched as strikers were arrested, bailed some of them out of jail, supported their efforts, then was sued by one of the manufacturers for conspiring to do damage to his business. Well-to-do women students from Vassar and Barnard supported the workers, joined them on the picket lines, and publicized the event in newspapers, keeping the strikers' goals on the front pages. The shirtwaist makers' strike was followed by a cloak-makers' strike in New York 1910, and the Chicago Clothing Workers Strike, led by a fifteen-year-old girl, Bessie Noramowitz, the same year.

Union members felt they had few alternatives to striking. Working conditions could be horrible, and a worker's recourse was limited. Many workers were underpaid, forced to clock in after they had really started work and to clock out before they were allowed to go home. Pay for overtime might consist of a piece of pie. Normal events such as staying home due to illness or leaving a machine to go to the bathroom could get a worker fired. There was no minimum wage paid and no maximum limit to the hours worked. No occupational safety laws protected workers. Lighting was often so poor that workers went blind from straining to see. Cotton dust filled the air in textile factories, and workers suffered and died from respiratory diseases. Many women workers feared sexual harassment, a constant problem with no legal recourse for victims.

Owners' responses to unions varied. They sued in courts, trying to sway public opinion against the unions. They used police to break the heads of union rank-and-file workers when they picketed. Owners broke up union meetings, had union organizers arrested, and fined and dismissed union organizers and participants who worked at their factories. In many cases, dismissed workers were replaced by other, more recent, more ignorant, and consequently more tractable workers, usually recently arrived young immigrant women. Taking advantage of racism and nativism, owners sometimes brought in black, Chinese, or other immigrant workers to replace those on strike, often paying them less than what strikers had made. Particularly in the South, where racism reached new levels of virulence and segregation became enshrined in Southern law, owners could often count on their workers' inability to rise above racial problems and work in concert against exploitation. Only one labor organization, the Industrial Workers of the World (IWW), called the "Wobblies," admitted African American workers on an equal footing with white workers. The Wobblies also sought women members, opposing their separation from the rank-and-file represented by the WTUL, arguing for the power of sexual integration.

The WTUL and the IWW, along with countless other labor organizations, not only fought for higher wages and benefits but also against unsafe working conditions. Company abuses against women workers led to one of the worst industrial accidents in U.S. history, the Triangle Waist Company Fire of 1911. On March 25, 1911, 600 women garment workers labored on the top three floors of a ten-story factory building. A fire broke out just before quitting time on a Saturday afternoon and soon turned into an inferno, spread by cotton dust in the air, cotton lint on the floor, and cotton fabrics used to make the shirtwaists. Five hundred young women, mostly Russian, Hungarian, Italian, and German immigrants, were still at work when the fire began. Some escaped, but 146 died, most of them by leaping out the windows to their deaths after the fire broke out.

The lives of these young women ended for several reasons, none of them good. The freight elevators in the building might have provided an escape, but one was not working, and the other failed after the fire began. The company had also locked the fire doors to prevent women from taking breaks and leaving the workrooms. Workers did not know about an escape route over the roof of the building, a route the owner took successfully. The Triangle fire was so horrific that, although the owners were acquitted of any wrongdoing, lawmakers responded to the disaster by passing the first of many reform bills to improve the safety of factories and their workers. Over the next three years, the New York state legislature would enact thirty-six worker safety laws, while lawsuits against the Triangle Factory were settled for seventy-five dollars per life lost. Button machine operator Rose Freedman, who escaped the fire by climbing up to the roof, would spend the rest of her life crusading for worker safety, until her death in 2001.

Women and the Mining Industry

Mining, particularly coal mining, was another industry ripe for reform. Dangerous, dirty work, it drew its labor force from immigrants and the uneducated. In 1890, a Knights of Labor trade group combined with the National Progressive Union of Miners and Mine Laborers to form the powerful United Mine Workers (UMW). Gruesome working conditions, including the use of child labor, attracted the attention of Mary "Mother" Jones, a volunteer who had risen above her own tragic past (she had lost her entire family to a yellow fever epidemic in 1867, and her business and home to the Great Chicago Fire of 1871), to help organize and fight, not only for miners, but also for railway workers, education projects, the Social Democratic Party, and for the goals of the IWW.

A volunteer organizer for the UMW in 1900, Mother Jones returned to her work as a paid organizer in 1911, in time to play a role in the Paint Creek–Cabin Creek strike in West Virginia. Coal had first been mined in West Virginia in 1883, and the industry attracted immigrants from Europe, as well as African Americans fleeing the poverty and racism of the South. The state had the roughest mines in the nation. Safety measures in the mines did not exist. One study showed that miners had a shorter life expectancy than soldiers in battle. Owners' corrupt practices included "cribbing," modifying the size of coal cars so that miners had to load in more coal than they were paid for, and inflating prices in the company stores, the only places in these isolated mining communities where women could buy supplies to feed their families. Company stores accepted only company scrip, the paper money that miners were paid with, and prices reflected that monopoly. Workers' housing that companies provided proved substandard at best and hazardous at worst.

The Paint Creek–Cabin Creek strikers fought for fair wages, an end to cribbing, alternate stores to shop in, freedom to organize and speak on union issues, and accurate scales to ensure accurate measurement of the coal the men mined. The mine owners hired private guards to intimidate union members by turning their wives and children out of their homes. Mother Jones arrived on the scene and fought back with ringing speeches against the mineowners and their hired thugs. She once led a parade of malnourished miners' children through the nearby capital city of Charleston to provide evidence of the want that miners' families suffered under greedy owners. Another protest led to her arrest, trial by a military court, and a short imprisonment on charges of inciting a riot. The governor freed her, fearing a Senate investigation into irregularities associated with Jones' conviction. She then traveled to Colorado to protest against working conditions there. Until she resigned from the UMW in 1922, Mother Jones continued to speak out against the exploitation of workers by owners of industries as varied as textiles, steel, railway cars, and mining.

The mining industry in the East held fast to an old Cornish superstition that women in the mines were bad luck. In the West, however, where mining began largely above ground during the California Gold Rush of 1849, a few intrepid women miners continued to be found, exploring the rich veins of gold, silver, and copper. Ferminia Sarras left her native Nicaragua to search successfully for silver in northern Nevada. After that commodity played out, she found copper with such success she became known as the "Copper Queen." Lillian Malcolm, a New York actress believed to be a Scottish immigrant, headed for the Klondike gold fields in 1898. In Nome, Alaska, she was repeatedly cheated out of her claims, and eventually left for the silver mines of Nevada. In 1911, Emma Stith worked alone near National, Nevada, first in open trenches and cuts, but eventually underground, successfully bringing out copper, gold, and silver. These unusual women broke cultural taboos by working in a male-dominated industry, as well as by dressing in men's clothing, since no one could successfully search for gold wearing the constricting garments of late-nineteenth and early-twentieth-century fashion. Women also assumed men's garb to disguise themselves, hoping to forestall sexual attacks. Their attempts at making their working lives easier were not universally approved. In California, women prospectors wearing pants were subject to arrest and fines. Miner Marie Pantalon (a name that, ironically, means "trousers" in French) was arrested because of her men's costume in San Francisco in 1871. She had better luck in Virginia City, Nevada, after she applied for permission from the city board of aldermen to wear men's clothing. Other women, some of whom were never found out by those who opposed their choices in fashion, maintained their disguises until they were ready to reassume their places in society as women rather than miners.

Women miners in mining camps were rare, although other women were not absent: prostitutes continued to ply their trade as they had since the days of the Gold Rush. One newspaper, *True Fissure*, in Candelaria,

Nevada, pointed out that women were uncommon enough, however, that their presence caused "more rustling, contention and petty jealousies" than anything else, except poker. Society at large was generally discomfited by women miners. These unconventional women were ostracized, particularly by the wives of clerks and other mine employees in the growing towns of the West. Women should be married, thought most Americans, and if they were not, they should occupy themselves in endeavors more suited to their delicate and feminine natures, such as teaching, nursing, or even, for the more progressive thinkers, social work. Even Dio Lewis, a physician and health reformer who promoted exercise, dress reform, and education for women (he had operated a school for young ladies in the 1860s where Angelina Grimké Weld taught history), argued that unmarried women would be better suited than men in occupations such as dentists and watch repairers because of their nimble fingers or as bank clerks and lawyers because of their higher moral standards. He did not envision women as miners, nor did anyone except the women who wished to pursue their goals of amassing wealth in the same manner that men did.

Protective Legislation

Notions that women had to be protected from inappropriate activities such as mining resonated with many Americans. Many states turned to legislative limits on women's work in the 1890s and early 1900s, usually beginning by limiting women's working hours. In 1908, in the landmark decision *Muller v. Oregon*, the Supreme Court codified such protection by approving Oregon's state law limiting women's workdays in laundries and factories to ten hours. Business owners opposed the law, arguing that such laws interfered with a person's ability to contract with an employer, and that these laws had nothing to do with the workers' health and safety. Illinois reformer Florence Kelley worked with Boston attorney Louis Brandeis, later a Supreme Court justice, to gather the scientific and social data needed to argue successfully that women workers needed protective legislation because they were women, and thus physically different from men. Medical belief at the time claimed long periods of standing were harder on women workers' bodies than on men's. But, more important, the court viewed all women workers as potential mothers. As Associate Justice David J. Brewer wrote in the Court's majority opinion: "as healthy mothers are essential to vigorous offspring, the physical well-being of woman becomes an object of public interest and care in order to preserve the strength and vigor of the race." Even if women had equal rights with men, the physical differences between the sexes could not be ignored.

The fact that legislation was passed, however, did not mean that it was enforced. In New York, for instance, despite legislation that regulated safety in factories and limited the workweek to 54 hours, girls in candy factories packed chocolates for 13 hours a day, working 65 to 78 hours a week. The laws did not apply to seasonal work, such as found in the canneries in Oregon's Willamette Valley, where women labored as many as 119 hours a week during harvest season. Former president Theodore Roosevelt, leader of the Progressive Party after he split from the Republicans in 1912, met with garment workers in 1913 and listened to tales of deplorable conditions. A young Spanish immigrant worked from 8 a.m. until 9 p.m. every day and made 36 kimonos (bathrobes) a day for 4¢ each. Out of that pay, she eventually had to reimburse the company for her $32 sewing machine. A young Jewish woman complained that she could never work a full week because Saturday was a workday, and that was her Sabbath. She made only $3.50 a week as a result. Another woman said she spent $2.75 of her weekly pay of $4.50 on food because, unlike the men who could go to a bar and get a free lunch with a nickel beer, she and her fellow women workers had to buy their lunches from pushcarts outside the bar, if they wished to remain respectable. Roosevelt, visibly angered by the girls' stories, declared he would push the New York state legislature to pass laws making the lives of women garment workers easier to bear. "This is crushing the future motherhood of the country," he said. "It must be stopped. It is too horrible for words."

Despite the public's growing acceptance of the need for protective legislation, controversy regarding its implications continued. Laws that presumed that all women were potential mothers did not make exceptions for women beyond the age of childbearing, or women who did not marry, or women who did not wish to bear children. Protective legislation proponents instead presumed that the majority of American women workers would marry and bear children, and they fought to protect those women. Others believed the only way to help women was to pass legislation for all workers, male and female, since legislation targeted at women allowed employers to discriminate against female employees. Their concern was justified, as some employers refused to hire women for jobs at their diners and bowling alleys, or at their industries that worked night shifts. Protective legislation remained a divisive issue among those concerned with working women's lives. Woman's rights advocates struggled over how much they should stress the differences between women and men (and their bodies) and how much they should emphasize their commonalities.

IMMIGRATION AND "AMERICANIZATION"

Many of the economic changes facing Americans at the turn of the twentieth century were part of worldwide trends. Industrialization, the expansion of commercial agriculture and mining operations, and the development of a faster, denser transportation network all resulted in an increasingly global economy. These changes caused economic and social disruption, and prompted millions to leave their homelands in search of a better life. Hoping for brighter prospects abroad, immigrants from regions of Europe, Asia, and the Western Hemisphere set forth for America. Traveling with their families or alone, sometimes to rejoin husbands and other kin who had immigrated earlier, women of diverse languages, faiths, and cultures made their way to America. When they arrived, most had few financial resources and spoke little English, but soon many had carved a place for themselves and their families in American life. The flood of immigrants provoked alarm among some with deeper roots in American soil. To these native-born Americans, the newcomers posed a threat to the nation's way of life. As a consequence, immigrants became the target of *Americanization* campaigns—programs to transform them into proper citizens of a modern democratic nation. Newcomers benefited from some of these efforts but resented and resisted those that smacked of condescension and discrimination. Immigrant women were key to forging communities that preserved and transformed their ethnic cultures.

The New European Immigrants

European immigration to America peaked in 1907, when 1.25 million immigrants came to the country. By 1913, nearly 15 percent of the U.S. population was foreign-born. After 1892, most immigrants entered America through Ellis Island in New York harbor, the first federal immigration station. There, officials inspected anxious men, women, and children for contagious diseases

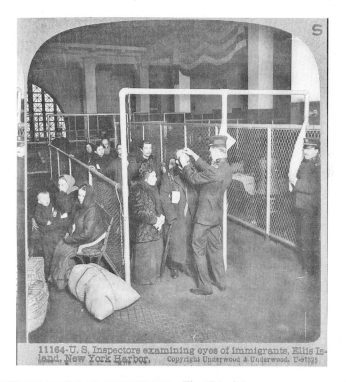

11164-U. S. Inspectors examining eyes of immigrants, Ellis Island, New York Harbor.   Copyright Underwood & Underwood. U-97328

IMMIGRANTS INSPECTED AT ELLIS ISLAND The United States saw an unprecedented rise in immigration during the end of the nineteenth and the early twentieth century. Here, a group of immigrants have their eyes inspected while waiting at Ellis Island in 1907, while another group waits with their children and belongings. This photo is from half of a stereoscopic card. Identical images were printed side-by-side, and a special viewer transformed the images into 3-D. Pictures such as these informed Americans about changes to their country as well as putting a face to immigration.

EMMA LAZARUS,
"THE NEW COLOSSUS"

In 1883, Emma Lazarus wrote a sonnet to celebrate the Statue of Liberty and to raise money for the pedestal on which the Statue of Liberty sits. While the last lines are those most often quoted, the image of a powerful mother created in her first few lines asserts the role women could play in a way that was different from that of men.

Not like the brazen giant of Greek fame,
With conquering limbs astride from land to land;
Here at our sea-washed, sunset gates shall stand
A mighty woman with a torch, whose flame

or any other characteristics that might prevent them from making a living, since they then might become an unwelcome burden on the state. The Statue of Liberty, whose shadow fell on the island, symbolized all that immigrants hoped for. A poem by popular writer Emma Lazarus, "The New Colossus," was engraved on a plaque at the base of the statue. The poem encapsulated both the desperate straits of those who came and poetic notions of what they expected life to be like in America, with phrases such as "Give me your tired, your poor/Your huddled masses yearning to breathe free/The wretched refuse of your teeming shore," and "I lift my lamp beside the golden door!" New Yorker Lazarus wrote this work partly as a response to anti-Semitic *pogroms,* the state-sponsored organized massacres in Russia and eastern Europe that had swept through Jewish communities in the 1880s and forced many Jews to emigrate to America just to survive (see Primary Source 7-1).

Between 1900 and 1910 alone, 8 million European immigrants arrived in the United States. While many hailed from countries that had sent large numbers of immigrants in the past, such as Germany, Sweden, Ireland, and England, most came from southern and eastern Europe: 2.1 million from the Austro-Hungarian empire, 1.6 million from lands controlled by Russia, and 2 million from Italy. Few of these newcomers were Protestants. Some cared little for organized religion of any stripe, but most were Catholic, many were Jewish, and a small number belonged to faiths, such as Islam, that lay far outside the mainstream of American culture. From 1900 to 1930, the United States also received nearly 2 million immigrants from the nation's neighbor to the north. All across the 49th parallel, English-speaking Canadian women found employment as maids and cooks in middle-class American homes, salesgirls in shops, and secretaries in offices. In New England, for example, women from the farms of Nova Scotia came to Boston to work as domestic servants, while French-speaking women from Quebec, both single and with their families, poured into the textile and shoe factories, taking jobs earlier filled by New England's own mill girls, then held by immigrants from Ireland. Farther west, Canadian women settled on family farms in the prairies and in growing urban centers such

Is the imprisoned lightning, and her name
Mother of Exiles. From her beacon-hand
Glows world-wide welcome; her mild eyes command
The air-bridged harbor that twin cities frame.
"Keep, ancient lands, your storied pomp!" cries she
With silent lips. "Give me your tired, your poor,
Your huddled masses yearning to breathe free,
The wretched refuse of your teeming shore.
Send these, the homeless, tempest-tost to me,
I lift my lamp beside the golden door!"

Source: Emma Lazarus, "The New Colossus," *The Magazine of Poetry* 5, no. 4 (1893), 379.

as Seattle. Some women from Canada were immigrants twice over: they first had come from Europe or Asia to Canada and then had moved once again to take up life in the United States.

Whole families as well as single women and men migrated to America, often timing their immigration to take advantage of instances when the American economy improved. Those who lacked English still knew quite a bit about America, learning from other immigrants and widely distributed literature. Still, many immigrants were taken advantage of as they searched for employment. Hiring agents dominated labor markets in New York, for instance, and received part of an immigrant's pay in exchange for finding a job. Railroad agents or employees took advantage of travelers seeking transportation to other communities, demanding extra money beyond the ticket price. Most immigrants settled down as quickly as they could in cities, searching for a community of their own to provide comfort in a strange new country. Ghettos and tenements grew crowded with ethnic groups. Tightly packed into small rooms, immigrants suffered from the lack of sanitation, light, privacy, and ventilation. Mortality rates soared in these squalid neighborhoods, particularly for children, as mothers watched 60 percent of their babies die before their first birthday.

The Settlement House Movement

To meet the needs of the influx of immigrants, reformers began the *settlement house movement*. Earnest middle- and upper-class workers moved into settlement houses, formerly private homes converted for the purpose, in poor urban neighborhoods. There they taught immigrants English and provided employment bureaus, as well as art galleries, theaters, music, and libraries. Children of immigrants had kindergartens and daycare facilities, playgrounds, and sports and summer camp programs. The settlement workers' goals were to teach children and their families proper "American" behavior—that is, behavior of the white middle class from which the reformers came.

In Chicago, home to hundreds of thousands of new immigrants, Jane Addams and Ellen Gates Starr created the most famous settlement house, Hull House. While many settlement house workers championed the contributions of immigrants to American life—their music, dance, and dress—Addams, Starr, and others thought it more important to educate immigrants to live successfully and healthfully in America as Americans. Hull House was part of the settlement house movement that included Lillian Wald's Henry Street Settlement, founded in 1895 in New York; Robert A. Woods's South End House in Boston; and the Ensley Community House in Birmingham, Alabama, an offshoot of the Methodist Church's Wesley House. Settlement house workers believed that the way out of poverty for most immigrants lay in becoming American in language, dress, and conduct. This acculturation could be fostered through services provided by settlement houses, which reformers believed worked better at ameliorating poverty permanently than the centuries-old practice of giving alms to the poor.

The houses met with mixed success. The community kitchens they set up to teach immigrant women how to cook American failed as immigrants preferred their own foods. The English classes and daycare provisions, however, were often gratefully accepted. Reformers also responded to the exploitation of immigrants by employers. Founding state and national organizations, settlement house workers fought for legislation to protect vulnerable immigrant workers. In Illinois, Addams and her fellow reformers founded the Immigrants Protective League to investigate suspect employment agencies, as well as the Juvenile Protective Association, a juvenile court to hear cases involving minors. At the national level, reformers successfully pressured Congress to create the Federal Children's Bureau in 1912, and to pass a federal child-labor law in 1916.

While settlement house workers sought similar goals, not all expected those whom they assisted to adopt white, Protestant, middle-class behavior. The National Council of Jewish Women (NCJW) founded Settlement House (later named Neighborhood House) in Seattle in 1906 to aid Jewish immigrants fleeing Russian pogroms. They provided a center to help arriving immigrants find work, medical care, legal services, and education. Even something as simple as a free public bath had real meaning to tenement dwellers who had only cold water at home. Young girls enrolled in sewing schools to learn a trade, and libraries provided additional educational opportunities. By 1916, the NCJW had eight classrooms, a clinic, social club rooms, and a place to teach English at night to workers in the Seattle area, all designed to help immigrants assimilate and to lessen anti-immigrant sentiments among Americans.

Asian Immigrants in the West

Anti-immigrant feelings often intensified into racism. In the western United States, racial discrimination against Asians who had emigrated to the Gold Rush fields and to work on railroad construction affected both men—the majority of immigrants—as well as women who tried to join husbands, fiancés, or male family members. Some discrimination mimicked that practiced against African Americans. Chinese immigrants were not allowed to testify against white Americans in court until 1872, and Chinese children were barred from San Francisco public schools. Chinese women faced additional discrimination based on anti-Chinese prejudice. American employers sought Chinese men as ill-paid, easily exploited, and often expendable workers, but did not want Chinese women to arrive and help those men set up households separate from company housing that cramped male workers into inexpensive bunk houses. Instead of encouraging single men to marry, employers often imported single Chinese women to serve as prostitutes. In 1875, Congress passed the Page Law to limit the practice, and many officials viewed any Chinese woman trying to immigrate to America as a prostitute. In 1880 California forbade interracial marriages, and in 1882, the Chinese Exclusion Law prohibited more Chinese laborers, women as well as men, from entering the country for ten years. All these limits guaranteed a gender imbalance in the Chinese community. Men who wanted families yet had wives still in China had to build second families in America when their first families were denied entry. Even that was difficult: by 1890 the ratio of Chinese men to women in America was 30:1, making marriage within the same ethnic groups nearly impossible. The federal government repeatedly renewed exclusion acts against Asian immigrants over the next sixty years, and anti-Chinese sentiments continued to be expressed in discriminatory incidents against individuals.

Discriminatory practices against Asians were met by the same sort of activism used by African Americans to help ameliorate and protest conditions. For example, members of the Gospel Society of San Francisco, much like members of the African American Phyllis Wheatley Homes, built a Japanese settlement house, set up by Japanese Christians, where Japanese immigrant women could meet, learn English, and reside in a boardinghouse atmosphere. Asian women's traditional subservience in Asian culture and limited numbers did not keep them from public activities and protests against mistreatment. Wives of ministers and women's auxiliary groups participated through clubwomen activities and organizations such as the Japanese Young Women's Christian Association in San Francisco. As the population of Asian women increased after the Progressive Era, their attempts to help those discriminated against by both government and culture in the United States would also grow.

Native American Women and Assimilation

Progressives' aim to reform all Americans meant continuing to try to assimilate Native Americans. Most white Americans still considered Indians "savages" rather than civilized, but had come to favor education over annihilation. Assimilationist Richard Henry Pratt opened the Carlisle Indian School in Pennsylvania in 1879, using military-style discipline to educate and socialize Native Americans so they behaved more as whites did. Pratt, like many others, argued that Indians must assimilate or they would be exterminated, especially as the great Indian wars of the 1870s and 1880s raged. In the 1890s, Congress authorized the commissioner of Indian

Affairs to require that Native children attend boarding schools similar to the Carlisle school, both on and off reservations. Families resisted, many hiding their children in the mountains or in camps out of reach of U.S. soldiers sent to enforce the mandatory education decree. When soldiers arrived to seize children, it caused, as one Indian agent put it, "quite an outcry. The men were sullen and muttering, the women loud in their lamentations, and the children almost out of their wits with fright."

White officials brought Indian girls and boys to boarding schools far from their home reservations. There, teachers dressed them in whites' clothing, cut their hair, and made them wear shoes, changing their physical appearance so the children would appear more white. Teachers forbade students to speak their native tongues. They faced disconcerting actions by whites. Zitkala-Sa, a Lakota Sioux forced to attend an Indiana Quaker missionary school miles from her South Dakota home, remembers being tossed up in the air by an excited school worker, happy to see her new pupil. "I was both frightened and insulted by such trifling," she recalled. "I stared into her eyes, wishing her to let me stand on my own feet, but she jumped me up and down with increasing enthusiasm. My mother [had] never made a plaything of her wee daughter." The Native girl interpreted the playfulness of her white teacher as disrespect. Such misunderstandings epitomized the relationship between whites and Native Americans in this era as in others.

Boarding schools off reservations taught reading, writing, and American values. In addition to academic lessons, girls learned domestic skills to prepare them to be maids or homemakers. Many girls found classroom performance difficult. Expected to rise and recite in the white style in front of a room filled with both boys and girls, Native American girls raised to be modest and unassuming found it hard to speak aloud in front of young men. The white Americans in charge, however, regarded assimilation as essential, and overrode such qualms, often with corporal punishment. In addition, teachers discouraged Indians from exhibiting any Native behavior and appearance. Students were beaten so severely for speaking their own languages that later many refused to teach them to their children.

After 1900, more schools were opened on reservations than off, and some of the worst abuses ended, but such experiences marked an entire generation of young Indians. Despite the difficulties Native American children had with the process, their educations sometimes proved invaluable. Anna Moore Shaw, the first Pima Indian to graduate from high school in Arizona, remarked that Pimas who attended schools learned to combine white and Native cultures, and made "a way of life different from anything the early Pimas ever dreamed of." Susan LaFlesche, an Omaha from Nebraksa, attended the Women's Medical College in Pennsylvania and became the first female Indian physician, combining white medicine with Indian ways to serve as a reservation doctor. She and her sister, Suzette, a nurse, also used their education to campaign for Indian rights to own land individually, to prohibit alcohol on reservations, and to eliminate political corruption that kept Indians dependent on the federal government.

By 1904, Commissioner of Indian Affairs Francis Leeup recognized Native Americans' resistance to assimilation, and began speaking of exercising influence over Indians, rather than working toward their trans-formation. As they had earlier in the nineteenth century, for example, Native women continued to participate in America's burgeoning market economy, but did so on their own terms. Tlingit women in Alaska sold baskets and other handicrafts to tourists, as well as processing fish in factory towns such as Sitka. In New England as well, women sold baskets to tour-ists, and young Native women worked in the textile mills of Lowell, Massachusetts, and Manchester, New Hampshire. Plains Indian women produced bead work and other handmade items for the national market. In the Southwest, Navajo women weavers, encouraged by entrepreneur Fred Harvey who worked tirelessly to bring tourists into the region, shifted from creating blankets for their own people to creating rugs for the tourist trade. The railroads, particularly the Santa Fe, also contributed to Native women's successes in the market economy by promoting tours in the Southwest and providing access to raw supplies, such as German aniline dyes for their weaving, as well providing as an inexpensive means to ship finished goods. Native American women's transformation of their tradi-tional women's work into moneymaking ventures often provided them the economic means to enable their communities to survive.

Hispanic Women in the Southwest

Hispanic women in the Southwest faced discrimination because of their skin color and language as well, made worse when Americans regarded a massive influx of Mexican immigrants after 1910 as a threat to their own economic stability. Over 1 million Mexicans arrived in the United States, fleeing revolution, hoping to take advantage of the growing U.S. economy. As the United States limited European immigration and banned most Asian immigration, Mexicans filled an important economic role, but white Americans sought to force Hispanic women to assimilate. In El Paso and Austin, Texas, for instance, the Methodist churchwomen organized and staffed settlement houses, determined to Americanize the women of the local Hispanic communities. Kindergartens, English language classes, working girls' clubs, Bible studies, all sought to turn Mexican and Hispanic women into recognizably middle-class Americans.

In northern New Mexico and Colorado, missionary women sought to train Hispanic women as domestic servants, assigning to them roles whites would be comfortable with, while ignoring the powerful economic position Hispanic women held in their communities. Hispanic men migrated to work, earning wages in mines and on railroads and cattle farms. They left women behind to run the villages and care for families. Over time, such villages became centers of Hispanic women's power. Instead of recognizing this, settlement workers pitied Hispanic women because they believed those women were forced to work outside the home because their husbands were gone. White women falsely assumed Hispanic women wanted to emulate Anglo patterns of employment, where men earned wages and women stayed home. Such cultural dissonance between settlement house workers and the people they tried to serve remained common.

REFORM RESULTS

Settlement houses were one of many methods designed to meet the needs of industrializing America, but other reform efforts continued. Three areas of activity attracted innumerable supporters. The women's club movement that had begun after the Civil War came into full flower in the Progressive Era and served as the foundation for settlement houses and other attempts to aid immigrants. A less traditional field of activity for women reformers came in the form of an *antilynching* campaign that arose as black Americans faced increasing levels of violent discrimination. Lastly, the temperance movement finally succeeded in reaching its goal of prohibiting the sale of alcohol to Americans.

The Women's Club Movement

Women of all backgrounds, in all the states and territories, joined women's clubs, and it seemed a rare woman who had no connection with one. Native American women in Oklahoma Territory, for instance, joined forces to form clubs to meet their needs. So did black Oklahoman women, beginning in Guthrie in 1906, a few years after white Oklahoman women founded their first club in Oklahoma City. Black women continued to form their own clubs in the South and North as they had done since the end of the Civil War, since the General Federation of Women's Clubs, which drew together women's civic clubs under a national umbrella organization in 1890, refused to include black women's clubs.

All women's clubs expanded their work following the end of Reconstruction in 1877. Reformers in Birmingham, Alabama, for instance, wanted to help immigrant families who had arrived to build the railroads and labor in the blast furnaces of Alabama's iron industry. As in cities in the North, immigrants to the South clustered together in ethnic enclaves, and native populations wondered if they could or should be brought into the mainstream of American life. One Methodist reformer and clubwoman, Mrs. S. A. Tyson, declared that immigrants had to be assisted to avoid anarchy. The Home Missionary Society of the First Methodist Church of Birmingham set up an industrial school to train immigrant children in trades in 1897, then set up Wesley Houses by 1908. By 1912, the group established a settlement house to aid Italian immigrant workers from the mills, where women taught sewing to immigrant women and girls, established a kindergarten, taught English in night schools, and eventually hosted twenty-two different clubs for men, women, and children. In Virginia, Richmond nurse Nannie J. Minor rented a house with a group of friends and opened the Nurses' Settlement, providing in-home nursing care, classes in baby care and hygiene, recreation, and cooking classes. The women helped develop practices of public nursing and social work in the city. Another group that shared an interest in helping Richmonders was the Instructive Visiting Nurses Association that provided industrial nurses for the growing number of factories, as well as organizing tuberculosis clinics to control the spread of disease.

Justifying clubwomen's public activities required some subterfuge on the part of Southern white women, since the Cult of White Womanhood that placed Southern Ladies on pedestals had not been completely obliterated by the war or the reconstruction of the South. Determined to promote child-labor restrictions, compulsory public education, prohibition, and other measures, however, Southern white women reformers used the effective technique of referring to the sacrifices made by the Confederate dead to rationalize their efforts. In one speech, for instance, Georgia reformer Rebecca Latimer Felton asserted that the soldiers who had died for the "lost cause" of southern independence would tell women that the greatest monument to that cause "would be institutions of learning in behalf of their country." Such a goal should excuse any un-"Lady"-like public efforts. In other cities, elite groups believed they could use indirect methods to accomplish their goals. The Richmond City Woman's Club supported the Nurses' Settlement house and used its influence with the city council to obtain annual funding. The work of such groups meant cleaner cities, increased numbers of parks and playgrounds, increased spending on education and public health, and a healthier urban environment that benefited both whites and blacks in the urban South.

Segregation of blacks from whites in the women's club movement, however, echoed southern society. Black codes restricting African Americans' lives in Southern states during Reconstruction were followed by Jim Crow laws afterward, codifying *segregation*. Such separation of the races became the law of the land after the Supreme Court decision of *Plessy v. Ferguson* in 1896. The Court held that segregated public accommodations—schools, hotels, restaurants, railway cars, and the like—were constitutional, as long as those accommodations were equal. The decision outraged many black Americans, who knew that segregated accommodations were inherently unequal, and accommodations for black were always second-rate. Some African Americans, however, saw some value in the supportive aspects of single-race institutions. Black women formed their own settlement houses for their own people, for instance. In 1893 in Kansas City, the Colored Women's League established an industrial home to teach young African American women sewing, cooking and "other useful employments." In 1896, not long after the *Plessy* decision, the Colored Women's League of Washington, DC, the Women's Era Club of Boston, and the National Federation of Afro-American women met to form the National Association of Colored Women (NACW) so that the 198 member clubs might fight together to improve the lot of black Americans. In addition to teaching members about child care, health issues, and domestic tasks, the clubs opened kindergartens, old folks' homes, orphanages, hospitals, and settlement houses, all designed to meet the needs of the black community. Their motto, "Lifting as We Climb," emphasized the communal nature of their struggle against racism, ever present. (See Primary Source 7-2.)

Even in the North, segregation between the races was the rule, but women leading northern black women's clubs and organizations did cooperate with white organizations on occasion. Phyllis Wheatley clubs, begun in Detroit in 1897, were sponsored by both the NACW and the white branch

FRANCES E. W. HARPER, *IOLA LEROY*

Frances Harper used her background as a clubwoman to become a speaker against racism. She wrote Iola Leroy *in 1892, the first novel by a black woman writer to have a marked political stance. The character, Iola, is an African American woman so light in skin color that she could "pass" for white, but she chose instead to remain an active member of her African American community. The popular novel criticized racism North and South.*

"As Iola wished to try the world for herself, and so be prepared for any emergency, her uncle and grandmother were content to have her go to New England. The town to which she journeyed was only a few hours' ride from the city of P—, and [her uncle] Robert, knowing that there is no teacher like experience, was willing that Iola should have the benefit of her teaching.

"Iola, on arriving in H—, sought the firm, and was informed that her services were needed. She found it a pleasant and lucrative position. There was only

of the YWCA when no black YWCA was present. Phyllis Wheatley clubs began as homes for elderly people, but evolved into clubs for young women to meet, socialize, and live independently. Likewise, the Bethlehem Settlement House in Houston, Texas, was run by a biracial committee and included a nursery, a kindergarten, and a self-improvement club for young black girls.

Despite reaching out to poor women in communities across America, clubwomen activities tended to be practiced by the middle and upper classes. The elite clubwomen in black society belonged to the NACW, in the same manner as white elite clubwomen belonged to the General Federation of Women's Clubs. In Orangeburg, South Carolina, members of the Sunlight Club, founded in 1910 as the local chapter of the South Carolina Federation of Colored Women's Clubs, declared that its membership was made up of "all interested women in Orangeburg," but in fact included only elite African American women. No middle-class or lower-class women were at the Sunlight Club meetings unless they were there as domestic servants. In many cities across the country, elite women, both black and white, brought with them to social reform a sense of *noblesse oblige*, of their obligation as the elites in society to care for those less fortunate.

The Antilynching Campaign

The discrimination faced by even elite African American women often presented additional obstacles to overcome. Many Americans refused to acknowledge the injustice African Americans faced under segregation. Ida B. Wells, who became an internationally known journalist, brought to light the terrible conditions faced by black Americans during this era. Wells, a teacher in Memphis, Tennessee, bought her ticket for the ladies' car and boarded a train in May 1884. The conductor ordered her to a segregated car, which had no separate areas for ladies. She refused, and when he grabbed her, she bit his hand. Railroad men removed her forcibly; she sued one drawback—her boarding place was too far from her work. There was an institution conducted by professed Christian women, which was for the special use of respectable young working girls. This was in such a desirable location that she called at the house to engage board.

"The matron conducted her over the house, and grew so friendly in the interview that she put her arm around her, and seemed to look upon Iola as a desirable accession to the home. But, just as Iola was leaving, she said to the matron: I must be honest with you; I am a colored woman.

"Swift as light a change passed over the face of the matron. She withdrew her arm from Iola, and said: I must see the board of managers about it.

"When the board met, Iola's case was put before them, but they decided not to receive her. And these women . . . virtually shut the door in her face because of the outcast blood in her veins."

Source: Frances E. W. Harper, *Iola Leroy, or Shadows Uplifted* (Philadelphia: Garrigues Brothers, 1892), 208–209.

the railroad and won. The state supreme court overturned her victory, but the conflict fed her interest in publicizing discrimination. She became editor of the *Evening Star*, a weekly African American newspaper, and wrote a column under the pen name "Iola." In 1889, she became owner and editor of the Memphis paper *Free Speech and Headlight* and wrote columns describing the inferior schools black children were forced to attend. Other black newspapers reprinted her writings, distributing her ideas nationwide.

In 1892, three friends of Wells were attacked after the grocery store they owned proved too successful for their local white competitors, and they had refused to shut their doors. Her friends were accused of raping white women and were lynched. Lynching, where mobs took it upon themselves to kill accused criminals without waiting for a trial, was a common method of dealing with those accused of particular crimes—particularly rape—not just in the South, but throughout the country. As was the case for most Americans, Wells had long believed newspaper reports she read of men who were lynched for attacking or raping women. But she knew these three men, and they had raped no one. They were lynched by a mob of whites angry both at their economic success and their resistance to being told to close their store. Wells began to investigate rape cases where the accused had been lynched. She published her findings in articles declaring that lynching was, as literary critic Emmanuel Nelson put it, "a racist device for eliminating financially independent Black Americans." Wells called on blacks to boycott white businesses and, later, to leave Memphis and take their money and businesses with them.

Wells left town as well, after writing in a column that many lynchings occurred after white women had been caught having consensual sex with black men. Her writings enraged the white community, and her newspaper office was burned to the ground. Wells traveled on to Europe, where she continued speaking out against lynching. She eventually settled in Chicago, where she married attorney Ferdinand Barnett and had four children. She continued to write, but admitted the difficulty of balancing family and work in a chapter titled "A Divided Duty" in her autobiography. Wells-Barnett protested against racial discrimination for nearly forty years, complaining that blacks were not represented at the Columbian Exposition of 1893, working to integrate the suffrage movement, and investigating race riots that occurred in the early part of the twentieth century. Her campaign against lynching failed to produce federal legislation; although the Dyer Antilynching Bill passed the House in 1922, it failed to pass in the Senate. The number of Americans lynched eventually reached nearly 5,000, and about 2 percent of the victims were women.

Segregation, lynchings, attacks by the Ku Klux Klan and other white supremacist groups, discrimination, and race riots drove many blacks north. Southern black sharecroppers and farmers also suffered an economic downturn after the boll weevil infestation devastated the cotton crops of

THE LYNCHING OF LAURA NELSON This photo shows what drove the antilynching campaign. Although most lynching victims were men, some women were killed as well. Laura Nelson was hanged from a bridge over a river in Oklahoma in 1911 after trying to protect her son from being arrested for stealing cattle. The lynching was a public spectacle; the bridge filled with men, women, and children come to see the hanging. Nelson's son was also hanged and the event was commemorated with a postcard so that onlookers could send a card to those unable to attend.

the South beginning in the early 1890s. The exodus from the South that Wells called for in the 1890s took place over the next thirty years. National organizations such as the National Association for the Advancement of Colored People (NAACP) founded in 1909 by Wells-Barnett, historian and activist William Edward Burghardt (W. E. B.) Du Bois, and others, began to pursue legal remedies for discrimination and segregation, but it would take over fifty years before segregation was outlawed. In the meantime, between 1900 and 1960, an estimated 5 million African Americans left the South for cities in the North and West, such as Chicago, Detroit, Cleveland, St. Louis, Los Angeles, and Oakland, California, and New York City, where they hoped to find communities more welcoming than the South.

Temperance

Mixed results were common for reform efforts, and opposition often derailed the most well-meaning and idealistic supporters. One reform movement of the Progressive Era that achieved its goal, however, was temperance. The Woman's Christian Temperance Union continued its push for prohibition under Frances Willard, who governed the organization until her death in 1898. Alliances among those advocating the abolition of alcohol were common. Because the WCTU embraced other causes, such as kindergartens, physical education, prison reform, and woman suffrage, many women involved in those reform efforts also supported prohibition efforts. Willard's successor, Lillian Stevens, used legislative means to achieve some of the WCTU goals. By 1901, for instance, every state was legally required to teach temperance in public schools. By 1910, the organization was distributing 50 to 60 million pages of literature every year, and by 1919 the nation agreed to try to go "dry," passing the Eighteenth Amendment to the Constitution ending the manufacturer, sale, importation, or exportation of "intoxicating liquors" in the United States (see Primary Source 7-3).

Not everyone associated with temperance reform went about their efforts so quietly. Between 1900 and 1910, one member of the WCTU, Carrie Nation, an imposing six-foot-tall woman from Kiowa, Kansas, took a hatchet to barrels in saloons and bars from Kansas to New York City. Scornfully dismissing her opponents as "rum-soaked, whiskey-swilled, Saturn-faced rummies," Nation fulminated against alcohol consumption. "A woman is stripped of everything by [saloons]. . . . Her husband is torn from her; she is robbed of her sons, her home, her food, and her virtue. . . . Truly does the saloon make a woman bare of all things!" Kansas passed a prohibition law in 1880, but Nation and her followers enforced the law after public officials winked at those who broke it. As one of Nation's followers pointed out in the *Kansas City Star* in 1901, "the men would not do it, [so] we women did it. . . . This conduct from us women means something." Nation called her followers "Home Defenders." They wore special buttons and sold miniature pewter hatchets to support Nation and to provide her bail money, as she was arrested more than thirty times. She eventually bought a home in Kansas City, Kansas, to provide a haven for women and children with drunkard husbands. Nation also supported dress reform, arguing against corsets

THE EIGHTEENTH AMENDMENT

Nebraska became the thirty-sixth and final state to ratify the Eighteenth Amendment in 1919, little more than a year after Congress had passed it. The "great national experiment" called Prohibition had begun.

"Section 1. After one year from the ratification of this article the manufacture, sale, or transportation of intoxicating liquors within, the importation thereof into, or the exportation thereof

as injurious to internal organs, refusing to wear one herself, and advising young men not to marry women who did. She crusaded against tobacco and was known to march up to men on the street, pull their cigars out of their mouths, and throw them on the ground and stomp on them. She supported woman suffrage as well, telling Kansas legislators that "You refused me the vote and I had to use a rock." Kansas granted women suffrage in 1912.

Although Nation's methods were extreme, she found supporters across the country. Many women preferred less aggressive methods of achieving temperance goals, however. African American author Frances E. W. Harper praised the power that came from women's enthusiasm for temperance, urging them to join together in a vast crusade. In contrast to the women's club movement, the WCTU allowed black women to join either existing groups or to form separate ones. After 1894, the WCTU gave black-only groups the same recognition and opportunities at the national level that white and mixed-race groups had. African American Sarah Jane Woodson Early was the National Superintendent of Work Among Colored People for the WCTU. In 1 year, she traveled 6,000 miles in 5 states, gave 130 lectures, met with 300 teachers and ministers, and distributed 10,000 pages of temperance documents, writing 800 pages of them herself. She linked participation in the temperance movement with black suffrage, a movement continuing in the South as Southern whites refuse to allow black men to vote despite the Fourteenth and Fifteenth Amendments, and called upon her fellow black citizens to help build the "highest interests of the institutions of this government." Other African American members who wanted to campaign for the cause found themselves limited by lack of funds, and many appealed for the national WCTU to do more to reach the 7 million African Americans who, they felt, needed to hear about temperance. The repeated defeat of temperance laws in southern state referendums was not the fault of the black voters, these women pointed out, when so little was being done to reach them.

By 1916, twenty-one states had banned saloons, and the elections that year returned a Congress where the majority of members supported a national amendment prohibiting alcohol. The Eighteenth Amendment to the Constitution passed in 1917 and was ratified in 1919, and the Volstead Act of 1920 provided mechanisms to enforce the amendment. A great national experiment in temperance had begun.

from the United States and all territory subject to the jurisdiction thereof for beverage purposes is hereby prohibited.

"Section 2. The Congress and the several states shall have concurrent power to enforce this article by appropriate legislation.

"Section 3. This article shall be inoperative unless it shall have been ratified as an amendment to the Constitution by the legislatures of the several states, as provided in the Constitution, within seven years from the date of the submission hereof to the states by the Congress."

NEW CENTURY, NEW WOMAN

Some of the impetus for reform in the Progressive Era came not only from the past, but also from an awareness of the future. The dawning of the twentieth century caught people's attention and inspired many who wanted to do more to make the world a better place. Senator Albert J. Beveridge of Indiana declared, "The twentieth century will be American. American thought will dominate it; American progress will give it color and direction; American deeds make it illustrious. Before the clock of the centuries strikes the half hour in the hundred years now beginning the American Republic will be the sought for arbiter of the disputes of nations, the justice of whose decrees every people will admit and whose power to enforce them none will dare resist. . . . The regeneration of the world, physical as well as moral, has begun, and revolutions never move backward." Many believed that women were going to have a powerful role in that regeneration of the world. At a dinner celebrating the arrival of the new century, Maud Nathan, reformer, suffragist, and president of the Consumers League of the City of New York, spoke. Until she pointed out the omission to the program committee, fifteen "representatives of the unfair sex" had been invited to speak at the dinner, but not a single woman. She agreed when they asked her to participate, she said, "because I do not believe a woman ought to neglect an opportunity to speak in public. A woman's tongue is her strongest weapon and she ought to use it at every opportunity." She went on to praise the number of occupations that had opened to women workers over the previous century, from 7 in 1840 to 336 by 1886. Who knew how many more jobs would become "women's work" in the twentieth century?

The new century demanded, it seemed to many, a New Woman: educated, confident, capable, athletic, flirtatious, and adventurous. She went to college or even graduate school. She might run her own business or work in one, but she valued her ability to care for herself economically as well as socially. She wore a shirtwaist and a gored skirt that allowed her to move easily and to play sports. She rejoiced in her sexuality, experimented with it, and considered True Womanhood hopelessly outdated. This new icon of the white upper and middle class combined some of the old virtues of True Womanhood with modern traits to represent a new ideal, as selectively desired and as attainable—or not—as the True Woman of the nineteenth century.

Education and Economics

Increasing numbers of women in the new century could attain an education, as the numbers of coeducational and women's colleges expanded between 1890 and 1920. In 1890, of the 1,082 institutions of higher education in the United States, 43 percent were coeducational and 20 percent were women-only. By 1910, 58 percent were coed, and the number of women-only institutions continued to decline as women students preferred coeducational institutions. The numbers of American women seeking higher education also increased. While in 1890 only 2.2 percent of college-age women in the country were enrolled in institutions of higher education, by 1920 it was 7.6 percent.

Most of the women who graduated went into teaching, permanently or until they married, and others used their educations to enter other fields of endeavor. Medicine, the law, the ministry, and academia, despite remaining male-dominated bastions, saw assertive women enter in small numbers. Far more women entered professions such as writing and journalism, the performing arts, social work, nursing, library science, and secretarial services. In many fields, the "first woman" had entered prior to 1890, and in the twentieth century, women continued to move into male-dominant professions. By 1910, for instance, there were at least 9,000 women physicians; ten years later, nearly 10 percent of general hospitals included women physicians on their staffs. By 1920, 1.4 percent of all lawyers were women, most practicing with their husbands or fathers. Those who could not join a law firm often used their training to accomplish other goals. Florence Kelley's training as a lawyer contributed to her success in her fight for social legislation in Illinois. Crystal Eastman used her degrees in sociology and law to work for victims of industrial accidents, leading to her appointment as the first woman member of the New York Employer's Liability Commission. She wrote the first workers' compensation law in the state, campaigned for woman suffrage, and, in 1913, became a founding member of the Woman's Peace Party.

Ida Tarbell, the sole woman graduate of her class at Allegheny College in Pennsylvania, became the most famous investigative journalist, or "muckraker," of her day. Tarbell's relentless search for the truth exposed the corruption of John D. Rockefeller's Standard Oil Company in publications that led to the Supreme Court's decision in 1911 to break up the company's trust. Her work on the tariff was so evenhanded that President Woodrow Wilson invited her to serve on the Tariff Commission. She declined, having never been comfortable with her career, and instead wrote articles advising women to stay home, out of the workplace. She could not reconcile the New Woman of the twentieth century with the True Womanhood ideal of her upbringing. Nellie Bly, another journalist of the era, had no such difficulty. As an undercover reporter for the *New York World*, she feigned insanity to write an exposé of an insane asylum, and traveled alone around the world in a stunt designed to beat the record set in Jules Verne's novel *Around the World in 80 Days*. She married a millionaire, then became president of Ironclad Manufacturing Company, and patented a steel barrel she invented. After her company went bankrupt, she returned to reporting, and even traveled to Europe to report on World War I.

Another New Woman comfortable in her expanded role was Maggie Lena Walker. Walker, a native of Richmond, Virginia, joined the Independent Order of St. Luke's, an African American mutual aid society that cared for sick and elderly people and provided money for burials among the black community. She began a newspaper and founded the St. Luke's Penny Savings Bank in 1903, becoming the first woman to charter a bank in the United States and the first woman to serve as a bank president. She also chaired the bank board, helped found a black-run department store, joined the NACW, served in the NAACP, and became president of Richmond's Council of Colored Women, which she founded in 1912. "If our women want to avoid the traps and snares of life, they must band themselves together, organize, acknowledge leadership . . . and make work and business for themselves," she said. Another African American entrepreneur, Sarah Breedlove, later known as Madam C. J. Walker, became one of those women making work and business for herself. Walker created a beauty business that sold hair products to the black community. By 1916, she employed 20,000 agents to distribute her wares. The first black woman millionaire, Walker declared the importance of women's economic self-sufficiency in speeches to groups such as the National Negro Business League. "I want to say to every Negro woman present, don't sit down and wait for the opportunities to come. . . . Get up and make them!"

Many a New Woman saw the importance of women's economic independence. Charlotte Perkins Gilman took a radical approach to women's work both inside and outside the home. In 1898 she published *Women and Economics: A Study of the Relation between Men and Women as a Factor in Social Evolution*. Influenced by advances in sciences and impressed with the possibilities of the new industrial age, Gilman argued that the social roles for men and women were artificial, out of date, and served only to hamper social progress. She advocated building houses equipped with communal kitchens, dining areas, laundries, and child care facilities so that women could be more independent, families could become more integrated with their neighborhoods, and waste could be reduced. The new age, she believed, brought with it an overabundance of consumption that imposed new burdens on women and made them more dependent on men. In 1915, Gilman articulated her vision of a better world in a novel, *Herland*. The work featured a society of women only, able to procreate without men, living in harmony with each other and their environment. The peace of their utopia is shattered with the arrival of three male explorers, who find the tranquility of *Herland* and the women's self-sufficiency stifling and threatening. Few women shared Gilman's views, but her provocative ideas on how women could fashion independent lives embodied the visionary thinking that characterized the dawning of the new century.

The Gibson Girl, Department Stores, and Domestic Servants

The new century brought not only a New Woman, but a new girl to the forefront in American culture. The *Gibson Girl* represented one version of the New Woman, immortalized in drawings by the man who named her, professional illustrator Charles Dana Gibson. Hair upswept, wearing a shirtwaist and a gored skirt, ready to play golf or tennis or perhaps even to ride that wonderful new invention, the bicycle, the Gibson Girl appeared in magazines, books, plays, and songs, and on china, tablecloths, fans, screens, umbrella stands, even wallpaper. The iconic image represented the modern woman, although without the need to work for a wage, without the interest in politics or the vote, and seldom in the company of a man or a child. Gibson's portraits instead were of upper-class women who might be found in public at balls, parties, or restaurants, or shopping in department stores.

Department stores, an urban invention designed primarily for women consumers, appeared after the Civil War. While there had been large stores called "emporiums" before the war, true department stores emerged only after the technology to support such massive merchandising endeavors developed. Department stores needed escalators and elevators, subways and railroads, omnibuses and paved sidewalks for customers to move easily and safely to their locations. The stores developed first in major cities such as New York (Macy's), Chicago (Marshall Field's), Philadelphia (John Wanamaker's), Seattle (Bon Marché), Atlanta (Rich's), and Detroit (Hudson's). Conspicuous consumption became the task of middle-class and upper-class housewives who patronized these establishments. Shopping became an end in and of itself, and passed for an entertainment. The interior design and decoration of stores was geared toward pleasing women with glass and marble display cases, distributed in high-ceilinged, cathedral-like spaces. Stores built lunchrooms or tearooms where women were allowed to dine alone, something not permitted at most restaurants because the management feared women on their own might be prostitutes. They also added restrooms. Giving women a place to go (and a place to "go") meant women could shop all day.

The success of stores also depended on a shift in the nature of cities' public spaces. Cities had to become places where women could be in public spaces, such as the sidewalk or the streetcar, by themselves without being threatened or being seen as morally deficient. The geographic spaces of the city, the stores, and even the offices had to become safe for women instead of being perceived as male spaces. The sidewalks of New York, or any other major city prior to the Civil War were gendered. Women who wish to be considered ladies, particularly white, upper- and middle-class women, did not often venture into cities on their own. They were driven, they were escorted, but they seldom went out without someone accompanying them to avoid being confused with lower-class women or, worse, prostitutes. Since department stores depended on upper- and middle-class women customers, public spaces that led to the stores had to be as available for these women to occupy as those spaces were for men. In addition, those stores also had to be places where women could safely have jobs as sales clerks, the majority of store employees. Clerking became women's work, despite its difficulty, with long hours, low pay, and demanding customers. While some women clerks might become buyers, managers were almost always men and clerking did not provide economic mobility or union protection. Overworked and underpaid, sales clerks wore the shirtwaists made by women workers in places like the Triangle factory, linking mass production with mass consumption, as women became the biggest consumers of the expanding panoply of goods in industrializing America.

Fatigued by her day of shopping at a department store, a Gibson Girl would head home. Domestic scenes in which Gibson Girls were portrayed made little mention of the army of domestic servants needed to maintain an upper-class, or even middle-class life. By the 1890s, one measure of middle-class status was being able to afford a "girl" to help with household chores. In the South, domestic service was almost always limited to black women. In the rest of the country, domestic service tended to be done by women from the immigrant group most recently arrived. Over 1.6 million women were domestics or "personal service" workers by 1890.

While some young women found domestic service to be a way to learn English and even to experience secondhand the pleasures of American consumption, women faced numerous difficulties in domestic service. Wages were low and hours were long. Women were expected to work seven days a week with Thursday afternoons and Sunday mornings off, but those could be canceled at the employer's whim. Servants were also at employers' beck-and-call, arising before their employers did and often ending their day after locking up the house and putting employers to bed. There was little chance for advancement except through the ranks of a large household. Sexual exploitation of young girls from the country or from a different country occurred frequently. Poor living conditions included tiny rooms, shared with others, that had no heat in the winter or cool air in the summer. Such difficulties led to what employers termed the *servant problem* of not being able to find or to keep servants. Because there was little economic mobility and few opportunities to marry and leave service work, domestic servants often changed employers with little notice, hoping for another position that might provide some small benefit in the form of a better room or slightly higher wages, or the presence of an attractive unmarried male servant.

Sports and Dress Reform

Gibson girls and other women also played more sports in the new century. The clubs to which women belonged encouraged the team-building needed for sports. Athletics generally became more popular in America and Europe in the Progressive Era, epitomized by the revival of the Olympics in 1896. Colleges had sports teams for men, and women's colleges embraced similar teams, but with competitions held in-house, rather than intercollegiately. Rules of play were also modified for women to account for physical differences. Baseball was thought too dangerous for college women after some women were injured during the sport's early years, but basketball and volleyball became particularly popular. Urban and working women also participated in team sports through the YWCA, the Young Women's Hebrew Association (YWHA), or by playing in industrial leagues organized by factory workers, or ethnic clubs to which they belonged, as well as with other organizations. Jewish women in Chicago, for instance, played on the Hebrew Maidens baseball team, organized by members of the Hebrew Institute. While women could participate in golf, field hockey, cycling, and tennis without risking life, limb, or modesty, considerable time was spent discussing the possible side effects of competition and athleticism on women's health and mental stability. Doctors advocated some exercise to offset such "female complaints" as menstrual irregularities, but while a little was regarded as beneficial, too much exercise or too much competition was seen as a precursor to women's masculinization. Moderation was the key, and most Americans approved of only moderate forms of athletic endeavor for women.

How women dressed affected their ability to play in sports as well. Reformers had long criticized women's clothing. The corsets women wore compressed their rib cages and even their internal organs into unnatural and dangerous positions, making breathing and other bodily functions difficult. Dresses and skirts could weigh upward of twelve pounds. The hoop skirt of the 1850s had been replaced after the Civil War by the bustle, with excess skirt fabric draped over a wire cage a woman wore strapped around her waist. Bustled skirts, popular until the early 1900s, were difficult to move in. The excess fabric was heavy and interfered with sitting; often the drape pulled the skirt's front material so tightly the wearer could barely walk. Collars and dress fronts also changed, from a fairly low or jewel neckline to a high, standing collar, starched so it would stand up even on a woman with a short neck. Playing sports in a bustle, while difficult, could be accomplished, but many women embraced instead split skirts, which resembled wide legged trousers with an overskirt, or gored skirts, that allowed greater freedom of movement with few underpinnings. Corsets, however, remained a part of every proper woman's wardrobe, even when swimming. Many believed only "loose" women failed to wear them.

Sexuality and Birth Control

Sexuality was another topic open for considerable discussion in the Progressive Era. More women in more public roles and more public places meant that tight control over women's bodies by a patriarchal culture was harder to achieve. Symbolically represented by shorter skirts and even the eventual elimination of corsets, the loosening of women's bodies from restriction also meant increased sexual freedom. For example, while southern women millworkers lived under company supervision in mill towns in much the same way as their northern counterparts had the previous century, the women working in northern and western factories were no longer under supervision within the company boardinghouses offered earlier in the century. They were more likely to establish sexually active relationships, and were, alas, more vulnerable to sexual exploitation. Young women without access to effective birth control suffered greatly from the social stigma associated with unmarried pregnancies.

Giving children up for adoption was one option for women who found themselves in such difficulties. Orphanages, run by Progressive women reformers, developed as large institutions to care for the growing population of illegitimate children within the cities. Other orphans were sent west on "orphan trains" to families in the Plains states who would take them in. Helen Macior left the New York Foundling Hospital and arrived in Chicago at age 3. The Polish immigrant family taking her in signed an indenture agreement, requiring that they treat Helen as a member of the family, and provide her a suit of clothes and one hundred dollars when she turned eighteen. In return, Helen had to be obedient. Adopted by her family, the Jazwiecs, Helen benefited from the arrangement, eventually marrying and opening her own insurance business. She was fortunate to have been rescued. Some women, unfortunately, saw so few choices for their own survival that they abandoned their children to the streets, resulting in a substantial population of children earning wages to keep themselves alive within the slums of major cities. Many of these children and their mothers turned to alcohol and drugs to ease the pain caused by their despair over the conditions of their lives, contributing to the growth of a large, impoverished, and often desperate underclass, documented in works such as *How the Other Half Lives,* by muckraker Jacob Riis, and the photographs of Lewis Hine, an investigative photographer for the National Child Labor Committee.

Women reformers, determined to break the cycles of poverty and despair caused by women having children they could not keep or did not want, worked to disseminate birth control information to all women, regardless of class. Upper- and middle-class white women had always had some access to birth control information, but for lower-class and immigrant women such information was seldom available. They depended upon knowledge passed on from other women to prevent or end pregnancies, or simply accepted their lack of reproductive control as their fate.

Margaret Sanger became the most notable reformer demanding birth control be made available. After the 1873 Comstock Law limited the distribution of birth control information, even upper- and middle-class women began to have difficulty controlling their fertility. Sanger, a nurse in New York City who blamed her mother's death at age 50 on her 18 pregnancies and 11 births, joined some of the more radical activist groups, including the New York Socialist Party, the Liberal Club, and the IWW, all of whom supported birth control. As a visiting nurse in some of the poorest areas of New York's lower East Side, Sanger saw firsthand the need that women had for accurate information about how to prevent unwanted pregnancies.

The turning point for Sanger came when one of her patients died after a miscarriage. The patient had asked her doctor how to prevent further pregnancies. He told her to tell her husband to sleep on the roof. Incensed by the doctor's dismissive attitude, in 1912, Sanger wrote a column for the New York *Call* titled "What Every Girl Should Know." State censors suppressed the column because it discussed sexually transmitted diseases. Sanger continued her crusade. In 1914, she wrote and published her own monthly paper, *The Woman Rebel*, that, along with articles promoting other feminist issues, discussed contraception and recommended that women use it. Three issues of the paper were banned, and Sanger was arrested and tried for violating the Comstock Law. She jumped bail, leaving behind 100,000 copies of an informative and explicit pamphlet called "Family Limitation" for her husband and friends to distribute, and fled to England.

In England, Sanger met noted European radical thinkers who also espoused birth control; she discovered the diaphragm on a visit to a Dutch birth control clinic. Convinced that it offered the most effective method (better than the douches and suppositories she had recommended in "Family Limitation"), Sanger returned to America to continue her work. Her trial on the charges connected with *The Woman Rebel* came to an end after the untimely death of her only daughter, five-year-old Peggy. The charges dismissed, Sanger then went on tour to promote her cause, giving speeches that described heart-rending cases from her nursing days. In 1916, she returned to Brooklyn and opened up the United States' first birth control clinic. Nine days later, the clinic was raided. Sanger was arrested, tried, and convicted, and spent thirty days in prison. The publicity surrounding the raid and her trial helped Sanger as she appealed her conviction as did the positive reception to her new monthly journal, *The Birth Control Review*. In the meantime, the New York state appellate court exempted physicians from the limitations on prescribing birth control. By 1923, Sanger was able to open clinics with licensed doctors instead of nurses, achieving her goal of making birth control more widely available, and established an organized birth control "movement."

Part of Sanger's argument for birth control was that the wealthy, who had always had access to the information, were not producing as many children as the poor. "All of our problems," she said in one speech in 1918, "are the result of overbreeding among the working class, and if morality is to mean anything at all to us, we must regard all the changes which tend toward the uplift and survival of the human race as moral. Knowledge of birth control is essentially moral. Its general, though prudent, practice must lead to a higher individuality and ultimately to a cleaner race." Sanger's view that America needed information about birth control to prevent the less "clean" race from taking over was termed *eugenics*. Sanger chose to emphasize eugenics in her argument to attract support from more conservative Americans, worried about immigration and its effects. Her prejudices, however, appalled many radicals who otherwise supported the birth control movement.

One reason why so many people opposed birth control was that allowing a woman to control her own fertility meant that she was less dependent upon a man. As women achieved more economic independence through increased educational and employment opportunities, men worried that they would become unnecessary to women. "Boston marriages," romantic relationships between single, educated women who lived together, flourished in the latter part of the nineteenth century and also contributed to the discussion of sexual issues that raised the hackles of many conservative men and women. Such public evidence of women living in nontraditional, non-patriarchal fashion, increased the desire of more conservative Americans to control women and to prevent disorder, just as they had attempted to do with limits on workers and immigrants, and as they would try to do on women in public.

PUBLIC POWER AND PUBLIC VOICES

The New Woman of the new century realized the importance of civic action. The more involved women became in civic action, the more important the vote became to them, especially when voting was linked to civic action

WHY WOMEN DESERVE THE VOTE, 1913 Some cartoonists supporting woman suffrage used nonthreatening images to evoke a childish truth: life should be fair. Women worked, paid taxes, and obeyed laws. They deserved the right to vote.

PRESIDENT OF THE NATIONAL ASSOCIATION OPPOSED TO WOMAN SUFFRAGE SEEKS SUPPORT

In 1917, NAOWS president Alice Hay Wadsworth sent a copy of the organization's beliefs to Illinois Representative Charles Fuller as she sought his help to defeat the proposed amendment. Many opponents of suffrage believed that the Constitution assigned to the states the task of determining who got to vote.

"Dear Sir:

"Your attention is invited to the following facts:

"1. The proposed Federal suffrage amendment positively destroys the right of the people to vote on the question of woman suffrage, as provided for in their State Constitutions, and allows woman suffrage to be forced on unwilling States by the Legislatures of other States.

"2. This proposal is a violation of the present Constitution of the United States, which provides that 'The powers not delegated to the United States by

through the rhetoric of domestic feminism and civic housekeeping. Most clubwomen, for example, belonged to several clubs at once, allowing them to make a concerted effort at social reform. After 1890, clubwomen began to rely more heavily not only on voluntary efforts, but also on political efforts. Despite more organized antisuffrage groups, the fight for the suffrage assumed a different aspect in 1890, becoming a mainstream issue as the NWSA and the AWSA finally joined forces in a last great push to amend the Constitution to allow women to vote. Suffragists would have to convince not only men, but also the women opposed to their cause as well, as antisuffragism found new supporters. A major war interrupted the drive for the vote again, as it had in 1861, but this time woman suffrage activities did not cease, and the final victory came in part because of women's actions during wartime.

Antisuffragism

The antisuffrage movement weakened after 1890, but still fought valiantly to limit women's exposure to politics and voting. At the Columbian Exposition in 1893, Thomas Edison exhibited the kinetoscope, the earliest motion picture device. Short films could be viewed for a quarter, and in 1894, the world's first kinetoscope parlour, featuring rows of the machines, opened in New York City. Films included antisuffrage dramas, where henpecked husbands cared for children while their wives went out to politick and vote. In addition to these graphic images, pamphlets, handbills, leaflets, cartoons, books, novels, even poems were used to publicize antisuffrage sentiments.

Much of the opposition came from the brewing industry. Brewers and bar owners alike feared that if women temperance supporters were given the constitution, nor prohibited by it to the States, are reserved to the States respectively, or to the people.'

"3. The people, through their State Constitutions, ratified by popular vote, have reserved the right to adopt or withhold woman suffrage by popular vote.

"4. This proposal asks you to rob the people of this right; to repudiate your party platform which recognizes the right of each State to settle this question for itself by popular vote.

"Every principle of patriotism, every ideal of self-government, and your oath to defend the Constitution, urges you to vote against the attempt to obtain woman suffrage in spite of the expressed will of the people. . . . Will you not defend the Constitution, your party platform and the rights of the people, rather than surrender to the futile threats and impotent dictation of the Woman Suffrage Machine and the Socialists, who are seeking this amendment precisely because they are not strong enough to carry woman suffrage in the majority of the States by popular vote?"

Source: Alice Wadsworth of the National Association Opposed to Woman Suffrage to Charles E. Fuller, December 11, 1917 (Petitions and Memorials Referred to Committees HR65A-H8.14), RG 233, National Archives, Washington, DC.

the vote, they would pass temperance laws and prohibit the sale of alcohol. In Colorado in 1893, for instance, as the state's campaign for woman suffrage came to its successful conclusion, the Denver Brewers' Association printed and distributed leaflets and pamphlets declaring that experience could provide true measures of the worthlessness of woman suffrage. Kansas, after all, had granted women municipal suffrage (the right to vote in town elections) and was, claimed the literature, "in worse shape than ever before." After twenty-four years of woman suffrage in Wyoming, pamphlets declared, no reforms had passed and women had been lowered "to the depths of all that low politics imply." In Utah came the "most striking example of what *women cannot do*"—despite having the vote—abolish polygamy, still practiced by members of the Church of Jesus Christ of the Latter-day Saints, or Mormons. One pamphlet complained that most women promoting suffrage, such as Susan B. Anthony, Emma Willard, and Kansan Mary Elizabeth Lease, did not have children (not true of Lease, who had four), and "in the absence of woman's proper occupations, they run the country over, reviling everything in general and men in particular, and such women as these are the ones who would rule under a regime of woman suffrage." To avoid such a calamity, men were urged to vote against suffrage. Many did, but woman suffrage passed anyway.

More formal opposition came from the National Association Opposed to Woman Suffrage (NAOWS), established in New York City in 1911. The group lobbied state and federal governments to oppose woman suffrage, arguing that "politics, factions and parties" would destroy "American Womanhood." (See Primary Source 7-4.) Meeting with little success in their attempt to downplay the power of the vote, by 1917 the antisuffragists proclaimed that passing woman suffrage would be seen merely as "an official endorsement of *nagging* as a national policy." The president of NAOWS insisted that the amendment "would give every radical woman the right to believe that she could get any law she wanted by 'pestering' her City Council, her Legislature, her Congressman or her President—no matter how the people voted, nor what national crisis existed. And if feminism can be put through by pestering, regardless of the will of the people, so can pacifism, socialism and other isms."

Such dismissal of concerned women suffrage supporters as nothing more than pests was a common tactic used by opponents of suffrage. Portraying suffragists as "hens," as women dressed in men's clothing, as sexless manhaters, as hysterics, or as mentally ill had been part of the antisuffrage movement since the 1840s. In the late nineteenth century, however, opponents added cries of "socialist" or "anarchist" to the attacks since Americans greatly feared both political philosophies, tied as they were to a confrontational labor movement and to political upheaval. As NAWSA continued to attract followers in the 1890s, the attacks became more shrill and more widely publicized, particularly through cartoons in widely read daily newspapers.

In the South, women formed their own Southern States Woman Suffrage Conference in 1913 to confront the special problems the region posed. The image of the Southern Lady worked against suffrage—Southern Ladies' interests were represented at the polls by the men in their lives, and Southern Ladies needed to avoid the muck of politics. Offsetting the black male vote by giving the vote to women was not necessary; white men had already accomplished that with poll taxes, literacy tests, and grandfather clauses, along with intimidating voters from even registering. Woman suffrage, thought most Southerners, was a Republican notion, and the South was solidly Democratic. The woman suffrage movement's historical link to the abolition movement did not help the cause, either.

NAOWS chapters in the South were joined by chapters of Men's Associations Opposed to Woman Suffrage. The groups faced great contradictions, however, in seeking support for their cause. They had to convince conservative women to act as political creatures to oppose suffrage to ensure that they did not have to become political creatures if suffrage were won. Southern NAOWS used moral suasion and education to attract adherents. Members argued that deciding who got to vote was a state issue, not one for the federal government. The power of the suffragists, however, was considerable. The result was, as one antisuffragist wrote, an unequal struggle: "The world, the flesh and the Devil against us, and not even the money to buy stamps to carry on the battle from our side."

At its height, between 1911 and 1916, NAOWS had perhaps 350,000 members. The NAWSA, on the other hand, claimed 3 million. Suffrage was not an accomplished fact, however, and the history of the final campaign for the passage of the Nineteenth Amendment made it clear that many Americans were uncertain about the effect of women voting.

The Final Fight for Woman Suffrage

In 1890, Elizabeth Cady Stanton presided over the united NAWSA; Susan B. Anthony took over in 1892 and served until 1900. These two veterans of the woman's rights movement persisted in their original goal to amend the U.S. Constitution to permit women to vote. In 1878, California senator Aaron Augustus Sargent had introduced the *Anthony Amendment*, a simple twenty-eight-word sentence declaring that citizens could not be denied the vote "on account of sex." In 1887, the Senate voted it down, but the amendment was reintroduced every year until 1896. Then, as activists concentrated on winning woman suffrage in the states, it vanished from consideration until 1913. Women received the vote in Colorado in 1893, Utah and Idaho in 1896, Washington State in 1910, and California in 1911. In 1912, Arizona became a state and enfranchised women; Kansas, already a state, did the same. In 1913, Illinois gave women the vote in most elections, the first state east of the Mississippi to do so, and in 1914, Montana and Nevada enfranchised women.

Western states successfully incorporated voting women into the body politic without the role reversals and social upheaval predicted by the antisuffragists. Suffragists emphasized the benefits of women voting, equating women's domestic skills with *civic housekeeping*, a term Jane Addams and others used. Cities suffered from problems that a good housekeeper could help solve. Women would be more interested in "domestic" matters such as sanitation, safety, and clean streets, Addams argued, since men were as indifferent to civic housekeeping as they were to "the details of the household" in their home lives. By using domestic imagery to push for women's involvement in the wider world, supporters saw opposition to woman suffrage decline.

By 1910, the old guard of suffragists was gone (Stanton died in 1902, Anthony in 1906). In its place, more pragmatic politicians such as Carrie Chapman Catt (1900–1904) and Dr. Anna Howard Shaw (1904–1920) assumed the presidencies of NAWSA. The movement also began to include more radical women, such as Alice Paul. In 1913, Paul formed the Congressional Union for Woman Suffrage, an organization with permanent offices in Washington designed to lobby Congress and to protest against the lack of woman suffrage on a daily basis. The day before Democrat Woodrow Wilson's inauguration as the nation's new president in 1913, he arrived in Washington expecting crowds to greet him. Alas, he was informed, the crowds were watching the suffragists' parade instead.

Paul was largely responsible for that parade. She, along with Lucy Burns and Olympia Brown, formed the more radical wing of suffragist activism. Paul had visited England in 1906 and participated in the radical techniques used by the English suffragettes: mass marches, hunger strikes, broken windows, and firebombs. She brought those ideas with her to Washington and began picketing the White House every day, taking exception to President Wilson's failure to support woman suffrage. The more radical approach Paul and her suffragette followers took appalled NAWSA leaders and members. In fact, the appearance of the radicals probably helped make mainstream suffragists perfectly normal by comparison. They, after all, did not picket, did not get arrested, and did not go on hunger strikes.

Paul and her associates did. Determined to shake things up enough to force Congress and President Wilson to listen to their demands, she encountered only minor resistance at first. After the United States joined World War I and she continued to lead pickets at the White House, however, the protests turned violent. Protesters carried banners calling for Wilson to be as fair to women as he was to Europeans. It seemed the height of hypocrisy to ask Americans to participate in what Wilson called a "war for democracy" while continuing the disenfranchisement of millions of women. Many Americans, however, viewed the suffragists as traitors for attacking the president during wartime. Paul and her fellow protesters were arrested frequently, and some spent months in the Occoquan Workhouse, a prison near the nation's capital. There, Paul and others went on hunger strikes. When newspapers reported scenes where these young women were tied down and force-fed, the public relations nightmare grew too large to ignore, and the government released the picketers.

In addition to opposition from NAWSA members over including radical suffragettes, the suffragist movement continued to suffer from a racial divide. Despite their racist language in the Kansas campaign in 1867, Anthony and Stanton had always had close friendships and working relationships with African American women. Hester Jeffries, for instance, an African American activist in New York, eulogized Anthony at her funeral. Jeffries later presented her African Methodist Episcopal church in Rochester with a memorial stained-glass window quoting Anthony: "Failure is impossible!" In 1913, however, fearing they would lose the support of white Southern women, NAWSA leaders asked African American women, including Ida B. Wells-Barnett, not to march with them in a suffrage parade. Wells-Barnett said nothing, but then quietly inserted herself into the line of marchers, integrating that particular march.

Most women of color had their own organizations supporting suffrage, however, led by the NACW, just as they had built their own organizations supporting the abolition of slavery in the previous century. They also had their own constituency to convince: not just women, but also men of color. Booker T. Washington, a leading African American and founder of the nationally known black college, Tuskegee Institute in Alabama, refused to support woman suffrage, despite being scolded for his position by activist Maud Nathan. Washington argued that the question of woman suffrage should be left to women alone, and that indirect influence over legislatures would achieve better results than the direct influence of the vote. Washington, seeking to avoid controversy, ignored the fact that without the vote, women could do little to change their circumstances beyond appealing to men. Nathan pointed out not only this, but also reminded Washington that the vote he enjoyed had been given for reasons of justice, not because of any indirect influence his people had on the white legislators in charge of changing things.

Many followers of Washington disagreed with Nathan. Washington's wife Margaret, a charter member of the Tuskegee Club, for instance, was well aware that in a society where black men were routinely lynched, public displays of support for woman suffrage were inadvisable. Race riots directed at black men, such as one in Atlanta in 1906, resulted in deaths as well as further limitations on black men's voting. Such racism and riots limited black women's ability to support suffrage publicly. Other prominent

African American men, such as W. E. B. Du Bois, the first black man to earn a Harvard PhD, supported woman suffrage but feared that the racist attitudes of white women, North and South, would limit black women's participation. Anna J. Cooper, an ardent suffragist, clubwoman, and writer, begged to differ. Author of *A Voice from the South*, Cooper declared that the time had come for black women's "political activity, and for a voice in the arrangement of her own affairs, both domestic and national." Most African American women's groups in the South, however, focused their efforts primarily on uplift and antilynching legislation, not on woman suffrage.

World War I

By 1914, a worsening economy and growing tension in international affairs often took precedence over Americans' interest in the suffrage movement. In 1913, the economy had collapsed for the fourth time in the new century, following financial panics in 1901, 1903, and 1907. Hard times followed each economic convulsion, and workers continued protesting their wages and the conditions under which they labored. Internationally, a series of alliances between European powers meant to prevent war began to collapse. In June of 1914, a Serbian nationalist assassinated Archduke Franz Ferdinand and his wife, the Grand Duchess Sophie, heirs to the throne of Austria. Austria responded by declaring war on Serbia in July. The alliances other nations had with each other soon brought all of Europe into the war. Austria-Hungary, Germany, Italy, Bulgaria, and Turkey formed one alliance, the Central Powers, and fought against the Allied Powers—Britain, France, Russia, Romania, Greece, and later Italy, which switched sides. The toll of warfare shocked many Americans, as millions died on both sides. The United States declared itself officially neutral, though economic and political support, especially from President Wilson, tilted toward the Allied Powers. U.S. neutrality did not last, however, when German U-boats attacked ships in the Atlantic and Americans lost their lives. In 1915, a German submarine sank the *Lusitania*, a passenger ship (which unknown to passengers was carrying war munitions). Nearly 1,200 died, including 123 Americans. The uproar over the sinking convinced the Germans to suspend such warfare for a time, but they resumed unrestricted submarine warfare in February 1917. The United States declared war on the Central Powers two months later, on April 6, 1917.

During World War I, women took on many tasks, as they had done in previous wars. Some 30,000 women served in the Army and Navy Nurse Corps, newly organized in 1901 and 1908, respectively. At least 3 earned the Distinguished Service Cross, the nation's second-highest military award, for their actions. Another 300 women served in the Signal Corps, after the American commander, General John J. Pershing, issued an emergency call for bilingual (French/English) operators to run switchboards connecting generals with troops in the field. Physical and occupational therapists served overseas as well, assisting soldiers wounded in battle. Seldom were any of these women recognized for their service (Signal Corps women finally were recognized by the army in 1978), but the government was certainly aware—and in need—of them.

As in earlier wars, women also came into the workplace to replace male workers who had joined the military. Jobs ordinarily performed by men might be dirtier, more dangerous, and more physically demanding than so-called women's work, but they also paid better, and women flocked to them. Some adjustments were made for women arriving at the factories: hairnets, protective sleeves and aprons, and eventually *womanalls* (a one-piece suit with pants attached to a shirt) replaced women's long skirts and full sleeves. Few other concessions were made. Women worked at armament factories, filling hand grenades with powder, making cartridges for machine guns, and making fuses for cannons and bombs. They worked in factories producing uniforms for men. They assembled cars, trucks, and tanks. They worked as clerks at the Treasury Department, and at warehouses for the Department of War. Black workers, migrating from a South still economically depressed, moving north and west to major American cities, increased the number of workers available for all kinds of labor. The war provided a domino effect: as white men left, black men and white women moved into their jobs, and left behind jobs for black women and other women and men of color. War-related industries boomed, while traditional jobs held by women workers went begging. As a consequence, workers struck for better wages and fewer hours and, occasionally, won. More often, worker protests were met with complaints from management that laborers had become little better than socialists and communists, or "reds"—an epithet used more often after the fall of Russia in 1917 to the Communist Bolsheviks, or "Reds," as the revolutionaries were called.

The U.S. government formed the Committee on Women in Industry to coordinate issues concerning women workers: productivity, labor conditions, and protection. Led by Mary Anderson, the committee worked to keep employers from increasing hours for women and to protect them from exploitation. It also collected information about women war workers and investigated sweatshops and outwork arrangements, common in larger cities as manufacturers continued to place profit above the health and welfare of their workers.

Not all women supported the war. Many groups pronounced their opposition to the war, concerned that it was a continuation of American imperialism. Imperialism, when a country extends its power and influence, usually through military means, had long been a feature of American foreign policy. The United States had used the Monroe Doctrine to respond to European activities in South America during the nineteenth century, and had gone to war with Mexico to relieve it of the Southwest territories. In 1893, Americans took over the Kingdom of Hawaii, removing Queen Liliuokalani from her throne with help from the U.S. Marines. The queen tried to regain her throne in 1895, but finally abdicated after her arrest. Her kingdom was forced to become an American territory in 1900. Another imperialist adventure, the Spanish-American War in 1898, brought the United States the Philippines, Puerto Rico, and Guam, as well as considerable influence over Cuba.

The Seeds *of* Victory
Insure *the*
Fruits *of*
Peace

WRITE TO THE
NATIONAL
WAR GARDEN
COMMISSION ~
WASHINGTON, D.C.
for free books on
gardening, canning
& drying.

"Victory Gardens Help *the* Hungry"
Charles Lathrop Pack, President

WORLD WAR I POSTER   Most women would never serve in the armed forces. The government found other ways to ask the women of America to support the war effort. Here, a poster asks women to plant their own vegetables to increase their domestic food production so that no one went hungry as soldiers ate the food that housewives could no longer purchase.

American women joined national protests against these imperialist actions. Katherine Lee Bates, a feminist and Wellesley College professor who wrote "America, the Beautiful" in 1895, also wrote poems protesting the Spanish-American War. The Anti-Imperialist League, arguing against the United States' involvement in the Philippines, provided a platform for women opposed to such adventures. The group elected Josephine Shaw Lowell, a reformer who created the New York Consumers' League in 1890, as vice president in 1901. Mary G. Pickering, another opponent of imperialism, funded the publication of *Liberty Poems*, a collection of poetry opposing imperialism penned by noted New England women authors. The Woman's Peace Party protested the warfare as well, and attracted numbers of supporters in the years immediately preceding World War I. This group included not only founder Crystal Eastman among the 3,000 women at is first meeting in 1915, but also Jane Addams, as well as fellow reformers Florence Kelley, Lillian Wald, and Dr. Alice Hamilton; suffrage leaders Carrie Chapman Catt and Dr. Anna Howard Shaw; economist Charlotte

THE NINETEENTH AMENDMENT

The Nineteenth Amendment is one of the shortest amendments to the Constitution, and one of the most transformative.

"Section 1: The right of citizens of the United States to vote shall not be denied or abridged by the United States or by any State on account of sex.

"Section 2: Congress shall have power to enforce this article by appropriate legislation."

Perkins Gilman; and the Montana woman who would become the first woman elected to the U.S. House of Representatives, Jeanette Rankin.

Passing the Nineteenth Amendment

Neither radical suffragists nor peace activists impressed President Wilson, but women serving their country in wartime did. In January 1918 he called for the enfranchisement of women as a "war measure." Part of Wilson's change of heart came when he saw women serving a country in which most could not vote. In his speech finally supporting woman suffrage, he said, "We have made partners of the women in this war; shall we admit them only to a partnership of suffering and sacrifice and toil and not to a partnership of privilege and right?" He convinced the House, but the Senate took more time. The House passed the bill again in May 1919 by a vote of 304 to 89; the Senate finally passed the Nineteenth Amendment on June 4, 1919. Three-quarters of the states ratified it quickly, adding it to the Constitution (see Primary Source 7-5).

The final and thirty-sixth state to ratify the amendment was Tennessee, which held its convention in August 1920. The vote was close. Antisuffragists and suffragists alike buttonholed legislators in the hot August days preceding it. In the end, it came down to one young man: Harry Burn, a Republican, and the youngest member of the legislature. He wore a red rose, signifying that he was an "Anti," but Harry had received a letter from his mother, Febb Ensminger Burn on the morning of the vote. Mrs. Burn wrote: "Dear Son: Hurrah, and vote for suffrage! Don't keep them in doubt. I noticed some of the speeches against. They were bitter. I have been watching to see how you stood, but have not noticed anything yet. Don't forget to be a good boy and help Mrs. Catt put the 'rat' in ratification. Signed, Your Mother." Burn switched his vote and the amendment passed. Yellow rose petals, the signifier of support for woman suffrage, flew like confetti onto the General Assembly floor. "I know," said Burn later, "that a mother's advice is always safest for her boy to follow, and my mother wanted me to vote for ratification." That simple act, reflected Carrie Chapman Catt in her book *Woman Suffrage and Politics*, ended a campaign that had run for seventy-two years. The struggle was over. A new era was begun.

THINK MORE ABOUT IT

1. Return to the opening vignette on the Women's Pavilion at the Columbian Exposition held in Chicago in 1893. This elaborate fair was meant to showcase American progress to the world, and the Women's Pavilion was designed to show that American women's endeavors and accomplishments were an integral part of the modern nation. In general, how did women's activities and efforts in the next two decades embody this sentiment that a progressive nation needed to accommodate a "New Woman"?

2. In what ways were women critical to the economy in late-nineteenth and early-twentieth century America? Be sure to pay attention to women as producers and consumers, as rural and urban residents, and as members of families, households, and other social groups. What particular economic problems faced women because of their gender?

3. When it was introduced in the early twentieth century, protective legislation for women proved controversial not only among employers (who wanted as complete control over their workers as possible), but among woman's rights advocates. In pressing for improvements in women's lives, the key question for them became to what extent they should stress the differences between women and men (and their bodies) and how much they should emphasize commonalities. As discussed throughout this book, this is a persistent issue for feminists. Explain the nature of this controversy as it pertains to protective legislation as well as to the ideas that feminists hold.

4. The United States became a more diverse place in the last decades of the nineteenth century and the first decades of the twentieth. Paying attention to women of varied economic, racial, and ethnic backgrounds, how did this increasing diversity affect relations among and between women? What were the consequences to women of specific backgrounds of the efforts to Americanize and assimilate them?

5. Describe the range of issues addressed by clubwomen and other women's associations in the late nineteenth and early twentieth centuries. How did the clubwomen's movement, the antilynching campaign, and the drive for temperance demonstrate both growing opportunities for women and continued inequalities among women?

6. What were the characteristics of the New Woman? How were they expressed in such arenas as education, the workplace, leisure time, consumerism, dress, and sexuality? Provide examples of those who embodied the image of the New Woman. To whom did this new ideal appeal and for whom was it attainable? With reference to particular women who embodied this image, discuss the effects of the emergence of this ideal for diverse women and for American society as a whole.

7. After the turn of the twentieth century, and in conjunction with the emergence of the New Woman, more women became involved in

civic action. Perhaps the most consequential of these became a renewed fight for woman suffrage. Discuss the various efforts of antisuffragists and prosuffragists to support their viewpoints. Describe the final fight for suffrage. What factors were responsible for victory in this long-fought battle? Pay attention to the strategies and tactics various suffragists pursued, the arguments put forward for gaining the vote, and the timing of the final suffrage campaign.

8. What did you learn in this chapter that you did not know before? How does this new information help you understand the overall story of women in American history? What topics would you like to explore further?

READ MORE ABOUT IT

Jane Addams, *Twenty Years at Hull-House*

James West Davidson, *"They Say": Ida B. Wells and the Reconstruction of Race*

Nan Enstad, *Ladies of Labor, Girls of Adventure: Working Women, Popular Culture, and Labor Politics at the Turn of the Twentieth Century*

Glenda Gilmore, *Gender and Jim Crow: Women and the Politics of White Supremacy in North Carolina, 1896–1920*

Jennifer Guglielmo, *Living the Revolution: Italian Women's Resistance and Radicalism in New York City, 1880–1945*

Joanne Meyerowitz, *Women Adrift: Independent Wage Earners in Chicago, 1880–1930*

Kathy Peiss, *Cheap Amusements: Working Women and Leisure in Turn-of-the-Century New York*

Stephanie J. Shaw, *What a Woman Ought to Be and to Do: Black Professional Women Workers During the Jim Crow Era*

KEY CONCEPTS

Columbian Exposition

New Woman

Panic of 1893

Women's Trade Union League (WTUL)

Muller v. Oregon

"Americanization"

settlement house

Chinese Exclusion Law

segregation

antilynching campaign

Plessy v. Ferguson

Gibson Girl

birth control movement

antisuffragism

Nineteenth Amendment

civic housekeeping

GOOD TIMES, HARD TIMES, WARTIME

Eleanor Roosevelt of New York and Washington

WOMEN IN WORLD WAR II

Rosie the Riveter
Women in the Armed Services
Internment
Women on the Home Front

THINK MORE ABOUT IT

READ MORE ABOUT IT

KEY CONCEPTS

When Eleanor Roosevelt married her cousin Franklin Delano Roosevelt in 1905, she was satisfied with her approach to the social work and reform activities she undertook to make the world a better place. She did not support suffrage for women. She had joined the National Consumers' League when she was only eighteen. She visited factories and sweatshops as she worked to improve health and safety standards for women. She joined the Junior League, teaching at the Rivington Street Settlement House in New York City. After her marriage to the up-and-coming New York politician, she curtailed her public activities at first, and had four children, one of whom died shortly after birth. By 1910, she began organizing social and political gatherings to support Franklin, now a Democratic New York state assemblyman, in his campaign against the then-current crop of corrupt politicians, and had two more children. When the United States entered World War I, Eleanor Roosevelt returned to her work to improve the lot of those less fortunate. She coordinated canteen activities at Washington's Union Station, where soldiers on their way to training camps passed the time between trains. She worked with the Red Cross. At the Department of the Navy, where her husband was assistant secretary, she supervised knitters making supplies for the war effort. She visited wounded soldiers in local hospitals and worked toward improving conditions at St. Elizabeth's Hospital for individuals who were mentally ill.

In 1920, after women got the vote, Roosevelt returned to New York and continued her reform efforts, but changed her tactics. She joined the newly created *League of Women Voters* and its legislative program, lobbying to help change state laws that needed to be modified to reflect women's new status as voters. In 1924, she led a delegation to the Democratic National Convention, where she worked to have the Democratic Party platform include issues such as the abolition of child labor and equal pay for women. She had learned, she later wrote, that "if you wanted to institute any kind of reform you could get far more attention if you had a vote than if you lacked one."

ELEANOR ROOSEVELT AT TODHUNTER SCHOOL Before becoming first lady, Eleanor Roosevelt, seated here giving a group of schoolgirls an impromptu lecture, taught American history, American literature, English, and current events at Todhunter School, a private academy in New York City. She sought to broaden the horizons of wealthy students, taking them on field trips to settlement houses. One of her essay exam questions read: "Give your reasons for or against allowing women to actively participate in the control of the government, politics and officials through the vote, as well as your reasons for or against women holding office in the government."

American women's lives transformed between 1920 and 1945. The impact of the vote could be seen in the lives of reformers such as Eleanor Roosevelt, who changed their tactics to include the power of the ballot, as well as the actions of politicians, who passed legislation to woo new voters. This impact of the so-called *women's bloc* of voters proved short-lived, however. After years of social, economic, and political upheaval, an influenza pandemic in 1918 that killed over 600,000 Americans in ten months, and a world war that killed millions in Europe as well as over 100,000 American soldiers, most Americans, male and female, longed for a return to "normalcy," as the new president, Warren G. Harding, put it. Reform efforts still went on and a new call for women's equality went out. An overheated economy provided both opportunities and demands for change. Fears of outsiders led Congress to limit immigration, but migration from the South to the North still changed the demographics of cities. Beyond it all, however, the cultural phenomenon known as the *Roaring Twenties* overshadowed everything else until the country collapsed into the Great Depression, an economic downturn unlike any other the United States had faced. Another international war, World War II, eased the Depression and provided new opportunities for women to play a role on the national and international stage.

THE "WOMEN'S BLOC" AND SOCIAL AND POLITICAL ACTIVISM

In Tennessee, seconds after Harry Burn's vote supporting the Nineteenth Amendment guaranteed women the right to vote, a fellow Tennessee legislator jumped to his feet to change his earlier "no" vote to "aye." Male politicians were unsure what their new constituents wanted, but they knew that their reelection chances now depended in part on women's votes, and they believed women would vote as a bloc. Legislation designed to appeal to women voters followed the Nineteenth Amendment's passage as surely as sunshine followed rain.

Congress began the process, establishing the *Women's Bureau* at the Department of Labor in 1920. It represented 8.25 million wage-earning women—nearly 20 percent of the American workforce—providing them with a voice in the formation of public policy. The bureau gathered statistics and information to improve working conditions and to help create opportunities for women to earn higher wages, as well as to promote the overall welfare of wage-earning women. Mary Anderson, a union member and founder of the Chicago Women's Trade Union League, became the Women's Bureau's first director (1920–1944). She pushed for protective legislation for women wage earners and conducted studies showing that the beliefs that women worked only for "pin-money"—or "extras"—and luxuries were myths. Most wage-earning women worked to provide for their families, and most faced a second shift of housework when they returned home from their jobs. In 1922, the bureau studied and reported on the difficulties African American women faced in industries; in 1924, on married women in industries; in 1926, on the effects of industrial poisons on women workers; in 1930, on women workers in Hawaiian canneries, on laundresses in twenty-three selected cities, on "Industrial Home Work" (formerly known as piecework), on women workers in five-and-dime stores, and on "Variations on Employment Trends of Women and Men." Congressional committees and activists for protective legislation used the evidence gathered in these reports and dozens of others to change public policy and to write new legislation affecting women wage earners.

Another area of concern for newly enfranchised women was maternal and infant health care. In 1921, Congress passed the Sheppard-Towner Maternity and Infancy Protection Act, the first federally funded act addressing the social welfare of the nation. It supplied matching funds to states to help provide prenatal and childhood health care. The bill was written by another Department of Labor bureau chief, Julia Lathrop of the U.S. Children's Bureau, and was introduced by Jeanette Rankin, the first woman member of the House of Representatives. American women desperately needed maternal and infant health care: one in six babies

ALICE PAUL, EQUAL RIGHTS AMENDMENT OF 1923

The original Equal Rights Amendment, which Alice Paul referred to as the Lucretia Mott Amendment, was introduced in every Congress from 1923 until a revised version passed in 1972. This one was never passed; the second version was never ratified.

"Men and women shall have equal rights throughout the United States and every place subject to its jurisdiction.

"Congress shall have the power to enforce this article through appropriate legislation."

Source: From Deborah G. Felder, *A Century of Women* (New York: Citadel Press, 1999), 270.

---

born died before his or her first birthday, and maternal death was second only to tuberculosis as the leading cause of death for women in the United States.

Small wonder that this was the first major piece of legislation women activists pushed Congress to pass after suffrage. Federal and state funds combined under the bill, funding itinerant nurses to travel with their "wellness tents," where they examined babies and taught mothers about cleanliness, nutrition, and when to seek medical help. The women's club movement actively supported the Sheppard-Towner Act, going door-to-door in cities, towns, and rural areas to gather information for the program, recording infant births and deaths, and then comparing statistics to show that infant mortality rates were even higher than previously thought. As useful as the legislation was, the American Medical Association opposed it, fearing both a "socialized" or state-run medicine program, as well as the economic impact of such clinics on their member doctors. Fiscal and social conservatives usually opposed such government intervention in the private sphere. The nation's second woman representative and the sole woman in Congress in 1921, Republican Alice Mary Robertson from Oklahoma opposed the bill as "an intrusion into women's lives." Activist women won their bill, but despite the success of the Sheppard-Towner Act, best shown by the fact that by 1930 the death rate for infants had been cut in half, Congress let its funding expire in 1929. They left it to the states to finance and administer the program.

The fate of the Sheppard-Towner Act symbolized what happened to women's issues generally in the 1920s. Great enthusiasm greeted the passage of suffrage, along with the sure belief that things were going to change because of the women's voting bloc. In the 1920 elections, not all eligible women could vote because the Nineteenth Amendment had not been ratified before the deadline for voter registration had passed in some of the states, particularly in the South. When the 1924 election came around, however, women activists were dismayed to discover that giving the vote to women did not seem to matter, since fewer Americans were

CHARLOTTE PERKINS GILMAN, "CHILD LABOR"

Gilman wrote essays, novels, and even doggerel such as the following short piece that quickly pointed out the unnaturalness of child labor. Upton Sinclair, a muckracking journalist who had exposed horrible working conditions in the meat-packing industry, included this poem in his anthology of writers seeking justice with their words.

voting at all. Only 25 percent of the general population—48.9 percent of eligible voters—took part in the presidential election, the lowest proportion ever. Compared to the 61.8 percent of the eligible voters participating in 1916, and even greater proportions in earlier presidential elections, the failure of women voters to seize the opportunity discouraged activists not yet satisfied with women's political participation. Activists also learned, by the next national election in 1928, that women voters did not vote differently from men voters. Their region, their economic class and interests, their ethnicity and religion, their family's traditional choice of political party, all apparently influenced women's voting decisions more than their gender.

The vision of a women's bloc uniting to support legislation promoting women's rights vanished in the aftermath of the ratification of the Nineteenth Amendment. By winning women the right to vote, suffragists had lost the great cause that had unified their voices for so many years. Dr. Anna Howard Shaw put it succinctly to a young women's rights activist, Emily Newell Blair, "I am sorry for you young women who have to carry on the work for the next ten years, for suffrage was a symbol, and now you have lost your symbol." Without that drive for the vote, the movement for women's rights splintered, and activists found it harder to accomplish their goals. The NAWSA became the League of Women Voters, and its membership dropped 90 percent within five years after winning the vote. The Women's Joint Congressional Committee formed in 1920, its members dedicated to shepherding legislation on women's issues through Congress. Alice Paul, who had coordinated efforts in the nation's capital to pass the Nineteenth Amendment, formed the National Woman's Party (NWP) in 1923. The NWP pushed for a constitutional amendment, the *Equal Rights Amendment* (ERA), to overturn the assorted state laws that prevented women from sitting on juries, receiving equal pay for the same work performed by men, or keeping their own property after marriage. (See Primary Source 8-1.) Future U.S. vice president Charles Curtis, Republican senator from Kansas, and Daniel Read Anthony, Republican representative from Kansas and nephew of Susan B. Anthony, successfully introduced the amendment in December, 1923, but it died for lack of support.

No fledgling feeds the father bird!
No chicken feeds the hen!
No kitten mouses for the cat—
This glory is for men.
We are the Wisest, Strongest Race—
Loud may our praise be sung!

The only animal alive
That lives upon its young!

Source: Charlotte Perkins, "Child Labor," *The Cry for Justice*, ed. Upton Sinclair (Philadelphia: John C. Winston Co., 1915), 662.

Women still interested in social activism, the social feminists, now could use the vote as a tool in their reform attempts, but the bonds forged in the fight for suffrage broke apart as women followed their different interests. Instead of equal rights, social feminists focused on gaining more protective legislation for women workers and banning child labor. Julia Lathrop, labor leader Mary Van Kleeck, and Frances Perkins, who would later become the secretary of labor and the first woman in a president's cabinet, argued that sexual differences between women and men should be recognized, respected, and protected. In opposition, Alice Paul and Maud Younger, leaders of the NWP, argued that equal rights were necessary for all women, and any protective legislation that infringed upon women's equality with men was not fair. This argument showed no signs of being settled as women moved into partisan political organizations as well as continuing their reform work. Both Democratic and Republican parties would eventually support the ERA in their party platforms, while the League of Women Voters would support protective legislation and oppose an equal rights amendment for years.

New possibilities opened for women eager to participate in existing political groups or to form new ones. Women interested in the peace movement could join national and international peace organizations, such as the Women's International League for Peace and Freedom, founded by Jane Addams and Emily Greene Balch. Women interested in women's health issues could join the American Birth Control League, led by Margaret Sanger, and work in the first legal birth control clinic in America. Women interested in children's issues could lobby for the Child Labor Amendment, passed in 1924, but still unratified. (See Primary Source 8-2.) Women appalled by the continued lynching of black men and women could join Jessie Daniel Ames, who founded the Association of Southern Women for the Prevention of Lynching. The group campaigned against a revival of lynching in the 1920s. Ames and her group contested the Cult of White Womanhood, decrying white men's violence against blacks, committed in the name of white women. She and her supporters, along with other anti-lynching advocates, worked so successfully that in the year 1940, for the first time in decades, no black Americans were lynched.

For women interested in traditional formal politics, newly founded women's legislative councils provided roles in state governments and politics. Women interested in partisan politics could also join the women's committees of national parties. Women also founded and joined groups within ethnic and religious groups, such as the Polish American Women's Political Club, and formed auxiliaries to men's groups such as the League of United Latin American Citizens. Other women devoted their time and efforts to preexisting labor organizations, such as the Women's Trade Union League, by 1926 led by Rose Schneiderman, or the International Ladies' Garment Workers Union (ILGWU) whose Education Department was led by Fannia Cohn. Cohn organized and promoted educational programs for workers and their families with classes in economics, history, and geography, as well as art, music, theater, psychology, and literature. The classes continued to promote the Progressives' goal of assimilating immigrants into American life and culture, helped to reinforce union ideas while educating young people, and made a liberal education available to thousands who had few educational resources. Winning the vote did not mean the end of women's voluntary organizations.

THE DESIRE FOR "NORMALCY"

The many choices women activists had were matched by the many opportunities for women to do something besides spend their time on politics and reforms. The preceding decades had been contentious and unsettling. The tumult of the late nineteenth century, of economic declines, strikes, and worker unrest, had been followed by America's participation in World War I, leaving many Americans disenchanted with international affairs. In 1918 to 1919, an influenza pandemic left 675,000 Americans dead, more than had died over the four years of the Civil War, and most in the prime of their lives. Twenty-six cities suffered from race riots and seventy-seven Americans were lynched by their fellow Americans in 1919. Bombs went off in eight cities in the summer of 1919, and communists, socialists, and anarchists were blamed and deported in the so-called Red Scare, when Americans feared a Russian-style communist revolution. Small wonder that the Republican presidential candidate Warren G. Harding ran on a platform of returning to normalcy in the 1920 presidential election. He sought to leave behind the exhausting and never-ending reforms of the Progressive Era, campaigning on the idea that Americans wanted "not revolution, but restoration; not agitation, but adjustment . . . not experiment but equipoise; not submergence in internationality, but sustainment in triumphant nationality." Harding's focus attracted those concerned about the economy and women's work, racism, nativism, and assimilation. The international vision of the Democrats and President Woodrow Wilson, who had unsuccessfully pushed America to join the international organization known as the League of Nations, was passé. Harding won in a landslide against Democratic nominee James Cox. The new president gained 16 million popular votes, about 60 percent of the total, and won the Electoral College, 404 to 127.

The Economy and Women's Work

Part of restoring normalcy was encouraging economic growth and opportunity. After the soldiers returned from World War I, women, thrown out of the better-paying jobs they had enjoyed during the war, did not go back into their homes. Women continued earning wages, moving back into jobs considered women's work: positions such as garment workers, domestic workers, laundresses, secretaries, and sales clerks. In 1910, they constituted 19.9 percent of the labor force, and in 1920 they were 20.4 percent. A slight recession in 1921 drove women out of some of the mechanized jobs in the garment industry, and declines in agriculture in the 1920s forced women out of wage jobs in that field as well, but the proportion of women earning wages in the national workforce increased by 1930 to 22 percent.

Some women moved into the economy as entrepreneurs. Helena Rubinstein, a Jewish immigrant from Poland via Australia, brought her beauty cream company to the United States in 1914. By the 1920s, she had successfully convinced upper- and middle-class women to buy not only her skin care products, but also entire beauty regimens that smacked of medical procedures. African American women enjoyed access to similar beauty products. Marjorie Stewart Joyner, a Chicago beauty salon owner, became director of Madame C. J. Walker's beauty colleges after Walker's death in 1919, and helped to write Illinois' first law regulating beauty shops in 1924. In 1928, she patented the first permanent-wave machine to replace old-fashioned curling irons and to help African American women achieve the smooth, wavy hairstyles then in fashion. Her invention did not make her rich, since Walker's company held the patent, but she took great pride in the enormous success her machine enjoyed.

Professions continued to open up to women, especially as the number of college graduates increased. By 1930, over 10 percent of American women ages eighteen to twenty-one were enrolled in college, representing nearly half of all college students. An expanded middle class whose members worked as doctors, lawyers, ministers, professionals, and teachers, and in businesses such as manufacturing, sent their daughters to colleges. College-educated women worked as librarians, social workers, and nurses, but a few also became physicians and lawyers. Changes in education that moved training for doctors and lawyers from apprenticeships to schools meant women could train at formal schools, instead of relying on the more informal and less accessible system of apprenticeship. Law schools slowly opened their doors to women. By 1915, the University of Michigan, Yale, Cornell, New York University, and Stanford all allowed women in their law schools. Howard University's law school allowed both black and white women to enroll, and the Portia Law School in Boston established a night school for women wanting to become lawyers. By far the vast majority of women college graduates, however, became teachers. Both white and black women entered the teaching profession in enough numbers to feminize it thoroughly at the lower levels. Women taught most often at the elementary levels; men were high school teachers, principals, and superintendents. Higher education reflected similar tendencies. Despite women making up nearly half of the number of college students, women were only 26 percent of faculty by 1920 (the same proportion as in 1980), and usually found only in the lower ranks.

As more and more women worked outside the home, *labor-saving devices* poured into the market. Electrical washing machines were patented in 1910, and electric vacuum cleaners in 1908. Anna Bissell's carpet sweeper provided a nonelectric solution for keeping carpets clean, as well as providing women in Grand Rapids, Michigan, with jobs assembling the sweepers. By 1905, electric-powered home sewing machines were available, and Helen Augusta Blanchard of Maine was busy patenting improvements for them, including a zig-zag stitch. Gas stoves with interior ovens and top burners were common by 1920. Lillian Moller Gilbreth of Rhode Island, an engineer, industrial psychologist, and mother of twelve children, studied time management to increase worker efficiency. She patented inventions such as a foot-pedal trash can, an electric food mixer, and shelves mounted on the inside of refrigerator doors. By 1920, her inventions could be found on some of the 200 different models of home refrigerators.

A 1922 model refrigerator had 9 cubic feet of storage and cost $714 (equivalent to over $8,000 today), at a time when a union plumber might earn $1.25 an hour for a forty-four-hour week ($55 per week or $2,860 per year). Most Americans could not buy such expensive home appliances, and only about 35 percent of American homes were wired for electricity. Still, many who could not afford to buy such commodities outright took advantage of the practice of buying "on time": taking home the item, then paying off the balance owed over months on easy credit terms. Conspicuous consumption reached middle-class America in the 1920s.

Labor-saving devices continued to be a double-edged sword for women. Expectations rose regarding what was seen as "normal" cleanliness. Because it was now easier to keep clothing and carpets clean, for example, people commonly expected they would be cleaned. Refrigerators and easier-to-use stoves and ovens meant people expected more complicated food dishes to be prepared, instead of one-pot meals. As the possession of consumer goods became a measure of one's status in society, more and more Americans found themselves living economically precarious lives, since easily available credit pressured buyers to maintain or improve their social status by purchasing items they could not really afford. In the volatile economy of the 1920s, economic choices grew increasingly complex and poor choices could have substantial repercussions.

Racism and Nativism

Racial discrimination against black Americans continued in the 1920s and 1930s, even when they had taken advantage of new opportunities to become well educated or trained to specific jobs. Academic training for black women reflected the cultural assumptions that they would most likely need domestic skills in their jobs, but included other topics as well. Black institutions offered courses in nursing, sewing, and hatmaking, for the professions that their students were most likely to enter, but they included courses in English, art, and music as well. College-educated black women who could not find teaching jobs usually wound up in domestic service, where they faced low wages and had few chances to improve their lot, and where unions were nonexistent. Union protection for any African American worker was rare, even in industries. Not until 1925 was the first African American union formed: the Brotherhood of Sleeping Car Porters and Maids, founded by A. Phillip Randolph. Sleeping car porters and maids cared for passengers traveling on railroad cars. Pullman Company, a Chicago-based manufacturer of railroad cars, was the largest single employer of black people in the United States. Despite the union's name, its focus was on the 15,000 black men working on Pullman cars, including college-educated men who could find no other jobs. While union women sought to organize alongside union men, many sleeping car maids feared retaliation for joining the union or lacked the time to participate.

The wives, sisters, and mothers of the union men formed the International Ladies' Auxiliary of the Brotherhood of Sleeping Car Porters and Women's Economic Councils to raise funds to assist the union's drive for recognition. "Labor solidarity meant family unity" was their motto. Better wages for men meant better lives for women and families. The women's groups set up consumer cooperatives to help cut costs for consumers and encouraged education by raising funds to provide college scholarships. Going beyond these bread-and-butter concerns, women in auxiliary groups also worked to pass federal and state legislation prohibiting lynching and attacking poll taxes, the fees people had to pay to vote that prevented most poor Southern blacks from voting. African American women activists also pushed for fairer wages for agricultural and domestic workers, the fields where two-thirds of all black Americans were employed by 1930.

Nativism, which sought to protect the interests of native-born American over those of immigrants, soared in the 1920s and 1930s. In the anti-immigrant climate of the 1920s, U.S. women married to foreign men sought protection from discrimination. After vigorous lobbying by women voters, in 1922 Congress passed the Cable Act (the Married Women's Independent Nationality Act), allowing women married to unnaturalized immigrants to retain their U.S. citizenship. The act served as a milestone in establishing the independent legal identity of married women. Prior to gaining the vote, American women who married alien citizens became alien themselves—no longer U.S. citizens—at marriage, sometimes to their dismay. Some women were, as Raymond Crist, U.S. Commissioner of Naturalization put it, "of perhaps Mayflower ancestry, whose forbears fought through the Revolution, and whose family names bear honored and conspicuous places in our history, who are thoroughly American at heart, and who perhaps have never left these shores," yet lost their citizenship when they married noncitizens. They objected to having to seek naturalization, "in the same manner as any lowly immigrant." When states began allowing women to vote, some judges objected to women voting, if they had been naturalized solely by virtue of their marriage to American men or to men who were naturalized Americans. The Cable Act met these objections by requiring women to apply for and be granted naturalization on their own merits, but also by allowing native-born American women to keep their citizenship regardless of whom they married.

Nativism, so evident in Crist's comments, used racism and religious bigotry to meet the challenge posed by economic competition. White Americans resented competing for jobs with immigrants from Europe and Asia. In 1924 the United States decisively slammed shut "The Golden Door" to immigrants, passing an immigration act that limited the total number of immigrants admitted per year. The act established quotas for each nation, determined by the population of immigrants already in the country at the turn of the century. These quotas drastically cut the numbers of southern and eastern Europeans admitted, and cemented the exclusion of almost all Asians, except Filipinos (who resided in an American territory). The act had immediate repercussions for many women. No Chinese women could enter the United States for permanent residence, even if their husbands already lived in the country. Not until 1929 did the Supreme Court rule that Chinese wives of Americans could join their husbands. Other government bodies also restricted immigrants. Western states passed laws restricting landownership by Asians. Mississippians drove the daughter of a Chinese grocer out of the "white-only" school. In Los Angeles, fourteen Japanese American college women started a Chi Alpha Delta, a Japanese sorority, when none of the campus sororities would allow them to become members.

The Ku Klux Klan (KKK), which campaigned for legally protected nativism, gained millions of adherents in the 1920s. Threatened and angered by immigrants, communists, Jews, Catholics, and African Americans, as well as labor unrest nationwide, 3 to 4 million Klan members, including women, marched and paraded in all major American cities. Klan members burned crosses at rallies, and lynched, beat, and flogged people who had, according to the Klan, committed crimes against the morals of "true" Americans. The Klan attacked mostly black, Jewish, and Catholic men, but they also attacked women for not living up to the Klan's behavioral standards. One Georgia woman, for instance, was given sixty lashes for not going to church and other "immoral" acts, her Klansman minister leading those carrying out the sentence. Another minister led the flogging of an Alabaman divorcée for remarrying. In Oklahoma, Klan members whipped young women caught riding in automobiles with young men; in California, the same was true. In an era when women were increasing their autonomy, the Klan rallied members around notions of "pure womanhood" and attacked women exhibiting independence.

The Women's Ku Klux Klan (WKKK), established in 1923, was a distinct group, rather than a women's auxiliary of the male Klan. The WKKK used many of the same symbols and political rhetoric as the KKK, but often attached different meanings to those than men did. Klanswomen were particularly opposed to miscegenation, or interracial sexual relationships and marriage. Unlike Klansmen who opposed such relationships because they were mixing "blood," Klan women feared losing their men to the mythical creature that was the exotic and sexually adventurous black woman, an image of African American women that survived from slavery days.

THREE GENERATIONS OF KLANSWOMEN JOIN A MARCH IN 1925 In support of white supremacy and nativism, a reinvigorated Klan viewed women's participation as a useful way to ensure the next generation of Americans would support their racist views.

The WKKK swore an oath to uphold the sanctity of the home and the "chastity of womanhood," and carried that into practice by providing social services, but only for their own members. They collected food to feed the families of Klansmen arrested for rioting and vigilante attacks, and ran homes for wayward girls. They opened a day nursery in Florida, complaining that the public school system had been ruined by Catholic teachers, and campaigned against "Catholic" encyclopedias in public schools, Catholic contractors working on publicly funded projects, and Jewish and Catholic vacationers at Protestant-mostly resorts. Klanswomen publicized the names of bootleggers who sold illegal alcohol during Prohibition. Violent opposition to that tactic led to the death of one participant. Myrtle Cook, a Klanswoman and WCTU president in Vinton, Iowa, was assassinated after she documented the names of bootleggers in her town. The Klan took over her 1925 funeral, serving as pall bearers and burning a cross at the head of her grave.

The women of the WKKK in the 1920s were not the same women the KKK swore to protect in the 1860s and 1870s. Then, the emphasis was on protecting white women from supposedly rapacious black males. In the 1920s, Klanswomen presented themselves as modern women. They even complained about women's historical exclusion from politics, and argued that the more Klan members involved in voting, no matter their gender, the better. Klanswomen also moved beyond the image of the Southern Lady, not only by including women of the North, but by using violence themselves against others, including women. In 1924 in Wilkinsburg, Pennsylvania, for instance, Mamie Bittner, a mother of three, was only one of thousands of Klanswomen carrying heavy wooden clubs to use against Irish Catholics on a march through town to protest the Irish celebration of St. Patrick's Day.

Public dismay at the excesses of nativism, such as lynching, immigration laws, and the Klan, led to some decline of these influences on American politics in the second half of the 1920s, as did activist individuals, judges, and opposition groups. For African Americans, however, racial segregation remained the norm, and as black Americans fled the poverty-stricken South for Northern cities, racism fanned the unrest that flared up in urban centers whenever the economy soured.

Assimilation

Many white, Protestant Americans, used to the assimilation efforts of the Progressive Era, continued to support Americanization efforts directed toward immigrants and Native Americans. Ethnic groups continued to resist, however. Native Americans in particular strongly resisted participating in the boarding schools that had caused so much destruction of their cultures in the Progressive Era. The harsh regimens and crowded conditions in the schools exacerbated the spread not only of childhood diseases but also tuberculosis, the eye disease trachoma, and, in 1918, the influenza that killed so many Americans nationwide. The Bureau of Indian Affairs' (BIA) Meriam Report of 1928 confirmed many of the horror stories of mistreatment Indian parents and students had been complaining about for years, and after 1933, a new commissioner of Indian Affairs, John Collier, began to close the boarding schools, converting some to day schools to better serve the children and their families. The government also provided federal funds to public schools for taking in Indian students.

By 1928, the majority of Native children attended public, rather than BIA schools, and federal officials hoped education would aid their assimilation. Federal attempts at assimilation continued to have mixed results. Zitkala Sa (Red Bird), called Gertrude Bonnin by whites, left the boarding school where her teacher had so frightened her when she arrived (see Chapter 7), and spent much of her career publishing articles about her people's heritage in popular magazines, determined to teach non-Indians the beauty and validity of her culture. She gave lectures, taught, and cowrote *The Sun Dance Opera*, which she premiered in 1913, playing a traditional Sioux flute. In the 1920s, she lobbied with her husband Raymond for a federal law allowing Indians to become citizens, a goal achieved in 1924. In 1926, the Bonnins founded the National Congress of American Indians, with Gertrude as president, to lobby Congress on Indian affairs, to be sure that Republicans and Democrats included them in their party platforms, and to keep Native American issues before the press in Washington. Bonnin offers merely one example of the way that Indians used their familiarity with white culture gained from boarding school educations to preserve and protect, rather than destroy, their culture and history.

Asians in America also faced hostility, particularly in communities where they were either few in number or a large enough proportion of the population to be viewed as an economic threat. After immigration limitations on Chinese laborers were implemented in 1924, American agricultural employers instead brought Korean, Japanese, and Filipino laborers to American territories, particularly Hawaii. By 1920, there were 110,000 Japanese in Hawaii. Many of the women workers there had emigrated as *picture brides*, coming to the United States as parties in arranged marriages, having never met their future husbands. The government and employers alike viewed these women as stabilizing influences among the workers, and hoped they would prevent labor unrest by dissuading husbands and fathers from protesting their working conditions. After a 1909 labor strike by these "stable" women workers, however, Filipino, Korean, and East Indian women were not so fortunate. Their menfolk emigrated without them. No longer able to bring their countrywomen to America, the men married Mexican, African American, or Native American women instead, often leaving behind their original wives and families.

Racial prejudice was rampant against all Asians, and only a few Asian women found ways to enter the professions. Instead, most worked as domestics, laundresses, housekeepers, clerks, gardeners, and storekeepers. Chinese immigrants and their families often lived in "Chinatowns" within cities, where shops, restaurants, and cultural events prevented much assimilation. As late as the early 1900s, wives of wealthy merchants in Chinatowns in San Francisco and Los Angeles remained confined to their homes except for special occasions, tottering around on bound feet, a mark of upper-class status imported from China. By the 1920s, few Chinese women had bound feet anymore, but segregation from white Americans was common for much of the Asian population, and Asian American women formed their own women's clubs to promote social reform within their communities.

Hispanics, particularly in Texas, continued to fight for their rights through women's clubs as well. In San Antonio, the *Cruz Azul Mexicana* Club, a women's club, built a free medical clinic and sponsored a library. The club also provided legal assistance to members and the community. Other Hispanics organized to fight against discrimination and racism. Los Angeles Hispanic women founded *La Sociedad de Madres Mexicanas* in 1926, and another, *Orden de Caballeros de América*, was founded three years later in South Texas by María Hernández and her husband, Pedro. Various groups in Texas formed the League of United Latin American Citizens (LULAC) also in 1929, to join forces in their fight against discrimination. Fair funding for schools, social programs to help children and elderly people, eliminating poll taxes and helping voters to register all were issues that these groups rallied around, evidence again of the ways in which all women activists continued their reform efforts after winning the vote.

THE POWER OF POPULAR CULTURE

Racism and efforts to assimilate immigrants persisted in part because of the power of the stereotypes used to represent various ethnic groups. Such stereotypes, not only of immigrants and ethnic groups but also of other cohorts within American culture, grew more popular in the 1920s as the technology used to promote them became more sophisticated and accessible. President Calvin Coolidge's view of American business being the business of men rather than women, for instance, derived in part from the popular stereotype of women in 1920: the *flapper*. The flapper represented the wild side of the New Woman. She had no interest in reform or politics, and could not have been further from the True Woman of the earlier century.

The Flapper

The flapper's physical characteristics exemplified the differences between her and previous images of women. She wore short skirts and rolled-down hose, and powdered her knees. She wore no corset, just a brassiere that de-emphasized her bust. She wore her hair short, or *bobbed*, and she used makeup—rouge (blush), powder, and lipstick—items previously worn primarily by actresses and prostitutes. Flappers inhabited speakeasies, drank bathtub gin, danced the Charleston, became sexually active, and rode alone or with men in automobiles.

While the flapper was based in part on the reality of the anonymous, young, single women who had moved from small towns and rural areas to enter the urban workforce, the stereotype came from the media's interpretation of the lives of college-aged single women and their collegiate boyfriends, portrayed in movies by women such as Louise Brooks and by Anita Loos. Loos was a best-selling author of the 1920s, whose book *Gentlemen Prefer Blondes* proved so popular that it was even serialized in Chinese. The book was the imagined diary of a flapper who traveled to Europe, met everyone who was anyone, and returned to America to marry a millionaire.

The flapper owed her existence to several factors. Prohibition, which prohibited the production, sale, and consumption of alcohol in the United States from 1919 until repealed by the Twenty-first Amendment in 1933, failed to end Americans' desire for alcohol. Instead, people made their own or smuggled supplies across borders. This massive resistance to the law led to a corresponding decline in their respect for law and order. In cities such as Chicago, organized crime took advantage of the situation to control drug trafficking and make inconceivable amounts of money, as well as to terrorize citizens and run the city. The flapper personified the decline in respect for the laws that accompanied Prohibition. She had no patience with chaperones or society's criticisms of her behavior. Flappers also existed because many young women were now earning enough in wages to live on their own, away from parental supervision and the protection of a parental home. The automobile, widely available by 1920 (Henry Ford's factories churned out thousands of Model Ts for $290 each), provided young women and their boyfriends with far more opportunities to explore other geographic locations, as well as the privacy to explore each other, an act less risky as access to and information about birth control increased. Along with this freedom came a culture of consumerism, where easy credit and payments for purchases over time were common. Flappers did not worry about to-morrow, but sought immediate gratification.

The popular culture that created the image of the flapper had new and highly effective methods of spreading itself. Five thousand radios existed in 1920, providing listeners with broadcasts from about 4 stations. By 1923, there were 508 stations, broadcasting to some 3 million radio receivers. Dozens of radio shows, from soap operas to comedies to adventure serials and mysteries, drew owners to their sets on a regular timetable. Movie theaters had grown from a handful in 1905 to 20,000 by 1928. Since mov-ies "talked" after 1927's *The Jazz Singer*, by 1930 nearly every small town had a movie theater, and the movies replaced the public lectures that had for so long entertained and informed Americans. Dozens of movies were now created in California in Hollywood and promoted in massive advertis-ing campaigns. Some actors and actresses made enormous salaries. In 1919, Mary Pickford, who made $350,000 a film, had enough money and business acumen to start United Artists, a movie company that would produce many of America's best-loved films for the next sixty years. By 1930, Clara Bow, the "'It' Girl" ("it" being sex appeal), made $7,500 a week—nearly $400,000 a year.

Images of women as flappers, homewreckers, vixens, and sweethearts became nearly universally accessible and universally understood. They were also nearly universally white. Flappers in movies were good girls who stayed chaste and married at the end. Non-American actresses often played the seductive women—the vamps—as did Polish actress Pola Negri and German actress Marlene Dietrich. Appearances by women of color on screen were also rare, except in the so-called race movies created specifi-cally for the black community. In mainstream films, Chicanas Dolores Del Rio and Lupe Vélez debuted in the mid-1920s; African American singing star Bessie Smith performed in *St. Louis Blues* in 1929; and Molly Spotted Elk, a Penobscot Indian, starred in *The Silent Enemy* in 1930. The majority of Americans saw movies that embraced cultural stereotypes and provided only limited roles for ethnic performers, those of chorus girl and flippant or incompetent servant. Images from the flickering screen proved both powerful and long-lasting. Various views of women in American popular culture became increasingly entrenched because of the ease with which they were disseminated.

The Harlem Renaissance

With the exception of Hollywood, the center for popular culture remained New York City. The Harlem Renaissance, an unparalleled flowering of music and literature created primarily by African Americans, was centered in the Harlem neighborhood of New York City during the 1920s and 1930s. Artists flocked to the area, producing brilliant music, art, and

ZORA NEALE HURSTON ON WRITING

In 1942, Harlem Renaissance star author Zora Neale Hurston described her view of the siren call that words exercised on her in her autobiography.

"I wrote *Their Eyes Were Watching God* in Haiti. It was dammed up in me, and I wrote it under internal pressure in seven weeks. I wish that I could write it again. In fact, I regret all of my books. It is one of tragedies of life that one cannot have all the wisdom one is ever to possess in the beginning. Perhaps it is just as well

literature. Musicians Duke Ellington, Ethel Waters, and Josephine Baker all soared to prominence and acclaim in the 1920s. Bessie Smith, known as the Empress of the Blues, enjoyed a career recording with stars such as Louis Armstrong and Benny Goodman. She eventually made $2,000 a week, a queenly sum.

Women musicians were the best-known participants in the Harlem Renaissance, but other artists flourished as well. Lois Mailou Jones and Meta Warrick Fuller represented African American women in the arts of painting and sculpture. Leading black writers such as Zora Neale Hurston rejected the dominant white cultural images of blacks as being one-dimensional. Hurston used funds from a white patron to visit the South, using sociological surveys she conducted of its black communities as the basis for her novels. Some black intellectuals criticized Hurston's work because her characters spoke in the dialect style that had traditionally been used by white writers, such as Harriet Beecher Stowe, to depict black life. But Hurston's novels also showed blacks developing communities that were alternatives to white societies—more communal with a sense of social equality. Her strongest characters were women. Hurston's male characters tended to die early because her female characters were struggling for the autonomy that they needed to define themselves. Hurston could not conceive, historian Nancy Cott wrote, of black women being able "to achieve full growth and become fully human" without writing out of the stories the black men who kept trying to define them. (See Primary Source 8-3.)

THE GREAT DEPRESSION AND A NEW DEAL

Another controversial artist in New York in the 1920s, Georgia O'Keeffe, filled her canvases with huge flowers that reflected the artist's concern that the era was too rushed and too pressured. It took time to see a flower, she wrote later, "like to have a friend takes time." That pressure and haste was about to come to a screeching halt in an economic crash that ended the Roaring Twenties and resulted in the Great Depression, an economic to be rash and foolish for awhile. If writers were too wise, perhaps no books would be written at all. It might be better to ask yourself Why? afterwards than before.... [T]he force from somewhere in Space which commands you to write in the first place, gives you no choice. You take up the pen when you are told, and write what is commanded. There is no agony like bearing an untold story inside of you."

Source: Zora Neale Hurston, *Dust Tracks on a Road: An Autobiography* (Philadelphia: J. B. Lippincott, 1942), 220–221.

downturn so profound that the federal government felt compelled to intervene, fearing the country would collapse along with its economy.

Crash and Depression

In the fall of 1929, the national economy was out of control. Speculation in stocks had run rampant the previous decade and buyers hoped stock prices would rise quickly enough that they could sell stocks they purchased on margin, a partial payment, for quick profits. The burgeoning economy, conspicuous consumption, easy credit, even a real estate boom in Florida all contributed to people's belief that the market would never stop growing. Eventually it did. By 1927, housing starts slowed and automobile sales lessened, inventories grew, and employment declined. People still bought, but wages were so low that many borrowed to buy their goods. The Federal Reserve Board increased borrowing rates and still people bought. Finally, in October 1929, it all came to a halt with a stock market crash that led to the Great Depression.

On Tuesday, October 29, the New York Stock Exchange saw 16.4 million shares traded, five times the usual amount, and the *New York Times* index of industrials dropped 43 points. The Dow Jones average of 381 on September 3, 1929, fell to 41 over the next three years. Personal incomes fell by more than half during the same period, from $82 million to $40 million. Over 9,000 banks failed, robbing savers of their hard-earned money. Factories and mines closed, banks foreclosed farms and sold them at auctions. People at every economic level were affected. Bonnie Baringer Coryell, recently married, believed her husband's small battery shop in eastern Kansas would survive, since farmers needed batteries to run radios, automobiles, and any electrical devices on farms. Those items became luxuries, however, and the farmers quit coming. Bonnie and her husband lost their savings and their shop, and found themselves moving to Oklahoma to live on his mother's farm. The worst economic depression the country had ever seen had begun.

The new president, Herbert Hoover, had been in office only seven months before the economy collapsed. Hoover, a mining engineer who had rescued Europe from starvation with his humanitarian efforts as director of the American Relief Administration after World War I, did not comprehend the scope of economic disaster that America faced, but few others did either. He urged business owners to keep shops and factories open and asked labor leaders to prevent strikes and higher wage demands. He continued to support funding for public works that created jobs, and pushed Congress to reduce taxes and the Federal Reserve to reduce interest rates, but Hoover preferred to rely on market forces to correct the economy.

The Depression in the United States was only part of the picture. Europe had yet to recover from World War I, and dictatorial leaders promising solutions for crises there began to appear. Despair fueled by economic depression and inflation in Germany combined to bring forth Adolf Hitler and the National Socialist Party, the Nazis, in 1920. By 1922, similar problems in Italy birthed Benito Mussolini and the Fascists. In Russia, the communist Bolshevik Revolution in 1917 had led to a civil war and by 1922, the Union of Soviet Socialist Republics (USSR) formed. By 1928, the USSR was under a Communist dictator, Josef Stalin. The strong, centralized power these dictators exercised did not appease market forces; neither did the laissez-faire attitude of the U.S. government. The economy simply was going to wind down and recover from its irrational exuberance of the previous decade by painful steps and slow.

In the agricultural sector, America's depression began some time before the stock market crash. Wheat that had sold for over two dollars a bushel in 1919 due to European demand brought only thirty-eight cents by 1932. Drought struck the middle of the country beginning about 1928, and created a Dust Bowl there by the mid-1930s. Topsoil blew away in ferocious windstorms that drove nearly a million people out of Oklahoma, Texas, Arkansas, and Missouri. Farmers complained bitterly of prices so low their products cost more to produce than they could sell them for, and dumped oceans of milk in protest. Others burned corn to stay warm. The militant Farmers' Holiday Association protested low prices with a blockade around Sioux City, Iowa, preventing produce from reaching markets. Activists threw up roadblocks, emptied dairy trucks, and occasionally broke heads trying to force the government to action. In Canton, New York, women joined men and children in a sit-down strike on the road leading to the Sheffield Farms Plant, protesting lower prices for the milk they sold to the plant.

Family farms suffered as well, as banks foreclosed on thousands of farm mortgages, and forced farmers out of their homes. "Okies," migrants whose harsh lives were captured in John Steinbeck's novel, *The Grapes of Wrath*, fled the state of Oklahoma for California and other western states, dispossessed by the catastrophe of the Depression. The pressure activists exerted did not improve farm prices, but several states did pass laws declaring moratoriums on foreclosures.

Others who fled from their homes included millions of black Americans who migrated north to escape the racism and discrimination of the South, as well as its unrelenting poverty. Still other African Americans, laid off by northern factories and shops, returned to the South in hopes of being taken in by relatives. The South's economy was already depressed because of the invasion of the boll weevil in 1915, an insect that destroyed the cotton crop. In Georgia alone, cotton cultivation dropped from 5.2 million acres

DOROTHEA LANGE, "MIGRANT MOTHER"   Dorothea Lange, a photographer who worked under the auspices of the New Deal's Farm Security Administration program, took this iconic photo of a thirty-two-year-old mother of seven, working as a pea picker in California.

in 1914 to 2.6 million by 1923. Even First Lady Lou Hoover's attempt to promote cotton as the fabric of choice for evening wear failed to increase prices. Because Southern agriculture relied on tenant farming and share-cropping, the less crops were worth, the harder times became.

Women struggled to care for their families. They relied on their own skills and ingenuity, but also on collective groups. Women's clubs such as Savannah's Federation of Colored Women's Clubs established the Cuyler Children's Free Clinic to provide free health care to children and, once a week, to adults. The Alpha Kappa Alpha Sorority formed the AKA Mississippi Health Project. Members worked several weeks each summer for years, providing health care in the Mississippi Delta. They had to. With only a few thousand black doctors and black nurses to care for a largely segregated population of nearly 10 million black Americans, voluntary organizations were a necessary part of health care for black Americans throughout the Depression.

Rural black women were especially hard hit at the beginning of the Depression. Often the last to be hired, they were the first to be fired. Forty percent of black women and girls worked in the labor force in 1929, about 4.3 million total, mostly in domestic service or in agriculture. By 1931, only 3 million were employed; by 1935, about 2 million. For African Americans,

MRS. M. A. ZOLLER PLEADS WITH THE PRESIDENT

After President Roosevelt's inauguration in March 1933, letters from constituents poured in offering advice and seeking aid. Letters such as the one following from a woman in Beaumont, Texas, pleaded for help. The economic collapse and the lack of old-age pensions, particularly for women who often earned no wages during their lifetimes, could mean complete destitution.

"July 13, 1933

"President Franklin Roosevelt

"Dear Sir:

"I write to ask your assistance in securing an old age pension for my mother Mrs. Martha Gilbert, wife of C. R. Gilbert (deceased since January 1920).

"She is helpless, suffering from Sugar Diabetes, which has affected her mind.

the racism that had reached new levels of virulence in the 1920s and 1930s was so entrenched that blacks and particularly black women were the worst off of all Americans, except Native Americans, when it came to unemployment. Thirty percent of whites lost their jobs, but over half of black women lost theirs. When the Depression hit, many white women who needed wages hired themselves out to do domestic work, displacing black workers who had traditionally occupied those jobs.

Some women, white as well as black, fled to urban areas to search for work. Some moved in with families or friends, combining households to save money. Some prostituted themselves. Some begged the federal government for assistance (see Primary Source 8-4). Government relief for white workers, male and female, was easier to get than for minorities. Asking for relief came at a price for many. Early on, a government report on unemployed Americans interviewed a Mrs. Amay who said, "We never asked help from no one. We couldn't bear to let no one, even our own people and they couldn't help us anyway, know of our trouble, but when the children needed food we had to tell some one."

Many women and men postponed marriage during the Depression, and divorce rates and childbearing rates both dropped. Married couples either pulled together during the crisis, or avoided the expense of divorce by deserting their families. A 1940 survey showed that 1.5 million married women had been deserted by their husbands. During the Depression, economic distress joined forces with Margaret Sanger's long crusade and the number of birth control clinics increased nationwide, as women tried to limit their fertility. Instead of the appeal to eugenics Sanger had used in the 1920s to argue that the "lesser" classes should be limited from having too many children, proponents of birth control now argued that preventing the mental and physical suffering that came with having more children than families could afford was critical if the nation was to recover. After the 1936 Supreme Court case, the *United States v. One Package* (of Japanese Pessaries,

She has to be cared for in the same manner as an infant. She is out of funds completely. Her son whom she used to keep house for is in a hospital in Waco, Texas—no compensation for either himself or her.

"I am a widow; have spent all my savings in caring for her. I have kept boarders & roomers in a private home to keep my four children for I have always been a lady, this is why I appeal to you to place your dear mother in my dear mother's place. With no money and no place to go unless it be to the poor house. I cannot rent my rooms now for she demands constant care & attention. Please do something about this request as soon as possible.

"She will be 82 years old on August 9th.

"Yours truly,

"Mrs. M. A. Zoller, Sr.

"I do not own my home & at present I cannot meet my bills (overdue). I don't know what to expect next.

"Thank you in advance."

Source: From www.socialsecurity.gov/history/lettertoFDR.html.

or birth control devices), physicians were allowed to discuss and disseminate birth control information, an activity the American Medical Association now endorsed.

Because everyone knew someone looking for work, public opinion polls and surveys found that Americans believed women should stay home if their husbands had jobs or wanted them to stay home. If married women continued to work, thought many Americans, they risked divorce or, at the very least, being thought "unwomanly." Women's magazines, which became increasingly popular during the Depression, reaffirmed the notion that a woman's proper place was in her traditional sphere, the home. *McCall's* magazine, for instance, published articles that made it clear that only as a wife and mother could any woman "arrive at her true eminence." A woman office worker, no matter how successful, was nonetheless, another article said, "a transplanted posey." Popular films portrayed working women as aggressive or flighty, and all were searching for the right man to care for them. After they found him, they would then give up their careers for marriage, as Rosalind Russell did in *His Girl Friday*, or give up their careers to placate their husbands, as Katharine Hepburn did in *Woman of the Year*. In movies, women resolved their problems by marrying men who had jobs, not by working themselves. Public opinion, expressed in films, wanted women out of the job market and into the home so that men could have jobs. The strategy never worked because women worked different jobs from men, and those were not the jobs lost in the Depression.

The Roosevelts and the New Deal

In 1933, with an anxious nation watching, Democrat Franklin Delano Roosevelt took his oath of office to serve as president of the United States, telling the country that the only thing Americans had "to fear was fear itself." He knew, he said in his inaugural address, that "a host of unemployed citizens face the grim problem of existence, and an equally great number toil with little return. Only a foolish optimist can deny the dark realities of the moment." Aggressive action was called for, rather than fearful timidity. He called upon Congress to enact legislation to centralize relief efforts, to help put people back to work, to support farmers and the agricultural sector, to end the mindless speculation that had led to the crash: in short, to transform America into a nation that recognized the interdependency of its people, "willing," he continued, "to sacrifice for the good of a common discipline." The administration had three goals with its program termed the *New Deal*: relief from the immediate economic problems people were facing, reform of existing institutions so current and future problems could be avoided, and the recovery of American business so that the country could return to prosperity. Most of the attempts to accomplish these goals were designed to get Americans working again, and most were *androcentric* (male-centered) in their assumptions and in their implementation.

Relief

During the first hundred days of FDR's administration, Congress enacted fifteen major bills that the president proposed. Much of the relief efforts took the form of what were called "make-work" jobs, federally funded projects designed primarily to get male breadwinners back on their feet. The government set up agencies such as the Civilian Conservation Corps (CCC) to plant trees, build roads, and work on federal lands. Over 2.5 million men worked for the CCC, along with 8,500 women. The Public Works Administration (PWA) and the Works Progress Administration/Work Projects Administration (WPA) provided make-work jobs as well. These infrastructure jobs employed mostly men to construct roads, bridges, dams, and other building projects. The Agricultural Adjustment Act (AAA), another relief project, provided farmers with federal cash subsidies, paying them not to grow crops. Here, again, the majority of recipients were men.

Federally funded national relief programs for women generally assumed that women worked only in traditional women's jobs, such as sewing, rather than in skilled crafts or construction. The WPA Milwaukee Handicraft Project in Wisconsin, for example, employed over 5,000 women from 1935 to 1941, manufacturing toys and dolls, quilts and weavings, fabric and furniture to use in schools and nurseries, hospitals and orphanages, and other state institutions. Professional women also benefited from the government's relief efforts. Historians and artists, for instance, received make-work jobs as well. Historians conducted oral histories, gathering firsthand accounts of historic events. One well-known collection of oral histories came from reminiscences by former slaves, interviewed by historians hired under the auspices of the WPA. Former bondsmen and women told their stories of life under slavery in their own words, weaving tales of horror and heartache, laying claim to their history.

The Public Works of Art Project and the Federal Art Project hired artists to create murals for walls in post offices, high schools, and public buildings of all kinds. About one-sixth of the commissions went to women and minorities. Verona Burkhard of Montana painted a lyrical portrait of miners in the mountains of Montana called *James and Granville Stuart Prospecting in Deer Lodge Valley—1858*. Sisters Jenne and Ethel Magafan installed their murals in Nebraska, Colorado, Texas, Utah, Oklahoma, Arkansas, and in Washington, DC. Many of the murals represented mythic versions of American history and stylized versions of American farming life, as the government sought to unify American culture during a time of great turmoil. Photographers, on the other hand, documented the lives of everyday Americans. Berenice Abbott, commissioned by the WPA to photograph New York City, wanted to provide Americans with a sense of hope, and to help Americans survive their economic hardships. "There is a need in America," she wrote, "for those who have a real love of America, to preserve such records of the evolution of our cities, which symbolize the growth of the nation, as yet—uncrystallized and unformed." Photographers also included pictures of the unemployed, the poor, and the destitute. Dorothea Lange's iconic photograph of a migrant mother, huddled in a tent, protecting her children from even the gaze of the camera, epitomized the desperation the country felt.

Other legislation reinforced the popular belief that if only women would stop working, the economy would improve. Section 213 of the 1932 Economy Act under President Hoover had prohibited more than one member of each family from working in federal civil service jobs, and 75 percent of those who resigned or were fired were women. That law was eventually modified under President Roosevelt, but many state and local laws prohibited hiring married women for local government jobs. Industries and businesses such as railroads, banks, insurance companies, and public utilities also had limits on married women working. By 1939, half the states in the country had bills pending to prohibit any married woman from working, whether or not her husband was employed. A National Education Association survey found that 75 percent of school boards would not hire married women as teachers, and most dismissed women teachers when they married. In response, many women teachers did not report their marriages and revealed them only if they became pregnant.

Despite the legislative limits on married women working, the number of married women in the workforce increased during the 1930s. In 1930, over 29 percent of women in the workforce were married. By 1940, and despite a lower marriage rate, 35 percent of women in the workforce were married. Wage-earning work was a necessity for most women, especially if their husbands were out of work. In addition, women worked in industries that were not as hard-hit by the Depression and in industries that recovered more quickly from hard economic times. Men worked in heavy industries such as the automobile, steel, and construction industries, all of which were greatly affected by the Depression. Women, on the other hand, worked primarily in sales, clerical, and service occupations. These jobs paid less, but because the work could not be easily mechanized or eliminated, people in these occupations lost their jobs less often. Women also earned money by doing what they had always done: expanding their domestic world to make it pay. They took in laundry; they took in boarders; they baked bread and sold it; they cooked for cash. Middle-class women also increased the amount of work they did at home, firing their domestic help and substituting their own labor for products they had been buying. Sales of Ball Company canning jars, for instance, soared as women learned to can food to help their families survive.

Despite public perception and government assumptions, the gendered nature of American employment meant men would not take women's jobs. Since employers sought the cheapest workers—women and children—women's employment did not disappear, even as child labor was limited in 1938 by President Roosevelt and Congress.

Labor and Union Resistance

Among all women workers, the Depression meant more competition for jobs as well as increased exploitation. Women's concentration in service jobs and their near-complete exclusion from heavy industries meant that they still remained outside of most union-protected industries, and continued to represent only 3 percent of the union members in the country. The total number of union members, women and men, had declined in the 1920s, as union growth in heavy industries, such as the automobile industry, slowed. "The chief business of the American people is business," said President Calvin Coolidge. "The man who builds a factory builds a temple. The man who works there worships there." Workers may have worshiped there, but many wanted to do so for fewer hours and with better pay.

Achieving those goals grew more difficult as the economy continued to struggle, and the competition for jobs strained race relations nationwide. Mexican workers, both those legally in the United States and those hired illegally during the boom times of the 1920s, were deported to Mexico during the Depression. A wholesale racist depopulation from the North, Midwest, and Southwest took place, and the Mexican population in the United States dropped by more than 40 percent—from 639,000 in 1930 to 377,000 by 1940. As Anglo-Americans moved into jobs formerly held by Hispanic women, Hispanic women who had not been deported moved into less desirable jobs with lower pay and poorer working conditions. Fighting exploitation, Chicana factory women in Los Angeles unionized, and in Texas, women struck at pecan-shelling factories and cigar-making factories. Emma Tenayuca, national committeewoman for the Workers Alliance of America, was jailed for her leadership in a strike in 1938 after pecan-shellers went from earning six or seven cents a pecan to earning only a penny.

Working women fought back against the discrimination they faced during the Depression. Feminists successfully used Women's Bureau statistics regarding married women's need for employment to lobby Congress to rescind section 213 of the Economy Act in 1937. Union activities and strikes increased as workers grew more desperate. In San Francisco, Chinese women workers joined forces with the International Ladies Garment Workers Union in a successful strike against Chinatown's largest garment manufacturer. In Elizabethton, Tennessee, thousands of women textile workers walked off the job as owners stretched-out the factory work, using the same technique that had caused women to strike in New England in the 1840s. In Gastonia, North Carolina, women organized by the National Textile Workers Union struck in the Loray textile mill. In 1934, the United Textile Workers Union led 400,000 textile workers off their jobs, many of them single women employed as spinners. The "Great Strike" asked employers for twelve dollars a week minimum wage. Governors of affected states called up the National Guard and hired strikebreakers. The strikers went back to work, but many lost their jobs and, blacklisted from the textile industry, were unable to find work. (See Primary Source 8-5.)

Conditions in industries that employed mostly male workers affected women as well. From December 1936 until February 1937, women joined their menfolk in supporting one of the largest sit-down strikes against General Motors in Flint, Michigan. Wives passed food to the strikers, despite tear gas attacks from the plant's owners. They brought their children to march in support of their fathers, and handed the children through the plant's windows so they could visit with their fathers for a bit. In January 1937, Flint police came to reinforce company guards trying to prevent food deliveries. They fired tear gas into the crowd and, after the union workers responded with milk bottles, lumps of coal, and two-pound auto hinges, the police opened fire. Genora Johnson, whose husband was one of the strikers inside, seized the union's sound truck microphone and shouted that the police were cowards, shooting unarmed men. "Women of Flint! This is your fight!" she shouted. "Join the picket line and defend your jobs, your husband's job and your children's home."

The Women's Emergency Brigade, 400 women strong, marched into the fray wearing red caps symbolic of international workers' rights, broke through the police line, and stood firm against them. The police, reluctant to fire on unarmed women, left the scene and did not return. After forty-four days of striking, the United Auto Workers (UAW) finally won the right to represent the workers. The Red Beret women of the Emergency Brigade are one example of the massive organizing in industrial unions that took place during the Depression, and that included the women in meatpacking, canning, and other industries. Union sympathizers also tried to organize groups as diverse as waitresses, elevator operators, and teachers.

Reform

The second component of the New Deal was to pass reform legislation to control the excesses of capitalism so that the disaster of the Depression might never happen again. Legislators designed reform measures to provide a safety net for workers. One of the first reform measures included unemployment insurance, providing cash to workers who had been laid off through no fault of their own. A law setting national minimum wages and

ELLA MAE WIGGINS, "TWO LITTLE STRIKERS"

Popular music was used to sway public opinion in favor of strikers and against exploitive conditions in factories. One such example is "Two Little Strikers," set to the tune of a Southern hymn. The author, Ella Mae Wiggins, was a union organizer. She was shot as she traveled to a union meeting during the Loray Mill strike in Gastonia,

North Carolina. Her killers were never convicted.

Two Little strikers, a boy and a girl,
Sit by the union hall door.
The little girl's hand was brown as the curls
That played on the dress that she wore.

the maximum number of hours that could be worked before overtime pay began was also passed. Such legislation had been a goal of the social feminists from the 1920s. It was adopted by the Roosevelt administration and designed by Frances Perkins, Roosevelt's secretary of labor.

President Roosevelt picked Frances Perkins to run the Department of Labor, a cabinet office whose power and importance had increased greatly during the country's economic crisis. Roosevelt had known Perkins, a Mount Holyoke graduate and a settlement house worker, from his days as governor of New York when he appointed her as the industrial commissioner for the state. As the first woman cabinet member, Perkins broke new ground and no one in the administration was sure how to treat her. She was placed with wives in formal state dinners instead of with the other cabinet officers. She was constantly called before Congress to testify, not surprisingly since labor was in so much trouble, but disproportionately all the same. Perkins resolved to succeed at her job by making some concessions to men's egos and to society's images of women. She used her maiden name instead of her husband's to avoid affecting his career. She presented her reform ideas as solutions to children's issues rather than women's issues to avoid opposition from those who believed women were already cared for. She reacted to the negative publicity engendered by her job by publicly declaring that she believed the happiest place for women was home. She also tended to relate to men as a mother figure rather than a peer or colleague, dressing dowdily and speaking softly, so as not to present a threat.

Perkins faced a monumental task and did a superb job as labor secretary. Her most important legislation was the Social Security Act of 1935, providing unemployment compensation, old-age pensions, and federal grants to the states to care for the homeless and destitute, as well as delinquent and disabled children. She helped provide federal grants to states for public health services, and for maternal and infant care. She orchestrated passage of the Fair Labor Standards Act of 1938 that provided protective legislation for all workers, not just for women. Minimum wages rose

The little boy's head was hatless,
And tears were in each little eye,
"Why don't you go home to your
mama?" I said.
And this was the strikers' reply:

"Our mama's in jail, they locked her up:
Left Jim and me alone,
So we've come here to sleep in the
tents tonight,
For we have no mother, no home.

"Our Papa got hurt in the shooting
Friday night,
We waited all night for him,
For he was a union guard you know,
But he never came home any
more."

Source: Ella Mae Wiggins in Vera Buch Weisbord's, "Gastonia, 1929: Strike at the Loray Mill," eds. Dan McCurry and Carolyn Ashbaugh, *Southern Exposure*, 1 (Winter, 1974), 1–23.

gradually to forty cents per hour, with maximum hours at forty hours per week. Under her leadership, the country finally outlawed child labor in industrial factories and limited children's exposure to dangerous jobs. Despite worries from opponents that raising wages would prevent an economic recovery, the legislation succeeded. Unemployment dropped from 19 percent in 1938 to 14.6 percent in 1940 to 9.9 percent in 1941.

Another area of reform centered around race relations, and involved the president's wife Eleanor and her good friend Mary McLeod Bethune. Eleanor Roosevelt remained a social activist during her years in the White House, and used her skills and connections with the social feminists she had worked with to promote their causes. She served as her husband's "legs" as she had since Franklin's paralysis from polio in 1921. Most Americans did not even know he was paralyzed from the waist down, and the press kept his secret, never photographing him in his wheelchair. Eleanor traveled everywhere she could, completely indefatigable, and reported back to Franklin at the White House. She took advantage of her role to promote her favorite humanitarian causes, and was often at odds with her husband's more politic approaches. She became a lobbyist for the poor and for relief organizations, and pushed particularly for the integration of African Americans such as Bethune into public policy discussions and programs. She brought Southern textile workers to White House dinners to sit next to the president and explain their plight. She attended a segregated Southern Conference on Human Welfare in Birmingham, Alabama, and placed her chair in the middle of the line dividing blacks from whites in the auditorium, dismaying officials who insisted the races could not sit next to each other. Her most famous act to promote racial integration came in 1939, when she resigned from the Daughters of the American Revolution after the group refused to allow African American contralto Marian Anderson to perform at Constitution Hall. Roosevelt arranged for Anderson to sing in front of the Lincoln Memorial instead. Her performance was a triumph.

Leading African American educator and political activist Mary McLeod Bethune enjoyed considerable access to the president because of her friendship with Eleanor. One of 17 children, Bethune was born in 1875 to two former slaves who had become sharecroppers. In 1904, she opened a school for black girls in Daytona Beach, Florida, on, as she put it, "$1.50 and faith." The school was so poorly funded that girls crushed elderberries for ink and used charcoal from the stove for pencils. The school eventually merged with a local boys' school, becoming Bethune-Cookman College in 1923. Bethune served as president until her death in 1955.

Bethune was also president of the National Council of Negro Women, an officer of the National Association of Colored Women and, at Eleanor Roosevelt's urging, was appointed by the president to serve as the head of the Negro Affairs section of the National Youth Administration, an organization providing federal work relief for teenagers. Bethune became part of FDR's "Black Cabinet," a group of black leaders brought into the administration to work on problems faced by African Americans during the Depression: higher unemployment rates, discrimination in the job market, and discrimination in relief programs.

Bethune was a pragmatist. She was most concerned with issues important to all African Americans, rather than focusing on issues important to black women, or indeed all women. She wanted the president to include black men as leaders in positions of power in the administration. She also pushed for increased student-aid funds for black youth and urged the federal government to help train teachers for rural black schools. While she saw the value of single-race groups and organizations, Bethune also fought for integration. For the federal government's National Youth Administration board, for example, she told white administrators they needed to include black members if they wanted to reach all Americans. "It is impossible for you to enter sympathetically and understandingly into the program of the Negro," she said, "as the Negro can do." Integrated boards were a must.

Limits of the New Deal

The Fair Labor Standards Act maintained the androcentric outlook of much of the New Deal's legislation. Minimum wages set a minimum wage per hour, but provided higher rates for men than for women, and exempted industries such as commercial laundries, cloakmaking, service industries, domestic service, and agriculture, all of which employed mostly women. The Social Security Act set up a trust fund that both employees and employers contributed to in order to help fund workers' retirements. As with the Fair Labor Act, there were limits: Social Security did not apply to many of the industries in which women predominated, most notably domestic service, canneries, and firms employing fewer than ten workers. Ironically, however, the act aided relatively few men at first, since one could not collect Social Security payments until age sixty-five, and that was the average life expectancy for males. For elderly women, on the other hand, it was a lifesaver. Widows who had tiny pensions or none and few resources during economic downturns could now be kept from utter destitution. The first woman to benefit from this was Ida May Fuller, of Ludlow, Vermont, a legal secretary who retired in November 1939. She began collecting her monthly Social Security benefits at age sixty-five in January 1940. Fuller lived to be one hundred, dying in 1975, drawing benefits for thirty-five years, having paid into the system for one year and eleven months.

Despite its androcentric outlook, the New Deal provided major benefits for women. The minimum wage was higher than what most women made before. Government assistance for technical improvement in factories meant that owners could fire skilled male workers, install new machinery, then hire unskilled, lower-paid women workers. For example, a cigar manufacturer could add machinery funded in part by the government, fire the men who had hand-rolled the cigars, and hire women to run the machines to roll cigars at lower wages. The administration also protected labor unions, convincing unions to try to enroll more members, including women. Women workers moved into what had been men-only unions, as well as strengthening their own women-dominated unions. The International Ladies Garment Workers' Union quadrupled in size by 1934; its umbrella organization, the Congress of Industrial Organization (CIO), had 2.6 million members by 1940. CIO unions supported gender equality in the workforce, opposing discrimination based not only on color and creed, but on sex as well. Despite this ideological stance, it would be years before women occupied executive roles in many unions and had their interests more often taken into account.

The New Deal of Franklin Roosevelt had some success in its attempt to help Native Americans during the Depression as well. The 1928 Meriam Report and John Collier's actions as head of the Bureau of Indian Affairs slowed attempts to assimilate Native Americans from the reservations into mainstream American society. In fact, Collier helped draft the Indian Reorganization Act (IRA) of 1934 that overturned the Dawes Act of the late nineteenth century, and strove to rehabilitate Indians both economically and spiritually. While some tribes refused to support the IRA and refused to accept citizenship granted by the Indian Citizenship Act of 1924 as well, 174 tribes did. Those who supported the IRA favored the act's provisions, which included self-government on reservations and allowing tribes to control their own lands, federal support for land management, and funding for public health, law enforcement, and scholarships. Most important to many Native women were government's efforts to respect Native economies, instead of forbidding them. Thus a Native woman could keep her traditional role as she saw fit, maintaining her religious practices and ceremonies, and producing her traditional crafts and taking part in the tribal economy in her traditional way. At the same time, Native women could choose to participate in the government-funded educational programs and modern health practices, if they desired. Many did: education rates went up, and both disease rates and death rates among Native Americans declined.

Of the seventy-eight tribes that rejected the IRA, criticism of the program centered around the notions of self-government. Alice Lee Jemison, a member of the New York Senecas, a congressional lobbyist, and a journalist, had complained as early as 1932 that Americans should realize that the Senecas were part of the Iroquois nation. Jemison, who also wrote articles complaining that Native American ironworkers and steel workers were discriminated against in New Deal projects, was a staunch supporter of Native American independence. The Iroquois considered themselves an independent sovereign power, governing themselves since 1848. Making all Native Americans citizens automatically, thought Jemison, violated that sovereignty. As Chief Clinton Rickard of the Tuscaroras put it, "Our citizenship was in our nations. We had a great attachment to our style of government. We wished to remain treaty Indians and preserve our ancient rights." Jemison helped found the American Indian Federation to campaign against the IRA, but the majority vote for the act meant its provisions would be carried out.

Recovery

The third component of the New Deal was recovery. By 1936, the numbers of unemployed Americans had declined from 12 million to 9 million and the average weekly paycheck was twenty-two dollars, up from seventeen dollars. Recovery was inextricably linked to the so-called alphabet agencies of Roosevelt's New Deal. The two components of the National Industrial Recovery Act (NIRA)—public works and the National Recovery Administration (NRA)—had provided not only new jobs but new rules and new expectations as well. Fairness in wages and competition meant workers enjoyed more purchasing power and a growing economy. Unions helped protect those basic standards of fair wages and hours. Other efforts by the government, such as the Tennessee Valley Authority (TVA), built dams and power plants, brought electricity to rural areas, and encouraged the government to form the Rural Electrification Administration (REA) to continue the process. REA-sponsored films portrayed farmers using electricity for milking machines and vacuum cleaners, linking electricity to both industry and consumption, all of which would draw the nation more closely together and improve the economy. A second term for Roosevelt in 1936 continued his policies. Roosevelt's refusal to support laissez-faire economic policies when the economy seemed to cry out for some government intervention, as well as his attempts to reach out to the poor, the destitute, and the forgotten, swept him into office again.

Roosevelt's second term began with an inaugural speech in which he challenged Americans to do better by the "one-third of a nation ill housed, ill-clad, ill-nourished" that he still saw after four years of reforms. He viewed his reelection as a mandate, but the Supreme Court saw it differently, and ruled against some of his reform measures in a series of court decisions. Roosevelt attempted to "pack" the Supreme Court with new justices to ensure that his programs would not be declared unconstitutional. The public outcry was intense, and Roosevelt faced strong opposition not only to his court-packing attempt, but also to his programs, as the economy underwent a recession and people feared a return to the worst days of the Depression.

Off-year elections in 1938 diminished Democratic power in the House of Representatives, and Roosevelt began to focus on making existing reforms work rather than proposing new ones. By the end of his second term, the nation and its government had been transformed into an amalgam of caretaking and capitalism, where the weakest in society would no longer be quite so vulnerable to the excesses of the latter. True economic recovery would not take place until wartime mobilization ended the Great Depression.

Women in the Government

Roosevelt's programs had not only benefited women, but he had also consistently appointed women to positions of power. Eleanor Roosevelt convinced her husband to appoint many women whom she knew could serve the government well, and her radio addresses and daily newspaper columns inspired others as well. Coya Knutson, eventually a representative from Minnesota, was inspired by hearing Mrs. Roosevelt give a 1942 radio address. "It was as if the sun burned into me that day," she recalled, responding to Roosevelt's appeal for women to become involved in civic affairs. Women had arrived in Congress prior to receiving the franchise, and kept coming afterward. As Eleanor Roosevelt understood, instituting reforms required not only the vote but active participation in government.

Thirty-eight women ran for Congress in 1936 alone. Many were Democrats and sought to ride FDR's coattails, and four succeeded. Democratic women from Oregon, Indiana, New Jersey, and New York served in the House, including Caroline O'Day who remarked during her campaign that women's "political apprenticeship" had ended. Republican Florence Kahn lost after five terms in the House, but Edith Rogers of Massachusetts was returned. Republican Margaret Chase Smith arrived, not as representative, but as a secretary to her husband, representing the state of Maine. She had been a reporter, president of the State Federation of Business and Professional Women's Club, and active in the Republican Party. When her husband died in 1940, Smith was elected to the House, where she served on the Naval Affairs committee. She won a Senate seat in 1948, and served until 1973. A liberal and an internationalist in foreign affairs, Smith fought for women's rights in the military, asking for a burial allowance for women killed in action.

By the second quarter of the twentieth century, only a few women had made it into the Senate. Hattie Wyatt Caraway of Arkansas, an independent Prohibitionist, was the first woman elected in 1932. Called "Silent Hattie" because she never made a speech on the floor of the Senate, she nevertheless became the first woman to chair a committee and the first woman to preside over the Senate (twice during her two terms in office). Five others served out terms vacated when senators died, usually their husbands. Far more women served in the U.S. House of Representatives in the years after they received the franchise. By 1940, twenty-three women had served as representatives and eleven others took office during the war years, including Frances Payne Bolton from Ohio, who served from 1940 to 1969.

Helen Gahagan Douglas, a former actress and opera singer, was elected in 1945. Active in California politics in various roles in the state's Democratic Party, she was appointed by President Roosevelt to the Voluntary Participation Committee in the Office of Civilian Defense. Once in office, Douglas used her glamour to win over colleagues while pushing for the completely unglamorous issues of civil rights, union and labor rights, and meeting the needs of migrant workers. (Not until 1965 would a woman of color, Patsy Mink, take a seat in the House of Representatives; not until 1993 would a woman of color, Carol Moseley Braun, arrive in the U.S. Senate.)

Women participated in state and local government as well. Bertha K. Landes was elected to Seattle's city council in 1924, and would become mayor of the city in 1926, running on a platform of municipal housekeeping. In 1925, Nellie Tayloe Ross became the governor of Wyoming, elected after her husband died. That same year, Miriam "Ma" Ferguson began her first term as governor of Texas, where she served two terms (1925–1927 and 1933–1935) as her husband's surrogate after term limits denied him another term. One state, Michigan, had a woman as lieutenant governor, Matilda R. Wilson, appointed in 1940 for one year. In 1938, Crystal Bird Fauset was the first African American woman elected to public office, serving in the Pennsylvania state legislature for a year, prior to her appointment to Pennsylvania's WPA program.

Chances for women to participate in government diminished with the onset of World War II. Many of the social programs that benefited women were suspended for the duration of the war. When it came to the government bureaucrats who ran the country during the war, women were appointed primarily to token positions. The War Manpower Commission had a Women's Advisory Commission, but advising is not running things. The head of the Women's Bureau, Mary Anderson, accused President Roosevelt of creating positions that excluded women from any real power. The president and the first lady fought over women's issues during the war, sometimes publicly, as Eleanor continued to push for social changes and women's issues in her books and newspaper columns, and Franklin focused on the war, which he saw largely as a male issue.

WOMEN IN WORLD WAR II

By the end of Roosevelt's second term, the international picture had once again grown dark with the storm clouds of war in Europe, Asia, and Africa. In Europe, Adolf Hitler and the Nazis had imposed a dictatorship on Germany, then invaded Czechoslovakia and Poland, claiming for their own the lands that they considered traditionally German. In Asia, Japan invaded China, seeking to establish hegemony over East Asia. In Africa, Italy invaded Ethiopia, a sovereign power and member of the League of Nations, and annexed it. Dictator Mussolini then returned to Europe to invade Albania. Civil War in Spain left Fascist dictator Francisco Franco in control.

Greece fell to dictator John Metaxas. Russia joined Germany in partitioning Poland, and the Japanese blockaded British and French ships on the Chinese coast. The League of Nations collapsed under the strain, and World War II was under way. In a time so unsettled, Roosevelt felt compelled to run for a third and then a fourth term as president.

World War II proved to be one of the most important factors in changing the roles American women played during the second half of the twentieth century. As had happened with other wars, women were invited into the workforce and even into the armed services for the duration. When the war was over, they were invited out. But each time this pattern occurred, it grew more difficult to put the genie back in the bottle. World War II would provide many women with long-term opportunities in the public sphere. As important as women were to the inner workings of government during the war as secretaries, aides, and administrators, the bulk of decisions were made by men and many of them no doubt believed wartime was a time for the girls to go home. But women did not go home, and as had been the case in every war, American women found varying ways to serve during wartime: in production, in the field, and in the home, caring for those left behind.

Rosie the Riveter

The United States entered World War II on the side of the Allied forces (Great Britain, France, China, and the USSR) after Japan attacked Pearl Harbor, Hawaii, on December 7, 1941, a date that would, as President Roosevelt put it, "live in infamy." Although the United States had been lending support since 1939 to the Allied powers, particularly Great Britain, which by 1940 was under siege by German bombers, the United States had stayed clear of outright involvement. That all changed one Sunday morning in December, as squadrons of Japanese fighter planes strafed the air field and bombed the fleet in Pearl Harbor, sinking five battleships and damaging others. The unprovoked attack on Americans brought the nation together, and Congress declared war on Japan the next day. Three days later, on December 11, Italy and Germany, the two remaining Axis powers, declared war on the United States. (See Primary Source 8-6.)

The production of war materiel—aircraft, ships, artillery, bullets, guns, tanks, chemicals, uniforms, bandages, and everything else—relied heavily upon women. With around 15 million Americans, most of them men, serving in the military over the next four years, it was imperative that women move into industries that had been male-dominated for years. The government mounted a concerted effort, led by the War Manpower Commission and its Women's Advisory Commission, to recruit women into the workforce using posters, magazine articles, and advertisements, as well as movie theater "shorts" shown before the regular film. Training, housing assistance, and daycare centers were offered in some areas, although chronic shortages of both workers and such assistance continued throughout the war. When housing for war workers near Portland, Oregon, ran out, shipyard owner Henry Kaiser built his workers their own city.

ELEANOR ROOSEVELT, "MY DAY," DECEMBER 8, 1941

Eleanor Roosevelt wrote a column called "My Day," six days a week from December 1935 until September 1962. Ninety papers carried it as she shared her activities and views with over 4 million readers. By 1940, the column was so popular that the United Features Syndicate that published it offered her a five-year contract to continue. The columns serve as the first lady's diary, since she did not keep a journal, and give modern readers insight on the political and social history of some of the most difficult times that this country went through. This selection, written the day after the Japanese bombed Pearl Harbor, which brought the United States into World War II, reflects the surprise nature of the attack, as Roosevelt describes hearing of the event on a peaceful Sunday afternoon after a family visit.

"WASHINGTON, Sunday—I was going out in the hall to say goodbye to our cousins, Mr. and Mrs. Frederick Adams, and their children, after luncheon, and, as I stepped out of my room, I knew something had happened. All the secretaries were there, two telephones were in use, the senior military aides were on their way with messages. I said nothing because the words I heard over the telephone were quite sufficient to tell me that, finally, the blow had fallen, and we had been attacked.

Vanport City's population was 40,000, of whom 15,000 were African American. The city included thousands of houses, 700 apartment buildings, a post office, as well as five grade schools and six nursery schools to care for the children of workers. These arrangements meant workers could focus on their tasks, but such concern for workers and families remained unusual. Only about 10 percent of children of war plant workers were in daycare by 1945. The majority of working mothers patched together child care as best they could.

The bulk of defense work took place on the East and West Coasts. Shipyards struggled to construct the 87,620 ships built over the course of the war, while other factories produced 296,429 aircraft. Additional war production factories were scattered across the countryside. In Huntsville, Alabama, the Huntsville Arsenal produced chemical munitions, including colored smoke munitions, toxic gases, and other articles of war. Nearby stood the Redstone Ordnance Plant, a facility that built the shells and loaded them with the chemicals. Between March 1942 and September 1945, women and men assembled and loaded a little over 45 million units of ammunition to ship to the front lines. Women were hired first as secretaries and skilled office personnel, but by 1945, more than 60 percent of the employees were women, working in every phase of production. So drastic was the need for workers that the factory even began hiring African American women, despite earlier racist opposition that reflected the Jim Crow laws of Southern segregation. It would be a problem to hire black women, claimed the factory managers, because the factory lacked "toilet

"Attacked in the Philippines, in Hawaii, and on the ocean between San Francisco and Hawaii. Our people had been killed not suspecting there was an enemy, who attacked in the usual ruthless way which Hitler has prepared us to suspect.

"Because our nation has lived up to the rules of civilization, it will probably take us a few days to catch up with our enemy, but no one in this country will doubt the ultimate outcome. None of us can help but regret the choice which Japan has made, but having made it, she has taken on a coalition of enemies she must underestimate; unless she believes we have sadly deteriorated since our first ships sailed into her harbor.

"The clouds of uncertainty and anxiety have been hanging over us for a long time. Now we know where we are. The work for those who are at home seems to be obvious. First, to do our own job, whatever it is, as well as we can possibly do it. Second, to add to it everything we can do in the way of civilian defense. Now, at last, every community must go to work to build up protections from attack.

"We must build up the best possible community services, so that all of our people may feel secure because they know we are standing together and that whatever problems have to be met, will be met by the community and not one lone individual. There is no weakness and insecurity when once this is understood."

Source: Eleanor Roosevelt, *My Day: The Best of Eleanor Roosevelt's Acclaimed Newspaper Columns, 1936–62*, ed. David Emblidge (NY: Da Capo Press, 2001), 59–60.

facilities to take care of race distinctions peculiar to the South," in the form of racially segregated bathrooms. Necessity would out. By the end of the war, about 11 percent of the workforce at the plant was African American.

The same conversion from largely white, all-male workforces to those integrated in race and gender took place elsewhere. Women worked as welders, electricians, and drill press operators in the Newport News, Virginia, shipyard. In Richmond, California, another Kaiser shipyard produced ships using assembly-line methods, speeding up construction from 245 days to 17. To keep up production, twenty-four-hour daycare was available, enabling more women to work. In Ypsilanti, Michigan, Rose Monroe riveted planes and starred in a short film promoting the sale of war bonds, about a "Rosie the Riveter," representing the American women who were doing their part for the war effort by working in war factories. Another "Rosie" appeared on the cover of the popular magazine, *The Saturday Evening Post*, as painted by Norman Rockwell. Mary Doyle Keefe of Nashua, New Hampshire, sat in front of an American flag, her penny loafers resting on a copy of Hitler's *Mein Kampf* (his book laying out his plans for conquering Europe and destroying the Jews), her riveting gun resting on her lap, along with her lunchbox. Her curly hair, only partially concealed by her bandanna, safety goggles, and mask, along with her lipstick and rosy cheeks proclaimed her underlying femininity, despite her muscular forearms and overall bulk. Hitler needed to watch out for this Rosie, was the message, and the image helped reconcile women and men to the heavy industrial labor that women undertook for the duration of the war.

Many women who worked in war factories enjoyed the work, finding excitement, female solidarity, friendship, and even romance. They also appreciated the pay, despite the fact that they earned less than men working the same jobs. The national average wage was between $12 and $17 at 30¢ to 40¢ per hour. Women in war-related heavy industries in 1944 earned on average $31.21 a week, while men doing the same jobs earned $54.65. Some women worked for short periods of time, while others stayed in the factories for the duration. By 1945, just before the war ended, some 5.4 million women had entered the workforce, half of them in manufacturing, and a total of 21.7 percent of all married women were earning wages. All told, women made up over one-third of the labor force. They left jobs as file clerks, stenographers, salesclerks, waitresses, and seamstresses to work in higher-paying, formerly male jobs as ticket takers, tax collectors, elevator operators, instrument builders, lab technicians, bank employees, and at other tasks in addition to working in war industries. Even the national pastime of baseball saw women assuming men's roles. The All-American Girls Professional Baseball League (AAGPBBL) formed in 1943 to fill major league ballparks after many teams disbanded when their players went to war. Recruited by professional baseball scouts, young women on teams such as the Rockford Peaches and the Milwaukee Chicks attracted fans and earned salaries of $45 to $85 a week. By the end of the war, nearly half a million Americans had seen the women of the AAGPBBL play.

Women in the Armed Services

The need to fill military ranks led thousands of American women into the armed services, where they served as auxiliaries to the existing military branches. Over the course of the war, some 340,000 women served in the armed forces. More than 150,000 women served in the Women's Auxiliary Army Corps (WAAC or WAC), the first group of women in the army who were not nurses. Colonel Oveta Culp Hobby, director of the WAC, chose mostly well-educated, middle-class women (white as well as women of color), to train at Fort Des Moines, Iowa, and at camps in Georgia, Massachusetts, and Florida. She fought hard to overcome suspicion from both the military and civilian powers that women were inadequate to the task or, far worse from the public's point of view, that women soldiers were lesbians who would lead to a breakdown of sexual morality. "Woman" and "soldier" were not categories that overlapped in the public imagination but Hobby compared women soldiers to women suffragists. "Just as a startled public was once sure that woman's suffrage would make women unwomanly," she said in an interview, "so the thought of 'woman soldiers' caused some people to assume that WAC units would be hotbeds of perversion." They were not. Some WACs were lesbian, discharged when discovered; all WACs simply wanted to serve their country.

Women soldiers worked as mechanics, photographers, teletype operators, parachute riggers, cartographers, and replacements for male

FIELD HOSPITAL NURSES IN MANILA, 1945   Thousands of young women worked near the front lines as nurses in World War II. Here, army nurses eagerly board transport home from Manila in the Philippines at war's end.

administrative and clerical workers who left for the battlefields. Racial segregation remained standard practice in the services, but some units were racially mixed. Puerto Rican women were segregated; Filipinas and Chinese American women were integrated into white units. Black women, many college-educated teachers, had their own units and accounted for 4 percent (about 6,500) of the total number of WACs by December 1944.

The majority of WACs served in the United States, but one white unit was integrated into the Fifth Army in northern Africa, and a black WAC unit, the 6888th Central Postal Directory Battalion, also went overseas to Europe. Racial discrimination against African Americans continued in the states, even against those women in service. A group of WACs in uniform were beaten by a mob in a bus station in Kentucky for breaking the Jim Crow laws of the state, then court-martialed by the army. The highest-ranking African American WAC, Harriet West, was denied admission to Constitution Hall in Washington in 1943 for a ceremony saluting women's services to the military because she was black. Mary McLeod Bethune and the National Council of Negro Women kept pressure on President Roosevelt and his administration to protect these women who were determined to serve their country.

While some women served as WACs, others joined the Women's Auxiliary Ferry Squadron (WAFS), led by Nancy Harkness Love. The WAFS flew planes from military aircraft production facilities to military bases. In

1943, that group was absorbed into the Women's Airforce Service Pilots (WASP), led by Jackie Cochran, the most famous woman pilot of the time. These pilots not only ferried planes, they also towed targets for aerial and ground practice, taught pilots in both flight and instrument training, and served as test pilots for new planes. Despite the dangers that the WASP had already faced and met, no one suggested that the group fly combat missions. Americans of the time would never have accepted that, even if three regiments of Russian women were flying combat aircraft in World War II.

The navy had the service of the Women Accepted for Voluntary Emergency Service (WAVES), patterned after the Women's Naval Reserve that had been created during World War I, as well as the Navy Nurse Corps. Mildred McAfee directed the WAVES, a branch of the naval reserves rather than an auxiliary, encompassing 8,000 officers and 76,000 enlisted women. They served primarily as radio operators and, by 1944, had joined nurses in serving overseas. The U.S. Coast Guard's women's reserve, named SPAR (from the coast guard motto "Semper Paratus"—Always Ready), was led by Dorothy Stratton. Relieving men on land from duties so that they could go to sea, some 11,000 women served with SPAR, mostly doing clerical work, but also serving as radio technicians, pharmacists' mates, parachute riggers, and control-tower operators. Unit 21 at Chatham, Massachusetts, was an all-female unit in charge of a Long-Range Aid to Navigation (LORAN) station used to track planes and ships. The Marine Corps also had women reserves, but used no acronym. They were simply the Marine Corps Women's Reserve, directed by Colonel Ruth Cheney Streeter. Formed in February 1943, within a year the reserves had 800 officers and 14,000 enlistees.

At the beginning of the war, the law prohibited all women's military units from serving overseas, except for the WACs and the Navy Nurse Corps. World War II required such a massive effort, however, and was fought on such a monumental scale that Congress passed legislation in November 1944, allowing women in all military organizations to serve outside the United States. They did not, however, provide servicewomen with military benefits such as combat pay, uniform allowances, or even burial costs. Of the thirty-eight WASP members killed in the line of duty, for instance, the vast majority had funerals paid for by their families or by collections taken up among their friends. While the Women Armed Services Integration Act (1948) allowed women to continue serving in the armed forces after the war, not until 1977 did Congress grant these women the status of military veterans with the benefits due them.

Internment

The burdens of war fell heavily on women who shared the same ethnic ancestry with the country's enemies: Japan, Germany, and Italy. The General Federation of Women's Clubs, among other groups, called for the *internment*, or imprisonment, of American immigrants who came from countries at war with the United States. While only legal aliens from countries at war with the United States could be interned, spouses and children often joined them, either voluntarily or because they feared that the separation might be permanent. Beginning in February 1942, the government interned 110,000 people of Japanese ancestry, two-thirds of whom were American citizens, in ten "war-relocation" camps in the isolated deserts of the West. Internees left their homes and businesses, selling property at prices far below its real value, or abandoning homes and goods entirely. *Nisei* (second-generation Japanese Americans) and their parents (*Issei*) lived behind barbed wire in crowded barracks. Former neighbors often scavenged what was left behind.

Life in the camps was familiar, yet difficult. Jeanne Wakatsuki Houston, imprisoned at Manzanar War Relocation Center in eastern California, recalls that the camp was much like any small American town. Children went to school, internees went to church, and women got their hair done at the beauty parlor. To survive, she wrote, "you learn to control your rage and your despair and you try to re-create, as well as you can, your normality." The strong patriarchal nature of the Japanese family began to break down as American officials separated *Nisei* children from their parents by allowing the *Nisei* to leave the camps, once their loyalty to the United States could be proven. Racial prejudice and discrimination followed those allowed to leave the camps, particularly as news regarding horrific treatment of American prisoners by the Japanese began to appear in the press. At one point, the governor of Idaho suggested sending all the "Japs" back to Japan and then sinking the island. Eleanor Roosevelt came to the defense of the *Nisei*, writing in *Collier's* magazine that Americans should allow them "a fair chance to prove themselves in the community."

About 40 percent of the *Nisei* who left the camps were young women. They joined the armed forces, went to college, or got jobs in factories or in domestic service. The army recruited fifty Asian American women, most of Japanese ancestry, to serve as translators. Parental authority over young Japanese women had not ended entirely—the army wanted 500 women as translators and blamed parental disapproval when they failed to meet their quota. After the war ended, some *Nisei* WACs continued their army careers. Eleven served in Japan as translators, clerks, and secretaries for General Douglas MacArthur during the American occupation after the war. Ironically, thirteen *Nisei* WACs sent by the army to Japan became cultural brokers, showing the Japanese the roles women played in America, in hopes of convincing the Japanese to allow their women a greater public role.

At the same time as Japanese internment, the government also interned some 11,000 "enemy aliens" of German descent. Some women enemy aliens were held in convents. Since the mid-nineteenth century, the order of Our Lady of Charity of the Good Shepherd built convents throughout the United States, dedicated to helping vulnerable girls and women, especially orphans and delinquent girls. During World War II, the government preferred the convents as a safe place to hold women

A GERMAN INTERNEE RECALLS
HIS WIFE'S ARREST

In an FBI raid in the middle of the night in December 1941, another German alien, Marie Theberath, was arrested and shipped to a detention camp in Georgia with her hus- *band Peter, their children taken from them. He wrote to his relatives six months later.*

"Marie was released on Feb. 11th [1942] but everything was gone, no

enemy aliens, rather than using the county jails. Anna Schafer from Milwaukee was arrested along with her infant son, Horst, and detained at a Home of the Good Shepherd convent, along with five other women. After repeated questioning by the FBI from December 1941 until April 1942, she was released. (See Primary Source 8-7.)

Many Germans were interned at Ft. Meade, Maryland. Others were sent to Ellis Island where they awaited deportation to Germany, often in exchange for Americans interned in Germany after the war began. Interning those used to American freedoms took a tremendous toll. Families were broken, living conditions were primitive, and reputations were destroyed. Some Ellis Island internees committed suicide by jumping into New York's harbor. Some German Jews were exchanged for Americans, and thus sent to their deaths in Nazi Germany's Holocaust, the organized genocide of millions of Jews and others. Frances Greis, a Milwaukee resident, had a nervous breakdown, and small wonder. Her husband, a German World War I veteran and paint chemist, had been taken away from the family's home on December 9, 1941, and held for four years. Frances, forced to care for herself and four children, finally joined her husband on Ellis Island to await forced repatriation to Germany. In April 1945, just as the European phase of the war was ending, the family was sent instead to Crystal City, Texas. Not until 1947 were they finally allowed to return to Milwaukee.

Italian resident aliens also faced internment. Some 10,000 Italian families, many in the fishing industry, were forced out of their Pacific Coast communities and had their boats impounded so that the navy could use them. Evicted from their homes, leaving behind most of their belongings, Italians were shipped to Ft. Missoula, Montana, or restricted from travel to militarily important areas, such as power plants, dams, and military installations. For Italian immigrant women focused on their families and surrounded by an enclave of fellow Italians, the separation from those with American citizenship was particularly difficult. Often these women did not even speak or read English. Coping with arrest, internment, or restrictions was beyond them. In Oakland, one Italian American remembered the women of the neighborhood gathered in the kitchen. They "would huddle together," she said, "talking and crying. They would soak the dish towels with tears." Ironically, Italians represented the largest single European children, no home. In one word every-thing robbed, the children placed in separate homes, the mother helplessly thrown *into the street*. . . . We arrived here on April 9th and no news yet from our family. The last time I saw John and Marie was in the prison on April 5th and I have not seen Gertrude and Friedrich since December 8th. These are ridicu-lous conditions. . . . All hope that the war will end soon."

Source: From www.traces.org/Vanished_panel_texts .htm.

ethnic group to serve in the military during the war. Over 500,000 women and men of Italian descent served in the armed forces. One Italian woman was ordered to evacuate her home on the same day that she learned of the deaths of her son and nephew at Pearl Harbor.

The large population of Italians on the East Coast made internment a logistical impossibility, so only smaller groups on the West Coast were interned. Not all East Coast Italians were safe from internment, however. Italian opera star Ezio Pinza, the leading bass in New York City's Metro-politan Opera and only four months shy of becoming an American citizen, was arrested and sent to Ellis Island. Leaving behind a sick daughter, his wife Doris traveled to Washington and spent eleven weeks seeking her husband's freedom. Even after Italian internees were freed and returned to their lives, they still lived under clouds of suspicion, resentment, and fear. Their stories, like those of the Japanese and Germans, remained largely unknown until brought to light by later generations, appalled at the whole-sale violation of civil rights that internship represented. In 1988, the federal government finally offered reparation payments to Japanese internees who still lived. In 2001, the federal government offered a report detailing the conditions under which Italians were interned and listing their names. In 2003, the House of Representatives supported a resolution for a national day of remembrance of the internment of Japanese, Germans, and Italians during the war.

Women on the Home Front

The majority of American women during World War II lived at home, caring for their families. Nevertheless, the war affected these women on the home front in a variety of ways. As was always the case during a major war, consumer goods grew scarce, and the government encouraged every-one to contribute to the collection of raw materials used to produce war materiel. Women saved paper, rubber, aluminum, tin cans, and even bacon drippings and grease that were used to make glycerin for explosives. Actress Rita Hayworth posed for a publicity photograph atop her car, minus its bumpers, to encourage people to hold scrap drives to collect unneeded metal parts of cars for recycling.

357

WOMEN AT WAR ON THE HOME FRONT   To convince women to join the "hidden army" of women workers in World War II, the government's War Manpower Commission issued posters designed to reassure women such actions were culturally acceptable, even by family members more used to being the only breadwinner.

In 1942, the government began rationing, limiting the purchase of food, gas, and even clothing. Ration coupon books provided a set number of coupons for each family, based on family size as well as occupation. Florence Lewis, a poultry farmer in Tulsa, Oklahoma, had a gas ration book allowing her to buy more gasoline than did a socialite in New York City, since Mrs. Lewis had to transport food to her customers and to the market. Rationed items included not only gas, but also sugar, butter, meat, canned goods, frozen and bottled items, even shoes and catsup. Women mixed yellow dye into margarine and used it instead of butter. They planted "victory" gardens so often that by 1945, 40 percent of the vegetables produced in the country were grown in some 20 million victory gardens. Women painted seams down the backs of their legs so it looked like they were wearing stockings, another rationed item nearly impossible to get, and attached new collars to old dresses to save fabric. They planned meatless meals, consuming cottage cheese, macaroni and cheese, or fish. Holiday celebrations often prompted women to combine rationing coupons with those of neighbors, hoping to create a festive meal.

Women invested their money, too. Half the population bought war bonds and stamps to help fund the war. The government's propaganda efforts, promoted in posters, advertisements, newsreels, and movies, made it clear to American women that they had a duty in this war and women understood they were to do that duty without complaining. Women with sons and daughters in the armed forces hung banners in their windows with a blue star for each child in service. Gold Star mothers were those who had lost a son or daughter. Gold Star wives, formed in December 1945 by four New York widows led by Marie Jordan and embraced by Eleanor Roosevelt, provided support for those who lost their spouses in the war, as well as activities for children and help navigating the system of government benefits for those left behind.

On May 8, 1945, victory in Europe was declared after the Germans surrendered. American joy was tempered with the knowledge of the continuing war against Japan and with the sorrow at the passing of Franklin Roosevelt, who had died in Warm Springs, Georgia, on April 12, 1945. His vice president, Harry S. Truman, assumed the presidency and guided the nation to victory against Japan after dropping two atomic bombs, one on Hiroshima, the other on Nagasaki. The Japanese surrendered on August 14, 1945. The next day, reported one employee of an electrical company, she was laid off. America was at peace, and America's women were going home.

THINK MORE ABOUT IT

1. Return to the opening vignette on Eleanor Roosevelt, who changed her views about women's suffrage once the Nineteenth Amendment was passed. How does her optimism about the possibility of women voters bringing about reforms square with the experience of women in the 1920s through World War II? In general, how consequential do you think this amendment was for women during this era?

2. Discuss the varied economic activities in which women engaged during the 1920s. Pay particular attention to the areas of paid work, unpaid work in the home, and consumerism. How were women's limited employment opportunities expanding? How did they continue to be constrained by race, ethnicity, nationality, and religion?

3. American culture during the 1920s mixed vibrancy and greater openness with prejudice and discrimination, a volatile combination that expressed itself in such diverse representations as the flapper and the Klanswoman. Examine at least three specific aspects of American

culture in the 1920s, emphasizing the ways in which women and women's organizations reflected and contributed to the growth of this changing culture.

4. Discuss the origins and extent of the Great Depression. How did this economic crisis affect women of different backgrounds and living situations?

5. Two major components of the New Deal were to provide relief to struggling Americans and to bring about reforms that would help the nation as a whole. How did these two components of the New Deal affect women? How did women contribute to the labor activism of the era? Be sure to use examples drawn from a range of New Deal programs and labor actions, and to recognize the limits of both government programs and labor unions to address women's economic situations and further women's interests.

6. During World War II, American women found varied ways to serve, including in paid work, in agriculture, in the home, in caring for those in need, in leisure-time activities, in raising funds for the war, and by participating more directly in wartime actions. Discuss and evaluate each of these areas of women's participation, using concrete examples to demonstrate your points. How did women of different backgrounds experience the war years? What were the long-term legacies of women's activities during wartime?

7. What did you learn in this chapter that you did not know before? How does this new information help you understand the overall story of women in American history? What topics would you like to explore further?

READ MORE ABOUT IT

Kristi Andersen, *Beyond Suffrage: Women in Partisan and Electoral Politics Before the New Deal*

Blanche Wiesen Cook, *Eleanor Roosevelt*

Susan Hartmann, *The Home Front and Beyond: American Women in the 40's*

Maureen Honey, ed., *Bitter Fruit: African American Women in World War II*

Kathy Peiss, *Hope in a Jar: The Making of America's Beauty Culture*

Vicki L. Ruiz, *Cannery Women, Cannery Lives: Mexican Women, Unionization, and the California Food Processing Industry, 1930–1950*

Cheryl Wall, *Women of the Harlem Renaissance*

Emily Yellin, *Our Mothers' War: American Women at Home and at the Front during World War II*

KEY CONCEPTS

League of Women Voters

Sheppard-Towner Maternity and
   Infancy Protection Act

Equal Rights Amendment

Women's Bureau

labor-saving devices

Cable Act

Women's Ku Klux Klan

flapper

Prohibition

Harlem Renaissance

stock market crash

New Deal

androcentric

"Rosie the Riveter"

WACs, WAVES, WASPS

internment

Chapter 9

COLD WAR, WARM HEARTH

Irene Morgan of Virginia and
Rosa Parks of Alabama

Native American Activism and Resistance
Asian American Women Activists

A NEW FRONTIER

The President's Commission on the Status of Women
> Primary Source 9-6: President Kennedy's Call for a National
> Commission on the Status of Women

Change on the Horizon

THINK MORE ABOUT IT

READ MORE ABOUT IT

KEY CONCEPTS

On June 3, 1946, the United States Supreme Court handed down a ruling in a case titled *Morgan v. The Commonwealth of Virginia*. Irene Morgan, the plaintiff, was a twenty-nine-year-old black woman from Virginia. Two years earlier, in July 1944, she had boarded a Greyhound bus in Gloucester, Virginia, for a trip to Baltimore, Maryland. She bought her ticket at the "colored" window, she sat in the bus in the colored section. At the next stop, the bus picked up a white couple and the bus driver strode back to where Morgan was seated and demanded that she stand so that the white couple could sit. She refused. The bus driver drove to the nearest police station, where Morgan was arrested for violating the segregation laws of the Commonwealth of Virginia. She was convicted, but appealed her case, which eventually came before the Supreme Court. Thurgood Marshall, an NAACP lawyer who later became the first black justice on the Supreme Court, argued that the segregation laws of Virginia unfairly interfered with interstate commerce. The Court agreed, and segregation on interstate bus lines was banned.

Nine years later, Alabama seamstress Rosa Parks attended a two-week session at Highlander Folk School in Monteagle, Tennessee. Highlander Folk School, founded in 1932 to support and train labor organizers, began to include civil rights work for African Americans in its curriculum in 1944. By 1953, the school was training men and women interested in achieving school desegregation and voting rights for blacks. Several months after her training session in 1955, Parks boarded a bus in Montgomery, Alabama, on her way home after a long day at work. The bus became full and she was asked to leave her seat in the colored section so the "whites-only" section could be expanded to accommodate the later arrivals. She refused. She, too, was arrested. She, too, was convicted. Her case provided an opportunity for the black community of Montgomery to make a public statement about segregation. A boycott of the buses followed Parks' arrest, and after more than a year, the system nearly bankrupt with the loss of riders, segregation on buses in the city of Montgomery ended. The next phase of the struggle for civil rights had begun.

Rosa Parks became an icon in American history for her resistance to segregation that eventually sparked a showdown over the issue. But Parks always pointed

ROSA PARKS   Rosa Parks heads the line to board a newly integrated city bus after the successful Montgomery Bus Boycott ended in December 1956. Parks became an icon of the civil rights movement after her arrest over a year earlier for refusing to give up her seat to a white person. Irene Morgan did the same ten years before to help overturn Jim Crow laws segregating black Americans on interstate buses.

out that she had not been the first to resist segregation. Women throughout the South, black and white, fought as they had fought in the years since *Plessy v. Ferguson* had legalized segregation in 1896 (see Chapter 7). They used activism, lawsuits, resistance, and personal and professional sacrifice to achieve their goals.

Except for the beginnings of the modern civil rights movement in the South, women's actions in the public sphere in the 1950s are often de-emphasized, in the same way that many women's abilities were dismissed by employers after World War II. Demobilization after the war left America with millions of unemployed men, and a strong cultural pronouncement that women belonged at home raising children and turning over their well-paying jobs to the returning soldiers. This pronouncement became even more powerful with the advent of television in the 1950s. The new medium helped to promulgate a mythic view of American women in weekly situation comedies and dramas that advertised both products and lifestyles no American woman would apparently want to live without. Conspicuous consumption in the 1950s rivaled that of the 1920s. Underlying both this consumerism and the back-to-home movement was Americans' deep desire for normal life again after years of depression and war, and now a new threat that possessed unimaginable destructive power, the atomic bomb. Yet, despite cultural constraints and expectations, American women again lived lives that did not match the images culture provided. American women took different paths after World War II, continuing their activism as well as embracing hearth and home in ways promoted by the dominant culture in their lives.

DEMOBILIZATION

After the war was over, Americans, women and men both, returned to their homes as part of a process called *demobilization*, where the government gradually discharged soldiers from their assignments. The process was slow: months after V-E Day, frustrated soldiers eager to return home rioted on overseas military bases. American armed forces, 12 million strong in June 1945, shrank to 1.5 million by June 1947. President Truman and his administration feared such rapid demobilization would lead to high unemployment and would compromise military strength. Nevertheless, Congress continued to dismantle the military machine that had won the war, shrinking the defense budget from $90 billion in January 1945 to $10 billion by 1947. America retained the largest army and navy in the world, as well as sole possession of the atomic bomb, but lost many experienced soldiers and military administrators who returned to civilian life.

The Armed Forces

Demobilization after World War II included both the armed forces and the civilian workforce. As clerks and secretaries, women processed the papers for the hundreds of thousands of returning soldiers. Women's military units created during the war—WACs, WAVES, SPARS, and women Marines—downsized drastically from their height of 400,000 women. The WASP had already disbanded in December of 1944 as soon as enough male pilots returned from European victories to take their place. The women pilots had flown 60 million miles and lost 42 women in service, but they received no veteran or survivor benefits for years. While government leaders failed in that regard, others praised women's service. General Dwight D. Eisenhower, who commanded the Allied forces in Europe, had been opposed to women in service before the war, but testified favorably in Congress about the possible formation of permanent women's organizations within the armed services. He said, "During the time that I have had women under my command, they have met every task assigned them. Their contribution in efficiency, skill, spirit and determination are immeasurable." Such support from the most popular general of the war (and a future president of the country) helped servicewomen in their struggle to become part of the permanent armed forces after the war.

The government also recognized and awarded women's contributions to the winning of the war in other ways. Medals went to 657 WACs, including Purple Hearts (for injuries from enemy actions) and Bronze Stars (for meritorious service overseas). By December 1946, WAC strength had fallen to less than 10,000 women, most of whom wished to stay in the army, a desire fulfilled when President Harry Truman created a permanent Women's Army Corps in 1948. Likewise, the WAVES of the navy did the same: most WAVES left the service, but a core group became the basis for a permanent branch of the navy. The Coast Guard's SPARs and women marines faced skeptics such as Marine Corps Brigadier General Gerald C.

Thomas, Director of Plans and Policies, who stated: "The American tradition is that a women's place is in the home . . . women do not take kindly to military regimentation. During the war, they have accepted the regulations imposed on them, but hereafter the problem of enforcing discipline alone would be a headache." Others accused or implied that women wanting to stay in the armed services were lesbians. During the war, such accusations against women were dealt with informally. After the war, as the services needed fewer women, lesbians more often faced formal action, such as "undesirable" discharges. More than 9,000 lesbians and gay men who served their country during the war were disqualified for veterans' benefits because of such discharges. Despite this kind of opposition, women in the coast guard and marines became part of the Armed Services of the United States, under the newly created Department of Defense, which replaced the Departments of the Army and Navy.

The Home Front

When World War II ended in August of 1945, millions of women war-plant workers had already lost their jobs as American industry prepared for returning veterans to assume their places in the workforce. In 1940, only 28 percent of the labor force were women. In 1944, women were 35.4 percent of the civilian labor force; in 1945, they were 36.1 percent. Of those women, 22.5 percent were married, and over 12 percent had children younger than ten years old. By war's end, 30 percent of women were employed in factories, and domestic employment had dropped from nearly 18 percent to only 9.5 percent. Women still earned less than men employed at the same tasks, but more than they had in low-paying, traditional women's work. As the war ended, surveys showed 75 percent of women wanted to keep their higher-paying wartime jobs.

Employers began firing women workers in the spring of 1945, anticipating victory in Europe (V-E Day). Millions of women were fired—first black women, then women belonging to nonwhite ethnic groups, then white women. At the Redstone Arsenal in Huntsville, Alabama, for example, the first 200 workers laid off in June 1945, after V-E Day, were primarily black women. In August, after the victory over Japan, V-J Day, 500 workers, mostly women, were furloughed from the facility. By the end of October 1945, no women production employees remained at the Arsenal. At the Brooklyn Navy Yard in New York, women workers had been aggressively recruited throughout the war and held over 6 percent of the jobs at the massive facility—some 4,657 out of over 71,000 workers were women. By the end of the war, nearly all the women workers were gone, replaced by men who held seniority rights in the unionized workforce or by male veterans who benefited from the government's policies of preferential hiring of returning soldiers.

The federal government watched veterans hunt for jobs with considerable concern. Firing women supposedly made room for men coming home from the war, but the rapid decline in military production meant there were few jobs available for men, either. So many men demobilized so rapidly from the army and failed to find jobs that unemployment threatened to

WOMEN AND MEN AND UNEMPLOYMENT As the war ended in 1945, women and men filed for unemployment benefits in Michigan. Similar scenes appeared across the country as both military and civilian workforces were demobilized.

send the economy into crisis. In 1944, hoping to avoid such problems, President Roosevelt had signed the Servicemen's Readjustment Act, better known as the G.I. Bill, to provide immediate unemployment insurance for veterans. The bill also provided funding for education, vocational training, and low-cost loans for veterans to buy houses or start businesses. While male veterans took advantage of the bill, one-third of women veterans did not even know of the bill and its provisions. Only about 64,000 women took advantage of the bill to attend college, compared to 9.2 million men who attended educational institutions or received on-the-job training.

Higher education leading to better jobs would take time, however. Fearing another Great Depression, President Truman proposed legislation to secure full employment as part of his domestic program called the *Fair Deal*. His "Full Employment Bill," attempted to even out the boom–bust business cycle that had plagued the American economy for years. By increasing federal spending and linking it to the unemployment rate, Truman hoped to guarantee full employment every year for Americans as a basic right that the power of the federal government would maintain. Such interference with market economics met with nearly universal dismay, and

DAUGHTERS OF BILITIS, STATEMENT OF PURPOSE

Lesbian women objected to their demonization by popular culture, but remained largely unorganized until the 1950s. The Daughters of Bilitis, a social group for lesbian women, first formed in San Francisco in 1955. Denigrated by the press and the public, fearful of persecution in the sexually repressive 1950s, founders Del Martin and Phyllis Lyon sought to contact and to educate other women to learn about and to accept their homosexuality. Their group published The Ladder, *a newsletter that printed their mission statement explaining their goals. They used the word* variant *instead of* lesbian, *as the latter word had negative connotations they wished to avoid.*

"Daughters of Bilitis—Purpose

"A women's organization for the purpose of promoting the integration of the homosexual into society by:

"(1) Education of the variant, to enable her to understand herself and make her adjustment to society . . . in all its social,

Congress transformed the bill into the Employment Act of 1946. This act set up a council of economic advisors to the president who suggested ways that he could promote policies resulting in "maximum employment, production and purchasing power," rather than guaranteeing jobs to all who wanted them.

Without that guarantee of full employment, the Employment Act of 1946 carried little meaning. It did, however, show that Presidents Truman and Roosevelt both wanted to prevent another economic depression. It also reflected the understanding many policy makers had gained from the economic turmoil of the 1920s and 1930s. Government failure to deal effectively with massive unemployment during those decades led to the rise of dictatorial regimes, such as those led by National Socialists in Germany and the Communist Party in the USSR. As the horrors of the Holocaust became increasingly apparent to Americans after men and women returned from the war in Europe, and as veterans and prisoners of war from the Asian theater told terrible stories of torture, killings, rapes, and other crimes, activists sought ways to ensure such tragedies would never happen again.

WOMEN ACTIVISTS FOR A BETTER WORLD

The United States enjoyed enormous power at the end of World War II. It possessed the largest army and navy, its infrastructure was largely undamaged by warfare, its population suffered little deprivation compared to those of other nations. Its greatest threat came from its former ally, the USSR.

civic and economic implications—this to be accomplished by establishing and maintaining as complete a library as possible of both fiction and non-fiction literature on the sex deviant theme; by sponsoring public discussions on pertinent subjects . . . by advocating a mode of behavior and dress acceptable to society.

"(2) Education of the public at large through acceptance first of the individual, leading to an eventual breakdown of erroneous taboos and prejudices; through public discussion . . . through dissemination of educational literature on the homosexual theme.

"(3) Participation in research projects by duly authorized and responsible psychologists, sociologists, and other such experts directed towards further knowledge of the homosexual.

"(4) Investigation of the penal code as it pertains to the homosexual, proposal of changes to provide equitable handing of cases involving this minority group, and promotion of these changes through the due process of law in the state legislatures."

Source: Marcia M. Gallo, *Different Daughters: A History of the Daughters of Bilitis and the Rise of the Lesbian Rights Movement* (Emeryville, CA: Seal Press, 2006), 11.

The USSR violated the international Yalta agreement of February 1945 that called for democratic elections in eastern European governments as they were restored after the war. By May 1945, British Prime Minister Winston Churchill warned President Truman that the Soviets were drawing an "iron curtain" across Eastern Europe, as the USSR moved to dominate the area. Before long, a cold war began between the United States and the USSR. As the USSR shut off its territories to free markets and emigration, as it achieved nuclear capabilities, and as it promoted atheism, the United States responded with attacks on "godless communism" within its borders. The cold war would dominate American foreign policy for the next forty years, pitting activists seeking alternatives to the forces that had led to World War II with those determined to promote the United States as a Judeo-Christian nation, rejecting not only communism and socialism, but also atheism and other religious traditions, as well as lesbianism and other so-called deviant behavior. (See Primary Source 9-1.)

Communists and Socialists

Women's activism after World War II took many forms. Some women looked toward the communism and socialism of the USSR as antidotes for the excesses of capitalism. Communists argued that collective ownership was necessary for a society to prosper. They drew upon the ideas of German political philosopher Karl Marx who held that individuals in society should both contribute to it as they could and receive from it what they needed. By 1949, the two major communist powers, the USSR and China, became communist dictatorships, but sympathizers saw them less as dictatorships and more as role models for how America should modify its capitalist

ELEANOR ROOSEVELT SPEAKS TO THE UNITED NATIONS

The former first lady and chairperson of the Commission on Human Rights spoke before the United Nations on March 27, 1958, to celebrate the tenth anniversary of the Declaration of Human Rights. Her ideas, embodied in the document, echoed a long trajectory of political theory that governments are duty-bound to respect the inalienable rights of those they govern. Roosevelt, however, emphasized the humanitarian aspect of equal rights and the community's role in protecting those rights.

"Where, after all, do universal human rights begin? In small places, close to

system. Labor union leaders supported some communist ideas, as did many of the rank-and-file of groups such as the United Electrical Radio and Machine Workers of America (UE). Because communists emphasized that workers or the state, rather than bosses, should own the means of production, their ideas appealed to labor supporters who had sacrificed during the war and now wanted to repair the years of economic restrictions on wages, prices, and supplies with changes that would benefit them.

In 1946, Betty Friedan, later a founder of the modern women's rights movement, began writing for the *UE News*, the union newspaper. She penned articles that supported not only communism, but also suggested automatic seniority in employment for African Americans in the union who had been discriminated against for years, child care support for women in the industry, and a pay-equity system that would help women workers overcome the discrimination that they faced in the union shops. She wrote articles describing instances of racism against African Americans and Latinas, and charged union officials as well as management with being both anti-Semitic and sexist. She documented the differences between management and labor with a portrait of each that delineated the wealth of the former and the poverty of the latter. Working-class women, she declared, did not even earn enough money to provide fresh vegetables or new clothes for their families, while their bosses spent extravagantly on consumer goods. Women were valued as customers, but not as workers. Friedan pointed out that advertisements glorified American women in "gleaming" General Electric kitchens, using Westinghouse appliances, watching Sylvania TV sets. Nothing was too good for the American woman, except decent pay and working conditions from General Electric, Westinghouse, Sylvania, and other corporations producing the goods she was expected to buy. While not a member of the Communist Party, Friedan believed that communism valued women for their labor.

Internationalists

While communism attracted some women activists, others participated in different international organizations. Eleanor Roosevelt, who left the White home—so close and so small that they cannot be seen on any maps of the world. Yet they are the world of the individual person; the neighborhood he lives in; the school or college he attends; the factory, farm, or office where he works. Such are the places where every man, woman, and child seeks equal justice, equal opportunity, equal dignity without discrimination. Unless these rights have meaning there, they have little meaning anywhere. Without concerted citizen action to uphold them close to home, we shall look in vain for progress in the larger world.

"Thus we believe that the destiny of human rights is in the hands of all our citizens in all our communities."

Source: Eleanor Roosevelt in *Activating Human Rights*, ed. Elisabeth J. Porter and Baden Offord (Bern, Switzerland: Peter Lang, 2006), 21.

House in April 1945 after her husband died, reemerged in the later 1940s and 1950s as an internationalist. Shortly after President Roosevelt's death, President Truman appointed Mrs. Roosevelt to the United States Delegation to the United Nations (UN), a newly formed organization dedicated to achieving world peace. While there, she chaired the Human Rights Commission to draft the Universal Declaration of Human Rights, a document that she hoped would be as important as the French Declaration of the Rights of Man and the U.S. Constitution's Bill of Rights. The General Assembly of the UN adopted the document in 1948, and Roosevelt remained prouder of that accomplishment than of any other achievement in her long career. Her humanitarian concerns, her warmth and humor, and her innate intelligence were made even more formidable by her steely resolve that humans—all humans—deserved to be treated with respect and dignity (see Primary Source 9-2). She debated the Soviets in the UN and in 1948 threatened to resign if President Truman refused to recognize and aid the controversial founding of the new nation of Israel, which she viewed as a haven for Jews after the horrors of the Holocaust.

In addition to her work in the international community, Roosevelt continued her activism on the national stage. She joined the NAACP board of directors and spoke out on the importance of civil rights. She helped create the group Americans for Democratic Action to push for social reform. She continued her service on the Women's Division of the Democratic National Committee until the party disbanded the committee in 1953, integrating women into the party structure. She interviewed world and national leaders on an educational television show called *Prospects of Mankind*, and served on presidential commissions not only on civil rights, but on women's rights as well.

Many women in the postwar years continued to join activist groups. The Women's International League for Peace and Freedom (WILPF) carried on the work it had launched at the beginning of the century. During World War II, it defended the war as necessary to aid the innocent victims of fascism, and in 1946, American Emily Greene Balch, its international secretary, received the Nobel Peace Prize, the second American woman to do so (the first had been Jane Addams in 1931). In her acceptance speech, Balch spoke for the entire organization in hoping that the year would be a turning point for peace, disarmament, and the "renunciation of power politics," but it was not to be. International tensions shifted the focus to Asia, as Communists in China, the USSR, and Korea fought for control of the Korean peninsula. War broke out in June 1950, and the United Nations joined the fray, sending troops to try to resolve the conflict. The WILPF opposed the war, and member Jeanette Rankin, who had cast the lone vote in the House of Representatives opposing the U.S. entry into World War II, spoke out against the Korean War and in favor of total disarmament and the end of war.

Another women's group active after the war was the Congress of American Women (CAW), founded in Paris in 1945 as the U.S. branch of the Women's International Democratic Federation, an antifascist, pro-Soviet, leftist organization. The group, a prolabor, antiracist organization that attracted a number of African American supporters among its officers and members, had more black women as officers than any other feminist organization before or since. CAW affiliated itself with numerous other national organizations to work for integration, against racism, for a higher minimum wage, against postwar inflation, as well as for child care for working mothers, job training and women's access to professional schools, and for laundries and kitchens in public housing projects. The group, a link to earlier suffragists and Progressive reformers, attracted numerous women eager to work in the wider world as they called for world peace as well as full economic, social, legal, and political rights for women.

Cold War Reactions

After only a year, CAW had 250,000 members. In 1947, however, the group, like so many other international groups after the war, came up against President Truman's containment policy, the Cold War, and the anticommunist hysteria of the late 1940s and 1950s, and was forced to defend itself against attacks from the administration. Truman, fearing the spread of communism through Soviet expansion into Europe and Chinese dominance in Asia, announced that the policy of the United States would be to contain that spread by helping any country trying to resist communism. Communism, declared Truman, was "based upon the will of a minority forcibly imposed upon the majority. It relies upon terror and oppression, a controlled press and radio, fixed elections, and the suppression of personal freedoms." The Cold War between the two systems of economy and government, capitalism and democracy versus communism (led by the United States and the USSR), led to an arms race as both sides manufactured increasingly destructive nuclear weapons. Civil defense against such weapons required the participation of every American, including women. The government urged women, as mothers and nurturers, to prepare their families for attacks. Its publications emphasized women's responsibility to control the fear and panic family members might feel while they simultaneously prepared for an attack. The government also encouraged women to

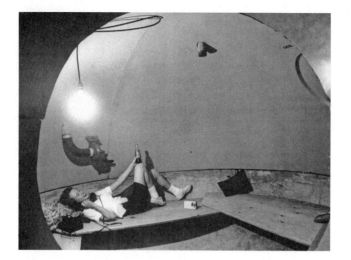

CIVIL DEFENSE BOMB SHELTER Frightened of nuclear war after the USSR announced it too had achieved nuclear capabilities in 1949, many Americans built underground bomb shelters. Above-ground testing of nuclear weapons caused radioactive fallout, so city dwellers relied on government-provided bomb shelters, stocked with emergency supplies, and often organized by women as volunteer civil defense wardens. Here, a young woman relaxes in a fallout shelter in 1961.

organize their homes in case of disasters, telling them that "good house-keeping is the first line of defense against fire," explaining how to stock first-aid kits, prepare basement shelters, and how to recognize the different air-raid alert signals that would alert Americans to a feared Soviet onslaught.

As the Cold War escalated, women's peace organizations such as CAW were criticized and linked to communism in ways that discredited their work. Groups lost members as the government called various groups to testify before Congress regarding their links to communism and, specifically, to the Communist Party of the United States of America (CPUSA). For example, in 1948, the House of Representatives' House Unamerican Activities Committee (HUAC) attacked CAW because it called for the United States to ban atomic bombs and to establish friendly relations with the Soviet Union. HUAC accused CAW of being an enemy agent of the government, despite a membership roster that included Susan B. Anthony II (the suffragist's niece), Elizabeth Cady Stanton's daughter Harriot Blatch, Women's Air Force Service Pilots' former director Jacqueline Cochran, Eleanor Roosevelt's daughter-in-law Faye Emerson, and Anne Carter Schneiderman, the national vice president of the American Jewish Congress. By 1950, membership had dropped to 3,000. Threatened with a $10,000 fine and five years' imprisonment each, officers of the group gave up, and the CAW disbanded, unwilling to register as an enemy agent of the United States.

Attacks on women's activist movements drove many women away from such groups. The HUAC, in particular, specialized in ruining lives and reputations. In the Senate, Senator Joseph McCarthy, chair of the Government Committee on Operations of the Senate, magnified the HUAC

MARGARET CHASE SMITH'S PRESIDENTIAL CAMPAIGN SONG

Sen. Margaret Chase Smith eventually ran for president in 1964. Lyrics to her campaign song reflect the cultural necessity of combining cultural standards of femininity with the unfeminine feat of running for president.

"Leave It to the Girls" by Hildegard (Gladys Shelley)

Leave it to the girls,
Where there's a frill,

findings with hearings that were televised, broadcast on the radio, and reported breathlessly in the press as uncovering communist infiltration everywhere. The hearings were nothing more or less than witch-hunts. McCarthy used lies, innuendos, gossip, and occasionally, though not often, facts to accuse hundreds of mostly innocent Americans of links to communism. Republican McCarthy, inspired by earlier trials of spies who had given the Soviet Union plans they used to produce atomic weapons (and afraid he would lose his Senate seat if voters discovered he had lied about his war record and was taking bribes from Pepsi-Cola), seized upon a friend's suggestion that he "find" communist subversives in the Democratic administration. He began his smear campaign in 1950, claiming to know of dozens of people in the State Department who were communists. When people responded with demands for proof, McCarthy suggested that asking for proof meant they were communists, too. One of his followers, Richard Nixon, used similar tactics in the California senatorial race of 1950. He accused his opponent, Representative Helen Gahagan Douglas, of being "pink," or communist, "right down to her underwear." Douglas failed to convince voters the attacks were false and lost the election.

Anti-Communist hysteria reached its peak in 1952. The McCarthy hearings were successful because Americans were worried. The war in Korea was going badly, China had become communist, the Soviet Union had "the bomb," and McCarthy seemed to have valid information that communist spies had infiltrated the State Department. He moved on to investigate the entertainment industry, American colleges, and anti-American library books. Union members and homosexuals came under attack as well. An enduring legacy of the Cold War era came in the form of an Executive Order that President Eisenhower signed in 1953 (and in force until 1975) mandating the firing of any federal employee deemed guilty of "sexual perversion," causing lesbians in all kinds of government employment—from clerical workers to supervisors in public agencies—to lose their jobs. Meanwhile the antihomosexual witch-hunt in the military escalated, with lesbians subject to incarceration as well as "other than honorable" discharges throughout the cold war era.

And a powder puff there's
greater skill
Leave it to the chicks
They've got a million magic tricks
To change the course of history
Their know-how is a mystery

Leave it to the girls
They're heaven sent
It could be that our next president
Will wear perfume and pearls

Be diplomatic in pin curls
For love and glory leave it to the girls

G is for the good in every woman
I is for ideals for which they stand
And r and l and s
And now, as you may guess,
When you spell girls, my friend
You spell success.

Source: © Gladys Shelley, from www.mcslibrary.org/program/library/song.htm.

Finally, in 1954, Sen. McCarthy attacked the U.S. Army and the secretary of the army, Robert Stevens. Televised hearings made clear to all who watched McCarthy's despicable actions. So did speeches by senators such as Margaret Chase Smith of Maine, the first woman elected to the Senate (see Chapter 8). She declared that as a woman, as a Republican, as a senator, and as an American, she was appalled at the tactics used by HUAC and McCarthy, even if at times the accusations were genuine. Americans needed to maintain their fairness and respect for others who held different beliefs, she said. At the same time, Smith proposed making the Communist Party illegal in a bill that she introduced in 1954. Like many politicians, Smith walked a fine line to preserve her office during a time when Americans greatly feared communism and the specter of atomic warfare. (See Primary Source 9-3.)

BACK TO THE HOME

The ruined reputations and lives of Americans accused of links to communism gave pause to many who might otherwise have involved themselves in the public sphere. Millions of American women had already made that choice, however, less for reasons of politics than for reasons of home and family. Promoted by the government and confirmed by popular culture, the back-to-home movement after World War II spawned suburbs, a baby boom, a culture of consumerism, and the revival of a cult of true womanhood, repackaged as the "Feminine Mystique."

The Government's Push for Domesticity

The federal government, concerned about the economic impact of demobilization, made a priority of convincing women working in war industries to give up their jobs to returning servicemen. While many women resented leaving good-paying jobs, others did not. The government used one wartime survey to promote a return to the home, since it reflected women's ambivalence about working. Of those women surveyed, 74 percent of women wanted to marry and become a homemaker while about 18 percent wanted marriage and a successful career. Government-sponsored newsreels interviewed working women eager for their men to come home and take over. Other newsreels showed children playing in the streets, and blamed working mothers for juvenile delinquency. Combined with the continued difficulty women had finding adequate daycare, many mothers would find it impossible to continue working after the war.

The government also contracted with the American Historical Association to find scholars to research and write forty-two pamphlets examining various issues important to the postwar world, including women working. The War Manpower Commission then distributed the pamphlets for discussion among soldiers to prepare them for their return home. One pamphlet asked soldiers, "Do You Want Your Wife to Work after the War?" The author and sociologist Clifford Kirkpatrick recognized that not all women were alike, any more than men were, and that many women enjoyed their jobs in wartime industries and might be reluctant to return to what

WOMEN'S FASHIONS FOR WOMEN'S NEW ROLE In 1947, after years of making do with made-over clothes and wartime uniforms, American women woke up to new possibilities of fashion with designer Christian Dior's "New Look." Characterized by fuller skirts, rich fabrics, and constricting construction, these clothes were made for women with new amounts of leisure time to spend, rather than laboring in factories. The look epitomized the return of the True Woman in twentieth-century style.

some viewed as the drudgery of housework. He suggested that returning veterans be open to discussion with their wives (making the assumption all veterans were men), and that they remember that many schemes had been suggested for solving what he termed the "woman problem," namely, that "women will continue to want babies and to want work that is satisfying." Husbands should recognize this and do their part, said Kirkpatrick, even if it meant doing the occasional dish. The *Christian Science Monitor*, among other popular publications, was not impressed with the War Department wasting its time producing a "booklet of instructions" for soldiers "on the mysteries of women!" Asking soldiers to help do dishes, one author remarked sarcastically, would "slow down demobilization." "G.I. Joe" had enough to worry about as it was, and the "military master of manners" who had come up with the idea ought to let him exercise his masculine prerogative and "splash in the dishpan" instead.

Women did leave their wartime jobs, but continued to work, filling jobs that had gone begging during the war, and seeing their income drop from an average wage of fifty to thirty-seven dollars per week. By 1947, there were more women working than before the war and more married women working as well. Seventy percent of professional women worked in fields traditional to women: teachers, nurses, and librarians. More white women went to college than before, but a greater proportion dropped out to marry—only 37 percent finished their degrees. Ninety percent of black women who went to college finished their degrees, but far fewer black women were able to attend institutions of higher education, and racial discrimination kept many African Americans out of the professions.

Numbers of African American farm women declined as well, as black southerners continued to migrate north and west. Near Las Vegas, Nevada, for example, thousands of black women, originally drawn to the city by war industries, settled into a substantial black community. Recruited by the Basic Magnesium Corporation that produced magnesium used in bombs during the war, whole families had migrated from towns in Arkansas and Mississippi. After the war, new employment opportunities became available for black women in the casinos and hotels of the growing Las Vegas area. They traded chopping cotton at $2.50 a week for, as one worker put it "eight dollars a day and working in the shade." Domestic work in the South paid only about $5.00 a week, and included ironing, cooking, child care, and serving, leaving workers little time to spend with their families. In Las Vegas, however, women's jobs such as cleaning hotel rooms were often protected by unions such as the Culinary Workers Union. Unions meant better wages, possible advancement, and leisure time after one's shift. Despite the discrimination that still existed in both jobs and housing, Las Vegas, along with other cities in the North and West, offered new possibilities to African American women fleeing the South's Jim Crow segregation and lack of economic mobility. The black population of Las Vegas climbed from 178 in 1940 to 16,000 by 1955.

Despite the millions of women who continued in the workforce after the war, however, the government and industry continued to portray working women as oddities. The government was anxious to prevent another depression; industry was anxious to increase consumer spending as they shifted from war materiel to consumer goods. Advertising agencies, in league with the government and manufacturers, made a concerted effort to inform American women that their proper place was in the home, consuming goods.

The Baby Boom, Suburbia, and Conspicuous Consumption

Returning veterans and the women in their lives began the road to conspicuous consumption by making babies and outfitting them with all the goods they could. The average age at first marriage dropped from 21.5 in 1940 to 19 in 1955, rising slightly to 20.3 in 1962. One-third of all women who married in 1951 were only 19. Women also began having children at younger ages. Between 1946 and 1960, on average, women had all their children before they turned 26. The birthrate climbed from 18.5 children per thousand women to 25.3 children per thousand women between 1933 and 1955. In 1940, only 2.6 million babies were born; by 1957, there were 4.7 million. The average family size grew as well because women wanted more children. Surveys taken by government agencies showed that over 40 percent of women in 1955 wanted four or more children, and nearly 60 percent wanted two or three. Fewer than 5 percent wanted no children, a choice made possible by easier access to birth control (Margaret Sanger's Birth Control League had become Planned Parenthood in 1942). By 1960, when birth control pills were first introduced, an even larger proportion of women wanted four or more children, and the majority of women still wanted at least two or three. Childbearing rates were even greater for women of color and immigrant women, as well as for rural women. Nearly all American women contributed to what was termed the *baby boom* in the years from 1946 to 1964.

Families with children needed places to live. Shortly after the war, responding to a critical housing shortage, the housing boom began in earnest. In Pennsylvania, halfway between urban centers of Philadelphia and Trenton, New Jersey, developer William Levitt built more than 17,000 single-family homes on some 5,500 acres. He patterned them after the government housing he had built for defense workers in 1941 near the naval shipyard in Norfolk, Virginia. Levitt went on to perfect his mass building techniques with other communities in New York, New Jersey, Puerto Rico, and in Pennsylvania. The planned communities included shopping centers, schools, churches, and recreational facilities—parks, ball fields, and community swimming pools. Suburbs such as Levittown provided white Americans with a respite from crowded urban living and left additional housing in cities available for immigrants and people of color. For as little as sixty-seven dollars a month, and with mortgages often subsidized by the G.I. Bill, suburbanites could own their own homes in the country, complete with developer-provided landscaping. Homes were standardized, with only a few models available. Levitt planned his houses with children in mind, using large open spaces, patio areas where adults could congregate while keeping an eye on the children, and modern kitchens with the latest appliances, as he advertised, to "take the labor out of housekeeping."

Advertisements for suburban housing were often directed at women. "When a woman goes house-hunting," read one ad for the General Electric appliances in a Levittown house, "the place she usually heads for *first* is the kitchen. This is where she spends so much of her day. This is where she's most likely to fall in love with the house, or reject it." Levittown's chief architect bragged that thanks to the number of appliances the houses contained, "the girls will have three hours to kill every afternoon." Time saved by appliances would be spent in shopping for additional consumer goods, sewing clothes and curtains, caring for more children, participating in various activities involving children, and planning events revolving around family life and children. The nuclear family, which had been disrupted by the Great Depression and World War II, reappeared as the norm.

The culture of conspicuous consumption and production, centered around the growing family, was further spurred by advertisements on television, the new medium of choice. There were 3 million televisions sets in America in 1950. By 1960 there were 55 million, and 530 television stations broadcast programs in the United States. Food was invented to serve while watching television—the frozen TV dinner, heated in the oven and placed on TV trays to eat while watching shows that glorified suburban life, such as *Father Knows Best* and *Leave It to Beaver*. Wives in the television shows dressed in the latest fashions, often cleaning in dresses and pearls. Husbands left home to go to "the city" for work, and returned to solve the dilemmas wives and mothers seemed unable to resolve. While occasionally screenwriters allowed women characters to vent their frustration at their never-ending round of domestic chores, the lack of appreciation for their work, and their limited options to change their lives, usually by the end of the half-hour show, women became resigned to their lives as housewives and embraced domesticity as what they and their families really wanted.

The Feminine Mystique

In many ways, the decade of the fifties represented a revival of the cult of domesticity that had characterized the first half of the nineteenth century, promoting many of the same ideas: the home is a woman's base of power and her true sphere for activity. The God-given task of all women became once again to be a wife and mother. Any deviation from that task would lead to unhappiness for women and the rest of society, including men and children. The education of women remained useful because it would help them rear children to be useful citizens of the nation. Once again as well, mothers were the religious leader of the family in that they were responsible for the morality of home and the religious upbringing of the children. Mothers achieved happiness and satisfaction only through service to others. A wife's task was to create a haven for her hard-working husband who worked hard in the public sphere. Feminists were neurotic, homosexual, envious of men, and wanted to be men. In the same way that the cult of domesticity and the ideals of True Womanhood were grounded in nineteenth-century white, middle-class America and assumed followers had an income that made it possible to pursue domesticity to the exclusion of earning a living, so did mid-twentieth-century domesticity. This time it had a different name: the *feminine mystique*.

The term feminine mystique was coined by Betty Friedan in her book of the same name published in 1963. It was a sociological survey of Friedan's former Smith College classmates in the 1950s. Friedan had earned her degree in 1942, then married and had children. While she had spent much of the 1940s writing for labor organizations, in her book she disguised or ignored that part of her life to focus instead on her life in suburbia. She emphasized that she had done much the same as many women of the period so that she could make a larger point: life in suburbia was stifling women by presenting them with a virtually unattainable role model.

Friedan had gone to graduate school to study sociology, but faced difficulties when the men in her department refused to take her or her work seriously because she was a woman. She also saw other women facing similar problems. Many of the women she interviewed during her research were bored with their suburban lives, the lack of challenge or chance to use their educations. Society recognized the problem Friedan described, that highly educated women were living limited lives and were denied any respect from society at large, despite the activities they undertook to raise the next generation safely and well. Instead, various experts told women that they "could desire no greater destiny than to glory in their own femininity. . . . All they had to do was devote their lives from earliest girlhood to finding a husband and bearing children."

According to the experts, devoting one's life to fulfilling one's femininity by marrying and bearing children was the highest goal that a woman could achieve. A woman who failed to accept that goal, who wished to have a career outside the home in addition to or instead of marriage and children, was always going to have and be a problem. Women who wanted careers were trying to be men, instead of housewives and mothers, their true destiny. Friedan argued that this belief—the feminine mystique—had limited women by declaring that those who did not live up to it were denying their femininity. She particularly objected to negative ways in which the image of a true American woman, one who believed and lived the feminine mystique, were promoted in popular culture.

One way the cultural myth of the feminine mystique was promulgated was by dressing it up using terms drawn from sociology, psychology, and psychiatry. One 1947 best-seller using such terminology was *Modern Woman: The Lost Sex* written by psychiatrist Marynia Farnham, MD, and sociologist Ferdinand Lundberg. In this antifeminist polemic, the authors divided mothers into two categories: those who produced normal children and those who produced neurotic children. Neurotic mothers produced neurotic children by rejecting them, overprotecting them, dominating them, and being overly affectionate toward them. Neurotic mothers also produced delinquents, children with difficult behavior problems, "some substantial" percentage of criminals, confirmed alcoholics, and general all-around troublemakers. The common factor that all neurotic mothers shared was the limited number of children they had—only one or two. The implication women could readily draw was that if they wished to avoid such problem children, they should have as many children as they could.

Popular Culture and Domesticity

The mass media also promulgated the feminine mystique in books, magazines, television, and the movies. In 1946, the Best Picture Oscar went to a movie called *The Best Years of Our Lives*. The story followed soldiers returning home from the war, looking forward to marriage and suburbia. The one character with a wife who did not want children divorced her in favor of the stay-at-home girl who did. Another Oscar-winning film, for best actress, featured Joan Crawford. In *Mildred Pierce*, Crawford played a successful career woman with a spoiled daughter. Mildred divorced her first husband, whom she emasculated by being more successful at her job than he was at his. The spoiled daughter then stole Mildred's second husband and later killed him, an unsubtle warning to women who put their careers before their families.

Women's magazines promoted home life—the elaboration of interiors, more complex cooking, more time-consuming chores, and home sewing. They printed interviews with doctors and psychologists on marriage and motherhood and published articles with titles such as "How to Help Your Husband Get Ahead" and "What Is a Well-Dressed Woman?" Romance novels promoted "happily ever after" endings. Best-sellers in the postwar era included advice books on homemaking, cooking, catching a husband, and raising a family. The most famous was Dr. Benjamin Spock's *Common Sense Book of Baby and Child Care*, first published in 1945, revised continually, translated into 39 languages, and selling over 50 million copies.

In the end, however, television had the greatest impact in promulgating the feminine mystique. The number one show in the nation in its time slot from 1952 to 1955 was *I Love Lucy*, starring Lucille Ball. Two-thirds of all Americans watching television at that moment were watching her situation comedy. The show had a domestic orientation—the story of a wife and her Cuban bandleader husband, played by Ball's real-life husband, Desi Arnaz. The wife in the show was childlike and economically dependent on her husband. The show revolved around Lucy's attempts to perform in her husband's club or take other jobs. Whenever Lucy tried to work, she failed because of incompetence, stupidity, or ignorance, or because she was discovered behind a disguise she had to assume in order to work because her husband did not think she should. To make society's point regarding working women even clearer, those women on the show who did work were portrayed as extremes: unattractive and bossy, or sexy, beautiful homewreckers.

Lucille Ball, ironically, was one of the most powerful women in Hollywood during and after the course of the show. She was an actress, singer, dancer, comic, radio star, a brilliant businesswoman, and the first woman to own a major studio. Her fans adored her and millions watched every week as she portrayed a woman incapable of functioning in a sphere other than the domestic one so many women occupied. Unlike the character she played, who had little interest in the world outside the domestic sphere, Lucille Ball's fame did not shield her from the larger political world. She was called before the HUAC to testify about her Communist Party membership in 1953. Apolitical, she had joined in 1936 to please her grandfather, a socialist. She disavowed any knowledge of the party in her testimony and provided, as historian Dan Georgakas put it, "garbled and meaningless testimony." Her husband Desi was quoted as saying the only thing red about Lucy was her hair and that was fake. Playing dumb—playing "feminine"—got her out of the HUAC hearing unscathed.

The feminine mystique, pervasive in so many ways, was hostile to powerful women and to feminism as well. Despite widespread activities by well-known women peace activists, the postwar period saw the collapse of the major political organizations for women. The leaders of the suffragist movement were retired or dead. The Women's Trade Union League disbanded in 1950. Goals many women's groups had fought had been achieved: the vote, the abolition of child labor, protective legislation. Another major goal of the feminists, the Equal Rights Amendment, had little support. Promoted by the National Woman's Party, approved by the Senate in 1950 and 1953, it was opposed in the House as well as by leading women's groups, such as the American Association for University Women (AAUW), the Young Women's Christian Association (YWCA), and the League of Women Voters, because it would mostly likely end protective legislation for women.

Even the White House had become less interested in women's issues. The New Deal's support for change that had come from Eleanor Roosevelt and the Democrats disappeared in 1952 with the election of the Republican president Dwight Eisenhower. Outgoing president Harry Truman's wife, Bess, had advised her husband behind the scenes. Eisenhower's wife, First Lady Mamie Eisenhower, however, was known better for her bangs and her love of pink than her activism. "Every woman over fifty," said Mrs. Eisenhower to the White House chief usher on her first day as first lady, "should stay in bed until noon," and so she did, reading and watching her favorite soap opera until lunchtime. Having spent years following after her husband and his military postings to various locales, Mamie Eisenhower was thrilled to settle into the White House and believed that women belonged primarily in the domestic sphere. While part of Mamie Eisenhower's reluctance to participate in politics was due to her health problems (heart disease, asthma, and Meniere's disease, which affected her balance), she also believed that women with careers were "unfeminine." In an article for *Today's Woman* magazine, she declared, "Our lives revolve around our men, and that is the way it should be. . . . Being a wife is the best career that life has to offer a woman. . . . [A] job that will take you out among people and give you extra money seems very desirable. But life will be far more rewarding if you do not yield to that temptation. If you do, you may find yourself with nothing but a job twenty years from now."

AFRICAN AMERICANS AND
THE CIVIL RIGHTS MOVEMENT

Where Mamie Eisenhower did take a stand on a public issue, unexpectedly, was with her quiet support for civil rights. African Americans had always resisted the constant pressure exerted by white society to limit their activities. Their successful participation in World War II, where they fought and died to free Europeans and Asians from the forces of Nazi Germany and Imperial Japan, combined with the rise of new leaders in the fifties to renew the fight for civil rights and against the segregation so institutionalized in the South.

Resistance to segregation and discrimination, as was true of resistance to slavery, took many forms. For some, like Mamie Eisenhower, it was largely symbolic, exemplified by her integration of the White House Easter Egg roll and her honorary membership of the National Council of Negro Women. For some in authority, such as her husband the president, it included forcing the integration of the Navy yards, veterans' hospitals, and public services in Washington, DC. For others, it might be an act fraught with the possibility of public humiliation, such as sneaking a drink from a "whites only" drinking fountain when no one was looking, or refusing to give up a seat on a bus—a seat paid for—to a white passenger, as Irene Morgan had done in 1946.

Desegregation and the Law

The civil rights movement in the second half of the twentieth century included both individual acts of resistance that blossomed into collective action, as well as concerted efforts in the courts to overturn *Plessy v. Ferguson*, the decision that legalized segregation as long as "separate but equal" facilities existed. In 1938, the Supreme Court ruled that an African American applicant to the law school of the University of Missouri had to be admitted, since there were no separate but equal law schools in Missouri for him to attend. In 1949, the Kansas State Supreme Court ruled that black children in a dilapidated ninety-year-old school building were not being treated equally with white students at a brand-new school and consequently should be admitted to the new school. In 1950, the U.S. Supreme Court ruled in favor of integration in similar cases in Texas and Oklahoma. *Morgan v. Virginia* (1946), with which this chapter began, overturned segregation in interstate transportation. *Smith v. Allwright* (1944) overturned the all-white primaries in the South. *Shelley v. Kraemer* (1948) struck down restrictive covenants that prevented homeowners from selling to minorities, restrictions all too common in postwar housing developments.

In 1954, Constance Motley, graduate of Columbia Law School and a lawyer for the NAACP's Legal Defense and Educational Fund (LDEF), worked with Thurgood Marshall, an NAACP lawyer and future Supreme Court justice, on the case of *Brown v. Board of Education of Topeka, Kansas,* the case that overturned legal segregation in schools. Motley had experience trying cases related to education in Alabama, Oklahoma, Texas, and Georgia. As a black woman lawyer practicing in the South, she faced discrimination and prejudice daily. LDEF lawyer Derrick Bell pointed out that to Southern male lawyers, African America women "were either mammies, maids or mistresses. None of them had ever dealt with a Negro woman on a peer basis, much less on a level of intellectual equality, which in this case, quickly became superiority." Motley, a native of Connecticut, found no housing but that provided by black Southerners sympathetic to her work, could not eat but in segregated restaurants, and typically was introduced or referred to by judges by her first name alone, all instances reflecting the casual white supremacist methods used in the South to oppress black Americans. In the end, however, she succeeded, not only in the *Brown* case, but in her career, becoming the first black woman federal court justice in the country.

The *Brown* decision in which Motley played such an important role revolved around Linda Brown of Topeka, Kansas, who wanted to go to a local school four blocks from her house, rather than the all-black school, a five-mile bus ride away. The local chapter of the NAACP helped the parents of Brown and thirteen other children file a class-action lawsuit against Topeka's Board of Education. When the case went to the Supreme Court, the justices ruled unanimously that the doctrine of separate but equal established by *Plessy v. Ferguson* was inherently unequal when it came to public schools. Topeka's elementary schools integrated peacefully; its middle and high schools were already integrated.

Desegregation and Nonviolent Protest

The court cases that culminated in *Brown* provided black and liberal white Americans with the legal ammunition to end segregation. Achieving that end, however, required popular protest as well. One example, the Montgomery Bus Boycott, began in December 1955 in Montgomery, Alabama. Rosa Parks had already been arrested and fined in 1943 for refusing to give up her seat to a white person when a bus driver ordered her to. In 1955, four other women, Aurelia Browder, Susie McDonald, Claudette Colvin, and Mary Louise Smith, were arrested on similar charges. These women would eventually file a lawsuit against the city. Parks tried a different tactic. After training in protest methods at Highlander Folk School in the summer, on December 1, 1955, she again refused to give up her seat in the colored section to a white man when the bus driver—the same who had done so in 1943, ironically— ordered her to. She was arrested and charged first with refusing to obey the orders of the bus driver and later with violating city ordinances that determined where she could sit based on her race. Black activist Edgar Daniel "E. D." Nixon, along with Virginia and Clifford Durr, liberal white supporters of civil rights who had urged Parks to go to Highlander, bailed the quiet, dignified, resolute woman out of jail. (See Primary Source 9-4.)

The night Rosa Parks was arrested, Jo Anne Robinson, an English professor at Alabama State College and president of the Women's Political

Council (WPC) of Montgomery, mimeographed 30,000 flyers calling for a bus boycott for distribution. Robinson's group, organized because the League of Women Voters in Montgomery remained all-white, had been active since 1946. In 1954, Robinson had written to the mayor threatening a boycott if the city's practices on buses did not change. The WPC not only wanted buses to stop at more corners as they did in white neighborhoods, but, more important, it wanted the city to eliminate the practice of blacks being forced to board and pay at the front, then get off the bus, walk to the back door, and enter from there, often being left behind after they had paid their fare. The mayor refused. Now, over a year later, came an opportunity for the black community to carry out its threat.

Some 200 volunteers distributed the flyers Robinson printed and the one-day boycott on December 5 was such a success that the president of the Montgomery Improvement Association, Dr. Martin Luther King Jr., called for it to continue. It did so, for more than a year. Seventeen thousand blacks formed car pools, walked, and received rides from sympathetic or, often, frustrated employers who wanted them doing their jobs. Dr. King promoted nonviolent, passive resistance to segregation laws, hoping to wear down those who opposed him and his followers, "by our capacity to suffer." Over one hundred people were arrested during the boycott, including Dr. King. His house and that of E. D. Nixon were bombed. The boycott spread to Tallahassee, Florida, where it lasted from May 1956 until 1958, and to Macon, Georgia, in 1962. Since African Americans were the majority of bus passengers, losing them as customers could bring a bus company to its knees.

On June 19, 1956, a federal district court ruled that segregated busing violated the Fourteenth Amendment, denying African Americans equal protection of the laws and due process. The class action lawsuit *Browder v. Gayle*, filed by the four women arrested prior to Parks, went to the Supreme Court and ended segregated busing. On November 13, 1956, the Supreme Court refused to overturn the lower court ruling. Montgomery and the state of Alabama appealed, but on December 20, the Supreme Court ordered integrated busing. After 381 days the boycott was over.

In her memoir, *The Montgomery Bus Boycott and the Women Who Started It*, JoAnn Robinson recalled that on the day of victory, "the black citizens were too tired to gloat, to lose their dignity in public rejoicing. The time was too sacred, the need prayerful, the masses tearful and filled with thanksgiving. For God had led them through the wilderness of discrimination and abusive treatment. . . . They could pay their fare as others did, take a seat, go to their destinations by bus with dignity and respect and be treated as human beings!" Rosa Parks recalled that she did not feel particularly victorious, either. "There still had to be a great deal to do."

Parks was correct. Segregation in public transportation had ended, but many other forms of segregation continued. The nonviolent resistance black Montgomerians practiced during the boycott proved difficult for white authorities to overcome, but the tactic took time. Black Americans grew impatient and sought a quicker way to end segregation. In January 1957, Dr. King and his followers met in Atlanta and formed the Southern Christian

THE SOUTHERN BELLE AND CIVIL RIGHTS

Southern white women who participated in the civil rights movement overcame not only racism but the ever-present mythic figure of the Southern Belle. Virginia Durr attended Wellesley College in the 1920s, a Southern belle and a bigot. There she learned racial tolerance and intellectual open-mindedness at the integrated tables of the college dining halls. After her marriage,

she and her husband worked in Washington as New Dealers. In 1938, Virginia helped found the Southern Conference on Human Welfare, and worked with Eleanor Roosevelt to lobby Congress to abolish the poll tax, designed to keep blacks from voting. The Durrs returned to Alabama in 1951 and joined the NAACP, wholeheartedly supporting the Montgomery Bus Boycott.

Leadership Conference (SCLC) to capitalize on the success of the boycott and coordinate efforts to continue the fight to desegregate America. The voter registration drive of the SCLC began shortly after Congress passed the Civil Rights Act of 1957. The act established a Civil Rights Commission and a Civil Rights Division in the Justice Department of the federal government. The latter would focus its work on cases of African Americans being prevented from voting or registering to vote. The SCLC seized the initiative and announced they would register 2 million voters.

Women in the SCLC included South Carolinian Septima Clark, who had worked with Thurgood Marshall and the NAACP to equalize teachers' salaries in South Carolina so that black teachers were paid the same as whites. Her salary tripled after the success of the court case in which she had participated. Interested in activities such as providing health care for poor children and providing scholarships for deserving students, Clark worked with various benevolent organizations, particularly interracial ones such as the Community Chest, as well as groups such as the Metropolitan Council of Negro Women. In 1954, after the *Brown* decision, Clark was fired from her teaching job for refusing to relinquish her membership in the NAACP. She was hired by Highlander Folk School as director of the workshops that would train so many civil rights activists. She viewed the work of the SCLC as parallel to her work with Highlander, where she worked until the state shut the school down in 1961 for making moonshine (illegal alcohol), selling chewing gum, and being entirely too successful at training activists who helped to register African Americans to vote.

Nonviolence Provokes Violent Resistance

While protesters against segregation led by King and the SCLC practiced nonviolence, those who resisted desegregation did not. African Americans continued efforts to integrate schools, assisted by the Supreme Court's ruling in 1955 that such integration should proceed "with all deliberate speed."

About her life as a Southern white woman activist, Durr liked the description in the foreword that Studs Terkel wrote for her autobiography.

"[T]here were three ways for a well-brought up young Southern white woman to go. She could be the actress, playing out the stereotype of the Southern belle. Gracious to 'the colored help,' flirtatious to her powerful father-in-law, and offering a sweet, winning smile to the world. In short, going with the wind.

"If she had a spark of independence or worse, creativity, she could go crazy on the dark, shadowy street traveled by more than one stunning Southern belle.

"Or she could be the rebel. She could step outside the magic circle, abandon privilege, and challenge this way of life. Ostracism, bruises of all sorts, and defamation would be her lot. Her reward would be a truly examined life. And a world she would otherwise never have known."

Source: Virginia Foster Durr, *Outside the Magic Circle: The Autobiography of Virginia Foster Durr*, ed. Hollinger F. Barnard (Tuscaloosa: University of Alabama Press, 1985), xi.

They met violent resistance in every state. In Little Rock, Arkansas, Elizabeth Eckford was one of nine students determined to desegregate the local high school. Governor Orval Faubus, who had actually desegregated public transportation and investigated integrating schools, responded to his white supremacist constituency. He declared that Central High School would remain segregated and that "blood will run in the streets" should any black students attempt to enter the school. Faubus called out the Arkansas National Guard to prevent Eckford and her classmates from entering the school, and an unruly mob greeted the students, jeering and spitting on them, shouting and threatening them. Eckford, alone because she had not been told her classmates were meeting together before attending school, remembered looking for a kind face in the mob and finding none, hearing only the words they shouted, "No nigger bitch is going to get in our school! Get out of here!" She fled to a nearby bus stop where she waited to ride a bus to safety. Newspapers published searing images: a fifteen -year-old Eckford carefully carrying her books as she walked through the crowd while behind her a young white woman shouts at her, her face twisted with hate; in another, a crowd of angry whites surrounded her as she waited quietly on the bus bench. The photographs brought home to the rest of America visual evidence of both the nonviolence Eckford practiced, and of the violence she faced.

President Eisenhower responded to the crisis by sending in federal troops to be sure the students safely arrived at the school. The troops remained in Little Rock for the entire school year, and the governor shut the schools down the following year. Not until 1959 did the schools reopen as the courts ruled against attempts in both Arkansas and Virginia to cut off state funding to public schools. Only the Deep South continued to hold out against integration. In 1960, six-year-old Ruby Bridges was guarded by federal marshals on her way to integrate her elementary school in New Orleans, Louisiana. The sight of the tiny girl escorted by white male guards inspired Norman Rockwell's famous painting of her called *The Problem We All Live With*.

INTEGRATION OF HIGHER EDUCATION IN THE DEEP SOUTH Surrounded by men, including National Guard troops, photographers, and Deputy U.S. Attorney General Nicholas Katzenbach, twenty-year-old Vivian Malone approaches Foster Auditorium to register for classes at the University of Alabama, the first African American woman to do so.

Bridges got in the door of her school safely, but other attempts at desegregating educational institutions were accompanied by violence. A federal court in Georgia ordered that Charlayne Hunter and Hamilton Holmes be admitted to the University of Georgia in 1961. Hunter, who lived in a dormitory on campus, survived a riot outside her dormitory where a mob smashed windows. She and Holmes were suspended for their own safety, and only reinstated after another lawsuit. James Meredith challenged the University of Mississippi's refusal to admit him and won in 1962, attending after federal troops arrived to keep him safe. A riot that killed 2, injured 160, and left 28 federal marshals shot did not prevent him from attending. In 1963, Vivian Malone became the first black woman to attend the University of Alabama, despite segregationist governor George Wallace's claim that he would not allow her in. A man who had vowed "Segregation now, segregation tomorrow, segregation forever!" at his inauguration, Wallace literally blocked her entrance to the school with his body until the federal government stepped in and he was forced to accept integration of the university. One day later, Medgar Evers, a prominent civil rights leader who had helped Meredith enter the University of Mississippi, was shot to death in his driveway while his wife and children watched from their home. His killer, a white supremacist, was finally convicted thirty-one years after the murder.

Women students were an important part of the civil rights movement in the South. Not only did they break the segregation barrier at universities, many of them took time away from their studies to protest segregation in other settings. In Greensboro, North Carolina, four students at North Carolina A & T conducted a "sit-in" at a lunch counter in a Woolworth's store that was willing to take blacks' money for merchandise but refused to allow them to eat at the in-house lunch counter. The young men were soon joined by African American women students from nearby Bennett College, as well as white women students from the University of North Carolina Women's College. Spelman College student Ruby Doris Smith organized Atlanta area students in sit-ins across Atlanta. By the spring of 1960, over 2,000 students had been arrested in demonstrations, boycotts, sit-ins, and other forms of resistance to segregation. Students in other parts of the country showed their support for desegregation by protesting at northern branches of national stores and chains that discriminated against blacks in the South.

While numbers of African American women participated in these acts of resistance, most played a supportive role, allowing black men to take the lead. Ella Baker, cofounder of In-Friendship, a group that aided victims of racial terrorism, epitomized the difficulties that many activist women experienced in the civil rights movement. King asked Baker to go to Atlanta to work for the SCLC in its Crusade for Citizenship, an educational program designed to help increase voter numbers. Baker went and worked, but clashed with ambitious young men in the movement who did not appreciate her ardor, her booming voice, her bluntness, nor her differing view of tactics. By mid-April, Baker had helped lead a conference at Shaw University and helped give birth to a new organization, the Student Nonviolent Coordinating Committee (SNCC), made up of students determined to forge their own paths and direct their own projects. SNCC preferred using nonviolence to achieve its goals, but also supported direct action, confrontation, and increased militancy if necessary. Baker pointed out that integrating lunch counters was all well and good, but that the movement was "bigger than a hamburger." It was also bigger than any leader. Baker believed in sharing power and participatory democracy, and often grew frustrated at the top-down approach of the SCLC. Nevertheless, the two organizations collaborated for years.

In the spring of 1961, SNCC activists undertook *freedom rides* to southern states to protest continuing segregation. Interracial groups of students shared bus seats to continue the process of integrating public transportation. White violence against freedom riders included mobs firebombing the buses, beating the escaping riders, and arresting them. The federal government sent in 400 federal marshals, but riders were still arrested and served time. SNCC members moved on to continue voter registration efforts in Albany, Georgia, but were stymied in their efforts to provoke the kind of response that would enable the federal intervention that the movement relied upon in order to generate real change. The activists moved on to Birmingham, Alabama, where, in 1963, after sit-ins and marches, SCLC leaders King and Ralph Abernathy were arrested.

King's arrest gave him time to pen a thoughtful treatise on the importance of direct action against racism. "All segregation statutes are unjust," he wrote in his famous *Letter from Birmingham Jail*, "because segregation distorts the soul and damages the personality. It gives the segregator a false sense of superiority and the segregated a false sense of inferiority." The SCLC, worried that the movement would lose momentum with Dr. King in jail, allowed a "children's crusade" in Birmingham on May 2 and 3, 1963, after training high school and college youth in nonviolent techniques. More than 1,000 young people marched on May 2 and were arrested. Even more showed up the next day to do the same, and the local sheriff, T. Eugene "Bull" Connor, ordered police dogs, clubs, cattle prods, and fire hoses turned on the unarmed marchers. Newspaper photographers and, more importantly, television news cameras captured the images of snarling dogs attacking women and men, and fire hoses, held by southern white men, knocking African Americans off their feet. The resulting outrage was international in scope. Martin Luther King's wife, Coretta Scott King, recovering from the birth of the couple's fourth child, called President John F. Kennedy and his brother Robert, the attorney general, for help. She feared that King would never leave jail alive. The Kennedys used their powers to force the city to meet with the federal attorney for civil rights to negotiate a settlement. On May 10, the SCLC and Birmingham's business community reached an agreement to desegregate public accommodations, to release jailed protesters, to set up a committee to oversee hiring practices in the city, and to ensure that black and white leaders would communicate to avoid further demonstrations.

The white community responded with violence to the "Birmingham Truce," bombing King's brother's house. President Kennedy sent in 3,000 federal troops to prevent further disturbances. The civil rights victory in the deepest part of the Deep South, and in Birmingham, a place King had once called "the most segregated city in America," provided inspiration for future laborers in the cause. In August 1963, civil rights leaders called for a March on Washington for Jobs and Freedom. Hundreds of thousands of marchers, perhaps half a million total, descended on the capitol city. Organizers originally planned to speak on economic issues, but a proposed civil rights bill before Congress changed the focus of the march. Speakers included the male leaders of the movement: Dr. King, Roy Wilkins of the NAACP, James Farmer of the Congress for Racial Equality (CORE), John Lewis of SNCC, Whitney Young Jr. of the Urban League, and A. Philip Randolph, president of the Brotherhood of Sleeping Car Porters.

Women of the movement had less prominent roles that day, but were praised in a "Tribute to Negro Women Fighters for Freedom" that introduced to the crowd Rosa Parks, Daisy Bates (the NAACP leader in Arkansas who organized the Little Rock students), Diane Nash (a SNCC leader from Tennessee), Gloria Richardson (a leader from Cambridge, Maryland), and to the widow of a man killed for trying to register to vote, a woman known only as Mrs. Herbert Lee. Tribute was paid as well to the absent Myrlie Evers, widow of Medgar Evers, slain two months before. In her speech to the crowd, Daisy Bates pledged to the leaders of the movement that women would join hands with the men to fight for civil liberties. "We will kneel-in, we will sit-in, until we can eat at any counter of the United States. . . . [W]e will walk until we can take our children to any school in the United States. . . . [W]e will lie-in, if necessary, until every Negro in American can vote," she declared. Singers Marian Anderson, Eva Jessye, and Mahalia Jackson provided music, and sixty-year-old entertainer and international star Josephine Baker proclaimed it "the happiest day of my life." The afternoon ended with a stirring speech by Dr. King, "I Have a Dream," which he delivered extemporaneously, departing from his prepared remarks to speak as a preacher would to a crowd of believers. His dream of racial harmony was saluted by the crowd, the press, and many in the nation. His words and his work, supported by countless women and men, paved the way for federal civil rights legislation to end racial discrimination.

ACTIVISM IN ETHNIC COMMUNITIES

The civil rights movement, revivified when ethnic minorities returned from their service in World War II, included other activists: Mexican Americans, Puerto Ricans, Native Americans, and Asian Americans. With similar goals, using similar tactics, ethnic minorities achieved similar results during the 1950s.

Mexican Americans Protest in the West and Southwest

As was true for African Americans, Mexican Americans returned to the United States after World War II with a new sense that they deserved better treatment. Over 350,000 Mexican Americans (Chicanos) had served in the war, and they had suffered proportionately greater casualties than any other group, as well as winning proportionately more medals for their service. During the war, thousands of Mexicans were brought into the country to work—some in well-paying war industries, but mostly as agricultural workers, living in appalling conditions, often without toilets, drinking water, or water for bathing. In 1943, outright attacks on minorities led to the so-called Zoot Suit riots in Los Angeles, where servicemen and civilians attacked young Mexican, Chicano, Filipino, and African American men, beating them and stripping them of their "zoot suits"—the fashionable and distinctive outfits they wore. The California governor had investigated and found substandard living conditions contributed to the unrest. Mexican Americans had long faced limited educational opportunities, discrimination in housing and employment, and racism. Activists seeking to end widespread discrimination against them founded the Community Service Organization (CSO) in California, and began its legal challenges. In 1947, California banned the segregation of Mexican, Asian, and Native American children into separate schools.

The CSO listed its goals in California in letters to the community: "improve living conditions, protect group and individual interests, protest, remedy and prevent violations of human rights, and provide a medium for social expression, leadership development, and inter-group cooperation." Much of its work focused on civil rights. With chapters in at least thirty-five different cities and with thousands of members, half of them women, the group focused on registration drives and voting rights. By 1949, their efforts had elected Edward Roybal, the first Latino to serve on the Los Angeles City Commission. As the organization grew, it established networks with other groups such as the AFL-CIO, and the Quakers at the American Friends Committee. It also enjoyed praise in newspapers, such as the *New York Herald* and the *Washington Post*.

Chicanas were the backbone of the CSO, raising funds, using their clerical skills to run meetings, record activities, make flyers, and stuff envelopes, feeding the crowds attending meetings, even campaigning for their husbands when they ran for office. Other women served as leaders. Hope Mendoza, an experienced labor agitator, used her skills advocating in labor disputes, as well as teaching CSO members about fair employment practices. The most famous woman in the CSO, former teacher Dolores Huerta, joined in 1955 after deciding she could do more for migrant workers by organizing them to fight for their civil rights than by teaching their children, who were often too hungry to focus on education. She moved to Sacramento to work as a labor lobbyist to the state legislature, founding the Agricultural Workers Association in 1960. In 1962, she formed the National Farm Workers Association (later the United Farm Workers) with Cesar Chavez, and they began a five-year boycott of California table grapes to try to convince the industry to treat workers fairly.

Huerta's career was remarkable. Latino mothers faced cultural pressures much stronger than those of Anglo women when it came to activism or work outside the home. Huerta had eleven children, and despite mothering them successfully, her two ex-husbands criticized her activism and blamed her actions outside the home for the end of their marriages. But in the *barrios* that were home to the Hispanics and Latinos in California, women activists such as Huerta proved invaluable registering new voters, conducting petition drives to improve public facilities such as sidewalks and streetlights in their neighborhoods, and lobbying for vaccinations and free hearing tests for Latino children in their schools. With so many Latina women active in the CSO, the organization was able to incorporate traditional women's issues into the goals it wished to achieve.

Another activist group, the G.I. Forum, was founded in Texas by Dr. Hector Garcia and Molly Galvan in 1947. The forum fought for the rights of returning Mexican American veterans. It wanted desegregated schools and hospitals and the abolition of the white primary and poll taxes that kept many Chicanos from voting. Working to provide scholarships for children, and seeking to influence the communities in which members lived through civic participation, Galvan and his followers also organized G.I. Forums in Colorado, as well as Utah, where members challenged the federal government's discriminatory hiring practices at Hill Air Force Base.

Beyond such organizations, Latinos and Hispanics also used labor strikes to protest segregation and discrimination as well as working conditions. In 1951 in Hanover, New Mexico, Empire Zinc mine workers struck for better working conditions. When the company invoked the federal Taft-Hartley Act of 1947 that forbade strikers from picketing, the wives of the strikers took up the picket line. When arrested, the women filled the jails and the men stayed home to care for the children. The company, nonplussed by women picketers who would not give up even if arrested, capitulated. Men who experienced firsthand the difficulty of caring for children under the substandard living conditions their wives faced at home, particularly the lack of running water, told the union to demand improvements in housing for workers' families. As a result, the company desegregated housing, the theater, and the pool, and provided running water to the Mexican Americans' houses as they had already done for whites (see Primary Source 9-5).

Puerto Rican Activism in the East and Midwest

Puerto Rican women and men, citizens of the United States since 1917, also participated in World War II—200 women served in the Women's Army Camps; 65,000 men served in Latin America, North Africa, and Europe. Those who returned rejoined their families, primarily in urban areas in the East and Midwest. Puerto Ricans had a long history of forming community associations to provide both aid and opportunities for socializing. Church groups and secular organizations such as the *Casita Maria* and the Puerto Rico Civic Club provided gathering places for thousands of Puerto Rican women who earned their wages in the textile and cigar factories in cities such as New York. Thousands of Puerto Rican women were hired after World War II, and while many belonged to labor unions to try to protect their rights, many more did piecework, now called "section work," to make a living.

By 1960, Puerto Rican women operated 25 percent of the sewing machines in New York City's garment industry. Many also worked for employers who paid less than the legal minimum wage in cramped workplaces called sweatshops, which were nonunion firetraps, with no safety features to protect workers. Dolores Juarbe, employed in a sweatshop, recalled the working conditions under which she labored. "There was not any union there. In that shop you had to sew, as fast as you could. And everyone smoked. The shop was in a basement. Once in a while the fire department would pay a little visit. The boss told us to stop smoking, that the fire department was on the way. The alerter heard that they were coming, you know, she used to pay them off. So then, they could knock real loud on the door: bam bam bam! And all the cigarettes would disappear." In contrast, in union shops where women served as chairs and organizers, working conditions improved. Rampant discrimination, however, both racial and sexual, kept women at the lowest rank in most union shops, as well as at the lowest pay rates.

Other Puerto Rican communities developed as contract labor workers, recruited by private companies as well as government organizations, arrived in cities such as Chicago; Buffalo; Philadelphia; Milwaukee; Gary, Indiana; and Camden, New Jersey. In Chicago, a private employment company agreed to recruit domestic and foundry workers for Puerto Rico's

THE SALT OF THE EARTH

Anita and Lorenzo Torrez were picketer and striker, respectively, at Empire Mine. A film based on their experiences, Salt of the Earth, *was produced in 1954 by filmmakers black-listed by Sen. Joe McCarthy's anti-Communist witch-hunts. In a 2003 interview with a journalist, the Torreses described the working conditions that led to the strike.*

"The conditions were harsh. Zinc mining is underground mining. The miners were Mexican Americans. We came back from World War II with the idea of democracy in our heads, and we found the same discrimination we faced before. We rebelled against it. We used the union to break the discrimination that had existed all along. We were determined to break through and be treated equally.

"This was a fight against racism and for equality. The union had 5,000 members. It was an amalgamated local of the Mine, Mill and Smelter Workers at six mines.

"Even the pay lines were segregated, one for the Anglos, the other for the Mexicanos. Housing was segregated. The movie theaters were segregated, with Mexicanos on one side and Anglos on the other. We couldn't sit together. The swimming pool was segregated. There was one day a week that the Mexicanos could go swimming, and then they would drain the pool and refill it.

"The Mexicanos were fed up. The Anglos were in the skilled jobs. The underground work was for the Mexicanos or African Americans—the dirtiest, the

Department of Labor. The women brought from the island to fill domestic jobs on the mainland were often under age. Wages were low, and from the $60 a month (plus room and board) that they earned, the agency deducted $10 a month to pay for their tickets from Puerto Rico as well as an additional $8.33 a month to bank for a return trip. Labor contracts did not limit hours, and many young women complained they were working fifteen hour days at wages far below the prevailing ones, as well as being transferred from one employer to another with little or no notice. Workers' complaints made their way back to Puerto Rico, and the Puerto Rican Assembly passed laws to limit these abuses. Women relied on the publicity that was generated by government reports to improve their working conditions because most unions were of little help, as was true for many women workers who did contract labor.

Native American Activism and Resistance

Native Americans had contributed to the war effort with nearly 50,000 men and several hundred women in the WACs, WAVES, Army Nurse Corps, and even the Marines, where Minnie Spotted-Wolf became the first Native American woman to serve in the Corps. Another 12,000 Native American women worked in war defense plants. Women left on the reservations took over traditional men's jobs, and many contributed money to the government. Alaskan women bought war bonds with earnings from trapping.

roughest jobs. Native American Indians, who had been brought in by the company to work the mines during the labor shortage of World War II, had been forced to move back to the reservations. The company pushed them out and tore down their housing after the war.

"[About the women's role in the strike:] if there was no picket line, the strike would be lost. There was a lot of discussion within the union. Someone said the women were not the ones on strike, so they could take over the picketing. Either you give up the strike or bring the women in. Some thought it was the only way, but others were opposed. The word leaked out that the women were going to picket, so we, the women, said, why not? A lot of them came to the picket line out of curiosity. Once they got there, they decided to join the picket lines.

"The law and the company were surprised and shocked that this was happening. They thought these women were crazy, that they can't survive, they can't last, it's not the proper thing for women to be doing. They took us to jail. As time went on, the company tried to start a 'back to work' movement. They hired people from out of town to cross our lines. That created violence. It had been decided that the men would not get involved, so women were going to fight it, the best way they knew how. When the women wouldn't get up, the police arrested them, but more women came to take their places. The jail was full."

Source: Libero Della Piana, Interview with Anita and Lorenzo Torrez, "History-makers Reflect on Salt of the Earth: Even More Relevant Now," *People's World*, www.peoplesworld.org/history-makers-reflect-on-salt-of-the-earth-even-more-relevant-now/.

The Red Cross and other volunteer organizations benefited from Native women's participation as well. While some Indian groups resisted any participation—the Iroquois challenged the right of the U.S. government to draft them—others participated at many levels. The Navajo basket weavers, for instance, signed a resolution that outlawed the use of the swastika, a broken cross motif that had been used for centuries by the weavers, but was later adopted by the Nazis as a symbol of their hatred.

After the war, however, Native Americans soon found themselves in worse straits than those they had occupied before the war. In 1945, John Collier left the Bureau of Indian Affairs, and the government decided to settle Indian claims against the government once and for all with an Indian Claims Commission. Collier's successor, Dillon S. Myer, the man in charge of relocating Japanese into internment camps during World War II, took office in 1950. He was determined to break Native Americans' reliance on the federal government. He planned to terminate the federal services provided to Indian tribes, and to relocate them to urban areas. Jurisdiction over Indian lands would pass to the state and local governments, and federal contracts, particularly for timber and other natural resources, would be terminated. So would the social services, such as hospitals, schools and other services paid for by those contracts.

It would be years before tribal communities recovered even partially from termination policies. Relocation efforts also failed. Many Native Americans had moved from reservations after the Indian Allotment Act (see Chapter 6) put them on small farms, and cities such as Denver, Chicago, Minneapolis, Los Angeles, and elsewhere had growing numbers of Native American blue-collar workers. Between 1952 and 1960, however, the Bureau of Indian Affairs, gave incentives to Indians to move to cities—one-way bus tickets, relocation centers, job training, free medical care, and a subsistence allowance until they were settled in. But the contrast between rural reservation life and the frenetic, capitalist competition of the cities made it difficult for Native Americans to survive and prosper.

Native Americans protested termination and relocation, forming support groups for the displaced "urban Indians" such as Chicago's All-Tribes American Indian Center and St. Augustine's Center for American Indians. The most important activist group was the National Congress of American Indians (NCAI), begun in 1944. In 1954, under the leadership of Executive Director Dakota Helen Peterson and Executive Secretary Cherokee Ruth Bronson, the NCAI stopped the federal government's termination and relocation program. The organization's Emergency Conference on Federal Legislation, held in Washington in late February, educated both Congress and the public about tribal opposition to termination, as well as providing an opportunity for Native Americans to construct a Declaration of Indian Rights. One outcome of this conference was a new policy of informed consent. Congress had to notify tribes and gain their consent before passing any legislation that would affect their rights.

The NCAI also lobbied for voting rights to oppose government dam-building on Indian lands. The dams flooded reservation lands and drove Indians away, destroying their traditional communities. The Yankton, Crow, Cheyenne, Seneca, Cherokee, and Mohawk nations all lost these battles against the federal government, but Native American resistance continued. Younger Indians, led by Mohawk Shirley Hill Witt, formed the National Indian Youth Council (NIYC) in 1961, a student organization that paralleled many of the efforts of the NCAI. Both groups fought against government policies that assumed, yet again, that Indians needed to assimilate to survive in America.

Asian American Women Activists

Asians and Asian Americans faced profound discrimination both during World War II and afterward. Many Americans dismissed all Asians as enemies during the war, and with the advent of Communist China, their racism knew few bounds. Despite changes after the war that included interracial marriage, relaxed immigration laws, and a growing population of Asians in America, most white Americans continued to expect that all ethnic groups would assimilate into American culture, and regarded those who did not assimilate with suspicion.

Japanese Americans refused to be branded traitors simply because of their race, both during World War II and afterward. Dillon Meyer's successful internment of thousands of Japanese in internment camps over the course of the war ended before the war itself did. Several Japanese Americans challenged their internment in court, and Mitsuye Endo, a twenty-two-year-old clerk in the Motor Vehicle Department of California, volunteered to serve as a test case. Like Rosa Parks, whose sterling character made her the perfect choice to battle segregation, Endo, who spoke no Japanese, had never been to Japan, and had a brother fighting in the American army, was the perfect choice to challenge the constitutionality, as well as the simple illogic, of internment. Her lawyer, James Purcell, filed a writ of *habeas corpus* in 1942, demanding that the government either release her or show the threat that she posed to the nation. Fearing a Supreme Court showdown, the government offered to release Endo anywhere but in the restricted military area of California. She refused the offer, and stayed imprisoned for another two years until December 1944, when the court ruled in *Ex Parte Endo* that loyal American citizens could not be held in detention camps against their will. She was released, but the legality of the internment of other Japanese was not decided by that case. By January 1945, internees had begun to return to their homes, and eventually the courts ruled that native-born citizens, such as Japanese Americans, could not be turned into enemy aliens.

Returning home, internees faced continued racism, discrimination, and attacks, even after V-J Day in August 1945. In Santa Ana, California, Mary Masuda, who had spent two and a half years in a relocation camp and whose brother had been killed in the service fighting in Italy, faced threats from locals. General Joseph Stilwell went to Masuda's home in person to award her brother's medal, the Distinguished Service Cross, in December 1945, in a well-publicized visit attempting to restore the peace and to prevent further incidents. The government also provided some remuneration for Japanese Americans who had lost everything when they were forced into the camps. Truman signed the Japanese American Evacuation Claims Act in 1948, which provided $38 million to reimburse those who were able to file claims, working out to about ten cents on the dollar for their losses. Many Japanese Americans never recovered economically from the war. Not until 1988 would the government apologize for the internment and offer reparations to the survivors.

After the war, when Asian women from other countries arrived in America, they also faced discrimination. In 1945, Truman signed the War Brides Act, temporarily allowing members of the armed forces who had married women they had met overseas to send for their wives. Unlike women from Europe who faced little resentment, Chinese, Japanese, Korean, and Filipino war brides faced a great deal. Some 72,700 women arrived from Asian countries between 1947 and 1964. In 1952, however, responding to the rising fear of communism, Congress passed the McCarren-Walter Act, adding Asians to the quota system that determined who was able to immigrate to America. The legislation further restricted Asian immigration. In all other instances, immigrants were defined by their country of origin. Asians, however, were defined by their race, thus limiting the total number who could immigrate to the United States.

The increase in the numbers and the visibility of Asian women in America worried many Americans, particularly given Japan's recent enmity, the fall of China to communism in 1949, and the Korean War, which lasted from 1950 to 1953. Writers for popular magazines such as the *Saturday Evening Post* called attention to the presence of war brides with articles such as "They're Bringing Home Japanese Wives," pointing out the difficulties Japanese women had adapting to cooking and cleaning in the American style. The article went on to examine whether white Americans were ready to "help them along." Some white Americans were. The Red Cross, for example, offered classes to aid assimilation, as did the YWCA, which had a War Brides program. Others were not. Racial restrictions on property sales, threats against Asian brides brought to American homes, and hand-wringing by the press continued. But Asians' decisions to assimilate and the lesser threat of their presence, compared to the more worrisome prospect of African American integration, eventually drove much of the racism against Asians to more subtle levels.

Changes in immigration policies and wartime marriages meant that the ratio of Asian women to men became more nearly equal. No longer was there a large male community of "bachelor societies," as had been the case after Chinese women were prohibited from immigrating to the United States in the nineteenth century. The shift in population meant more Asians could marry within their race if they desired. When California, the state with the largest Asian population, repealed its antimiscegenation law in 1948, marriage outside their race was easier for Asians as well. Consequently, Asians' ability to choose assimilation or not was easier for them to make. Given white American society's expectations of assimilation, and the pressure and hostility directed at Asians who chose otherwise, many Asians chose to deny their heritage. "I content to lose my Japanese blood stream in America," said Sachiko Pfieffer, war bride of a Chicago butcher. "I gonna die in America. This is my home forever."

A NEW FRONTIER

The years between the end of World War II and the election of 1960 had been ones of fear and uncertainty for many Americans, despite rising prosperity over the course of a decade and a half. Americans feared atomic warfare and fought to win the Cold War with the Soviet Union. Communism seemed so powerful there, as well as in China and Korea, that Americans feared Communists would infiltrate and corrupt American institutions. In domestic affairs, activists seemed determined to overturn white Americans' traditional positions so that they too could participate in the system. Resisting such efforts, many white Americans turned to a presidential candidate that promised to assuage their fears: Richard Nixon.

The conservative Republican nominee opposed many of the reforms put in place during the preceding decades, and enthusiastically supported the hunt for communists, even where they were not found. Democratic nominee John F. Kennedy, in contrast, was young, inexperienced, photogenic, and sold to American voters, claimed his wealthy father Joe, "like soap flakes." Kennedy's youth and charisma outshone Nixon's experience and tradition, particularly on television, the new medium of political communication. During the first televised debate between presidential candidates, 70 million viewers watched an attractive, poised Kennedy debate with a sweaty, nervous Nixon, sporting a heavy five o'clock shadow. Kennedy won the debate and his popularity continued to rise for the rest of the campaign, particularly after he came out in support of Martin Luther King Jr., who had been arrested in Atlanta for attempting to integrate a restaurant. The black vote helped Kennedy win.

Kennedy's speech accepting his party's nomination praised the past but focused on the future. Americans were standing, Kennedy said, at the edge of a "new frontier . . . a frontier of unknown opportunities and perils—a frontier of unfulfilled hopes and threats." He continued this theme at his inaugural address, saying "Ask not what your country can do for you—ask what you can do for your country" as he sought to shift Americans toward the issues that the country needed to resolve. The new administration had no election mandate—the election was the closest ever in American history to that point—but Kennedy's youth, optimism, and vitality inspired many throughout the nation to commit themselves to bettering the lives of those less fortunate.

The unrest in the South and continuing confrontations over the pace of integration prompted Kennedy, urged by his brother, Attorney General Robert Kennedy, to support Dr. King, particularly after attacks against civil rights marchers in Birmingham in May of 1963. He even endorsed a civil rights bill that would enforce rights guaranteed by the Constitution, but the bill did not make it through Congress. There were other areas that Kennedy pushed for change. He promised to nominate a woman to the cabinet, where only two women had served—Frances Perkins as secretary of labor under Franklin Roosevelt and Oveta Culp Hobby, secretary of health, education, and welfare under President Eisenhower. He failed to do so.

Kennedy, who retained a reputation as a ladies' man, retained as well the prejudices against women held by men of his class and time. In 1961, addressing a group of women delegates assigned to the United Nations, he responded awkwardly to a comment from a delegate from Burma. She had taken advantage of the president's welcoming remarks to suggest that when a woman was elected president of the United States, she would no doubt welcome the men delegates to the UN. Her unexpected comment met with his response, "I'm always rather nervous about how you talk about women who are active in politics, whether they want to be talked about as women or as politicians, but I want you to know that we are grateful to have you as both today." His gratitude, however, did not extend to inviting women to participate in his administration.

The President's Commission on the Status of Women

Kennedy's difficulty in seeing women as both women and politicians may have accounted for his failure to appoint women in roles of power. He did

PRESIDENT KENNEDY'S CALL FOR A NATIONAL COMMISSION ON THE STATUS OF WOMEN

President Kennedy's rationale for establishing a commission to examine the status of women in the country was laid out in Executive Order 10980 on December 14, 1961.

"WHEREAS prejudices and outmoded customs act as barriers to the full realization of women's basic rights which should be respected and fostered as part of our Nation's commitment to human dignity, freedom, and democracy; and

"WHEREAS measures that contribute to family security and strengthen home life will advance the general welfare; and

"WHEREAS it is in the national interest to promote the economy, security, and national defense through the most efficient and effective utilization of the skills of all persons, and

"WHEREAS in every period of national emergency women have served

not name a woman to his cabinet despite his promises, but made Elizabeth Rudel Smith U.S. treasurer. He also named Sarah Hughes as the first woman federal district judge in Texas, and appointed opera star Marian Anderson as a trustee of the American Freedom from Hunger Foundation. Most importantly, on December 14, 1961, Kennedy created the President's Commission on the Status of Women, chaired by Eleanor Roosevelt. In his statement setting out the rationale for the commission, Kennedy praised women participants in the public sphere for bringing "sensitivity to human needs," as well as "opposition to selfish and corrupt purposes," as the early suffragist leaders had promised they would. He also declared that women should not have to work unless they wanted to, nor be forced to give up their jobs "when unemployment rises or war ends." He hoped that the commission would reveal "what remains to be done to demolish prejudices and outmoded customs which act as barriers to the full partnership of women in our democracy" (see Primary Source 9-6).

As chairperson of the commission, Eleanor Roosevelt brought years of experience to the process of analyzing women's status in America. She described the commission's first meeting in her column "My Day," saying that Kennedy had joked that he had appointed the commission in self-defense. May Craig, a feminist newspaper reporter, often asked Kennedy in press briefings what he had done for women that day. On this day, wrote Roosevelt, Kennedy had appointed Esther Peterson, head of the Women's Bureau, to the commission. In the Women's Bureau, Peterson, a union activist who had organized teachers' unions and worked for the Amalgamated Clothing Workers of America, found herself with adequate funding, twenty-six nationally known leaders (fifteen women and eleven men), and participants who communicated their findings back to their organizations. The real goal of the commission, reported Roosevelt, was to ensure that with distinction in widely varied capacities but thereafter have been subject to treatment as a marginal group whose skills have been inadequately utilized; and

"WHEREAS women should be assured the opportunity to develop their capacities and fulfill their aspirations on a continuing basis irrespective of national exigencies, and

"WHEREAS a Governmental Commission should be charged with the responsibility for developing recommendations for overcoming discriminations in government and private employment on the basis of sex and for developing recommendations for services which will enable women to continue their role as wives and mothers while making a maximum contribution to the world around them:

"NOW, THEREFORE, by virtue of the authority vested in me as President of the United States by the Constitution and statutes of the United States, . . . [T]here is hereby established the President's Commission on the Status of Women."

Source: Barbara C. Burrell, *Women and Political Participation* (Santa Barbara, CA: ABC-Clio, 2004), 188–189.

women could reach their potential without interfering with their ability to care for their homes, husbands, and children. "We need to use in the very best way possible all our available manpower—and that includes womanpower," she wrote.

In April 1962, halfway through the commission's work, Roosevelt interviewed President Kennedy at the White House for her *Prospects of Mankind* television show. Kennedy reiterated that his primary interest was ensuring that women who worked did so for equal pay and under equal conditions. He maintained that women's primary responsibility, the home, took precedent in women's lives and presented women with special problems when they wanted to participate "usefully in public and private life." He also acknowledged the prejudice that Americans had against women working when unemployment rates were high, but pointed out that most women worked because they needed to "to maintain their families," and that most women "work in areas which are really more suited to them than to men." For her part, Roosevelt asked Kennedy why more women were not involved in politics, policy-making positions, and legislatures. Kennedy replied that he thought that women's careers were interrupted because of their families. He defended his appointment record, admitted the country had to do better, and acknowledged letters he had received "about getting women in these policy-making jobs . . . we are very conscious of that responsibility."

The commission's recommendations, published as the Peterson Report on American Women on October 11, 1963, found widespread discrimination against women in all aspects of American life, particularly in the workforce and in government. It laid out suggestions for a federal policy against sexual discrimination, called for affordable daycare options for women who worked, promoted expanded educational opportunities for women, and equal pay for women doing the same jobs as men (the Equal Pay Act of 1963 had been signed into law by President Kennedy on June 10). Perhaps most importantly, it called for the government to recognize that the Fourteenth Amendment guaranteeing equal rights to all citizens applied to women as well as men. The report led to the widespread creation of state commissions on the status of women, and provided concrete data that could be used by women activists at every level as they began to evaluate the discrimination they faced.

Change on the Horizon

The publication of the Report on American Women coincided with several other events that presaged an explosion of political activism by women for various causes in the coming decade. In 1961, the United States and the Soviet Union resumed atmospheric testing of nuclear weapons. Women grew greatly concerned with the radioactive fallout from such tests, particularly with strontium-90, a radioactive element that had begun showing up in their children's urine during medical examinations. Fearing their children might someday develop cancer, opponents of nuclear testing used their social and political connections, such as parent–teacher organizations, the League of Women Voters, the Women's International League for Peace and Freedom, unions, peace organizations, and every other means possible, including Christmas card lists, to ask women to take action in the form of a national one-day strike. On November 1, 1961, some 50,000 women in at least sixty cities walked out of their homes in protest, calling themselves the Women's Strike for Peace (WSP).

After the one-day walkout, a smaller group formed to continue organizing protests. Along with leader Bella Abzug, a civil rights lawyer defending victims of the McCarthy hearings, twenty members of the group were subpoenaed by the House Unamerican Activities Committee. At the hearing, nursing mothers brought their hungry babies along. The mothers testified, in between infants' cries, that they were not Soviet dupes, as the committee members seemed to believe. Rather, they wanted "Pure Milk, Not Poison." Between their thoughtful testimony and effective slogan, as well as their actions of nursing their children and bringing along playpens, they helped destroy much of the HUAC's credibility and its ability to limit dissent. The committee limped along until it died in 1975.

Partly as a result of the protests by Women's Strike for Peace and other groups, the Soviet Union and the United States signed a Limited Nuclear Test Ban Treaty to ban atmospheric testing in 1963. The nation became aware of the environmental effects of radiation, thanks not only to Abzug and her group, but also because Rachel Carson published her indictment of Americans' overuse of pesticides, *Silent Spring*, in 1962. Biologist Carson presented Americans with a readable synthesis of the effects of scientific "improvement" on the environment. The overuse of pesticides and herbicides, needed to make suburban lawns green and protect humans from the inconvenience of occasional insects, affected other animals as well. The whole ecosystem was at risk, warned Carson. Eventually springs would be silent, without the call of birds to mark the change of seasons. Her work would serve to launch an environmental movement in the decades ahead.

The environment of the cities also came under examination. In 1961, *The Death and Life of Great American Cities* by Jane Jacobs appeared. Jacobs, a reporter, writer, and editor of *Architectural Forum*, criticized the government's new initiative of modern urban planning, characterized by large-scale bull-dozing of so-called slums. While some slums featured buildings so decrepit that replacement was imperative, other slums were simply neighborhoods, often inhabited by minorities and third-generation white ethnic groups, living in nonnuclear households. These people had little recourse to stop governmental efforts at what was designated urban renewal that destroyed a variety of low-cost housing available to them. Mixed-use planning that preserved the diversity of homes and businesses made cities livable, argued Jacobs. There was an ecology to cities, she wrote, developing organically over time. "The more niches for diversity of life and livelihoods . . . the greater its carrying capacity for life." The cities of America had been left behind by middle-class whites fleeing to suburbs, and the ecology of cities were in danger. Her work would launch efforts toward urban renewal on a human scale.

Jacobs' critique of cities matched Betty Friedan's critique of suburbia in her 1963 book, *The Feminine Mystique*. She focused in part on the isolation women in the new American suburbs faced. "Each suburban wife struggle with it alone," Friedan wrote. "As she made the beds, shopped for groceries, matched slipcover material, ate peanut butter with her children, chauffeured Cub Scouts and Brownies, lay beside her husband at night—she was afraid to ask even of herself the silent question—'Is this all?'" For many women, it was not. The desire to do more and be more, to participate more in the public realm, prodded greater numbers of American women to action. The times were changing.

The greatest opportunity for activism still came in the American South, where Irene Morgan, Rosa Parks, and countless others had fought so long and so hard. Reactionary forces struggled to contain the forces of desegregation, as hundreds of cities saw thousands of protesters march, picket, boycott, and sit-in. On June 11, 1963, the sight of jeering white Alabamians protesting Vivian Malone's admission to the University of Alabama, of segregationist Governor George Wallace obstructing her passage into Foster Auditorium as she tried to register—the spectacle prompted President Kennedy to call for congressional action to prevent further violence as African Americans sought to exercise their civil rights. "We are confronted," he said to a national radio and television audience that same evening, "with a moral issue. It is as old as the scriptures and as clear as the American Constitution." He asked whether all Americans "are to be afforded equal rights and equal opportunities, whether we are going to treat our fellow Americans as we want to be treated." He cited statistics showing that blacks had a life expectancy seven years shorter than whites. They were half as likely to complete high school, one-third as likely to complete college or become a professional, and twice as likely to be unemployed as whites who had been "born in the same place on the same day," the president pointed out. Nine years after the *Brown* decision, black children still attended seg-regated schools. The problem of segregation was not regional or sectional, but national, Kennedy argued, and it was time for Congress to step in by enacting legislation that would speed the pace of school desegregation and give all Americans, regardless of race, the right to be served in public fa-cilities and to vote in safety. Everyone deserved those rights, Kennedy as-serted, and it was wrong to tell African Americans that "the only way that they are going to get their rights is to go into the streets and demonstrate. I think we owe them and we owe ourselves a better country than that."

The next day, June 12, civil rights leader Medgar Evers was assassinated in Jackson, Mississippi. Undeterred, Kennedy crafted a civil rights bill and sent it to Congress on June 19. Congressional hearings followed, but the bill soon stalled in a Congress where Southern Democrats remained largely opposed to such changes. The March on Washington later that summer inspired many. White supremacists were not impressed, however, and as desegregation orders continued, so did violence against blacks. In the early fall of 1963, the United States Fifth Circuit Court of Appeals ordered Birmingham, Alabama, to integrate its schools. A few days after the deci-sion, on September 15, a group of Klansmen exploded a bomb at the Six-teenth Street Baptist Church, a center for civil rights meetings. Four young girls attending Sunday school died in the blast: Denise McNair, age eleven; and fourteen-year-olds Cynthia Wesley, Carole Robertson, and Addie Mae Collins. The heinous nature of the crime shook the entire country. "The innocent blood of these little girls," said Dr. King, "may well serve as the

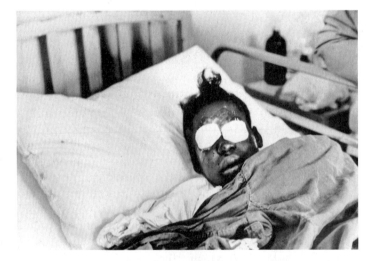

SARAH JEAN COLLINS, VICTIM OF THE BIRMINGHAM BOMBING By the time Ku Klux Klansmen bombed the Sixteenth Street Baptist Church of Birmingham, a center for civil rights activists, there had been so many attacks that the city had become known as "Bombingham." In September 1963, four young girls left their Sunday School room and were talking in the ladies' room of the church basement when nineteen sticks of dynamite stashed under the stairs went off, killing the girls and blowing a hole in the side of the church. Sarah Collins, sister of one of the dead girls, was partly blinded by glass from the blast; twenty more victims were taken to hospitals. Decades later, three Klansmen were finally convicted of the crime.

redemptive force that will bring new light to this dark city. . . . Indeed, this tragic event may cause the white South to come to terms with its conscience."

Kennedy's response was too slow and too measured for those angered by the blast. He sent FBI bomb experts and two special representatives, while black leaders demanded federal troops. Distracted by the Test Ban Treaty negotiations with the USSR, a coup in the Dominican Republic, a tax bill, and an eleven-state tour to support Democrats in the upcoming elections, Kennedy was also nonplussed by Alabama's announcement that state troopers had arrested men in connection with the bombing. The men were charged with the misdemeanor crime of possessing dynamite without a permit. Kennedy continued to push for his civil rights bill, but conceded by the middle of November that it would take another year to pass it. In a campaign speech to union supporters November 16, he said that creating jobs in a slow economy was even more important than civil rights. In the meantime, civil rights leaders continued to push both the president and the Congress to meet their responsibility to protect black Americans.

Despite congressional foot-dragging, the new frontiers Kennedy mentioned during his short presidency seemed destined to include civil rights. Events seemed to conspire in favor of change—the very air seemed ready

JACQUELINE KENNEDY AND LYNDON JOHNSON   A stunned Jacqueline Kennedy, her pink suit still spotted with the murdered president's blood, stands next to Lyndon Johnson as he is sworn in aboard *Air Force One* by Judge Sarah Hughes. Lady Bird Johnson, the new first lady, is on the president's right. The violent end of the Kennedy administration presaged a decade of unrest in the country.

for reform. As 1963 drew to a close, however, on a campaign visit to Dallas, Texas, President Kennedy was assassinated by Lee Harvey Oswald, an ex-marine, Castro supporter, and ne'er-do-well, who was himself killed by Dallas nightclub owner Jack Ruby while being taken to jail. The new medium of television brought the tragedy into everyone's homes—the death of the young president, then the murder by Jack Ruby, then First Lady Jacqueline Bouvier Kennedy and their two young children burying the president at Arlington National Cemetery. The nation paused to mourn. The violence in Dallas, however, foreshadowed the coming decade, when patience ran out and reform turned to revolution.

THINK MORE ABOUT IT

1. Return to the opening vignette on Irene Morgan and Rosa Parks. Detail the ways in which the actions of these and other women were critical to the growing civil rights movement during the post–World War II era. In what other ways did women of diverse backgrounds express activism in the public realm during these years? How does such activism contrast with the media's image of women's lives in this era?

2. Discuss the development of the Cold War between the United States and the Union of Soviet Socialist Republics and examine the various ways in which this conflict affected American women as activists, workers, consumers, and citizens.

3. Analyze the origins and varied aspects of the back-to-the-home movement that emerged after World War II. Whom did it benefit and in what ways? How did it constrain women and how did some evade or resist these constraints? How do statistics on women's postwar employment and educational attainments demonstrate the limits of this movement?

4. Explain the following statement: "in many ways the decade of the 1950s represented a revival of the cult of domesticity of the first half of the nineteenth century." How did the cultural myth of the feminine mystique become promulgated through science, advertising, and popular culture? How did this view of women undermine women's activism? Which groups of women proved the special targets of this revived, repackaged cult of domesticity?

5. What were the goals, tactics, and philosophies of civil rights activists and their organizations in the two decades following World War II? Be sure to pay attention to diverse activists and organizations. How successful were they, why, and at what cost?

6. What were the major findings and recommendations of the report issued in 1963 by the President's Commission on the Status of Women, chaired by Eleanor Roosevelt? How do these findings and recommendations recall those put forward by earlier groups promoting

women's rights and demonstrate both the advances American women had made over the centuries as well as the continued obstacles to their achievement of equal rights?

7. What did you learn in this chapter that you did not know before? How does this new information help you understand the overall story of women in American history? What topics would you like to explore further?

READ MORE ABOUT IT

Paula Barnes, *Subversive Southerner: Anne Braden and the Struggle for Racial Justice in the Cold-War South*

Vicki Crawford, *Women in the Civil Rights Movement: Trailblazers and Torchbearers, 1941–1965*

Sally Denton, *The Pink Lady: The Many Lives of Helen Gahagan Douglas*

Daniel Horowitz, *Betty Friedan and The Feminine Mystique: Labor Union Radicalism and Feminism in Cold War America*

Elizabeth Lapovsky Kennedy and Madeline D. Davis, *Boots of Leather, Slippers of Gold: The History of a Lesbian Community*

Joanne Meyerowitz, ed., *Not June Cleaver: Women and Gender in Postwar America, 1945–1960*

Sylvie Murray, *The Progressive Housewife: Community Activism in Suburban Queens, 1945–1965*

Barbara Ransby, *Ella Baker and the Black Freedom Movement: A Radical Democratic Vision*

JoAnne Robinson, *The Montgomery Bus Boycott and the Women Who Started It*

Amy Swerdlow, *Women Strike for Peace: Traditional Motherhood and Radical Politics in the 1960s*

KEY CONCEPTS

demobilization

consumerism

back-to-the-home movement

internationalism

anti-Communism

baby boom

feminine mystique

desgregation

Brown v. Board of Education of Topeka, Kansas

civil rights movement

sweatshop

President's Commission on the Status of Women

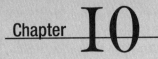

Chapter 10

FEMINISM AND FERMENT

Estelle Griswold of Connecticut

Primary Source 10-1: The Majority Opinion in *Griswold v. Connecticut*

WOMEN AND THE CIVIL RIGHTS ACT OF 1964
Economic Discrimination and the Equal Employment Opportunity Commission
The National Organization for Women
   Primary Source 10-2: NOW's Statement of Purpose

WOMEN'S RIGHTS WITHIN THE AFRICAN AMERICAN COMMUNITY
The Voting Rights Act of 1965
   Primary Source 10-3: Voting Rights Act of 1965
Women and the Radicalization of Civil Rights
   Primary Source 10-4: The National Black Feminist Organization's Statement of Purpose

NATIVE AMERICAN LIBERATION
The American Indian Movement
Women of All Red Nations

THE WOMEN'S LIBERATION MOVEMENT
The Vietnam War
Women and the Antiwar Movement
Consciousness-Raising
Birth Control and Abortion Rights
Local Feminist Groups and Goals
Cultural and Socialist Radicals
The Labor Movement
Hispanic Women in the Movement
   Primary Source 10-5: Dolores Huerta Calls for a Boycott

THE IMPACT OF THE WOMEN'S LIBERATION MOVEMENT

The Movement's Accomplishments

The Houston Conference

The Conservative Response

  Primary Source 10-6: Phyllis Schlafly, "What's Wrong with Equal Rights for Women?"

The Failure of the ERA

THINK MORE ABOUT IT

READ MORE ABOUT IT

KEY CONCEPTS

On November 3, 1961, at a little after two o'clock in the afternoon, two police detectives climbed the steps to the second floor of 79 Trumbull Street, New Haven, Connecticut. They entered the reception room of the Planned Parenthood League of Connecticut (PPLC). Dr. Virginia Stuermer was speaking to patients, instructing them on the various methods of birth control prior to fitting the women with diaphragms or prescribing birth control pills. The receptionist at the front desk left to find the clinic's director, Estelle Griswold. She came out, met the detectives and introduced herself, then invited them back to her office where, she said, she would be happy to give them whatever information they would like about the clinic and Planned Parenthood's work to prevent unwanted pregnancy.

Enthusiastically, Griswold shared with the detectives information about how the PPLC operated: their pamphlets and flyers; how they set fees for patients (maximum charge fifteen dollars); even how they fit diaphragms and showed women how to use spermicidal jellies. When she mentioned the last, Griswold cheerfully admitted that she realized she had just broken Connecticut state laws. One prohibited anyone from using "any drug, medicinal article or instrument for the purpose of preventing conception"; another punished "any person who assists, abets, counsels, causes, hires or commands another to commit any offense," such as breaking the law against using birth control.

After ninety minutes of discourse on birth control, the officers prepared to leave. Griswold, one detective recorded in his notes, "stated that . . . she welcomed arrest and a chance to settle the question of the Connecticut State Statute's legality." The clinic's medical director supported her. C. Lee Buxton, a Yale Medical School professor, had watched two of his patients suffer horribly from unwanted pregnancies. One woman died; the other suffered a series of strokes that left her paralyzed. The state law that prevented him from prescribing birth control left him frustrated and angry. He and Griswold had worked for years to overturn the law, as had countless others in Connecticut, but to no avail.

After the first police visit, Griswold and Buxton found two patients willing to turn evidence over to the police so the clinic directors could be arrested. One woman turned in a partially used tube of spermicidal jelly, the other, a partially used packet of birth control pills (she asked Griswold for a new packet—going to jail for the cause was one thing, she said, but getting pregnant quite another). With the evidence in hand, the police could act. Griswold put on one of her favorite hats and a coat with a fur collar and headed to the police station. There, she and Buxton were arrested and charged with the crime of helping "certain married women" to prevent pregnancies.

The arrests delighted birth control supporters. At last they had a test case that might overturn Connecticut's law, one of the strictest in the country and a direct throwback to the Comstock laws of the late nineteenth century that deemed birth control information to be obscene. Estelle Griswold saw birth control differently. Born in Hartford, Connecticut, in 1900, she studied voice and wanted to be a singer. Against her family's wishes, she went to Paris, where she did clerical work and fell in love. When her mother grew ill, she reluctantly returned to Hartford to assume the role of a dutiful daughter. In 1927, she married Richard Griswold and eventually started working as a medical technologist. After World War II, both Griswolds worked in Europe—Dick for the State Department, and Estelle for the United Nations Relief and Rehabilitation Association then later the Church World Service, relocating people displaced by the war. She learned firsthand the devastation poverty caused, and became interested in population control after visiting slums in Rio de Janiero, Algiers, and Puerto Rico. She believed that lack of access to information about birth control and uncontrolled fertility caused misery not only among those in foreign lands, but in America as well.

When Griswold returned to Connecticut in the 1950s, she needed a job. An old high school friend asked her to become director of Connecticut's PPLC. Because of Connecticut's law forbidding any contraception, the PPLC in the state worked primarily as a transportation service, shuttling women to and from New York, where they could meet with doctors and get birth control information and prescriptions. Despite years of lobbying the legislature and two appeals to the U.S. Supreme Court, Connecticut's law remained intact. The challenge of reviving the PPLC and of finding a way to change the law attracted Griswold. She raised money, made contacts, extended the group's reach to people beyond the upper and middle classes, found supporters—medical and legal—and bided her time until the opportunity presented itself to challenge the law successfully.

Griswold v. Connecticut reached the U.S. Supreme Court in 1965. Dean Thomas Emerson of the Yale Law School and Catherine Roraback, a civil rights attorney who had been the only woman in Yale Law School in 1948, argued the case against the Connecticut law. While the attorneys referred to President Lyndon Johnson's new program, the "War on Poverty" (and pointed out that "to fight poverty without birth control is to fight with one hand tied behind the back"), the attorneys focused their arguments on the right to privacy they thought implied in the Constitution, citing the Third, Fourth, Fifth, Ninth, and Fourteenth Amendments. "The sanctity of the home and the wholly personal nature of marital relations," said Emerson, were at the very core of the right to privacy in this case.

ESTELLE GRISWOLD AT PLANNED PARENTHOOD Estelle Griswold stands outside the Planned Parenthood Center in New Haven, Connecticut, the center of the law case that decided in favor of married women's right to have access to birth control.

On June 7, 1965, the Supreme Court ruled in favor of Griswold against the state of Connecticut's anticontraception statute 7 to 2. The Court established a right to privacy in marriage that was protected by the Constitution, despite there being no explicit mention of it because, as Justice William O. Douglas put it, "specific guarantees in the Bill of Rights have penumbras, formed by emanations from those guarantees that help give them life and substance. Various guarantees create zones of privacy," including the right for a marriage to be private. The Connecticut law forbidding the use of contraception, rather than limiting merely its purchase or sale, cast a forbidding specter: "Would we allow the police to search the sacred precincts of marital bedrooms for telltale signs of the use of contraceptives? The very idea is repulsive to the notions of privacy surrounding the marriage relationship" (see Primary Source 10-1). The law was declared unconstitutional. Estelle Griswold celebrated her sixty-fifth birthday the next day and returned to Hartford to open a new legal birth control clinic.

Griswold's fight to overturn the law through the use of civil disobedience echoed the techniques used by the civil rights movement. The cause for which she fought, however, centered on a woman's right to control her body, perhaps

THE MAJORITY OPINION IN *GRISWOLD V. CONNECTICUT*

Justice William O. Douglas enumerated a number of constitutional protections that guaranteed the privacy of individuals against governmental intrusion. By placing the Court's decision within the context of these protections, the Court recognized a right to privacy enjoyed by all Americans.

"[G]uarantees in the Bill of Rights have penumbras, formed by emanations from those guarantees that help give them life and substance. Various guarantees create zones of privacy....

"The Fourth and Fifth Amendments were described ... as protection against all governmental invasions 'of the sanctity of a man's home and the privacies of life. . . . [T]he right of privacy which presses for recognition here is a legitimate one.'

"The present case ... concerns a relationship lying within the zone of privacy created by several fundamental constitutional guarantees. And it concerns a law which, in forbidding the use of

the single most important right women could have. Access to legal, safe, and effective birth control transformed women's lives in the twentieth century. So did the Supreme Court's establishment of a right to privacy. Women gained those two rights and a host of others as legislation, protest, and rebellion transformed the political, economic, and social structures of the country.

The changes that continued in the 1960s came about through both peaceful and violent means, and women played major roles. Men dominated reform movements in ways that alienated many women, who began working for their own liberation in a movement they called the *Women's Liberation Movement*. The drive to change the way Americans treated women had enormous repercussions for all women's lives. In response, by the late 1960s and early 1970s, conservative activists tried to limit or turn back the changes that had transformed so many women's lives. They succeeded in one of their most important goals: blocking an attempt to amend the U.S. Constitution by codifying women's equality with the Equal Rights Amendment.

WOMEN AND THE CIVIL RIGHTS ACT OF 1964

After the tragic death of John F. Kennedy in November 1963, his successor, President Lyndon B. Johnson of Texas, was determined to carry forth the late president's vision of federal enforcement of civil rights. Democrat Martha Griffiths, a U.S. representative from Michigan since 1955, was largely responsible for including women in the legislation Congress proposed to guarantee civil rights for all Americans. Griffiths, a lawyer who had felt the sting of sexual discrimination in the earliest days of her career contraceptives . . . seeks to achieve its goals by means having a maximum destructive impact upon that relationship. Such a law cannot stand in light of the familiar principle . . . that a 'governmental purpose to control or prevent activities constitutionally subject to state regulation may not be achieved by means which sweep unnecessarily broadly and thereby invade the area of protected freedoms.' Would we allow the police to search the sacred precincts of marital bedrooms for telltale signs of the use of contraceptives? The very idea is repulsive to the notions of privacy surrounding the marriage relationship.

"We deal with a right of privacy older than the Bill of Rights—older than our political parties, older than our school system. Marriage is a coming together for better or for worse, hopefully enduring, and intimate to the degree of being sacred. It is an association that promotes a way of life . . . a harmony in living . . . a bilateral loyalty."

Source: From Kathryn Cullen-Dupont, ed., *Encyclopedia of Women's History in America*, 2d edition (New York: Facts on File, 200), 325–327.

when she was paid less than her lawyer husband for doing the same job, had responded by opening a private firm with him, then getting involved in politics to fight discrimination against women. She won election to the House in November 1954, and served for twenty years, focusing on social issues. Her proudest accomplishment came when she helped usher through the Civil Rights Act, successfully revising the legislation to include prohibiting discrimination based on sex.

When the Civil Rights Act came up for discussion in the House in February 1964, Virginia Democrat Howard W. Smith moved to amend it by adding the word *sex* to the list of categories protected from discrimination by the act. The new wording now prohibited discrimination based on "race, color, religion, sex, or national origin." Smith, a conservative Southerner opposed to civil rights for blacks, may have inserted the word to ensure that the bill would fail (as Griffiths later claimed), but he said that he had done it to fulfill a promise he had made to reporter May Craig, who regularly questioned presidents about women's issues. Craig had extracted that promise from Smith on the NBC television show *Meet the Press* two weeks before the vote. Smith also claimed that he favored equal rights for women as well, citing his long friendship with Alice Paul, leader of the National Woman's Party.

Regardless of Smith's motives, the debate following his proposed amendment to the bill left no doubt in the minds of U.S. congresswomen (now twelve in number) that many congressmen saw Smith's amendment as a joke. Smith himself began the debate by reading a letter from a woman constituent who complained that, according to the last national census, there were too many single women in America and that Congress should legislate a solution to this imbalance. He read it, he said jovially, to prove women had "real" grievances. Another representative said that while it was true that as the head of his house he always got the last word, his last word most often consisted of the phrase, "Yes, dear." Congressmen chortled.

Griffith and the other women representatives were not amused, angry at the trivialization of their concerns. The reports of the President's Commission on the Status of Women the House had recently received laid out the myriad ways that women faced discrimination, but Congress refused to take the topic seriously. Southern conservatives dismissed Smith's amendment out of hand, along with opposing the Civil Rights Act *in toto*. Assistant Secretary of Labor Esther Peterson, the highest-ranking woman in Johnson's cabinet, also opposed the amendment, believing that problems generated by sex discrimination differed enough from civil rights discrimination that they needed different solutions, preferably at the state level. Liberals who supported the rest of the Civil Rights Act feared supporting Smith's amendment would doom the entire attempt to limit discrimination, a fear that echoed the resistance that the supporters of black suffrage exhibited when considering woman suffrage in the nineteenth century.

Griffiths rose to her feet. "I suppose that if there had been any necessity to have pointed out that women were a second-class sex," she said "the laughter would have proved it." Then, using an argument similar to one used years before by supporters of woman suffrage and the Fourteenth Amendment, she pointed out that by not including the term *sex* in the Civil Rights Act, white women would have no protection against discrimination. "You are going to give the Negro man and the Negro woman rights, and down at the bottom of the list will be the white woman with no rights at all." She found it "incredible . . . that white men would be willing to place white women at such a disadvantage." Voting against the bill, she said, was voting against a daughter, a wife, a widow.

Other congresswomen joined Griffiths, some employing similar racist arguments. Rep. Catherine May of Washington called on members to not overlook the "white Native-born American woman of Christian religion." More facetiously, New York Rep. Katharine St. George asked the men of Congress, "We outlast you. We outlive you. We nag you to death. So why should we want special privileges? We want this crumb of equality." Not all congresswomen supported the amendment. Representative Edith Green of Oregon, who had authored the Equal Pay Act of 1963, argued against including the amendment, saying, "For every discrimination I have suffered, I firmly believe that the Negro woman has suffered 10 times," suffering "a double discrimination. She was born as a woman and she was born as a Negro." Protecting black women against race discrimination was more important to Green than ending sexual discrimination.

After hours of debate, the amended bill passed on February 8, 1964, by 168 to 133. President Johnson's support for Smith's amendment to the bill was less than Griffiths hoped for. Concerned more about racial discrimination than sex discrimination, Johnson responded to May Craig's question at a news conference by saying he would support the Democratic Party platform, which favored antidiscrimination legislation for women. He also hoped to do something about discrimination against women "in the next month." He did not come out directly in favor of the bill's amendment. In the end, however, the Senate passed a bill similar to the House's amended version. Griffith's determined efforts had kept the word "sex" in the bill, and President Johnson signed the Civil Rights Act into law on July 2, 1964.

In addition to the Civil Rights Act, Congress passed Johnson's Economic Opportunity Act of 1964 that summer. Its programs were designed to help poor and disadvantaged Americans, a group that had reached 20 percent of the population. Head Start (for preschoolers), Upward Bound (for college-bound teenagers), the Job Corps (for poor workers), and Volunteers in Service to America (for those who wanted to help the disadvantaged at home rather than abroad) symbolized Johnson's legislation, nicknamed the War on Poverty. The president brought African Americans into the process of designing and implementing the programs. He linked his call for economic justice with an end to racial discrimination, declaring at a speech in Ann Arbor, Michigan, that America needed a "Great Society" with "abundance and liberty for all" and an "end to poverty and racial injustice." After his landslide reelection in November, Johnson seized his mandate and sent legislation forward in the same manner as Franklin Delano Roosevelt had done in the Hundred Days after his election, thirty-two years before.

Hundreds of initiatives and bills came forth. Johnson formed a Department of Housing and Urban Development to spearhead urban renewal and repair the cities. Medicare (universal health care for elderly people) was passed, as was Medicaid (health care for the poor). Johnson signed a new education funding bill in the one-room schoolhouse that he had attended as a child. A new immigration act allowed more people to immigrate to America. Programs sought to improve health, education, nutrition, highway safety, air, and water. Administered in the form of Community Action Programs (CAPs), many programs were staffed by the poor—particularly women—who benefited greatly from the opportunity to work for wages. Johnson's Great Society held real promise out to poor Americans, particularly urban women, that the government was there to help them.

Economic Discrimination and the Equal Employment Opportunity Commission

Passing transformative legislation was only the first step to creating a fairer America. The government needed to enforce the legislation as well. Public or private jobs were not the only places women faced economic discrimination. Such discrimination took many forms. In many states, married women's property laws still limited women's ability to own property and control their wages. Women often could not get credit in their own names, and department stores that women frequented issued credit cards to married women based on their husbands' jobs and records, rather than allowing women credit independently of men. Buying a house was difficult, if not impossible, for single or divorced women, and single women often lived with their parents long after they were adults because credit proved so difficult to obtain on their own, and their paychecks could not support an independent life.

Most women earned wages in the service industry, where the earnings averaged $1.59 an hour. The top ten jobs for women workers in America remained low-paying. They included secretaries and other clerical workers, domestic employees, saleswomen, elementary school teachers, bookkeepers, waitresses, miscellaneous factory operatives, and registered nurses. Women were often legally or socially limited to certain jobs and when they protested, employers told them that women "didn't want" better paying jobs that might involve travel, working at night, or more physical exertion. They often faced being fired without recourse if they protested, joined a union (true for men as well), or if they resisted sexual harassment by their bosses.

The Equal Employment Opportunity Commission (EEOC) enforced the new antidiscrimination rules. Franklin D. Roosevelt Jr. served as chair, and Aileen Clark Hernandez, an African American woman who had most recently been the assistant chief of the California Fair Employment Practices Commission, represented all the women of America on the five-member commission. When the commission read reports and documents, they seldom discussed discrimination against women. The commission treated sex discrimination complaints filed under Title VII of the Civil Rights Act with the kind of trivialization often exhibited toward women's concerns. Men referred to Title VII as the "bunny law" and complained that they might have to look at knobby-kneed male Playboy bunnies. Middle-aged women bosses might chase their young attractive male secretaries around the desk. Men would even have to hire a woman who applied for a job as a pilot, if she showed up with the proper credentials. At the first White House conference on discrimination late in the summer of 1965, only nine among the seventy-five speakers were women and most of them participated on the same panel.

One of the earliest issues regarding Title VII came over a seemingly pedestrian issue: job advertisements in newspapers. Newspapers traditionally divided job ads by sex and race categories such as "Help Wanted, Female" or "Help Wanted, Male, Colored," and so on. Such limitations were clearly against the new law. While a majority on the EEOC voted to ban ads that discriminated by race, they allowed the ads separating men's and women's jobs to continue. Roosevelt, far more cautious than his mother had ever been, argued that enforcement of the sexual discrimination provisions of the Civil Rights Act needed to proceed gradually. He believed that Smith's amendment to the act was made, not as a serious demand for change, but rather to induce "ridicule and confusion." Since no congressional hearings had been held on the amendment itself to reveal what Congress wanted, Roosevelt knew not what to do. Caution became his watchword.

Outraged at the EEOC's blatant attempt to negate the law, Dr. Pauli Murray, a Yale law professor and a member of the President's Commission on the Status of Women, had a suggestion: that American women should march on Washington to demand equal opportunities. She joined attorney Mary Eastwood from the Justice Department to document discrimination against women. Of mixed-race ancestry—European, African, and Native

American—Dr. Murray was well aware of the dual discrimination women faced. Just because racial discrimination had been "more brutal" than the more subtle instances of sexual discrimination, she said, in both cases, "the rights of women and the rights of Negroes are only different phases of the fundamental and indivisible issue of human rights."

Despite such accomplished women as Murray and Eastwood demanding that officials enforce the law, the EEOC continued to trivialize or ignore women's concerns. Claims of discrimination against women in the form of protective legislation were ignored by the EEOC as well. Since the days of *Muller v. Oregon* in 1908 (see Chapter 7), employers had limited women workers as a class, presuming that all women were future mothers and therefore must be protected from harm. State laws limited women's work lives. They could not work in certain jobs, such as mining. They could not work as many hours as men, which meant no well-paying overtime work at overtime rates. They could not work at night in some industries, and could not lift a weight that might be equal to that of a toddler, yet exceeded a state's rules (fifteen pounds in Utah; thirty-five pounds in Michigan). Some states with protective legislation required employers to provide chairs or restrooms for any women they hired. Employers believed such amenities increased operating expenses, and consequently were less likely to hire women. Despite the EEOC's own study showing that protective legislation's restrictions were often irrelevant to modern women's lives and limited their abilities to work in better-paying jobs, the EEOC refused to strike down state protective laws. The commission argued it had no power to do so and left the matter up to the courts.

Women continued to file sexual discrimination complaints with the EEOC. Fully one-third of the complaints received by the EEOC by 1966 were from women, and many were not resolved for years despite EEOC provisions that required resolution within sixty days. In the late spring of 1966, Judith Evenson, a stewardess for Northwest Airlines, filed a complaint after she was fired for getting married. Men were not fired for the same act, she said, and the airline's insistence that stewardesses be young, attractive, and female was discriminatory. The EEOC was of no help, despite Martha Griffiths' impassioned speeches on the floor of the House to try to draw serious attention to a commission that was enforcing only the part of the law "that they are interested in." Aileen Hernandez eventually resigned, frustrated with the failure of the commission to enforce the law.

The National Organization for Women

June 1966 brought to Washington members of various states and cities for the Third Annual Conference of Commissions on the Status of Women, a follow-up conference to the one that had issued the Peterson report on the status of women in 1963. Many conference participants were frustrated in their efforts to confront discrimination at federal and state levels. Their livelihoods depended on their roles within male-dominated federal and state Bureaus of Labor or state-level commissions. Activism met resistance and repercussions could be severe—the Illinois state legislature, for instance,

NOW'S STATEMENT OF PURPOSE

On October 29, 1966, participants at the National Organization for Women's First National Conference in Washington, DC, adopted a statement that set out their beliefs and goals. The statement, some of which is reproduced here, was written by Betty Friedan, and included discussions of educational discrimination and cultural traditions that limited women's opportunities.

"The purpose of NOW is to take action to bring women into full participation in the mainstream of American society now, exercising all the privileges and responsibilities thereof in truly equal partnership with men.

"We believe the time has come to move beyond the abstract argument, discussion and symposia over the status and special nature of women which has raged in America in recent years; the time has come to confront, with concrete action, the conditions that now prevent women from enjoying the equality of opportunity and freedom of choice which is their right, as individual Americans, and as human beings.

---

cut off all funding to its women's commission after a state equal pay act passed. Many activists felt hamstrung by such retribution. Conference participant and best-selling author Betty Friedan suffered under no such limitations, however. *The Feminine Mystique* had come to represent a viewpoint for women activists to rally around. In a late-night session in her hotel room at the conference, Friedan and Kay Clarenbach, from the Wisconsin Commission on Women, met with a dozen or so other women fed up with the lack of progress. They argued about the best approach, and Friedan suggested founding a new activist organization for women, hoping to do for the women's movement what the civil rights movement had done for blacks. Needing, as one participant put it, "an NAACP for women," they founded the *National Organization for Women* (NOW).

NOW's straightforward goal declared the necessity of taking action, writing in its Statement of Purpose that it wished "to bring women into full participation in the mainstream of American society now, assuming all the privileges and responsibilities thereof in truly equal partnership with men." While Friedan's popularity with white, middle-class, college-educated women brought many of them into the organization, the membership of the founding board and the wide-ranging concerns expressed in the Statement of Purpose turned NOW into a human rights organization, recognizing not only professional and middle-class women's issues, but also labor issues and the double discrimination that poorly paid women of color suffered (see Primary Source 10-2). Finding a new home for her activism, Aileen Hernandez became an officer. "In many ways," she wrote of its founding, "NOW represents for me the beginning of the fulfillment of a dream I have long had that the women of the United States and the many racial and ethnic minorities which face similar discrimination would unite in their common cause."

In addition to discrimination in the workplace, NOW members sought redress for other areas where women suffered discrimination. The group

"NOW is dedicated to the proposition that women, first and foremost, are human beings, who, like all other people in our society, must have the chance to develop their fullest human potential. We believe that women can achieve such equality only by accepting to the full the challenges and responsibilities they share with all other people in our society, as part of the decision-making mainstream of American political, economic and social life.

"We organize to initiate or support action, nationally, or in any part of this nation, by individuals or organizations, to break through the silken curtain of prejudice and discrimination against women in government, industry, the professions, the churches, the political parties, the judiciary, the labor unions, in education, science, medicine, law, religion and every other field of importance in American society."

Source: Betty Friedan and Pauli Murray, "Statement of Purpose," in *It Changed My Life: Writings on the Women's Movement* (Cambridge, MA: Harvard University Press, 1998), 109–115.

recognized, for example, that women operated at a disadvantage in the criminal justice system. Women were punished disproportionately for crimes that they committed. In Pennsylvania, any woman convicted of a felony automatically received the maximum sentence allowed by law, unlike men, whose sentences might be less than the maximum depending on the circumstances. In other states, women who killed their husbands were charged with murder, while husbands who killed their wives were often accused of committing a crime of passion, and charged with manslaughter or lesser crimes, given lighter sentences if convicted, or not charged at all. Women prostitutes were arrested and charged; their male customers were usually let go. Women who were raped were usually regarded as having "asked for it," that is, for having brought on the attack by their behavior. Convictions for rape, a capital crime punishable by death in a number of states, were difficult to get. In New York, for instance, two witnesses had to be present at the rape for the crime to be prosecuted by the state. Few women reported rapes, not willing to undergo the demeaning process of trying to prove that a crime had been committed, nor the stigma associated with being its victim.

NOW attracted public attention to instances of sex discrimination in the workplace and elsewhere by using boycotts and demonstrations, as well as by attacking discriminatory laws and practices in the courts and the political institutions of the nation. In one of its earliest actions, NOW organized a boycott against Colgate-Palmolive, maker of households soaps and lotions used primarily by women. The company restricted women's employment by limiting them to jobs where they were not required to lift more than the state limit of thirty-five pounds. This kept women mainly in the secretarial pool and out of many higher-paying jobs, despite the fact many of those women had children they lifted who weighed more than thirty-five pounds. The group called on women to boycott Colgate products, picketed Colgate headquarters in New York City, and held a "flush-in," where protesters poured Colgate products into a toilet. In addition to boy-cotts, NOW also filed lawsuits. NOW attorney Sylvia Roberts showed that a secretary at Southern Bell telephone company, kept from a better-paying job as a "switchman" because of the thirty-pound weight limit, regularly had to move her typewriter that weighed more than that.

NOW members picketed men-only restaurants and clubs in a "Public Accommodations Week" in February 1969, objecting to restaurants and bars that discriminated against women. Some owners reasoned that single women might be prostitutes, and therefore barred them. The Palmer House Hotel in Chicago forced women to use a separate entrance. The famous New York restaurant "21" refused to seat any woman wearing pants, a policy that they quickly revoked after actress Judy Carne promptly checked her trousers at the coat check, then sat down at the table clad only in her long jacket top. NOW members also demonstrated at the White House, beginning their protest on Mother's Day and carrying placards calling for "Rights, Not Roses." Other members fought on college campuses to establish women's studies programs. Women students often learned little about women in their courses. In nearly every discipline, from anthropology to history to sociol-ogy, men were portrayed in textbooks as the "norm," while women were usually covered in a special chapter, regarded as the "other," despite the fact that women accounted for 51 percent of the American population.

NOW members also took on more radical causes. They fought to lessen restrictions against abortion, seeking the right to safe and legal abortions for all women. They supported lesbian rights for homosexual women, and cam-paigned for subsidized or free child care for women who were mothers. The organization reached what was perhaps the pinnacle of its success and activ-ism in 1970. During that year, it filed sexual discrimination complaints against 1,300 different U.S. companies for failing to file plans showing how they would meet federally required affirmative action goals, designed to help com-panies hire more women. It held a "Women's Strike for Equality" in August to mark the fiftieth anniversary of the passage of women's suffrage. Over 50,000 women marched down Fifth Avenue in New York City, and similar actions took place in 90 different cities and towns in 40 states. The group also enjoyed the success of intensive efforts to revive the Equal Rights Amendment. The bill finally moved out of committee, and the House of Representatives voted in favor of the amendment 354 to 24 in 1971. It also passed the Senate, 84 to 8, and was sent to the states for ratification in 1972. At long last, the dream of Susan B. Anthony and Alice Paul to embed the equal treatment of women into the Constitution seemed to be coming true.

WOMEN'S RIGHTS WITHIN THE AFRICAN AMERICAN COMMUNITY

The civil rights movement depended greatly on the time and talent of women (see Chapter 9). A young woman, Linda Brown, had begun school desegregation with her lawsuit in 1954. Vivian Malone had begun the desegregation of Alabama universities, which would gradually extend to universities across the South. The Montgomery Bus Boycott had been started by Rosa Parks and JoAnne Robinson. Septima Clark trained leaders for the civil rights movement at the Highlander School in Tennessee. But few of these women were well known outside the movement. The media and many followers portrayed the movement as a male-dominated and male-led movement, in which women played a minor, though important role. Dorothy Height, president of the National Council on Negro Women, a superb orator and a national civil rights activist since the 1930s, for example, was often cropped from media photographs showing male civil rights leaders such as Martin Luther King and John Lewis. Among civil rights advocates, black women suffered a dual discrimination—racism because they were black, sexism because they were women—but for the majority, racism needed to be overcome first. Their shift to the women's rights movement from the civil rights movement took a slightly different tack.

Following passage of the Civil Rights Act, black leaders shifted their focus from desegregation efforts to registering black voters. Ending segregation was important, but without a voice in the political system of the country, blacks could not hope to change the underlying causes of discrimination. The Freedom Summer Project began in 1964. After training at Western College for Women in Oxford, Ohio, nearly 1,000 young women and men—three-quarters of them white—drawn from the best American universities and colleges, traveled to the Deep South to register African Americans to vote. They met violent resistance.

The worst violence of the Freedom Summer occurred in Mississippi. Racists there, fearful of a race war led by Communists, as they called the young volunteers, reacted with great hostility to the "invasion." In June, three young men went missing: James Chaney, a twenty-one-year-old black Mississippian; and two white Jewish activists, Michael "Mickey" Schwerner, a twenty-four-year-old from New York; and Andrew Goodman, a twenty-year-old New York college student freshly arrived in the state. After a long search, their bodies were discovered buried in an earthen dam. They had all been shot by members of the Ku Klux Klan.

The tactical value of including white Americans in the drive for civil rights became apparent almost immediately. While at least five other black civil rights workers had been killed between the Birmingham church bombings and the deaths of these three men, the influential white families of Goodman and Schwerner demanded action. President Johnson, determined to show that he was a national rather than a Southern president, sent in the FBI, who found the bodies and the killers. Seven of the guilty were convicted, eight were set free, and three trials ended in deadlocked juries. (Forty-one years later, Edgar Ray Killen, an unrepentant Klansman, was convicted as well.)

The Voting Rights Act of 1965

The murders of these young men whose crime had been helping blacks register to vote gave added impetus to a drive for a voting rights act to guarantee black Americans the franchise by allowing federal supervision of registration and elections. That same summer, the Mississippi Freedom Democratic Party, led by Fannie Lou Hamer, Victoria Gray, Annie Divine, and Aaron Henry, elected delegates and traveled to the Democratic National Convention to try to unseat the all-white delegation elected by the white voters of Mississippi. Hamer, a granddaughter of slaves and now a field secretary for the Student Nonviolent Coordinating Committee (SNCC), protested vociferously when the white Democrats refused to seat the delegates at the convention. In 1962, Hamer had joined SNCC after the group came to Mississippi and informed her and her neighbors that they had a constitutional right to vote, something they had not known. Warned that she might be killed if she went to register, Hamer said later that "the only thing they could do to me was to kill me, and it seemed like they'd been trying to do that a little bit at a time ever since I could remember." She was arrested and severely beaten for helping others to register; she never fully recovered from her injuries. She testified to the Democratic National Committee (DNC) about the beating she suffered, about the beating another woman in jail with her suffered, about being told to leave Mississippi if she wanted to live. If her people were not represented at the DNC, if the delegation of which she was head was not seated at the DNC, she told the committee, "I question America, is this America, the

FANNIE LOU HAMER TESTIFIES   Fannie Lou Hamer testifies before the Credentials Committee of the Democratic National Convention in Atlantic City, New Jersey, August 1964. Hamer repeatedly protested the all-white delegation to the Democratic Convention to nominate candidates for president and vice president.

land of the free and the home of the brave where we have to sleep with our telephones off of the hooks because our lives be threatened daily because we want to live as decent human beings, in America?"

The delegation was not seated. Hamer rejected a compromise offer, brokered by liberal Minnesota Senator Hubert H. Humphrey, of two at-large seats in the convention as well as a promise that at the next convention in 1968, the Mississippi delegation would be integrated. She was "sick and tired of being sick and tired," she said, and so was the entire delegation, not just the two who were offered seats. Instead, she and many members of SNCC turned away from both the Democratic Party and cooperation with white liberals. Hamer later ran for the U.S. House of Representatives, began food and farm cooperatives to help blacks own their own land and, in 1971, helped to found the National Women's Political Caucus. Her appeal to the Democrats did not go unheard, however. Her spell-binding oratory attracted national support for the 1965 Voting Rights Act.

By the presidential election of 1964, civil rights and voting rights had become the primary domestic issue of concern to the nation. The Civil Rights Act had been passed in the summer, but a white backlash of attacks as well as black riots in cities far removed from the South were on the increase, as was a call for a voting rights act. Lyndon Johnson, a Southerner, knew he had lost his own region because of his support for civil rights. His opponent was arch-conservative Republican Senator Barry Goldwater of Arizona. Goldwater voted against the Civil Rights Act. He disapproved of Social Security and other federal programs, supporting only a strong military to fight against communism. He frightened many liberals with his declaration that "extremism in the defense of liberty is no vice; moderation in the pursuit of justice is no virtue," as well as his support of the "first-use" of tactical nuclear weapons. Johnson countered Goldwater's positions with negative campaigning, taking advantage of Americans' increased television ownership. The most famous campaign ad Johnson showed on TV was the so-called Daisy ad, where a little girl, innocently pulling off a daisy's petals and counting them was replaced by the image of an atomic bomb countdown. "These are the stakes," said Lyndon Johnson's voice, "to make a world in which all God's children can live, or to go into the darkness. We must either love each other, or we must die." The ad continued: "Vote for President Johnson on November 3. The stakes are too high for you to stay home."

The Daisy ad helped Johnson win the 1964 election handily, defeating Goldwater by 61 percent to 38 percent. Only the Deep South and Goldwater's home state of Arizona voted for him. In the election, one civil rights activist, Amelia P. Boynton, owner of an insurance and employment agency in Selma, Alabama, noticed that 77 percent of the black citizens of Alabama had not been able to vote because of white resistance to black voter registration. In Dallas County, where Selma was located, fewer than 350 of the 15,000 eligible black voters were registered. Attempts had been made to register black voters. Marie Foster and seven other African Americans created the Dallas County Voters League, held citizenship classes, demanded improvements in voter registration processes, and asked the local paper to

VOTING RIGHTS ACT OF 1965

The 1965 Voting Rights Act ended literacy tests used to prevent blacks from voting, and gave the federal government the power to register black voters, as well as to supervise southern states that tried to change laws to prevent blacks from voting. By the end of 1965, 250,000 African Americans were newly registered to vote. By the end of 1966, most Southern states had 50 percent or more of their black citizens registered to vote.

"AN ACT To enforce the fifteenth amendment to the Constitution of the United States, and for other purposes.

integrate its pages, rather than running a separate "colored" edition, so that African Americans would feel a part of the community. The group was so successful that the Ku Klux Klan threatened members of the League and the local district court judge forbade any gatherings of three or more people if the topic under discussion was civil rights.

By the spring after Johnson's reelection, Foster, along with Boynton, her husband Sam, and their friend the Reverend Frederick Reese, convinced Martin Luther King Jr. to come to Selma and lead a mass march to the state capitol, Montgomery, to protest their disenfranchisement. The march

THE MARCH FROM SELMA TO MONTGOMERY Both black and white women joined the civil rights protest, marching from Selma to Montgomery, Alabama. Demonstrators carried American flags to emphasize their beliefs that their actions were protected by the Constitution.

"Be it enacted by the Senate and House of Representatives of the United States of America in Congress assembled, That this Act shall be known as the "Voting Rights Act of 1965.

"SEC. 2. No voting qualification or prerequisite to voting, or standard, practice, or procedure shall be imposed or applied by any State or political subdivision to deny or abridge the right of any citizen of the United States to vote on account of race or color."

Source: From The National Archives, *Our Documents: 100 Milestone Documents from the National Archives* (New York: Oxford University Press, 2003), 242.

began on Sunday, March 7, 1965. As the marchers approached the Edmund Pettus Bridge outside Selma, police confronted the 525 marchers with tear-gas and clubs, beating many of them, trampling others under the hooves of police horses, and forcing the group back to Selma. The event, known as "Bloody Sunday," was televised to a national audience. Americans were horrified by the graphic violence against peaceful, well dressed, and orderly protesters. King and his followers seized upon this and rescheduled the march two days later, primarily for the publicity. They crossed the bridge again, but obeyed an injunction against the march and President Johnson's request to let things quiet down by merely praying at the other side, then returning to the city. That night, the Reverend James Reeb, a white Northern minister who had come to Selma to support the movement, was killed by white vigilantes. Protests began again. King organized his followers again for a third try and, after receiving a federal judge's permission to proceed, stepped off on March 21 with 3,200 supporters to walk all the way from Selma to Montgomery, fifty-three miles away. The marchers sang songs such as the civil rights anthem "We Shall Overcome" to keep up their spirits, camped by the side of the road, took handouts of food from sympathetic blacks along the route, and on March 25 stood at the end before the state capitol building, some 25,000 strong—women, men, and children. Congress took note, and passed the Voting Rights Act of 1965, making the federal government responsible for registering voters (see Primary Source 10-3). By 1968, Mississippi had registered 251,000 black voters, up from only 28,500 in 1964. While voting issues still remained, the era when white supremacists held absolute power over the vote in the South had ended.

Women and the Radicalization of Civil Rights

Despite the legislative victories won by black Americans in the form of the Civil Rights Act and the Voting Rights Act, some African Americans, particularly young black men and women in urban centers, grew increasingly tired of what they saw as a glacial rate of change and the failure of integration to achieve true economic, social, and political equality. They grew tired as well of King's nonviolent approach, arguing instead for achieving black power through black separatism. Critical of existing power structures and traditions, some groups even advocated using violence to achieve their aims. "Revolutions are based on bloodshed," declared Malcolm X, a leader of the Nation of Islam, an American-based Muslim group that did not believe that King's methods of nonviolence and integration would win African Americans equality. "The day of nonviolent resistance is over."

Practicing separatism instead of integration, the Black Power movement began in 1966 with Stokely Carmichael, the new head of SNCC, who promoted the ideas of electing blacks to political office to represent the interests of black Americans and to protect them from whites. Having given up on interracial collaboration, Carmichael dismissed SNCC's white staffers and broke away from any cooperative ventures with the Southern Christian Leadership Conference (SCLC), led by King and dedicated to nonviolent mass action. Many white women had already left SNCC. In May 1964, two white women, Casey Hayden and Mary King, had written a paper complaining about the treatment of women in the SNCC. As the Grimké sisters had done over a century before, the two women drew parallels between the treatment of blacks and the treatment of women. They declared that a "common-law caste system" existed that "at its worst, uses and exploits women." Because the caste system used traditional middle-class values to define "women's work," Hayden and King argued, it became a given that women would clean the so-called freedom house and do the secretarial work, while men would serve as leaders and spokesmen for the group. This thoughtful paper circulated at a retreat of SNCC staff, and, although he later denied it, Carmichael joked, "What is the position of women in SNCC? The position of women in SNCC is prone."

For white women, their position in the SNCC was soon vacant. Black women stayed longer, participating in ideological discussions about power, organizing, and protest. Frances Beal founded a Black Women's Liberation Committee in 1968. She published a critique of the difficulties black women faced in the civil rights movement in a 1970 essay, "Double Jeopardy: To Be Black and Female." In it, she discussed the link between racism and sexism for black women: "By reducing the Black man in America to such abject oppression," she wrote, "the Black woman had no protector and was used, and is still being used in some cases, as the scapegoat for the evils that this horrendous system has perpetrated on Black men." Black men who asserted their masculinity by forcing black women to accept a "domestic, submissive role" were eliminating what the black community needed most, the strong, black woman. As Beal put it, black liberation needed "our whole army out there dealing with the enemy," rather than "half an army." Beal and her followers soon broke with SNCC and the Black Panthers.

Not all black women left the radicalized civil rights groups that occasionally used acts of violence to achieve their goals. Angela Davis, for example, joined the Black Panthers. A Marxist philosophy professor at the University of California at Los Angeles, Davis protested that the American penal system was unfair to blacks, who made up half of all prison inmates.

The university fired Davis for her activism and Marxist views, but reinstated her after she sued. In 1970, she was arrested after Black Panthers used guns she owned to kill a judge in a failed escape attempt. She was tried and acquitted in 1972, and the defense committee organized to support her turned its efforts to work on behalf of others falsely accused, naming itself the National Alliance against Racism and Political Oppression.

Radical civil rights groups did not limit their activism to violent attempts to overthrow the corrupt political system that they opposed. The Black Panthers, for instance, also set up community outreach programs: a free breakfast program for children, free transportation for senior citizens, political education classes and voter registration drives, medical clinics, free clothing centers, legal aid, even community schools. Elaine Brown became the Black Panthers' chairperson in 1974, and Ericka Huggins directed its community school program in Oakland, California, for twelve years. Other black women activists preferred more traditional civil rights groups. The SCLC, for instance, continued to benefit from Septima Clark's leadership conducting voter registration drives throughout the second half of the 1960s.

Such drives remained difficult and dangerous. Clark recalled one trip to Jackson, Mississippi, where the town mayor waited with a tank to try to stop them. Despite her bravery, Clark received little public credit for her work in the civil rights movement. The men of the movement were lionized in the press as the real heroes, although Dr. King did acknowledge Clark's influence on him and his crusade and even asked her to travel with him to Sweden when he received the Nobel Peace Prize in 1965. Clark remained critical of men in the civil rights movement for failing to give women leadership roles and for failing to take many women workers seriously. "The civil rights movement," she said, "would never have taken off if some women hadn't started to speak up."

Sexism remained a problem in both radical and moderate civil rights groups. Even the Black Panthers, a party that prided itself on establishing a "classless" organization, calling its members "comrades" rather than by traditional titles, could not seem to eliminate sexism from its midst. Comrade Candi Robinson published a declaration in the August 9, 1969 issue of *The Black Panther*, the party's official newspaper, calling on women members to educate the men of the party. "We revolutionary men and women," she wrote, "are the halves of each other. We must continue to educate our men, and bring their minds from a male chauvinistic level to a higher level." Women played crucial supporting and organizing roles in all civil rights groups, in many cases doing most, if not all of the work required to keep organizations running. They still continued to face discrimination and even harassment, however, not only from government authorities, but also from men in the movement. Some women gave up and left the organizations to pursue careers, to concentrate on raising families, or to undertake community service. Still others remained, putting aside or ignoring sexism while striving for the end of racial oppression, while male chauvinism led still other black women to join other organizations (see Primary Source 10-4).

THE NATIONAL BLACK FEMINIST ORGANIZATION'S STATEMENT OF PURPOSE

In 1973, black women leaders met in New York City to form a new organization, the National Black Feminist Organization. Although the group lasted only three years, the statement of their beliefs encompassed many of the ideas that other women's groups from the era used: negative portrayals of women, systematic oppression caused by society's structures, and a call for Americans to recognize and fight against sexism.

"The distorted male-dominated media image of the Women's Liberation Movement has clouded the vital and revolutionary importance of this movement to Third World women, especially black women. The Movement has been characterized as the exclusive property of so-called white middle-class women and any black women seen involved in this movement have been seen as 'selling out,' 'dividing the race,' and an assortment of nonsensical epithets. Black feminists resent these charges and have therefore established The National Black Feminist Organization, in order to address ourselves to the particular and specific needs of the larger, but almost cast-aside half of the black race in Amerikkka, the black woman.

NATIVE AMERICAN LIBERATION

The question of where to put one's efforts—fighting racial discrimination or sexual discrimination—confronted Native American women in the 1960s as well. Discrimination against Native Americans remained common and, as was the case for other minorities, ranged in scale from the institutional—such as the forced relocation that had been practiced by the government—to the parochial: the Chamber of Commerce of Omak, Washington, refused to sponsor the county's preliminary competition for the Miss America beauty contest in 1948 when it learned that only white women could compete, because one-third of the town lay within the borders of the Colville Indian reservation. It is unclear whether any Native American women cared whether or not they could become Miss America, since many Indian groups had long resisted forced integration into white culture (by 1968, Native American women had their own pageant; prizes included college scholarships). Instead of seeking integration, most Native American activists concentrated on enforcing rights granted under various treaties and securing power for their nations.

As impatient young people in the black civil rights movement had split from the SCLC to form the more radical SNCC, so Native American students and young people began directing their energies to the more radical National Indian Youth Council (NIYC). The NIYC, founded in 1961, was led by Iroquois Shirley Hill Witt, Anishinabe Clyde Bellecourt,

"Black women have suffered cruelly in this society from living the phenomenon of being black and female, in a country that is *both* racist and sexist. . . . Because we live in a patriarchy, we have allowed a premium to be put on black male suffering. No one of us would minimize the pain or hardship or the cruel and inhumane treatment experienced by the black man. But history, past or present, rarely deals with the malicious abuse put upon the black woman. We were seen as breeders by the master; despised and historically polarized from/ by the master's wife; and looked upon as castrators by our lovers and husbands. The black woman has had to be strong, yet we are persecuted for having survived. We have been called 'matriarchs' by white racists and black nationalists; we have virtually no positive self-images to validate our existence. Black women want to be proud, dignified, and free from all those false definitions of beauty and womanhood that are unrealistic and unnatural. . . . We will strengthen the current efforts of the Black Liberation struggle in this country by encouraging *all* of the talents and creativities of black women to emerge, strong and beautiful, not to feel guilty or divisive, and assume positions of leadership and honor in the black community. We will encourage the black community to stop falling into the trap of the white male Left, utilizing women only in terms of domestic or servile needs. We will continue to remind the Black Liberation Movement that there can't be liberation for half the race."

Source: In Miriam Schneir, ed., *Feminism in Our Time: The Essential Writings, World War II to the Present* (New York: Vintage, 1994), 173–174.

and Cherokee Clyde Warrior, who also worked with SNCC. Radicalized by their experiences, militant Indian rights activists adopted the term *Red Power* by the mid-1960s. In 1968, urban Minneapolis Indians, led by Anishinabes Bellecourt, Mary Jane Wilson, and Denis Banks, formed the American Indian movement (AIM), which assumed much the same role for Indians as the Black Panthers did for African Americans. AIM offered Native Americans a path to achieve their radical reformation of American society by any means necessary, including violence.

Native Americans had much to complain about. Indians had ten times the unemployment rate, one hundred times the suicide rate, and twenty years less life expectancy than white Americans. The Democratic administrations of Presidents Kennedy and Johnson suspended Indian relocation, and Native activists seized the opportunity to protest the conditions under which most Indian nations lived. In Washington State, Natives held protests called "fish-ins" to protest government policies that tried to restrict Indian fishing rights that had been guaranteed by treaties. Salmon fishing in the Columbia River and along the coast was critical to the survival of the nations in the area. Pollution, dams, and commercial and sport fishing had decreased the salmon population, and Indians were arrested for fishing "out of season," despite nineteenth-century treaties that guaranteed them fishing rights. When state courts refused to grant them surcease, Indians protested, fishing anyway.

Heavily armed women protected fishermen from violence directed at them by state officials and by white vigilantes. The majority of protesters and half of the people arrested were women. Because women had always participated in the fishing done by Northwest coastal tribes, many of them viewed their actions as protestors as a continuation of their roles within their tribal culture. In 1964, determined to succeed in upholding their treaty rights despite arrests, Tulalip Janet Macleod and Pullyallup Tribal Chair Ramona Bennett founded the Survival of American Indians Association to raise the profile of the fish-ins to attract national attention, as well as to raise bail money for those arrested. The protests succeeded, and in 1974 Washington State was forced to recognize the treaty rights of Native Americans to fish their waters.

In the meantime, other Native protests—many led first by women—took center stage. In 1964, forty Indians organized by Lakota Belva Cottier claimed the island of Alcatraz in San Francisco Bay under their treaty rights to resume their possession of abandoned federal property. Alcatraz, site of the United States' highest level maximum-security federal prison, closed in 1963. The Indians wanted the island back for a cultural center and Native university. Their four-hour protest proved unsuccessful, but another long-term occupation began in November 1969 by a group naming itself Indians of All Tribes. Mohawk Richard Oakes, head of a Native American student group from San Francisco State College, and LaNada Means, a Shoshone Bannock who was head of the Native American Student Organization at the nearby University of California, Berkeley, established the occupation forces. They offered to buy the island from the federal government for $24 in glass beads and red cloth, totaling $1.24 an acre (this was more than the Europeans had paid for Manhattan in 1624, but land values, the Indians recognized, tongue firmly in cheek, had risen in the intervening centuries).

This time, the protest received worldwide notice. Publicity regarding the occupation usually ignored women protestors in favor of interviewing and profiling men, but throughout the occupation, women ran the day-to-day organization. The occupation forces created a small city. Dr. Dorothy Lone Wolf Miller, a Blackfoot, set up an island health clinic, printed the newsletter of the occupation forces, and received an education grant to start a school. Sac Fox Grace Thorpe, daughter of Olympic athlete Jim Thorpe, worked on the mainland to get a generator, water barge, and ambulance service for the island. Thorpe also coordinated publicity, attracting public support from Hollywood activists such as Jane Fonda, Candice Bergen, and Marlon Brando. Wilma Mankiller, who would later become principal chief of the Cherokee nation, visited the island to offer her support. Alcatraz, she later said, was why she became an activist. "It gave me the sense that anything was possible. Who I am and how I governed was influenced by Alcatraz."

The occupation lasted until June 11, 1971, when the protestors were removed by federal authorities. By then, the protest had run its course, and only a few Indians remained. They had achieved some goals: President Richard Nixon, elected in 1968, returned Mount Adams to the Yakima tribe in Washington, as well as Blue Lake and 48,000 acres of New Mexico land to the Taos Indians. A university for Native Americans was established near Davis, California, and in 1975, Congress eventually passed the Indian

Self-Determination and Education Assistance Act. Relocation efforts by the government stopped completely, and the Bureau of Indian Affairs (BIA) hired Native Americans to participate in establishing policy.

The American Indian Movement

The protest that garnered the most public awareness of injustices suffered by Native Americans came in 1973. That year, Native Americans occupied Wounded Knee, South Dakota. South Dakota was, as Oglala Sioux Russell Means described it, "the Mississippi of the north." Just as Mississippi had become the center for massive resistance against African Americans seeking their civil rights, so South Dakota became the center of white resistance to the Native American rights movement.

The Pine Ridge Reservation was run by a corrupt tribal chair, Dick Wilson, with a private army of his own and the tacit support of the BIA for his actions. In January 1973, a white man who had killed a Native American, Lakota Wesley Bad Heart Bull, was convicted of only involuntary manslaughter, rather than first-degree murder. Indians rioted in response to the verdict, and after another confrontation a few days later, Bad Heart Bull's mother Sarah was arrested for rioting. Tribal Chair Wilson made no attempt to see that justice was done, and instead threatened AIM members to keep them from protesting. Attempts to impeach Wilson failed, so women elders Gladys Bissonette and Ellen Moves Camp publicly picketed against him, trying to force him from office. When that failed, Bissonnette suggested that the Oglala Sioux Civil Rights Organization and AIM members protest by occupying the village of Wounded Knee on the Pine Ridge Reservation in South Dakota, site of an Indian massacre in 1890.

Native women were at the forefront of the occupation. During a ten-week siege, about 250 women and 100 men occupied Pine Ridge. The leaders declared their independence from the United States, forming the Independent Oglala Sioux nation. A media circus ensued as the federal government responded with a massive show of force. Phantom jets flew overhead, and half a million rounds of ammunition were fired into the compound. Two Indians were killed, and several more wounded. The media focused on the firefights rather than the legitimate complaints of the Indians, and on male leaders such as Russell Means, the national director of AIM, rather than the women who dug the bunkers, ran the medical clinic, carried weapons, and negotiated with the government.

The siege at Wounded Knee ended in early May 1973, as the Indians ran out of food and medical supplies. Despite an agreement signed with the government, nearly all AIM members were arrested. Male leaders received tougher sentences in court than did women activists, and a U.S. Senate subcommittee held hearings. Little changed on the reservation. Dick Wilson, still in charge of the tribal government, went on a rampage, killing hundreds over the next two years to consolidate his power. Gladys Bisonette, the elder who had called for the occupation, lost her son Pedro in October, killed by the BIA police. As her daughter Jeanette Bisonette came home from her brother's funeral, she, too, was shot dead. No one was ever indicted for the crimes; eventually Federal Judge Fred Nichol dismissed all charges against Wounded Knee participants because of government misconduct.

Women of All Red Nations

After Wounded Knee, AIM continued to exist, but its more radical actions were largely over, in part because so many male members of the group were either arrested or on the run. Remaining members focused on less violent means to achieve its goals, often using lawsuits to force the federal government to respect the treaties it had signed. They also worked to support Native culture and activities by promoting education, building schools and housing, and offering employment services. Many Native American women were skeptical of AIM's ability to move beyond political theater and confrontation to achieve lasting change. They felt their needs were not being met, so they established their own group to pursue their concerns. Women of All Red Nations (WARN), founded by Lakota Madonna Thunder Hawk, Tulalip Janet McCloud, Winnebago Lorelai DeCora and others, dealt with domestic issues facing women and their families.

In 1972, Native Americans had begun what was called "The Trail of Broken Treaties," a cross-country march that stopped at historical sites of Indian massacres, such as Sand Creek and Wounded Knee. The marchers planned their arrival in Washington, DC, in time for the national election in November to attract maximum publicity to their demands. The protest ended with a six-day sit-in at the BIA, the federal bureaucracy so ineffective at helping the Native population. After presenting a twenty-point document listing Native demands to President Nixon, leaders Russell Means and Madonna Gilbert Thunderhawk collected documents from BIA offices and left the occupation to return to the Midwest.

Some of the file documents Means and Thunderhawk liberated contained evidence of widespread involuntary sterilization of Native American women. The Indian Health Service (IHS), part of the Department of Health, Education, and Welfare begun by President Eisenhower in 1953, began counseling Indian women regarding birth control beginning in 1965, as new methods became available. But counseling soon turned into misinformation, as some doctors responded to what they perceived as too many Indian women with too many children by promoting sterilization as birth control. As was true for other minority women, the doctors and clinic workers provided inadequate, confusing, misleading, or no explanations of the procedures that Native women agreed to. For example, while in the hospital for alcoholism treatment, a twenty-year-old Native American woman was given a hysterectomy. Six years later, when she asked Choctaw/Cherokee Dr. Connie Pinkerton-Uri, a Los Angeles IHS physician for a "womb transplant" so she and her husband could have children, she was repeating what her original IHS doctor told her—that the procedure was reversible. Another case involved two fifteen-year-old Cheyenne girls in the hospital for appendectomies. They received tubal ligations as well, without their knowledge or the knowledge and consent of their parents. Coerced unknowingly into losing one's fertility in a culture that prized children had traumatic effects on the women involved: depression, guilt, alcoholism, divorce, even suicide sometimes followed the discovery they could not have children.

Dr. Pinkerton-Uri called public attention to the problem of forced sterilization and conducted research that concluded that, while the government had no comprehensive policy deliberately promoting sterilization of Indians, individual doctors, nurses, and social workers in the system pushed the idea to patients as a way to limit welfare costs, following what Pinkerton-Uri called "the warped thinking of doctors who think the solution to poverty is not to allow people to be born." Such a patronizing decision by doctors, mostly white men, did not take into account the importance of children to Native American women, not only for the joy they brought, and for the group's survival and economic well-being, but also to secure a woman's place in her tribe. As one Cheyenne tribal judge, Marie Sanchez, put it: "the Native American woman is the carrier of our nation." Many Native American women wanted large families because they believed there were not enough Indians left in America. Pressured by IHS doctors during delivery, during Cesarean sections, during discussions of how they would lose government benefits if they refused sterilization, Native American women consented to medical procedures that ignored IHS rules. By 1976, when Congress passed the Indian Healthcare Improvement Act, giving Native Americans control over IHS programs, estimates were that nearly 50 percent of full-blooded Native American women had been sterilized.

Native American women's focus on tribal matters and on their reproductive rights disappointed many white women activists, who wanted Native women to deal with what white women saw as a larger issue: the sexism of Native men. However, many Native women, as was true for many African American women, saw the preservation of their people as a far more important issue. They also did not necessarily define themselves as oppressed by men. "Indian women do not need liberation," said Lakota Bea Medicine, because "they have always been liberated within their tribal structure." White women activists and Native American women activists had little in common. White women worked for political rights within a system that Native women opposed. White women's fight for access to birth control and abortion held little appeal for Native women who had long practiced herbal forms of birth control and were suffering from the genocide of forced sterilization. Instead, Native women took a different path more meaningful to them.

THE WOMEN'S LIBERATION MOVEMENT

Social, economic, and political reforms that made up Johnson's Great Society and the fight for civil rights increased federal spending dramatically in the 1960s and 1970s. At the same time, Americans took on an expensive and ultimately futile war in Southeast Asia: Vietnam. At the beginning of

Johnson's tenure, Americans supported antipoverty programs. Over time, however, as the economy began a downward turn, as urban unrest led to violence in cities across the country, and as the war took more and more of the federal budget, Great Society programs were first underfunded and then unfunded. Women suffered the most from the cutbacks. Riots in Watts (a section of Los Angeles), Newark, Detroit, and Chicago exploded as the urban poor took to the streets to protest racial and economic discrimination. Opposition to the war grew as well, and sparked the formation of groups disaffected from traditional politics and culture.

The Vietnam War

The United States had been committed to keeping the country of Vietnam from falling under Communist rule after World War II. This practice was part of Truman's "containment" foreign policy to limit the spread of communism. In 1961, President Kennedy sent 400 Green Berets to South Vietnam to train Vietnamese soldiers to fight in the guerilla war being waged by Communist North Vietnamese. By 1963, Kennedy declared Vietnam a holding action against the forces of communism worldwide, saying in an interview, "If we withdrew from Vietnam, the Communists would control Vietnam. Pretty soon, Thailand, Cambodia, Laos, Malaya, would go." The fall of these countries, called the *domino theory*, had to be prevented. By the end of 1963, some 16,300 American military advisers were in Vietnam.

American involvement continued to escalate under President Johnson. In August 1964, with the cost of American support at 2 million dollars per day, Johnson claimed, to a national television audience, that the North Vietnamese had attacked two American destroyers in the Gulf of Tonkin, off North Vietnam's coast. In response, Congress passed the Tonkin Resolution, which Johnson used to send in additional troops and to begin sustained bombings of North Vietnam by American jet fighters. In March 1965, the first U.S. combat ground troops arrived, joining the 23,000 American advisors already there. In July, the president announced he would increase the size of the American force to 125,000 men, a demand that would be met by drafting young men.

Women and the Antiwar Movement

Protests against the war grew from a variety of sources, including religious groups and working-class and minority communities who were disproportionately affected by the draft, and disproportionately called upon to fight the war. The draft also greatly affected young men of college age who would lose their student deferments the minute they graduated. Students who had participated in the civil rights movement to protest segregation used similar tactics to protest the draft and the war. One of the best-known antiwar protest groups was Students for a Democratic Society (SDS), formed by Tom Hayden (civil rights activist Casey Hayden's husband) and Al Haber at the University of Michigan. SDS originally began in 1960, protesting against the materialism and loss of individual freedom in American life. The group's ideas struck a chord with other university students across the country. Other chapters of SDS and similar organizations formed, such as the Free Speech Movement at the University of California, Berkeley, and the Southern Student Organizing Committee, which sought links with civil rights advocates on the largely white college campuses of the South. Student groups called for more individual freedom, the abolition of dormitory regulations, curfews, and dress codes, more relevant classes, even lower movie prices, as well as advocating for community and union organizing, integration, and civil rights for all Americans.

When the draft was expanded, student groups expanded their protests as well. They marched against mandatory Reserve Officer Training Corps (ROTC) programs on campus, against the draft, and against the war itself. Professors opposed to the war and sympathetic to the plight of those soon to be drafted into service encouraged student resistance, holding "teach-ins" and participating in mass marches. Men burned their draft cards, refused to report for service, sought conscientious objector status, worked to fail the military physical, or fled the country to Canada or Sweden to avoid service.

The draft included only men, but the U.S. military presence in Vietnam included women as well. Army and civilian nurses and medical personnel served in the field hospitals and air bases around the country. Civilian secretaries and clerical workers labored for the armed forces. Some seventy women war correspondents filed pictures and stories. Entertainers traveled close to the front lines to give the soldiers a little relief, including Martha Raye, a comic who funded her own trips to spend up to six months at a time visiting soldiers. On one visit, when the enemy fired on the camp she was in, hitting the medic, Raye, a trained nurse, took over for him. She cared for injured soldiers for thirteen hours straight. The Green Berets made her an honorary member with the rank of lieutenant colonel. Other women entertainers, traveling with stars such as Bob Hope, focused more on entertaining the troops with their beauty, so the young men would "know what they were fighting for," as Hope put it.

In the United States, women opposed to the war participated actively in the antiwar movement. Because women could not be drafted, however, men often downplayed or disregarded their participation. Nevertheless, women continued their protests, burning others' draft cards, marching, submitting to arrest, and even fleeing the country. Some 26,804 women left for Canada to protest the war—nearly 1,000 more than male protestors. Women also joined antiwar organizations, but faced discrimination there as well. At one meeting at New York University, for instance, Leslie Cagan, a staunch opponent and leader of the antiwar protests, was told to sit quietly and listen to the men in the room. Since she was not subject to the draft, many in the antiwar movement argued that she and others like her were not qualified to talk about it.

That same second-class status for women showed up in student protest organizations such as SDS, as male leaders replaced participatory democracy and passive civil disobedience with violent and confrontational approaches. Leaders such as Hayden and Black Power advocates H. Rap Brown and Stokley Carmichael embraced militancy. Many activists particularly liked ideas expressed by the Leftist leader of the Russian Revolution of 1917, Vladmir Lenin. Lenin opposed capitalism and imperialism, and called for the violent overthrow of governments to overturn oppression. Revolutionaries adopted Lenin's ideas, calling themselves the "New Left," and blamed American capitalism and imperialism in Vietnam as the root cause for society's ills, becoming ever more militant by the late 1960s. The SDS chapter at Columbia University eventually kidnapped a dean, occupied the university president's office, and ransacked offices to protest the university's plans for a new gymnasium to be built on lands housing a black community.

At Harvard, Cornell, San Francisco State, Berkeley, and other schools across the country, students protested. Police were called, leading to often violent confrontations, alienating many women activists. In 1968, SDS splintered into groups such as the Weathermen (who firebombed buildings and other symbols of establishment power, injuring police and innocent bystanders) and the new Youth International Party, or "Yippies" (who called for the legalization of marijuana and psychedelic drugs, the abolition of schools, and free sex). During the Democratic National Convention in the summer of 1968, Yippies threatened to spike the Chicago municipal water supply with LSD. The police met protesters with force as they took to the streets. In 1970, student antiwar activists at Kent State in Ohio and at Jackson State in Mississippi were killed by National Guardsmen called out to protect the campuses.

Part of the capitalist imperialism that oppressed Americans, the New Leftists argued, included sexual restraints, and women activists in these groups faced increasing demands that they disavow sexual limitations as proof that they were full participants in resistance movements. One poster sold to raise funds for a group called The Draft Resistance showed three attractive young women, activist/singer Joan Baez and her two sisters, seated on a couch. The copy read, "GIRLS SAY YES to boys who say NO." The implication was that women should be willing to have sexual intercourse with men who protested the war. Such sexual objectification offended many women, as did men's assertion that women did not have a role to play in antiwar and civil rights protests beyond making coffee and typing papers.

Consciousness-Raising

As more and more American women joined the antiwar movement and faced similar experiences, they began to compare notes. In San Francisco, Bettina Aptheker, a leading activist with the National Mobilization Committee to End the War in Vietnam, watched as women did much of the work required for any protest to be successful, while men ridiculed the women's attempts to gain equality with men in the movement. Marian Gordon, who had worked in Mississippi during voter registration attempts, continued her activism with antiwar activities at California State University,

Los Angeles. Eventually she left to help form a women's organization, tired of having male activists treat her ideas so disrespectfully. Other women voted with their feet as well, and began organizing *consciousness-raising groups* where women assembled by themselves and spoke to each other of their experiences. In the South, one of the first women's liberation groups, Gainesville Women's Liberation (GWL), described how it operated at a national women's liberation conference. The group was small and women spoke about money, marriage, sexuality, racism, and capitalism, trying to relate their personal experiences to the political implications of their actions. "We speak 'pain to recall pain,'" the group declared, declaring that male domination oppressed women not occasionally, but systematically. Men's oppression of women was so systemic, the members thought the cultural and economic systems of America needed complete reorientation to liberate women. Two members of the GWL, Judith Brown and Beverly Jones, published "Towards a Female Liberation Movement," known as the *Florida Paper*, in 1968, calling for a women's liberation movement independent of other protest groups.

In consciousness-raising groups, women shared similar tales of being denigrated or dismissed because of their sex, of being sexually harassed or underpaid in their jobs, and of being denied opportunities in employment

WOMEN'S LIBERATION PROTESTORS Women's liberation incorporated many social issues that reflected the unequal status women had once they married. Here, protestors in 1970 declare their opposition to the very institution of marriage, along with the need to reform divorce laws.

and housing because they were women. Women participants in the civil rights, antiwar, and student protest movements learned of the commonality of their experiences, and many revealed a widespread desire to do something to make life better for all women. The women's liberation movement had begun.

In 1960, women made up 51 percent of the American population. Nearly 38 percent of women over age 16 were in the workforce, accounting for 33.4 percent of the total labor force. By 1970, those proportions would be 43.3 and 38.1 percent, respectively. The Civil Rights Act forbade discrimination against women because of their sex, yet women still faced discrimination, ranging from crippling financial limits on their freedom of action to petty annoyances. Married women still could not get credit in their own names, and single women—even well-off, fully employed women—usually were required to have a male cosign any credit applications, be they for cars, homes, or department store cards. Salesmen often ignored women shopping for major purchases alone, preferring to wait until a man came along, since he was presumed to be the decision maker. Married women could not get telephones on their own—their husbands had to be the account owners. Women's shirts cost more to dry-clean than men's, even if they were the same size, style, and fabric. At institutions of higher education, male professors often ignored women students. A woman might easily be denied admission to programs because of prevailing assumptions that she was just looking for her "Mrs." degree, rather than an academic degree, and that a man serious about his degree would be denied his rightful place if a woman was admitted. Women were expected to keep quiet when men were talking, to find happiness in housecleaning, to fulfill men's sexual desires while denying or second-guessing their own, and to accept a second-class, secondhand lot in life.

For women involved in the activism of the 1950s and 1960s, discovering the sexism inherent in reform movements came as a shock and served as an impetus for change. *The Feminine Mystique* had articulated the problem of sexism faced by women in the early 1960s. By the middle of the decade, radicals resurrected Charlotte Perkins Gilman's Progressive Era ideas about communal dining rooms and laundries, living communally, and rearing children collectively. Germaine Greer wrote *The Female Eunuch*, opposing marriage and arguing that many women sought economic and emotional security from an institution that cost them their personalities. In marriage, liberty of self was given up, she wrote, and at great cost. Marriage led to a war between women over the tasks of attracting, catching, and keeping a husband, and corrupted all involved. But for those women who avoided marriage and practiced sexual liberation and free love, she wrote, "Life is not easier or more pleasant—but is more interesting, noble even." Author Shulamith Firestone carried Greer's analysis forward: patriarchal families needed to end since they defined women primarily as mothers because of their ability to produce children. Just as early-twentieth-century revolutionary socialists argued that the workers needed to seize the means of production to free themselves from their oppression by the capitalist owners of those means, Firestone argued that women needed to seize control of their means of production—their reproductive capabilities. Only then could they free themselves from sexism, discrimination, and oppression.

Birth Control and Abortion Rights

Women's liberation depended in part on the ability of women to control their fertility. The single most important invention for women in history was safe, effective birth control. More information on birth control had become available, but the available techniques for preventing pregnancy were still limited in their effectiveness. Most couples practiced withdrawal (prior to ejaculation) or used douching immediately after intercourse. Condoms, far more acceptable since World War II when the government had distributed them to soldiers to prevent sexually transmitted disease (and, less importantly, pregnancies), were common but could still fail to prevent pregnancy 15 percent of the time. The most effective contraceptive method for women was the diaphragm, used with spermicidal jelly. It had been available since 1936, when Margaret Sanger successfully won her case, *The United States v. One Package*, in the U.S. Appeals Court. The package, seized by U.S. Customs, contained 120 diaphragms Sanger sent to Dr. Hannah Meyer Stone from Japan. The court ruled that the package could be sent, thus overturning the Comstock Law that prevented distribution of birth control information through the mails.

In 1950, Planned Parenthood began a study to develop an oral contraceptive, funded by Katherine Dexter McCormick, heir to the International Harvester fortune. Oral contraceptives had existed for centuries in one form or another. Indian women, for instance, ate papayas daily when they wanted to prevent conception. Other women drank pennyroyal tea. Researchers Gregory Pincus and Min Chueh Chang began their work to develop a contraceptive using synthetic progestin extracted from the Barbasco root, a wild yam also called *cabeza de negro*. Mexican women had eaten it for centuries to prevent conception. Drug trials were conducted by Dr. John Rock, a Catholic gynecologist who was searching for an acceptable method to complement the Catholic Church's "rhythm method," which limited sex to times during a woman's menstrual cycle when she was less likely to conceive. The "pill" was approved by the FDA in 1960, and America's sexual revolution began.

State laws still limited doctors' abilities to prescribe the pill, along with the IUD (intrauterine device) refined in the 1960s. *Griswold v. Connecticut*, discussed in the opening of this chapter, was followed by *Eisenstadt v. Baird* in 1972. That case followed the arrest of William Baird for distributing contraceptive foam during a lecture on population control in Boston. Massachusetts state law limited the use of contraceptives by single persons. Justice William J. Brennan Jr. wrote for the majority, striking down the law. "If the right of privacy means anything," he argued, "it is the right of the individual, married or single, to be free from unwarranted governmental intrusion into matters so fundamentally affecting a person as the decision whether to bear or beget a child."

Access to birth control as a matter of reproductive control included the right to abortion. Abortion, legal until the early 1800s, had been criminalized in the nineteenth century. Many early feminists were adamantly opposed to abortion, arguing that women should be allowed to learn about and gain access to contraception, since that would prevent pregnancy and the need for abortion. By 1965, every state banned abortion in all but a few situations: to save the life of the mother, to end pregnancies caused by rape or incest, or to end pregnancies when babies were afflicted with birth defects. At the same time that birth control and abortion were limited, the social stigma against having a child out of wedlock remained severe, and it was the mother, not the father, who suffered repercussions, such as being expelled from school, denied housing, and fired from employment. Illegal abortions were still performed, mostly on married women who did not want additional children, but some on young women who simply did not want to be pregnant—some 200,000 to 2 million in the 1950s and 1960s. These "back-alley" abortions, usually performed under unsanitary conditions by practitioners who might have no medical training at all, resulted in infections, sterility, and even the deaths of hundreds of women every year. In New York City in 1969, 23 percent of all pregnancy-related admissions to the city's hospitals were because of complications from illegal abortions. A woman desperate to end her pregnancy would insert a knitting needle into her uterus, trying to cause a miscarriage, but often perforating the organ. Others would swallow concoctions recommended by friends, throw themselves down stairs, ask their partners to punch them in the abdomen, or douche with lye solutions—all techniques exceedingly dangerous for the women trying to end their unwanted pregnancies.

In 1967, the NOW proposed a constitutional amendment to protect a woman's right to both birth control and abortion. Such an amendment was necessary, NOW reasoned, because, as the group put it: "There is perhaps no more fundamental human right, save the right to life itself, than the right to one's own physical person, a basic part of which is the right to determine whether or not one will give birth to another human being." The group passed a women's bill of rights in 1968, demanding an equal rights amendment, maternity leave, tax deductions for child care, enforcement of laws against sex discrimination in employment, equal education and job training and, last, "the right of women to control their reproductive lives." The degree to which politicians supported NOW's bill of rights helped determine how feminists voted in the 1968 elections.

In January 1969, NOW members in New York formed the first abortion law repeal group, based on the radical feminist belief that no woman should face restrictions to birth control or abortion. Later that month, the National Association for the Repeal of Abortion Laws (NARAL) was formed at a national conference in Chicago, where Betty Friedan spoke of safe and legal abortion as "a woman's civil right." In February, a group of activists protested a New York state legislative hearing where the panel's witnesses on abortion rights were fourteen men and one women—a nun. Concerted efforts by other groups at both state and national levels led to discussion of and action on abortion rights. In 1970, Hawaii and Alaska ended restrictions on abortions, and a Texas court overturned that state's restrictive laws. Other states faced similar challenges and found their laws overturned by the courts, usually on privacy or discrimination grounds. Finally, abortion was legalized nationally in 1973 by the Supreme Court case *Roe v. Wade*. Based on a woman's constitutional right to privacy first established by *Griswold v. Connecticut*, the ruling struck down all state laws prohibiting abortion in the first three months of pregnancy. During the second trimester, states were allowed to impose restrictions but only in ways that were designed to protect the woman's health. In the third trimester, when a fetus reached viability (the ability to survive outside the womb), states could regulate or prohibit abortions as they saw fit, unless an abortion was necessary to save the health or life of the woman. Opposition to *Roe v. Wade* began almost immediately and would eventually lead to restrictions on abortions, but the basic premise of a constitutional right to privacy held against later challenges.

Local Feminist Groups and Goals

NOW was only one of the many women's rights organizations founded in the late 1960s. Groups formed all over the country, all determined to reform society to meet the needs of women. One such group, the Chicago Women's Liberation Union (CWLU), created in 1969, recognized that changing women's position in American society required not only opening more jobs to women and providing child care and education for women—but also changes in the ways society distributed its power. The CWLU members considered themselves revolutionaries because they wanted "a total restructuring of society, not merely making room for more women within this structure." The group organized projects to fight discrimination on the job and in the unions, to distribute health care information gathered from a sexist medical establishment, to fight homophobia rampant in America, to protest against sexist policies by the Chicago public parks that blocked women's sports teams from using neighborhood facilities, and to develop a project named "Jane," which trained members to perform abortions safely in the days before abortion became legal. Another group, the Charlotte Perkins Gilman Group, formed in 1969 in Durham, North Carolina, sought to include working women—secretaries, lab technicians, and social workers employed by Duke University and the University of North Carolina—and their interests. A Nashville, Tennessee, group protested the poor treatment and pay for working women there as well.

Women's liberation groups sprang up in cities all over America and most had similar goals. The revolution that these women hoped to lead had a number of components. Activists worked for welfare reform, arguing that if the federal government was going to fight a War on Poverty then it ought to provide job training for women as well as men. They fought to extend Aid to Dependent Children, begun by President Roosevelt and expanded by Johnson's Great Society, so that women could care for their children and receive benefits whether or not fathers were present. Women's rights advocates pushed for affirmative action in hiring, arguing that women had been so short-changed in the market for so many years that if an employer's choice came down to an equally qualified man and woman, the woman ought to be the one hired. Activists suggested alternative living arrangements that might give women some freedom from domestic duties: communes, for instance, that had multiple people responsible for child care and domestic duties; and cooperatives in child care and food purchasing that allowed women's limited incomes to go further by exchanging individual baby care and grocery shopping for group care and group purchases.

The ideas of the women's liberation movement were disseminated not only by consciousness-raising groups and informal networks of women, but eventually by the popular press and other media. In 1972, the first mass circulation magazine to promote feminism and the women's liberation movement, *Ms.*, began. Its very title was an invention of the movement. Why should women be defined by their marital status as "Miss" or "Mrs." when men were not? "Ms." allowed women to define themselves as they wished, and the magazine that carried the same title, edited by leading activist Gloria Steinem, published articles about women's lives, legal and economic issues, history and popular culture, all designed to reach women in search of themselves.

Cultural and Socialist Radicals

A number of feminist groups were extraordinarily radical, pushing the envelope of possibilities for change. Cultural radicals, for instance, argued that gender issues affect every aspect of women's lives. Therefore, the patriarchal culture that had oppressed women through the centuries needed to change. Cultural radicals denounced marriage and romance as patriarchal inventions designed to keep women in chains. They advocated group marriage, celibacy, lesbianism, or free love. They also argued that women needed more legal control over their own bodies. Rape needed to be recognized as a crime, not some sort of passionate encounter. Rapes needed to be prosecuted, and rapists needed to be punished. The victims of rape should not be told that they should "lie back and enjoy it," or that they had caused the crime by wearing short skirts, or by walking along a public street. Sexual violence should be prevented if possible and prosecuted when it occurred, not dismissed with the excuse that "boys will be boys."

Cultural radicals taught people to look closely at American culture for stereotypes hostile to women, particularly in the media. One cultural phenomenon that attracted their criticism was the Miss America beauty pageant. Cultural radicals questioned why women had to stand in bathing suits before an audience made up largely of men in order to win a scholarship to go to college, while men did not. Any culture that promoted this, they argued, defined women first and foremost by their appearances, making for little difference between Miss America and a meat market. In 1968, women protestors from the New York Consciousness Awakening Women's Liberation Group and other groups on the East Coast draped themselves in pork chops and sausages, crowned a sheep, and marched on the boardwalk in

Atlantic City to protest the Miss America contest being held there. Into nearby trash cans went cosmetics, girdles (the "body-shapers" of the time), and a bra or two, all to protest women's imprisonment by the chains of appearance, as well as the pain women felt when they failed to measure up to the artificial beauty of the pageant's participants. Lindsy Van Gelder, the *New York Post* reporter covering the story, had been sent by her male editors to do a humorous piece on the protestors, but she wanted the women to be taken seriously. When she tried to link their protest to the antiwar tradition of burning one's draft card, however, the idea backfired. The "bra-burner" image appealed to the *Post*'s headline writers, and the most notorious stereotype of the women's movement was born: the *bra-burner*. By renaming women activists as bra-burners and "women's libbers," opponents trivialized protestors' concerns, diminishing their power.

In contrast to cultural radicals, socialist radicals blamed capitalism for the evils of the world, including women's oppression. Social inequities pervaded all human actions, particularly relations between men and women, thought socialist radicals, and those inequities were exacerbated by capitalism, which awarded some people more power and resources than others. Converting from capitalism to socialism could help to solve women's problems. An economic system where businesses, trade, and industries were owned and regulated by the community as a whole, rather than by private individuals, would change society's very structure.

Adherents of these radical philosophies formed groups to support their causes. The groups usually excluded men from membership, saw the primary issue to confront as being gender relations, and argued that the very basis for American civilization must change. As was true for the vast majority of protestors in the 1960s and 1970s, these radicals were trained by actions in the civil rights and antiwar movements. Heather Booth, for example, founding member of the Socialist CWLU, had registered voters in Mississippi, and then worked on child care issues in Chicago. Vivian Rothstein had gone to Vietnam in 1967 to protest the war, then returned to form a Liberation School in Chicago for women.

Cultural and socialist radicals argued that personal choices made by individuals had political implications for the rest of society. This idea, that the "personal is political," one that feminist Emma Goldman promoted earlier in the century, became a rallying cry for members of the women's liberation movement and feminists more generally. Carol Hanisch's essay, "The Personal Is Political," defended the practice of group consciousness-raising, arguing that one of the first things such groups discovered was that "personal problems are political problems." Hanisch belonged to the Redstockings, a radical anti-male group, whose manifesto included the statement: "In fighting for our liberation we will always take the side of the women against their oppressors. We will not ask what is 'revolutionary' or 'reformist,' only what is good for women." Other anti-male groups included the Society for Cutting Up Men (SCUM), and the Women's International Terrorist Conspiracy from Hell (WITCH), who on Halloween 1968 cast hexes on Wall Street firms and men-only bars to protest their exclusion from those places of power.

The anti-male rhetoric of the more radical reformers attracted some members but drove away more moderate feminists, even when their over-all goals were similar. Seeking to expand their influence, the largely white, upper- and middle-class organizers of radical liberation groups reached out to minority and labor groups, in hopes of attracting more members as well as finding supporters from lower economic classes who could benefit greatly from a decline in sexism and a radical restructuring of capitalism.

The Labor Movement

Labor organizations provided another route for activists to raise women's concerns. In 1939 in Atlanta, Georgia, Maria Getzinger had joined the International Typographical Union, the first union to require employers to pay men and women the same salary for the same jobs. When Atlanta women formed a chapter of NOW in 1968, Getzinger eagerly joined. She also traveled north to help found the Coalition of Labor Union Women (CLUW) in a Chicago conference in 1974. The CLUW sought to bring unorganized women into unions and to increase the participation of women already in unions, to promote affirmative action, and to increase women's participation in political activities and state legislatures. It lobbied for a higher minimum wage; educated workers on health and safety issues, par-ticularly lead exposure, which caused birth defects; and suggested ways that unions could negotiate for child care as a benefit. The CLUW supported the Equal Rights Amendment and convinced the AFL-CIO to do the same, then it refused to hold conventions in states that had not ratified the amendment.

Other women workers, isolated in secretarial pools or one-woman clerical positions, found most unions too male-dominated and too male-oriented to appeal to them or to pay attention to their needs. In 1972, Karen Nussbaum, a clerk-typist fed up with low pay and even lower respect for women clerical workers, got together with a group of women office workers in Boston to discuss some of the issues that they faced in the workplace: sexual harassment from bosses, balancing of work demands with family concerns, and unequal pay for comparable work. Traditional unions with their industrial workers did not seem to be the answer, but Nussbaum knew the value of collective action. The solution was a union-like associa-tion geared toward women who worked in offices doing clerical work. The women formed 9to5: Organization for Women Office Workers. Similar groups formed in other cities, and in 1977 an umbrella organization, Work-ing Women, established its headquarters in Cleveland, Ohio. The organiza-tion sought to document women's working lives to provide useful data as it worked for national goals of affirmative action, equal pay, and family and medical leave, as well as training older women entering the workforce, and eliminating racial and sexual discrimination.

Some women still entered traditional unions, as well. In Texas, Linda Chavez-Thompson, daughter of sharecroppers, began hoeing cotton at age 10, dropping out of school a few years later to contribute full time to her family's economy. After her marriage at age 19, she cleaned houses for a living, but eventually became a secretary to the local branch of the American Federation of State, County and Municipal Employees (AFSCME). Her bilingual skills led her to the job of international union representative in San Antonio because she could communicate with Spanish-speaking union workers. She also became active in the AFL-CIO, of which AFSCME was a part. In 1977, Chavez-Thompson became executive director of her AFSCME branch, one of the only women in America to occupy that position of power. She advocated legislative, political, and education programs, as well as conducting union members' grievance procedures. Chavez-Thompson would eventually become the international vice president of AFSCME and, finally, executive vice president of the AFL-CIO.

Hispanic Women in the Movement

The *Chicano Movimiento*, the civil rights movement for Americans of Hispanic descent, was inextricably linked to the labor movement, personified by women such as Dolores Huerta, labor organizer and feminist. Because so many Chicanos worked in low-paying agricultural jobs in states such as California, Washington, Texas, and Florida, the United Farm Workers (UFW) served as an organizing base for activists determined to improve the lives of their people (see Chapter 9). Using nonviolent protest, including hunger strikes, demonstrations, and boycotts against grapes and farmers using pesticides that injured workers, the UFW succeeded in greatly improving the lives of Chicano workers (see Primary Source 10-5).

The movement's political training translated well to political activism in government. In Crystal City, Texas, for instance, where 80 percent of the population was Mexican American since the 1930s, there were no Chicanos in office or on the school board. *La Raza Unida*, a political party dedicated to bringing more Chicanos into political office, ran slates of candidates for office, including a number of women. Chicana women activists, however, faced a problem similar to black women: activism was seen largely as the purview of men. Even though women were deeply involved in all levels of activism, the Chicano cultural construct of *machismo* (male chauvinism) allowed women little public recognition. *Machismo* had two definitions. The first definition portrayed a man as someone with an exaggerated sense of masculinity, stressing not only physical courage and strength, but also aggression, along with the sexual possession of women and domination over them. The second definition held that a real man was strong, responsible, and nurturing. The former definition was apparent far more often in the popular press and among activists as well.

In 1969, young Chicanos met in Denver in the National Chicano Youth Liberation Conference, seeking to coordinate the student activism that had spawned recent strikes and walkouts. Chicano students were protesting oppression, discrimination, and the lack of educational equality, primarily in southern California and Texas, areas with substantial Mexican American populations. Conference organizers announced a plan of action with seven goals at the end of the conference: unity, economy, education, institutions, self-defense, cultural, and political liberation. The few women attending

DOLORES HUERTA CALLS FOR A BOYCOTT

Inspired by fellow United Farm Worker leader Cesar Chavez's fast to protest conditions for farmworkers, Dolores Huerta thought the whole country could "do a little fast" to convince growers to treat their workers fairly. In February 1978, she recounted the importance of economic boycotts as a form of protest.

"Let's ask everybody not to eat grapes. That's kind of a simple thing, right? It doesn't take a lot, just don't eat grapes. And so we asked the whole country and the whole world not to eat grapes, and they didn't. And as a result of that, people not eating grapes, we had our first big national grape boycott and we got

the conference announced that Chicana liberation was unnecessary because Chicanas did not want to liberated, but that sentiment was not universal. As later meetings focused on oppression and discrimination against Chicano men and paid little attention to women's issues, Chicanas sought a voice. They held their own conference in Houston in May 1971. There, 600 Chicanas passed resolutions calling for less *machismo* and more support for reproductive rights, child care, an end to educational discrimination against women, an end to the sexual double standard, and more respect for women from men. The Catholic Church, which forbade female priests and kept women in inferior roles as laypeople and nuns, also came in for criticism from many Chicanas, who viewed the church as part of the oppressive forces women faced.

Student activists among Chicanos included the Brown Berets, comparable in many ways to the Black Panthers and the Red Power members of Native American groups. In each case, these more radical thinkers and activists wanted to push harder and faster for social, economic, and political changes. Here, too, the more radical Brown Berets disappointed many Chicana activists by ignoring their concerns. Chicanas, like African American women, also remained unconvinced that the Anglo women's liberation movement realized the role of racism in the discrimination that Chicanas faced. Organizations separate from Anglo groups would ensure Chicana voices were represented. The Southwest Council of *La Raza* formed to help Chicana community groups in 1968. By 1973, the council adopted a policy that half of its board would be women. Chicanas also formed their own groups to promote their agenda: reproductive rights, including abortion, and an end to forced sterilization for poor Chicanas; education and bilingualism to support women not yet conversant in English; equal pay for the same work that Anglos and Chicano men did; child care and respect for women as mothers; and recognition of spousal abuse and rape as crimes, rather than manifestations of *machismo*.

Other Hispanic women—Latinas from Puerto Rico, the Dominican Republic, Cuba, and Central American countries—made up a smaller our first contract. That was a really simple thing, but it had a tremendous impact. Because we were going to the heart of the growers, and that is in their pocketbook. . . . [W]hen you are dealing with a big social fight and trying to make changes, the people that you are dealing with are not going to be rational and they are not going to do things on the basis of justice—they respond to only one thing and that is economic power. So somehow, you have to hit them in that pocketbook where they have their heart and their nerves and then they feel the pain. Otherwise, they can give you a thousand arguments on why something can't be done. This is why . . . the Montgomery Bus Boycott was effective, right? Because it hit them where? In the pocketbook."

Source: Dolores Huerta, "Speech at UCLA, February 22, 1978," in A Dolores Huerta Reader, ed. Mario T. Garcia (Albuquerque: University of New Mexico Press, 2008), 245–246.

proportion of the U.S. population than Chicanos, but suffered the same effects of discrimination: racism, poverty, and limited educational and job opportunities. Organizations that represented Latinas' issues began as early as the 1930s when *El Congreso de Pueblos de Habla Española* (the Spanish-Speaking Peoples Congress), organized by Luisa Moreno, held a national meeting to call for an end to discrimination against Latinos. In New York City, where most Puerto Ricans lived, Dr. Antonia Pantoja founded the Hispanic Youth Adult Association in 1953, while still a student at Columbia University. By the 1970s, there were a number of women's organizations in New York, including the Latin Women's Collective formed under the leadership of Esperanza Martell. Cuban women in Florida, a large contingent of whom had migrated there after fleeing the Communist regime established on the island in 1959, had their groups as well. As was the case with Chicana groups, much of the work Latina activists did started with fighting against the discrimination suffered by both men and women, before shifting to an awareness of the double discrimination that Latina women felt.

THE IMPACT OF THE WOMEN'S LIBERATION MOVEMENT

The stories of reformers and activists illustrate the way that the women's liberation movement worked. Whether by demanding radical changes of the very structure of the country or by working for change by forcing traditional power structures such as unions to include women, the movement successfully brought society's attention to women's issues that male-dominated groups had heretofore largely ignored. Such inclusion allowed women to succeed in ways few women would have dreamed possible in the years before the women's liberation movement. Not everyone approved, however, and conservative opponents used an array of tactics to try to stem the tide of change.

The Movement's Accomplishments

The expansion of women's rights thanks to the women's liberation movement encompassed every aspect of American life and culture. A shift in the national consciousness between 1962 and 1977 led to widespread public support for the movement's key demands such as equal education, an end to overt discrimination in the workplace and in leisure activities, better health care, and more opportunities to participate in government. More women began to go to college, assisted by laws against discrimination and for affirmative action, the most important and effective of which was *Title IX* of the Education Amendment Act (1972). Title IX prohibited sex discrimination in colleges, universities, and graduate programs receiving any federal funds, including federal student loans—in other words, nearly every institution of higher education in America. In 1969 and 1972, Harvard and Princeton, which had relegated women students to women's colleges linked with their main male institutions (Radcliffe and Evelyn College, respectively), accepted women into their regular classes and onto their campuses. Other Ivy League schools also closed their coordinate colleges and finally admitted women into their institutions as equal students. The nation's military academies admitted women beginning in 1976. Law and medical schools opened their doors to more women students as well.

The influx of women into these bastions of power meant that when they graduated, they were able to use the invaluable connections of their college years to their benefit, just as men had done for centuries. The number of women entering the male-dominated professions rose substantially. Something as simple as the language used to describe professions changed to reflect the increasing number of women within the ranks: firemen became firefighters, policemen became police officers, mailmen became mail carriers, stewardesses became flight attendants, and chairmen and chairwomen became chairs.

Professional sports also experienced a sea change, thanks to Title IX, as more women participated in the college sports that fed women participants into the professional sports arena. The most famous woman athlete of the 1970s was Billie Jean King, a twenty-nine-year-old tennis player who in 1973 defeated fifty-five-year-old Bobby Riggs, an antifeminist tennis champion who boasted that any man could beat any woman. King, a Wimbledon champion and the first woman athlete to win more than $100,000 a year, was an ardent feminist determined to promote women's equality in sports. Riggs, who portrayed himself as a "male chauvinist pig" and wore a shirt with "Men's Liberation" emblazoned on it, played King before 30,000 viewers crowded into the Houston Astrodome, as well as 50 million more watching the televised match called "The Battle of the Sexes." The game's symbolic value to the women's liberation movement was to support the idea that women could do anything men could. King beat Riggs in straight sets (6–4, 6–3, 6–3) for a $100,000 paycheck.

Equality in health care was another goal for the women's liberation movement. Control over the health lives of women had largely passed into the hands of male doctors by the mid-twentieth century, and even women physicians were trained by male-dominated schools. In 1969, twelve women formed the Boston Women's Health Book Collective, and in 1970 they published a women's health manual, *Women and Our Bodies.* Through knowledge of their bodies and their sexuality, readers were invited to take control of their health and their lives. Three years later, Simon & Schuster, a mainstream publisher, brought out the book retitled *Our Bodies Ourselves.* It became a perennial best-seller and included topics important to women: childbirth, menstruation, and menopause, as well as masturbation, lesbianism, abortion, and rape. Trying to wrest control over women's medical lives away from male doctors and the male-dominated medical establishment and return it to women healers and women themselves, the book's authors encouraged midwifery, self-examinations, patient advocacy, and clinics run by women for women.

More women participated in state governments as a result of the women's movement as well, although national government was slower to change—Kennedy, Johnson, and Nixon had no women cabinet officers, for instance. When women took elective office, many used their power to change laws and expand women's legal rights. Discrimination against women in granting credit was abolished. Husbands with wives in the military received the same benefits as women with husbands in the military. Juries were to be selected from pools of women and men, not just men. State citizenship became personal, as national citizenship had become early in the century. A New York State resident, for example, would no longer lose her in-state tuition rates because she had married a man from New Jersey. Countless other laws passed codifying women and men's equal standing under the law.

The Houston Conference

In 1975, during the United Nations' International Year of the Woman, Congresswomen Democrat Bella Abzug from New York and Democrat Patsy Mink from Hawaii introduced legislation calling on the U.S. government to sponsor and fund a National Women's Conference. Two years later, nearly 20,000 people attended the conference held in Houston, Texas. Some came to celebrate the achievements of the women's liberation movement and to push for more changes, while others, about 20 percent of the delegates, came to criticize the effects the movement had on women's lives, and sought to slow or even reverse the pace of change. While cautioning voices would not win the day, the Houston Conference provided a platform and a gathering place for conservatives opposed to the women's movement.

The 2,000 delegates in Houston were charged with designing a National Plan of Action. Tying the conference symbolically to the first women's rights conference in the United States, a relay of women runners carried a torch from Seneca Falls to Houston. African American poet Maya Angelou wrote a new version of the Declaration of Sentiments modeled after the one produced over a century before. The torchbearers carried it on their journey as well, and thousands along the way signed the document. When the conference opened, the torch and the new Declaration were presented to three first ladies: Lady Bird Johnson, Betty Ford, and Rosalynn Carter, wife of the current president, Jimmy Carter. All three signed the Declaration and spoke to the convention about their lives as women, not just as the spouses of presidents.

After days of discussion, delegates passed twenty-six different resolutions dealing with the issues women faced. The National Plan called for better enforcement of existing laws as well as demanding a national health care system, peace and disarmament, and full employment. Of all the planks, only the one regarding equal credit passed unanimously. In particular, statements regarding the right to abortion, sexual preference, and the Equal Rights Amendment were rejected by about 20 percent of the delegates as too extreme if not downright immoral. Opposition to the women's liberation movement, particularly on these three key issues, was represented at the conference in significant ways. White social and political conservatives took over the state conventions in some southern states. The delegation from Mississippi, for instance, was completely white, despite Mississippi's 36 percent black population. That group's opposition to what they considered immoral, anti-family, "godless communists" running the Houston conference resulted in Mississippi state resolutions supporting gender differences and declaring that such differences were created by God and to go against them would destroy the nation.

The women's movement's support for abortion rights was particularly difficult for socially and religiously conservative women. These delegates did not believe that abortion was ever the solution to an unwanted pregnancy,

NATIONAL WOMEN'S CONFERENCE, 1977 Women's liberation supporters for the National Women's Conference in Houston in 1977 included women runners, shown here carrying the torch that they brought on a run across the country from Seneca Falls, New York, to Houston, Texas.

since all life was created by God, and no human had the right to play God by terminating a life. "Right to Life" supporters proposed prevention and adoption as alternatives, but given that even the best contraceptives could sometimes fail, abortion rights advocates maintained that a woman's right to choose an abortion to end an unwanted pregnancy was absolute. Battle lines between the two sides were drawn not only over whether the Supreme Court's decision legalizing abortion, *Roe v. Wade*, should be overturned, but also whether federal funds should be used to provide abortions for poor women whose health care was provided by Medicaid. Fifteen states (states administered federal Medicaid funds) had cut off that funding by 1977, and the Supreme Court had recently ruled they could do so as long as the health of the mother was not endangered by her pregnancy. Many of the more liberal delegates to the Houston Conference sought a definitive statement in the National Plan supporting abortion rights as well as public funding for abortions when needed.

Sexual preferences were another controversial issue at the conference. Lesbianism was not a new phenomenon in American culture, but public discussion of it was. Homosexuality and lesbian activism had become more public in the 1960s and 1970s as part of the general liberalizing trend during the era. Research in the 1950s had shown that homosexuality was widespread among both human societies and animal species. Alfred Kinsey's 1953 book, *Sexual Behavior in the Human Female*, an exhaustive study of the sexual lives of American women, showed that 2 percent of adult women defined themselves as exclusively lesbian and 13 percent of women had engaged in homosexual activities at least once during their lives. Despite social clubs, such as San Francisco's Daughters of Billitis, that provided a safe meeting place for gay women, most homosexuals maintained their privacy to protect themselves from abuse. In the 1960s, gay student groups formed on college campuses, and in 1969, at the Stonewall Inn in New York City, the gay clientele fought back against a police raid, finally fed up with the gay-bashing that was sport for police in many urban areas.

The Stonewall Riots marked a turning point for the gay community, leading to the formation of the Gay Liberation Front that sought toleration and even celebration of their sexuality. Leading feminists such as Betty Friedan, however, were opposed to including lesbian rights in any discussion of women's rights. She and others deemed lesbians the "Lavender Menace," convinced they would drive away mainstream supporters or enable opponents to dismiss all feminists as "man-haters." Lesbian activists had adopted the colorful title proudly, and wore lavender T-shirts when they appeared at the Second Congress to Unite Women in New York City in 1970. There, they explained to women's rights advocates how they, too, had been discriminated against and needed the support of the women's rights movement, since gay men were not interested in their goals. By the time of the Houston conference, lesbian rights were on the agenda. Lesbians wanted an end to discrimination against same-sex couples in child-custody suits, housing, employment, and credit, as well as the elimination of state laws that restricted "private sexual behavior between consenting adults." Despite recognizing that including lesbian rights might make the National

Plan more difficult to achieve, NOW leader Gloria Steinem pointed out later that support of lesbian rights was important for all women not only because it was just but also because, as she put it, "Any rebellious woman will be called a lesbian until the word lesbian becomes as honorable a word as any other." The plank was in.

The Houston Conference provided a gathering place for women's rights advocates as well as providing an opportunity for opponents to meet. About 20 percent of all Americans in 1977 opposed equal rights for women. Southerners and rural women, more conservative than the rest of the country, were most likely to oppose the Equal Rights Amendment, and fifteen states, mostly in the South, had yet to ratify the ERA, which needed only three more states to become part of the Constitution. Ironically, ratification of the amendment, which had seemed so probable after its passage in 1972, became less and less likely following the Houston conference, as conservatives rallied against the ideas expressed in the National Plan of Action.

The Conservative Response

The leading conservative spokesperson for opponents to the ERA and the women's liberation movement was Phyllis Schlafly, an Illinois lawyer. Schlafly had attended college, worked in a St. Louis ordnance factory during World War II, and later served as a policy analyst with a Washington, DC, think tank, the conservative American Enterprise Association (today, the American Enterprise Institute). After she married attorney Fred Schlafly, she worked in Republican party politics and wrote *A Choice Not an Echo* in 1964 in support of Barry Goldwater's presidency. In her book, she argued that Republicans gave too much attention to Eastern elites, who were merely Democrats in disguise, when choosing their Republican candidates for president. A true Republican came from the heartland and believed in limited government, low taxes, isolationism in foreign policy, and opposition to communism: in short, Barry Goldwater.

Schlafly was dismayed when Goldwater lost the election in 1964 and President Johnson expanded the reach of the federal government (and taxes) far beyond the parameters even of the New Deal. The president's foreign policy also grated against what Schlafly considered Republican values. While it was true that Johnson's war in Vietnam was against Communists, he had drafted men and taken them away from their families to fight a war against an enemy that had never attacked the United States. The next Republican president, Richard Nixon, also fell short of Schlafly's measure of good Republicanism by escalating the war in Vietnam, extending it to Laos and Cambodia, and visiting Communist China and the USSR. Perhaps even worse, he supported the ERA. Nixon's resignation in disgrace after a scandal known as the Watergate affair in 1974 was hard on Republicans and hard on the rest of the country. His vice president and former congressman Gerald R. Ford from Grand Rapids, Michigan, restored some luster to the Republican party, but he too supported the ERA, and took office with a staunchly feminist wife, First Lady Betty Ford. The president got all American troops out of Vietnam by 1975, which no doubt pleased

Schlafly, but he continued to talk with the Soviet Union, pursued an activist rather than isolationist foreign policy, and continued to push for ratification of the Equal Rights Amendment. Ford, thought Schlafly, was "overly influenced by his wife Betty," as historian Marjorie Julian Spruill put it.

Schlafly had decided the ERA was wrong in 1972, shortly after it passed the House of Representatives. She organized *STOP* (Stop Taking Our Privileges) *ERA* to lead a grassroots fight against the amendment. Schlafly and her followers argued that the ERA was not only unnecessary, but also unnatural, subverting the proper, God-given order of society. In 1975, Schlafly established a network of true believers called the "Eagle Forum" to promote her ideal. In 1981, she used a study by ACLU lawyer Brenda Feigen-Fasteau and Columbia Law School professor Ruth Bader Ginsburg (later the second woman justice on the U.S. Supreme Court) to suggest, often inaccurately, what would happen if the ERA was ratified. Women would be drafted and forced to serve in combat troops (the draft ended in 1973, and Congress could exclude women from combat if it so wished).

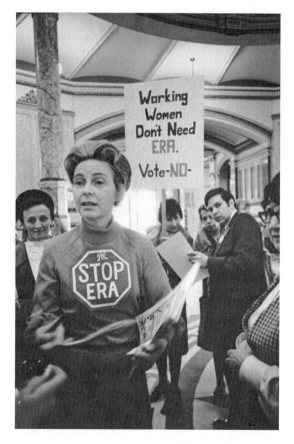

STOP ERA PROTESTORS IN ILLINOIS Phyllis Schlafly and other Equal Rights Amendment opponents lobby against the proposed amendment in the halls of the Illinois state legislature in 1975. The sign reflects the belief of many opponents that legislation protecting women workers would be overturned by the ERA.

PHYLLIS SCHLAFLY, "WHAT'S WRONG WITH EQUAL RIGHTS FOR WOMEN?"

In 1972, Phyllis Schlafly attacked the Equal Rights Amendment, declaring that the women's liberation movement did not speak for most American women, who preferred their lives as wives and mothers. Schlafly's proclamations relied on emotional appeals and a white, middle-class sensibility, ignoring the real discrimination cataloged by activists in the women's movement.

"In the last couple of years, a noisy movement has sprung up agitating for 'women's rights.' Suddenly, everywhere we are afflicted with aggressive females on television talk shows yapping about how mistreated American women are, suggesting that marriage has put us in some kind of 'slavery,' that housework is menial and degrading, and—perish the thought—that women are discriminated against. New 'women's liberation' organizations are popping up, agitating and demonstrating, serving demands on public officials, getting wide press coverage always, and purporting to speak for some 100,000,000 American women.

"It's time to set the record straight. The claim that American women are downtrodden and unfairly treated is the

The government would be required to extend "maternity leave" to fathers and call it parental leave (the government was not required to provide maternity leave, but if it did so, Ginsburg said the government needed to extend it to fathers as well). The concept of a breadwinner husband, dependent wife would be eliminated (the concept of the family structure that permeated U.S. laws, wrote Ginsburg, needed to be expanded to reflect the reality of a society in which 42.5 percent of the labor force was women, and over 50.2 percent of working women were married).

Schlafly used a highly effective combination of rhetorical techniques to dissuade people from supporting the amendment, and was well funded by insurance companies, who feared the impact on their bottom lines if they were forced to treat women equally, as well as liquor interests who feared a return to prohibition. She discussed some real effects of the amendment, exaggerated others, employed fear-mongering and religious proscriptions against equality, but also expressed concerns about the effects of the legislation on family and private life, as well as criticizing the governmental expansion that such a national amendment constituted. Schlafly and her supporters capitalized on the unsettled feeling many Americans had about the pace of social change engendered by the women's liberation movement, the antiwar movement, and the various civil rights movements of the previous decades (see Primary Source 10-6).

The Failure of the ERA

Leaders of the women's movement disregarded many opponents such as Schlafly and her Eagle Forum, or hoped that reasoned discussion and debate fraud of the century. The truth is that American women never had it so good. Why should we lower ourselves to 'equal rights' when we already have the status of special privilege. . . . Women's lib is a total assault on the role of the American woman as wife and mother, and on the family as the basic unit of society. . . . Women's libbers are promoting free sex instead of the 'slavery' of marriage. They are promoting Federal 'day-care centers' for babies instead of homes. They are promoting abortions instead of families.

"Modern technology and opportunity have not discovered any nobler or more satisfying or more creative career for a woman than marriage and motherhood. The wonderful advantage that American women have is that we can have all the rewards of that number-one career, and still moonlight with a second one to suit our intellectual, cultural or financial tastes or needs. . . . If the women's libbers want to reject marriage and motherhood, it's a free country and that is their choice. But let's not permit these women's libbers to get away with pretending to speak for the rest of us. . . . [D]egrade that role that most women prefer. . . . [D]eprive wives and mothers of the rights we now possess."

Source: From Phyllis Schlafly, "What's Wrong with Equal Rights for Women?" *Schlafly Report,* in *Debating the Conservative Movement: 1945 to the Present,* ed. Donald T. Critchlow and Nancy MacLean (Lanham, MD: Rowman and Littlefield, 2009), 199–200.

would change their minds. Many feminists failed to recognize the degree to which their opponents grounded their beliefs in religious ideals and morality, where compromise was impossible. In a country where religion had always played an important role in helping women define their actions, feminists seemed to dismiss the power of religion, at least conservative forms of religion, in shaping many Americans' reactions to the women's rights movement. They downplayed the legitimate fears many women held, ignoring the ever-present division even within the ranks of supporters, between women demanding equality with men and women who recognized that differences between the sexes might play havoc with notions of equality.

Feminists had good reason to dismiss their critics. Despite the impassioned nature of the opposition, after all, the ERA had been passed by overwhelming majorities in the House and Senate, and twenty-two states had ratified it in the year following its passage. But as had been the case for all constitutional amendments passed by Congress since Prohibition, the ERA was sent to the states with a seven-year deadline for ratification. By 1977, thirty-five of the needed thirty-eight states had ratified the amendment. Responding to strident opposition, however, Nebraska, Tennessee, and Idaho had voted to rescind their ratifications. Opposition from social conservatives and religious fundamentalists continued to increase, as did complaints from those opposed to what they saw as a federal power-grab and business interests opposed to the economic cost of equal rights.

The NOW began organizing marches, lobbying Congress for an extension of time to ratify the amendment, and boycotting states that had not ratified it. In the meantime, legal challenges to sex discrimination continued: a Rape Shield law (1978) passed, ending the use of a woman's sexual history in testimony in rape trials; the Pregnancy Discrimination Act (1978) passed, ending employment discrimination against pregnant women; proposed limits on Title IX (1979) were defeated; a drive defeated the so-called Human Life Amendment (1981) that would prohibit all abortions and ban some methods of contraception. New fields of endeavor for women also continued to open: in 1981, President Ronald Reagan, who had defeated President Carter in the 1980 election, appointed the first woman to the Supreme Court, Sandra Day O'Connor of Arizona.

The extension of time expired and so did the amendment, although it continued to be reintroduced annually in Congress. Opponents had revived the old doctrine of separate spheres in their portrayal of the effects of the ERA on American families and society at large. Phyllis Schlafly and her supporters included loaves of fresh-baked bread with their notes to legislators, claiming such home-baked treats would be no more should they vote for the amendment, since it would require all housewives to get jobs. The social changes that the women's movement had achieved were enough for many Americans and far too much for others. The ERA came to symbolize all of these changes. Constitutional scholars continue to debate the impact of the defeat of the ERA on the status of women under the Constitution. According to some theorists, women's rights under the Constitution are not yet equal. Others cite the Fourteenth Amendment to claim that they are. Regardless, the changes to American society and the fight over the issues represented by the ERA polarized Americans and began what were called the "culture wars" of the late twentieth century.

THINK MORE ABOUT IT

1. Return to the opening vignette on Estelle Griswold's successful fight to end the state of Connecticut's anticontraception law. How does the story of her struggle demonstrate both continuity with the concerns and tactics of women activists in the postwar period and anticipate key arenas of activism in the emerging women's liberation movement of the 1960s?

2. What were some of the most blatant forms of discrimination women faced at the time of the passage of the Civil Rights Act? In seeking enforcement of this act's provision against sex discrimination, Dr. Pauli Murray declared that although racial discrimination had been "more brutal" than sex discrimination, both were "only different phases of the fundamental and indivisible issue of human rights." Discuss Murray's statement in the context of the 1960s and 1970s movement for greater equality for women. How were women's concerns trivialized or ignored by individuals, governmental agencies, and overall public opinion?

3. Discuss the development of the NOW and the range of issues it addressed in the 1960s and 1970s. How did women fighting for civil rights (for various groups) contribute to the successes of that movement while continuing to face prejudice and discrimination within it? Discuss the tactics these groups pursued to press their cause, being careful to include examples from Native American groups.

4. What are some of the key reasons behind the emergence of the women's liberation movement? What role did consciousness-raising play in the movement's development? Discuss in detail at least three major issues supported by the movement and how differences in race, ethnicity, class, and sexualities led to divisions within it.

5. What does the precept "the personal is political" mean? Why is this insight about gender relations so important to feminism?

6. The women's movement of the 1960s and 1970s succeeded in changing the landscape of American life and culture, making sexism far more visible and expanding women's rights. Identify and discuss the impact of at least ten changes resulting from the women's movement.

7. Discuss the following statement: "The success of the effort to stop ratification of the ERA demonstrated that the changes in society brought about by the women's movement polarized Americans."

8. What did you learn in this chapter that you did not know before? How does this new information help you understand the overall story of women in American history? What topics would you like to explore further?

READ MORE ABOUT IT

Donald T. Critchlow, *Phyllis Schlafly and Grassroots Conservatism: A Woman's Crusade*

Judith Ezekiel, *Feminism in the Heartland*

David J. Garrow, *Liberty and Sexuality: The Right to Privacy and the Making of* Roe v. Wade

Cynthia Harrison, *On Account of Sex: The Politics of Women's Issues, 1945–1968*

Nancy Hogshead-Makar and Andrew Zimbalist, eds., *Equal Play: Title IX and Social Change*

Margo V. Perkins, *Autobiography as Activism: Three Black Women of the Sixties*

Ruth Rosen, *The World Split Open: How the Modern Women's Movement Changed America*

Benita Roth, *Separate Roads to Feminism: Black, Chicana, and White Feminist Movements in America's Second Wave*

Lynda Van Devanter, *Home Before Morning: The Story of an Army Nurse in Vietnam*

KEY CONCEPTS

Griswold v. Connecticut

Civil Rights Act of 1964

National Organization for Women (NOW)

Women of All Red Nations (WARN)

antiwar movement

consciousness-raising groups

Roe v. Wade

Ms.

cultural radicals

Coalition of Labor Union Women (CLUW)

machismo

Title IX

Houston Conference

"Lavender Menace"

STOP ERA

BACKLASH AND THE THIRD WAVE

Geraldine Ferraro of the House of Representatives

WOMEN IN POLITICS AND GOVERNMENT
Women Politicos
   Primary Source 11-5: Violence Against Women Act
Women and the Clinton Administration

THINK MORE ABOUT IT

READ MORE ABOUT IT

KEY CONCEPTS

On a cool July night in 1984 at the Democratic National Convention in San Francisco, Representative Geraldine Ferraro accepted the nomination of her party to serve as presidential candidate Walter Mondale's running mate in the race for the White House. Ferraro, a congresswoman from New York, had entered college in 1952 at age 16. She worked as an elementary teacher while attending Fordham University School of Law, completing her law degree in 1960. She married John Zacarro, then had three children while practicing law and working for her husband's real estate firm. In 1974, when her youngest child was in second grade, she became an assistant district attorney, heading a special victims' bureau that prosecuted crimes against elderly people and children. There, she found out the other bureau heads, all men, were paid more than she. When she asked her boss why, he said, "But Gerry, you have a husband."

Ferraro ran for Congress and won a House seat in 1978. In Congress she worked to pass the ERA and fought against budget cuts that disproportionately affected the poor, the aged, and women. Her service on the Budget Committee of the House of Representatives taught her a lot about the economic status of women, and she wrote legislation to make it easier for women to participate in pension plans, both as individuals and as widows. She was smart, talented, hard-working, and witty. "Anyone who can get a six-, a four-, and a two-year-old to share has the skills it takes to later succeed in Congress," she once said. In 1984, Mondale picked Ferraro as his choice to be the first woman nominated by a major political party to be vice president of the United States.

Despite the growing number of women in the political arena and in the workplace, Ferraro's candidacy raised eyebrows. After the 1980 presidential election, the Republican Party had been disturbed to discover the first "gender gap" in politics. More women had voted for incumbent Democrat Jimmy Carter than for conservative Republican Ronald Reagan. For the first time since women got the vote in 1920, a woman's bloc of voters had actually appeared. Ferraro's candidacy posed a threat to Republican ambitions to quash the gender gap, and Republican were unsure how to play politics with a woman. The normal free-for-all after candidates had been selected might backfire if voters thought attacking Ferraro was unfair or inappropriate. By the time of the vice presidential debates in October, however, Republicans had settled on a few tactics. One of them revolved around gender and the power a person has to name herself.

GERALDINE FERRARO MAKES HISTORY Signs supporting Geraldine Ferraro's vice presidential nomination, pictured here at the Democratic Convention, sometimes left off the name of her running mate, Walter Mondale, an indication of the history-making nature of her nomination.

Geraldine Ferraro had used her maiden name throughout her professional career. In the 1970s, feminists had designed the title "Ms." for women who did not care to share their marital status with the world, in the same way that "Mr." referred to both married and unmarried men. Ferraro preferred Ms. She explained to the *Washington Post* that while she was Mrs. Zacarro to the electric company and her children's teachers, she was "Congresswoman Ferraro when I run for reelection; Geraldine to my constituents; Gerry to my friends and Ms. Ferraro to just about everyone else. Modern life is confusing," she joked, "no 'Ms.take' about it." The use of Ms. grated on a lot of people, including the *New York Times* editorial staff. They were unable to reconcile the new term with their long-standing practices of referring to women as Miss or Mrs., according to their marital status. But Ferraro was neither Miss nor Mrs.—at least not as a candidate. The use of Ms. provided ammunition to opponents skeptical of women's liberation. Mississippi Republican representative Trent Lott, for instance, sarcastically referred to her as Ms. Ferraro Zaccaro.

For some time, the *Times* continued to name the candidate Mrs. Ferraro, but at the vice presidential debates in Philadelphia in October, the *Times* observed the power of naming as it related to gender. Vice President George H. W. Bush and Ferraro had agreed in advance that they would refer to each other by their professional titles: Vice President Bush and Congresswoman Ferraro. Bush, however, called the congresswoman "Mrs. Ferraro" throughout the debate. The *Times* noticed and commented on Bush's decision to ignore the agreement. Bush's action was further remarked upon unfavorably by *Times* columnist Sydney H. Schanberg a week or so later. By then, the vice president's wife, Barbara Bush, had escalated matters, reflecting the Democrats' belief that Republicans were "very uneasy" about Ferraro's historic candidacy. Mrs. Bush criticized Ferraro indirectly, quipping to reporters that Ferraro was, "I can't say it, but it rhymes with rich." Most Americans believed she referred to the term bitch, a word used only when criticizing a woman. She later apologized, arguing that she meant to say "witch," another derogatory term, also limited in use to the female gender. In the meantime, the vice president's press secretary had called Ferraro "too bitchy."

Using coarse and vulgar language highlighted Ferraro's gender, a technique the Republicans used to call into question her abilities. The gender issue continued as one reporter asked Ferraro if she thought the Soviet Union would take advantage of her "simply because you are a woman," and another asked her if she could "push the nuclear button," invoking a stereotype of noncombative women. Ferraro's answer was positive—she would do whatever was necessary to protect the United States—but the Republicans had clearly decided that raising various specters of less than ideal women—a timid woman, a bitchy woman, a married woman who refused to acknowledge her marriage with a traditional title—were all ways of diminishing the legitimacy of Ferraro's candidacy and the effectiveness of her campaign. They need not to have bothered. The Democrats did themselves in during the campaign without the need for outside help. Mondale told Americans flat out that he was going to raise taxes—something President Reagan had already done and would have to do again. The difference, said Mondale, was that Reagan would do it without telling the American public and would do it in a way that would benefit the rich.

Mondale's forthrightness won him little support. In addition, Ferraro faced unrelenting questioning about her spouse's finances (something no male candidate had ever dealt with), to the detriment of her campaign. In the end, Reagan and Bush won by a landslide. The Republicans took 59 percent of the popular vote, and the Mondale–Ferraro ticket carried only Mondale's home state of Minnesota and the District of Columbia, an area that was 70 percent African American in an election where 90 percent of black Americans voted for the Democrats. Even the *Times* remained unconvinced of the seriousness of Ferraro as a candidate, and the political sideshow of whether the leading newspaper in the country would respect a woman's right to name herself continued. Two more years passed before the *New York Times* began to use the title Ms. when naming women in its pages.

Ronald Reagan's presidency epitomized the conservative shift in America that took place in the 1980s as many Americans reacted to three decades of unrest and turmoil, including rapid and far-reaching social and political change. The Republican Party, in particular, had become a new home for religious, economic, and social conservatives, many determined to reverse some of the more radical changes that had taken place. The institutionalized nature of changes for women in American life made it difficult for conservative activists to achieve their goals, however, as did changes in the transforming economy, which shifted from one based on industry to one based on service. The social and economic dislocation caused by the decline of American industry paralleled that of the Industrial Revolution and the rise of big business in the nineteenth century. Changes in international affairs also disrupted American lives. The Cold War ended with the fall of the Soviet Union. Soon, the threat of mass destruction no longer came from a rival "empire," but from a host of smaller nation-states or from terrorist acts. Increased attention to international affairs and women's increased participation in all aspects of the public sector quieted much of the discourse about women's roles as they became—more than ever before—included in the national conversation. Yet conservatives continued to debate appropriate roles for women, and the images of women promoted by popular culture continued to affect their ability to take advantage of their expanded opportunities.

CONSERVATISM AND THE NEW RIGHT

Reagan's election in 1980 and the defeat of the Equal Rights Amendment two years later marked a turning point in the women's movement. Both events were reactions to the changes in the country that had occurred in the previous thirty years. In the next few decades, so-called Reagan conservatives sought to impose their vision of how Americans should live, in the same manner, they argued, that liberal Americans had done for some time. The roots of the contemporary conservative movement ran deep, stretching back at least to the 1960s, stemming not only from opposition to the various civil rights movements, but also from the failed war in Vietnam. Many Americans regarded the country's involvement in the Vietnam War as immoral, but many conservatives were enraged at the lack of support for American troops who fought and died to support the ideal of democracy in the Far East. Conservatives also viewed the Watergate scandal of 1972 to 1974, resulting in President Nixon's resignation, as an example of unwarranted interference by Congress in presidential matters. President Nixon's acts covering up a break-in at a Democratic campaign office and obstructing the investigation were illegal, argued one supporter, only because "he got caught." Conservatives viewed his resignation with dismay, did not care for his successor Gerald Ford, and thought the country was weaker under the Democratic president Jimmy Carter. They wanted a president who reflected their values.

Beyond politics, the economy in the 1970s and 1980s combined a high rate of inflation with stagnant growth. The press called it stagflation and it devastated American families' purchasing power. As had happened during the Great Depression, many conservatives thought women entering the workforce took jobs from men, preventing them from fulfilling their proper role of provider for the family. Vast social changes, most apparent in the area of race relations and in relations between men and women, alarmed conservatives. They felt that things had gone too far, and the country was on the road to ruin.

For many conservative Americans, one of the most regrettable ways life had changed was with regard to sexual activity outside of marriage. The development of the pill in the 1960s, the first relatively safe, effective,

THE REPUBLICANS MOVE RIGHT

The 1976 platform of the Republican Party proclaimed support for the Equal Rights Amendment, as it had for decades. By 1980, as a measure of the new power that Republican conservatives held, the party changed its course.

1976 Declaration

"Women, who comprise a numerical majority of the population, have been denied a just portion of our nation's rights and opportunities. We reaffirm our pledge to work to eliminate discrimination in all areas for reasons of race, color, national origin, age, creed or sex and to enforce vigorously laws guaranteeing women equal rights.

"The Republican Party reaffirms its support for ratification of the Equal Rights Amendment. Our Party was the first national party to endorse the E.R.A. in 1940. We continue to believe its ratification is essential to insure equal rights for all Americans. In our 1972 Platform, the Republican Party recognized the great contributions women have made to society as homemakers and mothers, as contributors to the community through volunteer work, and as members of the labor force in careers. The Platform stated then, and repeats now, that the Republican Party 'fully endorses the principle of equal rights, equal opportunities and equal responsibilities

cheap, and woman-controlled form of birth control, led to such a change in Americans' behavior that it was considered a sexual revolution. Protecting oneself from pregnancy had been declared a private right by the Supreme Court, and Planned Parenthood continued to grow as an institution dedicated to helping women define their reproductive lives. Along with a sexual revolution that allowed for sex without fear of pregnancy, there were "open" marriages, where partners were not exclusive; "swinging," where couples exchanged spouses to experience sex with others; and the growing visibility of and toleration for gays and lesbians.

At the same time, the divorce rate rose to about 50 percent by the 1980s, and many more couples lived together without bothering to marry. The latter became so common that the U.S. Census added the column, "Cohabitation by Persons of Opposite Sex Sharing Living Quarters" (POSSLQ) to categories of living arrangements for the 1990 census. Society allowed an increasing emphasis on individuality and the individual's fulfillment, and women's growing economic power now enabled them to leave bad marriages and still support themselves. Popular culture made these ideas easily accessible nationally. Television shows often portrayed parenting as a woman-only act. Highly rated shows such as *Maude, One Day at a Time,* and *The Partridge Family* featured single mothers raising children. The number one television show for years, *All in the Family,* portrayed men as buffoons and chauvinists who constantly battled feminists' suggestions that women were more than dishwashers and baby producers. By the 1980s, one of the more popular bumper stickers in America read: "A woman without a man is like a fish without a bicycle."

for women.' The Equal Rights Amendment is the embodiment of this principle and therefore we support its swift ratification."

1980 Declaration

"We acknowledge the legitimate efforts of those who support or oppose ratification of the Equal Rights Amendment.

"We reaffirm our Party's historic commitment to equal rights and equality for women.

"We support equal rights and equal opportunities for women, without taking away traditional rights of women such as exemption from the military draft. We support the enforcement of all equal opportunity laws and urge the elimination of discrimination against women. We oppose any move which would give the federal government more power over families.

"Ratification of the Equal Rights Amendment is now in the hands of state legislatures, and the issues of the time extension and rescission are in the courts. The states have a constitutional right to accept or reject a constitutional amendment without federal interference or pressure."

Sources: 1976 Declaration, from www.ford.utexas.edu/LIBRARY/document/platform/rights.htm; 1980 Declaration, from www.presidency.ucsb.edu/ws/index.php?pid=25844.

Conservative Americans, many of whom believed that a biblically defined patriarchy was the only appropriate style of family, were horrified by these changes. Political conservatives formed a political coalition known as the *New Right*, often joining forces with groups of Protestant evangelical conservatives called the *Religious Right* to oppose political and social issues that both groups believed were destroying America. The New Right, led by Phyllis Schlafly and her Eagle Forum, and the Religious Right, led by the Rev. Jerry Falwell, a Baptist minister who founded a group called the *Moral Majority* in 1979, entered American political life determined to restore the country to what they viewed as its true mission, to be an exemplar to the rest of the world as a Christian country.

Members of these groups appealed to people's emotions and religious beliefs. They began with an assault on the ERA, working both to defeat its passage in additional states and to have states rescind their earlier ratifications of the amendment. Between 1973 and 1979, five states voted to rescind their ratifications: Nebraska, Tennessee, Idaho, Kentucky, and South Dakota. Despite legal precedent holding that states could not rescind ratification of a constitutional amendment, and economic boycotts by NOW of the states trying to do so, opponents introduced rescission bills in twelve more states; all failed. Conservatives succeeded, however, in convincing the 1980 Republican National Convention's platform committee and presidential candidate Ronald Reagan to reverse the party's forty-year tradition of supporting the ERA (see Primary Source 11-1).

The conservative votes that swept Reagan into office in 1980 also came from Americans worried about the disastrous state of the national economy and American foreign policy. Presidents Ford and Carter had both faced insurmountable problems in the late 1970s. The domestic economy was in shambles, with a recession and accompanying inflation that had reached 18 percent by 1980. Foreign affairs gave no respite. Japan and Germany, rising industrial powers, brought new competition against American industries. Violence in the Middle East continued, and oil-producing countries there formed a cartel to raise prices, leading to American gasoline shortages and an energy crisis. The Strategic Arms Limitation Talks (SALT) with the USSR, designed to limit the nuclear arms race between the two countries, hit a snag when the Soviet Union invaded Afghanistan in 1979. Instead of continuing to move toward détente, the easing of international tensions with the Soviet Union that Richard Nixon had begun and Gerald Ford had continued, President Carter had to end consideration of the SALT II treaty and even stopped shipping grain to the Soviet Union in protest. Then late in 1979 came the Iranian hostage crisis, an alarming instance of a small group able to terrorize a world power. The U.S.-supported Shah of Iran, a corrupt and repressive leader, had tried to Westernize the country, but opponents led by Islamic fundamentalist Ruhollah Khomeini fought against modernization and what they saw as the secularization of the country. The Shah left the country in January 1979 for cancer treatment in the United States, and in November, Islamic radicals seized American diplomats and workers at the U.S. embassy in Tehran. The radicals wanted the Shah and his fortune returned to Iran in exchange for releasing fifty-three hostages, including two women.

Carter had few options in the Iranian crisis. He would not pay the ransom demanded by the radicals, and a military expedition to free them failed badly. His protests to the United Nations and the freezing of Iranian financial assets had little effect. He finally released several billions of dollars of assets to end the standoff. The Iranian hostage crisis lasted 444 days and cost Jimmy Carter the election. On January 20, 1981, as Ronald Reagan was being inaugurated, a plane holding the released hostages left Iran.

Ronald Reagan was an ironic choice for conservatives to support in the 1980 election. The divorced former actor seldom attended church, and had a family often estranged from him and his second wife Nancy, a former actress. Reagan had also been governor of a very liberal state, California, and had signed the state's liberal abortion rights law. However, his advisors packaged him and his campaign to appeal to conservative voters. Reagan stood for limited government interference in business, lower taxes, a strong military, and only limited support for women's rights. He opposed government regulation of industry, affirmative action, and other major social changes. He promoted his views with a sunny optimism that baffled his opponents for the next eight years. Charges of corruption, illegalities, conflicts of interest, discriminatory practices, and uncaring disregard for the less fortunate, all slid off the so-called Teflon President. Instead, Reagan's popularity soared as he worked closely with conservatives to turn back the changes that had taken place in American life. Three specific areas—his new direction for the economy, his lack of support for antidiscrimination legislation, and his positions on women's reproductive rights—had considerable impact on women's lives during his presidency and beyond.

WOMEN AND THE ECONOMY

During Ronald Reagan's two terms in office, greater numbers of women than ever before entered the American labor force. In 1980, 49.9 percent of women sixteen years of age or older were in the labor force. By 1990, that percentage had risen to 56.8 percent, with the largest increase among Native American and white women. About 60 percent of all Asian women and black women worked for wages by the end of the decade. Most American women, particularly women of color, continued to be employed in dead-end service jobs with low pay and few opportunities for advancement. Even college-educated women usually entered less lucrative fields such as education, foreign languages, health, the fine arts, and social sciences, while men usually chose better-paying fields, such as engineering, business, and the physical sciences. When women entered the workforce, they still worked disproportionately as administrative support staff rather than executives, as service workers rather than in precision production, and as nurses rather than doctors. And from birth until death, female Americans remained more likely to live in poverty than their male counterparts. By 1990, one-fifth of female children and nearly as many elderly women lived in poverty.

Women and the Conservative Economic Agenda

In the election campaign of 1980, Reagan appealed to voters by promising to lower taxes. In the years preceding the election, millions of Americans had migrated to the *Sunbelt*—to Southern states where hostility to taxes and big government was as natural as breathing. Reagan won the South, except for Carter's home state of Georgia, as well as gaining the votes of affluent suburbs across the nation. Once in office, and enjoying a Republican Senate for the first time since 1954, Republicans guided by Reagan began to implement his redesign for America. "Government is the problem," he declared, not the solution to the country's woes. He cut taxes drastically with the Economic Recovery Tax Act, lowering income taxes 25 percent across the board. The maximum tax rate was lowered from 70 percent to 50 percent. The capital gains tax on investments went from 28 to 20 percent. Reagan hoped that the tax cuts would end the stagflation that had continued through Carter's administration. Tax cuts for wealthier people would free up money so that the well-to-do would then spend their money to create more wealth that would "trickle down" to the rest of the country. Tax cuts, he believed, would also increase the supply of products by decreasing the taxes on them so that prices would fall, reducing inflation, thus making products more available to all. Supporters believed this idea, called *supply-side economics*, would reward both workers and investors.

The economy did not immediately improve, however, in part because nearly half of the federal budget was spent on programs that most politicians thought were political suicide to cut: Medicare and Medicaid, the Veterans' Administration, pensions, and welfare. Reagan and his followers, however, were determined to change America's support of the indigent. The safety net of welfare programs designed to relieve the ravages of the Great Depression had been greatly expanded during Lyndon Johnson's Great Society, and Reagan wanted to scale back the system. A man given to telling easily understood and often inaccurate stories to justify his actions, he told of a Chicago "welfare queen" who claimed extra welfare benefits while driving around in a "welfare Cadillac," a reference to a popular 1970s country song where the singer was collecting so many government benefits he could afford to buy his wife a fancy car. Such a story, widely reported in the media, was easy for many to believe, since women were by far the most common recipients of welfare payments. Playing the role of a benign patriarch determined to curb such abuses by undeserving women, Reagan proposed limiting Aid to Families with Dependent Children (AFDC) benefits to four months after the recipient had found a job, no matter what the job paid. Medicaid likewise would be severely curtailed for the working poor. He also cut domestic programs in education, health, housing, urban aid, food stamps, and school meals for a total of $35 billion in cuts, about 14 percent, that disproportionately affected women and their children. Women who wanted to stay home and care for their young children were among those hard-hit by these new policies. In a culture that criticized women, particularly single women of color with children, for even having children while unmarried, few options were available. As one mother put it, "I'm damned if I do and damned if I don't. In other words, if I stay home and care for my children I'm accused of freeloading, but if I work I not only face economic sanctions but a society that tells me I'm a bad mother for abandoning my children to child care and neglecting my responsibility."

The media search for the Welfare Queen proved unavailing; she could not be found. The cuts failed to lessen government spending because at the same time, trying to restore American prestige and international power, Reagan drastically increased military spending by $12 billion, about 7 percent more than earlier budgets. The recession continued and unemployment rose to 10.4 percent. By 1982, despite the Tax Equity and Fiscal Responsibility Bill Act of that year which "enhanced revenues" (raised taxes) by $98 billion, deficit spending became the order of the day, mostly to support the arms buildup. Reagan became enamored of a defense system nicknamed "Star Wars," a strategic missile defense system that would use lasers to shoot down incoming Soviet intercontinental ballistic missiles. The technological aspects of the system escaped most Americans. The nickname, however, referenced a popular movie of the day, and provided an image of a defensive shield to protect Americans far better than a policy of mutual destruction by atomic weapons which had long been characteristic of the Cold War. Numerous scientists, intrigued by the possibilities and attracted by the massive amounts of federal grant money available, eagerly joined the research, most ignoring that the economic well-being of poor women and children was being sacrificed to the Defense Department. Dr. Carol Rosin, however, a spokesperson for the peaceful development of space, responded to the Star Wars initiative by founding the Institute for Cooperation in Space. In consultation with the United Nations, she testified repeatedly against weaponizing space, and spoke in favor of converting military industry into space industry. Rosin was largely ignored, as were other protestors and peace activists such as the Women's Pentagon Action that marched repeatedly on the Pentagon to protest militarism, the growth of nuclear weaponry, and the escalation of the arms race (see Primary Source 11-2).

By the end of Reagan's first term, the economy had improved somewhat, largely because oil prices had declined, lowering energy costs. Restoring money to domestic programs was not on Reagan's agenda, however. Instead, the president continued to cut taxes with a Tax Reform Act in 1986, which simplified tax brackets and lowered the maximum rate again. The tax burden on the rich lessened, tax revenues continued to decline, and deficit spending soared to nearly $200 billion. The money went for military adventures in Central America, the Middle East, Lebanon, and Grenada. The arms race with the Soviet Union continued as well, and the money the USSR spent trying to keep up with the United States eventually led to its collapse.

In the meantime, the rate of poverty continued to climb, and women and children continued to be the largest segment of the poor in America. Geraldine Ferraro's work, prior to her nomination in 1984, centered on the Retirement Equity Act. This legislation allowed widows new economic power, including access to their deceased husbands' pension, a critical change at a time when 85 percent of women outlived their husbands, but only 9 percent received their husbands' pensions after death. It also forbade spouses from signing away their wives' or husbands' interests in their pensions, and allowed divorced partners access to pension rights earned during the marriage. Even the president applauded the act to remove economic discrimination against women, saying at the signing that "that parents who bear children [that would be women] and stay home to care for them in the early years" would no longer lose their pension credits.

Women, especially poor and nonwhite women, generally suffered more than men under Reagan's restructuring of the American economy, as some 60 percent of his budget cuts came from programs for the poor. Women were already disproportionately represented among the poor in a phenomenon known as the *feminization of poverty*. One cause of this came from liberalized divorce laws in many states, including California, where then-governor Reagan signed a no-fault divorce law in 1970. Rather than blaming one's spouse for actions that led to divorce, no-fault divorce meant that both partners were treated equally and property was divided equally. Spousal support, known as alimony, was usually limited, whereas before it could last the lifetime of a wronged ex-spouse. This meant that women who had been homemakers for twenty, thirty, or forty years could be divorced through no fault of their own, then be forced to seek employment with few skills and, in the poor economy of the 1970s and 1980s, fewer jobs available. In divorces, women usually were awarded primary custody of

CAROL SUE ROSIN IMAGINES SPACE WITHOUT WEAPONS

President Ronald Reagan's Star Wars initiative to militarize space sparked Carol Rosin to form an organization to suggest alternative uses for space. In a 1996 essay, she wrote the following:

"I know how to end war. I know how to transform the military-industrial complex. I know how we crones and all women of vision and action can create peace. . . .

We can create peace on earth through peace in space. . . .

"From 1974 to 1995, I played in the war game with the big boys, working within the military-industrial complex. That game is based on escalating the arms race into space. They aim to seize the high ground as they have always done on earth. Despite various peace actions, no current method of working for

children, while men were required to pay child support. In a time of fewer jobs and inflation, however, child support payments often never arrived. Even when the money was forthcoming, it was seldom enough to support children in families where mothers worked menial jobs in an inflationary economy. By 1978, single parents were raising 20 percent of families in the United States, and those parents were almost always the mothers. White women raising children were nearly six times more likely to be poor, and black women raising children were over ten times more likely to be poor than families headed by white men. Between 1980 and 1984, the number of Americans living in poverty had increased by 4 percent.

For many women raising children on their own, welfare often provided programs that were the only alternative to going hungry. Cutting welfare benefits or decreasing the welfare supplements workers used to get by while working (the benefit amount dropped some but did not end when recipients found jobs, since the jobs paid so little), destroyed most women's incentive to get off welfare and earn wages, when doing so meant they had less income than they would have while on welfare. Most welfare recipients cycled in and out of the system, and Reagan's budget cuts did not address the reasons why they did so: the state of the economy, the availability of low-skill, low-paying jobs, women's ability to care for their children or find decent child care, and their own health.

Many women still faced limited employment choices. Clerical workers were almost all women—in 1980, about 98 percent of all secretaries and typists were women. Women employed in the service sector continued to organize in hopes of improving their low pay rates. In Indiana, for instance, a group of waitresses formed a National Association of Waitresses to protest a new IRS tax regulation. The IRS required restaurants to assume waitresses received a predictable amount of income as tips. Their new rules required restaurants to report waitresses' income as if they had collected national defense or for peace will end wars. . . .

"My work in the belly of the beast taught me that the space frontier is the essential new element in our work for peace on earth. . . .

"Imagine we have put a literal lid on the arms race, once and for all time, by obtaining a good faith agreement from *all* the world's leaders stating they are willing to ban all space-based weapons.

"Imagine what humans can do in outer space instead of the current plan to build battle stations above all our heads with thousands of weapons pointed directly at us. . . .

"Imagine space craft, elevators and bridges to space with laser-powered rockets for transportation, space voyages through the universe; space-based hospitals, homes, schools, hotels, laboratories, industries, and farms with habitable ecospheres in space.

"Imagine all cultures and ages working, living and playing together on earth and in space."

Source: Carol Sue Rosin, "Imagine," *Crone Chronicles: A Journal of Conscious Aging* (Fall 1996), n.p.

tips enough to equal minimum wage even when they might not have done so. The rules, combined with withholding methods, meant many waitresses with poor tips in a poor economy earned less than $1.00 an hour some days, far below the minimum wage of $3.10, thanks to being taxed on the higher amount the government assumed they collected.

Reagan's ideas about America and about women's appropriate roles played an important part in his budget cuts. Along with the New Right and the Religious Right, Reagan viewed the patriarchal family as the only "normal" one. Husbands needed to support their wives and children. Poverty he saw as an individual's fault and a personal failure that government aid would not alleviate but only make worse. Reagan wanted poor people to pull themselves up by their bootstraps, accept responsibility for their poverty, and work their way out of it. Believing wholeheartedly in capitalism, free markets, and competition, he refused to concede that the playing field might not be a level one for all Americans. Even a spectacular stock market crash in 1987 failed to convince Reagan and his fellow Republicans that their economic ideas might not always succeed. His ideas attracted some bipartisan support and the long-term effects of Reagan's economic policies, especially his calls to cut taxes to stimulate the economy, remained part of the American economic and political landscape for years.

Women's Work, Education, and the Second Shift

In the last quarter of the century, women's roles in the American workplace expanded in number and variety as women took advantage of their increased educational opportunities. Working women with families still confronted difficulties balancing homes and work, and continued to face the so-called second shift, as corporate America remained fairly inflexible even as it moved from an industrial to a service economy. The "computer revolution," the expanding use of personal computers, enabled many women to enter higher-paying jobs, but often expanded work hours beyond the workplace as workers could use computers at home. The shift in the economy from a workplace outside the home to a workplace that often included the home made it all the more difficult for unions to attract workers. Nevertheless, unions responded to declining industrial membership, refocusing their efforts to attract women and to meet working women's demands.

More than any other single factor, the sheer number of women who moved into the labor force changed the United States in the last quarter of the twentieth century. The Women's Bureau of the Department of Labor still existed (see Chapter 8), and the statistics it gathered provided a snapshot of the changes in women's work and education. By 2004, women held half of all management and professional positions. Eleven percent of women between 25 and 64 years of age had college degrees in 1970; by 2004, that proportion had risen to 33 percent, and 72 percent of women high school graduates were likely to enroll in college. From 1979 to 2004, despite the fact that many women still labored in low-paying jobs, women's earnings had increased as a proportion of men's earnings, from 59 to 62 percent to somewhere around 80 percent. What appeared to be an economic gain for women, however, was actually a decline for men and society as a whole because men's jobs began to pay less as many manufacturing jobs were *outsourced*—transferred to countries with cheaper labor.

By 2000, nearly 58 percent of all American women—and 77 percent of women aged 25 to 44—were working full-time, year-round, compared with 41 percent some thirty years earlier, and compared to 72 percent of American men. The top ten jobs held by working women had not changed very much: they were secretaries and administrative assistants, nurses, cashiers, teachers, salesclerks, health aides, waitresses, and bookkeepers, but added to the mix now were customer service representatives, as well as supervisors and managers of retail sales workers. Women's median weekly earnings had also gone up. By 2006, the top ten jobs women held had a median wage of $550 a week, but if the best-paying positions of nursing and teaching were excluded, the median wage was only $463, barely above the federal poverty rate for a family of four. Nurses and teachers were paid far more than had been true in earlier decades, thanks to unions.

Black women continued to move out of domestic service into other better-paying jobs as they, like white women, became more likely to go to college and on to a career. Historically, a greater proportion of women of color than white women had worked for pay—in 1890, 40 percent of black women, but only 16 percent of white women worked for wages, and in 1950, the ratio was nearly 38 to 29 percent. However, by 1980, the ratio was nearly the same, and by 2006, about 62 percent of black women, 59 percent of white women, 58 percent of Asian women, and 56 percent of Hispanic women were in the labor force, and 75 percent of them worked full-time. Differences in unemployment rates remained consistent among women workers. Black women were always two to three times more likely to be unemployed than white, Hispanic, or Asian women. A pay differential remained a sign of continuing disadvantage for many women of color as well: black women, for instance, earned about eighty-nine cents for every dollar white women made in the same period.

Popular culture reflected the influx of women in the workplace with advertisers portraying the "Superwoman," who could work all day, then return to her home and continue her work as wife, mother, and consumer without missing a beat. In one way, the image did reflect the reality of many women's lives. Increasing numbers of women experienced the double duties of the second shift that had been characteristic of many women's lives, especially the poor, throughout the country's history. While the women's liberation movement had pointed out the inequity of household chores being done almost entirely by women, and while many men took on more chores when their wives or partners worked, a combination of cultural traditions and so-called labor-saving devices meant there was little real shift in the gendered responsibilities for housework. Women spent less time every week doing housework, declining from 30 hours to 17.5 hours by 1995, in part because they spent more time in the workforce; in part because devices such as microwave ovens made some chores, such as cooking, faster; in part because their standards of cleanliness declined as well. Men spent more time doing housework—up from 4.9 hours in 1965 to 10 hours by 1995. Women still did nearly twice as much, however, and men's housework tended to be once-a-week or other intermittent chores, such as lawnmowing or cleaning out the gutters, while women's housework continued to revolve around the daily duties of cooking, cleaning, and child care. The second shift women faced as they continued to move into full-time work for wages and demanding careers diminished only slightly.

The Computer Revolution

Many of the careers women entered came about not only because of additional education and despite the second shift, but also because of the advent of the personal computer. The first digital computer, capable of performing one complicated calculation every 15 seconds, was invented in 1939 by John Atanasoff at Iowa State University. World War II interrupted his research, but, more importantly, revealed the need for speedier calculations. Mathematicians such as Alice Burks, one of many women "computers" whose calculations created the firing and bombing tables the military used during the war, worked nonstop for the war effort, but the military needed faster calculations than the women computers could provide. Grace Hopper, a Naval reserve officer working at Harvard University, helped design a faster and more powerful computing machine to aid the war effort, the Mark I, and later invented the most widely used computer language, COBOL. The military commissioned an even larger computer, the ENIAC, completed shortly after the war ended, that could perform calculations 1,000 times faster than earlier machines. Despite their usefulness, computers such as ENIAC were enormous and expensive, and women operators had to physically reset switches in order to program them. Hopper's invention of COBOL, and Betty Holberton's development of keyboard input instead of switches made smaller computers possible and more user-friendly.

International Business Machines (IBM), Tandy Corporation (RadioShack), and Apple Computer developed computers for home use in the 1970s and 1980s. By the 1990s, the machines were widespread in nearly every profession and industry.

Computers lessened the need for manual labor and physical strength in many heavy industries, such as the automobile industry, that had long been dominated by male workers, and some women moved into those industries. More commonly, since computers required clerical skills to operate that women had long been hired for, employers quickly provided them for their clerical workers, replacing the typewriters and adding machines many women were familiar with. A division quickly arose between those who designed and programmed computers, primarily men, who were well paid for their work, and those who began using computers for repetitive office tasks, mainly women, who were paid less by employers who could hire less-educated employees to perform on the new machines. Computers also allow employers to keep tabs on job performance, counting keystrokes, break times, and mistake rates, and assessing penalties for workers who did not meet company standards for productivity, punitive measures that disproportionately affected women workers.

As they grew less expensive and more powerful, and as access to e-mail and the Internet increased, computers went home with workers. By the end of the century, workers were far more likely to interrupt their leisure time with work, and expectations grew in many service-oriented jobs that workers would be on call to their employers at all times, rather than simply when they were at their place of work. Computers also allowed women to work from their homes in lieu of going to a workplace. This choice, called *telecommuting*, combined benefits and drawbacks. Many women who had children to care for were able to work from home and balance their two tasks, but telecommuting jobs often paid less and were often regarded as piecework, the same types of jobs women had taken in the early nineteenth century when industrialization began. As was true for industrial jobs, computer piecework was less lucrative than a job requiring an appearance at a factory or office.

The computer revolution did not stop the second shift. Women continued to search for ways to earn money while still caring for their families. Another option that existed, although not commonly enough for many women workers with children, was *flex-time*, which allowed women to work hours more convenient for their family responsibilities, and *job-sharing*, where two workers shared one job. While these became more common options for women than previously, by 2001 only about 27 percent of women workers had flexible hours (over 30 percent of men did), and only 15 percent of American women workers spent at least one day at home, telecommuting to work.

Working conditions for women in a more service-oriented economy continued to convince women to join unions at increasing rates in the last part of the twentieth century. By the turn of the century, 55 percent of new union members were women. They continued to be underrepresented in union management; however, women who joined unions believed that they would help in the fight for not only better pay, but also for equal pay and other benefits such as health care, family leave, and child care. By including issues of importance to women, unions sought to reestablish their power in an economy where their traditional base of power, manufacturing, was vanishing. Unions' success at including women members and representing their interests was apparent in one strike in 2000. Verizon, a national cellular telephone company, required employees to accept forced overtime of up to fifteen hours a week. Such a demand wrought havoc in the lives of women workers with children. The union representing them, the Communications Workers of America, struck against the company and included reducing mandatory overtime among its demands. Aware of the need to recruit more women members and take their issues into account, the AFL-CIO issued a call to the unions under its standard to actively recruit women members, to adjust their negotiating demands to include women's issues, and to move beyond the "token woman" in upper levels in unions to make sure that more women took leadership roles.

DISCRIMINATION IN THE WORKPLACE

Despite the Equal Pay Act and Title VII of the Civil Rights Act passed in the 1960s, discrimination against women in the workforce continued. This was due in part to President Reagan's policies regarding affirmative action and sexual discrimination, which reflected his beliefs that everyone should be free to compete and that the market should be free to set wages and prices. Business deregulation, assumptions that businesses would voluntarily comply with antidiscrimination laws, proclamations against numerical "quotas" that Reagan believed were required to hire minorities under affirmative action, all marked the president's continuing attempts to restructure the American economy. While Reagan failed to achieve any real progress in eliminating protections for American women workers, employers were often reluctant to obey laws that the president claimed publicly were unfair and that he promised publicly were going to be changed. Such reluctance meant that widespread sex discrimination against women workers, in job opportunities and pay, continued throughout the 1980s, as did sexual harassment. Encouraging pay equity and flexible working arrangements for women met widespread resistance from Reagan conservatives, although many corporations discovered the benefits of these ideas.

Affirmative Action

By the time Ronald Reagan took office, the Supreme Court's decision in *Regents of the University of California v. Bakke* (1978) had brought a new term into the American lexicon: *reverse discrimination*. Allan Bakke, a white male, was an unsuccessful applicant to medical school in California despite higher scores than some minority candidates, admitted under the school's affirmative action policies. He sued, claiming reverse discrimination—that he had been denied admission because he was a white male. He won part of the suit as the Court agreed he ought to have been admitted. However, the Court also upheld the use of race in admissions decisions, as long as racial quotas were not used. Integration of both minorities and women had become important considerations for medical schools and other organizations, and affirmative action was a way to include minorities and women in what had traditionally been white male worlds of work and power. The government had encouraged affirmative action by requiring all companies with fifty or more employers conducting or wanting to do business with the federal government to have written affirmative action plans. Support for such policies in male-dominated industries was less than enthusiastic. Construction companies, for example, enjoyed a particularly lucrative relationship with the federal government. The law required that they hire women for about 7 percent of all jobs. By 1980, however, while the number of women in the construction trades had doubled, women were only 1.6 percent of the workforce.

While President Carter had issued executive orders creating a National Women's Business Enterprise Policy in 1979 that required government agencies to use affirmative action to support women entrepreneurs, Reagan viewed such efforts as "quotas" that demanded businesses hire a certain number of women and minorities, regardless of their qualifications. As president, Reagan set out to weaken federal requirements for affirmative action. He sought to decrease the number of companies affected by the legislation. He wanted to review their affirmative action plans every five years instead of yearly, and eliminate government reviews of companies' hiring practices before awarding contracts. Yet, ironically, even Reagan saw the value of affirmative action, as sociologist Judith Lorber pointed out in a letter to the *New York Times*. At a White House press conference in February 1986, Reagan had announced that there were a few new reporters in the room. Since they were new, he said, "to start with let me call on a couple of those . . . just two of them, and then we'll go on with the regular hands up." The incident, said Lorber, was a "perfect example of affirmative action, by proportional representation, to give newcomers to the competition a small advantage to get them started." Reagan's actions affirmed the legitimacy of the newcomers to the rest of the press corps and gave them a chance to enter their competitive field. Yet such behavior by employers (she pointed out the irony) would reflect "exactly the policy . . . objected to by the President."

Opposition from civil rights groups, Congress, and corporations meant Reagan's more extreme plans against affirmative action were never implemented, but they had a chilling effect in the workplace. Wider Opportunities for Women, an organization training women for jobs in nontraditional fields, found that most contractors, sure that affirmative action rules were going to be weakened or ended, did not bother to comply with them. As newspapers, magazines, advertisements, and other visual media portrayed women and minorities in nontraditional roles, many American grew to believe that economic assistance to women or minorities in the form of affirmative action was simply not needed anymore.

The attempt by Reagan and his conservative followers to destroy affirmative action failed in the end because the bureaucracy not only of the government, but also of many large corporations and organizations, already had affirmative action policies in place. Having committed themselves to diversifying their workforce, they discovered the inherent advantages of hiring women and minorities. Pollsters for *Money* magazine discovered that women were the primary purchasers in over one-third of American households, and that proportion continued to grow. Appealing to that large market made economic sense. In addition, by 1980 nearly 43 percent of American women were in the labor force. Women contributed so much to the American economy as customers and workers that to suggest that they not participate in order to reestablish a patriarchy would mean economic ruin.

Sex Discrimination

In 1972, Congress passed the Equal Employment Opportunity Act, giving the EEOC the power to sue unresponsive discriminatory employers. It made more employers subject to the law and allowed employees more time to file charges. It also made local, state, and federal governments subject to the act. President Carter gave the EEOC even more power in 1978, allowing the commission to coordinate efforts to prevent discrimination. In contrast, Ronald Reagan proposed legislation to limit the amount of back pay awarded to workers who complained of sex discrimination at their places of employment. He also weakened the EEOC by cutting its funding by 12 percent. Over 130 agency positions were cut, and for nearly four months in 1982, the commission could not even achieve a quorum so it could conduct business because Reagan had not yet filled a vacant commissioner's seat. He eventually appointed Clarence Thomas, a conservative black Republican who opposed affirmative action.

The Justice Department's Civil Rights Division, which pursued antidiscrimination cases for the EEOC, changed its tactics under Reagan. The division dropped class-action lawsuits, which had long been the preferred way to resolve cases of discrimination that affected large numbers of women. In 1970, for instance, the EEOC filed a class-action suit against AT&T. The mammoth telephone company, claimed the government, had discriminated against women for years. The government cited as evidence the fact that only 1 percent of the company's supervisory personnel were women, and there was not a single male operator. Three years later, women won the suit and $70 million in compensation, along with a promise by AT&T to promote more women. Suits filed by individual women affected by AT&T's discriminatory practices would have been far more difficult and time-consuming to resolve. The government's change in approach resulted in a backlog of cases that made it nearly impossible for women to get relief from discrimination.

Despite declining government support for prosecuting discrimination in the workplace, popular culture took note of those women who broke into new areas of endeavor and enriched the nation. Throughout the decades in the last third of the twentieth century, newspaper and magazine articles chronicled "first" women: the first Asian congresswoman, Patsy Takemoto Mink (1964); the first black federal judge, Constance Baker Motley (1966); the first black congresswoman, Shirley Chisholm (1969–1983); the first woman jockey in the Kentucky Derby, Diane Crump (1970); the first woman director of the New York Stock Exchange, Juanita Kreps (1972), who later became the first woman secretary of commerce under President Carter; the first woman rabbi, Sally Jean Priesand (1972); the first woman mathematician elected to the National Academy of Sciences (1975) and to the presidency of the American Mathematical Society (1983), Dr. Julia Robinson; the first Asian woman to serve as a network news reporter, and later anchor, Connie Chung (1984); the first woman to conduct at the Metropolitan Opera, Sarah Caldwell (1976); the first woman Supreme Court Justice, Sandra Day O'Connor (1981); the first American woman to serve as ambassador to the United Nations, Jeanne Kirkpatrick (1981); the first American woman astronaut, Sally Ride (1983); the first black Miss America, Vanessa Williams (1984); the first woman chief of the Cherokee nation, Wilma Mankiller (1985); the first black woman to host a television show, Oprah Winfrey (1986); the first Hispanic congresswoman, Ileana Ros-Lehtinen of Miami-Dade County Florida (1989), still in office twenty years later; and the first woman and the first Hispanic surgeon-general of the United States, Antonia Coello Novello (1990).

As long as these "first women" continued to appear in the chronicles of popular culture, many Americans could believe that the women's liberation movement had succeeded and was no longer needed, and that women were being treated equally with men, that sex discrimination was gone, and that women no longer needed protections from discrimination. However, popular culture also showed Americans the ways that things had not changed. An Academy Award–nominated film, *9 to 5* (1980), for instance, portrayed a divorced housewife's miserable experiences in finding and keeping a job, harassed by a male chauvinist boss. The comedy starred country singer Dolly Parton and well-known feminists Jane Fonda and Lily Tomlin. It explored issues such as on-site child care for employees, job-sharing so that women could work part-time, and women being passed over for promotion after training men who then climbed the corporate ladder. The film also dealt with the issue of sexual harassment; the character played by Parton had to constantly fend off her boss's advances.

Sexual Harassment

Despite its often comedic portrayal in popular culture, sexual harassment was no joke. One investigation by a congressional subcommittee in 1979 found that 40 percent of federal women workers had been harassed by their supervisors. Another study of 9,000 women found 90 percent had received unwanted attention from their male bosses and 75 percent of them felt intimidated, demeaned, and embarrassed by the harassment. Demands for sexual favors in return for promotions, crude language and insulting humor, attacks in the workplace, a "boys will be boys" attitude held by many supervisors to whom women appealed for redress, and a 440-day process of getting an appeal heard by the EEOC were all part of the picture of sexual harassment. Most women felt powerless to protest, needing their jobs to support their families. Women who complained could usually count on an escalation of the behavior, being fired, or worse.

The Women's Legal Defense Fund, founded in 1971, helped women who had been sexually harassed to file suit against their employers. They used antidiscrimination laws to justify their lawsuits, arguing that women who were harassed could not participate freely in the job market and were held to a different standard of behavior and expectations for employment than men in the same job. Women were expected to have sex with their supervisors to get or keep their jobs and be promoted whereas men were not. Thus, women were being discriminated against because of their sex.

Because harassing behavior usually took place in private rather than public, because many men and women believed that "boys will be boys" should excuse much, because many believed that women in nontraditional jobs were "asking for it" since women should not be in such roles in the first place, and because sexual harassment was such a constant in the lives of most American women (the lowest estimate in 1970s was that 70 percent of women were harassed on the job), most women were reluctant to file charges. Still, sexual harassment cases began to appear in the courts in the 1970s. Diane Williams, a public information specialist at the Justice Department, filed one. She described a "contest" among the men in her office as to who would take her out first. She refused to date her married supervisor, told him to stop asking her out, appealed to his supervisor when the harassment continued, and finally was fired a few days after filing a complaint. It took seven years to resolve the case, mostly due to the opposition of the Justice Department, where the man who harassed her was never fired or even punished. In her case, *Williams v. Saxbe* (1976), the courts finally ruled that sexual harassment was a form of sex discrimination prohibited under Title VII of the 1964 Civil Rights Act and enforceable by the EEOC under the provisions of the Equal Employment Opportunity Act of 1972. Williams testified before Congress, describing her experiences within the larger context of women's roles in the workplace. "We have accepted sexual harassment just as we have accepted the fact that women are expected to take notes at meetings and expected to make the coffee," she said. While her tormentors denied the seriousness of their acts, to her, sexual harassment "is not fun and games. It is a very emotional experience, a very degrading experience, a very humiliating experience."

Sexual harassment complaints and lawsuits accelerated in number and scope over the next thirty years. Courts found that *quid pro quo* sexual harassment, demanding sex in return for job benefits, was a form of discrimination. The Civil Service Reform Act (1978) forbade sexual discrimination in federal employment. In 1981, in *Bundy v. Jackson*, the courts said that sexual insults and propositions that created a "hostile work environment" were a form of sexual harassment for which employers could be held liable if they allowed it to continue. In various suits decided in 1983, the courts found that a woman's past behavior did not mean she could be sexually harassed; that it was sexual discrimination to reward one woman who had a sexual relationship with a supervisor and not reward women who did not; and that a tenant evicted by her landlord when she refused to pose nude for him had suffered sexual harassment forbidden by provisions of the federal Fair Housing Act that prohibited sexual discrimination.

The sexual harassment allegation that attracted the most national attention came in 1991. Thurgood Marshall, the sole African American Supreme Court justice, decided to retire. President George H. W. Bush, another conservative Republican who had succeeded President Reagan in 1988, nominated Clarence Thomas, former head of the EEOC, a conservative black forty-three-year-old Republican. Bush had made him a federal judge in 1989, and wanted a conservative voice added to the Court. During the Senate hearings on Thomas's appointment, Anita Hill, a law professor who had worked under Thomas at the EEOC, testified that he had sexually harassed her during her time at the agency, asking her for dates and discussing pornographic films with her, despite her requests that he stop. The televised hearings captured the nation's attention, and brought the subject of sexual harassment to the forefront of public conversation. Thomas dismissed the accusations angrily as nothing more than a "high-tech lynching." Hill's supporters decried both Thomas's attack on her veracity and the Senate's attack on her character, as senators questioning her implied that whatever took place, Hill had clearly "asked for it." The 98 percent male Senate voted to confirm Thomas on October 15, 1991, inspiring dozens of women who supported Hill to seek political office in the next election to help change the gender makeup of Congress.

Two weeks later, President George H. W. Bush's administration was further embarrassed when the Tailhook scandal broke. The Tailhook

ANITA HILL TESTIFIES BEFORE THE SENATE Despite testimony from a resolute Anita Hill on Capitol Hill about the sexual harassment she had endured from Supreme Court nominee Clarence Thomas, a majority of senators did not believe her and voted to confirm the former director of the Equal Employment Opportunity Commission to the Supreme Court.

Convention, held annually by a group of retired, reserve, and active duty U.S. Navy and Marine Corps members and defense contractors, gave junior members of the military the chance to interact with senior officers in a social setting, as well as to attend professional meetings. After-hours entertainment, usually cocktail parties, followed the day sessions. In 1991, a number of attendees indulged in what had become a tradition of drunkenness, strippers, public nudity, and even public sex acts. Eighty-three women and seven men were assaulted by others at the convention, which was paid for in part by the U.S. Navy. Most of the women victims were naval officers.

Over the course of the next few years, the U.S. Navy investigated the charges and eventually its own response. Part of the problem, testified one woman naval commanding officer, was that the U.S. Navy was hostile to women generally. Tailhook (named after the hook that caught and helped stop jets landing on aircraft carriers) had taken place after the Persian Gulf War (1990–1991), in the midst of a military "downsizing," and in the midst of congressional discussions about women in combat. Women naval personnel were perceived as threats, as persons who would take away spots from men on ships or in combat aircraft.

After years of investigations, most charges were dropped and the only person who resigned was Lieutenant Paula Coughlin, a helicopter pilot, who had been forced to run a gauntlet of drunken men who attacked her. Coughlin had been the first to complain. She was eventually followed by others, who had first been too afraid by what might happen to their careers if they testified. A few naval officers were censured, fined, or forced into early retirement (some in error), but none of the men accused of attacking women in the hotel were convicted of anything.

The real change after Tailhook came with public awareness of the military's hostility toward its woman members. The armed forces began to try to change that culture through education and training. A similar effort had taken place from the 1940s through the 1970s, when the armed services integrated black soldiers and sailors as equals. Whether or not they could do the same for their women members remained questionable, given women's exclusion from combat roles. Not until women were sent into combat alongside men in the 1990s were they regarded as truly equal in the armed services. In 1994, the navy allowed women to serve on combat ships. In 1997, it commissioned the USS *The Sullivans*, the first ship specifically designed for a coed force. Navy and Air Force women were part of the invasion force in 2001, when America invaded Afghanistan after terrorist attacks in New York and Washington, and in 2003, as the United States invaded Iraq in the second Gulf War. In the Army and Marines, women were forbidden from officially serving in combat roles, but as the wars changed from mass battles into house-to-house raids and small-scale attacks, women found themselves in combat whether or not they were supposed to be there.

Despite formal changes in the military, sexual discrimination against women soldiers continued. Sergeant Carolyn Schapper, a Virginia National Guard member and a military intelligence officer in Afghanistan and Iraq, went house-to-house, interviewing locals to gather military intelligence. She recalled in an interview that her reports were sometimes discounted when her male commanders debriefed her. "But it all turned around one day when one of my gunners got shot," she said, "and I took command of the convoy to get him back. And I got high praise from the infantry sergeant major when we got back, and that's when it turned around. So I had to prove myself to them that I was capable of doing the same job as a man." As was so often the case when women entered new fields of endeavor, it took time and effort to convince men to appreciate their work.

Among civilians, high-profile cases of sexual harassment continued to attract attention. As women moved into nontraditional roles and as women competed with men in the economy more directly than ever before, sexual harassment was a technique men could use to limit that competition. Despite federal laws against the practice, the very nature of sexual harassment, which was usually private and often a case of "he said, she said," continued to make cases difficult to prosecute. For many American women, sexual harassment became the price they paid to advance themselves economically. Elaine Ward, who graduated in 1990 from the Plumbers Apprenticeship Program run by her union in New York City, saw sexual harassment as "an attempt to really test my ability to persevere." What kept her going despite the intimidation was the increase in her pay—from $11.80 to $26.90 an hour—over twice as big a paycheck for what had been a man's job.

Pay Equity

The uncertainty of the economy in the 1980s meant that greater numbers of women of all ethnic backgrounds were in the labor force. Despite the expansion in the kinds of jobs women could take, on average, women continued to earn far less than men: about 59¢ for every $1.00 men earned. Statistics gathered by groups such as the National Committee on Pay Equity (NCPE) illustrated the challenges working women continued to face and fueled demands not only for support for affirmative action and an end to sex discrimination and sexual harassment, but also for *pay equity*, also called "comparable worth." Founded in 1979 under Democratic president Jimmy Carter, the NCPE members came from women's and civil rights organizations; state and local pay equity coalitions and commissions on women; religious, professional, legal, and educational associations and labor unions. The group devised a system of points that evaluators assigned to jobs, based on the level of skill, effort, and responsibility they required, as well as the conditions under which the work was performed. Compensating people based on those points, the group argued, would mean fairer wages for women and minorities.

Pay equity advocates highlighted links between the facts that women and minorities were still segregated in the job market and earned less than white men. Their studies also showed that the more a profession was filled with women and minority workers, the more likely it was to be poorly paid. In California, for example, women social service workers made $20,000 a year less than male probation officers, even though the point system measured the jobs as equivalent. In Hawaii, licensed practical nurses earned nearly $1,000 a month less than corrections officers. The Southern California Gas Company had appliance service representatives (men) and customer service representatives (women). The jobs were virtually identical, but men earned over $3,000 a year more. In Illinois, nurses finally sued the state after showing—with the state's own 1983 pay equity study—that their jobs scored 500 points more than electricians, yet they were paid nearly $12,000 less per year.

This long-standing prejudice—that women's work was simply less valuable than men's—proved difficult to overcome. One psychologist conducted a study that showed that students given an article to analyze rated it higher when they thought it had been written by a man. The more women a profession attracted, the more people devalued its status, while professions that attracted more men were more highly regarded. The connection between a worker's gender and salary was clear, but the solution to this economic inequity seemed intractable, since fixing it would cost a great deal of money.

Opposition to the mere concept of pay equity was intense. Opponents, many of whom came from the New Right, the Religious Right, and the Republican Party, argued that men and women viewed jobs differently, and that this fact accounted for differences in pay. Many women, for instance, took less demanding jobs so they had time and energy to care for their families. As had been true through the centuries, women at different points in their lifecycle tended to move in and out of the workplace, depending, for instance, on whether or not they had children to care for. Opponents also argued that women chose to go into what were coincidentally lower-paid occupations because they were pursuing their own interests—caring for others—instead of working for businesses and corporations where they would be making lots of money. Opponents to the idea of pay equity were aghast at the formulas developed by the NCPE, complaining that they were comparing apples to oranges and that the end result would be higher taxes and prices.

Supporters of pay equity, however, sued successfully in several arenas. In 1981, prison matrons in Oregon won pay comparable to what male prison guards made after the Supreme Court ruled in *Oregon v. Gunther* that they could sue despite the fact the jobs were slightly different. City workers went on strike in San Jose, California, in the same year for pay equity and won. In New York, emergency service operators (women) won equal pay with fire truck dispatchers (men). The state of Minnesota became a model for achieving pay equity after passing new legislation requiring it. Clerk-typists now made the same salaries as delivery truck drivers, instead of $500 a month less. The settlement was not without cost—the state's payroll increased 3.7 percent. But many believed the extra costs paying women equitably were justified. Despite opposition from Republican conservatives such as Clarence Pendleton, head of the U.S. Commission on Civil Rights who called pay equity "the looniest idea since Looney Tunes," several federal pay equity bills passed the House of Representatives, before the Senate defeated them.

SARAH BUESSING'S E-MAIL ON THE HARDEST THING ABOUT BEING A WOMAN

Sarah Buessing, a computer scientist at Google, answered the question of what she thought is the hardest thing women have to do. She e-mailed about becoming pregnant while working.

"Being pregnant right now, I'm sure my opinion on this is extremely influenced! However, I still think the hardest thing for a woman to do is balance her career with having children. In New York, most women wait until much later in life than they might normally wait to have kids, in order to establish their careers and get to a point they feel comfortable stepping back from them to have children. I love my job, but it still seems like the right thing to do to completely stop working and devote all of my time to the baby for a year after it's born. I don't feel like I can do that, because it becomes a sort of resumé scar. So instead I'll take off what little time I can and try to work from home and somehow do both. I've also managed to step into a loophole with FMLA [Family Medical Leave Act]—I had the same job for 7 years, and because of reorganizing, found out I'd be losing my job—after I was already pregnant. I got a new job, and even had 2 jobs for a week,

The "Mommy Track" and the Wage Gap

One of the criticisms that opponents of pay equity raised came from statistical studies that showed the wage gap between men and women workers was constant. The studies, critics charged, failed to take into account the various factors such as the higher levels of education men achieved, the time women took off to have children, the part-time work women sought instead of full-time work so they could have job flexibility. Such factors characterized the different job tracks men and women undertook in the economy, and explained the differences in men and women's pay. By 1987, enough women had scaled the corporate ladder to warrant commentary in pop culture. The popular film *Baby Boom*, nominated for two Golden Globe awards, featured Diane Keaton as a corporate executive with little time for a personal life who unexpectedly became the guardian of her young niece. The film portrayed the difficulties of balancing corporate demands with mothering a toddler, reflecting a difficulty that increasing numbers of women faced in real life because the structure of corporate America refused to change in response to women's changing work lives. The basic structure of American corporations reflected in the film had not changed much since the release of *9 to 5* in 1980. Women were now managers and executives as well as administrative assistants and secretaries, but still, by and large, they were expected to behave as men did, sacrificing family time to spend more time and energy working for their employers.

while I was taking vacation from one and starting the other. But, because I haven't been employed by my company for 1 full year, I don't qualify for their typical FMLA benefits of 4 weeks paid leave, and my pregnancy will be treated as a disability in which I can take a limited amount of unpaid time off.

"Now I'm new on the job and I can't help but fear my coworkers may start to see me like a time bomb. When I have the baby I know they will have to take on some of my work, and they are all young men, so I'm really not sure how understanding they will feel about that. The good thing about my company is that they offer the same amount of time off for fathers as for mothers, so maybe someday I can return the favor and cover for them.

"Pregnancy is just an inescapable divide, some men will understand, some will feel it's unfair if I get any special treatment. Hopefully my employer will be understanding and willing to work with me.

"I can understand why companies don't want to pay for salaried leave of women who were pregnant before they even started their job, but 9 months is a long time for unpredictability on the job. Granted I can see that it would be very silly for a company to hire someone 8 months pregnant, barely get them trained, and then have to pay them to not work right away. At the same time, pregnancy is an amazing experience, and worth a little unfairness."

Source: Sarah Buessing, e-mail message to Janet Coryell, October 14, 2007.

In 1989, Felice Schwartz, a long-time feminist and founder of Catalyst, a nonprofit organization dedicated to helping women reenter the workforce, examined the phenomenon. Schwartz had done research on job-sharing, maternity leave, parental leave, and dual-career couples, and warned corporate America that it made more financial sense to be flexible when dealing with women workers than to maintain a rigid corporate structure that discouraged them from having families or spending time with their children. She even devised a plan for a separate career track for women and men who had strong family priorities. The media labeled it "the mommy track," and feminists such as Gloria Steinem and Congresswoman Pat Schroeder excoriated Schwartz and her ideas.

Schwartz was a pragmatist. She knew that many women preferred flexibility in their work lives over more money if the flexibility guaranteed them the opportunity to care for their families. She knew that men and women worked in different ways, with more men than women willing to sacrifice family time to climb the corporate ladder. She also knew that some women chose not to have children, and that to assume all women wanted the same thing was nonsense. Schwartz sought to help businesses realize the absolute necessity of ending the female "brain drain" that corporations suffered as they continued to expect all women to work the same way or to work as most men did (see Primary Source 11-3).

Those who opposed Schwartz's idea argued that workplace flexibility ought to apply to both women and men workers. Economist Sylvia Ann

Hewlett, founder of the Center for Work-Life Policy, suggested that dual-career couples might instead follow a sequencing pattern of work: intense work on one's career, followed by a period of lesser intensity to care for family. However, she cautioned, as long as women were paid less than men for equal or comparable work, heterosexual couples would be more likely to choose women to assume family care since their economic sacrifice would be less than that of men.

Whether women followed the mommy track or not, women continued to earn less than men. In a long-term study on pay equity that finally took into account the different factors that affected the way men and women worked, psychology professor Dr. Hilary Lips showed that the wage gap between men and women had lessened somewhat during the 1980s, when many pay equity cases were won, but widened again in the late 1990s. She also discovered that the wage gap persisted across racial lines (in 2001, for example, black women earned only 84.8 percent of what black men earned), across education lines (women with high school diplomas, associate degrees, bachelor's degrees, master's degrees, doctorates—all earned about 75 percent of what men with similar education did) and, most important, across occupational lines. Women educated identically to men, working the same number of hours, in the same profession, still earned less than men. Only in the lowest-paid jobs ($25,000 to $30,000 annually) were pay rates equal. Women psychologists earned 83¢, college professors 75¢, lawyers and judges 69¢ for every $1 a man in the same position. She also found that being in a profession dominated by women did not erase the wage gap: elementary school teachers who were women earned 95¢ for every $1 men made; women secretaries—the overwhelming majority—earned 84¢ compared to every $1 earned by male secretaries.

Pay equity issues and the wage gap between men and women remain areas of contention in the American economy. Opponents of pay equity continue to assert the issue's intractability to solution. Supporters continue to argue that the economic success of women is critical to the nation as a whole, and that only when women are able to participate fully and as equal members of the national economy can they rise to their full potential as citizens.

REPRODUCTIVE RIGHTS IN A CONSERVATIVE ERA

The coalition represented by conservative Republicans, the New Right, and the Religious Right saw Reagan's presidency as an ideal opportunity to restrict women's reproductive rights, particularly their right to abortion. Long before the Supreme Court's decision upholding that a woman's right to privacy limited the state's ability to restrict abortion in *Roe v. Wade* (1973), abortion opponents had protested the procedure while supporters in favor of women's rights to safer, legal abortions countered their protests. The Catholic Church had forbidden all abortions in 1869 under Pope Pius IX. The church argued that a fetus was equivalent to a child, and because an abortion kills a fetus, abortions constitute murder. In 1962, abortion opponents hounded Arizonian Sherri Finkbine, host of a local television's children show, when she publicized an abortion she had after taking the drug thalidomide. She had hoped the publicity would warn other pregnant women of the dangers of the drug, which caused horrific fetal abnormalities. Instead, she lost her job, her husband was suspended from his teaching position, and her four children were harassed with death threats. In 1965, the *Griswold v. Connecticut* decision led abortion opponents to form "pro-life" groups to prevent changes to abortion laws that might use the constitutional right to privacy to lift restrictions. By 1973, after the Supreme Court legalized abortion, the U.S. Catholic Conference's Family Life Division, under the auspices of the National Conference of Catholic Bishops, organized the National Right to Life Committee. The NOW responded by protesting at the Vatican's embassy in Washington, DC, on Mother's Day, reminding the institution of America's constitutional separation of church and state. Catholic groups opposed to their church's stance, the Religious Coalition for Abortion Rights and Catholics for a Free Choice, became active supporters of women's rights to family planning and abortion.

Opposing sides quickly solidified over the issue of abortion. Republicans called for a constitutional amendment banning the procedure in their 1976 party platform, despite nominating pro-choice candidate Gerald R. Ford. Democrats adopted a pro-choice plank, despite their nomination of an evangelical Christian personally opposed to abortion, Jimmy Carter. The Supreme Court decided in *Planned Parenthood of Central Missouri v. Danforth* (1976) to nullify state laws that gave husbands veto power over their wives' decisions to have abortions. The Hyde Amendment, sponsored by conservative Republicans in Congress, prohibited the use of Medicaid funds for abortions unless a woman's life was in danger. Later that year, Rosie Jimenez, a poor, single mother of a five-year-old and a scholarship student six months away from completing her studies, died of an illegal abortion after the Hyde Amendment denied her access to a costlier but safe one.

Members of the New Right campaigned tirelessly for the return of abortion restrictions. Not content with peaceful protests, some members of the antiabortion community resorted to violence to convince women to stay pregnant. Beginning in 1977, violence against clinics performing abortions and providing birth control information, counseling services, and pregnancy testing began to increase. The Emma Goldman Clinic in Iowa City, Iowa, was firebombed. In Cleveland, an arsonist set fire to an operating room with a gasoline bomb while an abortion was in progress. Arsonists burned Planned Parenthood of St. Paul, Minnesota. NOW called upon both pro-choice and antiabortion groups to meet in 1979 to work together on lessening the need for abortion, but the organization would not compromise its stance that safe, legal abortion was the right of every American woman. By the year 2000, American abortion and reproductive service providers had suffered through 6,679 instances of hate mailings and crank calls; 33,235 instances of picketing; 836 acts of vandalism; 675 blockades resulting in 33,827 arrests; 365 invasions; 57 burglaries; 502 bomb threats;

77 attempted bombings or incidents of arson; 40 bombings; 406 incidents of stalking; 322 death threats; 112 counts of assault and battery; and 16 attempted murders. Three people had been kidnapped, one had been maimed, and eight had been murdered, all by so-called pro-life supporters.

Antiabortion groups used techniques borrowed from the civil rights movement, such as sit-ins and nonviolent protests, to shut down clinics in major cities, while NOW and other women's rights groups such as the National Abortion Rights Action League (NARAL) used lawsuits, mass marches, and counter demonstrations to protest pro-life actions. NARAL eventually used antiracketeering laws to hold one group, Operation Rescue, responsible for damages done by their members. Operation Rescue had "invaded" numerous cities, holding mass demonstrations and sit-ins, preventing clinic workers and patients from accessing clinics in violation of federal law, and costing cities enormous sums for police protection. NOW's successful lawsuit bankrupted the organization.

In the meantime, restrictions on both abortions and birth control gradually increased. Funding restrictions came first, limiting access to abortions for poor women and then limiting information clinic workers provided patients. In 1989, in the case *Webster v. Reproductive Health Services*, the Supreme Court allowed states to pass laws restricting abortions. In 1990, the Congress failed to override President Bush's veto of a law that would have allowed Medicaid to pay for abortions for women who had been victims of rape or incest—two of the common exclusions. By 1991, the government forbade family planning clinics that received federal money from even discussing abortion. Many physicians resisted what was termed the *gag rule*, viewing it as interfering with doctor–patient relationships as well as attacking their own freedom of speech. The Supreme Court ruled in *Rust v. Sullivan* (1991), however, that the rule did not violate freedom of speech, nor did it interfere with a woman's right to an abortion. More limitations followed. Some states also imposed age-related restrictions, prohibiting minors in some states from getting birth control or abortions unless both parents were notified, even in cases of abuse or incest.

In 1993, Bill Clinton, the first pro-choice president in twelve years, reversed many of his predecessors' limits on abortion funding and information. That same year, two doctors who had performed abortions were murdered. In response to increasing violence against clinics by antiabortion zealots, Congress enacted the Freedom of Access to Clinic Entrances Act (FACE) in 1994, making it a federal crime to interfere with either the providers or their patients and guaranteeing that women could not be prevented from entering clinics. The Supreme Court also ruled that antiracketeering laws could be used to prosecute groups whose mass action protests used intimidation, extortion, and barricades in their attempts to close down clinics. Conservative opponents of abortion continued to fight against the procedure, electing a staunchly conservative House of Representatives in 1994 that promptly passed bills attempting to ban abortion nationally. The president successfully vetoed the bills, but the violence continued.

In addition to fighting against abortion restrictions, abortion rights activists also worked to prevent pregnancy and thus to prevent abortions.

In 1998, health insurance plans for federal employees and their families finally added contraceptive coverage. NARAL changed its name to NARAL-Pro-Choice America and organized the 2004 March for Women's Lives in Washington, DC. There, 1 million protestors demonstrated in favor of freedom of choice and freedom of information regarding all contraceptive choices, including abortion. The group then turned its attention to emphasizing contraception as a way to prevent abortions, hoping to capitalize on the sentiments of a majority of Americans who were pro-choice yet still uncomfortable with abortion.

The issue of abortion affected all American women as it continued to raise ethical and moral dilemmas that for many Americans have no easy resolution—questions about when life really begins and whether it is right to force a woman to endure a pregnancy that she does not want. Most Americans regarded abortion as acceptable when pregnancy resulted from rape or incest, and some accepted abortion if the fetus suffered from serious birth defects. All but the most radical pro-life supporters viewed the continued good health of the mother or her survival as acceptable reasons to allow abortion as well. But for moral absolutists who made up the Religious Right, as well as many members of the New Right and the Catholic pro-life activists, a fetus was regarded as an unborn human with a soul who should be left to be born or not, as God willed. Choice advocates, in contrast, continued to favor allowing women to make such a personal decision about whether or not to bear a child themselves.

THIRD WAVE FEMINISM AND THE CULTURE WARS

By the 1990s, feminism had entered a new phase called the Third Wave. Many Americans approved of the changes that the women's movement had fought for as they continued to transform American society. Twenty states had embedded equal rights amendments into their constitutions, including states such as Louisiana and Virginia that had failed to ratify the federal equal rights amendment. Women moved toward new areas of endeavor and arenas made more equal because of the women's liberation movement, but many saw less need for activism, preferring individual empowerment instead. At the same time, the rise of conservatism polarized American political and popular culture in the 1980s and 1990s, a polarization so intense that it was deemed the *culture wars*. Conservatives painted feminists as radical extremists, out of touch with most American women.

The Fragmentation of Feminism

After the national ERA failed, the movement for women's rights splintered in much the same way that it had after women won the vote. Women have never constituted a single monolithic group, and individuals from differing backgrounds have different issues, goals, and interests. Varieties of feminism, many geared toward specific ethnocultural groups, continued to evolve in a third wave of feminism in the years after the failure of the ERA. In the 1980s and 1990s, many young women did not want to define themselves as feminists. They did not appreciate the strident militancy of their fore-mothers in feminism's second wave, in part because they were used to living in a world where the more visible instances of sexual discrimination had ended. When asked if they were feminists, many responded in the negative, "I'm not a feminist, but. . . ." Many saw no reason to join a women's movement (although NOW membership did nearly double to 260,000 in 1989 after the *Webster* decision limiting abortion rights), and directed their efforts toward reforming other aspects of American society. The federal ERA continued to be reintroduced in every session of Congress, but in the meantime, women used the sheer power of their numbers as well as existing laws to change their place in American society.

Black feminists in the 1970s expanded feminism beyond the white middle-class concerns of the original women's liberation movement. Angry about sexism and racism that doubled the discrimination they faced, black feminist authors such as Alice Walker and Ntozake Shange published books and plays examining the status of black women and the impact of sexism on them. By the late 1970s and 1980s, black lesbian feminists brought homosexuality and homophobia to the public discussion of black women's lives and roles, and organized groups to support their ideas. In 1991, black women academics, led by Elsa Barkley-Brown, a noted historian, formed African American Women in Defense of Ourselves, a group that took out a full-page ad in the *New York Times*, signed by 1,603 women of African descent to protest the smear campaign against Anita Hill during the Hill–Thomas controversy. Other black feminists began using the term *womanism* instead of *feminism*. Coined by Alice Walker, the term derived from the folk expression "womanish" that blacks used to describe courageous or au-dacious female behavior. Womanists insisted that the feminism of the wom-en's liberation movement was too white, too middle-class, and too focused on combat with men. Womanism recognized oppression but also celebrated women—their culture, their emotions, their strengths—as well as recogniz-ing and working for, as Walker put it, the "survival and wholeness of entire people—male *and* female." Black feminists and womanists expanded the interests and views of the feminist movement, hoping that it would grow more inclusive as a result.

Hispanic feminists continued their campaign against sexism as well and, like the womanists, were disinclined to use white middle-class measures of what their issues should be. Gloria Anzaldua, a lesbian/Chicana/feminist scholar, articulated Chicana concerns in 1987, writing that she abhorred "some of my culture's ways, how it cripples its women, *como burras* [like burros], our strengths used against us, lowly *burras* bearing humility with dignity. The ability to serve, claim the males, is our highest virtue." It was not enough to focus on just women, she continued, despairing of her cul-ture's tradition of *machismo* that "makes macho caricatures of its men." Rather than using others' definitions and concerns, she wrote, she would "stand and claim my space, making a new culture—*una cultura mestiza*—with my own lumber, my own bricks and mortar and my own feminist architecture." Another writer, poet Ana Castillo, cofounded a literary magazine, *Third Woman*, to provide an outlet for writings by women of color, who found it difficult to publish their work in the white mainstream press. Castillo saw most Chicana/Latina/Hispanic feminists turning from the white-dominated feminist movement as well, to focus on concerns that resonated more deeply in their lives. Castillo used a new term for Chicana feminists as well: *Xicanisma*, a word embracing the Mexican culture from where Chicanas came and which the white feminist movement largely ignored.

Native American women also differentiated themselves from the feminist movement. Continuing discrimination against all Indians limited the appeal of a woman-centered movement. Native American women activists often found other issues to focus on as they strove to improve the lot of all their people. For example, banker Elouise Pepion Cobell of the Blackfeet Tribe of Montana sought to force the government to live up to agreements it had signed with the tribe under the Dawes Act in 1887. Great-granddaughter of the legendary Blackfoot leader Mountain Chief, Cobell filed a lawsuit against the federal government in 1996 for mismanaging the resources of lands they had taken to hold in trust for the tribe since the breakup of the reservation system. Cobell noted that, according

ELOUISE COBELL WATCHES INTERIOR SECRETARY KEN SALAZAR TESTIFY When she began her investigation of the Bureau of Indian Affairs' (BIA) mismanagement of Indian trusts at age 18, a BIA representative told Eloise Cobell she wasn't "capable" of understanding the accounting. She became an accountant, a treasurer, a banker, a warrior, and a MacArthur "genius" Fellow. In 2009, she watched Interior Secretary Ken Salazar testify in favor of a proposed settlement in her fight to make the BIA accountable after more than a century of abuse.

to the trust provisions, the government was responsible for returning to the Indians "any revenues generated by mining, oil and gas extraction, timber operations, grazing or similar activities." The government, said Cobell, had not done so, and now owed the Native Americans upward of $176 billion. The government's lack of proper oversight and payment was clear. Land with five operating oil wells, for instance, brought the Native American who owned it a royalty check of only $30 a month at a time when domestic oil was sold for that much a barrel. Cobell worked on the discrepancies first as a tribal accountant. She then opened a Native-run bank after the government shut down the only bank on the reservation. As a banker, she used forensic accounting, accessing her customers' accounts, so she could gather the data she needed to win her case.

As a result of Cobell's years of detective work, the U.S. Court of Appeals issued contempt of court citations against successive secretaries of the Interior Department, beginning with Bruce Babbitt, who served under President Clinton. The lawsuit continued into the new century, with the federal government still dragging its feet, destroying files and records, intimidating witnesses, and exhibiting no intention of making a fair accounting of the monies. After a bench trial in 2007, U.S. District Judge James Robertson declared with disgust that the U.S. government had made it impossible to make any fair accounting of the tribal money and ordered the Interior Department to find a remedy. The case was finally settled for a fraction of what the government owed the Indians in 2010. The Blackfeet made Cobell a warrior, an unusual designation for a woman, and she became a hero to many not only for her fight to regain monies owed to Native Americans, but also for her work educating the people of her community about economics.

Other women worked on Native American issues in other ways. Many linked up with international groups such as the International Indigenous Women's Forum (1995) and the Indigenous Women of the Americas (formed in 2002) to work on issues that spanned the Western Hemisphere, hoping to amplify their voices as well by allying with the international indigenous women's movement. In 2007, these groups, along with the Continental Network of Indigenous Women of the Americas, called on member nations to vote in favor of the United Nations' 2006 document, the Declaration on the Rights of Indigenous People, which recognized the rights of Native women and men to self-determination, to the land, resources, and territories they depended upon for survival, and to their right "to live free from violence and discrimination."

Native Americans also grew increasingly concerned with the impact of governmental deregulation in the 1980s that relaxed environmental standards and affected many lands near their reservations. Anne Burford, President Reagan's appointee to head the Environmental Protection Agency, opposed strict regulation of air quality and toxic waste disposal, and James Watt, Reagan's secretary of the interior, increased mining and timber harvesting on public lands. Such actions had serious repercussions on the land. Ecofeminism, a belief that the oppression of women and nature were related, attracted many Native women as well as women from other interest groups and ethnic backgrounds. Ecofeminism attempted to link feminism and environmentalism to form a meta-feminism including politics, spirituality, feminism, and ecology. Many ecofeminists also believed in a woman-centered divinity, a trait they shared with many Native religions and that also helped attract Native American women.

Ecofeminists undertook a variety of specific reforms. In Arizona, they formed Feminists for Animal Rights, and focused on ending abuse against women, animals, and the earth. In Montana, Women's Voices for the Earth tried to help create a society that was both ecologically sustainable as well as socially just, publishing informative articles, such as ones linking chemicals to birth defects, that combined ecological and safety concerns with a feminist focus. One article, about the toxicity of nail polish and acrylic nails, noted that many nail artists were Vietnamese women immigrants working at sweatshop wages with poor ventilation of the toxic fumes emitted by the beauty products. These women suffered from asthma, headaches, nausea, and dizziness, and many had babies suffering from birth defects. In part because of ecofeminists' protests, the state of California finally passed a law to protect its 80,000 nail technicians, requiring beauty manufacturers to disclose harmful chemicals used in their products.

Women activists continue to form local grassroots organizations, and widespread use of the Internet allowed local and regional groups to circulate their ideas and calls for action nationally. Boston Ecofeminist Action promoted vegetarianism while providing online links to other organizations. The Southern Girls Convention held an annual conference to discuss everything from papermaking to car repair to breast-feeding to organizing a nonprofit film festival and promoting pro-choice policies to legislatures and governmental agencies. In Dallas and Salt Lake City, women joined revived chapters of the Brown Berets. These Hispanic activists were particularly interested in meeting the biggest threat that immigration reform might pose for illegal aliens—deportation. In the Midwest, Asian Women United of Minnesota provided counseling to women suffering from abuse, offering multilingual interpreters and community education about domestic violence. A similar group in Oregon, the South Asian Women's Empowerment and Resource Alliance, helped battered women and publicized other women's movements, including those in South Asia.

Lesbians had long been active in the feminist movement, organizing within broader organizations as well as mobilizing for their own rights. In 1965, one of the founders of the Daughters of Bilitis, Barbara Gittings, had helped organize the first demonstration in front of the White House to end the ban on lesbians and gays holding federal jobs (see Chapter 9). In the last decades of the twentieth century, lesbian women held hundreds of protests, vigils, and demonstrations throughout the nation, demanding equal treatment in employment and housing, fairer representations in textbooks and the media, and recognition for their relationships as lifetime partners and parents. In recent years, some of the most prominent of these marches have taken on a festive atmosphere. The annual Sistahs Steppin' In Pride March in Oakland, California, for example, celebrates the history and culture of the town's community of lesbian and bisexual women through chanting, drums, games, food vendors, and arts and craft displays. Such celebrations not only build community but also serve clear political purposes: to make lesbian and bisexual women visible as civic actors, deserving of human rights.

Lesbians were also key actors in promoting the cause of same-sex marriage to secure their legal, financial, and parental rights and to have the government recognize their full citizenship. By the 1990s, same-sex marriage had become an important constitutional question. Supporters argued that states should not forbid gay couples from marrying because that would deny them the equal rights all Americans enjoyed under the Fourteenth Amendment to the Constitution. Congress removed itself from the fight over gay marriage in 1996 after passing the Defense of Marriage Act that prohibited the government from recognizing gay marriage. States across the country followed, but some states began working toward laws legalizing gay marriage. Hawaii, California, Massachusetts, Vermont, Connecticut, Maine, and New Hampshire all passed laws supporting gay marriage, and lesbian couples who had lived together for years were thrilled to marry at last.

The techniques that women had learned in the early days of the women's liberation movement enabled them to form new organizations and to use the same skills to accomplish new goals. Many young women turned toward these smaller reform groups with more specialized interests. Even NOW recognized the importance of widening its appeal and expanded its efforts to incorporate more regional concerns. It formed new chapters that focused on women's interests within their own communities and geographic regions. In 1995, it ended its support of the ERA as written, and adopted a new text for a constitutional amendment that called for an end to all discrimination based on "sex, race, sexual orientation, marital status, ethnicity, national origin, color or indigence." NOW finished the century with 500,000 members and local chapters in every state and the District of Columbia. It continued to reach out to a broader constituency by expanding its statement of purpose to include fighting against racism, homophobia, violence against women, discrimination, and harassment, while continuing to fight for women's reproductive rights, including abortion.

The Culture Wars

As feminism achieved many of its most visible goals, many Americans, believing that oppression against women had largely ended, resisted any further changes and began to see continuing feminist demands as unreasonable. In 1991, Susan Faludi examined this phenomenon in her prize-winning book, *Backlash: The Undeclared War Against American Women*. She argued that conservatives had worked hard to promote myths about feminists. These included one that argued there was a "man shortage," and that a forty-year-old unmarried woman was more likely to be killed by a terrorist than to find a husband. Other myths proclaimed that professional women were jeopardizing their fertility and would never have children because they waited too long. The media, claimed Faludi, discouraged feminism by

CAGNEY AND LACEY AND THE WOMEN'S MOVEMENT   As the media expanded its roles for women, Tyne Daly (left) and Sharon Gless played two police officers on *Cagney and Lacey*, the first prime-time drama to star two women. The show's producer, Barney Rosenzweig, called on organized women's groups to support the show every time the network threatened to cancel it, which happened every time it dealt with controversial topics such as abortion clinic bombings.

promoting fashion featuring female models who appeared drug-addled or battered, or who wore miniskirts or baby-doll dresses, clothing of little practical use to women who worked. Television's leading shows changed from having strong women characters who worked as police officers (1982's *Cagney and Lacey*) to shows where women characters were happy only if they were homemakers and mothers, or, at best, part-time workers (1987's *thirtysomething*). Films portrayed women without men as needy and, even, in the case of the 1987's *Fatal Attraction* (nominated for six Academy Awards), as homicidal when rejected by a man.

Faludi's book sparked considerable discussion about the need for feminism and topped the best-seller list for nine months. Another work, Naomi Wolf's *The Beauty Myth* (1991), also examined the attacks against feminism and women that came from a beauty industry obsessed with tall, skinny models in a country where the average American woman was 5 feet 4 inches tall and weighed 140 pounds. Relentless advertising promoted from every conceivable source left many American women hating themselves and their appearances when they did not measure up to the air-brushed, computer-enhanced, professionally maintained American beauty. Feminists fought against the creation of beauty standards that derived in part from those images. They declared that women should not waste time making themselves pretty for men, that sexy clothing was a way to oppress women, and that natural beauty should be the order of things. Wolf and many other feminists blamed the decline of the feminist movement after the defeat of

CHRISTINA HOFF SOMMERS, WHO STOLE FEMINISM?

Christina Hoff Sommers, a philosophy professor at Clark University, published a best-selling critique of what she termed gender feminism. Gender feminists were radicals who hated men, claimed Sommers; equity feminists, such as herself, refused to accept that women suffered from ideological oppression. Such simplistic definitions of all feminists attracted considerable attention and strong reactions.

"American women owe an incalculable debt to the classically liberal feminists who came before us and fought long and hard, and ultimately with spectacular success, to gain for women the rights that the men of the country had taken for granted for over two hundred years. Exposing the hypocrisy of the gender feminists will not jeopardize those achievements....

"All indications are that the new crop of young feminist ideologues coming out of our nation's colleges are even angrier, more resentful and more indifferent to the truth than their mentors.

the ERA on younger women failing to understand how American culture used beauty and sexuality to oppress women.

Both Faludi and Wolf were vehemently criticized by antifeminists, including writers such as Professor Camille Paglia, a lesbian activist and art critic who labeled herself a "post-feminist," and argued that Faludi and Wolf presented women only as victims. Christina Hoff Sommers, a philosophy professor, also complained. Boys were being discriminated against, she wrote, not girls, and feminists ignored the gender differences that could not be assuaged by equal rights. The problems the authors discussed were in fact nothing new, as historians of women could attest: changes in the status of women have always met with resistance, and whether to treat women equally or differently because of their gender was not a new question. What was new was the primacy the media gave to women antifeminists criticizing women feminists, instead of male critics of feminists. The media relished the image of conservative women attacking what they termed "painfully outmoded" feminists, using intemperate language, complaining of being bullied by *feminazis*, as Paglia called feminists, who "crouch like cobwebby pouter pigeons ready to get their tiny claws into women students." A "war against women" became one more battle in America's cultural war between liberals and conservatives, with no victor in sight (see Primary Source 11-4).

WOMEN AND POPULAR CULTURE

The images of women in American popular culture always reflected a disconnect between those images and the realities of their lives. By the end of the millennium, the pervasiveness of outlets distributing popular culture made a difference in the numbers of women affected by these images. Some

"The large majority of women, including the majority of college women, are distancing themselves from this anger and resentfulness. Unfortunately, they associate these attitudes with feminism, and so they conclude that they are not really feminists. According to a 1992 *Time*/CNN poll, although 57 percent of the women responding said they believed there was a need for a strong women's movement, 63 percent said they do not consider themselves feminist. . . .

"The women currently manning—womanning—the feminist ramparts do not take well to criticism. How could they? As they see it, they are dealing with a massive epidemic of male atrocity and a constituency of benighted women who have yet to comprehend the seriousness of their predicament. Hence, male critics must be 'sexist' and 'reactionary,' and female critics 'traitors,' 'collaborators,' or backlashers.' This kind of reaction has. . . . alienated and silenced women and men alike."

Source: Christina Hoff Sommers, *Who Stole Feminism? How Women Have Betrayed Women,* (New York: Touchstone, 1995), 17–18.

of the changes were in delivery, from a popular culture controlled by a few powerful forces and corporations to a vast array of cultural images spread worldwide by a host of media outlets and the Internet. The number of television channels increased, as the television sets shrank in cost, and began appearing on the walls of bars, in beauty salons, and in waiting rooms, even in checkout lines at stores, where the images of women they put forth became nearly inescapable. The magazine and print industry also expanded exponentially in the 1980s and beyond, with well over half of magazine revenue coming from advertisements, most of them directed at women. Some of the changes were in content, with increasing conspicuous consumption of material goods and more explicit sexualization of nearly every commodity. "Image is everything," went the advertising copy for one product in the 1990s, and the idea seemed to be the watchword for the last part of the twentieth century.

Women's Television Roles

In 1950, only 9 percent of American households had television; by 1978, nearly 98 percent had television, 78 percent in living color. By 2000, nearly all—98.2 percent—of American households had at least one television and the average U.S. household had 2.24 sets, on for 6 hours and 47 minutes a day. Television became the most common medium to spread news and entertainment in the second half of the century, and the business as well as the shows themselves reflected the changes in society. In 1978, the Big Three television networks, CBS, ABC, and NBC, enjoyed 91 percent of the American audiences during prime time—8 to 11 p.m. Changes in regulation in the late 1970s, however, allowed for a proliferation of cable systems as well as televisions channels, and by 1993, the Big Three had only 61 percent of the market share, as Americans' viewing habits shifted, watching programming on dozens, then hundreds of other channels. With the exponential increase in the number of channels, advertising and television shows were directed at smaller and more specialized markets with niche networks, such as the Food Network or the Golf Channel. The cultural touchstone provided by network television shows in the 1950s and 1960s was gone.

Television shows reflected the changes in women's lives because of the women's movement. Barbara Walters is one example. In the 1960s, she was the decorative "Today girl" on NBC's morning show. At first, Walters was forbidden to ask guests questions about politics and economics because her bosses thought such "male" topics should be off limits to women interviewers. She persisted, however, asking her questions when her male counterparts were done, and her interviewing skills became formidable. She interviewed numerous world leaders and every president starting with Richard Nixon, whom she accompanied on his historic trip to China in 1972. Feminists rejoiced when Walters became the first woman news anchorperson, teamed with Harry Reasoner on ABC in 1976. But Reasoner made public his disapproval of what he considered a gimmick, refusing to even speak to Walters when the two were off the air. He also disliked the team approach, and Walters soon left for a more comfortable arena, interviewing diplomats, politicians, and celebrities in regularly scheduled shows for ABC. In 1977, she succeeded in arranging an interview with Egyptian president Anwar Sadat and Israeli Prime Minister Menachem Begin at a crucial time during peace talks that would eventually result in the Camp David accords between the two nations that President Carter brokered in 1978. By 1997, Walters created her own show, *The View*, where women commentators of different ages and backgrounds discussed current political and economic issues, as well as the social topics her earliest bosses thought she should stick to.

Mary Tyler Moore's career in television also reflected the changes in American women's lives during the decades of the last part of the twentieth century. In 1959, Moore, a dancer, took her first television role as a telephone receptionist on *Richard Diamond, Private Detective*. The role showed only her legs on camera, a gimmick it would be hard to imagine applying to a male actor. She quit the show, unhappy with the part's limits, and soon won a role as a housewife, Laura Petrie, on the popular *Dick Van Dyke* show. Like Lucy (see Chapter 9), the Laura character too found it impossible to balance a home life with a career, as one episode showed her failing when she tried to follow her old dream of being a dancer while maintaining her role as a full-time wife and mother.

Moore's success on the show led to an iconic series in the 1970s, the *Mary Tyler Moore Show*, revolving around the life of a single woman living and working in Minneapolis. Reflecting changes wrought by the women's movement, and unlike any earlier television series, Moore's show portrayed her character, Mary, as a person fulfilled by her career as a television producer and by her relationships with her friends. While the character dated and talked about wanting to marry, she had left her fiancé at the beginning of the series and did not have a husband or child by the end. The show's final episode in 1977, which allowed Moore to continue as a single woman rather than marrying her off to a man, reflected Moore's personal feminism. The success of the series made it easier for writers to portray women characters as something other than housewives or single women looking for mates, and the kinds of characters women played expanded as a result.

Women of Color on Television

Women of color, at least black women, benefited from the expansion of the media as well. *Julia*, a 1969 to 1971 series starring Diahann Carroll playing a nurse in a doctor's office, was a situation comedy that portrayed an African American woman in a nonstereotypical role. Carroll played, not a maid or a comic, but a woman raising her son alone after her husband had been shot down in the Vietnam War. Carroll's portrayal of a dignified black woman dealing with the problems of a working mother, such as finding decent child care, made the show a top-ten hit. At the same time, some blacks were angry that Carroll's character seemed to be thoroughly assimilated into white America, with no black neighbors, and no mention of the racial unrest of the times. However, as the mass-circulation *Ebony* magazine pointed out to its middle-class readers, the series provided Americans with an alternative image of blacks during the violence of the civil rights era, perhaps lessening some of the fear white Americans felt about integrating blacks into their communities.

The financial success of *Julia* encouraged other series, and the criticisms of the show led to more variety. *Good Times* (1974–1979), set in Chicago's public housing projects, revolved around a strong female character, played by Esther Rolle, with her husband present within the family, instead of the more stereotypical female-headed household. Rolle pressed hard for script changes to ensure that the characters were not caricatures, and even quit the show at one point to protest scripts that she thought offensive. *The Jeffersons* (1975–1985) showed an upwardly mobile black couple who had succeeded financially. Their neighbors were an interracial couple; their maid, however, was still black. Women of color were in short supply in other television shows. Most black entertainers with their own shows were men. Black comic Flip Wilson had his own show, where he played one character, Geraldine, in drag. Leading essayist Leoule Goshu argued that Wilson, by dressing up as a black woman, was asking the American public why this was one of the only images of black women on television. Playing bit parts or secondary characters remained the most common roles for black women, as well as for other women of color.

In the 1980s, Bill Cosby, a leading black comic and actor, created *The Bill Cosby Show* (1984–1992). Set in New York, the show personified for many Americans the changes in the lives of black women and men. The characters— Cliff Huxtable, an obstetrician, his corporate attorney wife Claire, played by Phylicia Rashad, and their five children—were bright, attractive, and intelligent. Claire was the epitome of the Superwoman: loving wife, caring mother, and income provider. The house was never messy, the children were never ignored, the husband was never resentful of his wife's career. While still a comedy, the show dealt directly with social issues, including racism, education, poverty, and protest. Black culture and history, particularly music and art, were incorporated in the show. Claire, a strong feminist, nevertheless was attractive and fashionable, as were her daughters. The *Cosby Show* became the top-rated show in the country for four years, despite cable television's splintering influence, and broke new ground with its successful portrayals of upper-class black professionals and beautiful feminists.

The most powerful black woman on television, however, came not from scripted situation comedies or dramas, but from the news and the talk-show circuit: Oprah Winfrey. A local news reporter and beauty pageant winner from Nashville, Tennessee, Winfrey imitated her role model, Barbara Walters, and taught herself to read the news and to interview well. She hosted talk shows in Baltimore and Chicago, where she became host of the *Oprah Winfrey Show*, the most popular daytime talk show in television history. Winfrey brought America and 117 other countries interviews with experts in finance, home decor, and relationships. Her production company produced films based on novels by African American authors, such as Zora Neale Hurston's *Their Eyes Were Watching God*, and Alice Walker's *The Color Purple*, in which Winfrey took a leading role. Her book club selections guaranteed best-selling status to authors whose work she selected. At age 34, she became the youngest and the first African American to win the Broadcaster of the Year award. By 1998, she had won so many Emmy awards from the National Academy of Television Arts & Sciences that she withdrew her name from any further consideration, so that others might win. In the same year she established a public charity with 100 percent of donations going to help children. By 2003, she was the first African American woman on *Forbes* magazine's annual list of billionaires, and in 2004 *Time* magazine named her one of the most influential people in the world. Winfrey's expanded role in television and in American culture is one measure of the ways in which women took advantage of new opportunities provided by the changes wrought by the women's movement.

WOMEN IN POLITICS AND GOVERNMENT

Many of those changes in American culture would stay, thanks to the arrival of women in powerful positions in politics and government, and despite attacks from the New Right and others who disapproved. At every level, women won elective office, and used their power to craft legislation supporting women's rights. In 1992, Democrats captured the White House again, turned back many of the conservative gains made during the previous Republican administrations, and doubled the number of women in Congress. Health and welfare reform, issues which often had the greatest impact on women, took center stage, until a sexual scandal involving President Bill Clinton shook the country and led to his impeachment and trial.

Women Politicos

In 1971, when the Texas Women's Political Caucus formed, only two women were in the state legislature. By 1977, at the time of the Houston Conference (see Chapter 10), there were fourteen. By 1998, Texas's thirty-two women legislators included blacks and Latinas, as well as whites. Earlier that decade, Democrat Ann W. Richards had become the first woman elected as governor since "Ma" Ferguson, who in 1924 had promised to listen to her husband when she made decisions. Richards did not see any necessity to make the same promise.

Other states followed similar patterns of women's increased participation in government after the 1970s. In 1978, Nancy Kassebaum was elected the first woman senator from Kansas and for a time was the only woman in the U.S. Senate. In 1991, Joan Finney became the state's first woman governor, and was followed in 2002 by another, Kathleen Sibelius, who later served as the cabinet secretary of health and human services. In 1999, Iowa had its first woman secretary of agriculture. By 2002, Michigan had had women in the posts of governor, lieutenant governor, attorney general, and secretary of state. That same year, 30 percent of the Minnesota legislature were women, as were 27 percent of the Illinois legislature. By 2007, there were nine women governors, eleven lieutenant governors, four attorneys general, twelve secretaries of state, twenty-one women working as state treasurers, auditors or comptrollers, and eleven women heading state commissions on education, insurance, labor, and the like across the nation, and one woman, Hillary Clinton, who was campaigning to become the next Democratic president. In the years since Geraldine Ferraro had run for vice president of the country, voters had obviously become far more comfortable with women serving in high office.

Nationally, women candidates benefited from groups such as the Women's Campaign Fund (1974), the first national political action committee with the goal of electing progressive women to office. EMILY's (Early Money Is Like Yeast) List formed in 1986 to elect pro-choice Democratic women, and soon became the largest financial source for liberal and minority women seeking office. The New Right continued to fund candidates through Phyllis Schlafly's Eagle Forum and another conservative group, Beverly LaHaye's Concerned Women for America (although LaHaye's website posted articles that bemoaned the lack of conservative women candidates running for office because it was so difficult to serve in office while raising a family).

Women interested in politics also benefited from presidential appointments. President Carter had appointed Patricia Roberts Harris as secretary of housing and urban development. The first black woman to serve as a cabinet secretary, she continued as secretary of health and human services in his administration. Carter also appointed Juanita Kreps his secretary of commerce and Shirley Hufstedler as head of the Department of Education. Conservative Republicans Reagan and George H. W. Bush appointed one

VIOLENCE AGAINST WOMEN ACT

In 1994, Congress passed the Violence Against Women Act, allocating more than $1 billion to fight violence against women. Each "title" of the act reflected the multitude of ways in which violence against women affected society. The legislation came about after 1992, deemed the Year of the Woman, when the number of women in Congress doubled virtually overnight. Once in office, women paid attention to women's issues to a far greater extent than male legislators had. In 2000 and 2005, the act was reauthorized; in 2009, Vice President Joe Biden, who *had drafted the original act, announced domestic violence expert Lynn Rosenthal's appointment as the first White House Advisor on Violence Against Women.*

"Be it enacted by the Senate and House of Representatives of the United States of America in Congress assembled. . . . The 'Violence Against Women and Department of Justice Reauthorization Act of 2005'

"Title I—Enhancing Judicial and Law Enforcement Tools to Combat Violence Against Women

woman between them: Elizabeth Dole served as Reagan's transportation secretary and Bush's secretary of labor (followed by Ann McLaughlin). Reagan also appointed Jeanne Kirkpatrick ambassador to the United Nations, the first woman to serve in that position, and Margaret M. Heckler as secretary of health and human services. Reagan's secretaries of commerce and labor were also women. Democrat Bill Clinton, who said he wanted a cabinet that looked "like America," put in only four women, although two were in particularly powerful positions: Madeline Albright was the first woman to serve as secretary of state, and Janet Reno became the nation's first woman attorney general. Clinton also appointed Supreme Court Justice Ruth Bader Ginsburg, who had written the analysis of the effect of the ERA back in the 1970s (see Chapter 10), and became the second woman on the Supreme Court.

Women and the Clinton Administration

When William Jefferson Clinton took office after his election in 1992, he brought with him an activist first lady, his wife Hillary Rodham Clinton. In the poisonously partisan atmosphere of the 1990s, Hillary Clinton became a lightning rod for much of the criticism surrounding the women's movement. Clinton's partnership with his wife—a vote for him, he said, would give Americans a "two-for-one" presidency—gave many conservative Americans pause. An attorney in her own right and an outspoken feminist, Hillary Clinton was an activist first lady the likes of which the country had not seen since the days of Eleanor Roosevelt. (See Primary Source 11-5.)

President Clinton came into office after a partisan election with unparalleled levels of rhetorical hostility toward feminists. The Religious Right, voting Republican, had solidified into a powerful and well-organized coalition. Pat Robertson, a television evangelist who regularly complained about the

"Title II—Improving Services for Victims of Domestic Violence, Dating Violence, Sexual Assault, and Stalking

"Title III—Services, Protection, and Justice for Young Victims of Violence

"Title IV—Strengthening America's Families by Preventing Violence

"Title V—Strengthening the Health-care System's Response to Domestic Violence, Dating Violence, Sexual Assault, and Stalking

"Title VI—Housing Opportunities and Safety for Battered Women and Children

"Title VII—Providing Economic Security for Victims of Violence

"Title VIII—Protection of Battered and Trafficked Immigrants

"Title IX—Safety for Indian Women

"Title X—DNA Fingerprinting

"Title XI—Department of Justice Reauthorization"

Source: From http://frwebgate.access.gpo.gov/cgi-bin/getdoc.cgi?dbname=109_cong_bills&docid=f:h3402enr.txt.pdf.

effects of the women's movement, declared in one 1992 political fund-raising letter for conservative Republican candidates that the ERA, still in the news ten years after its defeat, was supported by a feminist movement that was, in reality, a "socialist, anti-family, political movement that encourages women to leave their husbands, kill their children, practice witchcraft, destroy capitalism and become lesbians." Such vitriol found a ready audience, not only among the Religious Right but also among the news media that delighted in reporting the impolitic comments of men like Robertson, as well as others coming from the New Right. Despite such attacks, Clinton won the election, promising to cut taxes for the middle class instead of the rich, to cut the defense budget, and to fund social programs instead.

Once in office, Clinton discovered that his campaign promises could not be kept because of a massive federal budget deficit. He hiked taxes to erase the deficit, then proposed a stimulus package of spending programs to try to restore social programs cut by Republicans. The former passed, the latter failed in a deeply divided Congress. Clinton also tackled the thorny question of health care reform, turning much of the effort over to his wife. The first lady gathered experts and developed a plan, but did so behind closed doors, resulting in a public relations nightmare. Republicans complained about being left out of the process, then defeated the plan through a filibuster in Congress and using television advertising scare tactics declaring Clinton's plan to be "socialized medicine." The Democrats finally gave up. Instead of comprehensive health care, they settled for passing the Family and Medical Leave Act of 1993, which gave unpaid leave to workers to care for sick family members. By the end of 1994, Clinton was so unpopular that the Republicans won control of both the House of Representatives and the Senate in the fall elections.

Winning Republicans brought with them, they said, a *Contract with America*, which would dismantle the welfare state Democrats had designed

FIRST LADY HILLARY CLINTON TESTIFIES BEFORE CONGRESS In September 1993, First Lady Hillary Rodham Clinton testified before Congress about health care reform. A self-described policy "wonk" and chair of a task force to devise a plan to provide universal health care for all Americans, she faced Republicans who derided her efforts as "HillaryCare." Her efforts failed as those opposed decried the "big government" that would force all Americans to buy health care insurance. A similar proposal made in Massachusetts by a Republican governor—Mitt Romney— passed in 2006; a federal bill passed in 2010, while Clinton was still serving the government—as secretary of state.

to provide a safety net for America's poor. The plan failed. Many Americans saw the need for limits to government welfare, but few wanted a return to the days before Franklin Roosevelt's expansion of the federal government during the darkest days of the Great Depression. Instead, by 1996, Congress had increased the minimum wage to $5.15 and passed a measure, sponsored by Senator Nancy Kassebaum of Kansas, the only woman to head a U.S. Senate committee, making it harder for health insurance companies to deny coverage to sick Americans. President Clinton also signed a welfare reform measure, shifting much of the burden and control of welfare programs to the states, and requiring recipients to find jobs or get job training. Clinton's actions combining liberal support for welfare programs with conservative support for stricter rules and more accountability helped him win a second term. Many Democrats were horrified at the destruction of the welfare system, warning Clinton that it would push America's poor— still largely women and children—into utter destitution. Nevertheless, the reforms passed and aspects of them worked relatively well until the economy began to slide into recession after the turn of the century.

Clinton's problems with Congress and more liberal members of his party were soon dwarfed by sexual scandal and impeachment. In 1994, former Arkansas state employee Paula Jones accused President Clinton of sexually harassing her while he was governor of Arkansas. The charge was dismissed because Jones had suffered no discrimination in her employment with the state as a result, but the investigation of the incident led to further accusations, then to an investigation of whether or not Clinton had a sexual relationship with a White House intern, Monica Lewinsky. Clinton was forced to testify to a grand jury, and eventually had to recant his earlier assertions that he had not had an improper relationship with Lewinsky. The House of Representatives impeached the president in December 1998 for perjury and obstruction of justice. The Senate refused to repeat the party-line vote of the House, and Clinton escaped conviction.

The charges against the president gave many feminists pause. Delighted to have a Democratic president after so many years of conservative Republicans, many feminists had been dismayed by his domestic policies, particularly Clinton's failure to solve the issue of gays in the military (his final solution was to allow gays in the military as long as they did not admit to being homosexual), and his slow response to repeated violent attacks on abortion providers. Others thought his changes to the welfare program were unfair to women and children. For many feminists, the spectacle of Clinton's impeachment and trial for sexual dalliance with a White House intern in her twenties while First Lady Hillary Clinton kept a stiff upper lip and stood by her husband, meant suffering not only embarrassment and shock at his poor judgment, but a real sense of sorrow as they lost an opportunity to achieve feminist legislative goals. Feminist and Democratic Senator Dianne Feinstein of California called for the Senate to censure Clinton after his acquittal for his "shameful, reckless and indefensible" behavior. Senator Susan Collins, a Republican from Maine, voted to acquit the president, but was equally dismayed. "While it may not be a crime," she said, "he exploited a very young star-struck employee whom he then proceeded to smear in an attempt to destroy her credibility, her reputation, her life." Many conservative women rejoiced at Clinton's downfall. Still others were put off by the spectacle of a Congress that could not govern because of partisanship, and by the fact that in the interim between Clinton's impeachment and Senate trial, the Speaker-elect of the House, conservative Louisiana Republican Robert Livingston, was forced to resign because of his own sexual scandal.

As the century and millennium came to a close, the Clinton administration's scandal-ridden collapse gave Republican partisans additional ammunition to use against Democratic candidates in the election of 2000. Disassociating himself from the president as best he could, Vice President Al Gore of Tennessee ran on a platform of "prosperity, progress, and peace," and ignored the scandal to talk instead about job and wage growth, declining crime rates, and better health care, as well as a remarkably peaceful world. He faced George W. Bush, governor of Texas, a staunch conservative who ran on a platform similar to Ronald Reagan's: cutting taxes and increasing the size of the military. While political changes incorporated women at every level of government, enabling women to take ever-larger roles as part of the national conversation, in the last election of the millennium, over 200 years since the first American election, 80 years after women won the right to vote, in what would be the closest election in American history, the political choice still came down to two white men.

THINK MORE ABOUT IT

1. Return to the opening vignette on Geraldine Ferraro. How does the story of her candidacy for the vice presidency demonstrate the ways in which Americans debated appropriate roles for women and the obstacles that women still faced in acting in the public realm as late as the 1980s? To what extent do you think these debates and obstacles persist?

2. Discuss the restructuring of the American economy and accompanying changing governmental policies during the 1980s. How did these changes in the economy and public policy affect women, especially poor and nonwhite women?

3. What is the second shift? What conditions and attitudes account for its persistence? What factors might lead to its decline? Be sure to include a discussion of labor-saving devices and other new technologies (including the computer) in your discussion of these questions.

4. Discrimination against women in the workforce takes on many forms. Indicate the various forms of sex discrimination and discuss in detail at least two of them. To what extent and why do you think such discrimination persists?

5. By the late 1980s, as feminism achieved many of its most visible goals other than the ratification of the ERA, the women's movement fragmented, much as it had in the wake of the woman's suffrage amendment six decades previously. What were the effects of this fragmentation? Discuss in particular the rise of third wave feminism, including its precepts and the variety of forms it has taken, and the advent of the culture wars, as some Americans came to believe the women's movement already had accomplished enough and many more thought it had achieved too much.

6. In the 1980s and 1990s, women became more prominent in many arenas, from popular culture to public office. Yet for all the "firsts" for women during these years, barriers and obstacles remained. How do you account for this mixed legacy of the late twentieth century? Where have women made the most strides and which women have benefited most and least from these advances? Which areas of life seem most resistant to change for women? Be careful to take into account the longstanding argument about the extent and meaning of innate differences between women and men, particularly as it relates to sexualities.

7. What did you learn in this chapter that you did not know before? How does this new information help you understand the overall story of women in American history? What topics would you like to explore further?

READ MORE ABOUT IT

Gabriela Arredondo, et al., eds., *Chicana Feminisms: A Critical Reader*

Linda M. Blum, *Between Feminism and Labor: The Significance of the Comparable Worth Movement*

Stephanie Coontz, *The Way We Really Are: Coming to Terms with America's Changing Families*

Henry Etzkowitz, Carol Kemelgor, and Brian Uzzi, *Athena Unbound: The Advancement of Women in Science and Technology*

Neil Gilbert, *A Mother's Work: How Feminism, the Market, and Policy Shape Family Life*

Arlie Hochschild, *The Second Shift*

Louise Lamphere, *Sunbelt Working Mothers: Reconciling Family and Factory*

Karen J. Warren, *Ecofeminist Philosophy: A Western Perspective on What It Is and Why It Matters*

KEY CONCEPTS

stagflation	"Mommy Track"
the pill	pro-life
New Right	pro-choice
second shift	womanism
affirmative action	ecofeminism
sexual harassment	culture wars
pay equity	EMILY's List

EPILOGUE:
THE CONTEMPORARY ERA

Lilly Ledbetter

THE ELECTION OF 2000

WOMEN AND THE SECOND BUSH ADMINISTRATION
Women and the War on Terror
Women's Place in the House—and Senate

THE ELECTION OF 2008

THE FUTURE

For nineteen years, Lilly Ledbetter, a white woman in search of a decent job with benefits, worked at the Goodyear Tire & Rubber Company plant in Gadsden, Alabama. She started on the floor of the factory, then rose through the ranks until she became an area manager, the only woman among a number of men to hold that position. When she began her career, her pay was the same as the other male workers hired at the same time to do the same job. Over time, however, she heard rumors that her pay was never increased as much as male workers. She did not really understand why, since she was a hard worker, and a good worker, even receiving a "top performance" award from the management. The rumors about her lower pay bothered her, but she had signed a contract that forbade her to discuss her salary with any other employee of the plant. If she was paid less than men were for doing the same job, she figured that it was a "Southern thing," a "good-old-boy policy" at Goodyear, not a civil rights issue.

In 1998, not long before she retired, Ledbetter discovered the discrepancy in pay thanks to an anonymous note left in her mailbox. Her pay was $559 a month less than the lowest-paid male area manager, and lower than other male workers with less seniority and experience. She immediately filed a claim with the Equal Employment Opportunity Commission (EEOC), protesting the discriminatory pay. The company, just as promptly, retaliated by reassigning the then-sixty-year-old to a different job—lifting heavy tires. Ledbetter continued to perform the job, but took early retirement a few months later. She then filed a lawsuit against Goodyear. A jury awarded Ledbetter $3.8 million in back pay and damages; a judge later reduced the amount to $360,000. Goodyear appealed the decision, arguing that Ledbetter's lower pay was due to her lower performance evaluations.

The case eventually wound up before the Supreme Court. During the trial, Ledbetter said she was held to different standards in evaluations because she was a woman. "I'd been in meetings where higher people in my plant would say, 'We don't need women in this factory,'" she said, "but they knew the law required them to have some." Under the Equal Pay Act of 1963, the law also required Ledbetter to be paid equally with men doing the same job, if the job required, as the law put it, "substantially equal skill, effort and responsibility." But Ledbetter did not receive the same pay. She received smaller raises each time raises were given out, despite performing well. The discrimination had long-term effects. Lower paychecks over nearly the entire course of her career, lower than those of men who did the same job, meant Ledbetter's retirement benefits and social security payments would be lower as well. "I'm like a second-class citizen for the rest of my life," she pointed out. "I will never be compensated for my lower wages and my pension and Social Security wages are much lower, because Goodyear paid me less." In its effect, the discrimination she suffered during her career would never cease.

The Supreme Court took up the case in 2007. The court ruled, in a 5 to 4 decision, that Ledbetter filed her claim too late. She should have reported the discrimination within 180 days of the first time it occurred, rather than within 180 days of discovering the discrimination. This was despite the fact that Ledbetter was forbidden by the company she worked for to discuss or compare her compensation with anyone else in the plant. The conservative court, led by Chief Justice John Roberts, however, was determined to protect businesses from what it termed "frivolous" lawsuits, and decided to rewrite existing case law to reach its conclusion. Previous rulings had long held that, in the case of pay discrimination, each individual paycheck issued by a company constituted a new act of discrimination. Because pay discrimination is usually constant over time, rather than a single act of discrimination, this interpretation provided a worker with a new instance to cite when claiming long-term sex discrimination. However, according to the conservatives on the court, that was not what the statute said. On the contrary, it ruled, "current effects alone can't breathe life into prior, uncharged discrimination," even if the victim did not know the discrimination had taken place.

Justice Ruth Bader Ginsburg (see Chapters 10 and 11), the lone woman on the Court after Justice Sandra Day O'Connor retired in 2006, dissented, along with three other justices. She felt so strongly about her dissent that she took the rare step of reading it aloud from the bench. "In our view," she said, "the court does not comprehend, or is indifferent to, the insidious way in which women can be victims of pay discrimination." Companies, as was true of Goodyear, often forbade employees from discussing their salaries with anyone. New employees, especially women breaking ground as the "first woman" in a particular task or job, would be unlikely to make trouble by inquiring about others' wages in a search to be sure they were not being discriminated against in their first six months on a new job. The Court's ruling in Ledbetter v. Goodyear would allow companies to discriminate against women workers, as long as they did not get caught within the first 180 days of that discrimination.

Ledbetter was very disappointed with the result of the case, particularly, she said, since she had hoped that Justice Clarence Thomas, a fellow Southerner, an African American whom she assumed had felt the sting of discrimination himself, and the former head of the EEOC, would stand with her. He did not. Congress did, however, taking up the Lilly Ledbetter Fair Pay Act in 2007 and 2008. The AFL-CIO took up the cause, as did the American Civil Liberties Union. Democrats in the House of Representatives passed the bill in 2007, but Republican senators promptly filibustered it to death. In 2008, however, five Republican senators—four of them women—broke ranks with their party and voted in favor of the legislation: Kay Bailey Hutchison of Texas, Olympia Snowe and Susan Collins of Maine, Lisa Murkowski of Alaska, and Arlen Specter of Pennsylvania. The Lilly Ledbetter Fair Pay Act, allowing a person to file a complaint up to 180 days after any discriminatory paycheck, was the first bill signed into law by newly elected President Barack Obama, a Democrat.

Obama's election came after a landslide victory for the Democrats in the fall of 2008. A far more conservative Republican president, George W. Bush, had succeeded Bill Clinton in 2000. His attempts to turn back many of the gains made by the women's movement, particularly the freedom to enjoy reproductive rights, partially succeeded, but his domestic agenda was soon overwhelmed by foreign affairs, terrorism, and war. Bush's presidency encompassed

LILLY LEDBETTER   The nation's first African American president, Barack Obama, presents Lilly Ledbetter with the pen he used to sign the Fair Pay Act, which strengthened laws against wage discrimination by making each discriminatory paycheck a new act of discrimination, renewing the time for filing a pay discrimination claim. Senator Barbara Mikulski of Maryland is at front left; the first woman to be Speaker of the House of Representatives, Nancy Pelosi, is to the president's right.

two unpopular wars in Afghanistan and Iraq, eight years of continuing partisan bickering that grid-locked Congress, and finally, during his last few months in office, an economy in free-fall. This setting provided an opportunity for forty-seven-year-old Senator Obama, a Democrat from Illinois and perceived as an outsider to the entrenched powers in Washington, to win the presidency. In doing so, he defeated two women: Hillary Clinton, senator from New York, who had run for the Democratic nomination against him; and Sarah Palin, governor of Alaska, who ran as the Republican vice presidential nominee. Women voters provided a major base for Obama's victory over Republican presidential candidate John McCain, with more than two-thirds of all single women and women under thirty casting their votes for the first African American man elected to the presidency. An inspiring speaker and astute political analyst, Obama represented a decisive turn away from the past for many American voters as a record-breaking turnout elected him, and a record-breaking crowd viewed his inauguration in January 2009.

THE ELECTION OF 2000

The turn of the century did not eliminate the partisanship that had dominated American politics since the 1980s. The Republicans nominated a conservative Republican governor from Texas, George W. Bush, son of the former president George H. W. Bush. The Democrats picked Clinton's vice president, Albert Gore of Tennessee. The election was so close that the results were not made final for a month. Florida votes were key to the election, and difficulties with the state's election process were without number. Ballots were badly designed and poorly used. Voting machines broke down. Voters, particularly African American Democratic voters, declared that state electoral officials had committed fraud. They accused Florida officials, in a state governed by George Bush's brother Jeb Bush, of intimidating them with police officers at the polls and keeping them from voting by not having enough poll workers, voting machines, or voting materials available so that they could cast their ballots. Lines outside polling places were hours-long and many voters simply gave up.

After thirty-six days and countless motions before the Supreme Court, George Bush was declared the winner of the election, despite the inability of the state of Florida to count votes in a consistent manner across all counties. Democrats immediately declared the election "stolen" and used the Internet to publicize their claims, including attacks on Jeb Bush and Florida Secretary of State Katherine Harris, responsible for the recount. The partisan press labeled Harris "Cruella de Harris" (a reference to the villainess of Disney's movie *101 Dalmatians* who sought to make a fur coat out of puppies). For many, she became the representative of all that was wrong with the election, with the Republicans, and with the country. She managed to stoke the first charge herself. She had served as co-chair of Bush's election campaign while still secretary of state, a clear conflict of interest. She set arbitrary and seemingly capricious timelines during the election's recount, leading Democrats to accuse her of manipulating votes. She removed records from state computers during the recount, despite a state law that designated all records on state computers as public records. Harris denied all wrong-doing and became a hero to Republican partisans, later winning a seat in the U.S. House of Representatives despite failing to resign properly from her job as secretary of state before running. More important than anything else to her and the Republicans was that their goal of getting George Bush into the White House succeeded.

WOMEN AND THE SECOND BUSH ADMINISTRATION

George W. Bush prided himself on his bipartisan approach in governing Texas and declared that he wanted to be a "uniter, not a divider" in governing the United States. Despite his promise to use consensus and compromise to achieve his goals, however, Bush was not interested in alienating his conservative political base. The day after his inauguration, he restored the federal rules prohibiting any nongovernmental organization (NGO) from receiving money from the United States if the NGO performed abortions, or even if it just counseled women seeking abortions in cases of unwanted pregnancy.

Having thrown down that particular gauntlet, Bush made clear his positions regarding women's reproductive rights. His appointees to federal offices often faced what pro-choice advocates called a "litmus test" of support for antiabortion positions, and his decision a few weeks after his inauguration in January 2001 to use federal money to support faith-based community service organizations solidified his position with the New Right and Religious Right supporters who had helped elect him. He also appointed two conservative white men to the Supreme Court, Chief Justice John Roberts in 2005 and Samuel Alito in 2006. (Alito replaced Bush's earlier nominee, Harriet Miers, a Justice Department lawyer whom most conservatives viewed as unqualified for the high court, and whom many assumed Bush had chosen because of her personal loyalty to him.) The effect of Bush's conservative appointments was immediate in the area of reproductive rights, specifically regarding the abortion procedure of intact dilation and extraction (D&E), dubbed by its opponents "partial-birth" abortion to emphasize its medical technique. They highlighted the possibility of fetal dismemberment while medical experts testifying before Congress disagreed over whether the technique was ever necessary. Congress passed an act barring the procedure and Bush signed it into law.

In 2000, the Court had ruled a similar law was unconstitutional because it had no exclusion to allow the procedure if it was needed to save the health or the life of the mother, an exclusion that had always been the case for abortion procedures. After Bush's later appointments to the Supreme Court were confirmed, the court ruled 5 to 4 in *Gonzales v. Carhart* (2007) that the ban was constitutional. Despite the fact that the medical community had reached no consensus regarding the necessity of the procedure, Congress had. More shocking, the Court deferred to Congress and declared that there was no need for an exclusion to the law regarding its use to save the health of the mother. Justice Ruth Bader Ginsberg dissented vigorously, along with three other liberal justices. She read her dissent on that case from the bench as well, telling what the *Washington Post* described as a "stone-silent" courtroom, full of men, that "legal challenges to undue restrictions on abortion procedures do not seek to vindicate some generalized notion of privacy; rather, they center on a woman's autonomy to determine her life's course, and thus to enjoy equal citizenship stature." The decision, she said, "cannot be understood as anything other than an effort to chip away at a right declared again and again by this court—and with increasing comprehension of its centrality to women's lives"—the right for a woman to decide if she wants to continue a pregnancy or not. Bush and his antiabortion supporters then continued to seek cases that would give the Court an opportunity to overturn the *Roe v. Wade* decision that allowed women the right to an abortion.

Despite Bush's conservative beliefs that pregnant women's lives were secondary to the fetuses they carried, he exhibited some appreciation of women's skills in terms of running the country. During his two terms in office, the Departments of the Interior, State, Education, Labor, Transportation, Agriculture, and the Environmental Protection Agency were all headed by women. Karen Hughes, a conservative Republican from Texas and one of his closest advisors, served as counselor to the president and later as undersecretary of state for Public Diplomacy. Condoleeza Rice, an African American with a PhD from the University of Denver, served as national security advisor in Bush's first term, and became secretary of state in his second. Yet many wondered whether these highly visible women were only token appointments meant to give the appearance of a commitment to inclusion. Republicans faced a growing gender gap among the party's supporters, particularly as the Bush administration continued to cut funding for programs that feminists and progressive women considered critical to supporting women's rights. Nevertheless, the Republican Party won victories in the off-year elections of 2002, and kept control of both the House and Senate in 2004. Bush used those majorities to pass conservative legislation, including bans on certain kinds of abortions, bans on the use of most human embryos in stem-cell research, cuts in social programs, cuts in education programs, and changes in taxes and tax laws that primarily benefited the wealthy.

Women and the War on Terror

The conservative politics of Bush's first term received reinforcement from Americans frightened by terrorist attacks against the United States on September 11, 2001, and two resulting wars against Afghanistan and Iraq. Fundamentalist Islamic terrorists commandeered four planes and flew two into the twin towers of the World Trade Center in New York City, and another into the Pentagon. The fourth hit the ground in Pennsylvania after passengers attempted to free the plane from the hijackers' control. Thousands were killed—office workers and airline employees, passersby and safety personnel, moms and dads and children—all died on a heart-breakingly beautiful fall day. America's military response was swift: in October, Bush invaded Afghanistan, where the Taliban, another fundamentalist Islamic group, protected the attackers' leader, Osama bin Laden. In 2003, Bush also invaded Iraq, having linked—inaccurately, as was later revealed—that country to bin Laden's militant group Al Qaeda and the terrorist attacks of September 11.

The troops in Afghanistan and Iraq that made up America's invasion force contained many women in new positions in the military, which had changed its policies toward women soldiers because of the women's movement. In particular, the National Guard units that were called up to assist the U.S. Army in fighting the wars contained numerous women. By 2005, one of every seven U.S. troop members in Iraq was a woman—15 percent of the troops. This was an unprecedented change for the military, and became a serious issue in the countries where they fought, where fundamentalist Muslims viewed women as second-class citizens. As the nature of warfare had also changed, many more American women soldiers now came under direct fire, despite army regulations designed to keep them away from the front lines. Regardless of paper limits on their service, women in combat performed well, and some made the ultimate sacrifice: Private First Class Lori Piestewa, a Hopi Indian serving in the U.S. Army Quartermaster Corps, died of wounds suffered in an ambush in southern Iraq. On March 23, 2003, Piestewa became the first woman casualty of the war, and the first Native American woman to die in combat while fighting for American troops. Shoshana Johnson, another member of the same convoy, was wounded and captured—the first black woman prisoner of war in American history.

Women soldiers not only faced combat, but also dealt with sexual harassment and attacks from fundamentalist Iraqis aghast at women's presence as soldiers. They even suffered from attacks by some of their own comrades in arms as the war continued. Hearings in the House Armed Services Committee in 2008 estimated that over 30 percent of women soldiers were assaulted or raped by fellow soldiers during their service. Representative Jane Harman of California pointed out that this meant that "a female soldier in Iraq is more likely to be raped by a fellow soldier than killed by enemy fire." Few women filed complaints, afraid they would be removed from their units while their attackers would remain. Secretary of Defense Donald Rumsfeld charged the Defense Task Force on Sexual Assault in the Military Services (DTFSAMS), established in 2005, to recommend ways to prevent sexual assaults as well as improve conditions for sexual assault victims.

This was only one issue the armed services had to deal with as women became a greater proportion of the military. Women veterans injured by improvised explosive devices (IEDs), used commonly in the war, strained the resources of the Veterans Administration (VA) as it cared for injured soldiers, as women needed new types of health care and rehabilitation to treat their injuries. The VA needed more ob-gyn doctors; more privacy in their hospitals; more treatment for the different kinds of posttraumatic stress women suffered from. As the nature of military service changed to include more women, the armed forces continued to struggle to catch up to their desire to, as the DTFSAMS brochure put it, foster "dignity and respect for all who serve."

Women's Place in the House—and Senate

Dismayed with the cost of the wars, voters put the Democrats in control of the House of Representatives after the off-year elections in 2006. Once in power, Democrats elected Californian Nancy Pelosi as the first woman Speaker of the House of Representatives. A mother of five and grandmother of six who did not enter politics until her children were grown, Pelosi did not hesitate to refer to her experiences as a mother when talking about her goals and her methods in dealing with the politicians on Capitol Hill. When a microphone failed at her introduction, she quipped, "I could use my mother-of-five voice!" Calling her election an historic moment for American women, Pelosi said, "It is a moment for which we have waited over 200 years. Never losing faith, we waited through the many years of struggle to achieve our rights. But women weren't just waiting, women were working. Never losing faith, we worked to redeem the promise of America, that all men and women are created equal. For our daughters and our granddaughters, today we have broken the marble ceiling."

NANCY PELOSI, SPEAKER OF THE HOUSE   When Nancy Pelosi, third in line to the presidency, was sworn in as Speaker of the House, she chose to surround herself with her grandchildren as she took the oath of office. By doing so, she symbolized the combination of family and career common for so many women in the new century.

Pelosi's election to Speaker of the House, which made her third in line for the presidency of the country, marked the importance of women involving themselves in the public political world. Studies by political scientists have shown that women in Congress transformed the institution because they brought to the government an understanding of the commonalities they share with all women, regardless of class, race, region, or even political party. Congressional woman are more likely to use their personal experiences with issues such as child care and medical treatments and take gender into account when debating issues and crafting legislation. One study examined the increased money the National Cancer Institute spent on breast cancer research, which grew from $33.9 million in 1981 to $348.2 million by 1997. The difference could be attributed not only to widespread and vigorous public support for finding a cure to this terrible disease, but also to women legislators successfully channeling this support into advocacy. They did so in part by initiating one of the most important institutional changes in Congress—using congressional "earmarks" that allowed representatives to gain funding for pet projects without having to go through the normal appropriations process. Still a minority in the House and Senate, women legislators using earmarks could bypass male representatives' resistance to spending federal money on issues affecting primarily one gender, such as breast cancer research.

Both Democratic and Republican women sponsor more legislation on women's issues than do men. They seek to be put on committees, particularly those dealing with reproductive policy legislation, in order to influence the legislation, be it pro-choice or pro-life, often referring to the women's movement of the past to justify their actions in the present. Congressional staffers, many of whom are women, do much of the work on Capitol Hill, effecting change for women by promoting women's issues when presenting policy to representatives. Despite the elitist nature of the institution, women have been able to make changes to Congress by becoming part of the institution. After the 2008 election, there were seventeen women senators and seventy-seven women representatives in the 111th Congress, twenty-six of whom were women of color. Nancy Pelosi remained Speaker of the House, Democratic Senator Patty Murray of Washington was reelected Democratic Conference secretary (the fourth most powerful position among Senate Democrats), and Representative Cathy McMorris Rodgers, also of Washington, became vice chair of the Republican Conference, as well as co-chair of the Congressional Women's Caucus.

THE ELECTION OF 2008

The election of 2008 left no doubt that women in politics have become a accepted part of the national political conversation, as they entered races in every political arena. However, the election also revealed many Americans were still unable to view women separate from old stereotypes regarding their physical appearance, expected behaviors, and traditional roles.

Hillary Clinton, a former first lady and a second-term senator from New York, ran as a serious contender for presidential office, rather than as a token woman representing women's interests, as earlier candidates had been. When she began her campaign in 2007, she started as the front-runner, and many presumed she would be the eventual nominee. A talented politician, dedicated to public service, an experienced and hardworking legislator, Clinton epitomized the success of the women's movement. She had attended Wellesley College during the height of feminism's second wave, then went to Yale Law school in 1969, where she met Bill Clinton. She worked for the Children's Defense Fund and for the Judiciary Committee of the House of Representatives during the Nixon impeachment inquiry, then married Bill and moved to Arkansas, where she served as first lady of the state during Bill Clinton's governorship. She moved to the White House after his election in 1992. After his second term, she moved to New York, then won the 2000 U.S. Senate race after a long and thorough campaign during which she visited every county in New York State. She was, as she often described herself, a "policy wonk," who delighted in the hard work and details of legislation. She was also a staunch feminist, fighting at each stage of her career to protect and promote women's interests and their rights. With her talent, brains, and skills, and with a huge fund-raising machine behind her candidacy, she looked to be a shoe-in for the nomination.

Clinton's candidacy, however, met with stiff resistance from Republicans who detested both her and her husband, as well as antifeminists who did not yet accept that a woman should be president of the most powerful country in the world. Her rallies were often marred by misogynistic signs that attacked her femininity and appearance, rather than her political positions. She was called a shrew, a bitch, and a "ball-buster," and conservative media pundits spent much time fretting over the prospect of another Clinton in the White House. Her skills, competence, and experience were dismissed by opponents more eager to resurrect the frightening image of the evil that would befall the country should a woman involve herself in politics (see Chapters 4, 5, 6, 7, 8). Clinton won 18 million votes in the Democratic primaries, but could not overcome the lead Obama stacked up by the time of the nominating convention, and graciously conceded the race to the junior male senator from Illinois in June 2008. Although she had disparaged him during the primary campaign in ways that smacked, even to some of her supporters, of racism, at the convention she pleaded with her supporters to remain with the Democratic Party to defeat the Republicans, despite the fact the Democrats had nominated a man. Some supporters felt it was a case of history repeating itself, as when after the Civil War Wendell Phillips had told suffragists, "This is the Negro's hour," and women were asked to set aside their ambitions and support black suffrage over woman suffrage. Clinton did not view it that way. For her, Obama's progressive agenda, including support for key women's issues, was paramount.

In an effort to woo women voters disappointed at Clinton's defeat for the Democratic nomination, the Republican presidential nominee John McCain, the oldest person to ever run for the office and no friend of women's rights, chose Alaska governor Sarah Palin as his running mate.

Palin, a conservative Republican, evangelical Christian, pro-life, multitasking mother of five, including a newborn with Down Syndrome, took the media by storm and reenergized the Republican right wing who found McCain's candidacy dull at best. A former beauty queen and television sportscaster, Palin had long benefited from the feminist movement, but her political positions were in complete opposition to it. Most feminists were aghast at the pick, and many felt insulted by McCain choosing a woman with so little political experience (she'd been mayor of a small Alaska town with 6,300 residents, then governor of Alaska for nineteen months). Even many Republicans recognized that the only thing she had in common with Clinton was her gender. In her first campaign appearances, crowds of sympathetic and intrigued supporters declared their loyalty and affection for the folksy Palin, who winked and grinned, and proclaimed herself to be "just a mom," who could bring practical experience to Washington to solve the problems of the day.

As the campaign continued, however, Palin's lack of experience and ignorance of important domestic issues and foreign affairs quickly became evident. The glamorous image the Republican Party sought for her was soon replaced by the view that she was "stunningly uninformed," and, as one reporter put it, "the dim beauty queen, the kind of woman who floats along on a little luck and the favor of men." Her popularity among many conservatives did not wane, but in large rallies toward the end of the campaign, her vituperative and vicious, if not downright slanderous, attacks on Obama turned many undecided voters against the Republicans, as did concern that she might have to replace McCain during his term, given his advanced age and his medical history of cancer.

In the end, the election was decided by concern about the ongoing wars, but even more by an accelerating economic crisis. An economic downturn began in December 2007, and was finally labeled a recession by economists in early December 2008. Internationally, frightening increases in oil and food prices led to gasoline shortages and even food riots. The housing market, overvalued for years into a housing bubble, burst, with the United States leading the way in the collapse of home values. So many people lost jobs that by the end of the year—1 million in the final two months of the year—that there were more unemployed workers than at the end of World War II. Credit tightened, and banks and investment firms failed. The stock market crashed, losing about $1.3 trillion of wealth during the fall election campaign. President Bush seemed largely disinterested and disengaged, preferring first to allow the free market to settle the matter. He eventually signed an economic bailout of multinational corporations, since many economists feared bankruptcies of such large companies might destroy the economy completely. Both presidential candidates pushed their economic programs to solve the crisis. McCain held fast to the Republican tradition of cutting taxes, while Obama argued, as Franklin Roosevelt had during the Great Depression, that the federal government was the only entity large enough to provide an economic stimulus to salvage the tottering economy.

Obama won the election, capturing 9.5 million more votes than McCain, and winning 365 electoral votes to McCain's 173. The "solid

South" that had voted Republican in nearly every election since 1980 broke: Florida, Virginia, North Carolina, and New Mexico all went for Obama. The new president, a constitutional lawyer who had taught at the University of Chicago Law School and worked as a community organizer on the south side of Chicago, brought thoughtful, intellectual discourse to the presidency, and was determined to break the partisan gridlock if he could. His inauguration ceremony attracted nearly 2 million visitors to Washington, DC, as even those who had not voted for him celebrated America's step away from its racist past that his inauguration represented. His administration included a number of women: Hillary Clinton was the new secretary of state; Hilda Solis, the secretary of labor; Janet Napolitano, the secretary of homeland security; Lisa Jackson, the head of the Environmental Protection Agency; Susan Rice, the ambassador to the United Nations; and Valerie Jarrett, a long-time adviser and family friend, became a White House senior adviser. His first appointment to the Supreme Court was Sonia Sotomayor, who became the first Hispanic and the third woman on the Court; his second was Elena Kagan, building a Supreme Court that was one-third female.

Obama's first concern was the economy, which continued to worsen. He pushed an economic stimulus bill through Congress that passed, despite all Republican House members refusing to vote for it, because of the Democratic majority that had won both houses in the fall. He promised a troop withdrawal from Iraq and Afghanistan as quickly as was safe, and sought to overturn executive orders that the departing Bush administration had issued in a last-ditch effort to maintain a conservative hold on the country. Americans clearly wanted change, and two-thirds of the country was ready to move in a new direction. Obama signaled that concern for women's issues would be part of that new direction when he signed his first bill, the Lilly Ledbetter Fair Pay Act.

THE FUTURE

The economic downturn that began in 2008 had a monumental effect on American life. For the first time in the country's history, women workers passed the number of men in the workforce because layoffs in this downturn affected far more men than women. By November 2008, women already held 49.1 percent of jobs in the country. Of the millions of jobs lost by February 2009, 82 percent of them had been held by men, particularly in trades such as construction and manufacturing. Women's jobs, particularly in sectors such as health care and education, were less likely to disappear. Those jobs, however, almost always paid less than men's jobs, and women continued to suffer from the lack of benefits, such as health care, sick leave, and retirement, a lack of pay equity, and, as Lilly Ledbetter proved, outright pay discrimination. Now, however, many of these women became the sole financial support of their families, as men were laid off not only from blue-collar jobs, but from well-paying white-collar jobs as well.

Many men began to appreciate the economic limits that women faced in their jobs as they oftentimes had to rely on women's income until they found new jobs. Meanwhile, single women, including those with dependents to care for, continued to struggle with the consequences of unequal pay and benefits.

Beyond the economy, the new president faced monumental challenges in other areas. The war on terror continued on two fronts and U.S. armed forces suffered grievously as their extended tours of duty sapped military readiness. America's infrastructure, neglected for years as state and federal budget cuts postponed maintenance, required trillions of dollars in repairs to guarantee public safety. America's continued reliance on imported oil put its national security at risk, but the cost of shifting to renewable sources of energy was expensive, and much of the research needed to develop alternative sources of fuel had been badly underfunded as well. Social issues continued to divide the nation as well. In California, voters passed Proposition 8 in November 2008, restricting marriage to opposite sex couples after conservatives demanded that earlier court decisions allowing gay marriage in the state be overturned. A key component of Obama's agenda, national health care coverage, passed into law in 2010 after a bruising partisan fight. The plan was predicted to cost billions and raised conservative hackles as an unwarranted interference in the private lives of Americans.

American women will continue to use their political and economic power to play an ever-increasing role in the nation's life. As the economy changes in a seismic shift worldwide, as the political world responds to the demands for effective solutions, women's ability to make and to cope with those changes relies in part on their ability to access the sources of power—the courts and the legislatures, the marketplace and the family. American women's political and personal actions will continue to have repercussions in every sphere as they act both individually and within groups. As historian Mary Ritter Beard put it so well, women are a force in history.

CREDITS

PHOTO CREDITS

Chapter 10 p. 411, © Lee Lockwood/Time & Life Pictures/Getty Images; p. 422, Library of Congress Prints and Photographs Division Washington D.C. [LC-U9-12470B-17]; p. 424, Library of Congress Prints and Photographs Division [LC-DIG-ppmsca-08102]; p. 437, © Keystone/Hulton Archive/Getty Images; p. 450, © Steve Northup/Time & Life Pictures/Getty Images; p. 453, © Michael Mauney/Time & Life Pictures/Getty Images

Chapter 11 p. 461, © George Rose/Getty Images; p. 480, © Jennifer K. Law/AFP/Getty Images; p. 491, © Mark Wilson/Getty Images; p. 495, © Time & Life Pictures/Getty Images; p. 504, © Brad Markel/Getty Images

Epilogue p. 511, © Mark Wilson/Getty Images; p. 516, © Chip Somodevilla/Getty Images

LINE ART CREDITS

Chapter 1 p. 7, From Alan Brinkley, *The Unfinished Nation* 6e, p. 6, © 2010. Reproduced by permission of The McGraw-Hill Companies.
Chapter 3 p. 90, From Alan Brinkley, *The Unfinished Nation* 6e, p. 99, © 2010. Reproduced by permission of The McGraw-Hill Companies.
Chapter 4 p. 147, Courtesy of the United States Patent Office.
Chapter 5 p. 211, From Alan Brinkley, *The Unfinished Nation* 6e, p. 334, © 2010. Reproduced by permission of The McGraw-Hill Companies.

INDEX

INDEX

INDEX